Sixth Edition

Literacy Development in the Early Years

Helping Children Read and Write

Lesley Mandel Morrow

Boston   New York   San Francisco
Mexico City   Montreal   Toronto   London   Madrid   Munich   Paris
Hong Kong   Singapore   Tokyo   Cape Town   Sydney

Executive Editor: Aurora Martínez Ramos
Series Editorial Assistant: Kara Kikel
Executive Marketing Manager: Krista Clark
Editorial Production Service: Nesbitt Graphics, Inc.
Composition Buyer: Linda Cox
Manufacturing Buyer: Megan Cochran
Electronic Composition: Nesbitt Graphics, Inc.
Interior Design: Nesbitt Graphics, Inc.
Cover Administrator: Joel Gendron

For related titles and support materials, visit our online catalog at www.pearsonhighered.com.

Between the time website information is gathered and then published, it is not unusual for some sites to have closed. Also, the transcription of URLs can result in typographical errors. The publisher would appreciate notification where these errors occur so that they may be corrected in subsequent editions.

Library of Congress Cataloging-in-Publication Data
Morrow, Lesley Mandel.
Literacy development in the early years : helping children read and write / Lesley Mandel Morrow. – 6th ed.
    p. cm.
 ISBN 0-205-59325-9
1. Language arts (Preschool)–United States. 2. Reading (Preschool)–United States.
3. Children–Books and reading–United States. I. Title.
    LB1140.5.L3M66 2009
    372.60973–dc22   2007045147

Printed in the United States of America

        10 9 8 7 6 5 4 3 2 1 RRD–MO 08 09 10 11 12 13 14 15

Photo Credits: Lenore Arone, Susan Arone, Kate Brach, Douglas Bushell, Joyce Caponigro, Jenn Chiaramida, Lynn Cohen, Cheryl Devine, Tami-Lynne Eisen, Lisa Fazzi, Michelle Grote, Deborah Hanna, Lori Harrje, Katherine Heiss, Brent Horbatt, Pam Kelliher, Mary Jane Kurabinski, Kelly Lamar, Danielle Lynch, Milton E. Mandel, Howard Manson, Franklin A. Morrow, Lesley Mandel Morrow, Dana Pilla, Lisa Rosenfeld, Amy Sass, Andrea Shane, Kristen Valvanis

Allyn and Bacon
is an imprint of

www.pearsonhighered.com

ISBN 10:   0-205-59325-9
ISBN 13: 978-0-205-59325-5

**To Mary and Milton; Frank;
Stephanie and Douglas; James and Natalie,**

*my very special parents,
my very special daughter and son-in-law, and
my very special grandson and granddaughter.*

**Adorable,
Lovable,
Delightful**

**Hilarious,
Mischievous,
Luminous**

**Grandchildren
Natalie Kate
and
James Ethan
Priceless**

About the Author

Lesley Mandel Morrow is a Professor of Literacy at Rutgers University's Graduate School of Education, where she is Chair of the Department of Learning and Teaching. She began her career as a classroom teacher, then became a reading specialist, and later received her Ph.D. from Fordham University in New York City. Her area of research deals with early literacy development and the organization and management of Language Arts Programs. Her research is carried out with children and families from diverse backgrounds.

Dr. Morrow has more than 300 publications, including journal articles, book chapters, monographs, and books. She received Excellence in Research, Teaching, and Service Awards from Rutgers University. She was the recipient of the International Reading Association's Outstanding Teacher Educator of Reading Award and Fordham University's Alumni Award for Outstanding Achievement. In addition, Dr. Morrow has received numerous grants for research from the federal government and has served as a principal research investigator for the Center of English Language Arts, National Reading Research Center, Center for Early Reading Achievement, and currently for the Mid-Atlantic Regional Lab. She was an elected member of the Board of Directors of the International Reading Association (IRA), an organization of 90,000 educators in 100 countries, and she served as president of the organization in 2003–2004. She was elected into the Reading Hall of Fame in 2006. She is the extremely proud grandmother of James Ethan and Natalie Kate Bushell.

Contents

CHAPTER **10** Family Literacy Partnerships: Home and School Working Together   377

Foreword

Literacy Development in the Early Years: Helping Children Read and Write was published in its first edition in 1989. With the publication of this sixth edition in 2009, it celebrates its 20th anniversary. New features were added to each of the previous editions, as they are in this new edition. We have retained material covering what was sound and good practice 20 years ago, and have updated based on current research, policy, and practice. This text was one of the first on the topic of early literacy and has prevailed as one of the most utilized texts of its kind in the country.

The first edition of *Literacy Development in the Early Years* appeared when research on emergent literacy was just beginning to be implemented into practice. It was also a time when teaching whole language was the common practice. We once thought that children learned to speak and listen during their early years and later learned to read and write at five or six years of age. We also thought that early childhood was a time to learn to read and the elementary grades was a time to read to learn. We now know that children begin to develop early forms of language and literacy ability concurrently and from the day they are born. We have learned that learning to read and reading to learn go hand in hand. We have discovered that excellent strategies are good for all children at all ages. Excellent literacy instruction is created in literacy-rich environments in social contexts through immersion in literacy experiences, explicit instruction, practice, and modeling by teachers—all with constructive feedback.

Lesley Mandel Morrow based her book on her own research as well as that of others and her practical experience as a classroom teacher, researcher, mother, and now grandmother. She took a look at historical theories and philosophies about how children learn. As time passed and policy changes in teaching reading were legislated, Morrow took these developments into account and shared this very important information. With these new laws came new challenges, especially in the area of testing. She added more about assessment in her book to help teachers meet these challenges.

English language learners (ELL) make up a large portion of our school population. Morrow has added more material to the chapter dealing with diversity and has incorporated an ELL icon to indicate activities throughout the book that are particularly good for children who are English language learners.

Morrow demonstrates the value of involving children in many types of language and literacy experiences. She provides insightful examples of children's approximations of writing and reading as she establishes the necessity of giving them unlimited opportunities to practice. Further, she illustrates the ways in which adults provide models, explicit instruction, and feedback for young learners as they attempt to read and write. Morrow takes a comprehensive perspective toward literacy instruction by selecting the best techniques based on sound learning theories, such as a constructivist model or problem-solving approach to more explicit instruction.

Children's literature plays an important role in Morrow's literacy environment. Literature serves as a model for language learning and provides strong motivation for learning to read and write. It is a springboard for many literacy-related activities. Most important, literature is a way of knowing. It is shaped around story—a primary act of human minds. Morrow is also aware that in early literacy development, materials designed for instructional purposes are necessary for skill development and to attain national, state, and local standards for literacy learning.

Morrow recognizes the importance of parents, siblings, grandparents, and other caregivers reading to children and enjoying the books together. She shows how reading to babies influences their grasp of language and story patterns that serve them well as they learn to read and write. She illustrates how children learn concepts about print, book handling, and conventions of stories as they interact with books. Morrow establishes that adults teach by example as they enjoy shared reading and shared writing with children. She shows the impact of having a literacy center in a classroom and the effects of storybook reading aloud by a teacher. She illustrates that when children know authors and illustrators as real people, they want to read their work and write in a manner similar to them. Morrow states that storytelling is similar to reading aloud in its impact on children. She also recognizes the necessity of skills that involve learning concepts about print and books. For example, children need to develop phonemic awareness, alphabetic principles, and phonics for reading success. They also must learn to construct meaning from text by learning strategies for comprehension. Speaking from her own experiences as a teacher, researcher, parent, and grandparent, Morrow charts a path that leads to successful literacy learning.

Lesley Mandel Morrow has taken a long view of literacy development in the early years, showing its historical roots. She also knows and draws on the research of today's leaders because she is a member of that research community. She succinctly summarizes language theories and relates current research to shape sound practices. She has conducted much of the original research herself, testimony to the fact that she can bridge the gap among theory, research, and practice. Her examples are anchored in real classroom experiences—her own and those of other teachers with whom she works collaboratively. The examples are authentic and add credibility to the content of this book.

Morrow also spends a significant amount of time on organizing and managing language arts throughout the day. In case studies and outlines, she takes the reader step by step to show what exemplary literacy instruction looks like. Her book is filled with photographs, figures, and illustrations that take us into classrooms, and a new Strategies for the Classroom section that provides tear-out practical ideas and materials to take right to the classroom and use. The book also references online video clips where students can see strategies come to life in the classroom.

Dr. Morrow's treatment of literacy development is on the cutting edge of current knowledge. She is well informed about her subject and makes connections among all aspects of literacy learning. She is a sensitive observer and writer, letting children and teachers speak for themselves through their work.

Dr. Morrow states that few children learn to love books by themselves. Someone must lure them into the wonderful world of the written word. She shows us how to do that and enriches our lives and the lives of children through her work. Her contribution to the literacy development of children from birth through grade 3 is a lasting one.

Linda B. Gambrell
Distinguished Professor of Education
Clemson University

Preface

Literacy Development in the Early Years, Sixth Edition, is for teachers, reading specialists, administrators, students in teacher education programs, and parents. It is appropriate for graduate, undergraduate, and professional development courses in early literacy, and it complements texts on teaching reading in the elementary school, children's literature, child development, early childhood curriculum, and teaching language arts.

I wrote the book because of my special interest in literacy development in early childhood. I taught in preschool, kindergarten, and the primary grades; I was a reading specialist; and then I taught early childhood curriculum and literacy courses at the university level. My research has focused on instructional strategies in early literacy. Over the years, research in early literacy has generated new theory. It has implications for new instructional strategies and reinforces older practices based on little or no research to establish their validity. The book describes a program that nurtures literacy development from birth through third grade.

The ideas in the book are based on research. They have been tried and they have worked, but not all are appropriate for all teachers or all children. The good teacher functions most effectively with strategies he or she feels most comfortable with. The teacher needs to be a decision maker who thinks critically about the design of his or her literacy program and the selection of materials. Children come to school with diverse social, emotional, physical, and intellectual abilities and achievement levels. They have diverse cultural backgrounds, experiences, and exposures to literacy. All must be addressed appropriately.

Underlying this book is the merging of the art and the science of teaching. The science involves theories based on research findings that have generated instructional strategies. The book is also based on current standards for teaching literacy and current policy. Most of the book contains descriptions of strategies and steps for carrying them out. But the scientific research does not necessarily take into account individual differences among teachers and children. The art of teaching concentrates on those human variables. This book provides a comprehensive and balanced approach to early literacy instruction. Constructivist ideas that involve problem-solving techniques are blended with explicit direct instructional approaches so that teachers can decide what works best for the children they teach. There is a strong emphasis on learning to read through the integration of reading, writing, listening, thinking, and viewing. There is also a strong emphasis on the integration of these literacy skills into content area learning. Differentiation of instruction is a major theme. That theme suggests that teaching must be directed to the individual needs of every child and, in addition, there is a strong emphasis on the diverse nature of children.

The Introduction is a new feature that places you in an early childhood classroom immediately. Its purpose is to provide you with an exemplary model of excellent literacy instruction.

Chapter 1 provides a framework of theory, research, and policy from the past and present that has influenced strategies for developing early literacy.

Chapter 2 covers the important issues of assessment and provides the reader with concepts for authentic assessment, portfolio assessment, and standardized assessment. This chapter emphasizes how assessment must guide instruction and how they are connected. With this philosophy in mind, strategies for assessment are integrated into all chapters. In addition, a separate chapter is devoted to exploring the topic.

Chapter 3 is about the diversity in our classrooms. The chapter has been significantly expanded from the last edition because of the diverse nature of our children. There is an emphasis on English language learners in the chapter as well as discussion of special learning needs such as learning disabilities, physical disabilities, gifted children, and others. This chapter provides strategies for teaching children who are diverse in many ways. However, meeting the needs of these individuals is focused on throughout the book. An icon indicates that a particular strategy is important not only for native speakers but for English language learners (ELL) as well.

Chapters 4 through 8 deal with oral language and vocabulary development, word analysis, comprehension, writing, and motivating children to want to read. These chapters discuss theory and research—specifically, developmental trends, instructional strategies, and methods for assessment. The book views the development of literacy skills (reading, writing, and oral language) as concurrent and interrelated; the development of one enhances the development of the others. Furthermore, the theories, stages, acquisition, and strategies associated with each are similar, and it is difficult to separate them entirely. To make the volume more readable, however, I have treated the various areas of literacy in different chapters.

Chapter 9 provides the preparation and management of the components presented in the book that are organized to create a successful program. This chapter emphasizes the interrelatedness of the areas of literacy and describes how they can be integrated into the entire school day within content areas. Ways of organizing the school day are discussed, as are how to organize whole-group, small-group, and individualized instruction. An area of extreme importance to teachers is how children can learn to work independently at centers while teachers instruct small groups to meet achievement needs. This is accomplished through differentiation of instruction.

Chapter 10 discusses the strong influence of the home on the development of literacy, especially in a child's earliest years. It discusses broad perspectives concerning family literacy, such as integrated home/school programs, intergenerational programs, and sensitivity to cultural differences to provide programs that are not intrusive but build on the strengths of the families being served.

Each chapter begins with questions to focus on while reading the text. Important vocabulary in the chapter is listed under the Focus Questions. These Focus Questions are followed by a vignette from the classroom, theory and research, and then practice and assessment. Each chapter ends with suggested activities, questions, and ideas for the classroom written by classroom teachers for all children from all backgrounds. A new feature includes reference to MyEducationLab, which consists of online videos related to each chapter. The appendixes supplement the text with lists of materials that teachers use in carrying out a successful program to develop early literacy. Appendix G offers the instructor ideas for his or her college classroom. Key words dealing with early literacy development are defined in the glossary at the end of the book. The Strategies for the Classroom perforated pages at the end of the book include ideas for activities and center materials to create for field experiences, student teaching, or for your own classroom. An online Instructor's Manual is also available.

New Features of the Sixth Edition

New features of the sixth edition include:

- The book begins with a case study illustrating exemplary teaching of the language arts in an early childhood classroom. The purpose of the case study at the beginning is to set the stage for specifics to come in the rest of the book and provide a total picture of what a rich literacy environment looks like right at the start.

- A video component for every chapter is included in MyEducationLab. Students will have an ID number to allow them to go online and view videos illustrating strategies discussed throughout the book.

- Fifty-one new pages of classroom activities related to each chapter at the end of the book. The pages are perforated for students to take out and photocopy. These pages provide strategies and center materials to create and use in field experiences, student teaching, or their own classrooms.

- A new Integrated Language Arts Unit in the Appendix called *Animals around the World* has a strong multicultural theme.

- More extensive coverage of issues concerning English language learners within the chapter on diversity and throughout the book

- Continued emphasis on research on early literacy development, including findings from the National Reading Panel, National Early Literacy Panel, Preventing Reading Difficulties, Reading First, The Rand Report, and the implications of the No Child Left Behind legislation

- A significant number of new photographs, tables, and illustrations

- The methods chapters have been enhanced with more strategies and skills for literacy development related to language development, phonological awareness, phonics, comprehension, motivation, writing, and spelling development. Dialogue to help teachers deliver the instruction is provided.

- Updated appendixes for children's literature, children's television shows with associated books, early literacy software and websites for teachers and children

- New current children's literature added to activity samples in the book

- More discussion about the integration of the language arts into content area teaching and literacy and play

- More suggestions for how to organize differentiation of instruction through the preparation of activities and materials

- A strong emphasis on how to organize children with similar needs for small group instruction

Your Class. Your Career. Everyone's Future

MyEducationLab is a research-based learning tool that brings teaching to life. Through authentic in-class video footage, interactive simulations, rich case studies, examples of authentic teacher and student work, and more, MyEducationLab prepares you for your teaching career by showing what quality instruction looks like.

PEARSON
myeducationlab
Where the Classroom Comes to Life

MyEducationLab is easy to use! At the end of every chapter in the textbook, you will find the MyEducationLab logo with activities and exercises that correlate material you've just read in the chapter to your reading/viewing of multimedia assets on the MyEducationLab site. These assets include:

Video: The authentic classroom videos in MyEducationLab show how real teachers handle actual classroom situations.

Case Studies: A diverse set of robust cases illustrate the realities of teaching and offer valuable perspectives on common issues and challenges in education.

Simulations: Created by the IRIS Center at Vanderbilt University, these interactive simulations give you hands-on practice at adapting instruction for a full spectrum of learners.

Questions: A series of questions related to the videos help you reflect on them.

Readings: Specially selected, topically relevant articles from ASCD's renowned *Educational Leadership* journal expand and enrich your perspectives on key issues and topics.

Student & Teacher Artifacts: Authentic preK–12 student and teacher classroom artifacts are tied to course topics and offer you practice in working with the actual types of materials you will encounter daily as teachers.

Other Resources:

Lesson & Portfolio Builders: With this effective and easy-to-use tool, you can create, update, and share standards-based lesson plans and portfolios.

News Articles: Looking for current issues in education? Our collection offers quick access to hundreds of relevant articles from the New York Times Educational News Feed.

Acknowledgments

To the many individuals who helped in the preparation of the 6th edition, I extend my heartfelt thanks: Paula Batsiyan, Elizabeth Freitag, Lisa Fazzi, Kathy Minto, and Sara Stofik. Thanks also to those who who helped with the first, second, third, fourth, and fifth editions: Julie Anastasi, Lara Heyer, Kristen Valvanis, Patricia Addonizio, Susan Burks, Kathleen Cunningham, Katie Farrell, Donna Fino Nagi, Mary Ann Gavin, Laura Babarca, Tricia Lyons, Melody Murray Olsen, Michele Preole, Mary Joyce Santoloci, Sari Schnipper, Karen Szabo, Patricia DeWitt, Erica Erlanger, Michael Gravois, Katherine Heiss, Pamela Kelliher, Lisa Lozak, Stacey Rog, Monica Saraiya, Amy Sass, and Connie Zauderer.

I am grateful also to the teachers and administrators who helped with past editions and this new edition: Stephanie Adams, Ellen Abere, Bonita Bartholomew, Maxine Bell, Karen Buda, Pat Burton, Barbara Callister, Jennifer Castio, Mehzga Colucci, Tom DelCasale, Judy DeVincenzo, Fran Diamente, Tami-Lyn Eisen, Arlene Hall, David Harris, Lori Harrje, Catherine Hickey, Adriann Jean-Denis, Noreen Johnson, Tracy Kahn, Linda Keefe, Sheryl King, Penelope Lattimer, Gail Martinez, Nancy Mason, Joyce McGee, Carna Meechem, Dennis Monaghan, Stephanie Moretti, Joyce Ng, Susan Nitto, Ellen O'Connor, Catherine Ogletree, Lucy Oman, Barbara Oxfeld, Mary Payton, Tammye Pelovitz, Cynthia Peters, John Quintaglie, Robert Rosado, Sonia Satterwhite, Joyce Schenkman, Linda Schifflette, Christine Temple, Patty Thaxton, and Margaret Youssef.

Thank you, Andrea Shane, Milton Mandel, Howard Manson, Cheryl Devine, Kate Brach, Tami-Lyn Eisen, Danielle Lynch, Lynn Cohen, Lisa Fazzi, Lisa Rosenfeld, Jennifer Chiaramida, Kelly Lamar, and Amy Sass for many of the photographs, and to Pamela Cromey and Michael Gravois for many of the illustrations.

I'd like to extend my appreciation to Aurora Martínez, Executive Editor at Allyn and Bacon, for supporting the sixth edition of this book, and for the guidance she offered during the revision process. Aurora is an attentive editor with excellent suggestions, patience, and supportive comments.

Thank you, in particular, to the children I have taught, my college students, and the excellent teachers I have observed and from whom I've learned so much. I am grateful to the researchers in early literacy who have provided exciting information in the field. I consider this book a cooperative effort as a result of the contributions of so many in both direct and indirect ways. I would also like to thank those who work with Aurora: Judith Fiske, Kristina Mose-Libon, and Kara Kikel for their guidance. Thanks also to Linda Zuk for her work on production, and to Joel Gendron and Brent Horbatt for working with me on the cover.

To those who reviewed the sixth edition of the book and offered suggestions for what to include, I appreciate your careful analysis and thoughtful comments. To the college professors, college students, teachers, and parents who purchased the book and demonstrated their support for the publication, the sixth edition was made possible by you.

Finally, I think my parents, Mary and Milton Mandel, who provided a literacy-rich environment for me and a work ethic that gave me the ambition to take on this task. And to my family, specifically Stephanie Morrow and Doug Bushell for their love and friendship, and my grandson James and granddaughter Natalie for demonstrating the validity of many of the concepts expressed in the book.

L.M.M.

Introduction

A Look at an Exemplary Language Arts Classroom

Before you begin reading, carry out this activity from the Strategies for the Classroom section entitled Priorities in Teaching Early Literacy

Before you read the chapter, tear out the reproducible page in the Strategies for the Classroom section on page S-2 entitled *Priorities in Teaching Early Literacy*. Include your name and the date. List what you believe to be the most important elements in the teaching of literacy for young children from preK to grade 3. Keep the list brief. When your list is complete, go back and order it from the most important element ranked as #1 to the least important element. Keep this list and, when you finish reading the book, fill out the same form again: Compare the two. Have your ideas changed?

In this introduction I describe an early childhood teacher and her children in class at the end of the first-grade year. The purpose of this introduction is to give you a glance at what can be and should be an exemplary early childhood classroom. This will provide a framework for what you will read in the rest of the book. It is important to look at the whole picture at the beginning of the book, to study the parts through the middle of the book, and to go back to the whole again at the end. In the description of this classroom, many critical components, materials, and routines of exemplary literacy instruction are discussed. I recommend that the introduction be read again after reading the entire book.

Introduction to the Teacher and Students

Joan Fry has been teaching kindergarten for the past 7 years. Recently, she completed a master's degree, which also included a reading specialist certification. She teaches in a middle-income community. She has 22 students in her class, including 6 Caucasian children, 6 Asian American, 6 African American, and 4 Hispanic. Twenty percent of Suzanne's class speaks one of four languages at home: Spanish, Japanese, Hindi, or Mandarin Chinese. Thirteen students are boys and nine are girls. There is a full-time aide who is assigned to one student who is physically disabled and uses a wheelchair.

Joan's philosophy of teaching includes integration of the curriculum so that students can build connections between content areas. She purposefully integrates her literacy skill development in reading, writing, listening, speaking, and viewing with her social studies and science themes as much as possible. Her small-group literacy instruction emphasizes explicitly specific skill development.

Ms. Fry has a special interest in using informational texts. She recognizes that children gain background knowledge and vocabulary using expository material. She is aware that adults read informational text in a variety of forms such as how-to manuals, applications, instructions, and websites, and that children must be prepared for this at a young age.

Setting the Stage for Joan's Teaching

Joan's classroom is warm and inviting, with well-defined centers. The displays on the walls clearly reflect the theme being studied and show considerable evidence of the children's growing literacy development. The displays include charts that Joan has written with the children, samples of children's writing, or children's art-work. Joan has an easel with chart paper for the morning message, a calendar, weather chart, temperature graph, helper chart, a daily schedule, classroom rules, a pocket chart, and a word wall in the area where she teaches the whole group.

Joan's largest center is the literacy center, which has a rug for independent reading and is also used for whole-class meetings. The area includes lots of space for storing books. One set of shelves holds books organized in two different ways. There are baskets of books leveled for difficulty that coordinate with Joan's small-group reading instruction. For example, students reading books in the green basket during small-group instruction know that these books are ones they can read independently. Other shelves hold baskets organized by themes, such as dinosaurs, sports, and weather. Joan rotates books in the baskets monthly. Colored stickers on the books and baskets assist students in returning them to the correct spot. Student-made class books and stories are displayed in another basket. Books about the current theme are on an open-faced shelf.

The **literacy center** has flannel board characters and a flannel board, puppets, and props for storytelling. There is a rocking chair for the teacher and other adults to use to read to the class. The children use the rocking chair to read independently and to read to each other. The listening area in the literacy center has a CD/tape player for listening to stories. There are manipulative materials for learning about print, which include magnetic letters, puzzle rhyme cards, and letter chunks on small tiles for making words.

The **writing center** is an extension of the literacy center. There is a round table for small groups of children to meet with the teacher. Shelves hold many types of paper, lined and unlined, a stapler, markers, crayons, colored pencils, dictionaries, alphabet stamps, and ink stamp pads. A word wall in the writing center has each of the letters of the alphabet taped on horizontally. When the children learn a new word, it is written on a card and taped under the letter it begins with on the word wall. Children refer to the words when they need a spelling word or to practice reading. During instruction, children may be asked to think of words that begin with the same letter and sound as a word on the word wall or to think of words that rhyme with a word on the word wall. Joan places her students' names on the word wall and adds high-frequency sight words that her children are expected to learn.

Joan's *science center* provides a home for the class guinea pig, rabbit, and hermit crab. Equipment in this center includes plants, magnets, magnifying glasses, and objects that sink and float. Materials are added to match the themes being studied, and there are always new hands-on experiments for students to complete.

The *dramatic play center* includes a table and chairs and a bookshelf. Changes are made to the area to reflect the themes studied during the year. This center has been converted into a restaurant where children take orders, read menus, and check their bills. The restaurant helps with learning about multicultural food and customs. This year the class has had an Italian, Chinese, Mexican, Portuguese, Jewish deli, and Japanese restaurant. Dramatic play settings have also included a newspaper office, a post office, and a travel agency.

The *block center* includes wooden blocks of all sizes and shapes and other toys for construction such as Lego. There are toy trucks, cars, trains, buses, people, and animals in this area and labels designating where the different toys go. There are 5 × 8 cards and tape for labeling structures created by the children. There are several signs written by children such as "Please Save" on buildings under construction and signs naming finished structures. Children sign their names on the labels.

Located near the sink is the *art center*, which contains an easel, table and chairs. There are scissors, markers, crayons, and paper of many colors, types, and sizes. There are collage materials such as cotton balls, doilies, foil, wallpaper, stickers, and paste.

The *math center* contains math manipulatives for counting, adding, measuring, weighing, graphing, and distinguishing shapes. There are felt numbers to use on the felt board, magnetic numbers for magnetic boards, numbers to sequence in a pocket chart, and geometric shapes such as squares, triangles, cylinders, and rectangles.

The children sit at desks placed in pods of four. In a quiet corner of the room there is a round table, which Joan uses for small-group instruction. Shelves near the table have materials for small groups, such as letters of the alphabet, rhyming cards, leveled books, sentence strips, index cards, white boards, markers, and word-study games.

Center Management

Joan uses her centers daily, since primary-grade children learn best when they are manipulating materials and collaborating with peers. To ensure that students work at three specific centers each day, Joan designed a contract on which she indicates the centers where children are expected to work. The contract has the name of each center and an icon representing the center. These same labels are at the actual centers. When children complete work in a center, they check it off on their contracts. The completed work from a center is placed in the basket labeled Finished Work. At the end of each day, Joan reviews completed work from the centers and assigns centers for the next day. Any incomplete work, or work that indicates a child needs help with a concept, is placed in the Unfinished folder. Each day a time is set aside for completing unfinished work. If children have time after completing their three daily centers, they may choose other centers to work in. Thus, children have a combination of required activities in centers assigned by Joan and self-selected activities in centers of their choice.

Assessing Students to Determine Instructional Needs

To provide instruction to meet the varied reading and writing levels of her students, Joan spends considerable time assessing them with formal and informal measures. In September, January, and June, she assesses students' knowledge about phonics, the ability to read sight words, and their reading comprehension, fluency, and writing ability. She plans instruction based on the needs she identifies. Joan takes monthly running records for each child. This identifies the types of errors that children make, the decoding strategies they use, and their comprehension and reading level. A comparison of previous running records to new ones indicates student progress. Joan writes anecdotal notes about student behavior that indicate both achievement and where they may be having difficulties. She collects samples of children's writing, evaluates them, and places these materials in student portfolios. Joan also observes students for social, emotional, and physical development.

Small-Group Reading Instruction

Joan has developed a schedule that allows her to work with small groups of children to develop reading skills. Using the assessment information she collects, she places students with similar needs together for small-group instruction. As she works with children, she takes careful notes regarding progress in literacy and adjusts the members of her various groups as needed. While in small groups, Joan provides instruction in skills for the children she is working with. She works on phonics skills, comprehension, fluency, writing, and vocabulary development. She currently has four small groups and meets with each group three times a week. On Fridays she attends to children's special needs. Joan meets with those students who are struggling more often than are other groups.

Joan's Daily Schedule

8:45   When children arrive at school, they do the following:
        Carry out their jobs
        Make entries in their journals
        Complete unfinished work and practice skills needing extra attention

9:00   The group meets as a whole for the morning meeting
        Morning greetings are shared.
        The calendar and weather are discussed.
        The schedule for the day is reviewed.
        The morning message is read and added to.
        There are singing and movement activities.
        The teacher reads a book associated with the theme being studied.
        There is a whole-group minilesson on a skill outlined in the curriculum.

9:30   Small-group reading instruction and center activities

10:30   Snack

10:45   Writing block (interactive writing, mini-lesson, and writing workshop)

11:45   Lunch and indoor or outdoor play

12:40   Independent reading

1:00   Math

1:40   Theme-related activities in social studies or science in which reading and writing activities are used

2:15   Creative arts, music, or gym (specials)

2:50   Closing circle
        Reading aloud
        Sharing and reviewing activities of the day
        Planning for tomorrow

A Typical Day in Joan's Classroom

During this week, Joan and her children are studying dinosaurs. In her classroom, reading, writing, listening, speaking, and content area subjects are integrated into the dinosaur theme. On Monday she organizes activities for the week.

It is 8:45 on Monday morning and Joan's room fills with quiet chatter as her students arrive. Classical music plays in the background as children complete their morning routines. Children move their nametags on the attendance board from the side labeled *Not Here* to *Here* and place their name stickers into the *Buy Lunch* or *Milk* can. Some children cluster around the easel, where Joan has written the morning message and the question of the day. It says, "Good morning, children. Today is Monday, March 4th. We will have Art today as our special. Do you like dinosaurs?" *Yes* or *No* "If you said yes, why do you like them? If you said no, why don't you like them?"

Students are used to having *yes* or *no* questions and respond with tally marks, under the words *yes* and *no*. Students check the helper chart for jobs such as feeding the animals, watering plants, and recording the temperature and day's weather on the weather graph. The *zookeeper* reads the list posted by the animal cages to make sure he has completed all his tasks. Joan puts pictures next to each step to help with reading the chart. This is particularly useful with struggling readers and ELL students.

Students know it is time for writing their *weekend news* in their journals. Joan greets each child as she circulates among the writers, gently reminding some children about punctuation they might be missing, reminding them to use the word wall to spell needed words, and the like. As she listens to completed entries, she has the opportunity to chat with the children about their weekend. When the 2-minute warning bell rings, several children are already in the meeting area on the rug in the literacy center reading books, alone or with a partner. Those still writing begin to put away their materials and place their unfinished work in the Not Finished basket. They will be able to complete their entries later in the day during center time. Once the student in charge shakes the tambourine announcing morning meeting, everyone gathers and forms a circle on the rug.

The Morning Meeting

Joan says, "Good morning," and the children say good morning to each other and shake hands around the circle. Because they are beginning the new month of March, they echo read and then choral read a poem about the month. Joan wrote the poem on chart paper. At the end of the month the children will illustrate personal copies of the poem and place it in their Poem Books, along with other poems for each month. The *calendar person*, *weather reporter*, and *schedule person* lead the class in these activities. Joan records the attendance and lunch count, which the messenger takes to the office.

Joan leads the class in reading the *morning message* together. The children discuss the results of the tally of today's question, "Do you like dinosaurs?" For those who said no, they tell why they don't like dinosaurs. For those who said yes, they discuss why they like them. Sophia said she didn't think she liked dinosaurs because they looked scary. Kim thought they were interesting and couldn't believe there were so many kinds.

Joan asked the children to look at the morning message again. It said, *"Good morning, children. Today is Monday, March 4th. We will have Art today as our special. Do you like dinosaurs?"* Yes No *"If you said yes, why do you like them? If you said no, why don't you like them?"* She asked the children to identify the long and short vowels in the morning message by circling short vowels in red and long vowels in blue. They did so by volunteering. This led to a discussion about *r*-controlled vowels, since there were a few words, such as *Art* and *March*, in the message that make the vowel sound neither long nor short.

Joan has a poem about dinosaurs hanging on another chart for the theme being studied. After the first reading, the children echo read the poem with their teacher. Then she has them do an antiphonal choral reading: the boys read the first line and the girls read the second. Joan then covers a different word in each sentence of the poem with a Post-It. She asks the children to read a sentence and fill in the *blank* for the covered word. They go back to the beginning and read until the first covered word.

Joan: When I get all *blank* I just growl. What word could be placed in the blank space? Think what might make a dinosaur growl.

Student 1: When he gets all mad.

Joan: When I get all mad, I just growl. Does that make sense?

Class: Yes.

Joan: Does it match what you know about dinosaurs?

Student 2: Well, some dinosaurs get mad, but maybe not all of them.

Joan: So it does make sense.

Student 3: Yes it makes sense, but the dinosaur could be hungry too.

Joan writes the words *mad* and *hungry* on separate 5 × 8 cards and proceeds in the same manner until the class has four words on cards that could fit into the sentence. The words suggested were *mad, tired, hungry,* and *sad.*

Joan: Words need to make sense in the sentence and they need to match the letters in the words we are reading.

Student 3: You have to look at the letters to figure out the word, and the rest of the sentence helps you to figure out if the word you came up with makes sense.

Joan: Right. Let's check the letters and see which word matches.

They check *mad*, but none of the letters match; they check *tired* and nothing matches; they check *hungry* and all the letters match. The class continues with filling in the words left out on the chart. When all the words are figured out, Joan choral reads it with the children again. Before circle time ends, Joan puts on some music for the children to walk around the room acting like dinosaurs.

Center Time

Joan spends a few minutes reviewing the center activities and describing new activities placed in the centers for the exploration of dinosaurs. Centers have materials that are in place over a period of time, and they are enriched with activities that reflect the current theme and skills that need to be practiced. A description of what has been added to each center related to the dinosaur theme follows.

Writing Center: Dinosaur-bordered writing paper, dinosaur-shaped books, a dinosaur dictionary, a dinosaur-shaped poster with words about dinosaurs.

Literacy Center: Fiction and nonfiction dinosaur books, dinosaur books with accompanying CDs, a dinosaur vocabulary puzzle, a dinosaur concentration memory game, a teacher-made dinosaur lotto game.

Computer Center: *Eyewitness Virtual Reality: Dinosaur Hunter* (DK Multimedia) for printing dinosaur stationary, postcards, posters, and masks and for visiting a virtual museum exhibit about dinosaurs.

Science: Small skulls and old animal bones, along with a magnifying glass and rubber gloves to examine the bones and draw what they think the entire animal may have looked like; dinosaur pictures to sort into meat eaters and plant eaters; other pictures to be sorted into "walked on two feet" and "walked on four feet." There are recording sheets for all activities.

Math: Measuring tools in a basket and sheets to record the measurement of various plaster bones of dinosaurs; dinosaur counters; little plastic dinosaurs in an estimation jar; a basket containing 50 little dinosaurs numbered from 1 to 50 to be put in sequential order.

Blocks: Toy dinosaurs, trees, bushes, and some dinosaur books are placed in the block center.

Art Center: Dinosaur stencils and dinosaur stamps are added to the art center. There are clay models of dinosaurs and many pictures of dinosaurs to help students make their own sculptures.

Dramatic Play: The dramatic play area is transformed into a paleontologist's office with chicken bones embedded in plaster of paris. Students use carving tools and small hammers to remove the bones; they wear safety goggles. There are paper and pencils for labeling bones, trays to display them, dinosaur books, and posters of fossils and dinosaurs.

After Joan reviews center activities, her students look at their contracts and go off to do their activities. Activities that must be done are skills that students need practice in, such as matching pictures with letters to reinforce letter–sound knowledge. When they complete the *have to* activities, children may select any center, such as the block area or art. On their contracts, children check off centers that they worked in.

Small-Group Reading Instruction

The first group that Joan sees is reviewing a book they have read before. Joan does a walk through the book to introduce it to the children by looking at the pictures and talking about each page. During the book walk, the students are asked to find particular vocabulary words that are new to them and could cause some difficulty when first read. They also discuss the names of the animals in the book. As the group reads, Joan notices that one student read the book without any errors and read it quickly. Joan makes a note to think about moving him to a different reading group that would be more challenging. After the children finish reading, Joan asks everyone to turn to page 7. "I noticed that James read, 'We saw the pot bear' and then changed it to 'polar bear,' since he looked back at the letters and took into account the meaning of the sentence. He remembered that the words have to match the letters and what you read has to make sense."

While the children were reading, Joan did a running record on one child. She noted that this student read *seals* instead of *otters* and said *pander bears* instead of *bears*. Joan will help this child pay more attention to the print when working with him.

Joan's next group will be reading a different and more difficult book. This group is more advanced than the first. The group has worked with this book before; therefore, the lesson that Joan will carry out will help her children to become more independent readers. She will teach them how to figure out unknown words by using the meaning of a sentence and by looking at the letters in the words. They begin with a game called Guess the Covered Word, similar to an activity they used during the morning message. This time the covered word in the sentence "I can *blank* fast" is the word *run*. The children are encouraged to select a word that makes sense in the sentence and then to look at the letters in the word to see which is the correct word. Words generated for the missing word were *walk, eat, hop, sleep,* and *run*. The activity is repeated in other sentences throughout this book.

The next group is reading another book. In this lesson Joan will focus on looking at ending sounds to figure out words. Joan has written "I am *go* to the store" on the chart. She reads the sentence and the children quickly point out that it does not sound right. Joan writes a second sentence, "I am *going* to the store." They identify the difference in the two sentences by pointing to the words *go* and *going*. Joan reminds them how they have to look at the ends of words as well as the beginning of words when reading. They read the book with special attention to the word endings. After the first reading, she starts a discussion to demonstrate their ability to infer and asks them if they could think of another way to end the story.

Snack

For a snack there are dinosaur animal crackers and what Joan is calling dinosaur juice. Children read independently when finished with the snack.

Writing Workshop

The children gather for writing in the whole-class meeting area. Joan prepares them for a school-wide activity. They will survey all students in the school to find out what their favorite dinosaurs are. Joan uses a shared writing activity to draft a letter asking the teachers and children in other classrooms to participate. She begins by reviewing the format of a letter, which was introduced during a previous unit on the post office. They discuss how to begin a letter and how to end a letter. Using chart paper, Joan asks the children to offer suggestions to start the letter and write the letter. The children and their teacher compose the text. Joan types the letter and distributes it to each classroom. The original shared writing chart will be posted on the cafeteria door.

Next, Joan introduces the writing activity for the week. The children will be writing informational texts about dinosaurs. They are each to select the one dinosaur they like the most and answer the following questions before they do their writing.

What are the parts of your dinosaur? What does your dinosaur eat? Where did your dinosaur live? What else do you know about your dinosaur?

Each child selects a partner to work with and a dinosaur to study. Jamal and Damien chose a tyrannosaur. Joan has books to look up information in the categories outlined and has a website for children to review. Each child takes two sections of the book to write about and makes notes.

The children have learned from the writing process that brainstorming is crucial before you write. Brainstorming helps children decide what they will write. Tuesday they will continue to browse through dinosaur books for information and start to write. Children will write the facts collected into informational stories and illustrate them. When the activity is completed at the end of the week, children will share their informational dinosaur stories.

Lunch and Play

Lunch is in the cafeteria. After eating, if weather permits, the children play outside. If not, they play in the gym or their classroom.

Independent Reading

To instill the joy of reading, children can select from dinosaur books to read with a partner or alone. At the end of the independent-reading period, they fill out a card telling the book read and the number of pages read.

Math

There is a specific math curriculum that Joan follows in her school. But she also ties her math to her theme and literacy. Today the class gathers in the meeting area to brainstorm a list of as many dinosaurs as they can name. Using the index of a dinosaur encyclopedia to verify spelling and locate a picture of each dinosaur, the names are written on a large chart. They also search a dinosaur site on the Internet. After creating a list of 10 dinosaurs, children are asked to vote for their favorite dinosaur, while a student records the votes. Six dinosaurs received the most: Allosaurua, Iguanodon, Spinosaurus, Stegosaurus, Triceratops, and Tyrannosaurus.

Special Theme Activity and Center Time

Joan has planned an art activity that is theme related. Everyone will contribute to a mural and construct a habitat environment for dinosaur sculptures the children will be creating with the art teacher. To introduce the mural and habitat activity, everyone listens as Joan explains the details. Children talk about a piece of the mural they would like to work on, such as trees, vines, a cave, a river, or plants. Joan writes the children's names on a chart with the item they would like to draw with markers.

One third of the students remain on the carpet to work on the mural. These children huddle around books depicting plants and trees from the time of the dinosaurs. Animated discussions take place as each child draws food, shelter, water, and other elements necessary to sustain dinosaur life. The rest of the children use this time to complete unfinished journal writing or center work. If they have completed all their work, they can select any center activity they wish. This is a playful time of the day, and children build with blocks, play in the dramatic play area, do an art project, explore in the science area, or look at books. Students who did not get to work on the mural today will have a chance another day during the week.

Art, Music, Gym

At this time of day the class goes to a special teacher for art, music, or gym. Joan has coordinated with these teachers about the theme being studied, so the art teacher is working on paper mache dinosaur sculptures with the children, the music teacher has found some great dinosaur songs and one about habitats as well, and the gym teacher has thought of some movement activities to help the students walk like dinosaurs.

End of Day Circle Time

At the end of the day, students gather in the meeting area for a read aloud and a review of the day. Joan has selected an informational book about dinosaurs. This book will provide children with more facts and vocabulary that they can use in their writing and for the mural habitat they are creating. Before she reads the book, she points out some of the features of this informational book. There is a table of contents that includes each chapter and there is a glossary of new words. There are labels on figures, captions describing pictures, headings introducing new topics, and new vocabulary written in a bolder and bigger print than the rest of the words. Joan knows this book will introduce children to a topic not yet discussed in class: the differences between dinosaurs that were plant eaters and meat eaters. After reading, Joan helps children list the characteristics of plant eating and meat eating dinosaurs on an interactive writing chart. There were new dinosaur terms to learn, such as *armored plates, carnivore,* and *extinct.*

In another shared reading at the end of the next day, Joan focused on finding facts in informational text. When she read, she asked the children to listen for the facts about dinosaurs and the elements in the book that make it informational.

After reading Joan asked, "What elements made this book an informational story?"

Student 1: There aren't characters that have a story to tell.

Student 2: It is about real things.

Student 3: You learn a lot of facts.

After the discussion, Joan made a web that includes the facts in the text. She drew a circle on a chart with the word *dinosaurs* written in the center. Then she drew lines radiating out from the center circle. Next she drew smaller circles connected to each line radiating out from the larger circle. As children recalled facts about dinosaurs, Joan wrote the words in one of the smaller circles. After writing the web, Joan and the children read it: Dinosaurs: *Big, Scary, Vegetarians, Meat Eaters, Dangerous, Extinct.*

Joan talked about how informational texts are also called nonfiction because everything is real instead of make-believe. One student raised her hand and said:

Student 1: I think the book is make-believe, because the pictures are drawings. If it was an informational book, there would be photographs that we take with cameras.

Student 2: But they can't have real photographs because dinosaurs are dead, and they didn't have photographs since they had no cameras when they were alive. We don't have any more dinosaurs. What is that word, they are? Oh yeah, they are *extinct.*

Before the end of school the class reviews the activities of the day. They discuss those they liked best, and they plan for the next day.

Tuesday: Learning More About Dinosaurs

Tuesday's schedule remains the same as on Monday, but with new books and writing assignments. The rest of the week in Joan's classroom they followed the same routines with morning messages, shared storybook readings, whole-group skill lessons, small-group instruction, center work, independent reading, writing workshop, and theme-related activities in social studies, science math, art, music, and play.

Summary

Joan's classroom allows children to have the opportunity to explore and experiment, and they have explicit instruction. They are expected to complete work assigned to them during small-group instruction or during whole-group lessons. However, they also have choices in the selection of activities a few times during the day. A lot of information is introduced during whole- and small-group lessons, and information is repeated and reviewed all week long. Children's individual needs are met during small-group reading instruction, writing workshop, and center time. Reading and writing are integrated in content-area learning. Children in Joan's classroom read and write all day long during all content areas, and her classroom is arranged so that children have access to varied materials and books.

Focus Questions

- Several theorists, philosophers, and psychologists are mentioned in the chapter. Name and describe the unique contribution of each to early childhood education.

- Describe the major thrust in different approaches to early literacy instruction from the early 1900s to the present.

- The emergent literacy and whole-language philosophies are considered constructivist approaches to literacy instruction. Describe the characteristics of these constructivist perspectives.

- What does integrating the language arts using thematic instruction mean?

- Describe the characteristics of the explicit, direct skill instruction that are associated with behaviorist learning theory.

- What do we mean when we speak of a balanced perspective on literacy instruction?

- What implications does the No Child Left Behind legislation have for early literacy instruction?

- **VOCABULARY:** behaviorist approach, assimilation, accommodation, scaffolding, reading readiness, emergent literacy, whole language, explicit instruction, constructivist theory, balanced approach to literacy instruction

- **Strategies** Tear out Strategies for the Classroom activity for Chapter 1 on pages S-3 to S-6. It provides you with a plan and materials to carry out a lesson with behaviorist-explicit instruction as well as a constructivist component.

PEARSON myeducationlab **VIDEO PREVIEW: Developing a Philosophy of Education** (3:55 minutes). Before reading this chapter, go to www.myeducationlab.com. Under the topic "Becoming a Reading Teacher," access and watch the video "Developing a Philosophy of Education."

Foundations of Early Literacy Development

Surveying the Past to the Present

What a dangerous activity reading is: teaching is. All this plastering of foreign stuff. Why plaster on at all when there's so much inside already? So much locked in? If only I could draw it out and use it as working material. If I had a light enough touch, it would just come out under its own volcanic power.

—Sylvia Ashton-Warner
Spinster (1959)

Four-year-old James and his mother were driving in the car to do some errands. As they approached the mall, James said, "Look Mommy, I can read those letters. M-A-C-Y-S. Those letters spell Sears." James's mother smiled and praised him. "That was great, James. You got every letter right. Now I'll read the sign for you; it says Macy's. This is another department store like Sears. You did some good thinking when you tried to read that word."

Not too long ago we would have chuckled at James's remarks as cute but incorrect. Today, we realize that he is demonstrating a great deal of literacy knowledge that needs to be recognized. First, he knows what letters are, and he can identify the ones in the sign. Next, he knows that letters spell words. He knows that words are read and have meaning. Although he did not read the word correctly, he made an informed guess. James was aware from background knowledge that this building was a department store, but even though he had never been to this one, he called it by a store name he knew. He was trying out some of his literacy knowledge on an adult who he knew was interested and willing to interact positively with him. His mother offered positive reinforcement for what he did know and support by modeling the correct response when he needed some help.

Babies begin to acquire information about literacy from the moment they are born. They continue to build on their knowledge of oral language, reading, and writing as they go through early childhood and beyond. A great deal of attention is now being focused on literacy development in early childhood, an area somewhat neglected in the past. Teachers, parents, and administrators did not perceive preschoolers as readers or writers. Their emphasis was on oral language development and preparation for reading. Because of increased research, thinking about early literacy has changed: Very young children are now viewed as individuals with literacy skills. Although the literacy skills of preschoolers and kindergartners are not conventional like adults', they must be acknowledged because they have implications for instructional practice.

Like a child's first words and first steps, learning to read and write should be an exciting, fulfilling, and rewarding experience. This book draws on research and blends it with theory, policy, and practice that have proved successful in developing literacy. It presents a program for developing literacy in children from birth to 8 years. It takes into account the joint position statement of the International Reading Association (IRA) and the National Association for the Education of Young Children entitled *Learning to Read and Write: Developmentally Appropriate Practices for Young Children* (1998) and the position statement of IRA *Literacy Development in the Preschool Years* (2005). It also takes into account the National Reading Panel Report (2000) and *Put Reading First* (2001), published by the U.S. Department of Education, as well as other work that will be documented throughout. The book is based on the following rationale:

1. Literacy learning begins in infancy.

2. Families need to provide a literacy-rich environment and literacy experiences at home to help children acquire skills. Families need to be actively involved in their children's literacy learning when they enter school.

3. Teachers must be aware that children come to school with varying types of prior knowledge about reading and writing that differ from one child to the next.

4. Children need to continue to develop reading and writing skills through experiences at school that build on their existing knowledge.

5. Literacy learning requires a supportive environment that builds positive feelings about self and literacy activities.

6. Literacy learning requires an environment rich with accessible materials and varied experiences.

7. Adults must serve as models for literacy behavior by scaffolding and demonstrating strategies to be learned.

8. During their literacy experiences, children should interact within a social context to share information. Such interactions help motivate them to learn from one another.

9. Early reading and writing experiences should be meaningful and concrete and should actively engage children.

10. Early reading and writing experiences need to provide systematic and explicit instruction on skills.

11. A literacy development program should focus on experiences that integrate reading, writing, listening, speaking, and viewing and content areas such as music, art, social studies, science, and play.

12. Diversity in cultural and language backgrounds must be acknowledged and addressed in early literacy development.

13. Differences in literacy development will vary and must be addressed with small-group and one-to-one differentiated instruction. Struggling readers, for example, must be provided for in early intervention programs or inclusion-based classroom programs.

14. Assessment of achievement should be frequent, match instructional strategies, and use multiple formats for evaluating student behavior.

15. Standards for early literacy grade-level benchmarks should be tied to instruction and assessment and used as a means for reaching goals for all children to read fluently by third grade.

16. Programs should be designed that are appropriate for the development of children being taught, with high, yet achievable, expectations.

17. Programs should be research based. For example, from the results of the National Reading Panel Report (2000) we know some of the needed components in reading instruction to ensure student success. These include phonemic awareness, phonics, vocabulary development, comprehension, and fluency. We also have preschool literacy variables determined by the National Early Literacy Panel to predict later achievement in decoding and reading comprehension (National Center for Family Literacy, 2004).

This book incorporates the work of philosophers, educators, psychologists, and researchers who have described how young children learn and what they need to be taught. The book emphasizes that literacy development occurs in prepared, literacy-rich environments where planned experiences facilitate development in language, reading, writing, listening, viewing, and speaking in coordination with content-area subjects. Though some chapters concentrate on language, reading, or writing, an important concern at all times is the integration of all these literacy dimensions.

Literacy development early in life must focus on both learning and teaching. Teachers include some explicit instruction, and children are encouraged to be actively involved in learning with other children in social settings, using materials they can explore and experiment with. A major focus of the book is to motivate children to view reading as relevant and associate it with pleasure and a source of information.

Learning Theories, Research, and Philosophies That Have Shaped Practices

Several important philosophers, theorists, psychologists, and educators have addressed learning in early childhood, including the issue of appropriate educational practice. These ideas represent varying responses to the question of whether learning is primarily a matter of the nature or the nurture of the child. All have strong implications for planning early literacy instruction.

Theory and Philosophy from the 1700s and 1800s

ROUSSEAU. Jean-Jacques Rousseau (1762) strongly recommended that a child's early education be natural. That is, children should only be asked to learn things for which they are developmentally ready. Rousseau advocated abandoning contrived instruction and instead allowing children to grow and learn with the freedom to be themselves. He believed that education follows the child's own development and readiness for learning. According to Rousseau, children learn through curiosity. He believed that children have individual ways of learning and that formal instruction can interfere with development. Rousseau's philosophy suggests that the role of the educator is to use strategies that mesh with the child's readiness to learn and that require as little intervention by an adult as possible.

PESTALOZZI. Johann Heinrich Pestalozzi (Rusk & Scotland, 1979) was influenced by Rousseau's natural learning ideas, but he added a dimension to them. He started his own school and developed principles for learning that combined natural elements with informal instruction. He found it unrealistic to expect children to learn totally on their own. Although Pestalozzi felt that children may be able to teach themselves to read, for example, he also felt that it was necessary for teachers or parents to create the conditions in which the reading process grows. He believed that the potential of a child develops through sensory manipulative experiences, so he designed lessons that involved manipulating objects he called gifts. Children learned about them through touch, smell, language, size, and shape.

FROEBEL. Friedrich Froebel's ideas (1974) were similar to his predecessors'. Like Rousseau, he believed in the natural unfolding of a child and followed Pestalozzi's ideas by providing plans for instructing young children. He is best known for emphasizing the importance of play in learning. He specified that the benefits of playing-to-learn require adult guidance and direction and a planned environment. Froebel saw the teacher as a designer of playful activities

According to Pestalozzi, Froebel, Dewey, and other philosophers and theorists, learning in early childhood occurs when youngsters have the opportunity to explore, experiment, and play at real-life experiences.

and experiences that facilitate learning. He was the first educator to design a systematic curriculum for young children, which included objects and materials. In handling and playing with these materials, children used psychomotor skills and learned about shape, color, size, measurement, and comparison. Many of his strategies are used in preschools and kindergartens today, such as circle time when the class sings songs and learns new ideas through discussion. He coined the term *kindergarten*, which means "children's garden." The phrase illustrates his philosophy that children, like plants, grow only if they are tended to and cared for. He referred to the child as a seed being cared for by the gardener, or teacher.

Moving into the Twentieth Century

English Language Learners

DEWEY. John Dewey's (1966) philosophy of early childhood education led to the concept of the child-centered curriculum, or *progressive education* as it was called. Dewey believed that the curriculum should be built around the interests of children. He agreed with Froebel that children learn best through play and in real-life settings. He maintained that social interactions encourage learning and that interests are the vehicles for learning information and skills. Dewey rejected the idea of teaching skills as ends unto themselves. He also believed that learning is maximized through integrating content areas.

Dewey significantly influenced programs in U.S. early childhood education throughout the twentieth century, especially from the 1920s through the 1950s. During these decades, preschools and kindergartens typically had different centers for different activities. Shelves in a "block corner" held various sizes and shapes of blocks, toy cars, trucks, and wooden figures of people. An art area contained easels with watercolors, crayons, paper, paste, scissors, construction paper, clay, and scraps of interesting materials, such as fabric, plastic foam, and pipe cleaners for making collages. The dramatic-play corner was set up like a kitchen, with sink, oven, refrigerator, empty food boxes, table and chairs, telephone, mirror, dolls, and some clothing for dressing up. Still another area held manipulative toys that taught concepts about color, shape, and size. A science area revealed a water-play table, shells, interesting rocks, plants, a class animal, magnets, and magnifying glasses. The music area usually had a piano, rhythm instruments, and at that time a record player. There was a rug for children to sit on when they came to sing by the piano. One corner of the room had a shelf of children's literature and soft pillows to lie on when looking at books.

The daily routine was similar in most of these settings. As children entered the classroom, they played with quiet toys. The teacher then called them to circle time to talk about the weather and the calendar. The conversation soon focused on a topic in social studies or science—animals or community helpers, for instance—with perhaps a song in keeping with the theme. Circle time was commonly followed by a long period called free play in which children could use the materials in the different areas of the room. There was minimal guidance during free play; children could explore and experiment with the materials. A snack, sometimes followed by a rest period, was an integral part of the daily routine. The day might also include a special lesson in art, social studies, or science appropriate to the unit being studied. Outdoor play allowed children to run, climb, play in sandboxes, and use riding toys. The teacher read a story daily, probably at the end of the day, often relating it to the topic being studied.

Reading and mathematics were not taught formally or as isolated skills. Instead, the teacher might ask a child to count out enough cookies for all the children in the class, to name the date on the calendar, or to compare the sizes of different children. There were no workbooks or commercial reading materials. Teachers led some informal activities that could eventually lead to reading, but they did not attempt to teach children to read. The letters of the alphabet might be found strung across the wall, the days of the week pointed out on a calendar, children's names written on their cubbies, and some other items in the room labeled with words. The general atmosphere was relaxed. The goal was to accustom children to school routines and make them comfortable in the school environment. The focus was on social, emotional, and physical development. There was no place in these programs for formal reading and writing instruction.

SKINNER AND BEHAVIORISM. According to behaviorists, the outcome of learning is a relatively permanent change in behavior that is caused by an individual's response to an experience or stimulus (Slavin, 1997). Behaviorists suggest that we learn through imitation and association and through conditioning, or a series of steps that are repeated so that the response becomes automatic. Skinner (1954) realized that human learning is not all automatic and unintentional. People themselves operate on their environment to produce learning. These purposeful actions are called *operants*. The individual learns to behave in certain ways as he or she interacts with the environment. Skinner also discovered in his research that positive reinforcement for a desired behavior increased the frequency of use of that behavior. From a behavioristic point of view, skills are acquired in a series of steps, small enough to avoid failure and frustration, with rewards at each level. Learning with a behavioristic perspective includes an organized program presented in a systematic and direct manner. Learning requires time on task, structure, routines, and practice. Behaviorist programs are skill based, with little time or concern for social, emotional, or physical development. The main concern is the acquisition of cognitive skills. The materials in behaviorist programs can be rated according to difficulty, can include programmed sequential lessons, and can have scripted guides for the teacher. In these programs, guides for teachers give the objective for learning for a specific page and then provide a script for the teacher similar to the following:

Teacher: ch, ch, ch: What sound is this?
Wait for Response: ch, ch, ch. Good.

Teacher: ch, ch, ch. Tell me ch.

Wait for Response: Yes ch, ch, Good.

(From S. Englemann and E. C. Bruner, Distar Reading I, An Instructional System. *Copyright 1969 by Science Research Associates. Reprinted with permission of McGraw-Hill Education.)*

Reading programs that use some behavioristic methods are DISTAR: Direct Instruction System for Teaching Arithmetic and Reading (Engleman & Bruner, 1968), Programmed Reading Series (Sullivan & Buchanan, 1963), and Success for All (Slavin, 1998).

MONTESSORI. Maria Montessori (1965) created a method of instruction that departed from the educators and philosophers mentioned thus far. Although she believed in the use of the senses to promote learning, her emphasis on the senses was not based on the natural unfolding of the child, the child's interests, or play. She believed that children needed early, orderly, systematic training in mastering one skill after another, so she supplied her teaching environment with materials for learning specific concepts to meet specific objectives and ways of using them. The use of the materials is modeled by the teacher and then provides the source of learning for the child. Children educated themselves by using these manipulatives, and because the materials were self-correcting, the children could determine their own errors and make corrections independently. All materials in the classroom were stored in their own containers, on a particular shelf, and in order of difficulty. According to Montessori, it is the role of the teacher and parent to watch for the child's sensitive periods for learning and take advantage of them by preparing the environment with appropriate materials and experiences for learning. In short, according to Montessori, the teacher is a guide who prepares an environment for learning. But unlike the educators already discussed, Montessori carefully designed learning materials to teach specific skills. These materials are attractive and sturdy and have influenced manipulatives we use for learning today. In Montessori's curriculum, children work with practical life materials first, which include activities such as buttoning clothes, pouring water, and scrubbing tables. There are precise steps to complete each task correctly. The second area of learning is called sensorial. Through the senses of touch, taste, smell, hearing, and sight, children learn about size, color, shape, and the like, by manipulating materials designed to teach these skills. Finally, the early childhood curriculum includes the learning of reading and math, which are taught using manipulative materials as much as possible. In math education, Montessori is well known for her colored beads that teach counting, addition, subtraction, multiplication, and division. Early reading instruction includes learning the sounds of letters with the help of beaded letter cards that are traced by the child as they make the sound. Sight words are taught using real objects and pictures. In the Montessori curriculum, which is drawn from behavioristic theory, children's natural curiosity and exploration are of less concern than their ability to work with specific materials to achieve a particular goal and do it correctly. Play is not as important as work, because it might waste precious opportunities for goal achievement. Montessori promotes independent learning and respect for the child. She insists on a systematic organization of the school day.

PIAGET. Jean Piaget's theory (Piaget & Inhelder, 1969) of cognitive development describes the intellectual capabilities of children at their different stages of cognitive development. The cognitive stages of development he describes include the following:

1. Sensorimotor period (0–2 years): Thinking is determined by a baby's sensory explorations related to what he hears, sees, tastes, and feels.
2. Preoperational period (2–7): A child's language develops and she begins to organize her world. The child's thinking is concrete.
3. Concrete operational period (7–11): The child begins his thought processes in the concrete. With the use of concrete objects, the child is able to move from there into some abstract ideas.
4. Formal operations period (11–adult): In this highest level of thinking, the person uses language to deal with abstract thoughts.

Trying to involve children in abstract thinking experiences during the pre-operational stages would be considered inappropriate. Piaget believed that a child acquires knowledge by interacting with the world. Educators who have applied his theories involve children in natural problem-solving situations where they learn through assimilation and accommodation. **Assimilation** means that the child incorporates new information into already existing schemes. That is, she interprets new information in terms of other information she has from the past. For example, when Michael saw a cat for the first time he said, "Look at the dog, Mommy." Michael used what he knew about four-legged animals from his past experience with dogs and applied it to the cat, an animal he had never seen before. **Accommodation** requires changing existing schemes to incorporate new information. A child accommodates when a new situation is unfamiliar. In this situation the child has to create a totally new response. For example, consider Michael, whose structure of meaning with respect to the class concept of dog is limited to what dogs do and look like, such as bark and have four legs. When he perceived a cat to be a dog, he had assimilated the new experience with reference to his present comprehension level. The complementary process of accommodation may be engaged when the child finds that the object is not a dog, rather a cat, and that the cat meows and doesn't bark. His conceptual understanding of cat must be refined to handle this apparent incongruity; he accommodates his reference system to fit the external reality more accurately.

According to Piaget, children need to be active participants in their own learning, constantly changing and reorganizing their knowledge. Piaget stressed that learning occurs when children interact in their environment with peers and adults. Educators who have incorporated Piaget's theories in curricula for early childhood education have designed constructivist-type programs: a setting with many real-life materials, including the opportunities to play, explore, experiment, and use language. A Piagetian preschool curriculum, called *High Scope*, encourages decision making, problem solving, self-discipline, goal setting, planning one's own activities, and cooperating with teachers and peers. Piaget agreed that young children should use their curiosity, inquisitiveness, and spontaneity to help themselves learn. Unlike Dewey, Piaget's theories interpreted into classroom practice do not stress content-area centers such as math and science. The Piaget curriculum has centers that involve children in cognitive activities such as these:

Piaget stressed that learning occurs when children interact with peers and adults in a social setting as they act on the environment.

1. *Language development:* Talking, listening to stories, describing, and the like.

2. *Classifying:* Children describe attributes of objects, notice sameness and differences, sort, match, and the like.

3. *Seriating:* Children arrange objects by color, size, shape, or other feature.

4. *Representing in different modalities:* Learning about something in many different ways; for example, to learn about an apple. We can eat it, make it into applesauce, draw an apple, write and read the word *apple,* sing a song about apples, and so on.

5. *Spatial relations:* Children are asked to put things together, take things apart, rearrange things, reshape things, see things from a different point of view, describe direction or distance, and so on.

VYGOTSKY. Lev S. Vygotsky's (1981) general theory of intellectual development, like Piaget's, suggests that learning occurs as children acquire new concepts or schemas. A *schema* is a mental structure in which we store information we know. We store information and call it to mind when we have to make predictions, generalizations, or inferences.

According to Vygotsky, all types of mental functions are acquired through social relationships. To extend or build a new concept, children must interact with others who provide feedback for their thoughts or help them to complete a task they could not do on their own. Children need to talk about new ideas in order to understand them. Parents and teachers provide the language children need to help them solve a problem. Children learn by internalizing the activities and language of others into their world. Vygotsky speaks of the "zone of proximal development," the period of time when a child can do some parts of a task, but not all. This is a sensitive time for learning and growth. The child needs the help of a more knowledgeable person to *scaffold* the new ideas. Adults scaffold by showing children how to complete a task or modeling what a particular behavior looks like. Scaffolding talk gives information about finishing a task and directs a child's attention to what she needs to know. When the help a child receives is internalized, he or she is capable of performing the new task alone. At this time, the teacher or parent must step back and allow the child to perform and practice the new skill independently.

The learning theories of the individuals discussed have contributed to the way we look at literacy development in early childhood education. Their ideas are the basis for early literacy instruction as it is described in this book. Particularly applicable among their concepts are the following:

1. Concern for a child's level of development—physical, social, emotional, and intellectual

2. Concern for prepared environments in which learning can take place

3. Emphasis on learning and on teaching

4. Emphasis on social interaction with supportive adults

5. Focus on learning through real experiences in meaningful and natural settings, as well as in settings for explicit teaching

6. Focus on actively engaging students in their own learning and the use of manipulative materials and experiences that are functional and interesting

7. Practicing and repeating skills learned

Practices in the Past: Early 1900s to the End of the 1950s

READING READINESS. Judging from the professional literature of the early 1900s, little attention was paid to a child's literacy development before he entered school. It was generally assumed that literacy began with formal instruction in first grade. A strong influence on reading instruction came from developmental psychologists like Gesell (1925), who advocated maturation as the most important factor in learning to read. Reading instruction was not given until the child was ready to read. Preschool and kindergarten teachers generally avoided reading instruction. Typically, they read to children; encouraged play, exploration, and problem solving; and led songs and discussions in circle times based on unit themes. Methods were child centered, with great concern for social, emotional, and physical development. This perspective was based on a constructivist learning theory.

Influenced by the climate of the times, Morphett and

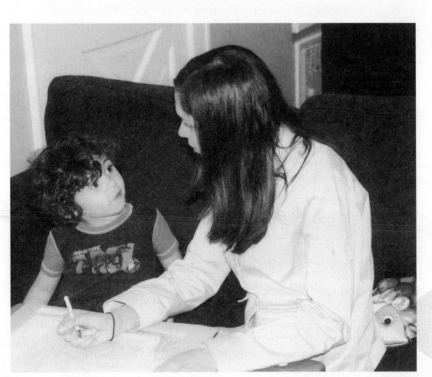

This child needs a more knowledgeable person to model and help with new tasks.

Washburne (1931) supported the postponement of reading instruction until a child was developmentally "old enough." Their study concluded that children with a mental age of 6 years, 6 months made better progress on a test of reading achievement than younger children. Although many educators believed that natural maturation was the precursor to literacy, others grew uncomfortable with simply waiting for children to become ready to read. They began to provide experiences that they believed would help children become ready for reading.

The growing popularity of testing during the 1930s and 1940s helped educators in this effort and affected the next several decades of early childhood reading instruction. Generally, the standardized tests served the prevailing concept of maturation by indicating whether a child had reached the maturity she needed to be able to learn to read. The tests usually included sections on specific skills. These skills were viewed as elements that would help children become ready to read. The term **reading readiness** became popular during this time, and instead of waiting for a child's natural maturation to unfold, educators focused on nurturing that maturation through instruction in a set of skills seen as prerequisites for reading. Readiness skills include (1) **auditory discrimination:** the ability to identify and differentiate familiar sounds, similar sounds, rhyming words, and the sounds of letters; (2) **visual discrimination:** including color recognition, shape, and letter identification; (3) **visual motor skills:** such as left-to-right eye progression, cutting on a line with scissors, and coloring within the lines of a picture; and (4) **large motor skills:** such as skipping, hopping, and walking on a line. The reading-readiness model implies that one prepares for literacy by acquiring a set of prescribed skills needed for learning to read. These skills are taught systematically on the assumption that all children are at a similar level of development when they come to preschool or kindergarten. The system does not consider experiences or information that a child may already have about literacy.

Literacy Research and Practice from the 1960s to the Present

In the 1960s through the 1980s, researchers investigating early childhood literacy development brought about many changes in practice. Investigators looked at the cognitive development of the child using varied research methodologies for data collection. There were experimental studies with treatment and control groups, correlational research, interviews, observations, videotapes, and case studies. The research was done in diverse cultural, racial, and socioeconomic settings. The research was field based, taking place in classrooms and homes, rather than in laboratories as in the past. Research in the areas of oral language development, family literacy, early reading, and early writing had a strong impact on our understanding of how children learn and consequently how we should teach reading and writing. This research is reviewed in the appropriate chapters.

The findings of the research from the 1960s through the 1980s enabled us to understand more of the processes involved in becoming literate. To acquire skill in oral language, writing, and reading, children need models to emulate and the freedom to create their own forms of reading, writing, and speaking. The work that was done brought about the emergent literacy perspective in early literacy instruction.

Emergent Literacy

Research concerning early readers and what they learn about books, print, and writing before going to school has changed attitudes and ideas about early childhood strategies for literacy development. One such concept is **emergent literacy**, a phrase first used by Marie Clay (1966). Emergent literacy assumes that the child acquires some knowledge about language, reading, and writing before coming to school. Literacy development begins early in life and is ongoing. There is a dynamic relationship among the communication skills (reading, writing, oral language, and listening) because each influences the other in the course of development. Development occurs in everyday contexts of the home, community, and school through meaningful and functional experiences that require the use of literacy in natural settings. The settings for the acquisition of literacy are often social, with adults and children interacting through collaboration and tutoring. Literacy activities occur and are embedded purposefully within content areas such as art, music, play, social studies, and science to ensure that meaning is involved. For example, in art, children should have a recipe to read in order to be able to make play dough.

Children at every age possess certain literacy skills, although these skills are not as fully developed or conventional as we recognize mature reading and writing to be (Baumann, Hoffman, Duffy-Hester, & Ro, 2000; Morris & Slavin, 2003). Emergent literacy acknowledges a child's scribble marks on a page as rudimentary writing, even if not one letter is discernible. The child who knows the difference between such scribbles and drawings has some sense of the difference between writing and illustration. Similarly, when children narrate familiar storybooks while looking at the pictures and print and give the impression of reading, we acknowledge the activity as legitimate literacy behavior, even though it cannot be called reading in the conventional sense. Literacy development approached in this manner accepts children at any level of literacy at which they are functioning and provides a program for instruction based on individual needs. The emergent literacy perspective exposes children to books early; it is a child-centered approach with more emphasis on problem solving than on direct instruction of skills.

Definitions of Whole Language

Whole language is similar to the emergent literacy perspective, but considers all children at all ages. Advocates of whole language support the constructivist and natural approaches to learning fostered by many of the early philosophers, psychologists, and theorists already discussed. From a content analysis of 64 professional articles related to whole language, Bergeron (1990) composed this definition:

> Whole language is a concept that embodies both a philosophy of language development as well as the instructional approaches embedded within, and supportive of, that philosophy. This concept includes the use of real literature and writing in the context of meaningful, functional, and cooperative experiences in order to develop in students motivation and interest in the process of learning. (p. 319)

From my perspective, whole language is a philosophy about how children learn, from which educators derive strategies for teaching. In a whole-language

Children need to be exposed to books and writing early in life. Early attempts at literacy should be encouraged and rewarded.

approach, literacy learning is child centered because it is designed to be meaningful and functional for children. The purpose and significance are drawn from the child's life experiences at home or those created in school. For example, if a beehive is discovered at school and removed by an exterminator, children may be interested in discussing, reading, or writing about bees. Although learning about bees is not built into the prescribed curriculum, the teacher allows children to pursue this spontaneous interest (Collins & Shaeffer, 1997; Dunn, Beach, & Kontos, 1994; Fingon, 2005).

Literacy activities are purposefully integrated into the learning of content-area subjects such as art, music, social studies, science, math, and play. The use of social studies and science themes, such as the study of ecology, links content areas and literacy experiences. Equal emphasis is placed on teaching reading, writing, listening, and oral language, because all help create a literate individual. In the past, this program has been referred to as an *integrated* language arts approach. Varied genres of children's literature are the main source of reading material for instruction. This method is called *literature-based* instruction. Classrooms must be rich with literacy materials for reading and writing throughout the room and also housed in special literacy centers. This design is often called the *rich* literacy environment.

In a classroom that uses holistic strategies, teachers place more emphasis on learning than on teaching. Learning is self-regulated and individualized, with self-selection and choices of literacy activities. Rather than only teaching lessons in literacy, teachers are more likely to provide models of literacy activities for children to emulate. There is adult and peer interaction as children observe one another and adults engaged in literacy acts. There is opportunity for peer tutoring and collaboration with each other in active literacy experiences. Children also can learn through practice by engaging in long periods of independent reading and writing and sharing what is learned—by reading to others and presenting written pieces to an audience. A major objective for literacy instruction is the development of a desire to read and write.

In classrooms that use holistic approaches, skills are taught when they are relevant and meaningful; for example, when studying a theme such as dinosaurs, the teacher may focus on some letters and sounds in the initial consonants found in the names of dinosaurs. In early implementation of whole-language programs, some thought that skills were not to be taught in any systematic way and that children would acquire those that they needed by being immersed in experiences with reading children's literature and writing.

Certainly, skills are assimilated through this immersion, but specific skills, such as how to use decoding strategies to figure out unknown words, require some explicit instruction by the teacher.

In a whole-language approach, assessment is continuous and takes many forms: Teachers collect daily performance samples of work, they observe and record children's behavior, they audio- and videotape them in different situations, and they build a portfolio filled with information about each youngster. The evaluation process is for both teacher and child, and conferences are held to discuss progress.

In a whole-language orientation, teachers along with children are the decision makers about instructional strategies, the organization of instruction, and the instructional materials used. Commercial materials do not dictate the instructional program, although they may be used if desired. Literacy learning is consciously embedded throughout the curriculum in the whole school day. Large blocks of time are needed for projects. Children are able to read and write independently for long periods of time.

Integrating the Language Arts with Thematic Instruction

With whole language based strongly on authentic, relevant learning, the integrated language arts concept combined with thematic instruction became important to the literacy curriculum. In classrooms that use an integrated language arts approach, literacy is taught not as a subject, but as a mechanism for learning in general. Literacy learning becomes meaningful when it is embedded into the study of themes and content-area subjects.

The main goal of thematic units is to teach content information and literacy skills in an interesting way. Thematic units use a science or social studies topic and consciously integrate literacy into all content-area lessons, including music, art, play, math, social studies, and science. Many selections of children's literature are used as a major part of the unit; however, the literature does not drive the unit—the topic of the unit is the main focus. In this type of unit, the classroom centers are filled with materials that relate to the topic, including literacy materials to encourage reading and writing. In all science and

Thematic units often use a science or social studies topic, and teachers integrate literacy activities into content-area lessons.

social studies lessons, reading and writing are purposefully incorporated. Skills are taught when they seem appropriate; for example, in the unit on the farm, when the class hatches baby chicks in an incubator, journals may be kept on the progress of the chicks, and the digraph *ch* could be emphasized. Topics may be predetermined by the teacher, selected by the children and teacher, or spontaneously based on something of interest that occurs in the school, in someone's home, or in the world. Chapter 9 elaborates on the use of thematic units. A description of how units are implemented throughout the school day is also included. Appendix A provides a list of popular early childhood unit topics with related selections of children's literature to use when studying these topics.

Explicit Instruction and Constructivist Approaches: Phonics and Whole Language

Some problems evolved with the whole-language and thematic instruction. Schools did not provide adequate staff development, materials, and in-class support for the ambitious changes proposed in classrooms. Many misunderstood the philosophy when interpreting it. Many thought that whole language meant teaching children only in whole groups. Thus, teachers stopped meeting with small groups of children for instruction to meet individual needs. Many thought that whole language meant that one could not teach phonics. This was not the case at all. The manner in which phonics was to be taught involved immersion into literature and print, together with spontaneous and contextual teaching of skills. As a result of the misinterpretations, many children received little or no instruction in phonics. Many schools did not follow a scope or sequence of skills and did not monitor skill development. Because of misinformation, misinterpretation, and incorrect implementation, many children did not develop skills they needed to become fluent, independent readers.

The pendulum began to swing again to those who favored an approach to early literacy development with more explicit use of phonics, and they cited many studies to substantiate their claims. According to Juel (1989), as children first begin to experiment with reading and writing, they need to focus on the sounds that make up words. Knowing that words are made up of individual sounds and having the ability to segment these sounds out of the words and blend them together is called **phonemic awareness**. According to research, phonemic awareness instruction in preschool, kindergarten, and first grade strengthens reading achievement. Phonemic awareness is also thought to be a precursor to phonics instruction (Byrne & Fielding-Barnsley, 1993, 1995; Stanovich, 1986). With phonemic awareness, children can learn principles of phonics including (1) alphabetic understanding (knowing that words are composed of letters) and (2) cryptoanalytic intent or sound–symbol relationships (knowing that there is a relationship between printed letters and spoken sound). Research also suggests that knowledge of sound–symbol relationships, or **phonics**, is necessary for success at learning to read and write (Anthony & Lonigan, 2004; Lonigan, 2006).

Those who propose a behaviorist or explicit-skills approach for literacy instruction have argued for a strong phonics program in early literacy. The materials for instruction are systematic and provide direct instruction of skills with scripted manuals for teachers to use. On the other side of the

Strategies

debate are the constructivists, who propose natural settings for literacy instruction based on function and meaning and the integration of skill development. The constructivists prefer children's literature as the source for literacy instruction. (See Strategies for the Classroom for Chapter 1 on page S-3.)

Politics, the U.S. economy, and the statistics about how children are doing in reading determine the type of reading instruction that is adopted. The First Grade Studies (Bond & Dykstra, 1967a, 1967b) tried to answer the question of which method was the best for early literacy instruction. This exemplary piece of work found that no one method was more effective than another. It seems certain to me that this debate will continue.

Balanced Literacy Instruction

ELL

English Language Learners

A position statement by the International Reading Association, entitled *Using Multiple Methods of Beginning Reading Instruction* (1999), suggests that no single method or single combination of methods can successfully teach all children to read. Teachers must know the social, emotional, physical, and intellectual status of the children they teach. They also must know about the many methods for reading instruction. Only then can they develop a comprehensive plan for teaching reading to meet individual needs.

This perspective on literacy instruction, which emerged as a result of the whole language versus phonics discussion, is a balanced approach. A balanced perspective includes careful selection of the best theories available and use of learning strategies based on these theories to match the learning styles of individual children to help them learn to read (Figure 1.1). More skill-based explicit instruction or some holistic and constructivist ideas, which include problem-solving strategies, might be used (Morrow & Tracey, 1997). According to Pressley (1998), explicit teaching of skills is a good start for constructivist problem-solving activities, and constructivist activities permit consolidation and elaboration of skills. One method does not preclude or exclude the other.

A balanced perspective is not a random combination of strategies. A teacher may select strategies from different learning theories to provide balance. One child, for example, may be a visual learner and not benefit much from instruction in phonics; another child, whose strength may be auditory learning, will learn best from phonics instruction. The balanced approach is a thoughtful and mature approach. It focuses more on what is important for individual children than on the latest fad in literacy instruction.

Balanced instruction is grounded in a rich model of literacy learning that encompasses both the elegance and complexity of the reading and language arts processes. Such a model acknowledges the importance of both form (phonics, mechanics, etc.) and function (comprehension, purpose, meaning) of the literacy processes and recognizes that learning occurs most effectively in a whole–part–whole context. This type of instruction is characterized by meaningful literacy activities that provide children with both the skill and desire to become proficient and lifelong literacy learners. A balanced program includes the components in Figure 1.1.

Figure 1.1   Strategies and Structures in a Comprehensive, Balanced Literacy Program

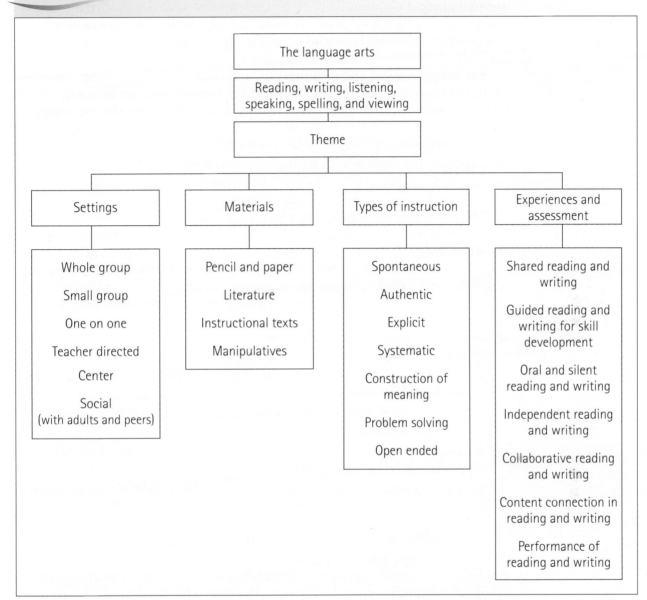

Source: Adapted from L. M. Morrow, D. S. Strickland, & D. G. Woo, *Literacy Instruction in Half- and Whole-Day Kindergarten: Research to Practice* (Fig. 2, p. 76). Newark, DE: International Reading Association. Copyright © 1998 by the International Reading Association.

Reading First and Scientifically Based Reading Research

In January 2002, the No Child Left Behind Act was passed. This act proposes that every child in the United States has the right to become a fluent reader by grade 3. The legislation was designed to help close the gap in literacy development between the rich and the poor and prevent problems before they occur. Grants from the federal government called *Reading First* are intended to help accomplish the goal. The funding is for kindergarten through grade 3 children from at-risk school districts. To qualify for grants, states and school districts must identify the reading assessments and programs they will use and demonstrate that the programs are reliable and valid.

For the assessment and programs to be considered reliable and valid, scientifically based reading research has to have been carried out on them. Requirements of scientifically based reading research include the following:

- Randomly chosen subjects in the experiment
- Experimental designs with treatment and control groups
- Research published in a peer-review journal

The states that are funded must base their reading programs on the findings of the National Reading Panel Report (2000) and studies that are scientifically based.

A broader definition of research has been offered by those in the field of education. It is called evidence-based research as opposed to scientifically based research. Evidence-based research is all of the following:

- Objective   Data are identified and interpreted similarly by any evaluator.
- Valid   Data adequately represent the tasks that children need to perform to be successful readers.
- Reliable   Data remain essentially unchanged if collected on a different day or by a different person.
- Systematic   Data are collected according to a rigorous design of either experimentation or observation.
- Refereed   Data are approved for publication by a panel of independent reviewers.

Evidence-based research will use both qualitative and quantitative designs in studies. The results of this research are considered valid for designing instructional programs in reading as long as the investigations follow the definition described above (International Reading Association, 2001).

National Reading Panel Report (2000)

English Language Learners

The National Reading Panel Report (2000) presents findings about the most effective strategies for teaching children to read. The panel reviewed more than 100,000 studies to come up with their results. They admit, however, that some areas that may be important to literacy instruction, such as writing development and motivation for reading, were not studied because of a lack of adequate numbers of high-quality investigations to analyze. In addition, only experimental studies with treatment and control groups were selected for analysis. Other research designs, such as qualitative or case study and correlational research, for example, were not included.

The results of the report indicate that teaching the following elements is crucial to reading success in early literacy:

- Phonemic awareness
- Phonics
- Vocabulary
- Comprehension
- Fluency

National Early Literacy Panel Report (2004)

English Language Learners

The National Early Literacy Panel of the National Center for Family Literacy studied existing scientifically based research to identify the skills and abilities of young children from birth through age 5 that predict later achievement in reading, such as the ability to decode and comprehend. After identifying the variables, it was the panel's task to determine environments, settings, programs, and interventions that contribute to or inhibit the skills that are linked to later outcomes in reading. The variables the panel has identified thus far include the following:

- Oral language development: expressive and receptive vocabulary
- Alphabetic code: alphabet knowledge, phonological and phonemic awareness, invented spelling
- Print knowledge: environmental print, concepts about print
- Other skills: rapid naming of letters and numbers, visual memory, and visual perceptual abilities

It appears that involving children in appropriate activities that will help them develop these areas is an important recommendation. Schools where children do not score well on testing measures will be identified as in need of help.

The research, theory, philosophies, and methods through the years have helped us to understand that children learn in situations that are significant and purposeful. They develop literacy in social and cultural contexts and through interaction with adults and other children. The instruction they receive should reflect on their background knowledge and be sensitive to a child's stage of development socially, emotionally, physically, and intellectually. We have also learned that organized, systematic presentation of skills is necessary to literacy development. Here is an outline for teachers to follow when planning lessons.

- Explicit modeling and scaffolding of lessons to be learned
- Guided practice
- Independent practice
- More time on task
- More structure and routines
- More structured routines
- Differentiation of instruction to meet individual needs

- More feedback for children
- Time to explore
- Time to experiment
- Time to collaborate in social settings
- Time for problem solving

Throughout the years there has been a great deal of interest in early literacy. Trends in thinking about early literacy development change often. In the mid-1990s a change occurred that moved away from incidental teaching of skills to more systematic teaching of skills in early literacy. Taking a balanced perspective, the International Reading Association along with the National Association for the Education of Young Children worked on a document called *Learning to Read and Write: Developmentally Appropriate Practices* (1998). Box 1.1 is a section of the document that lays out goals for preschool through grade 3 instruction and describes the roles of children, teachers, and parents.

Box 1.1

Continuum of Children's Development in Early Reading and Writing

Note: This list is intended to be illustrative, not exhaustive. Children at any grade level will function at a variety of phases along the reading/writing continuum.

Phase 1: Awareness and exploration (goals for preschool)

Children explore their environment and build the foundations for learning to read and write.

Children can

- enjoy listening to and discussing storybooks
- understand that print carries a message
- engage in reading and writing attempts
- identify labels and signs in their environment
- participate in rhyming games
- identify some letters and make some letter–sound matches
- use known letters or approximations of letters to represent written language (especially meaningful words, like their name and phrases such as "I love you")

What teachers do

- share books with children, including Big Books, and model reading behaviors
- talk about letters by name and sounds
- establish a literacy-rich environment
- reread favorite stories
- engage children in language games
- promote literacy-related play activities
- encourage children to experiment with writing

What parents and family members can do

- talk with children, engage them in conversation, give names of things, show interest in what a child says

- read and reread stories with predictable texts to children
- encourage children to recount experiences and describe ideas and events that are important to them
- visit the library regularly
- provide opportunities for children to draw and print, using markers, crayons, and pencils

Phase 2: Experimental reading and writing (goals for kindergarten)

Children develop basic concepts of print and begin to engage in and experiment with reading and writing.

Kindergartners can

- enjoy being read to and can themselves retell simple narrative stories or informational texts
- use descriptive language to explain and explore
- recognize letters and letter–sound matches
- show familiarity with rhyming and beginning sounds
- understand left-to-right and top-to-bottom orientation and familiar concepts of print
- match spoken words with written ones
- begin to write letters of the alphabet and some high-frequency words

What teachers do

- encourage children to talk about reading and writing experiences
- provide many opportunities for children to explore and identify sound–symbol relationships in meaningful contexts
- help children to segment spoken words into individual sounds and blend the sounds into whole words (for example, by slowly writing a word and saying its sound)
- frequently read interesting and conceptually rich stories to children
- provide daily opportunities for children to write
- help children build a sight vocabulary
- create a literacy-rich environment for children to engage independently in reading and writing

What parents and family members can do

- daily read and reread narrative and informational stories to children
- encourage children's attempts at reading and writing
- allow children to participate in activities that involve writing and reading (for example, cooking, making grocery lists)
- play games that involve specific directions (such as "Simon Says")
- have conversations with children during mealtimes and throughout the day

Phase 3: Early reading and writing (goals for first grade)

Children begin to read simple stories and can write about a topic that is meaningful to them.

First graders can

- read and retell familiar stories
- use strategies (rereading, predicting, questioning, contextualizing) when comprehension breaks down
- use reading and writing for various purposes on their own initiative

(continued on next page)

Box 1.1

Continuum of
Children's
Development in
Early Reading
and Writing

(continued from previous page)
- orally read with reasonable fluency
- use letter–sound associations, word parts, and context to identify new words
- identify an increasing number of words by sight
- sound out and represent all substantial sounds in spelling a word
- write about topics that are personally meaningful
- attempt to use some punctuation and capitalization

What teachers do
- support the development of vocabulary by reading daily to the children, transcribing their language, and selecting materials that expand children's knowledge and language development
- model strategies and provide practice for identifying unknown words
- give children opportunities for independent reading and writing practice
- read, write, and discuss a range of different text types (poems, informational books)
- introduce new words and teach strategies for learning to spell new words
- demonstrate and model strategies to use when comprehension breaks down
- help children build lists of commonly used words from their writing

What parents and family members can do
- talk about favorite storybooks
- read to children and encourage them to read to you
- suggest that children write to friends and relatives
- bring to a parent–teacher conference evidence of what your child can do in writing and reading
- encourage children to share what they have learned about their writing and reading

Phase 4: Transitional reading and writing (goals for second grade)
Children begin to read more fluently and write various text forms using simple and more complex sentences.

Second graders can
- read with greater fluency
- use strategies more efficiently (rereading, questioning, and so on) when comprehension breaks down
- use word identification strategies with greater facility to unlock unknown words
- identify an increasing number of words by sight
- write about a range of topics to suit different audiences
- use common letter patterns and critical features to spell words
- punctuate simple sentences correctly and proofread their own work
- spend time reading daily and use reading to research topics

What teachers do
- create a climate that fosters analytic, evaluative, and reflective thinking
- teach children to write in multiple forms (stories, information, poems)
- ensure that children read a range of text for a variety of purposes
- teach revising, editing, and proofreading skills
- teach strategies for spelling new and difficult words
- model enjoyment of reading

What parents and family members can do
- continue to read to children and encourage them to read to you
- engage children in activities that require reading and writing
- become involved in school activities
- show children your interest in their learning by displaying their written work
- visit the library regularly
- support your child's specific hobby or interest with reading materials and references

Phase 5: Independent and productive reading and writing (goals for third grade)

Children continue to extend and refine their reading and writing to suit varying purposes and audiences.

Third graders can
- read fluently and enjoy reading
- use a range of strategies when drawing meaning from the text
- use word identification strategies appropriately and automatically when encountering unknown words
- recognize and discuss elements of different text structures
- make critical connections between texts
- write expressively in many different forms (stories, poems, reports)
- use a rich variety of vocabulary and sentences appropriate to text forms
- revise and edit their own writing during and after composing
- spell words correctly in final writing drafts

What teachers do
- provide opportunities daily for children to read, examine, and critically evaluate narrative and expository texts
- continue to create a climate that fosters critical reading and personal response
- teach children to examine ideas in texts
- encourage children to use writing as a tool for thinking and learning
- extend children's knowledge of the correct use of writing conventions
- emphasize the importance of correct spelling in finished written products
- create a climate that engages all children as a community of literacy learners

What parents and family members can do
- continue to support children's learning and interest by visiting the library and bookstores with them
- find ways to highlight children's progress in reading and writing
- stay in regular contact with your child's teachers about activities and progress in reading and writing
- encourage children to use and enjoy print for many purposes (such as recipes, directions, games, and sports)
- build a love of language in all its forms and engage children in conversation

Source: From *Learning to Read and Write: Developmentally Appropriate Practices for Young Children.* Copyright © 1998 by the International Reading Association and National Association for the Education of Young Children. All rights reserved.

An Idea from the Classroom

Preschoolers Go Restaurant Hopping
(Constructivist Theory)

ELL

English Language Learners

As part of a unit dealing with nutrition, I have individual conferences with my preschoolers to help them create their own restaurant menus to be used during dramatic play. This activity is great for diverse learners because it celebrates cultural differences, engages the universal theme of food, and is hands-on and tailored to individual ability levels. The children can write their menus themselves (any form of early writing will be accepted, from drawing a picture, to scribble writing, to random letters), or they can dictate their menus and I will write them down. Their menus contain such savory items as fried chicken on the bone; apple juice; pink ice cream with sprinkles, whipped cream, and chocolate sauce; and cherry tacos. The children decorate covers for their menus and choose a name for their restaurant. The children have the opportunity to discuss and share their menus with the class during our Morning Message time.

The next step is to transform our housekeeping area into a restaurant. The play food and utensils are already there. We add items such as a tablecloth, serving trays, and small writing pads and pencils for taking orders. I've made large signs with every child's restaurant name on it. I rotate the names so that each child has a chance for his or her restaurant to be the restaurant of the day. When the children come to school, the first thing they do is rush over to the play area to see whose restaurant sign is posted.

During a typical playtime, a great deal of literacy behavior occurs. Children read menus and take orders. They discuss the specials of the day and how the food tastes, and they pay the check. This science unit on good nutrition is conducive to providing meaningful literacy experiences for young readers and writers.

Meeting with each child individually in a conference allows me to identify and deal with his or her needs. The needs span from finding strategies for early reading and writing that suit a child's learning style to realizing that each child can share his or her diverse background. For example, in addition to traditional hamburger and pizza places, we had a Japanese restaurant, a Mexican restaurant, and a Jewish deli.

Marcia Wesalo, Nursery School Teacher

Strategies   For materials to use to design a restaurant, use the Strategies for the Classroom Chapter 8 activity on page S-42.

An Idea from the Classroom

English Language Learners

Learning the Initial Consonant *P* (Explicit Instruction)

Explicit modeling for children

Teacher: Today we are going to learn about the sound of *P*. Who has a name that starts with a *P*?

Peter: My name does.

Teacher: You are right. Let's everyone say Peter.

Class: Peter.

Teacher: Now put your hand up to your mouth and say Puh, Puh, Puh.

Class: Puh, Puh, Puh.

Teacher: How did it feel?

Nancy: I felt air and it was warm.

Teacher: Good. I'm going to tell you a story that has a lot of *P* words in it. I will use felt figures to tell the story. Listen and remember your favorite two *P* words so you can tell your neighbor about them after the story. You might hear pig, party, pizza, panda, plums, or purple. The story is called *The Pig's Party*. (See the characters in Figure 1.2. Photocopy, color, laminate, and put felt on the back for use on a felt board or magnets for use on a white board.)

> Pink Pig was having a party. He wanted it to be a perfect party. He had invited Patty Pig (Figure 1), his favorite pig person, Panda Bear (Figure 2), and Proud Peacock (Figure 4). He had petunias on the table and there were pizza and popsicles for dessert. Panda Bear came to the party first, and Pink Pig asked, "How can I look special for Patty Pig?" Panda Bear said, "Borrow my panda bear suit and you will look perfect." So Pink Pig put on panda bear's suit and he thought he looked perfect (Figure 3). Then Proud Peacock came to the party. Pink Pig asked him, "How can I look perfect for the party?" Proud Peacock said, "Take my purple plumes and put them on and you will look perfect." So he did (Figures 4, 5, and 6). Everyone agreed he looked perfect. Patty Pig (Figure 7) knocked on the door. Pink Pig opened it. She screamed when she saw Pink Pig; she thought she saw a monster with his purple plumes and panda bear suit, and she ran away. Pink Pig gave back his suit to Panda Bear, and Proud Peacock his purple plumes and took a petunia to run to find Patty Pig (Figures 1 and 8). He found her hiding behind the porch. When she saw Pink Pig she said, "Thank goodness it is you Pink Pig," and they went inside and had a perfect party.

Guided Practice

Teacher: Tell your partner the two words you liked the most that started with a *P* in the story.

Josh to Jen: I liked plumes and Patty.

Figure 1.2   The Pig's Party

Jen to Josh: I liked petunia and pizza.

Teacher: How many of you had the same two words? (Only a few children raise their hands.) How many of you had one word the same? (A few more raise their hands.) How many had two different words? (Most of the class raise their hands).

Independent Practice
Teacher: I will put the pig story and the felt characters in the literacy center in this plastic baggie and you can tell the story or read the story and write down the *P* words you remember and like the most. There is paper for you to write your words on.

Activities and Questions

1. Answer the focus questions at the beginning of the chapter.

2. Select from the National Reading Panel's list to develop such skills as phonemic awareness, phonics, vocabulary, comprehension, or fluency. Create an experience for an early childhood classroom that combines the doctrines of Piaget and Vygotsky when teaching your selected skill. Create three additional experiences using the same skill with the doctrines of Montessori, Dewey, and Skinner. In other words, teach the same lesson four different ways based on four different approaches.

3. Observe an early childhood classroom (preschool through second grade). Decide which theoretical influences have determined the type of practices carried out. Document your findings with specific anecdotes illustrating the theory.

4. **Strategies** Tear out the Strategies for the Classroom activity for Chapter 1 on pages S-3 through S-6. It provides you with a plan and materials to carry out a lesson with behaviorist or explicit instruction and a constructivism component as well. Photocopy the figures (enlarge if you wish), color them or copy on colored paper, laminate, cut them out, and paste felt on the back. Tell the story using the figures and a felt board. Have children retell the story. Have children cut sequence strips. Mix them up and then assemble them in the order in which the events in the story happen. Ask the children to tell the story again using the characters and to create a new ending.

myeducationlab

VIDEO EXERCISE

Developing a Philosophy of Education (3:55 minutes)
Now that you have the benefit of having read this chapter, return to the www.myeducationlab.com topic "Becoming a Reading Teacher" and watch "Developing a Philosophy of Education" one more time. You may complete the questions that accompany it and save or transmit your work to your professor, or complete the following questions, as required.

1. Summarize Joyce Madsen's philosophy of education in one sentence.

2. Summarize Leonia Townsend's philosophy of education in one sentence.
3. Summarize Lynda Hootman's philosophy of education in one sentence.
4. Summarize Trent Eaton's philosophy of education in one sentence.
5. Revisit your answers to the first four questions. Were there similarities in the philosophies of these four teachers? How do you explain the differences?
6. In what ways do teachers' philosophies affect students' learning? Can you identify the components of these teachers' philosophies that may have led to the impact you experienced?

Focus Questions

■ Define authentic assessment and identify some measures.

■ Describe the nature of standardized tests and standarized testing.

■ What is meant by high-stakes assessment?

■ What are the pros and cons of authentic assessment and standardized measurement?

■ What do we mean when we speak about standards for early literacy development and standardized tests?

■ How can we tie together standards for instruction and assessment?

■ **VOCABULARY**: authentic assessment, running record, informal reading inventory, standardized tests, high-stakes assessment, standards

■ **Strategies** After giving the interviews from Strategies for the Classroom for Chapter 2 on pages S-7 and S-8, reflect upon the type of reader and writer the child is based on your discussion with him/her.

myeducationlab VIDEO PREVIEW: Using Assessments to Inform Instruction (5:32 minutes); Designing Developmentally Appropriate Days (4:18 minutes); Observing Children in Authentic Contexts (6:03 minutes). Before reading this chapter, go to www.myeducationlab.com. Under the topic "Assessment, Remediation and Diagnosis," access and watch the videos "Using Assessments to Inform Instruction," "Designing Developmentally Appropriate Days," and "Observing Children in Authentic Contexts."

Assessment in Early Literacy

A Guide for Designing Instruction

On the test there was a picture of Sally and Tom. Sally was giving Tom something. It looked like a baloney sandwich. Underneath it said:

Sally is taller than Tom. ____

Tom is taller than Sally. ____

Jim wondered what being tall had to do with getting a baloney sandwich. And was it really a baloney sandwich? It might be tomato. Jim took a long time on that one.

—Cohen, 1980, pp. 9–10

When the teacher passed out the standardized test booklets, Rosa was confused and frightened. She had been in her present second grade for just 4 months. She had been learning English, but her ability was limited. She could read Spanish quite well and was capable of decoding printed English, but with little comprehension. As she looked at the test, she knew that she could not understand the questions or answers. She decided the only thing to do was to fill in the answers by marking an *X* in a box for each question. She appeared busy at work filling in all the boxes without reading one question or answer. She felt better about doing this than letting the teacher know that she could not read the test.

In her book *First Grade Takes a Test,* Miriam Cohen describes the experience of a first-grade class taking a standardized test, as well as the consequences of the test results for the dynamics of the interpersonal relationships within the class. In one section of the account she writes:

> George looked at the test. It said: Rabbits eat
>
> ☐ lettuce   ☐ dog food   ☐ sandwiches
>
> He raised his hand. "Rabbits have to eat carrots or their teeth will get too long and stick into them," he said. The teacher nodded and smiled, but she put her finger to her lips. George carefully drew in a carrot so the test people would know. (1980, pp. 5–6)

In both incidents, children answered questions incorrectly on the standardized tests given to them but for different reasons. Rosa could not read the test in English. Although she was reading at grade level in Spanish, she was jeopardized because of her cultural background. George, relating his own experience to the question at hand, actually had a more sophisticated answer than those provided. His answer was marked incorrect because his background experience with rabbits was different from that of the person who wrote the test. In addition, George may not have understood how to take the test, that is, to fill in the box beside the best answer provided. In both incidents, children answered incorrectly, but not because they did not know the answer.

This chapter deals with critical issues facing early childhood educators today: achieving standards by assessing the needs of children. Assessment must be sensitive to children's different backgrounds and abilities. Only when we recognize individual differences based on our assessment of special needs can appropriate instructional strategies be planned and standards be achieved.

In this chapter, I will introduce the topic of assessment. Some basic assessment instruments will be described. The practical applications for assessment of children's performance will be discussed in the chapters that deal with the various skills and instructional strategies. The main purpose for assessment is to help the teacher prepare and guide instruction for children to meet their individual needs.

Theory and Research on Assessing Early Literacy Development

Early literacy educators, with their concern for children's interests, learning styles, and individual levels of ability, have made us begin to take a closer look at our methods for assessing performance. It is apparent that standardized group paper-and-pencil tests are not always sensitive to strategies drawn from early literacy constructs. In addition, it has become clear that one measure cannot be the main source for evaluating a child's progress. Rather than testing children, we need to assess their performance for growth in many areas and under many conditions. Assessment should help the teacher, child, and parent determine a child's strengths and weaknesses and plan appropriate instructional strategies. Assessment should match educational goals and practices. To meet the needs of the different populations in our schools, assessment measures need to be diverse because some children perform better in some situations than in others.

The International Reading Association (IRA) and the National Association for the Education of Young Children's (NAEYC) joint position statement on learning to read and write (1998) makes the following recommendations: "Use evaluative procedures that are developmentally and culturally appropriate for the children being assessed. The selection of evaluative measures should be based on the objectives of the instructional program and should consider each child's total development and its effect on reading performance." Quality assessment should be drawn from real-life writing and reading tasks and should continuously follow a range of literacy activities.

The type of assessment referred to is often called **authentic assessment**. There are many definitions for the term, but one that seems to capture its essence is *assessment activities that represent and reflect the actual learning and instructional activities of the classroom and out-of-school world*. Several principles emerge from an authentic assessment perspective (Johnston & Costello, 2005; Purcell-Gates, Duke, & Martineau, 2007; Ruddell and Ruddell,1995).

Objectives for Assessment

1. Assessment should be based on observations and evaluation of a variety of measures, rather than relying on one assessment approach.

2. Assessments should be observations of children engaged in authentic classroom reading and writing tasks and on more formal tests as well.

3. Assessment should focus on children's learning based on the goals of the curriculum.

4. Assessment should be continuous and over a substantial period.

5. Assessment should take into account the diversity of students' cultural, language, and special needs.

6. Assessment should be collaborative and include the active participation of children, parents, and teachers.

7. Assessment must be knowledge based and reflect our most current understanding of reading and writing processes.

To accomplish these goals, assessment must be frequent and include many types. The main goal is to observe and record actual behavior that provides the broadest possible picture of a particular child. Every chapter in this book that deals with a specific area of literacy development contains a section with suggestions for collecting material related to assessment for this particular skill. A list of authentic assessment measures that will help paint a comprehensive picture of a child is provided in this chapter.

Authentic Assessment: Measures and Strategies

ANECDOTAL OBSERVATION FORMS. Prepared forms or teacher-made forms may be used for observing and recording children's behavior. Observation forms usually have broad categories with large spaces for notes about children's activities. Goals for observing should be planned and forms designed to meet the goals. Teachers can write down interesting, humorous, and general comments about the child's behavior in the classroom. Observations should focus on one particular aspect of the child's performance, such as oral reading, silent reading, behavior while listening to stories, or writing. Within the descriptions of behavior, dialogue is often recorded. Figure 2.1 presents a sample observation form that can be used for several different types of observations.

Figure 2.1

Sample Observation Form

Teacher's Name:_____

Date:_____

Time:_____

Location:_____

Classroom or Setting:_____

Purpose of Observing:_____

Prediction or Expectation during Observation:_____

Significant Events during Observation:

Reflective Analysis of Significant Event (this reflection should include what you have learned):

List at least three ways you can use or apply what you observed to your future teaching:

Source: George S. Morrison, *Fundamentals of Early Childhood Education,* 5th Edition, © 2008, by permission of Pearson Education, Inc., Upper Saddle River, NJ.

Figure 2.2

A Daily Performance Sample of Nicole's Writing at the End of Her Kindergarten Year

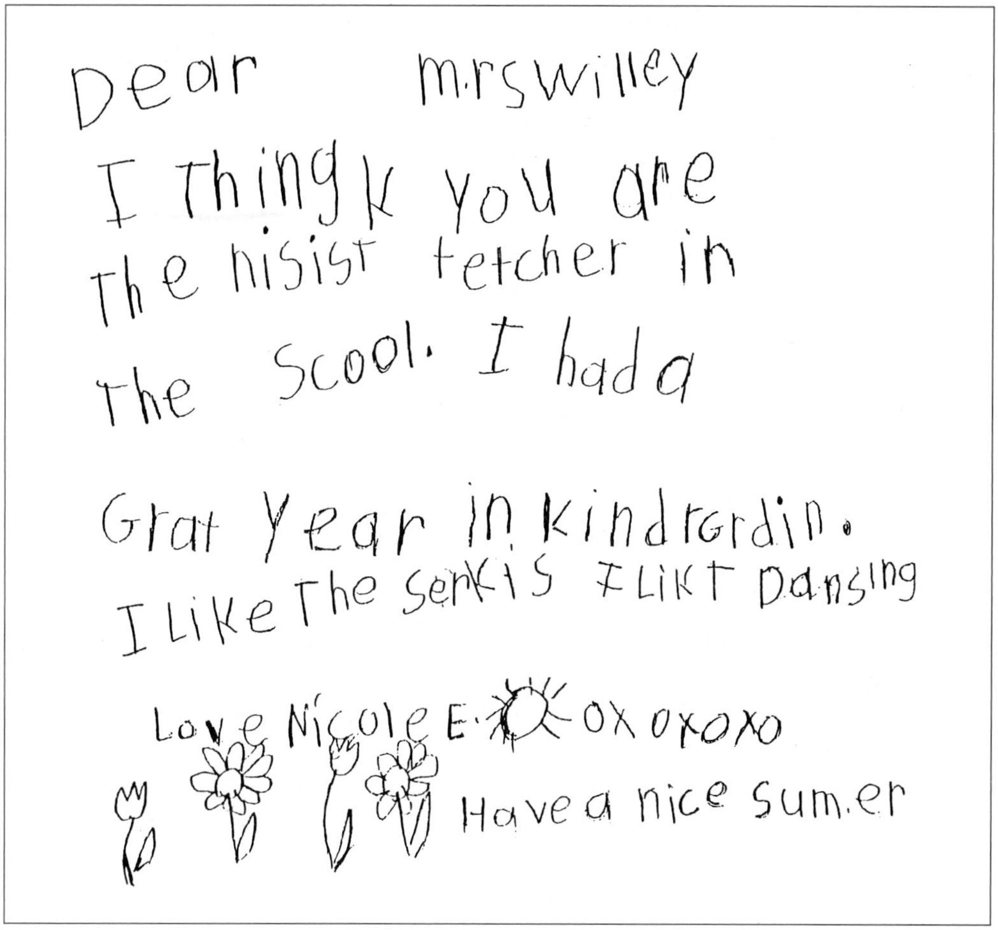

> Dear   mrswilley
> I thingk you are
> The hisist tetcher in
> the scool. I had a
>
> Grat year in kindrerdin.
> I like The senkis I likt Dansing
>
> Love Nicole E. OX OXOXO
> Have a nice sumer

DAILY PERFORMANCE SAMPLES.   These are samples of the child's work in all content areas that is done on a daily basis. Various types of samples should be collected periodically. Samples of writing, artwork, and science and social studies reports can be collected throughout the school year (Figure 2.2).

AUDIO RECORDING.   Whether on CDs or DVDs, recordings are another form of assessment that can be used to determine language development, to assess comprehension of story through recorded retellings, to analyze progress in the fluency of oral reading, and so on. They can also be used in discussion sessions related to responses to literature to help understand how youngsters function in a group and the types of responses they offer. Children can listen to their own recordings to evaluate both their story retellings and fluency. In Chapter 6 there is an evaluation of story retelling that requires a recording for evaluation of the student's performance.

VIDEOS.   Videos relate information similar to that in recordings, with the additional data that can be gained by seeing the child in action. Videos can be used for many different purposes. Therefore, they should be done with a purpose in mind and evaluated with a checklist or observation form. Videos of the teacher can be used for assessing their own performance.

Strategies

SURVEYS AND INTERVIEWS. Surveys can be prepared by teachers to assess children's attitudes about how they think they are learning or what they like or dislike in school. Surveys can be in the form of questionnaires or interviews with written or oral answers. Chapter 8 provides a **motivation survey** to be administered to children. It is a multiple-choice questionnaire that also asks for open-ended responses from the child. See Strategies for the Classroom for Chapter 2 on page S-7.

TEACHER-MADE PENCIL-AND-PAPER TESTS. These tests will probably match instruction better than measures designed by commercial companies; therefore, teachers need to provide this type of experience for children.

STUDENT EVALUATION FORMS. Authentic assessment must involve the child. Forms are prepared for children to evaluate their own performance (see Figure 2.3). Children should regularly evaluate their performance by collecting samples of their work and discussing them with the teacher and other children. Children are an integral part of the assessment process.

PARENT ASSESSMENT FORMS. Authentic assessment also involves parents as evaluators of their children. Parents may be asked to collect work samples from home and to write anecdotes about behavior. It is good to provide

Figure 2.3

Children's Self-Evaluation Form

Name _____ Date _____

1. I know all the letters of the alphabet. yes ☐ no ☐

2. I can write the letters. yes ☐ no ☐
   Here is a sample of some letters I can write:

3. I know letter sounds. yes ☐ no ☐
   Here are some letter sounds I know:

4. Letters I need help with are:

- -

1. I like to read: yes ☐ no ☐ Why?

2. Things I like to read are:

3. The things I do well in reading are:

4. The things I need to learn how to do better in reading are:

- -

1. I like to write: yes ☐ no ☐ Why?

2. Things I like to write are:

3. The things I do well in writing are:

4. The things I need to learn how to do better in writing are:

parents with forms for observing and recording behavior. Children should talk about their work with their parents. The parent is an important resource for providing more information about the child from the home perspective. (See Figure 10.3 for a parent assessment form entitled Observing My Child's Literacy Growth.)

CONFERENCES.   Conferences allow the teacher to meet with a child on a one-to-one basis to assess skills such as reading aloud, to discuss a child's progress, to talk about steps to improve, to instruct, and to prescribe activities. Children should take an active role in evaluating their progress and are equal partners in the assessment process. Parents also are involved in conferencing with teachers about their child's progress. They meet with teachers alone and with their child. They bring materials they have collected at home to add to the packet of information.

CHECKLISTS.   Inventories including lists of developmental behaviors or skills for children to accomplish are a common form of authentic assessment. The list is prepared based on objectives a teacher may have for instruction. Therefore, the inventory is designed to determine whether goals set forth have been accomplished. Box 2.1, on the developmental characteristics of children (page 60) can be used as a checklist to determine how children are developing socially, emotionally, physically, and cognitively based on their age. In several chapters in the book, checklists for skills are presented.

Running Records and Informal Inventories

Marie Clay (1993a) created **running records** for closely observing and recording children's oral reading behavior and for planning instruction. In the analysis, what a child can do and the types of errors the child makes when reading are recorded. Running records also determine the appropriate material for instructional purposes and for independent reading. In addition, a student's frustration level can be identified. Determining the level of material for instruction and the types of strategies for instruction based on errors made is crucial for productive guidance in reading to occur. Running records spend more time indicating the types of errors students make in oral reading than evaluating their ability to comprehend text.

In taking a running record the child is asked to read a short passage of 100 to 200 words. Younger children have shorter passages, and older children have longer ones. The teacher has a copy of the passage, and as the child reads the teacher uses the prescribed coding system to indicate on a running record form whether words are read correctly and what types of errors are made. The types of errors recorded are insertion of a word, omission, deletion, repetition, substitution, reversal, refusal to pronounce a word, and an appeal for help. Self-corrections are recorded, but are not considered errors. As the child reads, the teacher records that the reading is accurate with a check over each word or the type of error (see Figure 2.4).

If a child reads 95 to 100 percent of the words correctly, the material is at his or her independent level; if 90 to 95 percent of the words are correct, the material is at the instructional level; less than 90 percent of the words read

Figure 2.4   Running Record Coding System

Type of error or miscue	Code	Description
Accurate reading	✓ ✓ ✓ ✓	For each word read correctly a check or dash is placed above the word. Some prefer no marking to mean accurate reading.
Self-correction (not counted as an error)	his | sc / her |	Child reads the word incorrectly, pauses, and then corrects the error.
Substitution (counted as an error)	boat / barge	The student substitutes a real word that is incorrect.
Refusal to pronounce told word (counted as an error)	– | / table | T	The student neither pronounces the word nor attempts to do so. The teacher pronounces the word so that testing can continue.
Insertion (counted as an error)	at / —	The student inserts a word or a series of words that do not appear in the text.
Omission (counted as an error)	– / rat	The student omits a word or a continuous sequence of words in the text, but continues to read.
Repetition (not counted as an error)	◄———— The horse ran away |	The student repeats one or more words that have been read. Groups of adjacent words that are repeated count as one repetition.
Reversal	he\said / was	The student reverses the order of words or letters.
Appeal for help (counted as an error)	– | App | / house | T	Child asks for help with a word he or she cannot read.

Source: Adapted from A. P. Shearer & S. P. Homan, *Linking Reading Assessment to Instruction.* Mahwah, NJ: Erlbaum, 1994.

correctly suggests the child's frustration level. Calculations for running records for percent of accuracy rate follow:

1. Record the number of words in a testing passage (for example, 70).
2. Count the number of errors made by the child and subtract that from the total number of passage words (for example, 5 errors subtracted from 70 equals 65).
3. Divide that number (65) by the total words in the passage (70).
4. Multiply that by 100; the result equals the percent of accuracy for the passage read (about 93 percent in this example).

An important part of a running record is to analyze further why errors are being made. This is done by classifying them one step further as M for meaning, S for structure, or V for visual. To determine the type of error, go back to

Figure 2.5

Running
Record Form

Name_____   Date_____

Book_____   Book level_____

Words: Error rate: Accuracy rate:

Errors:

Self-correction rate:

| | | | Cues used | | | | | | |
| | | | E—errors | | | SC—self-correction | | |
E	SC	Text	M	S	V		M	S	V

M—meaning, S—structure, V—visual, E—error, SC—self-correction

Reading level
Independent: 95% to 100% accuracy
Instructional: 90% to 95% accuracy
Difficult (or Frustration): 89% or less accuracy

Reading proficiency: fluent _____   word by word _____   choppy _____

Retelling

Setting: characters _____   time _____   place _____

Theme: problem or goal _____

Events: number included _____

Resolution: solved problem _____   achieved goal _____   ending _____

Source: Adapted from M. Clay, *Running Records for Classroom Teachers.* Auckland, New Zealand: Reed Publishing (NZ) Ltd., 2000.

the text and look at the error and predict what it might be. Here are some examples:

1. A child makes a meaning error when the word read is incorrect, but the meaning of the text is intact and makes sense. For example, if a child reads, "This is my house," instead of "This is my home," although the word is not correct the meaning is intact. This error should be marked with an M.

2. A child makes a structure error when the word in the sentence sounds correct in the sentence, but was not read correctly. For example, if a child reads, "I went to the zoo," instead of "I ran to the zoo," the English grammar or syntax is correct, but the word is not. Therefore, the error is marked S for structure.

3. The last type of error is visual. Here the child might say "spilt" for "spill," because the words look similar and he or she is not looking carefully enough.

For kindergarten and first-grade children, the running record can start with a letter-recognition test. This test shows the letters of the alphabet printed out of order in upper- and lowercase. Children are asked to read the letter names one row at a time. The teacher records letters correct and incorrect. The test can go one step further, to determine whether students know sound–symbol correspondence, by asking children if they know the sound that particular letters make and a word that begins with each letter or sound and then recording their responses. In addition, high-frequency word-recognition assessment can be done. Figure 5.2 on page 151, is a high-frequency word list. The list can be divided by grade level according to which words are considered most difficult. The teacher asks children to read words from the list beginning with what are considered to be the easiest first. If they are successful, the next group of words for the next grade level is tried.

Running records should be done about once a month for all early childhood students. The teachers should talk to children about the types of errors they make in a running record to give them strategies such as listening to the meaning of a sentence and looking at the letters in the word to figure out a word.

There is a place on the running record form to indicate if the child's reading was fluent, word by word, or choppy. Teachers can ask children to retell stories read to determine comprehension of text (Harp, 2000; Hasbrouck & Tindal, 2006; Kuhn, 2007; Stahl & Heubach, 2005).

Informal reading inventories (IRI) similar to running records are tests to determine a child's instructional level. IRIs consist of paragraphs of graded reading materials for children to read silently. After reading, the students answer comprehension questions. IRIs can be carried out when students read aloud. Errors are counted and an accuracy

Running records document children's oral reading behavior and help teachers to plan instruction.

percentage calculated, which indicates if the child reads at the independent, instructional, or frustration level. Errors typically are not analyzed for type, for example, to determine whether a child has a decoding problem or one that involves the use of context or meaning from text. IRIs do reveal the material that is suitable for a child's instructional level. IRIs can also include graded word lists for students to read (Combs, 2006; Gunning, 2003; Hasbrouck & Tindal, 2006; Tompkins, 2007).

Another quick way to determine reading level is as follows: 0 to 3 errors in the passage are considered independent level; 4 to 10 errors, instructional; and 11 or more errors, frustration. If a child is at the frustration level with the first book he or she tries, for kindergarten to first grade, stop testing. If the child is at the frustration level for grade 2 to 3 material, use K to 1 material to test.

Portfolio Assessment

A portfolio provides a way for teachers, children, and parents to collect representative samples of children's work. The portfolio can include work in progress and completed samples. It provides a story of where children have been and what they are capable of doing now, to determine where they should go from this point forth. The teacher's portfolio should include work selected by the child, teacher, and parent. It should represent the best work that children can produce and illustrate difficulties they may be experiencing. It should include many different types of work samples and represent what the child has been learning.

The physical portfolio is often an accordion-type folder with several pockets to hold work. The folder can be personalized with a drawing by the child, a picture of the child, and his or her name. Because portfolios often are passed on to the next grade, the pieces collected need to be carefully selected to limit the size of the folder. The portfolio should include different samples representing different areas of literacy and the best work the child has to offer. For example, the following should be included:

- Daily work performance samples
- Anecdotes about behavior
- Audiorecordings of oral reading
- Language samples
- Story retellings
- Checklists recording skill development
- Interviews
- Standardized test results
- Child's self-assessment form
- Journals
- Expository and narrative writing samples
- Artwork

Figure 2.6   Schedule for Collecting Portfolio Samples and Tests

Student_____   Grade_____

School_____   Teacher_____

Tests are given in September, January, and May. Record the test when given in the space provided.

Grade	Sept. Pre-K	Jan. Pre-K	May Pre-K	Sept. K	Jan. K	May K	Sept. 1	Jan. 1	May 1	Sept. 2	Jan. 2	May 2
1. Child interview												
2. Parent interview												
3. Self-portrait												
4. Concepts about print test												
5. Story retelling/ reenactment												
6. Written retelling*												
7. Free writing												
8. Letter recognition												
9. Running record*												
10. High-frequency sight words												
11. Observation comments												

*Not applicable for Pre-K.

Source: Adapted from South Brunswick, New Jersey, public schools portfolio.

Some schools have formal schedules for collecting portfolios and administering tests (see Figure 2.6). A portfolio also should be prepared by the child with the teacher that he or she can keep and take home at the end of a school year (Gunning, 2003.)

Throughout the chapters of this book, assessment will be discussed at the end of sections that deal with specific skill development. Multiple measures will be offered to include a portfolio of assessment materials for children. These materials should help teachers create appropriate instructional strategies, help parents understand their child's development, and make children aware of their strengths and weaknesses and how they can improve.

Standardized Tests

Standardized tests measure what students have learned. Standardized tests are prepared by publishers and are norm referenced; that is, they are administered to large numbers of students to develop norms. Norms are the average performance of students who are tested at a particular grade and age level. When selecting a standardized test, it is important to check its validity for your students. That is, does the test evaluate what it says it tests for, and does it match the goals you have for your students? The reliability of the test is important as well. That is, are scores accurate and dependable?

Other features of standardized tests are as follows:

1. *Grade-equivalent scores* are raw scores converted into grade-level scores. For example, if a child is in first grade and receives a grade-equivalent score of 2.3, his performance would be considered above grade level.
2. *Percentile ranks* are raw scores converted into a percentile rank. They tell where the child ranked as compared to all children who took the test at the same grade and age level. Therefore, if a youngster received a percentile rank of 80, it would mean that this student scored better than or equal to 80 percent of students taking the test at the same grade and age level and that 20 percent of the children taking the test scored better.

Although many criticisms are associated with standardized measures, they do present another source of information about a child's performance. Parents like receiving the information from the test because it is concrete information regarding where their child ranks among others in the same grade. It must be realized, though, that it is just one type of information that is no more important than all the other measures discussed earlier. Taking a standardized test does expose children to another type of literacy situation that they are likely to encounter in later years both in and out of school. Many question, however, whether it is necessary to use standardized tests with very young children. A well-known standaradized test for early literacy is entitled DIBELS, Dynamic Indicators of Basic Early Literacy Skills (R. H. Good, III & A. R. Kaminski, 2003. Longmont, CO: Sopris West Educational Services).

Concerns Associated with Standardized Testing

A number of problems are associated with standardized tests. We must recognize that they represent only one form of assessment; their use must be coordinated with that of other assessment measures. Some standardized tests for early literacy evaluate children on skills such as auditory memory, rhyme, letter recognition, visual matching, school language, and listening. By contrast, practices that nurture early literacy that may not be included in the test emphasize children's prior knowledge, book concepts, attitudes about reading, association of meaning with print, and characteristics of printed materials. One child might pass all portions of a standardized test, yet not be able to begin to read, whereas a second child might not pass any portion of the test, but may already be reading.

Some standardized tests do not match the instructional practices suggested by the latest research and theory on early literacy. Because school districts are often evaluated on how well children perform on the standardized tests, teachers may feel pressured to teach for the test. This situation is often referred to as **high-stakes assessment,** because major decisions are being made from the results of one test score. Teachers who succumb to this temptation could use inappropriate strategies for teaching young children. In addition, such teachers spend a great deal of time preparing children for standardized tests by drilling them on sample tests similar to the real ones. The sample tests are graded, and instruction is geared to remedy the student weaknesses indicated. If teachers do not prepare children for the test with practice sessions and do not teach to the test, their children may not score well. Aside from the content of the test, the knowledge of how to take the test is crucial for success. Thus, teachers may feel they are jeopardizing their own jobs if they refuse to teach to standardized tests. It is a difficult dilemma.

Another high-stakes issue with standardized tests is that the results of such tests are commonly used in placing children in specific classrooms and reading groups. Once placed, a child may never be moved to a different group. Yet the standardized tests on which placement decisions are based can yield inaccurate information. Figure 2.7 illustrates hypothetical subscores and overall percentile ranks of three kindergarten children on a typical standardized test.

Student A scored well in auditory and visual skills and poorly in language skills. The child's overall score is at the 50th percentile. Student B has good auditory skills, poor visual skills, and good language skills and also scored

Figure 2.7

Hypothetical Subtest Profiles on Three Kindergarten Children Achieving about the Same Test Performance Rating

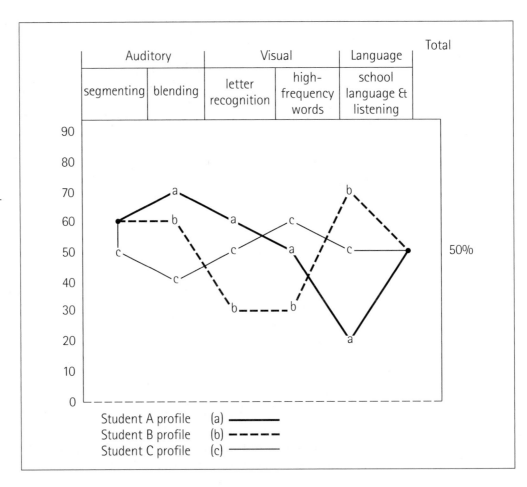

overall at the 50th percentile. Student C scored fairly consistently across visual, auditory, and language skills and likewise scored overall at the 50th percentile. All three children will go to the first grade and could be placed in the same reading group, even though Student A has a possible language deficit and is missing one of the most important ingredients for reading success—a strong language base. These three children are very different in ability, yet have scored at the same overall percentile on a standardized test. It is very unlikely that the three will achieve similar success in reading, although they might be expected to on the basis of their test scores.

Another concern with standardized tests is bias. For example, standardized test scores are less reliable with younger children than with older children. Furthermore, some standardized tests are still biased in favor of white, middle-class children despite genuine attempts to alleviate the problem. Their use tends to place rural, African American, and bilingual youngsters at a disadvantage. Prior knowledge plays a large role in how well children will do on the test. Children from white, middle-class homes tend to have experiences that lead to better achievement on the tests. In addition, following test directions such as "Put your finger on the star" or "Circle the goat that is behind the tree" is often a problem for the young child. Children who have never seen a goat may not circle anything, because the animal on the page might look like a dog to them.

The joint IRA/NAEYC position statement *Learning to Read and Write: Developmentally Appropriate Practices for Young Children* (1998) suggests that evaluative procedures used with young children be developmentally and culturally appropriate and that the selection of evaluative measures be based on the objectives of an instructional program and consider each child's total development and its effect on reading performance. Various steps can be taken to remedy the abuse of standardized testing in early childhood education. Administrators and teachers must understand the shortcomings of standardized tests and that the use of multiple assessment tools given frequently throughout the school year would tend to prevent undue emphasis on standardized test results.

Standardized tests are a source of concern with young children; however, if they are used, teachers need to help youngsters learn about them. Children need to learn how to follow the directions and how to fill in the answers. Children must have the advantage of knowing what the test is like before they are faced with taking it.

Finding suitable tests is a difficult task. However, some test makers are becoming aware of the discrepancies between new instructional strategies and the design of the present tests. There are tools for assessing many aspects of early literacy that acknowledge and reflect the instructional strategies we evaluate today, specifically Clay's (1979) Concepts about Print Test. This test evaluates what the child knows about print and how it is used in books. In addition to any standardized test, authentic assessment measures, such as interviews, anecdotal records, collection of work samples, and others described throughout the book, should be used frequently.

According to recommendations by the International Reading Association (1999) concerning high-stakes assessment in reading, teachers should:

- Construct rigorous classroom assessments to help outside observers gain confidence in teacher techniques.
- Educate parents, community members, and policy makers about classroom-based assessment.

Standards and Standardized Tests for Reading and Writing

With the call for all children in the United States to be fluent readers by the end of third grade, professional literacy organizations have outlined standards for achievement. **Standards** define what students should know about and be able to do with reading and writing. The purpose of standards is to articulate what students need to learn at each grade level in the English language arts—reading, writing, listening, speaking, viewing, and visually representing.

To determine whether children have learned the standards, tests are now being given at the third- and fourth-grade levels. These standardized tests could represent high-stakes assessment for school districts and children, because the scores might influence promotion decisions and ratings of districts and could put jobs at risk for principals and teachers. One test should never be the determining factor for important decisions such as these. Nonetheless, to be successful in these tests and, more importantly, to help students become fluent readers, schools must begin with a set of standards for children to achieve from preschool to the third grade. In reality the test is not a fourth-grade test, but rather an accumulation of specific behaviors learned from the beginning of a child's school experiences. The creation of standards helps develop fluent readers who will accomplish the goals.

The *Standards for the English Language Arts* (1996), a project of the International Reading Association (IRA) and National Council of Teachers of English (NCTE), suggests that standards are needed to do the following:

1. Prepare students for literacy now and in the future with specific concerns about how technology will change the manner in which we deal with literacy in the future.

2. Ensure that students attain the vision of parents, teachers, and researchers about expectations for their achievement in the language arts.

3. Promote high expectations for literacy achievement among children and bridge inequities that exist in educational opportunities for all.

General standards were articulated by IRA and NCTE and, since this first endeavor, many states have adopted their own standards for the English language arts. These state standards and others being generated by various groups are extremely specific. They list expectations for reading and writing for every grade level. In addition, standards, instruction, and assessment are being linked to ensure accountability for achieving the goals that have been set forth.

The National Center on Education and the Economy (NCEE) and the Learning Research and Development Center (LRDC) at the University of Pittsburgh developed a document entitled *Reading and Writing Grade by Grade: Primary Literacy Standards for Kindergarten through Third Grade* (1999). A set of general standards for all grade levels is followed by specifics outlined for each level. For early literacy the standards are linked to instruction and assessment. In kindergarten, for example, one standard is the acquisition of phonemic awareness, more specifically the ability to segment and blend sounds. The standard is even more detailed and suggests that it is expected that by the end of kindergarten children be able to do the following in the area of phonemic awareness:

produce rhyming words and recognize pairs of rhyming words;

isolate initial consonants in single-syllable words (for example, /t/ is the first sound in *top*); when a single-syllable word is pronounced (for example, *cat*), identify the **onset** (/c/) and the **rime** (-at) and begin to segment, or separate, the sounds (/c/-/a/-/t/) by saying each sound aloud; and

blend onsets (/c/) and rimes (-at) to form words (*cat*) and begin to blend separately spoken phonemes to make a meaningful one-syllable word (for example, when the teacher says a word slowly, stretching it out as "mmm–ahhh–mmm," children can say that the word being stretched out is *mom*). (p. 54)

Instructional activities are being presented with standards to help teachers achieve these goals with children. In addition, a means for assessing the standard is provided. Standards may differ somewhat from one state to the other. However, there are a great many similarities among them as they are adopted throughout the country. The *Primary Literacy Standards* (NCEE/LRDC, 1999) mentioned suggest the areas for the development of literacy in grades K through 3. For each different area, specific expertise for each grade level is suggested. The following is the general outline for reading and writing:

READING STANDARDS

Print—Sound Code

Knowledge of letters and their sounds.

Phonemic awareness: The ability to hear the different sound segments at the beginning, middle, and end of words and say, or blend, separate phonemes to make meaningful utterances.

Reading words: The ability to figure out words from knowledge of the alphabetic principles and the ability to read words learned by sight.

Getting the Meaning

Accuracy and fluency when reading: Accuracy is the ability to recognize words correctly. Fluency is the ability to read aloud with appropriate intonations and pauses, indicating that students understand the meaning.

Self-monitoring and self-correcting strategies.

Comprehension.

Reading Habits

Reads a lot.

Discusses books.

Has a large vocabulary.

WRITING STANDARDS

Habits and Processes

Writing Purposes and Resulting Genres

Sharing events, telling stories: narrative writing.

Informing others: report or informational writing.

Getting things done: functional writing.

Producing and responding to literature.

Language Use and Conventions

Style and syntax.

Vocabulary and word choice.

Spelling.

Punctuation, capitalization, and other conventions.

In each chapter dealing with reading and writing, objectives for instruction that match standards will be listed.

Prekindergarten standards are being written for literacy development of 3- and 4-year-olds. We are recognizing that children this young are capable of learning many literacy skills and enjoy learning them if engaged in activities in an appropriate manner. The following are representative of some prekindergarten literacy objectives being created by different groups.

Listening Comprehension

Listens with increased attention.

Listens for different purposes.

Understands simple oral directions.

Listens to and engages in conversation.

Listens to tapes and responds to directions on the tapes.

Speech Production and Discrimination

Identifies differences between similar sounding words (e.g., *tree* and *three*).

Produces speech sounds with increased ease and accuracy.

Experiments with language.

Vocabulary

Shows an increase in listening and speaking vocabulary.

Uses new vocabulary in daily communication.

Refines understanding of words.

Increases listening vocabulary.

Verbal Expression

Uses language for a variety of purposes.

Uses sentences of increasing length and grammatical complexity.

Uses language to express routines.

Tells a simple personal narrative.

Asks questions.

Begins to retell stories in sequence.

Phonological Awareness

Begins to identify rhymes.

Begins to attend to beginning sounds.

Begins to break words into syllables or claps along with each syllable.

Begins to create words by substituting one sound for another.

Print and Book Awareness

Understands that reading and writing are ways to obtain information and knowledge and communicate thoughts and ideas.

Understands that illustrations carry meaning, but cannot be read.

Understands that letters are different from numbers.

Understands that a book has a title and an author.

Understands that print runs from left to right and top to bottom.

Begins to understand basic print conventions (e.g., letters are grouped to form words, words are separated by spaces).

Letter Knowledge and Early Word Recognition

Begins to associate letter names with their shapes.

Identifies 10 or more printed letters.

Begins to notice beginning letters in familiar words.

Begins to make some letter–sound matches.

Begins to identify some high-frequency words.

Motivation to Read

Demonstrates an interest in books and reading.

Enjoys listening to and discussing books.

Requests being read to and rereads the same story.

Attempts to read and write.

Knowledge of Literary Forms

Predicts what will happen next in a story.

Imitates special language in a book.

Asks questions about the information or events in a book.

Connects information and events in books to real life.

Written Expression

Attempts to write messages.

Uses letters to represent written language.

Attempts to connect the sounds in a word with its letter forms.

Begins to dictate words and phrases to an adult who records them on paper.

Stages of Child Development

Early childhood education has always been concerned about the physical, social, emotional, and cognitive development of the child. The curriculum, therefore, should emphasize all four areas. One cannot discuss early literacy without being concerned with the total child. This information is needed when preparing instructional environments and activities. This knowledge will also help determine whether children have special needs related to learning disabilities, giftedness, or communication disorders, for example. Considering the total development of the child, and not just the cognitive, has been and always should be a hallmark in early childhood education and must influence early literacy development as well. Box 2.1 describes the developmental characteristics of children from birth through 8 years (Seefeldt & Barbour, 1997, pp. 63–69). It can be used as a reference throughout this volume, in teaching and assessing child development. The chart can be used as a checklist for evaluating child development.

Box 2.1

Developmental Characteristics of Children during Stages of Development

Birth through Twelve Months

Physical

Develops rapidly.

Changes from waking because of hunger and distress to sleeping through the night with two naps during the day.

Changes eating patterns from every three hours to regular meals three times a day.

Develops control of muscles that hold up the head. By four months enjoys holding up head.

Focuses eyes and begins to explore the environment visually.

Begins to grasp objects at about sixteen weeks. Can grasp and let go by six months.

Rolls over intentionally (four to six months).

Holds own bottle (six to eight months).

Shows first tooth at about six months. Has about twelve teeth by age one.

Sits well alone, can turn and recover balance (six to eight months).

Raises body at nine months. May even pull self up to a standing position.

Starts to crawl at six months and to creep at nine or ten months.

May begin walking by age one.

Social

Begins to smile socially (four or five months).

Enjoys frolicking and being jostled.

Recognizes mother or other significant adult.

Notices hands and feet and plays with them.

By six months likes playing, alone or with company.

Begins to be wary of strangers.

Cooperates in games such as peekaboo and pat-a-cake.

Imitates actions of others.

Emotional

Differentiates crying according to specific discomforts, such as being hungry, cold, or wet.
Shows emotions by overall body movements, such as kicking, arm waving, and facial expressions.
Begins to show pleasure when needs are being met.
By six months shows affection by kissing and hugging.
Shows signs of fearfulness.
Pushes away things not liked.

Cognitive

First discriminates mother from others; later discriminates familiar faces from those of strangers.
Explores world through looking, mouthing, grasping.
Inspects things for long periods.
As a first sign of awareness, protests disappearance of objects.
Discovers how to make things happen and delights in doing so by repeating an action several times.
Between six and twelve months becomes aware of object permanency by recognizing that an object has been taken away and by looking for a hidden object.
Begins intentional actions by pulling at an object or removing an obstacle to get at an object.
Becomes increasingly curious about surroundings.

One and Two Years Old

Physical

Begins to develop many motor skills.
Continues teething till about 18 months; develops all 20 teeth by age 2.
Develops large muscles. Crawls well, stands alone (at about a year), and pushes chair around.
Starts to walk at about a year to fifteen months.
Places ball in and out of box.
Releases ball with thrust.
Creeps down stairs backward.
Develops fine motor skills. Stacks two blocks, picks up a bean, and puts objects into a container. Starts to use spoon. Puts on simple things—for instance, an apron over the head.
By end of eighteen months, scribbles with a crayon in vertical or horizontal lines.
Turns pages of book.
During second year, walks without assistance.
Runs but often bumps into things.
Jumps up and down.
Walks up and down stairs with one foot forward.
Holds glass with one hand.
Stacks at least six blocks and strings beads.
Opens doors and cupboards.
Scribbles spirals, loops, and rough circles.
Starts to prefer one hand to the other.
Starts day control of elimination.

Social

At age one, differentiates meagerly between self and other.
Approaches mirror image socially.
By eighteen months, distinguishes between terms *you* and *me*.
Plays spontaneously; is self-absorbed but notices newcomers.
Imitates behavior more elaborately.

Identifies body parts.

Responds to music.

Develops socialization by age two. Is less interested in playing with parent and more interested in playing with a peer.

Begins parallel play, playing side by side, but without interaction.

By age two learns to distinguish strongly between self and others.

Is ambivalent about moving out and exploring.

Becomes aware of owning things and may become very possessive.

Emotional

At age one is amiable.

At eighteen months is resistant to change. Often suddenly—won't let mother out of sight.

Tends to rebel, resist, fight, run, hide.

Perceives emotions of others.

At age one, shows no sense of guilt. By age two, begins to experience guilt and shows beginnings of conscience.

Says *no* emphatically. Shows willfulness and negativism.

Laughs and jumps exuberantly.

Cognitive

Shows mental imagery: looks for things that are hidden, recalls and anticipates events, moves beyond here and now, begins temporal and spatial orientation.

Develops deductive reasoning: searches for things in more than one place.

Reveals memory: shows deferred imitation by seeing an event and imitating it later.

Remembers names of objects.

Completes awareness of object permanence.

By age two or three distinguishes between black and white and may use names of colors.

Distinguishes one from many.

Says "one, two, three" in rote counting, but not often in rational counting.

Acts out utterances and talks about actions while carrying them out.

Takes things apart and tries to put them back together.

Shows sense of time by remembering events. Knows terms today and tomorrow, but mixes them up.

Three to Four Years Old

Physical

Expands physical skills.

Rides a tricycle.

Pushes a wagon.

Runs smoothly and stops easily.

Climbs jungle gym ladder.

Walks stairs with alternating feet forward.

Jumps with two feet.

Shows high energy level.

By four can do a running broad jump.

Begins to skip, pushing one foot ahead of the other.

Can balance on one foot.

Keeps relatively good time in response to music.

Expands fine motor skills, can do zippers and dress oneself.

Controls elimination at night.

Social

Becomes more social.

Moves from parallel play to early associative play. Joins others in activities.

Becomes aware of racial and sexual differences.
Begins independence.
By four shows growing sense of initiative and self-reliance.
Becomes aware of basic sex identity.
Not uncommonly develops imaginary playmates (a trait that may appear as early as two and a half).

Emotional

Begins enjoying humor. Laughs when adults laugh.
Develops inner control over behavior.
Shows less negativism.
Develops phobias and fears, which may continue until age five.
At four may begin intentional lying, but is outraged by parents' white lies.

Cognitive

Begins problem-solving skills. Stacks blocks and may kick them down to see what happens.
Learns to use listening skills as a means of learning about the world.
Still draws in scribbles at age three, but in one direction and less repetitively.
At age four, drawings represent what child knows and thinks is important.
Is perceptually bound to one attribute and characteristic. "Why" questions abound.
Believes everything in the world has a reason, but the reason must accord with the child's own knowledge.
Persists in egocentric thinking.
Begins to sort out fantasy from reality.

Five and Six Years Old

Physical

Well controlled and constantly in motion.
Often rides a bicycle as well as a tricycle.
Can skip with alternating feet and hop.
Can control fine motor skills. Begins to use tools such as toothbrush, saw, scissors, pencil, hammer, needle for sewing.
Has established handedness well. Identifies hand used for writing or drawing.
Can dress self, but may still have trouble tying shoelaces.
At age six begins to lose teeth.

Social

Becomes very social. Visits with friends independently.
Becomes very self-sufficient.
Persists longer at a task. Can plan and carry out activities and return to projects next day.
Plays with two or three friends, often for just a short time only, then switches play groups.
Begins to conform. Is very helpful.
By age six becomes very assertive, often bossy, dominating situations and ready with advice.
Needs to be first. Has difficulty listening.
Is possessive and boastful.
Craves affection. Often has a love-hate relationship with parents.
Refines sex roles. Has tendency to type by sex.
Becomes clothes conscious.

Emotional

Continues to develop sense of humor.
Learns right from wrong.
At age five begins to control emotions and is able to express them in socially approved ways.
Quarrels frequently, but quarrels are of short duration.

At age six shifts emotions often and seems to be in emotional ferment.

New tensions appear as a result of attendance at school all day. Temper tantrums appear.

Giggles over bathroom words.

At age five develops a conscience, but sees actions as all good or all bad.

At age six accepts rules and often develops rigid insistence that they be obeyed.

May become a tattletale.

Cognitive

Begins to recognize conservation of amount and length.

Becomes interested in letters and numbers. May begin printing or copying letters and numbers. Counts.

Knows most colors.

Recognizes that one can get meaning from printed words.

Has a sense of time, but mainly personal time. Knows when events take place in the child's own day or week.

Recognizes own space and can move about independently in familiar territory.

Seven and Eight Years Old

Physical

Great variation in height and weight, but rate of growth slows.

Masters physical skills for game playing and enjoys team sports.

Is willing to repeat a skill over and over to mastery.

Increases in fine motor performance–can draw a diamond correctly and form letters well.

Has sudden spurts of energy.

Loss of baby teeth continues and permanent teeth appear.

Physique begins to change. Body more proportionately developed and facial structure changes.

Social

Beginning to prefer own sex—has less boy/girl interaction.

Peer groups begin to form.

Security in sex identification.

Self-absorption.

Begins to work and play independently.

Can be argumentative.

At seven still not a good loser and often a tattle teller.

By eight plays games better and not as intent on winning.

Conscientious—can take responsibility for routine chores.

Less selfish. Able to share. Wants to please.

Still enjoys and engages in fantasy play.

Emotional

Difficulty in starting things, but will persist to end.

Worries that school might be too hard.

Beginning of empathy—sees other's viewpoint.

Sense of humor expressed in riddles, practical jokes, and nonsense words.

Discriminates between good and bad, but still immature.

Is sensitive and gets hurt easily.

Has sense of possession and takes care of possessions (makes collections).

Cognitive

Attention span is quite long.

Can plan and stay with a task or project over a long period.

Interested in conclusions and logical ends.

Aware of community and the world.

Expanding knowledge and interest.

Some sevens read well and by eight really enjoy reading.

Can tell time—aware of passage of time in months and years.

Interested in other time periods.

Conscious of other's work and their own. May comment, "I'm good at art, but Sue is better at reading."

Differences in abilities widening.

Source: C. Seefeldt and N. Barbour, *Early Childhood Education: An Introduction*, 4th ed., pp. 63–69. © 1998. Reprinted by permission of Pearson Education, Inc., Upper Saddle River, NJ.

An Idea from the Classroom

English Language Learners

Reviewing What Was Learned Today

I like my second-grade students to reflect on and evaluate what they have learned on a daily basis, so I created a way for them to maintain an ongoing record that chronicles knowledge they have constructed over time. I created a chart that hangs on the wall with one pocket for each student on the chart. There is a stack of index cards in a pocket for this purpose. At the end of each day I allow 10 minutes for the children to complete the evaluation task. They are to take an index card and for 2 to 3 minutes review the learning activities that took place that day. Then they are to take 2 to 3 minutes to write down key concepts learned. Students should write down only three to five concepts. After they write these concepts, they "pair and share" with a partner. Each one reads what he or she wrote. When the children leave the class to go home, they put the index cards into their pocket on the chart. On occasion I have the students review the cards. I also review the cards; reviewing gives me insight into what concepts the children have understood and recalled correctly.

Cards are sent home at the end of a week so parents may be kept up to date about what their child is learning. Encourage children and parents to discuss the contents of the cards and to extend the learning at home. For young children, draw pictures to represent learning for the last few days and have them circle what they have learned.

Christine Zehnder, Graduate Student at Rutgers Graduate School of Education

An Idea from the Classroom

English Language Learners

You Write, I Write: Using Interactive Writing as a Means of Authentic Assessment

During journal time, I pull aside one student or a small group of students to conduct an interactive writing activity in my first-grade class. This activity is beneficial to ELL students because it is collaborative and provides excellent teacher support for individualized instruction. Have the students bring their journals and materials for drawing and writing. Give the students 2 to 3 minutes to select what they want to write about from three topics you present. Some will start by drawing a picture. Others will begin writing. Interact with the children as they write. Ask them to tell you about what they are writing and prompt them at their point of need. For example, "What sound do you hear at the beginning of that word? What letter makes that sound? Can you hear any sounds at the end of the word? How about in the middle?" For more fluent writers, encourage them to elaborate on their ideas. For example, "If you added some describing words, I would be able to clearly see that picture in my mind."

Encourage the children to do as much of the problem solving and writing as possible. They may refer to word walls, charts, and other print sources in the classroom. When a child needs more support, write what the child could not write using a felt-tip pen. For example, a child may be able to record beginning and ending sounds in words, but is developing hearing middle sounds. A word in their journal may look like the following: h**ear**t (bold print is the teacher's writing). You may note other areas in the journal entry where strong teacher support was required by marking a dot at the beginning of the passage and a dot at the end, indicating where you helped the child. Make sure to use lots of specific, positive praise in your interactions. For example, "Placing the exclamation point at the end of that sentence was perfect. I could tell you really were surprised when you found what the tooth fairy left for you."

By looking over the children's journals, you can see both progress over time and the children's areas of need. You may, for example, see the need to teach certain sight words, punctuation usage, or prefixes and suffixes. These can be addressed in whole-group shared reading and writing lessons or in a one-on-one context. As the year progresses, it is rewarding to both the children and the teacher to see the student's participation in the interactive writing increase while the teacher's decreases.

Susan Yoder, Kindergarten Teacher

Activities and Questions

1. Answer the focus questions at the beginning of the chapter.

2. Select a child from your field placement or from your own classroom. The child can be a relative or a friend's child. The child should be between the ages of 3 and 8. Begin a portfolio for this child with pieces of work you collect, such as a language sample, a writing sample, a running record, and a sample that reflects word study and comprehension abilities. Evaluate the child's ability in each area and design instruction for the child based on the assessment findings. In the supplementary section at the end of this book, there are perforated pages with the forms you will need to take out to evaluate your child.

3. Parents in your district are not pleased with the authentic measures for assessment being used. They want to know if their children are doing as well as others. Based on a test, they want to know if their child is above, below, or at grade level. You are convinced that authentic assessment is the right way to evaluate children. What can you do to help parents understand and accept the authentic assessment strategies? Plan a parent workshop to inform them about standards and how you link your instruction and assessment to them.

4. **Strategies** Administer the reading and writing interview on pages S–7 and S–8 to a selected child. Reflect on the type of reader and writer the child is based on your discussion.

PEARSON myeducationlab

VIDEO EXERCISE

Now that you have the benefit of having read this chapter, return to the www.myeducationlab.com topic "Assessment, Remediation and Diagnosis" and watch "Using Assessments to Inform Instruction," "Designing Developmentally Appropriate Days," and "Observing Children in Authentic Contexts" one more time. You may complete the questions that accompany them online and save or transmit your work to your professor, or complete the following questions, as required.

Using Assessments to Inform Instruction (5:32 minutes)

1. What is a running record, and how does it identify a reader's strengths and weaknesses?
2. When should a teacher perform a running record? Why?
3. Perform a running record on a child. Afterward, discuss your findings with the teacher and determine if he or she concurs with your results. Summarize the discussion here.

Designing Developmentally Appropriate Days (4:18 minutes)

1. When determining the developmental level of a child, what are four kinds of skills you should consider?
2. Why is it important for teachers to have knowledge of developmental patterns in young children?
3. One teacher mentions the importance of viewing children holistically. Explain this in terms of Bloom's three developmental domains: psychomotor, cognitive, and affective.

Observing Children in Authentic Contexts (6:03 minutes)

1. What techniques did the teacher use to observe children in this clip?
2. What are the advantages and disadvantages of the observation techniques used by the teacher?
3. What additional tools could the teacher use to enhance the observation process?
4. How can observations be used to inform or enhance future curriculum planning?

Focus Questions

- How do we plan for early literacy instruction with children from diverse cultural backgrounds in our classrooms?

- What do we need to plan for children who are English language learners?

- What is meant by early intervention programs?

- What is meant by inclusion?

- Describe the multiple-intelligence theory and how it relates to literacy instruction.

- How do we deal with children who have physical impairments in the regular classroom?

- **VOCABULARY:** cultural diversity, English language learners (ELL), gifted, learning disabled, inclusion, early intervention, pull-out programs

- **Strategies** Are children learning English words used in school and common phrases as a result of hanging the Spanish words and picture cards shown on Strategies for the Classroom pages S-9 through S-11.

myeducationlab VIDEO PREVIEW: Teaching to Diverse Learning Styles (4:20 minutes); Inclusion in an Early Childhood Class (2:52 minutes). Before reading this chapter, go to www.myeducationlab.com. Under the topic "Differentiating Instruction," access and watch the video "Teaching to Diverse Learning Styles." Under the topic "Special Needs," access and watch "Inclusion in the Early Childhood Classroom."

Literacy and Diversity
Meeting Needs of Children with Special Concerns

3

Thomas Jefferson articulated three fundamental beliefs about literacy and education that have become part of our national ethos: (1) the ability of every citizen to read is necessary to the practice of democracy, (2) it is therefore the duty of the general public to support the teaching of reading for all youngsters, and (3) reading should be taught during the earliest years of schooling. Among the reasons he cited, "none is more important, none more legitimate, than of rendering the people safe, as they are the ultimate guardians of their own liberty."

—Thomas Jefferson
The Life and Selected Writings of Thomas Jefferson

Quality literacy instruction is appropriate for all children. Small-group settings are particularly good for children with diverse needs. Small-group settings encourage communication and meaningful, natural conversation. ELL students will pick up a lot of English from informal conversations and interactions with their peers. More capable children will help struggling readers to learn in small groups, as we see in the following examples during literacy center time in three different classrooms.

> *Mr. Abere's second-grade children were working independently and in collaboration with each other during a literacy center time. He described the following incident with an English language learner. Juanita would never speak in class. One day during class, Mr. Abere observed Juanita acting as a teacher with a group of children she had organized. She had the group of three sitting in a circle. Each had a copy of the same book. Juanita called their names and asked each to take a turn reading.*
>
> *Mrs. Nash had a literacy center time in her classroom where small groups of children had the opportunity to work together and be independent of the teacher. She had modeled the materials for the children so they would know how to use them.*
>
> *It became apparent when speaking with Mrs. Nash that children with special needs gained a lot from the independent work during literacy center time. Mrs. Nash described an incident involving a struggling reader in her classroom who was well below grade level in her work. According to Mrs. Nash, Charlene never read aloud. One day Mrs. Nash noticed her reading aloud to a rag doll while another child was listening. Mrs. Nash offered positive reinforcement to Charlene very quietly, and the reading aloud continued daily during literacy center time.*
>
> *Marcel was a gifted child in Mrs. Rosen's classroom with mostly low achievers. He worked alone most of the time. About 2 months after literacy center time was initiated in his classroom, he was able to participate with other children in literacy activities. The first time I observed him with others, he was reading the newspaper and checking out the weather in other parts of the country. Patrick asked Marcel if he could look too. Marcel was pleased, and then David joined them. Together they read and discussed how hot and cold it was in Florida, Colorado, and so on.*

Numerous anecdotes from literacy center time describe how children are able to find a way to participate in spite of special problems. One teacher commented, "There seems to be something that every child can find to do during literacy center time."

Theory and Research about Literacy and Diversity: Addressing Children's Individual Needs

Many of the theoretical and philosophical perspectives presented in Chapter 1 and throughout the book discuss the necessity of differentiating instruction to meet the individual needs of children. Early childhood education has always been child centered and concerned about the social, emotional, physical, and intellectual needs of children. In early childhood, every youngster is seen as a unique individual; however, there is greater diversity than ever in classrooms today, and there are more and more individual needs to meet.

Identifying special needs is the first step in dealing with diversity. Identification makes us more aware that differences exist and then helps us determine the educational implications for instructional programs.

I had a difficult time deciding whether to have a separate chapter about diversity or to integrate strategies for teaching diverse students throughout the book. The latter was my first inclination. Our classrooms, however, are so diverse and teachers are so concerned about meeting the needs of these children that I decided to do both. This chapter begins the discussion and introduces you to the types of diversity teachers might find in their classrooms. Some strategies are discussed here. In addition, throughout the book, strategies are discussed that are designed to meet individual needs. Since issues of diversity such as teaching English language learners and students at risk are of particular interest, from here to the end of the book I have provided an ELL icon that indicates when particular strategies are especially good for the students discussed in this chapter. Many different types of diversity are represented in our schools today. It has been found that good instructional techniques for all children will be appropriate, with some modifications for those with special needs (Delpit, 1995).

English Language Learners

Addressing the Literacy Needs of a Diverse Multicultural Society

The demographics of the U.S. population are becoming more racially and ethnically diverse. Current statistics show that one in every three children is from a different ethnic or racial minority group. The United States at this time is serving more than 14 million children who come from households in which English is not the primary language. It is projected that by 2030, 40 percent of the school-age population of U.S. schools will be English language learners. Over 400 different languages are reported to be spoken in the United States. Spanish is the most widespread, but there are other languages such as Korean, Arabic, Russian, Navajo, Mandarin, and Japanese, to name a few (Brock & Raphael, 2005; Miramontes, Nadeau, & Commins, 1997).

Much of the research on academic achievement in U.S. schools demonstrates that if English is not a child's first language the child is less likely to be successful (Rossi & Stringfield, 1995). Some reasons for this problem are the lack of support for the home culture provided by schools, the complex nature of learning a second language, and the low socioeconomic status of many of the families who do not speak English as a first language (Banks & Banks, 1993; Connell, 1994; Garcia & McLaughlin, 1995).

In the past, diversity was disregarded in the United States, and children were expected to ignore their cultural backgrounds and language differences and learn English and American customs on their own. If we are to live in harmony in a pluralistic society, it is imperative that educational leaders accept the charge to provide a culturally relevant education for all students. We must be sensitive toward cultural and language differences and recognize that children can and should maintain their cultural heritage and that they can still be considered American and learn English and American culture and customs without abandoning their native language (Templeton, 1991).

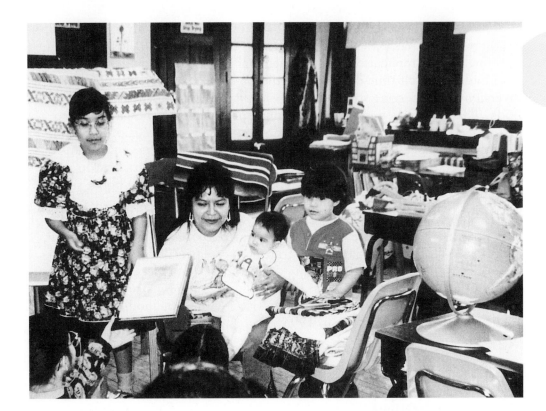

Diversity in language and heritage should be shared in classrooms to enrich the class-room experience.

Cultural Diversity

Multiculturalism is a complicated issue, referring not only to race and ethnicity, but also to class, religion, sex, and age. The multiracial, multiethnic, multicultural, and multilingual nature of our dynamic society mandates that we teach tolerance and understanding of differences as an ongoing process involving self-reflection, self-awareness, increasing knowledge, and developing relevant skills (Schickedanz, York, Stewart, & White, 1990). We need to welcome diversity in our schools. It adds a rich dimension to the classroom and to topics of study. By recognizing students' diverse backgrounds, we will enhance their self-image. Differences should be the norm, rather than the exception. Differences in cultural backgrounds often provide explanations of why children behave as they do. Behaviors that are acceptable in one culture might be thought of as disrespectful in another. Goals for classrooms in our multicultural society need to be as follows:

1. An improved understanding of cultural differences and their effect on lifestyle, values, worldviews, and individual differences

2. An increased awareness of how to develop strategies to enhance learning in a multicultural environment

3. A framework for conceptualizing ways to create a climate conducive to learning and development

The goals we need to pursue for children in ethnically diverse classrooms and for children whose language is other than English are as follows:

1. Children need to learn to accept and be comfortable with their ethnic identities.
2. Children need to learn to function in other cultures, particularly in the dominant culture.
3. Children need to relate positively with individuals from varied ethnic backgrounds.
4. Children who do not speak English or standard English must learn English, but also need to retain and value their first languages.

Teachers need to develop their own understanding of the multiethnic groups they serve. They must recognize that the children they deal with are multiethnic. They must respect the ethnic identities, heritages, and traditions of others. Teachers must be aware of their own ethnic heritages, traditions, and beliefs (Barone, 1998; Schickedanz, York, Stewart, & White, 1990; Tabors, 1998).

Helping English Language Learners in Your Classroom

A major instructional concern in early childhood literacy programs is the varied language backgrounds of the children who come to day-care centers, preschools, kindergartens, and first, second, and third grades. Any given group may contain children using words, syntax, and language patterns very different from those of standard English. Particularly in the United States, there are many different forms of English usage, for example, distinct grammars in rural New England, Appalachia, and some African American communities. There are children whose families have immigrated from Latin America, the Middle East, or Asia. The following categories represent the diverse language abilitites of young children (Fromkin & Rodman 1998; Galda, 1995).

DIVERSE LANGUAGE ABILITIES OF CHILDREN

1. Children who are recent immigrants with little or no English.
2. Children who come from homes in which the language is something other than English, but who speak some English because of their experiences with television and their contacts outside the home.
3. Children who speak both English and another language fluently. Such children are usually easily assimilated into the majority group. Often English becomes the major language with which they communicate. They then risk losing the advantages that bilingualism gives them.
4. Children who speak mainly English but who have poor skills in their parents' or family's language. Often these children speak English at home, but their parents speak to them in another language.
5. Children who speak nonstandard English because the English spoken at home is not fluent or is a dialect. Although they need to learn a more standard English at school, they must not be made to feel that their home language is inferior.
6. Children who are monolingual in English.

All six categories represent major concerns because a firm base in oral language is strongly linked to literacy development. In addition to skill development, we need to think about emotional concerns. Unfortunately, we have often looked down on children with language differences and classified them as students with potential learning problems. We have come to realize, however, that differences do *not* mean deficits. Linguists have found, for example, that black English is a systematic, rule-governed dialect that can express all levels of thought. Teachers must be sensitive to the differences in language among youngsters in their classrooms. Children must not be embarrassed or made to feel inferior because they do not speak standard English. Teachers need to respect language differences and help children take pride in their backgrounds. Diversity in language and heritage should be shared in classrooms to enrich the classroom experience (Neuman & Roskos, 1994).

Children's Responses to Language Differences

Children tend to choose playmates who speak the same language, presumably because it is easier to communicate. They usually do not reject those who speak a different language, however, and will use gestures and other means of communication when interacting with them. Bilingual children will often act as interpreters for their parents and friends who are less skilled in the language of the classroom. Although children are curious about differences in speech and will often "correct" one another, they have not developed the biases that adults have toward nonstandard usage.

Preschool and kindergarten children will acquire the language easily when immersed in language-rich classrooms where there are good models of English and sensitive teachers. This is mostly true with children whose native language is well developed and not necessarily so with children whose first language is not well developed.

How Many English Language Learners Are in our Classrooms?

According to the Census Bureau, about 400 languages are spoken in the United States (Gollnick & Chinn, 2002). The number of students who are English Language Learners is growing constantly. According to estimates from the National Clearinghouse for English Language Acquisition and Language Instruction Educational Programs (NCELA, 2006), there are about 4.7 million ELL students in the United States. Some researchers have estimated that by 2050, 40 percent of the children coming to U.S. schools will speak a language other than English (IRA, 2001). Teachers today must

If teachers become familiar with their students' cultures, the teachers are more likely to respond effectively to the students' needs.

face the reality of having students in their classroom whose primary language is not English. Right now a disparity exists between the student and teacher populations because 86.5 percent of teachers are white (Gollnick & Chinn, 2002). It has been found, however, that most good strategies for teaching early literacy development to native English speakers are also good strategies to use with ELL.

Respecting Family and Cultural Heritage

It is crucial that teachers show that they respect the cultural heritage and value the native language of their students from the moment the students walk into their classrooms. Imagine how scary it is for a young child to come into a place where everyone speaks a different language. Teachers should show interest in their students' native languages and try to learn at least a few key phrases in each of the languages represented in their classrooms (Xu, 2003). It is helpful to talk with parents about their child's level of familiarity with English. Teachers can invite parents to bring a translator to their initial conference or can provide one if the parents wish. Whenever possible, schools should consider the parents' preference for their child's literacy instruction to determine whether the child should be taught with English-only instruction or in the family's primary language (International Reading Association, 2001). Parents should be encouraged to participate in the classroom as much as possible and to share their culture and language with their child's class.

The classroom should have plenty of texts in the native languages of the ELL students. These include translations of favorite books, newspapers, menus, and other everyday texts that a student might encounter at home. Teachers should do everything they can to create a connection between each child's home and school literacy experiences. This is especially challenging because different cultures and communities embrace different approaches to literacy (Espinosa & Burns, 2003; Xu, 2003). Again, communication with parents about their children's home literacy practices will help teachers to improve instruction with ELL students. A teacher can also ask parents to introduce new concepts from the classroom in the child's native language, further enhancing the connection between home and school. If teachers become familiar with their students' cultures, the teachers are more likely to respond effectively to the students' needs. In some cultures, for example, children are encouraged to participate in classroom discussions; in others, children are encouraged not to speak in class. In some cultures we teach our children to look at us when they speak; in others it is considered impolite and children are to bow their heads. In some cultures children eat with their hands; in others, with forks, knives, and spoons; or chopsticks. If we don't know the cultural traditions, we might interpret child behavior as rude or indifferent. Therefore, it is crucial to understand the behaviors of the children in our classrooms in order to respond to them in an appropriate manner (Hadaway & Young, 2006).

Hadaway, N. L., & Young, T. A. (2006). Changing classrooms: transforming instruction: In T. A. Young & N. L. Hadaway (Eds.) *Supporting the Literacy Development of English Learners: Increasing Success in all Classrooms,* pp. 6–18. Newark, DE: International Reading Association.

The questionnaire shown in Figure 3.1 should be helpful in getting information from parents about their children that will provide you with information that will help you better understand their culture and make the child feel more comfortable in your classroom.

Figure 3.1   Helping Me Learn about You and Your Child

Child's name:_____

Father's name:_____

Father's country of origin:_____

Mother's name:_____

Mother's country of origin:_____

What name do you use for your child?_____

Does your child's name have a particular meaning or translation?_____

Where was your child born?_____

Where else has you child lived and when?_____

How long has your family lived in (name your community)?_____

What language or languages do you use to speak to your child?_____

    Father:_____

    Mother:_____

What languages do you speak?_____

    Father:_____

    Mother:_____

Who are the immediate members of your family that your child lives with or spends a lot of time with, such as siblings, grandparents, aunts, uncles, cousins? List:

Name	Relationship	Language used with your child
____	____	____
____	____	____
____	____	____

If English is not your home language, estimate how many English words your child knows. (Circle one)

Fewer than 10   10 to 50   50 to 100   More than 100

If you belong to a particular religion, respond yes or no. If you wish, you can list the religion.

_____

List the food that your child usually eats and likes. _____

List the food that your child cannot eat because of religious or other reasons. _____

What food does your child not like to eat? _____

What does your child usually eat with?   a. Fingers   b. Chopsticks   c. Fork and spoon

Complete the sentences:

When my child is with a group of children, I would expect my child to _____

When my child is misbehaving in class, I would expect the teacher to _____

If my child is unhappy in class, I would expect the teacher to _____

The three most important things my child could learn in school this year would be

(1)_____

(2)_____

(3)_____

Source: Adapted by permission from P. O. Tabors (1997). *One Child, Two Languages.* Baltimore, MD: Paul H. Brookes Publishing Co., Inc.

Instruction Appropriate for English Language Learners

Three well-known types of instruction for English language learners are (1) English immersion, (2) bilingual education, and (3) primary language programs. English immersion, or English-only instruction, may work for younger students who are able to acquire new languages more easily. Students may learn English through interaction in their regular classrooms or be pulled out for an **English as a second language** (ESL) program, in which they are taught English. English immersion instruction does not help maintain or further develop a child's native language (Espinosa & Burns, 2003).

There are several approaches to bilingual education. The *transitional approach* promotes subtractive bilingualism, in which English eventually replaces the student's native language. The goal of the *maintenance approach* is additive bilingualism, which means that students learn English while maintaining their first language. The two languages have equal value. The *two-way bilingual approach* can be used in classrooms with a mix of English speakers and non-English speakers (Espinosa & Burns, 2003; Gollnick & Chinn, 2002). Roughly half of the curriculum is taught in English and half is taught in the other language. This approach benefits ELL students, who acquire English, and English speakers, who learn a second language.

Primary language instruction for ELL students develops literacy in the primary language first, before shifting to bilingual or English-only instruction. Children are taught concepts, knowledge, and skills in their primary language as English skills are gradually incorporated into instruction (Gollnick & Chinn, 2002). Research shows that programs that provide initial literacy instruction in a child's primary language and promote long-term primary language development have proved the most effective with English language learners (Espinosa & Burns, 2003; International Reading Association, 2001). The Committee on the Prevention of Reading Difficulties in Young Children recommends that children learn to read in their first language while learning to speak English over time (Snow, Burns, & Griffin, 1998). Two-way bilingual instruction, for example a mix of English and Spanish, has also been successful.

People naturally learn spoken language before they learn to read and write. Therefore, it is beneficial if students become proficient with oral skills in English before they have formal English instruction for reading and writing (Espinosa & Burns, 2003; Gunning, 2003). Because there are many factors at play in each ELL student's educational development, there is no one perfect method of instruction for all ELL students. Teachers need to decide with other professionals and parents what is best for different children.

Good Strategies for Teaching Reading to English Language Learners

Teachers who have ELL students in their classrooms must find as many creative ways as possible to encourage their students' language and literacy development. There are numerous strategies for attending to English language learners in the classroom. Many of these strategies for promoting English language development are strategies for all students, not just second-language learners. Good literacy practice is good practice for all.

ELL students may be very timid and nervous when they first enter an English-speaking classroom, so it is crucial that teachers immediately foster a sense of belonging for these students. Teachers may want to have someone who speaks the child's language record a welcoming greeting to be played on the first day of class. Teachers can help their students develop empathy for the ELL students by having someone come into the class and teach a lesson in an unfamiliar language (Shore, 2001). This experience will help the students to better understand how an ELL student feels in an English-only classroom. Some key elements to helping ELL students feel comfortable are:

- Make classrooms predictable with routines that will help ELL students to feel safe and confident in their new environment.
- Be sure you and your students are accepting of all children.
- Assign a classmate (ideally a bilingual student) as a buddy of each ELL student. This buddy should be friendly, knowledgeable, respectful, and eager to show the ELL student around and assist the student when necessary.
- Engage ELL students in peer-assisted learning, with older children working with younger and more advanced peers paired with others to guide them.
- Provide intensive small-group language and literacy instruction.

Dramatic play with stories, rhymes, and props is helpful with ELL students.

- Tasks should involve students as active participants. For example, assign English language learners nonverbal class jobs, like passing out folders or watering the plants, at the beginning of the school year so that they can contribute to the classroom despite the language barrier.
- Activities should maximize the opportunity for language use.
- Instructional interactions should provide support for student understanding.
- Instructional content should utilize student diversity.

Sources: Freeman & Freeman, 2006; Parker & Pardini, 2006.

To help English language learners with language and literacy development:

- The classroom library should contain a variety of texts in English and a variety of books in the primary languages of all the students.
- Have examples of other languages in your classroom, such as books, newspapers, printed songs, menus, and signs.
- Teachers need to provide daily and extensive vocabulary instruction. Vocabulary development is the key to learning English and learning to read. Do not introduce too many words at a time. Less is more. Select words that convey key concepts, and work with words for a long period of time. Use visuals, such as pictures and graphic organizers, when possible to help teach words.
- Teach basic greetings and expressions, such as hello, good-bye, thank you, you're welcome, and excuse me.
- Make a point of teaching school-related vocabulary to the ELL students so that the students can navigate their way through the classroom and school. Words such as playground, cafeteria, bathroom, gymnasium, centers, books, paper, pencils, pens, and crayons are first words to learn. Children can collect this new vocabulary in their **Very Own Words** container. It is helpful if the Very Own Words index cards have the word in both English and the child's primary language and have an accompanying picture. (See Chapter 5 for a description of Very Own Words and the glossary.) See Strategies for the Classroom page S-13.

Strategies

Because original text is not bogged down in unfamiliar vocabulary, syntax, or cultural references, it is easier for ELL students to embrace and try to read.

- Teachers can use a technique called *sheltered English,* which involves using simple language, slow and repeated phrases, gestures, and visual references (Shore, 2001).

- Teachers should avoid using idioms if possible, as well as other culturally specific expressions.

- Teachers can also help their students follow instruction by previewing all reading selections for vocabulary, syntax, semantics, cultural references, or background knowledge that may be challenging for ELL students (Gunning, 2003). After a thorough preview, teachers will be able to preteach new vocabulary and go over any possible difficulties with a text ahead of time. Texts with a universal knowledge base, like informational or concept books, are especially beneficial to ELL students because they are not culturally specific (Xu, 2003).

- Use high-interest picture books. Books with predictable patterns are also particularly useful for the literacy instruction of ELL students. Teachers should give children as many language clues as possible through visuals, gestures and expressions, and repetitive phrases. Repetition should be encouraged, through predictable books as well as fun songs and rhyming games. Dramatic play with stories, rhymes, and props is helpful with ELL students.

- Involve ELL students in creating their own texts about subject matter that is familiar to them. Original text is not bogged down in unfamiliar vocabulary, syntax, or cultural references, so it is easier for ELL students to embrace and to attempt to read (Gunning, 2003; Xu, 2003).

- Buddy writing and reading are useful, especially when one person is proficient in English and has some knowledge of the language spoken by the ELL child. Children will build on the language and ideas of their classmates as they create a text together.

- Teachers can take dictation from English language learners and write down their stories when they cannot write them down themselves. Stories can include a mixture of English and the native language of the children. This tendency should be allowed and might help their English language development (Gunning, 2003).

- Use of manipulative materials in the form of games, puppets, and visual figures is helpful with ELL students' vocabulary development.

- ELL students need to learn our alphabet and the new code they have to deal with. It does take time, with a good deal of exposure through language games, books, and access to print (Adams, 1990).

- Basic literacy lessons need direct instruction, modeling, picture cues, and picture walks through books (that is, reading the pages by using the pictures).

- Children need to practice the skills learned over and over again, first with guidance and then independently.

- Use the cloze proceudre. Write a sentence or two and leave out a word or put the first letter of the word and leave the rest out. Have the children figure out the word from the meaning of the sentence. For example, after reading a simple story, have the children fill in the the missing words.

  > Once upon a time there were _____ little pigs.
  >
  > They lived with their Mother and _____, but wanted to leave home.
  >
  > They said good-by and went out to build themselves a_____.
  >
  > The first pig built a house of _____.
  >
  > The second pig built a house of _____.
  >
  > The third pig built a house of _____.

- Engage students in repeated readings of storybooks.

- Record simple stories and have ELL students follow simple texts as the story is read.

- Cut up short stories into sentences for children to sequence.

- Cut up sentences into words to be sequenced into the sentences.

- Show similarity between some English and Spanish words

Accident	Accidente
Intelligent	Intelligente
Marvelous	Maravilloso

- Involve parents as much as possible by demonstrating strategies and encouraging them to help.

Sources: Akhavan, 2006; Capellini, 2005; Gersten et al., 2007.

English Language Learners

Throughout the book, at the end of each chapter, one or more ideas have been provided that are especially appropriate or helpful with English language learners. Most good early childhood strategies for native English speakers will also be good for students learning English. In the rest of this text, when an activity or strategy is particularly good for an ELL student, there will be an ELL icon to indicate this.

Resources to Learn More about English Language Learners

Understanding and teaching English language learners is a key issue in our society today and a difficult one. There are books completely devoted to dealing with this issue. Some are listed next as resources for the preservice and inservice teacher to consult for additional information.

Akhavan, L. L. (2006). *Help! My kids don't all speak English: How to set up a language workshop in your linguistically diverse classroom.* Portsmouth, NH: Heinemann.

Bouch, M. (2005). *Comprehension strategies for English language learners.* New York: Scholastic.

Capellini, M. (2005). *Balancing reading and language learning: A resource for teaching English language learners, K–5.* Portland, ME: Stenhouse; Newark, DE: International Reading Association.

Freeman, Y. S., & Freeman, D. E. (2006). *Teaching reading and writing in Spanish and English in bilingual and dual language classrooms* (2nd ed.) Portsmouth, NH: Heinemann.

Gersten, R., et al. *IES Practice Guide: Effective Literacy and English Language Instruction for English Learners Elementary Grades.* Washington, DC: NCEE 2007-4011, U.S. Department of Education, Institute of Education Sciences: National Center for Education Evaluation and Regional Assistance.

Parker, E. L., & Pardini, T. H. (2006). *The words came down: English language learners read, write, and talk across the curriculum, K–2.* Portland, ME: Stenhouse.

Gifted Children, Learning Disability, and Attention Deficit Hyperactivity Disorder

Gifted youngsters are often identified as having an intelligence quotient (IQ) of approximately 130. Those who develop other skills in addition to academic skills, such as playing a musical instrument at an ability level far above that expected of a same-age child, are also considered gifted. Gifted children are often leaders. These special talents need to be encouraged, but not at the expense of recognizing the social, emotional, and physical needs of the child. Differentiating assignments to make them more challenging for the ability levels of these children will accommodate their special talents.

Learning disabled youngsters are those who perform at a level below what is expected for their age or grade. Children are learning disabled for a variety of reasons. They are usually of normal intelligence, but performing below their level of ability. Learning disabled children cannot process language properly. That is, they have trouble speaking, writing, or understanding language.

Some conditions associated with learning disabilities are perceptual problems, dyslexia, or some type of brain injury causing minimal brain dysfunction. Children with these conditions are often easily distracted and have short attention spans.

Attention deficit hyperactivity disorder (ADHD) is a condition affecting children who have trouble focusing, paying attention, sitting still, and staying on task. The problem is usually due to a chemical imbalance and causes learning problems.

Programs for the learning disabled and children with ADHD need to be highly structured, with short periods of direct instruction. In addition, programs must provide students with materials that will be of interest to them. Many of the strategies throughout the book will be good for teaching disabled children.

Students Who Are at Risk

Children considered at risk are affected by several factors that have been identified. The areas under discussion in this chapter often put students at risk. Such students may come from diverse backgrounds, speak a language other than English, have physical difficulties, or live in poor, disadvantaged homes. Poverty does not mean that children can never be successful in school; however, research about literacy achievement illustrates that about 55 percent of children below the poverty level read below grade level (Donahue, Doane, & Grigg, 2000).

According to the report of Snow, Burns, and Griffin (1998), good strategies are good for all children. Good strategies usually consist of a **balanced approach to literacy instruction** with some **explicit instruction** that follows a systematic sequence of skill development, allowing time for problem solving and providing real-life materials and **experiences.** We have learned from brain research and from research dealing with the fact that children who attend preschool are more successful in school that we need to start early. Many at-risk children are already behind at 3 and 4 years of age. Teachers need to select activities in which children can experience success. When you

If children who are at risk and already behind at age 3 and 4 attend preschool, their chances for success in school are significantly improved.

are successful, you want to try more. If you are not successful, you often want to quit.

At-risk children lack background experiences, and this limitation affects their vocabulary and language development, which in turn affects their literacy learning. Many have no books or printed matter in their homes. Providing experiences that cause talk are helpful in building vocabulary. Having access to books in your classroom is crucial.

Multiple Intelligences and Literacy Development

Howard Gardner (1993) has discussed the concept of multiple intelligences. His theory suggests that some people have all seven types of intelligences that he outlines and others have fewer. I have placed this topic in this chapter because it has to do with diverse learning styles. Gardner believes that most people can acquire a type of intelligence in which they may not be strong. Therefore, we need different learning experiences—some that foster our strengths and some that help us develop skills in other areas. Gardner's list of intelligences follows, along with the types of activities appropriate for each intelligence (Armstrong, 1994).

> **Linguistic:** lectures, discussions, word games, storytelling, choral reading, journal writing
>
> **Logical mathematical:** brain teasers, problem solving, science experiments, mental calculations, number games, critical thinking
>
> **Spatial:** visual representations, art activities, imagination games, mind mapping, metaphor, visualization
>
> **Bodily kinesthetic:** hands-on learning, drama, dance, sports that teach, tactile activities, relaxation exercises
>
> **Musical:** rapping, songs that teach
>
> **Interpersonal:** cooperative learning, peer tutoring, community involvement, social gatherings, simulations
>
> **Intrapersonal:** individualized instruction, independent study, options in the course of study, self-esteem building

When we teach children to read, we need to remember that not all children learn in the same way. We should therefore think about the different intelligences and provide many experiences to meet individual needs.

Children with Physical Impairments

Physical impairments include visual or hearing impairments, communication disorders, and orthopedic impairments. **Inclusion** is a term that suggests that children with impairments become a part of the regular classroom, even if they have severe problems, with the necessary assistance provided. Children with *visual impairments* are legally blind, have no useful vision, or have very limited sight. For these children, strategies that include auditory and tactile experiences are important. Learning materials are available in large print for low-vision children. Children with no vision must learn to read through the use of braille, a system of reading for the blind consisting of characters represented by raised dots on paper. These materials are available in basal readers from the American Printing House for the Blind (Ward & McCormick, 1981). For the most part, only children with minimal visual problems will be present in the regular classroom.

Children who are *hearing impaired* are completely deaf or have some useful limited hearing. Some of these youngsters can be helped through the use of a hearing aid, which amplifies sounds for them. Children who are hearing impaired and likely to be included in regular classrooms will be those with some hearing ability. Visual and tactile methods for learning are encouraged with these students. Those who are deaf or have very limited hearing may use sign language to communicate. Some knowledge of signing would be helpful for classroom teachers.

Mobility impairment in this context refers to handicaps that are often congenital or acquired during childhood through such diseases as cerebral palsy, muscular dystrophy, spina bifida, and rheumatoid arthritis. Children who suffer from these problems to a severe degree are not usually in regular classrooms; however, those with mild cases may be included. Children with these problems may have normal intelligence, but often need help with mobility. Learning strategies will be similar to those used with all children. If the ability to use fine motor control is compromised, alternative methods for writing need to be found, such as using a computer or having a teacher or peer take dictation. Youngsters with diseases that cause mobility problems may need more time to complete assignments, not necessarily because of their intellectual ability, but because of motor coordination problems. Because their disability is more obvious than others, an important goal with these youngsters is helping non-special needs children feel more positively toward them so that all are comfortable in one another's presence. Discussing the problems, how they occurred, and how everyone feels about them will often help.

Children with *communication disorders* are likely to be a part of the regular classroom. These children have speech or language difficulties. Speech impairments include problems in articulation, voice disorders (abnormal loudness, pitch, or voice quality), and fluency disorders such as stuttering.

Children with *language disorders* have difficulty acquiring and using language. Delayed-language children are significantly behind their peers in both the production and comprehension aspects of language development. These children will go to special classes for help with their problems. For the most part, strategies that are appropriate for all children will be appropriate for these youngsters in the regular classroom. Chapter 4, which deals with language development, discusses instructional contexts appropriate for children with minimal language problems.

Techniques for instruction need to be concrete and include active involvement. Helping these youngsters stay on task is an important goal.

Activities that will grasp their attention are those that are most likely to be successful. Working with them on an individual basis is crucial to finding out the best ways for these children to learn. As with the gifted child, differentiating regular classroom activities to meet their ability levels will accommodate their needs.

When trying to meet the special needs of children, focusing on the instructional goal rather than activities is important. A team of school personnel needs to be involved in preparing plans for disabled youngsters. This team needs to figure out how to help these children compensate for their disabilities and therefore be able to carry out activities successfully. For example, a child who has an attention deficit disorder and moves too quickly during independent center work from one task to the next can be paired with a peer who is known to be able to stay focused. This peer can read directions for the student who has the disability, thus providing explicit instruction about the activity.

Parents can be an excellent resource for informing the teacher about a child's strengths, weaknesses, and interests. The collective guidance of other children, special education consultants, and aides also can help support the engagement of children with special needs.

All those involved in dealing with children with special needs must have tolerance for differences. Thinking of children with differences as less fortunate is not conducive to learning. The attitude must be how we help children compensate for their disabilities so that they can learn to function independently (Erickson & Koppenhaver, 1995).

Following are some instructional guidelines that can prove helpful when dealing with children who have physical impairments or developmental learning differences, whether they are learning disabled or gifted (Ruddell & Ruddell, 1995).

1. Observe students on a regular basis for indications that they may have some physical impairment or developmental learning differences. For example, a child who seems to have difficulty seeing the chalkboard, who copies things incorrectly, and who squints to see things may have a visual problem that needs attention.
2. Seek help from your district's support services with children you find are experiencing problems. Be sure you have suspected problems identified and appropriate assistance given to children in need.
3. When you find out the nature of the problem a child may be experiencing, become informed about it by discussing it with special education teachers and other staff members.
4. Use learning principles that are successful with all youngsters, such as encouragement, praise, and positive feedback.
5. Adapt instruction to meet special needs. Good strategies are often good for all children, with some adaptations to meet their individual differences.
6. Involve parents with children who have special needs. Discuss the help the school is providing, inform them of additional help they might seek outside the school environment, and enlist their help with activities they can do with their youngsters at home.

Intervention and Differentiation of Instruction

Differentiation of Instruction

Meeting individual needs is a major concern for teachers. In this chapter we have discussed English language learners, children who are gifted, those with learning disabilities, those who are struggling readers, and children with physical disabilities. Except for the gifted children, all the others are at risk for success at learning to read, and all the children, including the gifted, need differentiated instruction to meet their individual needs. Many programs have been used throughout the years to help these youngsters, and it has become apparent that meeting individual needs requires time with a teacher and child working together. When a teacher has this time with the child, he or she is able to assess the child and differentiate instruction to meet the child's needs.

> Savannah is reading at a second-grade level and is very immature. She has a single mom who works long hours and doesn't read to Savannah or take her to the library. Savannah only reads in school. Jose just came from Mexico and speaks no English. He knows only math facts and has no access to books. Nathaniel reads at the fourth-grade level. His mom and dad are both teachers and provide lots of literacy experiences for him. He has a large collection of books at home and goes to the library often. He has many experiences with his family on vacation and at museums and reads a lot at home. Ashley is an excellent creative writer who reads at the third-grade level. She often doesn't pay attention to what is going on at school and does her own thing. Finally, Jenny is a struggling reader with language and visual processing problems. She is not fluent in Engish. All these children are in the same classroom, Ms. Callihan's second grade. There is no way these children can be taught as a whole class all the time. They are in need of differentiated instruction.

When we differentiate instruction, teaching is flexible and

- Assesses students to design the instruction to meet their needs
- Responds to student differences
- Responds to student interests
- Responds to student achievement levels and learning needs

When teachers differentiate instruction, they begin with high-quality, whole-group instruction that builds on background knowledge, is linked to standards, is research based, and includes a variety of activities to learn one skill. This is often referred to as *tier one* teaching.

Differentiation of instruction also includes targeted instruction, referred to as *tier two*, which includes:

- Small groups
- Working directly with the teacher
- Accelerated work for those who are most capable

- Reinforcement of particular skill needs for those who are struggling
- Materials for instruction selected for children's interests, achievement level, and needs
- Instruction tailored to student's learning styles

The most intense approach for the students most in need of differentiated instruction is *tier three*, the most targeted approach, or a safety net. At this level

- Children receive small-group systematic and explicit instruction.
- It is aimed at preventing children from needing special education services by providing more flexible regular education options.
- Students receive their regular reading instruction, but in addition either more small-group literacy in their classroom or in a pull-out setting.

The goals for all children in differentiating instruction are similar for their grade level; however, the difficulty with which they are expected to achieve is different. Materials teach the same concepts, but those more capable can be challenged by them and those who need more help can be successful with them as well. An example of a material that allows for differentiated instruction is finding little words in big words. Assume the word is *Thanksgiving*. The more capable children will find more words and more difficult words; the less capable will find fewer words and less sophisticated words, but the activity is the same and the goal is the same.

Teachers believe that differentiation of instruction is important. However, many feel they lack appropriate materials, time, and professional development and need additional help in the classroom to carry it out.

Intervention Program

Early intervention programs are a form of differentiating instruction, but they are concerned with being preventive, rather than trying to fix the problem when it is too late. These programs are based on the premise that more can be done and needs to be done in school to support young children's literacy learning. Many children from at-risk populations could be successful if early intervention were available (Hiebert & Taylor, 1994; Tomlinson, 2003; Walpole & McKenna, 2007).

The term **early intervention** refers to programs that encourage instruction that is developmentally appropriate as far as reading and writing experiences are concerned. The purpose is to improve and enhance the literacy development of children entering school who have not achieved early literacy abilities similar to their peers. In programs that have been implemented, it has been found that children can be prevented from falling behind their peers and from experiencing failure (O'Connor, Harty, & Fulmer, 2005; Slavin & Madden, 1989; Stanovich, 1986).

Educators have questioned whether it is more appropriate for early intervention to occur in the classroom with the support of special teachers who work with the classroom teacher or whether **pull-out programs** are more successful, in which youngsters go to a special teacher to work on skill improvement. The ultimate goal of such programs is to provide supplemental instruction to accelerate literacy development with the use of quality instruction in reading and writing. There is a movement toward integrating the intervention into the regular classroom, rather than taking children out of class. The rationale for this trend toward *inclusion* is to limit the movement of children in and out of the classroom during the school day and for the special instruction to be an integral part of the regular classroom instruction. In this way, children do not miss what is going on in the regular classroom. The instruction is coordinated with their classroom instruction. The stigma of being taken out for special help is eliminated, and the classroom teacher and special teacher work together toward helping children.

A well-known early intervention pull-out program is **Reading Recovery**, developed in New Zealand (Clay, 1987) and studied extensively at Ohio State University (Pinnell, Freid, & Estice, 1990). Reading Recovery is a program for young readers who are having problems in their first year of reading instruction. Children receive daily 30-minute, one-to-one instructional sessions in addition to their regular classroom reading instruction. Reading Recovery lessons are tailored to the special needs of children, contain authentic literacy experiences that are collaborative and active between teacher and child, and use specific skill instruction. Some Reading Recovery strategies within a lesson include the following:

1. The child reads a familiar story to enhance fluency and experience success.
2. The teacher introduces a new book, and teacher and student walk through the book together, looking at the pictures and predicting what the book is about.
3. The child reads the new book without assistance from the teacher.
4. The teacher takes a running record to check the child for types of errors made and comprehension through a retelling.
5. The teacher carries out a lesson that helps the child with word-analysis strategies by looking at onsets of words and letter chunks or rimes at the end of words.

To make the experience more concrete, the teacher engages the child in the use of manipulating letters and chunks that are magnetic on a magnetic board. The child is asked to use words learned by writing them on a slate within a sentence. Also, sentences from the book are written on sentence strips for children to put into sequence, and sentences are cut into words for children to identify out of context and to sequence into context. These familiar activities are repeated in different lessons.

Teachers who participate in Reading Recovery receive special training to help develop their ability to observe and describe the behavior of children when they are engaged in literacy acts. Reading Recovery teacher training emphasizes how to respond to children with appropriate modeling and scaffolding to help them progress. Another feature of the program is the use of authentic literacy experiences balanced with skill development. Reading Recovery has demonstrated increased performance by at-risk children. In addition, Reading Recovery strategies have been adapted for small-group guided reading instruction within the classroom.

Many schools and commercial programs are creating early intervention programs with high-quality instructional strategies used to work with children who are not performing well. It is very likely that, if a teacher works with a student on a one-to-one basis or in small groups with no more than three children using good strategies, the child should improve because of the extra and personal help received. A brief description of two intervention programs designed for at-risk children by school districts follows.

The Early Intervention in Reading program was designed for first-grade children in diverse communities. The purpose was to supplement instruction provided by their teachers for groups of low-achieving students. Teachers took 20 minutes a day to provide supplemental reading instruction to a group of five to seven children. Children in the program demonstrated improved literacy skills (Hoover & Patton, 2005; Taylor, Strait, & Medo, 1994).

An early intervention program entitled A Storybook Reading Program was incorporated into a regular class for kindergarten children identified as at risk. In addition to traditional instruction with a skills-based program, the following were added to their literacy program:

1. Directed listening and thinking activities when reading to children
2. Retelling of stories read to the children
3. Repeated readings of storybooks so that children could engage in attempted readings of these stories from hearing them frequently
4. Active discussions to construct meaning from stories read to the children
5. Provision for classroom reading and writing centers containing materials that encourage literacy activity
6. Time for children to engage in periods of independent reading and writing to practice skills learned (Morrow & O'Connor, 1995)

Work took place in whole-class, small-group, and one-to-one settings when teachers worked with children to discover their strengths and weaknesses. Basic-skills teachers worked along with the classroom teachers in the room during the small-group and one-to-one periods to help with instruction. Students in this program made significant improvement over children also identified as at risk who did not have the advantage of the intervention described.

When deciding to implement intervention programs, consider the children involved, the resources you have, and how best to use the talent within your own school. Recognizing that special needs exist and what they are is the most important step for a teacher. Next is to respect and accept differences that exist in the children whom you teach.

In a speech given at a National Reading Conference meeting, Lisa Delpit (1995) spoke about teaching "other people's children." She discussed general characteristics for a successful literacy program in urban school settings with children from diverse backgrounds and disadvantaged backgrounds. Some of the main points in her presentation were as follows:

1. Learn and respect the child's home culture.
2. Do not teach less content to children from disadvantaged backgrounds. They can learn as all other children learn. Teachers, parents, children, and the community should recognize children's ability and teach them accordingly.
3. Whatever instructional program or methodology is used, critical thinking should be a goal. Children achieve because of teachers who believe in them

and have a vision for them. Poor children practice the use of critical skills on a regular basis, because they have had to be independent and have many responsibilities at home.

4. All children must gain access to basic skills and the conventions and strategies that are essential to succeed in U.S. education and life. Adults need to help children learn the skills they need to succeed outside school.

5. Help children view themselves as competent and worthy.

6. Use familiar metaphors and experiences from children's lives to connect what they already know to school knowledge. If you cannot justify what you are teaching, you should not be teaching it.

7. Create a sense of family and caring in your classroom. Make the children your own while you have them. Tell them they are the smartest children in the world and expect them to be. Then they will learn for the teacher, not just from the teacher.

8. Monitor and assess needs and then address them with a wealth of diverse strategies.

9. Recognize and build on strengths that children and families already have.

10. Foster a connection between the child and the community so that there is something greater than themselves to use for inspiration. Help them understand that they go to school for their community and predecessors. If they fail, they fail not only for themselves but for their community as well; if they succeed, they succeed for everyone, including themselves.

Put Yourself in the Place of the Child

It is difficult for us as adults to understand and appreciate the various processes involved in learning to read and write because, as adults, we have been reading and writing for many years. Reading is a complex process and to the novice it is overwhelming. For children who have additional problems, such as visual impairments, or those who are English language learners, think how difficult it will be. To understand better the nature of learning to read or write, put yourself in the place of the learner. With a contrived alphabet called the Confusabet, I have taken college students and parents back to when they were 5 and 6 and first taught to read and write (Figure 3.2). Whole words are introduced in the unfamiliar alphabet, accompanied by picture clues and context clues. They are reinforced with worksheets. After being introduced to about 25 words, the students are given a book containing pictures and stories that use these words. They are called on to read just as they were in a reading

Figure 3.2

The Confusabet

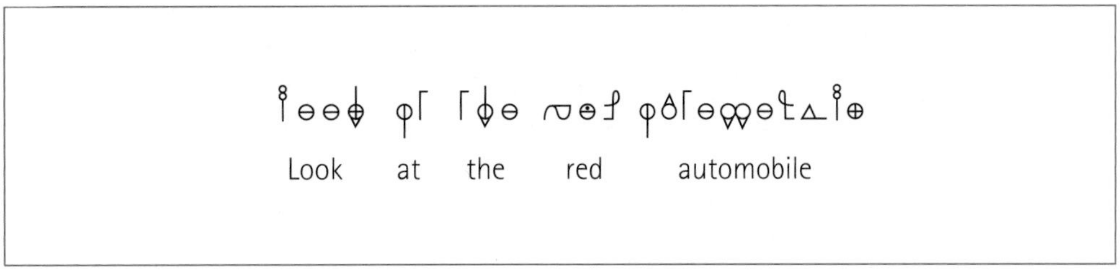

Look   at   the   red   automobile

group in an early childhood classroom. They are also asked to write one sentence about what they read in the Confusabet alphabet.

After the lesson we discuss how they have just learned to read and write with the Confusabet. Students consistently report similar strategies: They try to relate information they already know about writing and reading to the situation. They realize quickly that Confusabet words have the same number of letters as words written in our regular alphabet, and their knowledge of words in general helps them make sense of Confusabet words. Certain similarities in letter forms help them figure out words. They use context and picture clues as much as possible. Their knowledge of syntax (language structures) and the meanings of words surrounding an unknown word helps them determine words they cannot otherwise identify. They skip around within a sentence looking for words they might know. Some rely on the first letter of a word to identify it. Many try to memorize words by the look–say method. Most agree that words with unusual shapes or lengths are easy to identify. They acknowledge that to learn they have to involve themselves actively in the reading process. In short, they guess, make mistakes, and correct themselves.

In addition to the strategies just described, my observations of the students' behavior during this class experience revealed another powerful strategy: the natural tendency to collaborate and cooperate with one another during learning. The students discussed successes and failures with those around them. They wanted to talk about the words they had figured out and share that excitement with others. They spontaneously expressed frustration when they experienced difficulty, and they sought help of those nearby. Some said that they were experiencing such difficulty that they wanted to stop trying and just quit. The room was noisy at times because of the social interaction of the literacy-learning experience. At times, two or three of them disagreed about a particular word, finally arriving at consensus. Sometimes problems were solved through peer tutoring, with one student helping another who was having trouble. They demonstrated a natural curiosity as they flipped eagerly through new materials.

All the students agreed that working together gave them a sense of security, provided easily accessible sources of information, and made the task more fun. They were almost unaware of their socially cooperative behavior until I pointed it out to them. Most commented that seeking and relying on social interaction when trying to learn to read with the Confusabet seemed to be a natural inclination.

In their descriptions of how they learned to read and write with the Confusabet, the students used problem solving and some behavioristic-type strategies. In all cases they sought meaning. They approached a printed message looking for visual clues and auditory cues, and they looked at the total piece, trying to draw on past experience as well as the help of one another. They guessed, predicted, and invented to construct meaning. They also used strategies such as trying to decode words by focusing on the first letter, using context clues, and using the sight–word approach. The many different approaches that were used by the college students to try to learn to read indicated the diversity among them. Regardless of the difficulties a child may have, each is entitled to instruction that suits his or her individual needs. (The Confusabet lesson can be found in Appendix G.)

An Idea from the Classroom

English Language Learners

Where in the World Are You From?

At the beginning of the school year, I send a notice home with my first graders with the heading "Where in the World Are You From?" The parents are asked to fill in information about their heritage and the heritage of their child. They are to do this with their child. The responses have been more than I anticipated. Parents have been happy to cite the countries of origin and to offer information about these lands. This exercise has helped me begin my year with a clear view of the cultural diversity within my class.

From the information returned, I found that one of my students was related to Daniel Boone and another had a grandfather who was one of the first African American pilots in the U.S. Air Force. One child, who was adopted from Peru, had an American father, his mother was German, and his brother, who was also adopted, was from Colombia. I had several children from Hispanic backgrounds and from many different countries. There were some Asian children as well. I received photographs and artifacts from the various countries. With this information, I was able to use books and activities that represented the diversity within my class. I also had parents come to school to share information about their heritage.

We began a class book about the countries represented by the heritage of the children and called it *The Passport*. I met with all children on a one-to-one basis about their page in the book for which they could write things about their backgrounds. In addition, I featured one child a week on a small bulletin board where I placed a photograph of the child with information about his or her heritage. I tried to include things that are interesting to children, such as food, stories, songs, dances, and clothing pertaining to the featured child's heritage. A map showing the country of origin was also included. Parents were invited to share their backgrounds.

This project gave me an immediate wealth of knowledge about my class and a glimpse into each child's background. It was a wonderful way to celebrate diversity, involve parents, read, write, and be involved with social studies within a meaningful context.

Katherine Heiss, First-Grade Teacher

An Idea from the Classroom

A Multicultural Bakery in the Dramatic-Play Area

In coordination with a unit on Community Helpers, we set up a bakery in the dramatic-play area. Materials included a baker's hat and apron, cookie cutter, rolling pin, mixing bowls, measuring spoons, and trays and boxes with labels for baked goods, such as donuts, cookies, cakes, and pies. Some classroom recipes that had already been made were hung in the area, and pens, pencils, and books with recipes for baking were also placed in the area. A disk for the computer in the bakery has recipes recorded. The Internet is consulted if a new recipe is needed. Children were encouraged to bring recipes from home, especially recipes from their cultural background, such as strudel from Germany, biscotti from Italy, or a Jewish challah bread.

For buying and selling baked goods, which were actually made, there were an ordering pad, a cash register, receipts for purchases, number tickets for standing in line, and name tags for the baker and salesperson.

To guide the children in their play, on different days I modeled the behavior for a salesperson, a customer, and the baker. This was a popular play area in which a great deal of literacy behavior occurred. For example, the salesperson took orders on the phone and in person and wrote them down, the bakers followed recipes in the cookbook and on the wall, and the customers counted out money and read the labels naming the baked goods. Children participated in behaviors that I modeled and generated their own ideas when participating in play in the bakery.

Joyce C. Ng, First-Grade Teacher

Activities and Questions

1. Answer the focus questions at the beginning of the chapter.

2. In this chapter the term *diversity* applies to children who are English language learners (those who are non–English speaking or have limited English proficiency); children with learning differences (gifted, learning disabled, ADHD); children who are at risk; children with physical impairments (visual, hearing, mobility, communication disorders); and children from different cultural backgrounds. Select one of these areas of diversity and describe a theory that you feel has implications for instructional strategies appropriate for a child with that special need. Outline the strategies for learning.

3. Throughout the book, strategies will be presented for teaching literacy learning in classrooms. At all times, have the interest of children with special needs in mind and decide the strategies appropriate for these youngsters.

4. **Strategies** Enlarge and photocopy word cards on pages S-9 through S-11, color or run off on colored paper, laminate, and cut. Hang on the wall and discuss the words when you put them up and afterwards.

PEARSON myeducationlab

VIDEO EXERCISE

Now that you have the benefit of having read this chapter, return to the www.myeducationlab.com topic "Differentiating Instruction" and watch "Teaching to Diverse Learning Styles" one more time. Under the topic "Special Needs," watch "Inclusion in the Early Childhood Classroom" one more time. You may complete the questions that accompany them online and save or transmit your work to your professor, or complete the following questions, as required.

Teaching to Diverse Learning Styles (4:20 minutes)

1. What techniques does this teacher use to ensure that all students are able to comprehend when reading? Why do you think she chose these particular techniques?
2. Why is it important to vary the teaching methods, particularly when you have children with learning disabilities in the classroom?

3. Interview teachers and/or administrators at a school regarding the roles that special educators, classroom teachers, and reading specialists play in literacy instruction for students with special needs. Summarize your findings here.

Inclusion in an Early Childhood Class (2:52 minutes)

1. What are the benefits of inclusion in preschool for a child with special needs and for that child's peers?
2. Many states have a special education category called *developmentally delayed* that can be used to identify students needing special education services up to age 9. Why do states have such a category, and how can it be useful for early childhood teachers?
3. As a student with special needs progresses from the early childhood classroom through the grade levels, how might the benefits and limitations of inclusion change for the student?

Focus Questions

■ According to the theorists described in this chapter, how is language acquired?

■ What is important to know about how the brain develops and how it relates to language and literacy development?

■ How does language develop and progress from birth to age 8?

■ What do we mean when we speak of children with language differences?

■ What are some practical activities that demonstrate how we respect different cultural backgrounds in our classrooms?

■ What classroom practices are particularly good for helping children to learn English?

■ What are the objectives for language development in early childhood?

■ What strategies can teachers and parents carry out to encourage language development from birth to age 2?

■ What strategies can teachers and parents carry out to encourage language development from preschool through third grade?

■ Describe specific strategies for building vocabulary and word meaning for second and third grade.

■ What techniques can be used for a portfolio of materials that assesses children's language development?

■ **VOCABULARY:** zone of proximal development, neural shearing, synaptogenesis, phonemes, syntax, semantics, *dialect, receptive language, expressive language,* aesthetic talk, efferent talk, t-unit

■ **Strategies** Ask a child to create a story with the figures provided on page S-12 of Strategies for the Classroom. How well does the child do?

PEARSON myeducationlab VIDEO PREVIEW: An ESL Vocabulary Lesson (4:55 minutes). Before reading this chapter, go to www.myeducationlab.com. Under the topic "English Language Learners," access and watch the video "An ESL Vocabulary Lesson." Consider whether or not you think the teacher's methods are appropriate.

Language and Vocabulary Development

"The time has come," the Walrus said,
"To talk of many things:
Of shoes and ships and sealing-wax,
Of cabbages and kings"

—Lewis Carroll
"The Walrus and the Carpenter"

From the moment of birth, the infant is surrounded by oral language. The development of language is one of the child's first steps toward becoming literate; it helps make reading and writing possible. Using research methods that involve close observation of children, investigators have been able to describe the strategies by which youngsters learn and use language. Among the many things these researchers have observed is that children are active participants in their learning of language. To learn, children involve themselves in problem solving, first creating hypotheses based on background information that they already have and then interacting with the individuals around them who are generating language. These strategies have implications for initial instruction in early literacy.

A parent of a child in one of my kindergarten classes related a conversation she had had with her daughter Melody. Mrs. Tracey said they were outside looking at the sky one evening, and she noticed that the moon was full. She said to her daughter, "Look, Melody, the moon is full tonight." Melody looked up at the moon with a slightly confused expression on her face and said, "Why is it full, Mommy, did the moon eat too much for dinner?" Melody used her background language information to help her understand her mother. Until this time the word *full* meant filled up with food, and Melody made sense of the discussion with what she knew. Her mother explained what she meant by a full moon and that the same words can have different meanings depending on the situation in which they are used.

Children do not learn language passively; they actually construct—or reconstruct—language as they learn. In another one of my kindergarten classes, we were talking about what the children wanted to be when they grew up. It was Michael's turn. He started by telling us that his dad is a doctor and recently he had taken him to see the operating room where he works. Michael said, "I liked the people and all the machines that my daddy uses and so when I grow up, I want to be an *operator,* just like my daddy." Michael selected a word for the situation that made wonderful sense under the circumstances.

Although language acquisition is based somewhat on developmental maturity, research has found that children play an active role in their acquisition of language by constructing language. They imitate the language of adults and create their own when they do not have the conventional words they need to communicate their thoughts. Their first words are usually functional words, and they are motivated to continue generating language when their attempts are positively reinforced. Children who are constantly exposed to an environment rich in language and who interact with adults using language in a social context develop more facility with oral language than children lacking these opportunities (Cazden, 2005; Dickinson, McCabe, & Essex, 2006; Gaskins, 2003; Morrow, 2005; Morrow, Kuhn, & Schwanenflugel, 2006).

Findings from research on language acquisition motivated investigators to carry out similar studies of how reading and writing were acquired. Because reading and writing involve the use of language, many believed that the acquisition of oral language, reading, and writing might share some similarities.

Language Development and Reading

Now that language processes are commonly recognized as the basis for learning to read, *language learning* is considered an important part of *learning to read*. Reading has been defined as the use of one's language ability to decode and comprehend text (Roskos, Tabors, & Lenhart, 2004; Ruddell & Ruddell, 1995; Vukelich, Christie, & Enz, 2002). Reading is the interaction between the reader and written language. It is the attempt by a reader to reconstruct the author's message. The graphic sequences and patterns that appear as print represent the oral sequences of language. In the process of reading, we look and listen for recognizable grammatical sequences and patterns that trigger appropriate phrasing. Using what we already know of language structure, we then test how each word fits into the context of what we are reading. As readers, we use syntactic and semantic cues that enable us to predict what comes next. Our skill in processing semantics (meaning) and syntax (language structure) makes us more adept readers. The reader who encounters unfamiliar language structures and unfamiliar concepts in material to be read has difficulty understanding it. Familiarity with both syntax and semantics enables even very young readers to anticipate the format and content of sentences in print. Past theory held that it was our accumulation of letters and words that led to competent reading. Now we realize that our ability to understand what we are reading is based on our *reconstruction* of the meaning of the printed word. Such understanding is based on our previous experience with the topic, our familiarity with its main concepts, and our general knowledge of how language works.

The relationship between reading and language is evident in studies of children who are early readers. It has been found, for instance, that early readers score higher on language screening tests than children who were not reading

Book language takes children beyond their own language patterns.

early. Early readers come from homes where rich language and a great deal of oral language are used (Dickinson & Tabors, 2001). When interviewed, parents of early readers revealed that their children tended to use very descriptive language and sophisticated language structures. The youngsters invented words, used humor, and talked a lot. The mother of a 4-year-old early reader reported that while watching the first snowfall of the year, her youngster said, "The snow is swirling down and looks like fluffy marshmallows on the ground." One spring day a few months later, the same child noted, "Look, Mommy, the butterflies are fluttering around. They look like they are dancing with the flowers." Children whose language is not appropriately developed by age 3 because of lack of experiences or exposure to language are already at risk. But with quality preschool that emphasizes language and literacy they can catch up.

Halliday (1975) notes that, among other functions, language helps children learn how to determine meaning from the world around them. Early readers demonstrate an awareness of story language. They can retell stories using such literary conventions as "Once upon a time" and "They lived happily ever after." When telling stories, they tend to use delivery and intonation like those of an adult reading aloud. This "book language" takes children beyond their own language patterns and is distinctively characteristic of early readers (Burns, Snow, & Griffin, 1999; Dickinson & Tabors, 2001).

Theory and Research on How Children Acquire Language

Although we do not have all the answers about language acquisition, many theories help explain how babies learn to speak. Knowing how language is acquired has strong implications for providing environments that promote language development. It also implies how reading and writing skills develop.

The Behaviorist Theory

The **behaviorist approach** has influenced our thinking about how language is acquired. Although behaviorism does not present the total picture, it still offers ideas about language acquisition that should be considered for instruction. Skinner (1957) defined language as the observed and produced speech that occurs in the interaction of speaker and listener. Thinking, he said, is the internal process of language; both language and thought are initiated through interactions in the environment, such as those between a parent and a child. According to behaviorists, adults provide a language model that children learn through imitation. The child's acquisition of language is enhanced and encouraged by the positive reinforcement of an adult (Cox, 2002).

Early attempts at language are often rewarded, and this reinforcement leads to additional responses by children. These attempts are also *interactive;* that is, the language is mediated by adults through interactions designed to elaborate and extend meaning (Hart & Risley, 1999). When newborns coo or make other verbal sounds, most parents are delighted and respond with gentle words of encouragement. The infant, in turn, responds to the positive reinforcement by repeating the cooing sounds. As babies become able to formulate consonant and vowel sounds, they try them out. It is not uncommon to hear a 10-month-old playing with sounds such as *ba, ba, ba,* or *ma, ma, ma.* The responsive interactive parent perceives such sounds as the child's first words and assumes that the child's *ma-ma* means *mommy.* The delighted adult says more warm and loving things to the baby and adds hugs and kisses. The parent might say, "Come on, now say it again, *ma, ma, ma.*" The baby is pleased with the warm reception and tries to repeat the sounds to receive additional interaction and positive reinforcement.

Unfortunately, the converse is also true. If a baby's babbling is considered annoying, if the parent is aggravated by the sound and responds with negative reinforcement by telling the baby in harsh tones, "Be quiet and stop making so much noise," the child is less likely to continue to explore the use of language.

It is evident that children imitate adult models and are motivated to continue using language because of positive reinforcement. Children surrounded by rich language begin to use the language they hear, even though imitation sometimes occurs with erroneous comprehension or no comprehension at all. A child can imitate the sounds of the "words" of a familiar song, for instance, with no concern for meaning. A 3-year-old girl sang "My country 'tis of thee" as "My country tis a bee." She imitated what she heard. She also substituted a similar-sounding word that had meaning for her from her own experience, that is, the word "bee" instead of the word "thee," which she had never heard.

The Nativist Theory

Chomsky (1965), Lennenberg (1967), and McNeil (1970) have described the **nativist theory** of language acquisition. They contend that language develops innately. Children figure out how language works by internalizing the rules of grammar, which enables them to produce an infinite number of sentences. They do so even without the practice, reinforcement, and modeling offered by adult language, which are considered necessary by the behaviorists. The ability to learn language must be innate to humans, the nativists believe, because almost all children develop and use language in the first few years of their lives. Language growth depends on maturation: As children mature, their language grows. Children learn new patterns of language and unconsciously generate new rules for new elements of language. The child's rule system increases in complexity as he or she generates more complex language. Lennenberg (1967), an extreme nativist, finds nothing in the child's environment to account for language development. Rather, language acquisition is motivated *inside* children; learning language is a natural ability (Pinker, 1994). Although maturation does play a role in language development and it is innate to humans, newer theories offered by Piaget and Vygotsky have come to be the more accepted ideas concerning language acquisition.

Piagetian and Vygotskian Theories

Piaget's theory of *cognitive development* is built on the principle that children develop through their activities. Children's realization of the world is tied to their actions or their sensory experiences in the environment. According to this theory, children's first words are egocentric, or centered in their own actions. Children talk about themselves and what they do. Their early language and their general development relate to actions, objects, and events they have experienced through touching, hearing, seeing, tasting, and smelling (Piaget & Inhelder, 1969).

Vygotsky's theory of *basic learning* also has implications for language development. According to Vygotsky, children learn higher mental functions by internalizing social relationships. Adults initially provide children with names of things, for instance; they direct youngsters and make suggestions. Then, as children become more competent, the adults around them gradually withdraw the amount of help they need to give. Vygotsky (1978) describes a **zone of proximal development,** a range of social interaction between an adult and child. Theoretically, the child can perform within that range, but only with adult assistance. Proximal development ends when the child can function independently. The implications for language instruction are clear: To promote language development, adults need to interact with children by encouraging, motivating, and supporting them (Sulzby, 1986a).

As a child builds an oral vocabulary, he or she tries words more frequently. Children will point to a toy and name it. While playing with a ball, a child may say the word *ball* over and over again. The attentive parent now interacts with the child by expanding and extending the original language (Burns, Snow, & Griffin, 1999). After the child says *ball,* the parent may say, "Yes, that is a nice, big, round, red ball." Through such *expansion* and reinforcement of words by the adult, the child acquires new language. The adult often *extends* on the baby's words by asking questions, for instance, "Now what can you do with that nice red ball?" Such extension requires the child to think, understand, and act. Positive interactions encourage practice, which helps continue language development (Dickinson & Tabors, 2001).

The Constructivist Theory

The more contemporary perspective of language acquisition is the **constructivist theory** emerging from the work of Piaget and Vygotsky and described and supported by those who have studied language development (Brown, Cazden, & Bellugi-Klima, 1968; Halliday, 1975). Constructivists describe children as the creators of language on the basis of an innate set of rules or underlying concepts. They describe language as an active and social process. The child constructs language, often making errors. But making errors is a necessary part of learning how language works. We need to accept language errors in a child's first years.

The implications of the constructivist theory are important for early literacy development. Even though language development charts show when to expect certain stages of development on average, we do not discipline babies who have not uttered their first words at 8 months or their first complete sentences by two and a half years. Sometimes we find their errors cute. We seem to respect their individuality and their right to grow at their own pace. Yet when children enter school, we neglect to recognize developmental differences; we prescribe tasks based on a curriculum, not on the child.

The process of acquiring language is continuous and interactive; it takes place in the social context of the child's interacting with others (Hart & Risley, 1999). Children also learn by playing with language themselves. They try out new words, involve themselves in monologues, and practice what they

Children learn language from social interaction with an adult who provides a language model and positive reinforcement for the child's early language attempts.

have learned. The acquisition of language varies from child to child, depending on each child's social and cultural background (Au, 1998). Children's remarks illustrate that they do not *simply* imitate adult language. It is as if children need to express themselves, but do not have sufficient conventional language to draw upon, so they create their own based on their backgrounds and their awareness of semantics and syntax.

A 3-year-old girl saw a freckled youngster for the first time and said, "Look, Mommy, that little girl has *sprinkles* on her nose." A 4-year-old boy observed an elderly man with deep wrinkles and said, "I wonder why that man has *paths* all over his face." A father and his 3-year-old daughter were toasting marshmallows; the little girl said, "Mmmm, I can smell the taste of them." After a quick summer rain, a 3-year-old boy observed the sun returning to the sky and the water evaporating all around him. "The sun came out and ate up all the rain," he observed. Toward the end of the winter as the snow was melting, a 4-year-old girl noted, "See how the grass is peeking out from underneath the snow."

Halliday's Theory of Language Development

Halliday (1975, p. 7) describes language development as a process by which children gradually "learn how to mean." According to his theory of developmental language, what a child can do during interactions with others has meaning, and meaning can be turned into speech. In other words, children's initial language development is based on *function:* What can be said reflects what can be done. Language is learned when it is relevant and functional. The seven functions evident in the language of young children that Halliday (1975, pp. 19–21) identifies are found in the following list, with examples.

Halliday's Functions of Language

1. *Instrumental:* Children use language to satisfy a personal need and to get things done.
   Example: Cookie Mommy.

2. *Regulatory:* Children use language to control the behavior of others.
   Example: No sleep now.

3. *Interactional:* Children use language to get along with others.
   Example: You want to play?

4. *Personal:* Children use language to tell about themselves.
   Example: I'm running now.
5. *Heuristic:* Children use language to find out about things, to learn things.
   Example: What are cows for?
6. *Imaginative:* Children use language to pretend, to make believe.
   Example: Let's play space.
7. *Informative:* Children use language to communicate something for the information of others.
   Example: I'll tell you how this game works.

The theories just discussed explain how language is acquired. Each has something to offer, but none by itself presents a complete picture. We *do* know, however, that children's language grows according to their need to use it, their interests, and the meaning it has for them. Children's language is acquired through exploration and invention and is controlled by their own maturity, the structure of the language, and its conventions. Language acquisition is fostered by positive interactions regarding language between the child and an adult.

Brain Development and Language and Literacy Development from Birth to Age 3

The study of brain research has made it very apparent that what happens to a child from birth to age 3 can affect his or her language and literacy development. Babies are programmed to learn. Every minute, they search to learn about the environment they are in and to connect with the experiences it has to offer.

When a child is born it has about 100 billion neurons. This is all the neurons or brain cells it will ever have. For learning to take place, neurons must make brain connections. Brain connections that are repeated and used become permanent; when brain connections are not used, they disintegrate and vanish. This is referred to as **neural shearing,** the loss of brain cells (Shaywitz, 2003). At birth, the baby's billions of neurons or brain cells have already formed 50 trillion connections, or synapses. By 1 month of age, they have formed 1,000 trillion brain cell connections. The connecting of the brain cells is called **synaptogenesis,** or the rapid development of neural connections. The brain connections form as a result of experiences the baby has and become permanent when those experiences are repeated. The permanent connections mean that learning has occurred (Berk, 2004; Newberger, 1997; Vukelich, Christie, & Enz, 2002). The right experiences must occur to help with language and literacy development, and these experiences need to begin at birth.

Different parts of the brain are responsible for different kinds of development: The motor cortex is responsible for the control of movement; the cerebellum for the development of motor skills; the temporal lobe for auditory processes of hearing including learning, memory, and emotion; Wernicke's area for language understanding; Broca's area for speech production; the frontal lobe for planning, reasoning, and emotional expression; the somatosensory cortex for body sensations, touch, and temperature; the parietal lobe for perceptions and special processing; and the occipital lobe for visual processing. There are specific periods of time when the different areas in the brain are most sensitive for development. For example, the first year of life is the most critical time for language to be learned. During this time, the auditory channels for language develop. At birth, the child has neurons waiting to be connected for every language in the world. Neuron shearing occurs as early as 6 months of age, when the baby can no longer recognize sounds of languages it has not heard. By 1 year, babies are programmed to listen to and learn the language they have heard and are no longer programmed to hear those they have not been exposed to. Those neurons no longer remain (Berk 2004; Karmiloff & Karmiloff-Smith, 2001; Kuhl, 1994).

What does this mean for families and child-care providers who are engaged with children from birth to age 3? What experiences do they need to provide to create a strong base for language and literacy development so that neurons for language and literacy connect and remain permanent? From the time the child is born through age 3, family members and child-care providers need to do the following:

Provide love, food, and clothing.

Talk to them.

Use sophisticated vocabulary.

Use complex sentences.

Respond to cries, smiles, and so on.

Be playful with language, such as using rhymes.

Play with different toys.

Sing songs.

Read books.

Play many different types of music.

Stages in Language Development

Children acquire language by moving through predictable stages. In doing so, they discover the rules that govern the structure of languages, specifically, those of phonology (sound), syntax (grammar), and semantics (meaning).

There are 44 separate sounds, or **phonemes,** in English. With them we produce oral language. Children who grow up in a language-rich environment can learn these sounds very easily. They learn appropriate articulation, pronunciation, and intonation. *Intonation* involves pitch, stress, and juncture. *Pitch* refers to how high or low a voice is when producing a sound; *stress,* to how loud or soft it is; and *junctures,* to the pauses or connections between words, phrases, and sentences (Berk, 1997; Berk 2004).

Syntax refers to the rules that govern how words work together in phrases, clauses, and sentences. Internalizing the syntactic rules of language helps children understand what they hear and what they read. Syntax includes rules for forming basic sentence patterns, for transforming those patterns to generate new sentences, and for embedding, expanding, and combining sentences to make them more complex. Brief examples follow:

1. Some Basic Sentence Patterns
   a. Subject–verb: *The girl ran.*
   b. Subject–verb–object: *The girl ran the team.*
   c. Subject–verb–indirect object–direct object: *Susan gave Lynn a dime.*
   d. Subject–to be–noun or adjective or adverb complement: *Tom was the captain. He was happy. He was there.*
   e. Subject–linking verb–adjective: *Jane is tall.*
2. Some Basic Sentence Transformations
   a. Question
      (1) Kernel: *Jim went to the store.*
      (2) Transformation: *Did Jim go to the store?*
   b. Negative
      (1) Kernel: *Jane is a cheerleader.*
      (2) Transformation: *Jane is not a cheerleader.*
   c. Passive
      (1) Kernel: *Jennifer gave Lisa some bubble gum.*
      (2) Transformation: *Some bubble gum was given to Lisa by Jennifer.*
3. Some Embeddings (sentence expansion and combination)
   a. Adding modifiers (adjectives, adverbs, adverbial and adjective phrases)
      (1) Kernel: *The boy played with friends.*
      (2) Transformation: *The boy in the red pants played with three friends.*
   b. Compounding (combining words, phrases, or independent clauses to form compound subjects, verbs, etc.)
      (1) Kernel: *Jane ran. Jane played. Jack ran. Jack played.*
      (2) Transformation: Jane and Jack ran and played. (Morrow, 1978; Tompkins, 2007)

Semantics deals with the meaning that language communicates, through both content words and function words. It largely governs vocabulary development. *Content words* carry meaning in themselves. *Function words* have no easily definable meanings in isolation, but they indicate relationships between other words in a sentence. Function words include prepositions, conjunctions, and determiners (Fields, Groth, & Spangler, 2004; Pflaum, 1986; Tompkins, 2007).

Although we have identified stages of language growth, the pace of development may differ from child to child. An individual child's language development also tends to progress and then regress, so the stages of growth are not always easy to recognize. However, language development has been studied to the extent that it can be described generally.

From Birth to Year 1

In the first few months of infancy, oral language consists of a child's experimenting or playing with sounds. Infants cry when they are uncomfortable and babble, gurgle, or coo when they are happy. Parents are able to distinguish cries. One cry is for hunger and another is for pain, for instance. Infants learn to communicate specific needs by producing different cries. They communicate nonverbally and by moving their arms and legs to express pleasure or pain.

When babies are about 8 to 10 months old, their babbling becomes more sophisticated. They are usually capable of combining a variety of consonant sounds with vowel sounds. They tend to repeat these combinations over and over. It is at this stage that parents sometimes think they are hearing their child's first words. The repeated consonant and vowel sounds, such as *da, da, da* or *ma, ma, ma* do sound like real words. Most parents reinforce the child's behavior positively at this stage. Repetition of specific sounds and continued reinforcement lead the child to associate the physical mechanics of making a particular sound with the meaning of the word the sound represents.

From 8 to 12 months, children increase their comprehension of language dramatically; their understanding of language far exceeds their ability to produce it. They do, however, tend to speak their first words, usually those most familiar and meaningful to them in their daily lives: *Mommy, Daddy, bye-bye, hi, baby, cookie, milk, juice,* and *no,* for instance. As they become experienced with their first words, children use holophrases—one-word utterances that express an entire sentence (Hart & Risley, 1999; Vukelich, Christie, & Enz, 2002). For example, a baby might say "cookie," but mean "I want a cookie," "My cookie is on the floor," or "I'm done with this cookie."

From Age 1 to 2

A child's oral language grows a great deal between the ages of 1 and 2. Along with one-word utterances, the child utters many sounds with adult intonation as if speaking in sentences. These utterances are not understandable to adults, however. Children begin to use telegraphic speech from 12 months on, the first evidence of their knowledge of syntax. Telegraphic speech uses content words, such as nouns and verbs, but omits function words, such as conjunctions and articles. In spite of the omissions, words are delivered in correct order, or syntax: "Daddy home" for "Daddy is coming home soon," or "Toy fall" for "My toy fell off the table."

Language grows tremendously once the child begins to combine words. By 18 months most children can pronounce four-fifths of the English phonemes and use 9 to 20 words (Bloom, 1990).

From Age 2 to 3

The year between ages 2 and 3 is probably the most dramatic in terms of language development. Typically, a child's oral vocabulary grows from 300 words to 1000. The child can comprehend, but cannot yet use, 2000 to 3000 additional words. Telegraphic sentences of two or three words continue to be most frequent, but syntactic complexity continues to develop, and the child occasionally uses such functional words as pronouns, conjunctions, prepositions, articles, and possessives. As their language ability grows, children gain confidence. They actively play with language by repeating new words and phrases and making up nonsense words. They enjoy rhyme, patterns of language, and repetition (Bloom, 1990). Consider the following transcription of Jennifer's dialogue with her dog. Jennifer was 2 years, 10 months at the time. "Nice doggie, my doggie, white doggie, whitey, nicey doggie. Good doggie, my doggie, boggie, poggie. Kiss doggie, kiss me, doggie, good doggie." Jennifer's language is repetitive, playful, silly, and creative, demonstrating some of the characteristics of language production typical for a child her age.

From Age 3 to 4

A child's vocabulary and knowledge of sentence structure continue to develop rapidly during the fourth year. Syntactic structures added to the child's repertoire include plurals and regular verbs. Indeed, children of this age are prone to overgeneralization in using these two structures, mainly because both plural formation and verb inflection are highly irregular in the English language (Jewell & Zintz, 1986; Otto, 2006; Vukelich, Christie, & Enz, 2002). Four-year-old Jesse illustrated both problems when he had an accident in class and came running over very upset. He said, "Mrs. Morrow, hurry over, I knocked over the fishbowl and it broked and all the fishes are swimming on the floor." Jesse knew how to form the past tense of a verb by adding *ed*, but he did not know about irregular verbs such as *broke*. He also knew about adding an *s* to form a plural, but again was unaware of irregular plural forms such as *fish*.

As they approach age 4, children *seem* to have acquired all the elements of adult language. They can generate language and apply the basic rules that govern it. However, although their ability with language has grown enormously and they sound almost as if they are using adult speech, children have acquired only the basic foundations. Language continues to grow throughout our lives as we gain new experiences, acquire new vocabulary, and find new ways of putting words together to form sentences. At the age of 3 to 4, children talk about what they do as they are doing it. They often talk to themselves or by themselves as they play. It seems as if they are trying to articulate their actions (Roskos, Tabors, & Lenhart, 2004; Seefeldt & Barbour, 1986; Strickland & Schickedanz, 2004). While painting at an easel, 4-year-old Christopher said to himself, "I'm making a nice picture. I'm making colors all over. I'm painting, pit, pat, pit, pat. I'm going back and forth and up and down. Now I'm jumping as I paint." As he talked and painted, he did exactly what he said, words and actions coinciding.

From Age 5 to 6

Five- and six-year-olds sound very much like adults when they speak. Their vocabularies are always increasing, and so is the syntactic complexity of their language. They have vocabularies of approximately 2500 words, and they are extremely articulate. Many, however, still have difficulty pronouncing some sounds, especially *l*, *r*, and *sh* at the ends of words. They become aware that a word can have more than one meaning. When they are embarrassed or frustrated at misunderstanding things, they say something silly or try to be humorous. They also tend to be creative in using language. When they do not have a word for a particular situation, they supply their own. Adults often find the language used by children of this age to be amusing as well as delightful and interesting (Krashen, 2003; Seefeldt & Barbour, 1986; Weitzman & Greenberg, 2002):

> *Benjamin ran into school very excited one morning. "Mrs. Morrow," he said, "you'll never believe it. My dog grew puppies last night!"*
>
> *My husband and I were going to a formal dance one evening. My 5-year-old daughter had never seen us dressed up like this before. When I walked into the room wearing a long gown and asked Stephanie how I looked, she said, "Mommy, you look soooo pretty. What is Daddy's costume going to be like?"*
>
> *Escorted by her mother, Allison was on her way to her first day of kindergarten. She seemed a little nervous. When her mother asked her if she was okay, Allison replied, "Oh, I'm fine, Mommy. It's just that my stomach is very worried."*

There are other characteristics of kindergarteners' language. Kindergartners have discovered bathroom talk and curse words, and they enjoy shocking others by using them. They talk a lot and begin to use language to control situations. Their language reflects their movement from a world of fantasy to that of reality.

From Age 7 to 8

By the time children are 7 years of age, they have developed a grammar that is almost equivalent to that of adults. Of course, they do not use the extensive numbers of grammatical transformations found in adult language, nor do they have the extent of vocabulary found in adult speech. Seven- and eight-year-olds are good conversationalists who talk a lot about what they do.

Helping English Language Learners in Your Classroom

English Language Learners

The number of English language learners (ELL) with different languages and different language proficiency in American classrooms is increasing rapidly. There are children who do not speak any English; these children come from homes where English is not spoken at all. And there are children with very limited English proficiency; the English proficiency of this group of youngsters varies. Many of them are more proficient in the home language than in English. The goal is for them to become truly bilingual, that is, equally proficient in English and the home language.

Children also come to school speaking different dialects. A *dialect* is an alternative form of one particular language used in a different cultural, regional, or social group (Jalongo, 2007; Leu & Kinzer, 1991; Otto, 2006). Such differences can be so significant that an individual from a region with one English dialect may have difficulty understanding someone from another region because the pronunciation of letter sounds is so different. Dialects are not inherently superior to one another; however, one dialect typically emerges as the standard for a given language and is used by the more advantaged individuals of a society. Teachers must be aware of different dialects and help youngsters with the comprehension of standard dialects. Children are not to be degraded or viewed as less intelligent for speaking different dialects. Although it is important for children to achieve a level of standard English to help them succeed in society, emphasizing the need to become a standard English speaker before learning literacy in their first language is inappropriate and likely to create difficulties for the children by slowing their literacy development.

There are general strategies that will support the first language of students in regular classrooms. It is helpful when there is someone in the school who speaks the English language learner's first language. It could be a child or adult in the school who can speak the home language of ELL children to provide translation. The following strategies expose children in the class to other languages, thus creating an interest and appreciation for different backgrounds:

- Include print in the classroom that is from children's first language.
- Suggest that ELL students create books in their first language and share their stories.

Assign an English-speaking child as a buddy to help with the English language learner's English.

■ Be sure that children from different language backgrounds have the opportunity to read and write with others who speak their language, such as parents, aides, and other children in the school (Freeman & Freeman, 1993; Griffin, 2001; Otto, 2006; Roskos, Tabors, & Lenhart, 2004).

Along with the support of children's first language, it is also important to support the learning of English. Assign an English-speaking child as a buddy for the English language learner to help with that child's English. A few strategies that are helpful with young ELL students are included in the **language experience approach** (**LEA**). The following types of activities are used in this method.

■ Allow children to talk.

■ Have routine story times.

■ Provide thematic instruction that elicits talk, reading, and writing and heightens interest in exciting topics.

■ Write charts based on talk about children's home life and experiences in school.

■ Encourage children to copy experience charts, have them dictate their ideas for you to write, and encourage them to write themselves (Leu & Kinzer, 2003; Lindfors, 1989; McGee & Morrow, 2005; Miramontes, Nadeau, & Commins, 1997).

In the discussion of diversity in Chapter 3, the topic of English language learners was dealt with in more depth. Throughout the book, icons indicate when a strategy is especially good for ELL children.

Strategies for Language Development

A review of theory and research suggests how we can help children acquire and develop language pleasantly, productively, and appropriately. Children acquire language by emulating adult models, interacting with others when using language, and experiencing positive reinforcement for their efforts. If language is innate, it can develop naturally as individuals pass through common stages of development at certain times in their lives. As children mature, they become capable of generating ever more complex language structures. They learn language by doing, by acting on, and within familiar environments. Their first spoken words are those that are meaningful for them within their own experiences. Their earliest language is an expression of needs. They learn language through social interaction with individuals more literate than they, whether adults or older children. Children also create their own language, play with it, and engage in monologues.

Using what we know of language acquisition and developmental stages as guidelines, we can begin to create appropriate materials, activities, and experiences in a suitable atmosphere to nurture children's language development. The following objectives are formulated for a program fostering language development in children from birth to age 8.

Objectives for Receptive Language Development

1. Provide children with an atmosphere in which they will hear varied language frequently.

2. Allow children the opportunity to associate the language that they hear with pleasure and enjoyment.

3. Give children the opportunity to discriminate and classify sounds they hear.

4. Expose children to a rich source of new vocabulary on a regular basis.

5. Offer children the opportunity to listen to others and demonstrate that they understand what is said.

6. Provide children with opportunities for following directions.

7. Provide children with good models of standard English, and allow them to hear their home language in school.

Objectives for Expressive Language Development

1. Encourage children to pronounce words correctly.

2. Help children increase their speaking vocabularies.

3. Encourage children to speak in complete sentences at appropriate stages in their development.

4. Give children opportunities to expand their use of various syntactic structures, such as adjectives, adverbs, prepositional phrases, dependent clauses, plurals, past tense, and possessives.

5. Encourage children to communicate with others so that they can be understood.

6. Give children the opportunity to use language socially and psychologically by interpreting feelings, points of view, and motivation and by solving problems through generating hypotheses, summarizing events, and predicting outcomes.

7. Give children opportunities to develop language that involve mathematical and logical relations, such as describing size and amount, making comparisons, defining sets and classes, and reasoning deductively.

8. Provide children with the opportunity to talk in many different settings: in the whole group with the teacher leading the discussion, in teacher-led small groups, in child-directed groups for learning, or in conversation in social settings.

9. Give opportunities for children to use their own language freely at any stage of development. This could be a different dialect or mixtures of English and Spanish. Their desire to communicate should be encouraged, accepted, and respected.

Language is best learned when it is integrated with other communication skills and embedded within topics or content areas that have meaning and function for children. Children are constructive learners; they are active meaning makers who are continuously interpreting and making sense of their world based on what they already know.

Language is the major system by which meanings are communicated and expressed in our world. Language is best understood when it is related to some meaningful context. Language is learned through use, as part of our daily social activities. In addition to being aware of all these things, we need to accept language differences and help youngsters with special needs acquire skills and develop, enhance, and practice language (Au, 1998).

Strategies for Language Development from Birth to Age 2

"Hi, Natalie. How's my great big girl today? Let's change your diaper now, upsy-daisy. My goodness, you're getting heavy. Now I'll put you down right here on your dressing table and get a nice new diaper for you. Here, want this rubber ducky to hold while I change you? That's a good girl. You really like him. You're really lucky; let's clean you up now. This is the way we clean up Natalie, clean up Natalie, clean up Natalie. This is the way we clean up Natalie, so she'll feel so much better. You like that singing, don't you. I can tell. You're just smiling away, and cooing. Want to do that again? This is the way we clean up Natalie, clean up Natalie, clean up Natalie. This is the way we clean up Natalie, so she'll feel so much better. Wow, you were singing with me that time. That's right, ahhh-ahhh-ahh, now do it again. Mmmmm, doesn't that smell good? The baby lotion is so nice and smooth."

DEVELOPING LANGUAGE IN THE CHILD'S FIRST YEAR.   My grandbaby Natalie was 4 months old when I had that conversation with her. In print, it reads like a monologue; in reality, Natalie was a very active participant in the conversation. She stared intently at me. She cooed, she waved her arms, she smiled, and she became serious. I was providing a rich language environment for her. I encouraged her participation in the dialogue and acknowledged her responsiveness in a positive way. I provided her with the environmental stimuli necessary for her language to flourish. I engaged her in this type of conversation during feedings and while changing, bathing, and dressing her. I talked to her even when she was in her crib and I was in another room or while in the same room but involved in other things. The baby knew that communication was occurring because she responded to the talk with body movements, coos, babbles, and smiles. When she responded, I responded in turn.

SURROUND INFANTS WITH SOUNDS.   Infants need to be surrounded by the sounds of happy language. Whether from mother, father, or caregiver at home or a teacher or aide in a child-care center, sounds and interaction should accompany all activities. Adults responsible for babies from birth through the first year need to know nursery rhymes, chants, finger plays, and songs. It is important for children to hear the *sounds* of language as well as the meanings. Thus, adults can make up their own chants to suit an occasion, as I did when I spontaneously adapted "Here We Go Round the Mulberry Bush" while changing my granddaughter's diaper. Such experiences make the baby conscious of

Providing children with rich sources of new words in storybook reading, for example, will develop receptive language and vocabulary

the sounds of language. Children learn that they can have control over language and that oral language can be a powerful tool as well as fun.

In addition to the conversation of nearby adults, infants should experience other sounds and other voices, such as lots of different kinds of music, including classical, jazz, popular, and so on. Babies need to hear the sounds of "book language," which differs in intonation, pitch, stress, juncture, and even syntax from normal conversation. They need familiarity with language in all its variety so that they can learn to differentiate among its various conventions and patterns. Speaking to infants, singing to them, reading to them, and letting them hear the radio and television provide sources of language that help their own language grow. In addition, there are sounds in the immediate environment that need no preparation and are not the sounds of language, but that provide practice in auditory discrimination—the doorbell ringing, teapot hissing, clock chiming, vacuum cleaner humming, a dog barking, a bird singing, a car screeching, and so on. Bring them to the baby's attention, give them names, and heighten the child's sensitivity to them.

SURROUND INFANTS WITH SENSORY OBJECTS.   In addition to hearing a variety of sounds, babies need objects to see, touch, smell, hear, and taste. Objects should be placed in the baby's immediate environment—the crib or playpen. They will stimulate the baby's activity and curiosity and become the meaningful things within the environment from which language evolves. Some of the objects should make sounds or music when pushed or touched. They can have different textures and smells. They should be easy to grab, push, kick, or pull. They can be placed so they are visible and within the child's reach, and at least one item should be suspended overhead: stuffed animals, rubber toys, music boxes made of soft material, mobiles that can be kicked or grasped, mobiles that hang from the ceiling and rotate by themselves, and cardboard or cloth books with smooth edges. Books can be propped open against the side of the crib or playpen when the baby is lying on its back or against the headboard when the baby is on its stomach. Certain familiar objects should always remain, and new objects frequently should be made available. In addition to allowing the child to play independently with these objects, the adults in charge need to talk about them, name them, occasionally join the child in playing with them, and discuss their characteristics.

From 3 to 6 to 12 months, the baby gurgles, coos, begins to laugh, and babbles. Adults or caregivers should recognize an infant's sounds as the beginning of language and reinforce the infant positively with responses aimed at encouraging the sounds. When the baby begins to put consonants and vowels together, again adults should reinforce the behavior, imitating what the baby has uttered and urging repetition. When the babies become aware of the ability to repeat sounds and control language output, they will do these things. Babies also will begin to understand adult language, so it is important to name objects, carry on conversations, and give the baby directions. At the end of its first year, assuming he or she has experienced both appropriate sounds of language encouragement and pleasant interaction, the baby will be on the verge of extensive language growth during its second year.

LANGUAGE DEVELOPMENT AT AGES 1 AND 2. Through the second year of a child's life, the adults in charge need to continue the same kinds of stimulation suggested for developing oral language during the first year. However, because the baby is likely to develop a vocabulary of up to 150 words and to produce two- and possibly three-word sentences during the second year, additional techniques can be used to enhance language growth. One- and two-word utterances by children at this age usually represent sentences. When a 12-month-old points to a teddy bear and says "bear," the child probably means "I want my bear." Parents and caregivers at home or in child-care centers can begin to expand and extend the child's language by helping increase the number of words the child is able to use in a sentence or by increasing the syntactic complexity of their own utterances.

SCAFFOLDING TO HELP LANGUAGE DEVELOP. One method for helping a child develop language ability is a kind of modeling called **scaffolding** (McGee & Richgels, 2000; Otto, 2006; Soderman & Farrell, 2008). In scaffolding, an adult provides a verbal response for a baby who is not yet capable of making the response itself. In other words, the adult provides a language model. When the baby says "bear," for instance, the adult responds, "Do you want your teddy bear?" or "Here is your nice, soft, brown teddy bear." In addition to expanding on the child's language, the adult can extend it by asking the youngster to do something that demonstrates understanding and extends his or her thinking. For example, "Here is your nice, soft, brown teddy bear. Can you hug the teddy? Let me see you hug him." In addition to questions that require action, the adult can ask questions that require answers. Questions that require answers of more than one word are preferable, for example, "Tell me about the clothes your teddy is wearing." *How, why,* and *tell me* questions encourage the child to give more than a yes or no answer and more than a one-word response. *What, who, when,* and *where* questions, however, tend to elicit only one-word replies. As the child's language ability develops, the adult provides fewer and fewer such scaffolds; the child learns to build utterances along similar models.

NEW EXPERIENCES HELP DEVELOP LANGUAGE. Adults should select songs, rhymes, and books for 1- to 2-year-olds that use language they can understand. They are capable of understanding a great deal of language by now, and the selections should help expand and extend their language. Both vocabulary and conceptual understanding are enhanced by experiences. For the 1- to 2-year-old, frequent outings, such as visits to the post office, supermarket, dry cleaners, and park, provide experiences to talk about and new concepts to explore. Household tasks taken for granted by adults are new experiences that enrich children's language. Adults should involve toddlers in activities. For example, an 18-month-old can put a piece of laundry into the washing machine or give one stir to the bowl of food being prepared. During such daily routines, adults should surround the activity with language, identifying new objects for the baby and asking for responses related to each activity (Hart & Risley, 1999).

OVERGENERALIZATIONS AND LANGUAGE DEVELOPMENT.   As children become more verbal, adults sometimes want to correct their mispronunciations or overgeneralization of grammatical rules. The child who says, "Me feeded fishes," for instance, has simply overgeneralized the rules for the following:

Forming most past tenses (*feeded* for *fed*)

Using pronouns (objective *me* for subjective *I*)

Forming most plurals (*fishes* for *fish*)

Children also can overgeneralize concepts. A child who has learned to associate a bird with the word *bird* might see a butterfly for the first time and call it a bird, thinking that anything that flies is a bird. Correcting such an overgeneralization is best done positively rather than negatively. Instead of saying, "No, that's not a bird," it is better to refer to the butterfly as a *butterfly,* commenting on its beauty, perhaps, and thus expanding the child's verbal repertoire. Eventually, with positive reinforcement and proper role models in language, the child will differentiate between birds and butterflies, as well as between regular and irregular grammatical conventions and forms.

Correcting overgeneralizations negatively as absolute error, alternatively, is not likely to help young children understand the error or use proper tense and plural forms. Rather, it is likely to inhibit the child from trying to use language. In learning, children need to take risks and make mistakes. Hearing good adult models will eventually enable them to internalize the rules of language and to correct their errors themselves. At least until age 5, children should be allowed to experiment and play with language without direct concern for 100 percent correctness in syntax and pronunciation. The English language is extremely complex and irregular in many of its rules; in time, children will master these rules in all their complexity, if they have good adult models and plenty of verbal interaction. At the same time, encouraging "baby talk" simply because it is cute, for instance, is likely to inhibit growth because children will use whatever language they believe will please the adults around them.

MATERIALS FOR LANGUAGE DEVELOPMENT AT AGES 1 AND 2.   Materials for the 1- to 2-year-old should be varied and more sophisticated than those in the first year. Now that the baby is mobile in the home or child-care center, books need to be easily accessible to the child. Toys should still include items of various textures, such as furry, stuffed animals and rubber balls. Other toys should require simple eye—hand coordination. Three– to five–piece puzzles, trucks that can be pushed and pulled, dolls, a child-size set of table and chairs, crayons and large paper, and puppets are examples. Choose objects that require activity, for activity encourages exploration, use of the imagination, creation, and the need to communicate. The number of books in a child's library should be increasing. Those they are allowed to handle and use alone should still be made of cloth or cardboard.

Strategies for Language Development in Early Childhood Classrooms

From ages 3 to 8 a great deal of language development occurs. Children should continue to hear good models of language. They need constant opportunities to use language in social situations with adults and other children. Their oral language production must be reinforced positively. They must be actively involved in meaningful experiences that will expand their knowledge and interest in the world around them. Language should be purposeful and its development integrated with other subjects, rather than taught separately.

To accomplish these continuing goals, early childhood teachers provide an environment in which language will flourish. They organize centers of learning, one for each content area, that include materials for encouraging language use. A science center, for instance, can include class pets such as a pair of gerbils. Gerbils are active, loving animals that are fun to watch and handle. Children surround the cage often and generate talk just from watching the animals. Gerbils reproduce in 28-day cycles. When litters arrive, the birth process can be observed. The new babies cause much excitement and generate questions, comments, and unlimited conversation.

In my own classroom, our parent gerbils reproduced a second litter 28 days after the first and before the first babies had been weaned. The mother looked tired and thin from feeding and caring for 10 baby gerbils. One morning one of the children noticed that the mother was not in the cage. We could not imagine what had happened to her. A few days later, we found her hiding behind the refrigerator in the teachers' room. We never figured out how she got out of the cage, but we hypothesized all kinds of possibilities, and there was lots of discussion about why she left. No teacher alone could provide a lesson in which language flourished and grew the way it did during that incident, simply because gerbils were part of the classroom.

English Language Learners

CENTER MATERIALS FOR LANGUAGE DEVELOPMENT. Here are some examples of learning centers and appropriate materials in early childhood classrooms that will help generate language.

Science: aquarium, terrarium, plants, magnifying glass, class pet, magnets, thermometer, compass, prism, shells, rock collections, stethoscope, kaleidoscope, microscope, informational books and children's literature reflecting topics being studied, and blank journals for recording observations of experiments and scientific projects.

Social Studies: maps, a globe, flags, community figures, traffic signs, current events, artifacts from other countries, informational books and children's literature reflecting topics being studied, and writing materials to make class books or your own books about topics being studied.

Art: easels, watercolors, brushes, colored pencils, crayons, felt-tip markers, various kinds of paper, scissors, paste, pipe cleaners, scrap

materials (bits of various fabrics, wool, string, and so forth), clay, play dough, food and detergent boxes for sculptures, books about famous artists, and books with directions for crafts.

Music: piano, guitar, or other real instruments, CD and/or tape players, and tapes and CDs of all types of music, rhythm instruments, songbooks, and photocopies of sheet music for songs sung in class.

Mathematics: scales, rulers, measuring cups, movable clocks, stopwatch, calendar, play money, cash register, calculator, dominoes, abacus, number line, height chart, hourglass, numbers (felt, wood, and magnetic), fraction puzzles, geometric shapes, math workbooks, children's literature about numbers and mathematics, writing materials for creating stories, and books related to mathematics.

Literacy: multiple genres of children's literature, CD players or tape recorders, headsets and stories on tape or CDs, pencils, writing paper, stapler, construction paper, 3 × 5 cards for recording words, hole punch, letter stencils, computer, puppets, storytelling devices such as felt-board and roll movies, stationery with envelopes, letters (felt, wood, and magnetic) and letter chunks for building words, sets of pictures for different units (seasons, animals, space exploration, and so on), rhyme games, color games, cards for associating sounds and symbols, alphabet cards, and pictures and words representing out-of-school environmental print. (The literacy center also includes a library corner, a writing center, oral language materials, and language arts manipulatives, all of which are described in later chapters.)

Dramatic Play: dolls, dress-ups, telephone, stuffed animals, mirror, food cartons, plates, silverware, newspapers, magazines, books, telephone book, class telephone book, cookbook, notepads, cameras and photo album, table and chairs, broom, dustpan, child-size kitchen furniture such as refrigerator, sink, ironing board, and storage shelves. (The dramatic-play area can be changed from a kitchen to a grocery store, beauty shop, gas station, business office, restaurant, or the like, with the

A Winter Experience
We mixed Ivory Snow with water.
We spread it with our hands on blue paper.
It felt: gooky soft
Sticky yucky slimy
gluey gushy icky
smushy warm mushy

We did this because it's winter, and it's snowy, and Ivory Snow and real snow are white.

Experiences related to themes generate oral language that can be written down and then read.

addition of materials for appropriate themes when they are studied. Include appropriate materials for reading and writing related to the theme of the dramatic-play area.)

Block Area: blocks of many different sizes, shapes, and textures, figures of people, animals, toy cars, trucks, items related to themes being studied, paper and pencils to prepare signs and notes, and reading materials related to themes.

Workbench: wood, corrugated cardboard, hammer, scissors, screwdriver, saw, pliers, nails, glue, tape, and work table.

Outdoor Play: sand, water, pails, shovels, rakes, gardening area and gardening tools, climbing equipment, riding toys, crates, playhouse, balls, tires, and ropes.

Children need opportunities to use such areas for interacting with one another and the teacher. They should be given enough time to touch, smell, taste, listen, and talk about what they are doing. Exploring and experimenting with the materials in the centers are creative, imaginative, problem-solving, decision-making experiences in which children use language. The opportunity to *use* language is one of the key elements in language development.

Some materials remain permanently in the centers; others are replaced or supplemented occasionally so that new items of interest become available. Materials added to the centers are often coordinated with thematic units of instruction. For example, if a unit on Native Americans is introduced, Native American dolls and artifacts are added to the social studies center and books about Native Americans to the literacy center. The different content-area centers provide sources for language use and development; the literacy center is devoted *primarily* to language development. Thematic units of instruction that integrate all areas make learning more meaningful and expand concepts. (Interdisciplinary instruction is described more fully in Chapter 9.)

Block play encourages discussion as the children talk about the animal pens for their zoo.

DEVELOPING LANGUAGE WITH STRATEGIES USED IN THEMATIC UNITS.   Each new unit of instruction offers specific language experiences that expand vocabulary and develop syntax, pronunciation, and the ability to understand others and be understood. Again, these experiences should incorporate all content areas and make use of the senses (Antonacci & O'Callaghan, 2004; Combs, 2006; McGee & Morrow, 2005; Spencer & Guillaume, 2006; Tompkins & Koskisson, 1995). The suggestions that follow can be used each time a new theme is initiated. They reflect or describe activities designed to aid language growth in early childhood classrooms. For purposes of illustration, assume that the topic throughout these suggestions is *winter.*

English Language Learners

Discussion: Hold discussions about the unit topic. What is the weather like in winter? What kind of clothing do children need to wear in winter? What fun things can they do in winter that they cannot do at other times of the year? What problems does winter bring? What is winter like in different parts of the country, for example, New York, Florida, and California?

Word Lists: Ask the children to name words that make them think of winter. Your list might include *snow, ice, cold, white, wet, freezing, sleds, snowman, mittens, scarf, hat, slush, skiing, ice skating, snowballs, fireplace,* and *snowflakes.*

Classify the words on the list into how winter feels, looks, smells, sounds, and tastes, or what you can and cannot do in winter. List the words on a chart, and hang the chart in the room. Leave the chart hanging when you go to the next unit. When the wall gets too crowded, compile the charts into a class book.

Pictures: Provide pictures of winter scenes for discussion, each depicting different information about the season.

Sharing Time (Show and Tell):   Hold a sharing period during which children bring things from home related to the topic. Give all the children an opportunity to share if they wish, but assign different children for different days, because sharing by more than five or six children in one period can become tedious. Sharing objects from home is an important activity. It gives children confidence, because they are talking about something from their own environment. Even the shyest children will speak in front of a group if they have the security of sharing something familiar from home. Encourage

Food preparation can be a source of new vocabulary, especially because many of its terms take on special meanings—*stir, blend, boil, measure.*

children to relate the items to the unit topic, if they can. Model language for children to encourage them to speak in sentences. Coordinate the activity with parents, informing them of their children's scheduled sharing and the general topic under discussion.

Experiments: Carry out a science experiment related to the topic being studied. Involve the children actively. Discuss the purpose and hypothesize what is likely to happen. Encourage children to discuss what they are doing *while* they are doing it. When the experiment is complete, discuss the results with the class. (Example: Allow water to freeze, then melt. In warm climates use the freezer for freezing the water.)

Art: Carry out an art activity related to the topic. Allow children to create their own work, rather than making them follow specific directions that yield identical results. Discuss the project and the available materials before the activity. Provide materials that children will want to touch, describe, and compare. While children are creating, encourage conversation about what they are doing. For example, provide blue construction paper, tinfoil, white doilies, cotton, wool, tissue paper, and chalk for a winter collage. Discuss why these colors and objects were selected. What is there about them that makes people think of winter? Suggest creating a picture that makes one think of winter. Discuss the textures of the materials and what can be done with them.

Music: Sing songs about winter, such as "It's a Marshmallow World in the Winter." Music is enjoyable, and lyrics help build vocabulary and sensitivity to the sounds and meanings of words. Listen to music without words, music that creates images concerning the topic. Ask the children for words, sentences, or stories that the music brings to mind.

Food Preparation: Prepare food related to the unit. Make hot soup, flavored snowballs, or popcorn. Discuss food textures, smells, taste, and appearance. Follow recipe directions, thus learning about sequencing and quantity. Allow children to help prepare the food and enjoy eating it together, encouraging discussion and conversation throughout. Food preparation can be a source of new vocabulary, especially because many of its terms take on special meanings: *stir, blend, boil, measure, dice,* and so on.

Dramatic Play: Add items related to the topic to the dramatic-play area—mittens, hats, scarves, boots for dress-up—to encourage role playing and language about winter. Introduce the items by placing each in a separate bag and asking a child to reach in, describe what it feels like, and identify it without peeking. The sense of touch elicits descriptive language.

Outdoor Play: Encourage spontaneous language and frequent problem-solving situations during outdoor play. For example, provide snow shovels, sleds, pails, and cups during playtime in the snow. Discuss outdoor play before going out and again after coming in.

Morning Message: Discuss weather and the calendar in a daily morning message. Encourage children to share news about themselves: a new pair of sneakers, a birthday. Make plans for the school day.

Class Trips: Take the class on a trip, bring in a guest speaker, or show a film. All three activities can generate language and encourage its use.

Read Stories: Read stories to the children about the topic under study. Books such as *Katy and the Big Snow* (Burton, 1943) enhance information and expand vocabulary.

Create Stories: Provide the children with a title, such as "The Big Winter Snowstorm," and let them think of a story about it.

Retell Stories: Ask children to retell stories. This activity encourages them to use book language and incorporate it into their own. Retelling is not always an easy task for young children, so props can be helpful—puppets, felt boards and felt characters, roll movies, and pictures in a book. With these same props, children can make up their own stories as well.

Very Own Vocabulary Words: In any of these activities, children should be encouraged as often as possible to select their favorite Very Own Words about winter. Favorite Very Own Words can be selected from discussions, art lessons, science experiments, songs, books, poems, cooking experiences, or any other activity. After a particular experience, ask children to name a favorite word. Record children's favorite Very Own Words for them on 3 × 5 cards and store them in each child's own file box or on a binder ring. When children are capable of recording their own words, assist them with spelling when they ask for help. Favorite Very Own Words enhance vocabulary and are a source for reading and writing development.

Word Walls: As the class learns new words that are especially related to themes, the teacher can place them on a word wall for use. Word walls have many purposes. They are mostly for reading grade-level, high-frequency words. These words should be separated from the new vocabulary-themed words by color. That is, all high-frequency words may be in red and all new thematic words in blue. The new vocabulary on the word wall is used in different activities, such as alphabetizing words or using them in sentences and stories.

Summary of the Day: Summarize the day's events at the end of the school day, encouraging children to tell what they liked, did not like, and want to do the next day in school.

English Language Learners

CHILDREN'S LITERATURE AND LANGUAGE DEVELOPMENT.   Among more general suggestions, select and offer children's literature that represents varieties of language and experience. Some children's books, such as the classic *Strega Nona* (dePaola, 1975), feature not only sophisticated, interesting language, but wonderful rhymes that Strega Nona sings throughout the book. The book is excel-

A felt board with story characters helps children use book language as they recall stories.

lent for vocabulary development, developing syntactic complexity through the use of adjectives and adverbs, and an emphasis on rhyming words. The book *How Do Dinosaurs Eat Their Food?* is composed of questions throughout the book that teach punctuation and sentence structure.

Craft books require children to follow directions. Wordless books encourage them to create their own stories from the pictures. Concept books feature words such as *up, down, in, out, near,* and *far* or involve children in mathematical reasoning. Realistic literature deals with death, divorce, loneliness, fear, and daily problems; discussion of such themes leads to sociopsychological language, interpretation of feelings, sensitivity to others, and problem solving. Books of riddles, puns, jokes, and tongue twisters show children how language plays on meaning in certain situations. Poetry introduces children to rhyme, metaphor, simile, and onomatopoeia, and encourages them to recite and create poems. (Children's books are listed by these and other categories in Appendix A.) When children hear and discuss the language of books, they internalize what they have heard; the language soon becomes part of their own language. Research studies have found that children who are read to frequently develop more sophisticated language structures and increased vocabulary (Beck & McKeown, 2001).

Two anecdotes illustrate how children incorporate into their own language the language of books that have been read to them. My kindergarten class was playing on the playground one early spring day. A few birds circled around several times. Melissa ran up to me and said, "Look, Mrs. Morrow, the birds are fluttering and flapping around the playground." Surprised at first by Melissa's descriptive and unusual choice of words, I thought for a moment, then remembered. The words that Melissa was using came directly from a picture storybook we had read shortly before, *Jenny's Hat* (Keats, 1966). In the book, birds *flutter* and *flap* around Jenny's hat. Melissa had internalized the language of the book and was able to use it in her own vocabulary.

One day after a big snowstorm, my daughter asked, "Mommy, can I go out and play? I want to build a smiling snowman." I was surprised and pleased with this sophisticated language being uttered by my 4-year-old. *Smiling snowman,* after all, represents a participle in the adjective position, a syntactic structure usually not found in the language of children before the age of 7 or 8. Then I noticed that Stephanie had a book in her hand, *The*

Snowy Day (Keats, 1962). In it Peter goes outside and builds a *smiling snow-man*. Stephanie had used the book's language and made it her own.

The activities just suggested can be repeated throughout the school year with each new theme that is studied. Such adaptation and repetition make it possible to introduce children to hundreds of new vocabulary words, concepts, and ideas. They will assure children of opportunities to participate in new kinds of spontaneous language as topics and structured experiences change. Word lists and other materials produced during each unit can be maintained and made available for review and reuse.

Most of the suggestions can be followed at home as well as at school. Parents should not be expected to create elaborate centers or carry out units of instruction. But daily living offers holidays, seasons, family events, and other topics and events of special interest. Parents can tap such meaningful occasions for their potential enhancement of language development. They can discuss events, list words, help children collect favorite Very Own Words, involve children in cooking and household chores, take trips, read stories, sing songs, and generally encourage the use of language as a pleasurable activity and a useful skill.

In the learning environment described throughout this chapter, language development is spontaneous and also encouraged. Modeling, scaffolding, and reinforcement make this environment interactive between child and adult, and they guide and nurture language development to an extent that children are not likely to achieve on their own. The strategies discussed are appropriate for children who have language differences and minimal language disorders. These youngsters, however, may need additional attention on a one-to-one basis from the classroom teacher or a resource-room teacher. See page S-12 in Strategies for the Classroom for characters for children to use to create their own stories.

 **Strategies**

Expanding Vocabulary and Word Meaning in Second and Third Grades

I have suggested many strategies to develop vocabulary for children from birth through the early childhood grades. Following are strategies for children in second and third grades to help them increase their vocabulary and make connections with the meaning of words when reading text. These strategies also should enhance vocabulary used in their writing.

Semantic Maps: Semantic maps are diagrams that help children see how words are related to one another (Fisher & Frey, 2006; Johnson & Pearson, 1984; Otto, 2006). To enrich vocabulary development and the meaning of words, try the following:

1. Choose a word related to a student's interests or a theme that is being studied.
2. Write the word on a chalkboard or a piece of experience chart paper.
3. Brainstorm other words that are related to the key word.
4. Create categories for the new words that emerge and classify them into these categories (see Figure 4.1).
5. Use the words to create a story. (Cox, 2002)

Figure 4.1

Semantic Map about Transportation

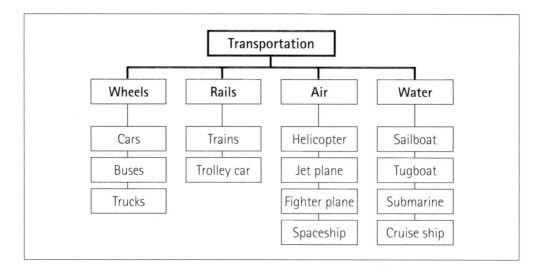

Context Clues: Using clues from surrounding text is an important way of figuring out word meanings. Leaving blanks in sentences for children to determine the appropriate word is an activity that helps them understand how to use context to find word meanings. Just looking to other words in a sentence to determine meaning is helpful as well. Students need to know that this is one of the best ways to learn new words because they are embedded in meaningful text. The clues they use are other words or phrases in the sentence that tell something about unknown words. Clues can be before or after the unknown word and are usually close to the word. They could also be in sentences before or after. Have students guess the meaning of the word from the clues and then discuss if the guesses are correct. The following sentence is from the book *Swimmy* (1975) by Leo Lionni. The unusual words that Lionni uses can be grasped from the words surrounding the more difficult ones:

"One bad day a tuna fish fierce, swift, and very hungry came_____ through the waves."

    The teacher left a blank in the sentence for a word that was difficult, but could be figured out. It was for the word darting. *She read the sentence to the children with the blank and asked what word they thought fit there. They suggested that the word could be* swimming, rushing, shooting out, jumping, pushing. *None said* darting, *since it was not familiar to them. The teacher praised their choices and put in the word* darting *from the story. She asked the children what they thought it meant. They agreed it meant* pushing, shooting out, *and maybe* rushing, *which were words that they had already generated and that defined the unknown word* darting.

Vocabulary Books: Children can keep a new vocabulary book for the school year. There is a pattern to the book. The new word is written in the middle of the page. A synonym for the word is written in the upper-right corner and its definition in the upper-left corner. The student writes a sentence using the word, along with an illustration, in the lower-left corner. In the lower-right corner, the student chooses a classification for

English Language Learners

the word (e.g., a *poodle* is a dog, *orange* is a color). This book grows throughout the year as new words are added.

Word Parts: Learning word parts is a way for second and third graders to build vocabulary and meaning. Choose word parts that are well-known prefixes and suffixes and commonly used roots of words. With knowledge of a few of these, children can begin to build their own words. Teach children to talk through the use of word parts to get the meaning. For example, when students learn word-part meanings they can talk through their word building as follows: "I know that the prefix *dis* means "not," and I also know that the word *content* means to be happy or pleased. If I add *dis* to the word *content* it would be *discontent.* Now it would mean that someone was not happy.

The Dictionary: Using the dictionary is another way to add to a student's repertoire of strategies to find and check meanings. Students must learn that words have many meanings, and they may all be listed in the dictionary. Therefore, when using the dictionary, they need to select the meaning for the word that makes sense in the context in which it occurs. Dictionaries prepared for young children should be used in the primary grades (Graves, Juel, & Graves, 1998).

Vocabulary-rich second- and third-grade classrooms have many materials to enrich language and vocabulary development. These classrooms, like those in earlier grades, should display new words and have many dictionaries. In the library corner, there are riddle books, joke books, and books with puns. There are many genres of children's literature, such as fiction and nonfiction. There are word games such as Boggle, Pictionary, Scrabble, and crossword puzzles (Blachowicz & Fisher, 2002).

Formats for Promoting Language and Vocabulary Development in the Classroom

By the time children come to school, they have had varied opportunities for talk in their daily lives. Most of the talk is spontaneous and deals with real-life experiences. With their parents, talk has included questions and answers, with parents directing the discussion or the children playing a more active role. I have discussed strategies that initiate talk. Here I will offer organizational structures in classrooms that will provide different types of talk experiences. These include teacher-directed question and answer discussions, small-group conversations to give and receive information, and spontaneous discussions that are led by the teacher or children in social settings. In addition, conversations that include different types of talk will be described. In structured question and answer discussions, teachers need to provide open-ended questions that will encourage talk such as "What would happen if?" "What would you do if?" and "Tell us why."

Conversations occur best in small-group settings that include three to six children. Any number beyond that can no longer be considered a conversation, but rather a large-group discussion. Guidelines, such as those that follow, need to be established for conversation to be productive.

Guidelines Small-Group Conversations with the Teacher

1. Children should listen to others during conversations.
2. Children need to take turns talking.
3. Students should raise hands, if necessary, to ensure everyone gets a turn, and individuals do not interrupt each other.
4. Everyone should keep talk relevant to the topic of conversation.
5. Teachers need to help redirect conversation to its stated purpose should it stray.
6. Teacher talk should be kept to a minimum as the teacher becomes a participant. Teachers should follow the same rules as the children: Listen to others when they are talking, take turns, do not do all the talking, and so on.

Guidelines Formal Conversations without the Teacher

A group leader needs to be selected to help direct the conversation when children are in charge of their own discussion. All the same guidelines for productive conversation when the teacher is present apply when children direct conversations themselves.

1. Children should listen to others during conversations.
2. Children need to take turns talking.
3. Students should raise hands, if necessary.
4. Everyone should keep the talk relevant to the conversation's purpose.

English Language Learners

Informal Conversations without the Teacher

Children need time to talk without leaders or specific outcomes. This type of conversation is likely to occur during free-play periods, center time, or outdoor play. Although classrooms that encourage this type of talk can be noisy, it is important for children to have the opportunity to use language in social settings at school.

In addition to learning the types of organizational structures in which talk should take place, students need to engage in different types of talk, including aesthetic talk, efferent talk, and talk in dramatic activities.

Aesthetic talk typically revolves around children's literature. In this talk, children have the opportunity to interpret what they have read or listened to. Children can participate in aesthetic talk when discussing literature, telling stories, and participating in Reader's Theater. These activities will be discussed further in Chapter 8, which deals with using children's literature in the classroom.

Efferent talk is used to inform and persuade. Efferent talk occurs in discussion of the themes being studied. It also occurs in situations such as show-and-tell, oral reports, interviews, and debates. These types of interchange are

more formal than previously discussed and often require preparation on the part of the child.

Dramatic activities provide another avenue for different types of talk. When children participate in dramatic activities, they share experiences, explore their understanding of ideas, and interact with peers. Dramatic experiences can include informal role playing in dramatic-play areas of the classroom. Use of props and puppets to act out stories provides another avenue for talk. Look at the Strategies for the Classroom activity for language development on page S-12.

A teacher who uses these organizational frameworks for language and has children engage in the types of activities that motivate talk will be providing a classroom rich in experiences and topics to talk about. In turn, language development will be enhanced.

Assessment of Children's Language Development

It is important to assess children's language to determine if it follows expected stages of development. Assessment also determines how much a child has progressed. The word *assessment* suggests several rather frequent measures by which to judge progress. Assessment should reflect instructional objectives and strategies. It should include evaluation of a wide range of skills used in many contexts. A certain child, for example, may perform better in an interview than on a pencil-and-paper test. Both kinds of evaluation, therefore, should be used. Literacy includes a wide range of skills; it is important to evaluate a child for as many as possible to determine strengths and weaknesses. Unfortunately, many assessment instruments are narrow in scope and frequently do not measure a child's total abilities.

There are some basic concepts to employ when assessing language and vocabulary so that we have a broad perspective. The following are some guidelines:

- Use tools that reflect your instruction.
- Incorporate student self-assessment.
- Assess words students need to know.
- Assessment tools for vocabulary should evaluate what it means to know the word.
- Vocabulary assessment should be systematic.
- Assess explicitly taught vocabulary.
- Children should be involved in assessing their vocabulary alone or with other students or the teacher.

Children should be encouraged to engage in conversation as they work together in small groups.

CheckList   Assessing Language Development

Child's name _____ Date _____

	Always	Sometimes	Never	Comments
Makes phoneme sounds				
Speaks in one-word sentences				
Speaks in two-word sentences				
Identifies familiar sounds				
Differentiates similar sounds				
Understands the language of others when spoken				
Follows verbal directions				
Speaks to others freely				
Pronounces words correctly				
Has appropriate vocabulary for level of maturity				
Speaks in complete sentences				
Uses varied syntactic structures				
Can be understood by others				

Teacher Comments:

There are several ways to measure children's language development in early childhood, which are similar to those used for measuring literacy development described in Chapter 2.

Checklists are practical because they provide concise outlines for teachers and appropriate slots for individual children. They are most effective if used periodically during the school year. Three to four evaluations during the year can provide sufficient data to determine progress. Program objectives offer criteria to include on checklists.

Anecdotal records are another form of language assessment. They tend to be time consuming but can reveal rich information. Loose-leaf notebooks and file cards offer two means for keeping anecdotal records. These records require no particular format. Rather, the teacher or parent simply writes down incidents or episodes on the days they occur. Samples of a child's language and situations involving language can be recorded. Like checklists, anecdotal samples are necessary periodically to determine growth over a school year.

Audio Recordings are another means of evaluating language. The process can take the form of an open interview or a hidden recording. (Video equipment can serve the same purposes, but may not be readily available in most early childhood classrooms.) Children who are unaware that their conversation is being recorded are likely to be more spontaneous and uninhibited (Genishi & Dyson, 1984; McGee, 2007; Otto, 2006).

It is often difficult, however, to place a tape recorder where it will record language clearly enough to transcribe and analyze. Interviews with children can be more natural when an adult familiar to the child does the interviewing. Or it is also helpful to allow the tape recorder to become such a familiar tool in the classroom that the child uses it often in the language arts center. Under such circumstances the machine is not threatening when used in an assessment interview.

To record samples of natural language, discuss the child's experiences. Ask about home, favorite games or toys, favorite TV programs, brothers and sisters, trips taken, or birthday parties recently attended. You should try to collect a corpus of spontaneous language that provides a typical sample of the child's ability with language.

Record audio assessment samples three or four times a year. Let children hear their own recorded voices and enjoy the experience. Then, for assessment purposes, transcribe the recordings and analyze them for such items as numbers of words uttered and numbers of words spoken in a single connected utterance (for example, "Tommy's cookie" or "Me want water"). The lengths of such utterances can be averaged to determine mean length. Length of utterance is considered a measure of complexity. When children begin to speak in conventional sentences, such as "That is my cookie," measure the length of the t-units. A **t-unit** is an independent clause with all its dependent clauses attached, assuming it has dependent clauses. It can be a simple or complex sentence. Compound sentences are made up of two t-units. Length of t-units, like length of utterances, is a measure of language complexity. It typically increases with the user's age and usually the more words per unit, the more complex the unit (Hunt, 1970).

Further analysis of taped utterances and t-units can determine which elements of language a child uses: number of adjectives, adverbs, dependent clauses, negatives, possessives, passives, plurals, and so on. The more complex the transformations, embeddings, and syntactic elements used are, the more complex the language overall (Morrow, 1978). Data from several samples over a year can be most revealing.

The following is a verbatim transcription of a recorded language sample from a 7-year-old boy in the second grade. The child was presented with a picture book and asked to tell a story from the pictures.

> *He's getting up in the morning and he's looking out the window with his cat and after he gets out of bed he brushes his teeth then when he gets done brushing his teeth, he eats he eats breakfast and then when he after he eats breakfast he he gets dressed to play some games then in the afternoon he plays with his toys then in the afternoon he plays doctor and early in the day he plays cowboys and Indians then when it's in the afternoon close to suppertime he plays cops and robbers when he's playing in his castle he likes to dream of a magic*

carpet he's driving his ship on the waves he's uh circus uh ringmaster he's lifting up a fat lady I mean a clown is standing on a horse a clown is on a high wire somebody fell and then hurt their head the cowboy is bringing some ice cream to the hurt man that night he goes in the bathroom and gets washed and then he goes to bed then he dreams I don't know what he's dreaming I will think of what he's dreaming he's dreaming of going to play and he's playing the same things over

After the sample is transcribed, the language is segmented into t-units. Following is a sample of the segmented sample of t-units:

1. He's getting up in the morning.
2. And he's looking out the window with his cat.
3. And after he gets out of bed, he brushes his teeth.
4. Then when he gets done brushing his teeth, he eats.
5. He eats breakfast.
6. And then (when he) after he eats breakfast he (he) gets dressed to play some games.
7. Then in the afternoon he plays with his toys.
8. Then in the afternoon he plays doctor.
9. And early in the day he plays cowboys and Indians.
10. Then when it's in the afternoon close to suppertime he plays cops and robbers.
11. When he's playing in his castle he likes to dream of a magic carpet.
12. He's driving his ship on the waves.
13. He's (uh) circus (uh) ringmaster.
14. He's lifting up a fat lady.
15. I mean a clown is standing on a horse.
16. A clown is on a high wire.
17. Somebody fell and then hurt their head.
18. The cowboy is bringing some ice cream to the hurt man.
19. That night he goes in the bathroom and gets washed.
20. And then he goes to bed.
21. Then he dreams.
22. I don't know what he's dreaming.
23. I will think of what he's dreaming.
24. He's dreaming of going to play.
25. And he's playing the same things over.

Standardized Language Assessment

Assessment for language development thus far has been a discussion of informal measures. There are standardized measures used for different purposes and age levels from preschool through the primary grades. The following are some standardized measures: The *Peabody Picture Vocabulary Test: 2 years to 18 years* (Dunn & Dunn, 1997), the *Test of Language*

Development: Primary, 4 through 8 years (TOLD) (Hresko, Reid, & Hammill, 1999), and *Expressive One-Word Picture Vocabulary Test, 2 to 18 Years* (EWPVR) (Brownell, 2000). These tests provide information for the teacher about children's vocabulary development and their use of complex sentence structure (McGee, 2007).

I have discussed oral language separately from the other communication skills in this chapter in order to describe its developmental stages and the theories of how it is acquired. This separation is somewhat artificial, however, because oral language is as important to literacy development as are reading and writing. We know that communication skills develop concurrently, each helping the growth of the others. Coordination and integration of the several communication skills in a single program are described in Chapter 9.

An Idea from the Classroom

English Language Learners

Using Props for Oral Language Development

Children's books that lend themselves to storytelling with props are always beneficial to ELL students because the props make the language visual, hands-on, and specific. Some good stories to use with a first-grade class include *The Jacket I Wear in the Snow* (Neitzel, 1991), *A Letter to Amy* (Keats, 1968), and *Peter's Chair* (Keats, 1967). After first reading one of these stories aloud, have the children create or gather the props needed to tell the story. For example, after reading *The Jacket I Wear in the Snow*, discuss the articles of clothing that were mentioned in the story and add to the list if necessary. Distribute the articles of clothing to the students so that each has one item. Read the story a second time. This time, pause when an article of clothing is mentioned in the story. Encourage the children to hold up their item and name it when it appears in the story. For example, you will read, "This is the (sweater) I wear in the snow." The child who has the sweater will hold it up and say "sweater." Encourage the children to join in by chanting the repetitive phrases and the names of the articles of clothing as they are repeated in the story. This activity can be adapted for any story that provides opportunities for hands-on materials and repetition. The class participation using these props allows ELL students to make a connection between a tangible, familiar object and its English name.

Gina A. Goble, ESL Teacher, Grades K–3

Activities and Questions

1. Answer the focus questions at the beginning of the chapter.

2. What strategies are good for teaching language and literacy skills to English language learners?

3. What cultural concerns do teachers need to recognize when teaching English language learners?

4. Select an objective for language development listed in the chapter. Prepare a lesson that will help a child achieve the goal. Identify the theories of language acquisition used in your lesson.

5. Tape-record children at play or working in a group. Identify which characteristics of their language can be described by various theories of language acquisition. For example, imitation could be explained by the behaviorist theory.

6. Begin a thematic unit that you will continue as you read this book. Select a social studies or science topic. Select three objectives for language development, and describe three activities that will satisfy each objective using your theme. An example follows:

Content Area: Science

Theme: Creatures That Live in the Sea

Objective for Language Development: Develop new vocabulary

Activity: Read *Swimmy* by Leo Lionni. Ask the children to remember two new words they hear in the story. After reading, list words that the children mention on a chart, and discuss their meaning.

7. Observe a preschool, kindergarten, or first- or second-grade class for about 3 hours. Note the amount of time children are given to talk, the amount of time the teacher talks, and the amount of time during which there is no verbal interaction. Compare the three figures. Then classify talk in the classroom into the following categories:
   a. Questions and answers
   b. Whole-class discussion
   c. Small-group discussion led by the teacher
   d. Interactive discussion among children
   e. Interactive discussion between teacher and children

Based on the results of this ministudy, determine how often we allow children to use language and in how many different contexts or situations.

8. Plan an activity that will elicit aesthetic talk and one that will involve efferent talk. How is the language in each setting the same, and how is it different?

9. Continue the collection of assessment materials for the child for which you began a portfolio in Chapter 2. Collect one language sample from a child age 2 through 7. Elicit the language by showing a picture to discuss or asking the child to talk about favorite TV shows, pets, friends, family members, or trips. Tape-record the sample and transcribe it.
   a. Check the characteristics of the child's language development according to the descriptions in this chapter and the checklist provided to decide whether the child is above, below, or at a level appropriate for his or her age. Compare with other members of the class who have studied different age groups.
   b. Divide your language sample into t-units and determine the average length per t-unit; then count the number and type of syntactic elements used. Compare your sample to someone else in the class who is working with a child of a different age.
   c. Collect three additional language samples for the same child at different times in the year. Evaluate the new samples as you did the first time and check for growth.

10. 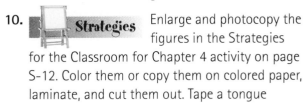 Enlarge and photocopy the figures in the Strategies for the Classroom for Chapter 4 activity on page S-12. Color them or copy them on colored paper, laminate, and cut them out. Tape a tongue

depressor to the back of each figure to create a stick puppet. Create an original story using the characters provided. Ask the children to do the same after you have modeled the activity. If nec-

essary, help the child start by saying, "You can begin your story with 'Once upon a time there was a girl and a boy. They decided to take a walk in the woods.' "

myeducationlab

VIDEO EXERCISE

Now that you have the benefit of having read this chapter, return to the www.myeducationlab.com topic "English Language Learners" and watch "An ESL Vocabulary Lesson" one more time. You may complete the questions that accompany it online and save or transmit your work to your professor, or complete the following questions, as required.

An ESL Vocabulary Lesson (4:55 minutes)

1. What was the purpose of the vocabulary activity at the beginning of the video?
2. What is automaticity, and what is its role in vocabulary acquisition?

3. Next step: The activities discussed were all pre-reading activities. Design a postreading activity that could be used with these children to reinforce the vocabulary words.
4. Next step: Vocabulary in content-area reading can sometimes be a greater challenge to limited-English-proficient students than new vocabulary in literature. What strategies would you recommend to teach content vocabulary to elementary school English language learners? If you were fluent in the children's native language, how might your strategies be different?

Focus Questions

■ Children demonstrate an interest in function, form, and the conventions of print. Discuss the implication of this statement for classroom instruction.

■ Describe the concept of reading readiness.

■ Define the following emergent literacy strategies and describe how to teach them to enhance knowledge about print: (1) environmental print, (2) Very Own Words, (3) language experience approach, and (4) context and picture clues.

■ Define high-frequency words and how they are taught.

■ Define the following terms: (1) phonemic awareness, (2) phonological awareness, (3) alphabetic principle, (4) phonics, (5) phoneme—grapheme correspondence, (6) digraphs, (7) consonant blends, (8) long and short vowel sounds, and (9) inflectional endings.

■ Describe the characteristics of commercially prepared materials designed for literacy instruction.

■ How much time needs to be spent on word study?

■ Where do you fit word study into your program?

■ **VOCABULARY:** word-study skills, phonemic awareness, phonological awareness, environmental print, sight words, high-frequency words, language experience approach (LEA), phonics, *vowels, consonants*

■ **Strategies** See pages S-13 through S-21 in Strategies for the Classroom for activities dealing with word study. How do you evaluate the value of these activities in helping children with the strategies involved?

PEARSON myeducationlab VIDEO PREVIEW: **Teaching Phonics** (6:14 minutes); **Word Chunking** (1:00 minute); **Phonics Instruction** (4:43 minutes). Before reading this chapter, go to www.myeducationlab.com. Under the topic "Phonics/Phonemic Awareness," access and watch the videos "Teaching Phonics," "Word Chunking," and "Phonics Instruction."

Strategies to Figure Out Words

Phonological Awareness, Phonemic Awareness, and Phonics

Young children are more interested in the functions of literacy first and the form later. The first words a child says, reads, and writes are those with meaning and function in his or her life, such as family names, food labels, and road signs. After function, the child becomes interested in the forms of print, which include names of letters and their sounds. Finally children learn conventions of print. This is the recognition that punctuation serves a purpose in reading and writing, and that spaces demarcate letters and words and words are written and read from left to right.

—Frank Smith (1971)

Mrs. Abere's class was studying nutrition. The dramatic-play area was set up like a supermarket with products displayed separately in food groups: dairy products; breads and cereals; meat, poultry, and fish; and fruits and vegetables. To connect the learning of sound–symbol relationships and letter names with the unit, three letters were featured: *m* for meat, *f* for fish, and *d* for dairy. In addition to creating funny stories using the featured letters, such as *Fanny the Fish was a Friendly Flounder who liked to Flip her Flippers as she Fluttered through the waves,* the children were to collect things that began with the featured letters and place them in boxes labeled with the appropriate symbol. These experiences caused them to talk about letters, sounds, and words in spontaneous play. Kathy and Kelly were pretending that they were shopping in the dramatic-play store. Kathy picked up a can of tuna fish and said, "Kelly, let's see how many foods we can find that begin with the letter *f*." They looked around, and Kathy found a box of Frosted Flakes and some French Fries. Kelly found a can of Fruit Cocktail, Fruit Loops cereal, and a container of Frozen Yogurt. The girls were excited when each found some food that began with the letter *f*. They said each word with a strong emphasis on the beginning *f* sound. Another activity the children were asked to do was to copy the names of the food that began with *f*. Mrs. Abere told them to do the same activities for the other featured letters in the unit, *m* for meat and *d* for dairy. Mrs. Abere does many mini-lessons such as this with the entire class. However when she works with the children in small groups she will focus on individual needs based on achievement. Some children will not be ready for sound–symbol correspondence; others will be looking at onsets and rimes in words.

Theory and Research Concerning the Acquisition of Literacy by Figuring Out Words

Becoming literate is a process that begins at birth and continues throughout life. Children differ in their rates of literacy achievement; they must not be pressured into accomplishing tasks or placed on a predetermined time schedule. Researchers have found that children learn that print has *functions* as a first step in reading and writing (Goodman, 1984; Mason, 1980; Smith, 1971). The first words a child says, reads, and writes are those with meaning, purpose, and function in his or her life, such as family names, food labels, road signs, and names of fast-food restaurants.

After function, the child becomes interested in the *forms* of print. Details about names, sound, and configurations of letters and words now serve the child's learning more than simple understanding of how print functions.

A child then learns the *conventions* of print. This process involves recognition that we read and write from left to right, that punctuation serves a purpose in reading and writing, and that spaces demarcate letters and words. Although recognition of the function of print dominates the first stages of reading and writing development, children acquire an interest in and notions about the form and conventions of print at the same time, but to a lesser degree.

Researchers warn that children do not systematically go from one developmental stage to the next in early reading and writing; they can take one step forward and, the next day, one step backward. For example, if you test a child's knowledge of the alphabet and she can identify 15 letters, the next day she may only identify 12.

In a study of what children know about reading and of their skill in letter and word recognition, McCormick and Mason (1981) established three developmental levels in word recognition. Children first identified words through context, then used letter-sound cues, and finally relied on sounding out words.

Studies of young children's responses to story readings also reveal developmental trends that follow McCormick and Mason's basic three-strand paradigm. Children's initial questions and comments during story readings are related to the pictures and the meanings of the stories. As they gain experience with story readings, their questions and comments begin to concern the names of letters, the reading of individual words, or attempts to sound out words (McAfee & Leong, 1997; Neuman & Roskos, 1998). The function of print dominates early responses; the form of print becomes more important in later responses.

Some children have considerable information about reading and writing before they enter school for formal instruction. Some can read and write before they come to school; others have had little exposure to literacy. Some children come to school with almost no exposure to print and have no books in their home. Children who have had exposure to print and a literacy-rich environment know the difference between drawing and writing, and they associate books with reading. They can read environmental print, and they realize the functions of reading and writing. Because their knowledge about literacy to this point is based on meaning and function, they expect that reading and writing will be activities that make sense. Children without this exposure do not have these concepts about books and print.

Efforts to expand children's reading abilities into reading fluency initially need to build on their strengths and on what they already know and expect of reading (Harste, Woodward, & Burke, 1984; Kuhn et al., 2006). Early writing, similarly to early reading, is embedded in real-life experience. Many families do things together that involve meaningful literacy. They write each other notes, lists, holiday greetings, and directions. Many children, however, do not have these same opportunities and therefore will not have the same skills developed at the same age.

Children are likely to become involved in literacy activities if they view reading and writing as functional, purposeful, and useful. Studies of early reading and writing behaviors clearly illustrate that young children acquire their first information about reading and writing through their functional uses (Cook-Cottone, 2004; Morrow, 2004; Ollila & Mayfield, 1992). Grocery lists; directions on toys, packages, household equipment, and medicine containers; recipes; telephone messages; school-related notices; religious materials; menus; environmental print inside and outside the home; mail; magazines; newspapers; storybook readings; TV channels;

telephone numbers; conversation among family members; letters and their names represent but a sample of the functional literacy information with which a child comes in contact daily. Children are familiar with these forms of literacy, they participate in them, they pretend to use them at play, and they understand their purposes. Parents and child-care providers and preschool and kindergarten teachers need to provide experiences with reading similar to experiences children have already had. In her research with preschool and kindergarten children, Goodman (1984) found that some already knew certain things necessary for reading. These children knew the difference between letter characters and pictures in books, how to handle a book, and how to turn pages. And they knew that books are sources of meaning through printed words. Her work also concerned children's awareness of environmental print in familiar contexts and suggested that literacy-rich environments can make learning to read as natural as language acquisition.

Psycholinguistic Cueing Systems

According to psycholinguistic theory, language and literacy are acquired as a result of children having the ability to use three cueing systems to figure out new and unknown words to grasp meaning.

1. **Syntactic cues:** Using the grammatical structure or syntax of language
2. **Semantic cues:** Using the meaning of words and sentences
3. **Graphophonic cues:** Using the visual cues of letters and print and associating them with letters, letter clusters, and corresponding sounds

Along with these cueing systems, the psycholinguistic definition of reading also recommends capitalizing on children's prior strengths, knowledge, and past experiences. Goodman (1967) described reading as a psycholinguistic "guessing game" in which the child attempts to reconstruct, in light of his or her own knowledge, what the author has to say. Young children bring to school concepts and understanding from past experiences. Their awareness and use of oral language are particularly helpful.

Reading is an active process. Therefore, when children try to read, they need to anticipate what the written message is likely to say. They need to search the printed page for cues based on what they already know. They need to use the three cueing systems.

There are syntactic cues such as *The boy walked down the*   . The child's internalized knowledge of syntax indicates that the word to place in the blank must be a noun such as *hill, stairs,* or *street.* A verb would make no sense: *The boy walked down the jumped.*

Semantic cues help children determine which words would make sense in a particular slot and which would not. Few would guess that the sentence reads *The boy walked down the butter,* for example. It just doesn't make sense.

Graphophonic cues enable the child to determine words by looking at the visual cues of letters and letter clusters and associating them with their corresponding sounds.

Using the syntactic, semantic, and graphophonic cues, children can predict, guess, expect, make associations, and correct themselves to derive meaning from the printed page. The meaning comes from what they know about language and from their own experiences.

Word-study skills and knowledge about print involve learning strategies that will help children figure out words and become independent readers. Word-study skills for decoding words include the use of context and syntax, the development of a sight vocabulary, the use of the configuration or the shape of a word, and structural analysis (attending to different parts of words, such as prefixes, suffixes, or the root). The best-known word-study strategy is the use of phonics, which involves learning letter sounds and combinations of letter sounds (referred to as *phonemes*) associated with their corresponding letter symbols (referred to as *graphemes*). One problem with phonics is that the English alphabet has at least 44 different sounds, and sound–symbol correspondence is not consistent—there are many irregularities and exceptions to many rules.

Phonemic awareness, which will be discussed in more depth in this chapter, is the ability to recognize that words are made up of individual speech sounds. This is different from phonics, which includes knowledge of the relationship between letters and sounds.

Phonological awareness, which is different from phonemic awareness, involves identifying and manipulating larger parts of spoken language such as whole words, syllables, initial consonants, and word chunks at the end of words, referred to as onsets and rimes. These are considered to be precursors to phonics; that is, they are needed in order to learn phonics. Phonics has received attention as an important skill for reading success to a greater and lesser extent over the years. There is no doubt that research has demonstrated its importance. However, it is the concurrent use of several of the word-study skills mentioned that creates a proficient reader (Bear, Invernizzi, Templeton, & Johnston 2008; Ehri & Roberts, 2006; Reutzel & Cooter, 2000).

Research concerning early literacy has demonstrated the importance of meaningful experiences in instruction (Teale, 2003). We also have considerable research that demonstrates that to become a proficient reader language codes need to be learned. This is true not only in English-speaking countries; there is considerable evidence from both experimental and longitudinal studies from many countries that phonemic and phonological awareness and knowledge of phonics are necessary for success in learning to read and write alphabetic languages (Adams, 1990; Juel, 1994; McNaughton, 2006).

Concerns about word study in early literacy deal with questions such as exactly what skills should be taught, when to introduce them, how to teach them, and how much time to spend dealing with them. Although there are no definitive answers to all these questions, we have found that teaching word-study skills in a variety of ways seems to be the best approach. For example, there should be some direct systematic instruction, some spontaneous instruction, and teaching and practicing skills in meaningful settings.

English Language Learners

Standards, Skills, and Objectives for Word Study

State and U.S. National Standards dealing with word-study skills have been written for Pre-K through grade 3. The purpose of standards is to provide benchmarks for achievement and to account for what should be learned. These may differ in different areas of the country, but not to a great extent. The following are objectives for word study to enhance literacy development that reflect standards. The child should be able to do the following:

1. Demonstrate that print is read from left to right.
2. Demonstrate that oral language can be written down and then read.
3. Demonstrate what a letter is and point to one on a printed page.
4. Demonstrate what a word is, point to one on a printed page, and know there are spaces between words.
5. Demonstrate that print in the environment has a message, and read some of this print on signs and logos.
6. Recognize high-frequency words and other words by sight.
7. Identify rhyming words he or she hears and make up a rhyme.
8. Identify and name upper- and lowercase letters of the alphabet.
9. Blend and segment phonemes in words.
10. Associate letters with their initial and final corresponding consonant sounds, including sounds of the same letter (such as hard and soft *c*—cat, city; and hard and soft *g*—goat, George).
11. Associate letters with corresponding long and short vowel sounds (*a*—acorn, apple; *e*—eagle, egg; *i*—ice, igloo; *o*—oats, octopus; *u*—unicorn, umbrella).
12. Read fluently at instructional level.
13. Blend together consonant blends *bl, cr, dr, fl, gl, pr, st,* and others (consonant blends are two or three letters that when placed together blend into one sound that represents the two or three letter sounds).
14. Identify consonant digraph sounds *ch, ph, sh, th,* and *wh* (digraphs are two letters that when placed together make a new sound unlike the sounds of either letter).
15. Use context, syntax, and semantics to identify words.
16. Divide words into syllables.
17. Attempt reading by attending to picture clues and to print.
18. Predict words based on a knowledge of phoneme–grapheme correspondence.
19. Identify different structural elements of words, such as prefixes, suffixes, and inflectional endings *-ing, -ed,* and *-s* at the end of a word.
20. Apply the following phonic generalizations:
    a. In a consonant–vowel consonant pattern, the vowel sound is usually short (bat, bet, but, bit).
    b. In a vowel–consonant–e pattern, the vowel sound is usually long (cake, cute).

As children gain experience with story readings, their questions and comments begin to focus on names of letters, the reading of individual words, or attempts to sound out words.

   c. When two vowels come together in a word, the first is usually long and the second is usually silent (train, receive, bean).

21. Identify common word families, referred to also as rimes or phonograms, and build words by adding initial consonants (called *onsets*) to word families (*it, an, am, at, ite, ate,* and so on).

Chapter 7 on writing discusses the development of spelling. Spelling also is learned as sound–symbol relationship patterns are acquired. As you use the strategies discussed for the acquisition of phonics, have children practice these word patterns frequently by using them in their writing to help with spelling.

Teaching Strategies for Figuring Out Words

Instructional activities designed to help youngsters learn emergent literacy skills and about the function, form, structure, and conventions of print should involve a wide variety of learning experiences. Children need to be socially interactive when they are learning about print; they need direct instruction with models to emulate, and they need to learn through experiences that are meaningful, that are connected with real life, and that incorporate what children already know. If children see a need or usefulness attached to a reading skill, the skill probably will be learned without difficulty.

In the sections that follow, strategies are described to help children learn about print in direct, meaningful, and functional ways. Each strategy is appropriate for youngsters from preschool through third grade; teachers simply adjust the activity to the age groups they are working with. Learning these skills should be connected to content-area material and functional activities. Activities such as reading to children, pointing out words in the environment, noting their letters and sounds, taking a child's dictation, encouraging children to write in their own way, allowing youngsters to see the print as it is read from a Big Book and tracked from left to right across the page, and using predictable books that rhyme or have patterned language and that allow children to guess and share in the reading all help youngsters learn about print (Invernizzi, 2003). Through these experiences, children learn that print is read from left to right, that words in a book are oral language that has been written down and can be read, that letters have sounds, that letters make up words, that words have meaning, that pictures hold clues to what the print says, and that words can be predicted based on the meaning of the text. In addition, direct instruction in phonological and phonemic awareness, alphabetic knowledge, and phonics is needed.

When teaching all skills as discussed previously in the book, begin by

- Telling the child what skill is being taught and what it is used for
- Modeling and scaffolding the skill explicitly to demonstrate what it is and what it is used for
- Allowing time for guided practice with the teacher
- Allowing for independent practice
- Reviewing the skill often

Reading Readiness Activities

As noted in Chapter 1, early childhood researchers and teachers believed in the natural unfolding of the child. At a certain level of maturity, they felt, a child was ready to read, instruction was then appropriate, and the child would learn to read. Some educators became impatient with the notion of simply waiting for maturation, even though they thought that certain levels of maturation were necessary before reading could be taught formally without detriment to the child. This attitude led to instructional programs in reading readiness.

Reading-readiness programs include the social, emotional, physical, and cognitive competencies necessary for formal reading instruction. Strategies for readiness instruction depend on lists of skills in the four areas of development. The skills for reading readiness are included in the checklist on page 144.

Social and emotional development was and still is enhanced with periods of play during which children can select from materials placed in classroom centers. Centers may be for dramatic play, art, science, library, or outdoor play and may contain blocks and manipulative toys. The goal is for children to learn to share and cooperate, to develop self-control and a good self-concept, and to learn about appropriate school behavior. Discussions often will focus on the topic of sharing and getting along with others. There will almost always be a unit focused on All About Me, which emphasizes building self-confidence and positive self-esteem. Food plays an important role in the curriculum; a healthy snack is served daily, and snack time is considered a time to socialize and learn to get along with others.

English Language Learners

- *Physical development* of large and fine motor control was and is seen as a factor in literacy development.
- For **large motor development,** teachers should have indoor and outdoor periods designed to allow children to practice hopping, skipping, galloping, jumping, and throwing a ball. Often there is music to accompany these activities.
- To develop **fine motor coordination,** children can use clay and play with toys that require fitting pegs into holes or snapping things together.

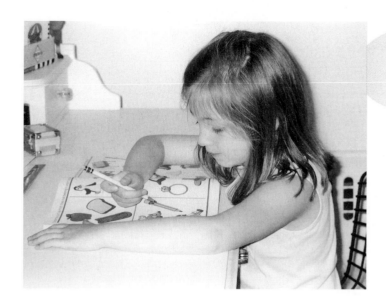

The use of an occasional worksheet will help to reinforce skills taught.

These activities supply the strength that little hands need to develop the coordination necessary to write letters. Teachers ask children to trace around lines of a particular illustration to develop eye–hand motor control. Children practice cutting and trace pictures and letters with their fingers.

- *Cognitive development* activities in reading-readiness programs include work with auditory and visual discrimination skills.

- **Visual discrimination** activities involve children in seeing likenesses and differences in shapes and pictures. In the past, worksheets were used to help children develop this skill. For example, a worksheet may picture a line of flowers that all look the same with one slightly different from the rest. Children are to find and circle or color the flower that is different. An occasional worksheet such as this can be useful in helping children follow directions. The activity is more useful with real objects in which we discuss similarities and differences. Another visual discrimination activity is color identification. Here children are asked to classify objects into color groups or to make a collage of pictures cut from a magazine that are all, for example, red, blue, or green. Identifying like and different shapes, such as squares, circles, and rectangles, is another activity used for developing visual discrimination. Finally, children are taught left to right eye progression because the skill is necessary for reading. After working with these visual discrimination skills, teachers work on identification of the letters of the alphabet.

- **Auditory discrimination** prepares children for learning to use auditory decoding skills. Teachers ask children to identify sounds that are alike and different. In the past we asked children to circle pictures on a worksheet that represented animals that make different or like sounds. Listening to rhymes, identifying rhyming words, and creating rhyme word lists is another auditory discrimination activity. Next the teacher progresses to associating letters with their sounds. Some activities that help children perform this task include collecting objects that begin with the sound featured and asking children to cut pictures from a magazine to make into a collage for the letter *M*, for example. Figure 5.1 shows a typical reading-readiness worksheet that asks the child to circle pictures that begin with consonant sounds *d*, *p*, and hard *c*. These worksheets can be confusing because the deer could be considered a moose or antelope based on experiences children have had. A child could identify an illustration as

CheckList Reading Readiness

Child's name _____ Date _____

Social and Emotional Development	Always	Sometimes	Never	Comments
Shares				
Cooperates with peers and adults				
Demonstrates confidence, self-control, and emotional stability				
Completes tasks				
Fulfills responsibilities				

Physical Development	Always	Sometimes	Never	Comments
Demonstrates large motor control by being able to run, hop, skip, trot, gallop, jump, throw, and walk a straight line				
Demonstrates fine motor control by being able to hold a pencil properly, color within lines, and cut with scissors				
Demonstrates eye–hand coordination				
Can write name, copy letters, and draw a human figure				
Is generally healthy and vigorous				
Shows no visual or auditory defects				
Has established dominance (hand, eye, foot)				

Cognitive Development	Always	Sometimes	Never	Comments
Demonstrates auditory discrimination by identifying familiar sounds, differentiating sounds, recognizing rhyming words, identifying initial and ending consonant sounds, and possessing an auditory memory				
Demonstrates visual discrimination by understanding left to right eye progression; recognizing likenesses and differences; identifying colors, shapes, letters, and words; possessing visual memory; and showing a sense of figure–ground perception				

Teacher Comments:

Figure 5.1

Reading-
Readiness
Worksheet for
Sound–Symbol
Relationships

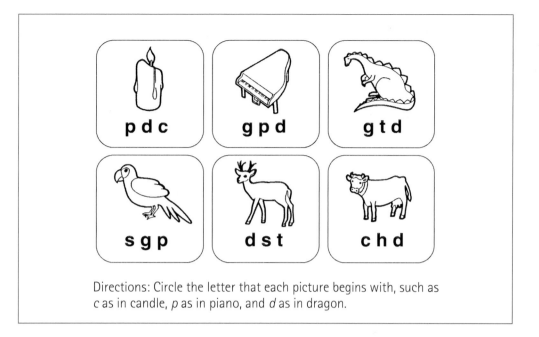

Directions: Circle the letter that each picture begins with, such as
c as in candle, *p* as in piano, and *d* as in dragon.

something different from what the artist had in mind and circle the wrong letter. Therefore, if this type of activity is used, teachers *must* identify picture names for children. Reading-readiness skills are important for children to learn, along with emergent literacy skills.

Using Environmental Print

English Language Learners

Several researchers have found that children as young as 2 can read familiar environmental print (Orellana & Hernandez, 1999; Strickland & Snow, 2002). Others, however, have shown that a child often is reading the sign rather than its print. When the print is separated from its familiar environmental context, the young child sometimes can no longer identify it (Hiebert & Raphael, 1998). Even so, when very young children associate the McDonald's logo with the word *McDonald's* and try to read it, they are learning that a group of letters makes up a word that can be read and thus provides information. The ability to read environmental print also gives the child a sense of accomplishment and usually elicits positive reinforcement of the child's achievement by caring adults.

Parents can make children aware of environmental print from the first year of life. During daily routines, parents need to point out and read words and labels on food boxes, road signs, stores, and restaurants. The world is filled with environmental print. Our early childhood classrooms need to have environmental print brought in from outside, and teachers need to label items in their child-care centers, nursery schools, kindergartens, and first and second grades. The print should be traced and copied. Such print, once familiar, becomes part of a child's sight vocabulary.

The environmental print that children tend to know best appears on food containers, especially those for cereal, soup, milk, and cookies, and on detergent boxes and bottles. Among common signs, they recognize fast-food logos, road signs, traffic signals, and names of popular store chains, supermarkets, and service stations. Collect such logos and trade names and make them available in your classroom by posting them on charts, pasting them onto index cards, and creating loose-leaf books of environmental print. Most firms distribute various printed materials free, complete with logos. Photograph environmental print in your neighborhood and bring the photos to your classroom. Suggest that children read the words, copy them, and write them in a sentence or a story.

Start including environmental print in your classroom at the beginning of a school year with only a few signs, such as children's names on their cubbies, and the words **Block Center** to identify that area of the room. Make labels with 5 × 8 index cards and dark felt-tip markers. Begin each word with a capital letter and continue with lowercase script, thus providing youngsters with configuration clues. Hang labels at heights easy for children to see. Point out the labels to the children, and suggest that they read them to friends and copy them. As the school year progresses, label new items that are added to the classroom. Refer to the labels as part of your normal routine so that they are used and will then add to the child's sight vocabulary. Label items because they are of interest to the class and serve a function, such as identifying important classroom materials and learning centers. Use labels for relating messages such as **Wash Your Hands Before Snack.** Refer to the labels often so that the children will identify them as useful and functional.

Label items related to content-area topics. If you are studying dinosaurs, a popular topic in early childhood, display model dinosaurs and label each with its name. Even long, difficult words such as *brontosaurus* and *tyrannosaurus* immediately become sight words for many early childhood youngsters. It is common to observe preschool, kindergarten, first-grade, and second-grade children reading labels to themselves or to each other. I observed a kindergarten class after the teacher had posted two new labels in the science center, which featured a lesson involving listening to sounds and identifying them after shaking a canister. I watched Jovanna take Juan by the hand and heard her say, "Listen Juan, when I shake this it sounds like there is sand inside. You try it. See, the word says *sand*." Juan continued the conversation as he picked up another canister and shook it. "Listen to this one Jovanna, this sounds like stones. This sign must say *stones*. Hey look, *sand* and *stones* both begin with an *s*," said Juan. The children shook the canisters and pointed to the appropriate label and said *sand* or *stone*. They repeated the sequence several times and switched canisters as well.

English Language Learners

THE MORNING MESSAGE.   Another way to make print part of the classroom environment is to communicate with it, even with preschool children. Post messages and assignments for children daily. Select a permanent spot on the chalkboard or on chart paper. Use rebus or picture writing along with print to help children make sense of the message. Here are a few examples of appropriate messages:

> *Today is Tuesday.*
> *It is raining outside.*
> *We are learning some more about spiders today.*
> *I have some new spider books to share.*

This routine will teach children to look automatically at the chalkboard each day for a special message. From the messages they will learn that print carries meaning that is interesting and useful. Some teachers refer to this practice as the **morning message** and have formalized it into a lesson when the school day begins (Morrow, 2003).

Morning messages are used at morning meetings, when the class gets together to discuss what will happen in school on that day. Write at least some of the message with the children watching so that you provide a writing model for them. Use the message to develop various concepts about print. Emphasize specific words or letters, pursue questions about meaning, or let children add sentences to the original message.

Have children find letters in their name on the message; look for similar word endings. For example, in the message above *day* appears three times at the end of words.

When working with 7- and 8-year-olds, the contents of the morning message and the environmental print displayed in the room will be more sophisticated than when working with younger children. They can be used to point out sound–symbol relationships or phonic generalizations that are appropriate to deal with in first and second grade. For example, a morning message such as the following is a perfect opportunity to point out the *sh* digraph:

Shelly is wearing shiny new shoes.

In another message, such as the following, there are five examples of the phonic generalization that, in a vowel–consonant-*e* pattern, the vowel is usually long.

Kate told us that her birthday cake was made in the shape of a kite.

This is a perfect opportunity to observe and discuss this letter–sound pattern.

Teachers use morning messages to teach letter writing by writing some of the messages in the form of a letter and pointing out the elements of the format. Teachers also sometimes purposefully make spelling or punctuation errors in messages and ask the children to be detectives to find the mistakes.

Letters of the alphabet can be left out of words to be filled in, or complete words can be left out for children to figure out from the context of the sentence. Some teachers embed the class spelling words or new words into the message. They include words that demonstrate skills being taught, such as words with long *a* sounds or short vowel sounds or words with digraphs or blends. Children are asked to identify and circle the featured words, vowels, and so on.

In Mrs. Youseff's kindergarten they had a morning message time daily. The message was similar every day to help learn words, letters, and sounds. Today it said:

> *Dear Boys and Girls,*
> *Today is Monday January 4, 2010.*
> *The weather is cold, and it is raining.*
> *We are learning about reptiles. We talked about*
> *snakes, lizards, and alligators.*
> *Love,*
> *Mrs. Youseff*

Since the message is similar every day, the children begin to read it. Soon Mrs. Youseff leaves out a part of a word for the children to identify what is missing, for example:

> *Today is Tues _____ January 5, 2010.*
> *The weather is c_ _ d and it is rai_ i _ g again.*

She will leave endings off words such as *day* in the word *today*. She will leave off the year on the date, and so on.

Developing Sight Vocabulary

English Language Learners

In *Teacher* (1963), Sylvia Ashton-Warner described **Very Own Words** as a method for developing sight vocabulary. She encouraged children to write their favorite words from a story or content-area lesson on 5 × 8 cards, each word on a separate card. Very Own Words are often from a child's home life: *Mommy, Daddy, Grandpa, Grandma, cookie.* They also reflect emotional feelings: *naughty, nice, good, punish.* After Very Own Words are recorded on index cards, they are stored in a child's file box, in a coffee can, or in a plastic baggie hanging on a loose-leaf ring.

A good way to start Very Own Word collections is through a discussion of favorite things to do at home or favorite pets, toys, friends, and the like. Let children know that after this discussion you will ask them to name their favorite word based on the discussion. For example:

The teacher held up an index box of her favorite Very Own Words and said

Teacher: This is my Very Own Word box. I collect words about my family, friends, things I like to do, and new words I learn. See, this one says bicycle. I like riding my bicycle, so I put that word in my box. On one side you can see the word; on the other side is the word with a picture of the bicycle. What are your favorite people, things, pets, toys?

During the morning message, the morning news is reported and written down.

Jamal: I love my grandma; I would like to have the word *grandma*.

Kim: I love chocolate chip cookies, I want that word.

Amad: I like it when my mom reads books to me. I want the word *book*.

Their teacher had cards ready and a marker and wrote Grandma for Jamal with a picture of a lady's face; on the other side she just wrote Grandma without a picture. She wrote Chocolate Chip Cookie for Kim on one side with a picture and on the other, just the words. For Amad she wrote Book with a picture and on the flip side only the word.

The activity should be a pleasant one that produces interesting language, perhaps about popping corn or making play dough. Children also can choose a favorite word in a storybook or words generated from the study of social studies and science units. Soon children will request their Very Own Words without being asked.

Encourage children to do things with their words—read them to friends or to themselves, copy them, dictate them to the teacher, and use them in sentences or stories. Because words are based on a child's expressed interests in situations at home and in school, the collection of Very Own Words is a powerful technique for developing sight vocabulary.

Seven- and eight-year-olds also enjoy and learn from collecting Very Own Words. They should alphabetize them and store them in a file box. Teachers can encourage children to study the letter patterns in their Very Own Words. They can discuss consonant and vowel sounds, blends, digraphs, and structural elements such as prefixes and suffixes, as well as phonic generalizations that may be evident. When a child studies letter patterns in words he or she has selected, it will mean more than doing the same task with words selected by the teacher or found in a textbook.

Very Own Words are also useful with bilingual children. The index card should include a child's Very Own Word in English and can also have the word written in his or her native language.

HIGH-FREQUENCY WORDS AS SIGHT WORDS.   A group of words, **sight words,** found frequently in reading materials for young children need to be learned for quick recall. These words do not carry meaning, but they hold sentences together. They are often difficult to decode because they have irregular patterns in their spelling. It is helpful for children if they do not have to spend time segmenting these words as they read; they should be

Very Own Words are a source for personal sight vocabulary. Teachers should encourage children to copy them, write them, and read them.

able to read them easily because they have been learned by memory or sight.

Sight words are often taught in a systematic and direct manner. The teacher selects a few of these words for the children to learn each week. To learn these words, the following activities are used:

- Words are said aloud and used in a sentence.
- The sentence is written on a chalkboard or flip chart and the sight word is underlined.
- Features of each word, such as the letters or its similarity to other words, are discussed. The teacher also points out any regular or irregular patterns the word may have.
- Children are asked to spell the word aloud, spell the word in the air with their finger, and write the word on paper.
- Children chant the letters as they spell words.
- The teacher has a high-frequency word box. While sitting in a circle, each child has a turn to pick a word, say it, use it in a sentence, and show it to the group.
- The words can be written on index cards similar to Very Own Words and stored with the child's other cards.

Figure 5.2 shows a list of **high-frequency words** (Fountas & Pinnell, 1996). Teachers in grades K, 1, 2, and 3 need to make sure these words are learned by sight over this period of time. According to Adams (1990), the following 13 words are 25 percent of the words children find in early literacy texts. These should be first on the list to learn: *a, and, for, he* (or *she*), *in, is, it, of, that, the, to, was, you.* To ensure that children are acquiring sight recognition of high-frequency words, they should be tested on their ability to read them. The teacher should ask them to identify the words with flash cards and find them in context within passages to read. This testing can be done several times during the school year (Allington & Cunningham, 1996).

Figure 5.2

Frequently Used Words

a	boy	going	into	my	run	two
after	but	good	is	no	said	up
all	by	had	it	not	saw	us
an	came	has	just	now	see	very
and	can	have	keep	of	she	was
am	come	he	kind	old	so	we
are	could	her	know	on	some	went
as	day	here	like	one	that	were
asked	did	him	little	or	the	what
at	do	his	look	our	then	when
away	don't	house	looked	out	there	where
back	down	how	long	over	they	will
be	for	I	make	people	this	with
because	from	if	man	play	three	would
before	get	I'm	me	put	to	you
big	go	in	mother	ran	too	your

Source: Reprinted by permission from *Guided Reading* by Irene C. Fountas and Gay Su Pinnell. Copyright © 1996 by Irene C. Fountas and Gay Su Pinnell. Published by Heinemann, Portsmouth, New Hampshire. All rights reserved.

English Language Learners

WORD WALLS TO TEACH HIGH-FREQUENCY AND OTHER MEANINGFUL WORDS.   **A word wall** typically has the letters of the alphabet posted across a wall at a child's eye level. As high-frequency words are featured, they are posted under the letter where they belong in alphabetical order. The featured words are ones teachers select as being a priority to learn. Others may be ones that children are having difficulty with reading and spelling. The words are placed on index cards. Children are asked to spell the words out loud, trace them in the air, and copy them. Sometimes words are written and then cut out into the shape of the word, providing visual configuration clues for remembering it. Before putting words up, note their characteristics, such as their pronunciation, spelling, and letter patterns. Suggest to children that the word wall can be used as a dictionary when writing.

The word wall can be used to play word-study games. For example, if the teacher wants to work with substitution of sounds, he or she points to a word such as *went* and says, "This word says *went.* If I take away the *w* and put in a *b,* what does it say?" or "This word rhymes with *look* and begins with a *b.* Can you find it on the word wall?"

Word-wall words can be sorted by word families, or word endings, by moving the words around the wall or writing them down on a sheet of paper.

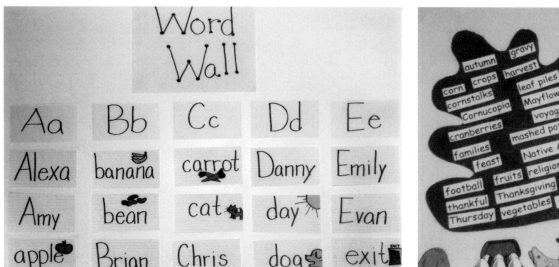

Word walls feature high-frequency words (left) and theme-related words for autumn (right) and from other units of study in science and social studies.

Many different lessons for using the wall independently should be provided (Cunningham, 1995; Moustafa, 1997).

Although the word wall was designed to teach high-frequency words, teachers use it for new words learned in themes, from books read, and from daily discussions. With very young children, the first words on the word wall will be their NAMES. The number of words on the wall with preschoolers is kept limited.

Some additional word-wall activities that the teacher can lead are as follows:

- Have students sort words by pattern, for example, words with the letters *an* or *at*.
- Classify words into colors, names, animals, or the like.
- The Secret Word game with the word wall provides the student with a series of clues such as these:

    The secret word has an at *pattern at the end.*
    It has three letters.
    It is an animal.
    It has fur and little pointy ears.
    They live in people's houses.
    It likes milk. It is a ___ at.

English Language Learners

USING THE LANGUAGE EXPERIENCE APPROACH.   The **language experience approach (LEA)** has been used for many years in reading instruction. It can help children associate oral language with written language, teaching them specifically that what is said can be written down and read. It illustrates the left to right progression of our written language. In practice, it demonstrates the formation of letters plus their combination into words; it helps build sight vocabulary; it is a source for meaningful teaching of phoneme–grapheme correspondence, as well as other knowledge about print; and it is based on the child's interest and experiences.

Many educators have been associated with developing and articulating the language experience approach, among them R. V. Allen (1976), M. A. Hall (1976), and J. Veatch and co-workers (1973). The LEA is based on the following premises from the learner's point of view:

What I think is important.

What I think, I can say.

What I say can be written down by me or by others.

What is written down can be read by me and by others.

The interests and experiences on which the LEA builds come from children's lives both at home and at school. The LEA is particularly suited for use with ELL students. It is about their lives; the vocabulary comes from them; they make their own books with their own words. In school, the teacher needs to plan experiences, for example, class trips, cooking projects, use of puppets, guest speakers, class pets, holiday events, or the study of topics that are exciting to young children, such as dinosaurs, outer space, and other cultures. The language experience lesson is usually carried out with an entire class, but it also can take place with a small group or an individual child.

An LEA lesson begins with oral language. A discussion is usually generated from an interesting or exciting class experience, for instance, a recent trip to the zoo or the pet gerbil's new litter. To begin the discussion, ask open-ended questions that will encourage descriptive responses rather than yes or no answers. For example, if the topic is a trip to the zoo, ask children to name their favorite animal. Why was it their favorite animal? What did the animal look like? What did the animal do while they were watching it at the zoo? It is important to accept all the children's responses. Accept nonstandard English without correction, but provide a language model by using standard English to paraphrase what the child has said.

After a discussion has generated several ideas, write them down. With the whole class, write the ideas on a large sheet of lined newsprint paper (approximately 24 × 36 inches), which becomes an experience chart. It can be taped to the wall or mounted on an easel. Print with a dark felt-tip marker of medium thickness, allowing ample spacing between words and between lines so that the chart is very readable. Use manuscript in upper- and lowercase letters, following the conventions of regular print and thus giving configuration to words that the use of uppercase alone cannot give. Word configuration aids children in word identification.

In recording language on experience charts, teachers should write quickly and legibly, providing good manuscript samples for children to read and copy. As you write what children dictate, use their language unless it is difficult for others to understand. When dictation is difficult to understand, ask a child to restate an idea or, if necessary, help the child restate it. It is important to include the comments of as many children as possible. When creating a new chart, try to remember which children have not contributed in the past and

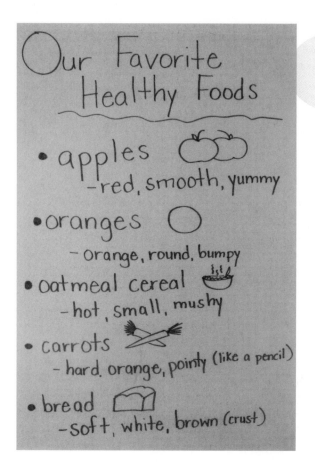

Experience charts, dictated by the children and written by the teacher, develop oral language and encourage reading and writing about what is being studied.

encourage them to contribute to the new chart. It is a good idea to identify who said what. The chart is more interesting to those whose names are included. For example:

Jacob said, "I liked the gorilla at the zoo. He jumped around and made funny faces." Jovanna said, "I liked the baby deer. They had big, bright, black eyes, wet black noses, and shiny brown fur." Try to accompany each sentence with an illustration; this will help children read the charts.

Experience charts dictated by 2- and 3-year-olds can be simply lists of words, such as names of animals with illustrations next to them. Lists of words make appropriate charts for older children as well. They are a quick way to record and reinforce new vocabulary associated with topics being studied. While writing a chart, take the opportunity to point out concepts about print: "Now I am writing the word *gorilla—g-o-r-i-l-l-a*. See, it begins here with a *g* and ends here with an *a*." Mentally note which letters or sounds interest children. Ask children to point out on the chart where you should begin to write. Like directed listening (or reading), thinking activities, and the morning message, the LEA lesson should have a specific skill objective.

The last step in the LEA lesson is to read the chart to the class and with the class. Use a pointer to emphasize left to right progression. Let the class read the chart in unison, or ask individual children who contributed different sentences to read them. Leave the chart in a visible spot in the room, and encourage the children to read it and copy parts of it, copy words they like, or add to their Very Own Word collection from the chart. Vocabulary charts and experience charts representing different topics discussed in school can be left hanging in the room if space permits and then made into Big Books for children to look at through the school year. If a laminating machine is available, it is wise to preserve charts. Children's dictated stories, books, and class books can be placed in the class library for others to read. Those made by the class often become the most popular books in the room.

Pocket chart activities are associated with the language experience approach. Words associated with experiences the class has had are featured in the chart. Short stories, poems, and songs that students chant can be printed on individual sentence strips. Ask children to copy the charts to practice their writing. In addition, the sentence strips can be scrambled and sequenced into

How to Talk to Your Snowman

Use words that are pleasing,
Like: freezing
And snow,
Iceberg and igloo
And blizzard and blow,
Try: Arctic, Antarctic,
Say: shiver and shake,
But whatever you never say,
Never say: bake.

by Beverly McLoughland

Ms. Burk wrote a poem on chart paper and then on sentence strips for children to sequence.

the pocket chart. Sentence strips can be cut up into the individual words for students to work on the word level, to identify and practice placing them into sentences.

When teaching a unit about animals featuring animal sight words, Ms. Macki selected the anonymous poem "Good Morning" and read it to her kindergarten class to reinforce their ability to read the animal names. The text of the poem is as follows:

> *I say good morning to the birds*
>
> *Good morning to the bees*
>
> *Good morning to the pigs in the pen*
>
> *I say good morning to the ducks*
>
> *Good morning to the geese*
>
> *Good morning to the happy little hen*

Ms. Macki wrote the words to the poem on chart paper and then on sentence strips. She drew a picture of each animal at the end of each line. She cut a second set of sentence strips into individual words. In this way she provided the children with four activities:

1. Read the poem.
2. Sequence whole sentences into a story.
3. Build sentences from individual words by using the syntax and semantics of the text.
4. Identify the sight words: birds, bees, pigs, ducks, geese, and hen.

Pocket chart activities are often used to practice skills during independent center time.

The language experience approach, which is appropriate throughout early childhood and beyond, can be used similarly in the morning message and Very Own Words for noticing phonic generalizations and sound–symbol correspondences. Learning about print in this situation is done with material that is familiar and meaningful. Occasionally, prepare a chart in the language of bilingual children in your class. If necessary, solicit help from bilingual parents or colleagues. This strategy will guide bilingual youngsters in making connections between their language and English.

LEA materials are inexpensive and easy to use. They include chart paper, markers, colored construction paper, white paper, index cards, scissors, staplers, pencils, and crayons. With directions from the teacher, these simple classroom materials record the precious words and pictures created by children from their own meaningful, real-life experiences. The LEA should be central, not supplemental, to literacy instruction in early reading programs.

Using Context and Pictures to Figure Out Words

Experiences with literature can lead children to use contextual clues and illustrations to figure out words and recognize that they have meaning. Literature experiences can take place in whole-class, small-group, or one-to-one settings, using directed listening (or reading) and thinking activities, shared book experiences, and repeated readings of stories. For example, select a story that is predictable, in which the text and illustrations are closely related. Ask children to look at the pictures on a page before reading it to them. Ask them what they think the words will say. Then read the page to demonstrate that print and illustration are closely related and that the pictures provide information that can help the children as they read the story.

The syntax and semantics of a sentence (its grammatical structure and meaning) also help children identify words. Encourage children to use these elements of written language by stopping your oral reading at predictable points in a story and asking them to fill in words. For example, when reading *The Three Little Pigs* (Brenner, 1972), first read the complete repetitive phrases,

> *"Little pig, little pig, let me in," said the wolf. "Not by the hair of my chinny, chin, chin," said the first little pig. "Then I'll huff and I'll puff and I'll blow your house in," said the wolf. The second time say, "Little pig, little _____ let me come in." "Not by the hair of my chinny chin _____." Then I'll huff and I'll _____ and I'll blow your _____ _____," and so on.*

This technique is most effective with a Big Book because you can point to the words as the children say them. As the children begin to understand the concept of filling in words, choose more difficult passages for your pauses. Prepare charts and sheets with predictable text, and leave out words to be filled in as you read. Children use their prior knowledge of syntax and context in predicting words. They assimilate and use the strategy when they read themselves.

In addition to these general suggestions, specific experiences to figure out words can be varied so that students have many different strategies for using context. A common way to determine words from context is through the meaning of the text. For example, in the sentence that follows, it is apparent that the missing word is *Queen*. We can show children how to use the meaning of the text to figure out a word that might be unknown to them.

The King and _____ *lived in the castle together.*

Another context clue exercise involves a series of related words. To help with this exercise or other context clue exercises, the initial consonant can be included. For example:

*My favorite kinds of fruit are apples, b*_____*, pears, and oranges.*

A gamelike context clue activity involves the use of scrambled letters, as in the following sentence:

I am always on time, but my sister is always _____ *(alte).*

When working with context clues, teachers can choose to omit all nouns, verbs, every fourth word, and so on. There are endless ways to use this strategy, and each contributes to helping children figure out unknown words. This approach is referred to as the *cloze procedure*.

Phonological Awareness and Phonemic Awareness

Phonological awareness and phonemic awareness instruction in early literacy lead toward helping students to become independent readers. Teaching these skills to children should be done concurrently with other strategies for learning to read, such as acquiring sight words and learning how to use context clues and picture clues. Children need to have a holistic view about books and reading, as well as the more abstract skills, as they work on decoding unknown words. Phonemic awareness is the ability to recognize that words are made up of individual speech sounds (Burns, Snow, & Griffin, 1999; Soderman & Farrell, 2008; Strickland & Schickedanz, 2004; Tompkins, 2003). The words *hat* and *chat* contain three speech sounds referred to as phonemes. The phonemes are not letters; they are sounds. This is different from phonics, which includes knowledge of the relationship between letters and sounds. Phonological awareness is different from phonemic awareness. It is the awareness of the sound structure of language. Phonological awareness involves identifying and manipulating larger parts of spoken language such as whole words, syllables, initial consonants, and word chunks referred to as onsets and rimes. The segmenting and blending of these sounds is the important skill children need to develop.

Phonemic awareness is a subset of phonological awareness. Phonemic awareness and phonological awareness are considered precursors to phonics and are needed to learn phonics. They are important to achieve successful reading ability. However, they are one part of a comprehensive program in learning to read (National Reading Panel Report, 2000). It is the concurrent use of several word-study skills that creates a proficient reader (Reutzel and

Cooter, 2004). According to the National Reading Panel Report, 18 hours of teaching phonemic awareness in the kindergarten year is needed for a child to learn the skills. In a 180-day school year, that would be about 6 minutes a day.

Phonemic and Phonological Awareness Instruction

Instruction in phonemic and phonological awareness should be playful as teachers read stories, tell stories, play word games, and use rhymes and riddles. Instruction in the area should be purposeful and planned; we cannot leave it to chance. In the past this instruction was spontaneous and incidental. Of course, it can still be spontaneous when the moment arises and should be; however, it must be systematically written into daily plans. Try as much as possible to make your instruction meaningful and with a purpose (Adams, 2001; Cunningham, 2005; Gambrell, Morrow, & Pressley, 2007).

It is easiest for young children to learn to deal with larger parts of words or whole words first and then smaller parts. A skill to begin with in phonemic awareness is exposing children to rhyming activities. This is considered to be the easiest task, since it is deals with a whole word. Rhyming activities can be done in preschool and kindergarten. Simply chanting nursery rhymes or reading stories that rhyme helps children develop the skill. Next children can deal with segmenting sounds, such as listening for and counting syllables in words. Have children learn about segmenting sounds in words by clapping the sounds in their name. The most difficult skill dealing with phonological awareness is segmenting and then blending words together using onsets and rimes. An *onset* is the beginning sound in a word; the *rime* is the ending chunk or group of letters in a word. Work in this area; for example, ask children to listen for the beginning sound in the word *cat*, which is *c*, and then to put it together with its ending chunk *at* to make the whole word *cat* (Yopp & Yopp, 2000). When teaching activities that help to learn rhyming, segmenting, and blending, we ask children to match sounds, to work with sounds in isolation, and to make sound substitutions and sound deletions. These activities help children learn about sounds in words. Remember that phonological awareness involves saying sounds and not identifying them with the letters. They are oral exercises. The following activities ask children to match, isolate, substitute, and delete sounds from words.

When asking children to match, say "Which words have the same sound at the beginning, *big* and *boy* or *house* and *go*?

When working with words in isolation, we will say to the children, "What sound do you hear at the the beginning of the word *cow*?" (We are not asking for the letter name; we are asking for the sound.)

When we ask children to substitute sounds, we say, "Listen to the word *bat*; it has a *buh* sound at the beginning. Can you say it, *buh*, *bat*? Now see if you can make a new word if we say *mmm* at the beginning instead of *buh*. Everyone *mmmmat*. That was great. What word did we make? *Mat*."

When we ask children to delete, we might say, "Tell me what word we have when we say the word *snowman* without the *man*, or *hat* without the *h*." In a lesson we can say, "When it is rainy outside, we wear a rain-coat. If you take the rain away from the word, what word do you have left?" The children answer *coat*.

The easiest phonemic awareness task is working with rhymes. Teachers can help children to hear, identify, and match to similar word patterns such as rhymes. Early work in this area should be playful. Exposing children to books that contain rhymes, such as *Green Eggs and Ham* (Seuss, 1960), *Goodnight Moon* (Brown, 1947), and *The Queen of Hearts* (Hennessy & Pearson, 1989), helps develop the skill. Teachers can recite rhyming and nonrhyming words from the books and ask children to differentiate between them. For additional practice with rhyme, you can ask children to do the following:

Can you think of words that rhyme with your name? My name is Ann and *fan* rhymes with Ann.

Sing songs that rhyme, such as "Hickory Dickory Dock," and separate out the rhyming words.

Act out well-known nursery rhymes, such as "Jack and Jill," and identify the rhyming words.

Make up new rhymes in a story such as *I Know an Old Lady*. Let the children decide what else she could swallow and what would happen to her if she did. For example, "I know an old lady who swallowed a frog; she began to jog when she swallowed a frog."

It is a good idea to have some routine rhymes and songs that the class chants repeatedly. The chant should allow children to change the rhymes and to match and substitute rhymes. The following chant will allow children to make up rhymes and substitute rhymes:

Let's Make a Rhyme

When it's cold outside, and you want to play,
Let's make a rhyme, my teacher would say.
    Did you ever see a dog
    Pushing a log
On a cold and winter's day?

When it's cold outside, and you want to play,
Let's make a rhyme, my teacher would say.
    Did you ever see a moose
    Pushing a goose
On a cold and winter's day?

The next step is for each child to think of an animal to make a rhyme with, for example:

Did you ever see a cow
Saying bow-wow
On a cold and winter's day?

Segmenting is an important skill that is more difficult than rhyming for children. It is easier for a child to segment the beginning sound or onset and then the ending chunk or rime. If this is done with the word *man,* for example, the child should be guided to say *mmm* for the onset /m/ and then *annn* for the rime /an/.

Syllabication is a way of segmenting words or working on phonological awareness. Children can clap the syllables in their names and in the names of their friends.

Name Chant

If your name has a beat and the beat is one,
 Say and clap your name and then run, run, run.

If your name has a beat and the beat is two,
 Say and clap your name and hop like a kangaroo.

If your name has a beat and the beat is three,
 Say and clap your name, then buzz like a bee.

If your name has a beat and the beat is four,
 Say and clap your name and stamp on the floor.

After segmenting words, ask children to blend them back together again. The goal is for children to be able to identify each sound within a word, know the number of sounds heard, and blend the word back together. We can ask them to stretch the word out like a rubber band, which would be asking them to segment and then say it really, really fast as the elastic springs back to blend. The following are some activities that will help children learn to segment and blend:

Sing the song "Bingo." In the song each letter is chanted and then blended together. Change the words from "There was a farmer had a dog and Bingo was his name" to "There is a pretty girl (or handsome boy) that I know and Jenny is her name-o, J-e-n-n-y, J-e-n-n-y, J-e-n-n-y, and Jenny is her name-o."

Play a riddle substitution of onsets game. Say "I'm thinking of a word that sounds like head, *but begins with the /buh/ sound," or "I'm thinking of a word that sounds like* fat, *but has an /mmm/ sound at the beginning."*

A good song for segmenting and blending goes to the tune of "This Old Man." You can use the name of the letter featured or use the letter sounds. This song does name the letter that we will create words with, but it is an oral activity, not matching a letter seen to the sound it makes.

This Old Man

This old man sings N songs
He sings N songs all day long
With a Nick, Nack, Nakie Nack
He sings his silly song
He wants you to sing along

This old man sings B songs
He sings B songs all day long
With a Bick, Back, Bakie Back
He sings his silly song
He wants you to sing along

Now make up your own verse with a new sound.

Figure 5.3   Word-Study Game

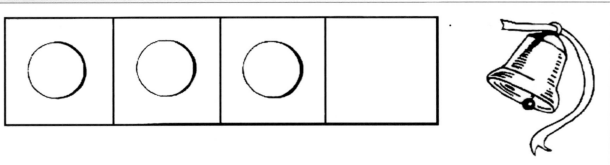

Directions: Let's figure out how many sounds are in the word *bell*. I'm going to say it again, B-E-LL. Put a chip in the squares for each sound you heard in the word *bell*. How many chips did you use? Now look at the letters in the word *bell*. How many do you count (4)? A word can have different numbers of letters and sounds.

Elkonin boxes are used to engage children in segmentation and blending (Figure 5.3). Select and write words on a piece of paper. Draw square boxes next to each word. Have chips for students to put into the squares. Say the word on the paper, such as duck *and have the children put the number of chips in the boxes that represent the number of sounds in the word. For the word* duck, *children would put three chips into the boxes because the second ck in the word has one sound (Fitzpatrick, 1997; Invernizzi, 2003; Johns, Lenski, & Elish-Piper, 1999).*

Learning about the Alphabet

English Language Learners

Many young children who cannot yet identify individual letters of the alphabet are able to read. As noted, they read sight words from environmental print, from classroom labels, and from Very Own Words lists. They learn other sight words from repeated readings and shared book experiences. It is not necessary to be able to identify and name the letters of the alphabet in order to develop an initial sight-reading vocabulary. It is easier for a young child *initially* to learn whole words already familiar through oral language, rather than learn abstract letters. Familiar words carry meaning for them, whereas isolated letters do not.

Children need to learn the alphabet to become independently fluent readers and writers. Traditionally, the alphabet has often been the first thing parents try to teach their children at home, and it is usually high on any list of reading-readiness skills in preschool and kindergarten curricula. It has been demonstrated by research to be a predictor of reading success.

Allow children to explore letters by using manipulative materials available in the literacy center. Be sure to include in the center alphabet puzzles, magnetic upper- and lowercase letters with an accompanying magnetic board, a set of wooden upper- and lowercase letters, tactile letters made of sandpaper, alphabet games, felt letters and an accompanying felt board, letter stencils, alphabet flash cards, and a long alphabet chart posted along the wall of the classroom at the children's eye level. In addition to these materials, a large supply of alphabet books and taped songs about the alphabet should be in the classroom library. (See Appendix A for a list of alphabet books.) Be sure that every child has a baggie in which you place letters of the alphabet in their name and in other words they have learned. These letters can be written on the computer, and with a paper cutter you can easily make multiple sets of upper- and lowercase letters for everyone. As time goes on, every child will have a complete alphabet in a baggie.

Encourage children to explore these materials first through play. Later they will begin to identify the letters they are playing with and teach letters they know to other children. Provide chalk and a chalkboard so they can make letters themselves. Children also enjoy finger-painting letters, painting them on easels, and shaping them out of clay. They like to eat alphabet soup and alphabet cookies and pretzels. Shaping letters with their fingers and whole bodies is an activity often used in early childhood rooms.

Systematic teaching of the alphabet, one letter per week, is not as successful as teaching children letters that are meaningful to them. Many teachers help children identify the letters in their own names first. When teaching thematic units, select a few letters to feature that are used in the context of the theme. For example, in a unit on transportation, feature *b* for boat and *t* for train. When children have learned to identify several different letters, ask them to look for the same letters in other contexts, such as magazines, newspapers, and books. Check children individually by using flash cards to determine which letters they know and which they do not know. Ask children which letters they would like to learn next from their Very Own Words. Give children flash cards of the letters they choose to learn, and encourage them to use these letters in all the activities just mentioned. Letters also need to be practiced all year through.

Additional ideas for learning and reinforcing what is known about the alphabet include the following:

- Sing the alphabet song and point to the letters on a poster as they are sung.

- Play letter bingo, which involves cards filled with letters and markers to cover them. Call a letter and hold up a card with the letter on it to help children with letter identification. When a child covers one row of letters on the card, he or she gets bingo.

- Provide children with alphabet journals. Each page has another letter of the alphabet. On the different pages children can trace the letter, write the letter, and find words in a magazine that use the letter and paste them on the page.

- Create an alphabet center with many different alphabet materials such as those already mentioned (magnetic letters, wooden letters, matching letter games, alphabet puzzles, alphabet books, alphabet stamps, alphabet flash cards). Children will identify this area with the alphabet and should be encouraged to use the materials often.

State standards expect preschool children to know about half of the alphabet before going to kindergarten. Kindergarteners must be able to name and recognize all the letters of the alphabet by the end of that year. Teachers need to check children's knowledge of the alphabet and provide instruction based on the findings. If more explicit instruction is needed to help students, it should be provided one-on-one or in a small group. The letters of the alphabet must be practiced regularly. Students should be exposed to letters on a daily basis and in different settings. Figure 5.4 illustrates a commonly used form to record children's letter knowledge. Eventually, children need to learn the alphabetic principle: knowing that words are composed of letters and that there is a systemic relationship between the letters and the sounds they hear.

Strategies for Teaching Phonics

Phonics is the best-known word-study strategy. Quite simply, phonics is the connection of sounds and symbols. The use of phonics requires children to learn letter sounds and combinations of letter sounds (referred to as phonemes) associated with their corresponding letter symbols (referred to as graphemes). In the English language there are 26 letters in the alphabet; however, there are at least 44 different sounds. Sound–symbol correspondence is not always consistent in English; there are many irregularities and exceptions to many rules, which are difficult for children to learn. Therefore, we must help children learn words by sight that cannot be sounded out, and we need to give them strategies for figuring out words.

There is a recommended sequence for teaching phonics. However, when teachable moments occur, teachers should take advantage of them whether or not they are within recommended sequences.

Consonants

We begin teaching phonics with the most commonly used initial consonant sounds, such as *f, m, s, t,* and *h,* and then use these same sounds in ending word positions. The next set of initial and final consonant sounds usually taught is *l, d, c, n, g, w, p, r, k,* then *j, q, v,* final *x,* initial *y,* and *z.* Most consonants are quite regular and represent one sound. Some consonants have two sounds, such as *g* as in the words *go* and *girl,* often referred to as the hard *g;* and *g* as in *George, giraffe,* and *gentleman,* referred to as the soft *g.* Other consonants with two sounds are *c* as in *cookie, cut,* and *cost,* the hard *c* sound; and *c* as in *circus, celebrate,* and *ceremony,* the soft *c* sound. The letter *x* has a *z* sound at the beginning of a word, as in *xylophone,* but has the *x* sound as in the word *next.* The letters *w* and *y* say their names at the beginning of a word and act as consonants, as in *was* and *yellow.* In the middle or at the end of a word, *w* and *y* act as vowels, as in *today* and *blow.* Learning the consonant sounds begins in preschool in a limited way; more instruction occurs in kindergarten; and they are mastered in first grade.

Consonant blends and consonant digraphs are pairs of consonants that make new sounds. The blends are clusters of two or three consonants in which the sounds of all the consonants are heard, but blended together, as in

Figure 5.4   A Form to Record Children's Letter Knowledge

Letter Identification Score Sheet

Child's name _____   Age _____   Date _____

Recorder _____   Date of birth _____

	A	IR		A	IR
A			a		
F			f		
K			k		
P			p		
W			w		
Z			z		
B			b		
H			h		
O			o		
J			j		
U			u		
C			c		
Y			y		
L			l		
Q			q		
M			m		
D			d		
N			n		
S			s		
X			x		
I			i		
E			e		
G			g		
R			r		
V			v		
T			t		

Confusions:

Letters unknown:

Comments:

A = Alphabet response: (✔); IR = Incorrect response: record what the child says   **Test Score:** ☐

the words *blue, true, flew,* and *string.* Consonant digraphs are composed of two consonants that when put together do not have the sound of either one, but rather an altogether new sound, such as *th* in *three, sh* in *shoes, ch* in *chair, ph* in *photograph,* and *gh* at the end of a word, as in *enough.*

Vowels

The next phonic elements we teach are the vowels, which are *a, e, i, o,* and *u.* We teach the short vowels first: *a* as in *cat, e* as in *bed, i* as in *hit, o* as in *hot,* and *u* as in *cut.* Next we teach the long vowels: *a* as in *hate, e* as in *feet, i* as in *kite, o* as in *boat,* and *u* as in *cute.* Long vowels have the sound of the name of the letter. As mentioned earlier, *w* and *y* act as vowels in the middle and at the end of words. The letter *y* has the sound of a long *e* when it comes at the end of a word as in *baby.* The *y* has the sound of a long *i* when it is at the end of a one-syllable word such as *cry, try.*

Vowels change their sound when they are *r*-controlled. They become neither long nor short, as in *car* and *for.* As with consonants, there are vowel pairs that we teach. The first vowel pair is called a vowel digraph (two vowels represent a single sound such as *ai* in *pail* and *ea* in *seat*). The next vowel pair is called a diphthong. Diphthongs are a combination of two vowels that form a gliding sound as one vowel sound blends into the other, such as *oy* in toy and *oi* in *oil.*

Vowels can be difficult for children to learn, since they have many sounds and combinations of sounds that make the sounds change. The vowel sounds can begin to be taught in kindergarten; however, direct and systematic instruction occurs in first grade.

The phonic elements to deal with next include some structural aspects of words. At each grade level, teachers should review what has been learned and add on additional work in medial consonants, variant consonant sounds and blends, compound words, syllabication, contractions, prefixes, suffixes, synonyms, antonyms, and homonyms.

Children find it easier to learn about word patterns or chunks rather than individual sounds. Word patterns help in decoding many different words that contain the same patterns, but may have a different beginning or ending sound. Teachers should help students to learn familiar word patterns, often referred to as phonograms, chunks, or word families. These groups of letters when at the end of a word are referred to as rimes. There are many common rimes. A list is provided in Figure 5.5.

There are many phonic generalizations or rules. Most of them only apply to a few words and therefore are not worth learning. Three are consistent and are therefore worth teaching:

Figure 5.5

Common Rimes Used in Early Literacy

ack	al	ain	ake	ale	ame	an	ank	up	ush
at	ate	aw	ay	ell	eat	est	ice	ick	ight
id	ill	in	ine	ing	ink	ip	ir	ock	oke
op	ore	or	uck	ug	ump	unk			

Children sort words and make words to learn about word patterns with manipulative materials.

When a one-syllable word has only one vowel and the vowel comes in the middle of two consonants, the vowel is usually short, such as *hot, cut,* and *bet.* This is called the CVC pattern rule.

When there are two vowels in a word with one syllable, and one of them is an *e* at the end of the word, the first vowel is long and the *e* is silent. This is called the CVCe pattern or the final *e* rule. Some words that demonstrate the rule include *plate, cute,* and *bone.*

When a consonant is followed by a vowel, the vowel is usually long, as in *be, go,* and *because.* This is called the CV rule.

Earlier in the chapter, I discussed the necessity for teaching phonics within meaningful contexts, along with a systematic and direct presentation of skills. It is also important that children have continual practice to learn sound–symbol relationships; rarely is a single lesson sufficient. Therefore, teachers should provide several experiences with letter and letter–sound combinations and review them with children as often as possible. Consonant sounds and long and short vowel sounds are now being taught in kindergarten. They must of course be reviewed thoroughly in first grade.

Meaning-Based Strategies

English Language Learners

How can we help children recognize the sound–symbol relationships of consonants and vowels in a meaningful context? Science and social studies themes lend themselves to featuring letters that appear in units. For example, when studying farm, pet, and zoo animals, feature the letter *p*, because it is used frequently with this context. The following types of activities then can follow and be used with other consonants as well:

1. Read *The Pet Show* (Keats, 1974) and *The Tale of Peter Rabbit* (Potter, 1902), for example, during the unit, and point out words that begin with the letter *p* in these books.
2. Make word charts using words from the books that begin with the letter *p*.

3. On a field trip, bring peanuts to the zoo to feed the animals.

4. Make lists of animals that begin with the letter *p*, such as peacock, panda pear, pig.

5. Read the book *Animalia* (Base, 1987) and point out the *p* page, which says "Proud Peacocks Preening Perfect Plumage."

6. Collect sensory items about animals that begin with the letter *p*, such as Puppy Chow to smell, peanuts to eat and to feed to elephants when you visit the zoo, peacock plumes to touch, a purring kitten to listen to, and the book *Petunia* (Duvoisin, 1950) to look at and read.

7. List words from the unit that begin with the letter *p*.

8. Write an experience chart of activities carried out during the unit, and highlight the letter *p* when it appears in the chart.

9. Ask children to add to their Very Own Word collection with favorite words from the unit that begin with the letter *p*.

10. Make a collage of pictures featuring things from the unit, and mark those that begin with the letter *p*.

11. Print on a chart the song "Peter Cottontail." Sing the song and highlight the letter *p* when it appears.

12. Have children help you make up nonsense rhymes for featured letters and chant them, such as the following:

    My name is P*enelope* P*ig.*
    I p*ick* p*etals off of* p*etunias.*
    I p*lay* p*atty-cake*
    and eat p*retzels with* p*ink* p*unch.*

13. Add a page for the letter *p* to a class Big Book entitled *Our Own Big Book of Letters, Sounds, and Words.* Have children draw pictures or paste in pictures of words that begin with the letter *p*. (Directions for making a Big Book are in Chapter 6, page 191.)

14. Complete a worksheet for the letter *p* that requires students to trace the letter, write the letter, and circle pictures that begin with the letter *p*, such as *pig* and *popcorn*.

15. Encourage children to write about their experiences during the unit, such as their visit to the zoo, the books they read, and the songs they sang. In their writing they will be using the letters emphasized and, although their writing may not be conventional, through the use of their invented spellings, they are indirectly enhancing their phonemic awareness. When children write, they have to face the problem of mapping spoken language into written language. This process can lead to an understanding of the structure of spoken language. The more children write, the better they become at segmenting sounds in words. This point is demonstrated in this example of Justin's story about *the panda bear at the zoo.* He wrote, "*I saw a prte panda ber pik up her babi panda at the zooo.*"

Children's literature is an excellent source for featuring letters attached to themes. Be careful not to abuse the stories by overemphasizing the sounds featured; however, do not pass up the opportunity to feature letters in this natural book setting. For example, in a unit on food, Ms. Fino, a first-grade teacher, featured the letter *b* and read *Blueberries for Sal* (McCloskey, 1948), *Bread and Jam for Frances* (Hoban, 1964), and *The Berenstain Bears and Too Much Birthday* (Berenstain & Berenstain, 1987).

These and similar activities can be carried out for any initial consonant. Whenever letters being featured in a thematic unit appear in a language experience chart or a piece of children's literature, point them out to the children. Alphabet books generally use sound–symbol relationships as they introduce each letter, as do picture storybooks that use a particular letter prominently. (See Appendix A for children's literature for building sound–symbol relationships.)

When we read, we use several skills concurrently to decode and derive meaning from the printed page. We therefore need to encourage children to use multiple skills, rather than isolated skills, in their approach to reading. Children should be taught to use context clues and phonic clues simultaneously. One strategy that accomplishes this goal has already been suggested— reading a sentence in which you pause and leave a "blank" to be filled in by the child. For example, say, "The b⸻ flew up to the tree and landed on a branch." Supplying the initial consonant for the word, either by sound or by sight, draws on a child's skills with phonics, context, syntax, and semantics.

Whenever possible, take advantage of spontaneous situations to help children learn about print, as in the following example:

> *Christopher, a child in first grade, had just written his name on a picture he drew and exclaimed, "Wow, the word* STOP *is right in the middle of my name. See Christopher." He pointed to the letters in his name that spelled* STOP. *He continued, "But that doesn't make sense, then I should say my name Chri-STOP-her." The teacher immediately seized the opportunity to point out the* ph *digraph and explain to Christopher that the word* STOP *was in his name, but when the letters* p *and* h *come together, they make a new sound as heard in Christopher, like the sound of* f. *She mentioned other words such as* photograph *and* phantom *that illustrated the* ph *sound.*

Explicit Word-Study Activities

Based on research about how children learn and how the brain works, activities with word families, also called *phonograms* and *word chunks,* that include building words and sorting words into different patterns help children learn letter–sound relationships and consequently how to decode unknown words. Word sorts and word building with *onsets* (the initial letter or letters before the first vowel) and *rimes* (the vowel and what follows) allow children to look at bigger chunks of words. When children learn how to figure out new ones by looking at and using the patterns in words, they have developed a strategy to deal with other unknowns. According to research, the brain looks for known patterns when involved in learning. It takes what is known and tries to apply it to the unknown. Patterns such as familiar word endings help children deal with unknowns (Strickland & Snow, 2002).

MAKING WORDS.   Making words is a gamelike activity in which children learn to look for patterns in words and ways to make new words by changing one letter or more. Children use magnetic letters, wooden letters, felt letters, or letter tiles. In this activity, the teacher asks children to make words from a real word selected from a story, new vocabulary, themed words, and the like. The word can be scrambled or spelled correctly (Gunning, 2003).

Another popular type of word-making activity uses onsets and rimes. With younger children, the teacher provides a few well-known rimes, such as *at, an,* or *in,* and asks the children to make as many words with these endings as they can think of by adding different initial consonants or consonant blends to the beginning of the rimes. With the rime *at,* for example, children could create the following words: *cat, sat, mat, rat, hat, fat, vat, pat,* and *bat.* With the letters *a, d, n, s,* and *t,* children can be asked to do the following:

Use two letters to make *at.*

Add a letter to make *sat.*

Take away a letter to make *at.*

Change a letter to make *an.*

Add a letter to make *Dan.*

Change a letter to make *tan.*

Take away a letter to make *an.*

Add a letter to make *and.*

Add a letter to make *sand.* (Cunningham & Cunningham, 1992)

Change a letter to make **word sorts.** After words have been made, they can be sorted in many different ways, or teachers can provide words for sorting. For example, if children make little words from the bigger word *Thanksgiving,* such as *thanks, giving, sing, sang, hang, king, thanking,* and *having,* they can be asked to sort the words that all have the *-ing* ending, words that rhymed, words ending with the consonant *g,* words beginning with the consonant *s,* and so on. Sorting words for blends, digraphs, and numbers of syllables is another way to help students see patterns. Words also can be sorted for meaning by categories, such as colors and types of food.

Using phonograms, or rimes, is an important way for children to sort and make words. A list of the most commonly used rimes for children to learn is presented in Figure 5.5

TEACHING CHILDREN HOW TO DEAL WITH NEW WORDS.   When children learn new words, they need to look at the elements within the word to help them understand its parts. Figure 5.6 is a word-study guide for young children to use when they are introduced to new vocabulary.

When working with manipulatives, it is very important for children to write down the words they create some of the time so that you can see if they understand what they are doing.

A Center for Word-Study Activities

A center that contains materials for word study is necessary in early childhood classrooms. The activities for making and sorting words discussed earlier can be gamelike if they are presented with interesting manipulative materials. With onsets and rimes as well as scrambled words, teachers can

ELL
English Language Learners

Figure 5.6

Tell It to Yourself
and a Friend
Word-Study
Guide

- The word is _Hat_ _____
- When I say and stretch the word, it sounds like this:_____
- The number of letters I see in the word is_____
- I hear this number of sounds in the word:_____
- The spelling pattern in the word is_____
- This is what I know about the vowel in the word:

  _____

- Other words with the same sounds are

  _____

- A sound box for this word looks like this:

  _____

have children use magnetic letters and a magnetic board for making words. Students can use movable wooden letters, rubber foam letters, or flash cards with letters on them. Flash cards can have word endings on them or initial consonants or consonant blends. All onsets can be written in one color and rimes in another. The flash cards can be used to make words on a table or a pocket chart. To make this activity even more interesting, letter stamps and white slates with magic markers will work for making words. Some teachers use manipulatives such as movable wheels for making words. Board games such as bingo, lotto, concentration, and Candyland and card games can be constructed so that children have to make words within the rules of the game. Figure 5.7 illustrates some sample word-study games to place in centers.

Games for centers can be purchased from stores for teachers and large school-supply companies. Teachers also can create numerous word-study activities that children learn from, use to reinforce what they know, and use independently when teachers are engaged in small-group instruction. Teachers can make materials and seek the help of parents, aides, and upper-grade children to make materials. The following is a list of books that contain ideas for word-study center materials:

Bear, D. R., Invernizzi, M., Templeton, S., & Johnston, D. (2003, 4th edition). *Words their way.* Upper Saddle River, NJ: Prentice Hall.

Cunningham, P. (2005, 4th ed.). *Phonics they use.* New York: Harper-Collins.

Cunningham, P., & Hall, D. (1994). *Making words.* Torrance, CA: Good Apple.

Hill, S. (1997). *Reading manipulatives.* Cypress, CA: Creative Teaching Press.

Marriott, D. (1997). *What are the other kids doing?* Cypress, CA: Creative Teaching Press.

Figure 5.7   Word-Study Games

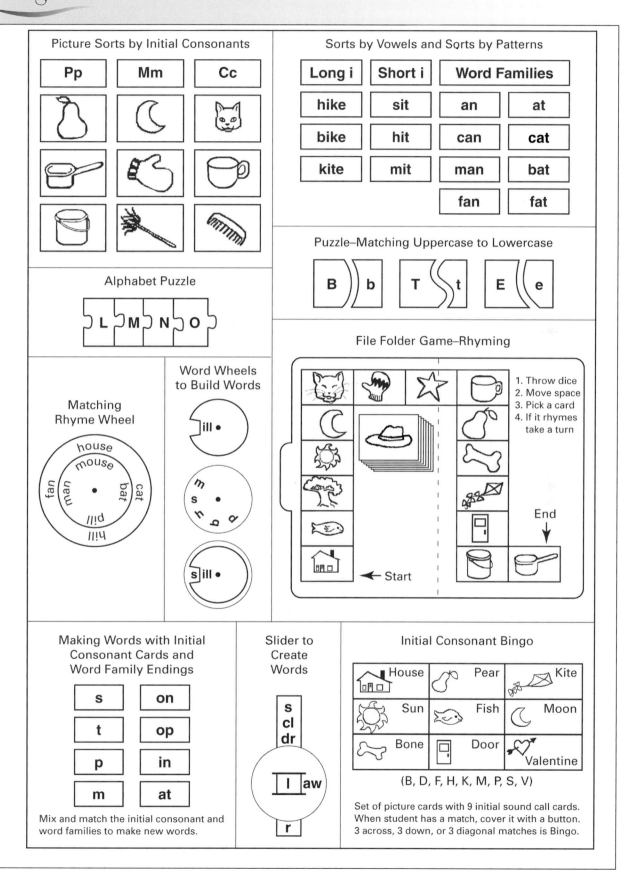

Picture Sorts by Initial Consonants

Pp	Mm	Cc

Sorts by Vowels and Sorts by Patterns

Long i	Short i	Word Families	
hike	sit	an	at
bike	hit	can	cat
kite	mit	man	bat
		fan	fat

Puzzle–Matching Uppercase to Lowercase

B b   T t   E e

Alphabet Puzzle

L M N O

File Folder Game–Rhyming

1. Throw dice
2. Move space
3. Pick a card
4. If it rhymes take a turn

End

← Start

Matching Rhyme Wheel

house
mouse
fan man cat bat
pill hill

Word Wheels to Build Words

ill •

m s h p d

s ill •

Making Words with Initial Consonant Cards and Word Family Endings

s	on
t	op
p	in
m	at

Mix and match the initial consonant and word families to make new words.

Slider to Create Words

s
cl
dr

l aw

r

Initial Consonant Bingo

House	Pear	Kite
Sun	Fish	Moon
Bone	Door	Valentine

(B, D, F, H, K, M, P, S, V)

Set of picture cards with 9 initial sound call cards. When student has a match, cover it with a button. 3 across, 3 down, or 3 diagonal matches is Bingo.

Morrow, L. M. (2002, 2nd ed.). *The literacy center: Contexts for reading and writing.* Portland, ME: Stenhouse.

Rosencrans, G. (1998). *The spelling book: Teaching children how to spell, not what to spell.* Newark, DE: International Reading Association.

USING A WORD-STUDY CENTER.   After children have been introduced to the use of materials, their teacher Mr. Rosen is able to assign word-study activities for them to work on while he works with small groups in guided reading instruction. The following explains the activities the children engaged in during center time.

Four children made as many words from the word *Thanksgiving* as they could. The letters of *Thanksgiving* had been cut up and placed in plastic baggies for each child. In addition to manipulating the letters to create words, the children wrote the words on an activity sheet.

With magnetic letters and their own individual magnetic slates, children created word ladders. They started with one-letter words, then two, then three, and so on. Each child also had a 5×8 index card to write his or her word from the bottom of the card up the ladder. A partner checked the words.

Another group of four children worked with ending phonograms or chunks, as Mr. Rosen called them, by creating words with onsets or initial consonants. He had prepared sliders, which are oak tag circles that have ending phonograms, with a slide of onsets to create words. Children created words with the sliders and wrote them down. They wrote additional words thought of as well.

Finally, children created sentences with letter and word stamps. The stamps had familiar words for the children to create the sentences.

All these activities were manipulative. They involved children working with words from individual letters, to letter chunks, beginnings and ends of words, and total sentences. They also required children to work together, check each other's work, and collaborate. All the activities had a pencil-and-paper component for recording what was done; for example, the little words made from the big word *Thanksgiving* were written on a sheet of paper provided. This way the teacher has a record of work done with manipulatives, and the students are responsible for completing tasks. All children have the opportunity to use every material during this period. Worksheets to be used with the manipulatives are important and provide practice. We have looked upon worksheets as materials that were not very useful; however, as long as children are involved in learning through multiple strategies, an occasional worksheet provides practice and reinforcement. Consult Strategies for the Classroom to tear out of the book and use with children.

Strategies

Concerns about Phonics

There are several concerns about teaching phonics. A major problem is that so many rules for the English language have exceptions. For example, the sound of *k* in the word *kite* is its usual sound, but when *k* is followed by *n* it becomes silent as in the word *knot*. I believe that we should teach fewer rather than more rules, because the ability to apply them is so limited for young children. Exceptions can be dealt with when they occur in print or be treated as sight words when they are uncommon. In early childhood, our main concern should be with sound–symbol relationships and generalizations that rarely have exceptions.

Another problem when dealing with sound–symbol relationships is dialects. If a teacher from upstate New York taught in South Carolina or Georgia, he or she would teach long and short vowels with different sounds than those taught by a teacher who was from the South. Children in most parts of the United States live in communities comprising youngsters who speak many different dialects and attend the same school. These children may have difficulty dealing with sounds regardless of where their teacher is from.

In addition, there are different types of learners. There are auditory learners and visual learners. A child who is weak in auditory discrimination is not likely to master phonics and is best taught to his or her strength, rather than to a weakness. The skills a child acquires as a result of learning phonics are important for becoming a proficient reader; alternatively, it is just one strategy within the total picture of literacy development, and we need not overemphasize it.

Oral Reading to Check Word Study Knowledge

We ask children to read orally in early literacy classrooms for many reasons. We can determine their reading level, the types of strategies children have for decoding and comprehending text, the types of errors they make, and strategies they need to develop. Oral reading tells us about children's reading **fluency,** which is determined by the rate of reading, accuracy, expression used, and phrasing. Children who are fluent readers use verbal expression and intonation that conveys the meaning of the text, and they attend to punctuation.

The accuracy with which children read particular passages determines their reading level. Reading level indicates which materials should be used for instructional purposes, which for independent reading, and which will be too difficult. When children read orally, we can also find out if they self-monitor their own reading. For example, when they make an error, do they correct that error on their own? Do they search through the text to figure out words?

When we listen to children read orally, we can provide needed strategies for independent reading. The following are prompts for strategies students can use when they have difficulty decoding. The prompts should help children gain meaning from the text. These prompts are adapted from those presented by Fountas and Pinnell (1996).

Prompts to support the reader's use of sources of information

Check the pictures.

Does that make sense?

Does that word sound right?

What's wrong with this? (Repeat what the child said.)

Try that again and think of a word that makes sense.

Do you know a word that starts with those letters?

Do you know a word that ends with those letters?

Prompts to support the reader's use of self-monitoring or checking behavior

Were you right?

Why did you stop?

Would _____ fit here?

Would _____ make sense?

Check it. Does it look right and sound right to you?

You almost got that. See if you can find what is wrong.

Try that again.

Prompts to support the reader's self-correction behavior

I liked the way you worked that out.

You made a mistake. Can you find it?

You're nearly right. Try again.

What else can you do to try and get the words right?

Prompts to support phrased, fluent reading

Can you read this quickly?

Put your words together so it sounds like talking.

Source: Adapted by permission from *Guided Reading: Good First Teaching for All Children* by Irene C. Fountas and Gay Su Pinnell. Copyright © 1996 by Irene C. Fountas and Gay Su Pinnell. Published by Heinemann, division of Reed Elsevier, Inc., Portsmouth, New Hampshire.

Published Materials for Literacy Instruction

When we discuss the development of skills, it is natural to talk about published materials. Published materials have been available for many years and have played an important role in literacy instruction. The materials have been referred to as basal readers. In the early 1990s when whole language was the model for instruction and children's literature the main source for literacy development, basal readers were referred to as anthologies of children's literature. These prepared reading instructional materials have been more popular at some times than at others, depending on the focus for literacy instruction. The programs are used by most school districts and probably will continue to be used, because they provide a complete package of instructional materials and are revised to include new findings in early literacy development. Some general rules should be applied to the selection and use of materials.

1. Study the objectives for the published program and determine if they incorporate the latest findings on strategies for nurturing early literacy.

2. Determine if the program matches the goals for standards set forth by the district or state where the material will be used.

3. Determine if the program includes developmentally appropriate practice as you view it in your district.

4. Ensure that the materials suit the needs of the children you teach.

5. Urban and rural children may need materials different from children in suburban settings. Are there materials suited for children who speak English as a second language?

6. Examine the materials for clarity, appeal to children, and durability.

7. Analyze the teacher's editions for clarity of objectives, descriptions of plans, suitability of lesson content, and flexibility for teachers in using the material. The program should put the teacher in charge of the materials; the materials should not dictate to the teacher.

8. Ensure that leveled little books to match instruction to children's reading ability are included.

In addition, ask the following questions about the published materials:

1. Are technology components available?

2. Are there practice materials?

3. Do the books have adequate multicultural representation?

4. Are a variety of genres, including ample expository, narrative, fables, folktales, poetry, and so on, presented in the books?

5. Do the stories link to other content areas?

6. Are there manipulative independent activities for centers and independent work?

7. Does the assessment component meet district needs?

8. Are there plans for organizing and managing the delivery of the program?

9. Are there ample leveled books at all grade levels to meet the different skills needs of all children?

10. Does the teacher have to follow a script or can he or she use the materials to meet the needs of his or her class?

11. Does the publishing company provide adequate staff development with the program?

Published materials have improved over the years. They use real literature to help children learn to read from authentic meaningful text. The issue of the type of text to use for literacy instruction has always been of concern. Texts developed to teach specific skills often lack meaning and literary qualities. They do, however, provide a sequenced plan for helping young children understand what they read, with repeated vocabulary, limited vocabulary, phonetic elements, picture clues, and so on. Another type of text proposed by some educators is called *decodable text,* which has several definitions. Some suggest that with decodable text all skills needed to read are taught before giving a child the material to read. In this text about 75 percent of the words include letter–sound patterns that are familiar to children and are taught until the text is given to the child to read. The main focus of the text is phonetically regular patterns. When introducing phonetic elements such as initial consonants *d, r,* and *m* and the *an* phonogram, decodable text might read:

Dan ran after the man.

Before reading the text, the word *the* would be taught as a high-frequency word and the word *after* as a sight word.

Basal materials always have had grade designations. One problem with grade designations is that, although the material is probably appropriate for instructing most children in a particular grade, some students will be reading above the level or below the level of their designated grade. For instruction to be useful, the level of the material is critical.

Many teachers figure out the difficulty level of books and select them to match the instructional level of the small groups they teach. Commercial publishers also level their materials. The leveled books are typically little paperbacks. Publishers may designate the grade level or give them a letter level, such as A, B, or C books. The purpose of leveled books is to disregard the grade assignment completely and to determine a child's level of reading and then select the appropriate book for instruction. Books are leveled for difficulty based on the following factors (adapted from Fountas & Pinnell, 1996):

The length of a book, including number of pages and words

The size and layout of the print

The patterns, predictability, and structure of language

Text structures and genres used

Phonetic patterns in the words

How well illustrations support the text

Teachers working together have leveled collections of their books based on these criteria. They test the books by having children read them to determine how difficult or easy they are to read. To enhance collections, teachers use central areas for storing leveled books so that they have access to those needed for their students.

Publishers also create sets of leveled books, making purchasing easier for teachers if funds are available. Publishers level books based on many different criteria. One publisher may level books with specific repeated vocabulary, introduction of specific phonetic elements, and the like. Some companies that create leveled books for instruction are the following:

Benchmark Word I.D., 2107 N. Providence Road, Media, PA 19063

Rigby, 500 Coventry Lane, Suite 200, Crystal Lake, IL 60014

Scholastic, Inc., 555 Broadway, New York, NY 10012-3999

Sundance Publishers, 234 Taylor Street, Littleton, MA 01460

The Wright Group, 19201 120th Avenue NE, Bothell, WA 98011-9512

William H. Sadlier, 9 Pine Street, New York, NY 10005-1002

Selecting the appropriate book for instruction also can be done with the use of the running record described in Chapter 2 about assessment. The test is administered with leveled material. When a child scores 90 to 95 percent with a particular book, the level of that book is his or her reading instructional level. If the child scores higher than 95 percent, the book is for independent reading, and a score below 90 percent indicates the book is too difficult for the child to read.

Each teacher needs to make critical decisions about the use of materials in his or her instructional program. You should be in control of published materials and not allow the materials to dictate to you. For example, select sequences to use from the material that seem most appropriate. You need not start at the beginning of a book and follow it page by page to the end. Eliminate sections that you feel are inappropriate for your children. Repeat material when necessary. We have not found one published program that will determine the success or failure of literacy development with all young children. It is how you use the materials along with your basic philosophy and organization of the entire literacy program that will determine success. Commercially prepared instructional materials are only one part of literacy development. Many school districts use published materials, and many teachers depend on them as organizational tools. As a teacher you must decide on the design of your literacy instruction, the materials you use, and how you use them. Over and over again in research investigations, when the teacher is included as a variable when testing different types of methods, he or she is found to be the most important element for literacy success. The basals cannot stand alone as the only material for literacy instruction. They are a jump-off point for the teacher, and he or she has to supplement them with literature, poetry, magazines, and the like.

Assessing Knowledge of Word-Study Skills

Numerous word-study skills are discussed in this chapter. Initially, teachers should be concerned with a child's phonemic awareness. The Yopp–Singer Test of Phoneme Segmentation (Yopp, 1992), in Figure 5.8, is widely used to determine how well children can segment phonemes in words. The directions specify to ensure that the child says the sounds, not the letters in the word, because these are two different skills.

Figure 5.8 Yopp-Singer Test of Phoneme Segmentation (Yopp, 1992)

Child's name _____ Date _____
Score (number correct) _____

Directions: Today we're going to play a word game. I'm going to say a word and I want you to break the word apart. You are going to tell me each sound in the word in order. For example, if I say "old," you should say /o/-/l/-/d/." *(Administrator: Be sure to say the sounds, not the letters, in the word.)* Let's try a few together.

Practice items: *(Assist the child in segmenting these items as necessary.)* ride, go, man

Test items: *(Circle those items that the student correctly segments; incorrect responses may be recorded on the blank line following the item.)*

1. dog _____

2. keep _____

3. fine _____

4. no _____

5. she _____

6. wave _____

7. grew _____

8. that _____

9. red _____

10. me _____

11. sat _____

12. lay _____

13. race _____

14. zoo _____

15. three _____

16. job _____

17. in _____

18. ice _____

19. at _____

20. top _____

21. by _____

22. do _____

Source: Hallie Kay Yopp, "A Test for Assessing Phonemic Awareness in Young Children," *The Reading Teacher* 49(1), September 1995, pp. 20-29.

Fluency, self-monitoring, accuracy, level of text, knowledge of basic phonics when reading, and types of errors made can all be determined with the running record. A description of the purpose of a running record and how it is administered and scored is in Chapter 2.

In addition to daily performance samples of children's writing and activity sheets, observations and descriptions of children's reading behaviors should be included in word-study assessment. Checklists (like the one on pages 179–180) are also important materials for testing children on word-study

CheckList   Assessing Concepts about Print and Word Study

Child's name _____ Date _____

	Always	Sometimes	Never	Comments
Knows print is read from left to right				
Knows that oral language can be written and then read				
Knows what a letter is and can point one out on a page				
Knows what a word is and can point one out on a printed page				
Knows that there are spaces between words				
Reads environmental print				
Recognizes some words by sight and high-frequency sight words				
Can name and identify rhyming words				
Can identify and name upper- and lowercase letters of the alphabet				
Can blend phonemes in words				
Can segment phonemes in words				
Associates consonants and their initial and final sounds (including hard and soft *c* and *g*)				
Associates consonant blends with their sounds (*bl, cr, dr, fl, gl, pr, st*)				
Associates vowels with their corresponding long and short sounds (*a*-acorn, apple; *e*-eagle, egg; *i*-ice, igloo; *o*-oats, octopus; *u*-unicorn, umbrella)				
Knows the consonant digraph sounds (*ch, ph, sh, th, wh*)				
Uses context, syntax, and semantics to identify words				
Can count syllables in words				

(continued)

	Always	Sometimes	Never	Comments
Attempts reading by attending to picture clues and print				
Guesses and predicts words based on knowledge of sound–symbol correspondence				
Can identify structural elements of words such as prefixes and suffixes, inflectional endings *-ing, -ed,* and *-s,* and contractions				
Demonstrates knowledge of the following phonic generalizations:				
a. In a consonant–vowel–consonant pattern, the vowel sound is usually short				
b. In a vowel–consonant–e pattern, the vowel is usually long				
c. When two vowels come together in a word, the first is usually long and the second is silent (train, receive, bean)				
Uses word families often referred to as rimes and phonograms, such as *an, at, it, and ot,* and initial consonants to build words, such as *man, can, fan, ran*				

Teacher Comments:

skills. For example, to test for knowledge of the alphabet, the teacher can name particular letters and ask a child to circle them on a sheet of paper containing upper- and lowercase letters. Teachers can also use flash cards of letters for students to identify. Basic sight words are checked similarly to alphabetic knowledge by circling on a sheet of paper or with flash cards. To determine the ability to rhyme, the teacher says pairs of words and asks children to identify which rhyme and which do not. Knowledge of phonetic sounds such as consonants is checked by having the child circle a picture that begins with a particular letter. Sometimes the teacher will say a word and ask the child to identify the letter it begins with. When asking children to determine the beginning letter of an object in a picture, ensure that the object is clear and easy to identify. For example, some children may mistake a donkey for a horse and choose the initial letter *h,* instead of *d.* Besides the assessments mentioned, some of the same gamelike activities used for instruction and practice materials for reinforcement are used for assessing children's knowledge of word-study skills.

When Do I Teach Word Study in the School Day? How Much Time Do I Spend Teaching Word Study? How Do I Differentiate Instruction to Meet All Achievement Levels?

Word-study skills are taught to help children to become independent, fluent readers. The skills should be mastered by third grade, with attention then shifted mostly to comprehension development. Comprehension skills are also taught in preK and kindergarten through grade 2, but in addition there is a strong emphasis on learning to decode. There should be a daily lesson based on standards and your school curriculum dealing with word study for the entire class. Take advantage of teachable moments when they occur to reinforce the skills being taught. Purposefully integrate whatever skill you are emphasizing into science, social studies, math, play, music, and art. For example, if you are learning the initial consonant *t* and learning about the temperature in different seasons in a science unit, point out the consonant *t* in the word *temperature* and remind the children that they were discussing this in their phonics lesson.

It is crucial to teach in small groups to determine individual needs. Small groups allow you to find out what students have learned and what they need to learn. Small groups allow you to differentiate instruction. When differentiating instruction, you have similar goals for all children in the different groups, but lessons are designed for the students needing more challenging or easier work. Small groups meet individual needs.

There is a formal time in the day to teach word study in a whole group, there is informal teaching embedded into content-area teaching, and there is a formal time for small-group instruction to meet individual needs. The length of lessons depends on the age of the children. They are shorter with younger children and longer with older ones. Materials selected for instruction should always challenge the child but be easy enough for them to succeed. For example, children who are working with onsets and rimes using magnetic letters and phonograms will make fewer words and more familiar words than those who are moving along more quickly. The materials and skill are useful for all these children. Small-group instruction with materials that can be used for differentiation of instruction is important for English language learners. In some cases, differentiation of instruction may mean that a small group is so advanced or so challenged that they are working on different skills than the majority of the class.

An Idea from the Classroom

English Language Learners

Strategies

Ideas Using Alphabet Books

I have a collection of alphabet books I find very useful for teaching the alphabet with my kindergarten children. I read different books throughout the year, and we do different activities based on the book. One of my favorites is *Chicka-Chicka-Boom-Boom* (Archambault & Martin, 1989). To help my students with learning the alphabet, they each make a sign for one letter of the alphabet. They write both the upper- and lower-case letters. When I read the story, the children put their signs around their neck and pop into the story when their letter is called. Each letter is mentioned in the story twice. When we read the book again, the children trade signs. I have photographed as the story is read and then made a book of the photos for them to read their own live version of *Chicka-Chicka-Boom-Boom*.

In addition, the teacher can have each child make his or her own alphabet book. Make a cover of colored $8\frac{1}{2} \times 11$ paper and write: My Very Own Alphabet Book by _____. Put a line at the bottom for the child to write her or his name on and paste a photo of the child on the cover. Using the pictures on the perforated pages at the end of the book, write and photocopy for each child a book that says _____ has an apple. Do this for each page of the alphabet. Take the 26 white sheets of paper with the sentences at the bottom and fold in half horizontally and staple into a book. Do one page at a time with the children, such as _____ has an apple. The child cuts and pastes the apple on the page and fills in his or her name. This is done for every letter of the alphabet. Children can also write the letter (see Figure 5.8). Use the pictures on page S-15 in Strategies for the Classroom.

Some other excellent alphabet books I use with my students are the following:

The Handmade Alphabet (Rankin, 1991) is an alphabet book in which hands sign each letter. I do the same with the children I teach.

Potluck (Shelby & Travis, 1991) is about children going to a picnic and each bringing something. It starts with Acton who appears with asparagus soup, and then Ben who brought bagels. It ends with Yolanda bringing yams and yogurt and Zeke and Zelda zooming in with zucchini casserole. We make food in our class based on the book.

Where Is Everybody (Merriam, 1989) is about different animals in different familiar places in the neighborhood doing different familiar things. For example: "Bear

Figure 5.9   My Very Own Alahabet Book

My Very Own Alphabet Book

Aa

apple

By: _James_

James has an apple.

Bb

ball

James has a ball.

Cc

car

James has a car.

is in the bakery, Cat is at the computer, Dog is at the day-care center." We act out what the letters and animals are doing.

Alphabestiary (Yolen, 1995) is a collection of poems by several different authors for every letter of the alphabet.

Ruth Mandel,
Kindergarten Teacher

An Idea from the Classroom

My Very Own Alphabet Book

I made an alphabet book for my grandson. Each page featured him in a photo that represented the letter. For example, on the *A* page, I put at the top *Aa* and the word *Apple* under the letters. Below is a picture of James holding an apple. At the bottom of the page it says, *James has an apple.* I did the same for every letter of the alphabet. For example, *Bb, Ball,* a photo of James holding a ball, and a sentence that says *James has a ball.* C is *James has a car,* and so on. I thought every child should have his or her *Very Own Alphabet Book* so I started one for you to complete.

On the cover is a picture of a girl and a boy, and the title of the book, *My Very Own Alphabet Book.* Under the pictures is the word By: _____ with a line for the child to write his or her name. The teacher should get a photo of the child and paste it on the boy's face or the girl's face, as appropriate. The teacher can continue to put the child's face on every page or just the cover. Use clip art or the pictures in the supplementary section of this book for Chapter 5, where there is one for every letter of the alphabet. Cut it out and paste it on the page. You can make one book for all children by simply photocopying it again and again. This is something a child will keep forever. See sample pages on page 183.

Lesley M. Morrow
Teacher, Mother, and Grandmother

Activities and Questions

1. Answer the focus questions at the beginning of the chapter.

2. Observe the environmental print in an early childhood classroom. Note what you think could be added to it, both from within the classroom and from the outside world.

3. Select three children from prekindergarten through second grade whose scores on standardized tests are available. Observe the children for oral language ability, competence in comprehension, and print knowledge. Compare what

you observe concerning the children's literacy ability with their test results.

4. Write an experience chart dictated to you by children in an early childhood classroom. If you do not have access to children, do this exercise in your college classroom with your peers dictating the contents for the chart. Critique the appearance of your chart and note problems you encountered while writing it. Use your self-evaluation for ideas for improvement.

5. Select five children from an early childhood classroom in which the students have collected Very Own Words. List all the words in the children's collections. Compare the list with the words you found in basal reading material for the age of the children you selected. How closely do the basal words and the children's Very Own Words match each other?

6. Select three initial consonants other than *p*. Design classroom experiences that will teach and reinforce the sound–symbol relationships

of each. Connect the letters to a thematic topic that is commonly studied in science or social studies in early childhood classrooms. Use traditional and authentic experiences.

7. Create a lesson to teach high-frequency words using a word wall.

8. Create lessons to teach phonic skills using your morning message words. With a pocket chart and word cards, have children:
   a. Make words from onsets and rimes.
   b. Sort words with similar patterns into piles.
   c. Make little words from a big word.
   Use sheets to create materials for the lessons provided.

9. **Strategies** There are several activities for phonemic awareness and phonics in Strategies for the Classroom for Chapter 5. Enlarge the figures and letters on the pages if necessary, color or copy on colored paper, laminate, and cut. Then do the activities.

PEARSON myeducationlab

VIDEO EXERCISE

Now that you have the benefit of having read this chapter, return to the www.myeducationlab.com topic "Phonics/Phonemic Awareness" and watch "Teaching Phonics," "Word Chunking," and "Phonics Instruction" one more time. You may complete the questions that accompany them online and save or transmit your work to your professor, or complete the following questions, as required.

Teaching Phonics (6:14 minutes)

1. Teaching phonics as an isolated activity is not recommended. Why does this teacher spend the time teaching the silent *e* rule to these children? How does she move the students from sounding individual words to using the rule in context?
2. Over the years there have been various schools of thought on the use of phonics to teach reading. What role do you think phonics should play in a reading program?
3. Two primary approaches to teaching phonics are analytic and synthetic. Explain the difference between these two approaches.

Word Chunking (1:00 minute)

1. What reading strategy is demonstrated by the student in this example, and how is the teacher supporting the student's development of this strategy?
2. You may notice that the teacher is introducing words that the student is likely to recognize. Why is it a good strategy to focus on high-frequency words at this level?
3. Choose a nursery rhyme that repeats a pattern (e.g., Hey Diddle Diddle), and develop an activity around it. How does this activity benefit beginning reading?

Phonics Instruction (4:43 minutes)

1. What skills related to letter–sound knowledge are being taught?
2. Distinguish between phonemic awareness and phonetic analysis. Name one activity that focused on each concept.

Focus Questions

- What are the objectives for teaching concepts about books and comprehension of text for your children?

- What experiences enhance a child's concepts about books?

- Define the term *comprehension of text*.

- Describe the types of read-aloud experiences and how they are effectively carried out to promote comprehension.

- Identify and describe strategies that develop comprehension, such as the use of graphic organizers and summarizing techniques.

- How should comprehension strategies be taught?

- List and define the structural elements in good narrative text.

- What are the structural elements found in good expository text?

- What is meant by an aesthetic stance and efferent stance when discussing text?

- **VOCABULARY:** comprehension, metacognition. expository text, narrative text, directed listening and thinking activity (DLTA), directed reading and thinking activity (DRTA), shared book experiences, graphic organizers (e.g., webs and maps), literature circles, buddy reading, partner reading, think, pair, share, K-W-L, fluency, mental imagery, think-alouds

- **Strategies** Take the activities from Strategies for the Classroom dealing with journal entries about books read, literature circles and building fluency. Do students enjoy this work?

PEARSON myeducationlab VIDEO PREVIEW: Defining Reading Comprehension (1:58 minutes); **Contextual Analysis and Story Dramatization** (3:36 minutes). Before reading this chapter, go to www.myeducationlab.com. Under the topic "Comprehension," access and watch the videos "Defining Reading Comprehension" and "Contextual Analysis and Story Dramatization."

Developing Comprehension
of Text and Concepts
about Books

6

*Few children learn to love books themselves.
Someone must lure them into the wonderful
world of the written word, someone must show
them the way.*

—Orville Prescott
A Father Reads to His Child (1965)

For several months, Mrs. Johnson has been discussing different authors and illustrators with the children in her first-grade class. A class chart in the room lists their favorite authors and illustrators. Today Mrs. Johnson asked the children to add names to the list because they had recently read stories by authors and illustrators who were new to them. First she asked for authors, and the following names were mentioned: Ezra Jack Keats, Tomie dePaola, Leo Lionni, and Arnold Lobel. Next she asked if they could name some illustrators, and students came up with the following names: Dr. Seuss, Eric Carle, and Maurice Sendak. Jamie raised her hand and said, "Hey, something weird just happened. I noticed that all of the authors named are also illustrators and all of the illustrators are all authors too." Christopher raised his hand and said, "That's not so weird, I know a bunch of people who are authors and illustrators at the same time. There's me, and Josh, Jennifer, and Patrick." Christopher was looking around the room and naming all the children in the class. When he finished naming his classmates, he continued, "We're all authors and illustrators. We all write books and illustrate them. They are published and they are in our classroom library. How could we forget that?"

Mrs. Johnson made a **t-chart** on the whiteboard. (See Figure 6.1). On one side she wrote "Dr. Seuss," and on the other side, "Ezra Jack Keats." She explained to the children that the t-chart was a strategy to help organize and understand information read. The t-chart would help them to compare and contrast the characteristics of the authors and illustrators to find out what they had in common and what characteristics were different. She then guided the children by modeling how to use the t-chart. She asked them to list characteristics of each author's illustrations first and then list characteristics of their stories. When they finished, they looked for characteristics in common and those that were different. On another day, Mrs. Johnson did this activity with the whole class again with two of the other author–illustrators. She then had pairs of children work on another author–illustrator pair doing their own t-chart as she walked around the room to help. Finally, for the last pair of author–illustrators, children were expected to do a t-chart on their own during independent center work. When completing this task, children were encouraged to use the books of the author–illustrators to help with the characteristics list. As she taught this comprehension strategy, Mrs. Johnson first explained the strategy and what it was for. Next she modeled the use of the strategy. The third step was to have the students use the strategy in a cooperative setting with a partner, and Mrs. Johnson walked around the room to answer questions and generally help to guide the students as they practiced the new strategy. Finally, she gave the students the opportunity to perfect the skill and practice it more in independent application.

Figure 6.1

t-charts

Authors		Illustrators	
Dr. Seuss	**Ezra Jack Keats**	**Dr. Seuss**	**Ezra Jack Keats**
Rhymes	No rhymes	Bold colors	Bright colors
Characters	Real characters	Watercolor	Collage
Imaginary	Real-life story	Cartoons	Realistic
Made-up words	Real words		

Concepts about Books

When children are very young, teachers discuss how to handle books, the parts of a book, and the difference between pictures and print. Children with early book experience are aware of many of these concepts. Those who are not need to be taught. Knowledge of concepts about books is important along the road toward becoming literate.

OBJECTIVES FOR DEVELOPING CONCEPTS ABOUT BOOKS
A child who has a good concept of books

1. knows that a book is for reading.
2. can identify the front and the back of a book as well as the top and the bottom.
3. can turn the pages of a book properly in the right direction.
4. knows the difference between print and pictures.
5. knows that pictures on a page are related to what the print says.
6. knows where one begins reading on a page.
7. knows what a title is.
8. knows what an author is.
9. knows what an illustrator is.

Activities That Develop Concepts about Books

English Language Learners

We often assume that children know the concepts about books just outlined. However, to many 2- to 6-year-olds these concepts are totally unfamiliar. About 1000 books need to be read to a child before he or she enters kindergarten to help the child acquire concepts about books so he or she is ready for experiences in reading and writing. To help children learn concepts about books, point the concepts out at every opportunity when you read to them. You can introduce a story, for instance, by pointing appropriately as you say,

> *"The title of the story that I'm going to read is* Harriet, You'll Drive Me Wild *[Fox, 2000]. This is the title on the front cover of the book. The author of the book, or the name of the person who wrote the book, is Mem Fox. Here is her name. And the illustrator, the person who drew the pictures, is Marla Franzee. Here is her name on the book. All books have titles and authors, and if they have pictures they also have illustrators. The next time you look at a book, see if you can find the title. It is always on the front cover. And look for the names of the author and illustrator. For some books like this one,* No David *[Shannon, 1998], the person who wrote the book is the author and is also the person who drew the pictures, and his name is David Shannon."*

The repetition of such dialogue familiarizes children with the concepts, which they will eventually understand. Similar dialogue helps to explain other concepts. Point to a picture, then point to the print. Identify each, then ask, *"Which do we read, the picture or the print?"*

As you get ready to read to them, ask children to point out the top and bottom of the book and where you should begin reading on a page. Not only will you give the children the opportunity to learn the concepts, but at the same time you can determine which children understand the concept and which need help. These discussions can be carried out during story readings to small groups or with individual students. A child's independent exploration of books will reinforce what you have pointed out or explained. As a result of this type of teacher behavior, the following will begin to happen when reading stories to children.

After I read *Knuffle Bunny* (Willems, 2004) to a 4-year-old, she said to me, "Show me where does Trixie say Aggle Flaggle Klabble? I want to see it in the book." When I showed her the words, she repeated them while pointing to them and then asked to see them again in another part of the book. She proceeded to search through the book, trying to find the line "Aggle Flaggle Klabble" again.

English Language Learners

Big Books are an important part of early literacy instruction. They are oversized picture storybooks that measure from 14 × 20 inches up to 24 × 30 inches. Holdaway (1979) suggested that the enlarged print and pictures in these books help get children involved with concepts about books, print, and the meaning of text. Big Books are appropriate from preschool through third grade. Active involvement is encouraged when using Big Books in small- and large-group settings. When using a Big Book, a teacher places it on a stand because it is difficult to handle otherwise. An easel is usually used for a Big Book stand and makes the print and pictures visible for the children. Class Big Books can be made as well as purchased. When they are made, children become even more aware of book concepts because they are engaged in creating a book. Figure 6.2 provides directions for making a Big Book.

Big Books are effective for developing concepts about books mainly because of their size. As the teacher reads the book and tracks the print from left to right across the page, children see that books are for reading, and they see where a person begins to read on a page. They also learn to differentiate the print from the pictures. The connection is made that the oral language they hear from their teacher is being read from the print on the page in the book. The correct way to turn pages is easy to see with Big Books because they are so enlarged. The title of the book is prominently displayed on the front of the book and on the title page, as is the name of the author and illustrator.

In Mrs. Johnson's first grade, children are always encouraged to read the title of a book and the name of the author and illustrator before starting to read the text. One day during an independent reading and writing period, Damien placed the Big Book *My Friend and I* (Jahn-Clough, 1999) on the Big Book stand. He had gathered three children to sit in front of him to read to. He started by saying, "The title of the book I'm going to read is *My Friend and I.*" He turned the first page and began reading the text. Patrick popped up and said, "Damien, you can't read the book yet; you forgot to read who the author and illustrator are." Damien pounded his fist to his forehead, looked somewhat annoyed with himself, and said, "How could I forget that? Let's see, here is the name of the author and it must be the name of the illustrator too since there is only one name. Mrs. Johnson can you help, I can't read the name?" Mrs. Johnson came over and read, "The author and illustrator is Lisa Jahn-Clough."

Figure 6.2

Instructions for
Making a Big
Book

Materials

- 2 pieces of oak tag for the cover (14" x 20" to 20" x 30")
- 10 pieces or more of tagboard or newsprint the same size as the oak tag used for the cover to be used for the pages in the book
- 6 looseleaf rings (1¼")
- Hole punch

Directions

- Punch three sets of holes in top, middle, and bottom of the cover and paper that is to go inside the book.
- Insert a looseleaf ring in each hole. The Big Book should have a minimum of 10 pages.
- Print should be 1½ to 2 inches high.

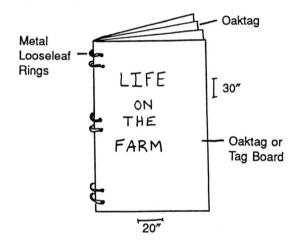

Theory and Research on Comprehension of Text

Comprehension is the ability to read or listen and understand text. Understanding what is read is one of the major goals for reading instruction. The English poet Samuel Taylor Coleridge wrote the following short piece entitled *On Reading Comprehension:*

> There are four kinds of readers. The first is like an hourglass, and their reading being as the sand, it runs out, and leaves not a vestige behind. A second is like the sponge, which imbibes everything and returns it in nearly the same state, only a little dirtier. The third is like a jelly bag, allowing all that is pure to pass away, and retaining only the refuse. And the fourth is like the workers in diamond mines, who cast aside all that is worthless and retain only pure gems.

How do we get children to cast aside unnecessary information and retain only the pure gems when reading or listening to a passage?

Pressley and Afflerbach (1995) have outlined the characteristics of the kind of skilled readers who comprehend well, the kind of readers we hope to create:

- Good comprehenders read materials from the beginning to end and also jump around looking for information that might help with clarification.
- Good comprehenders slow down their reading when they come to information that is relevant to what they want to remember.
- Good comprehenders anticipate the content of the text based on prior knowledge about the topic.
- Good comprehenders reflect on ideas in the text by creating summaries about what they have read.
- Good comprehenders refer to the text about important information to clarify issues.

Definitions of comprehension emphasize that it is an active process. In this process, the reader or listener interprets and constructs meaning about what he or she reads or listens to based on prior knowledge about the topic, thereby making connections between the old and the new (Pressley & Hilden, 2002). This concept arises from research on schema theory that suggests that that we have schemata (background knowledge) for certain information based on prior experience with a given topic. That schema is never complete because more can always be learned about a subject. For example, if someone told us something about the circus, we would gain one bit of information; if we saw pictures of the circus, we would have additional information; and if we went to see the circus, we would know even more. Then when we read about the circus or listen to a story about it, the new information would expand and refine what we already know. Comprehension of a narrative or expository piece that is read or listened to involves a child's integration of his or her prior knowledge concerning a topic with the new text to create new knowledge (Pressley & Hilden, 2002).

Comprehension development is enhanced as a result of children's social interactions with others during reading and writing experiences (Rand Reading Study Group, 2002). For example, children benefit from early experiences with books that are mediated by an interactive adult who provides problem-solving situations. The child is asked to respond, and the adult offers information when necessary. In such situations, children and adults interact to integrate, construct, and make relationships with printed text.

Comprehension greatly depends on how the difficulty of the text matches the ability of the listener or reader. Therefore, it is important to keep in mind when reading to children, or when they read themselves, the following characteristics about the text that will determine how well they will comprehend:

- The familiarity of the content in the text
- The background knowledge required to understand the text
- The quality of the writing
- How interesting the topic is to the listeners or readers
- The syntactic complexity of the sentences
- The amount and difficulty of vocabulary included
- The length of a selection that is read or listened to (Graves, Juel, & Graves, 1998)

Comprehension is an active process through which readers and listeners interpret and construct meaning about what they read or listen to.

Developing metacognitive abilities is an aid to comprehension. **Metacognition** is one's own awareness of how his or her learning is taking place. When it comes to comprehension, it means that students can articulate how they are able to comprehend and the problems they have comprehending and then can discuss how the problems might be solved. When students engage in metacognition, or self-monitoring, they can choose the appropriate comprehension strategy for the text and can regulate, check, and repair their reading processes as they go (Gunning, 2003).

In an important and well-known piece of research by Dolores Durkin (1978–1979), it was found that comprehension was rarely taught in the primary grades. During the 1980s, a great deal of research about comprehension was carried out by the Center for the Study of Reading at the University of Illinois in Urbana and, as a result of that work and other work that followed, more attention has been paid to teaching comprehension in the primary grades. A report entitled *Reading for Understanding: Toward a Research and Development Program in Reading Comprehension*, created by the Rand Reading Study Group (2002) and published by the U.S. Office of Educational Research and Improvement in Washington, D.C., and the National Reading Panel Report (2000), discusses the comprehension strategies that need to be taught to students and how they should be taught. Both reports draw on research about successful comprehension practice. The objectives and strategies discussed in this chapter to a large extent reflect the findings of these reports.

Objectives and Standards for Developing Comprehension of Text

Individual states as well as national organizations have created standards for comprehension development. Getting meaning from text is the ultimate goal. When getting meaning from text, children are expected to have competence in self-monitoring and self-correcting strategies. When children self-monitor their reading, they use syntax to help figure out the meaning of new words. They raise questions about what the author was saying.

When children demonstrate comprehension

- They can comprehend text when reading books that have subplots as well as a main plot
- They understand nonfiction that contains concepts with subordinate and coordinate structures presented in complex and compound sentences.
- They grasp meaning from figurative language such as similes and metaphors.

- They compare one text to another text they have read or heard.
- They explain motives of characters. (National Center on Education and the Economy and the Learning Research and Development Center at the University of Pittsburgh, 1999)

A child is accomplishing objectives set forth in comprehension of narrative and informational text when he or she completes the activities shown in Box 6.1.

Box 6.1

Objectives for
Comprehension
of Narrative and
Expository Text

1. Attempts to read well-known storybooks that result in the telling of a well-formed story.
2. Participates in story reading by saying words and narrating stories as the teacher reads.
3. Participates in cooperative learning activities to construct comprehension of text.
4. Monitors his or her comprehension (metacognition):
   Think about your thinking;
   Know what you understand;
   Know what you don't understand;
   Use strategies to help understand what you don't know.
5. Answers questions and participates in discussions and activities involving
   a. literal thinking that asks the reader to identify details, such as who, what, when, where, and to classify, sequence, and find the main idea.
   b. inferential and critical thinking that asks the reader to predict, interpret (put yourself in the place of the characters), draw from background knowledge, make connections from text to the child's life, make connections from the text to the world, make connections from one text to another, evaluate, compare and contrast, determine cause and effect.
6. The child generates questions, discussions, and activities involving
   a. literal thinking that asks the reader who, what, when, where to classify and sequence.
   b. inferential and critical thinking that asks the reader to predict, interpret (put yourself in the place of the characters), draw from background knowledge, connect text to life, evaluate, compare and contrast, determine cause and effect, apply information and problem solve.
7. Uses graphic organizers:
   a. Maps
   b. Webs
   c. KWL
   d. T-charts
   e. Venn diagrams
   f. Graphs
   g. Charts
8. Recognizes and understands features of and structures in expository text such as the following:
   a. Features in expository text
      (1) Table of contents
      (2) Headings
      (3) Glossary
      (4) Index
      (5) Diagrams
   b. Structures in expository text
      (1) *Description:* Gives the reader a picture of the subject based on story observation.
      (2) *Sequence:* Explains the steps that produce a certain product or outcome.

(3) *Comparison and contrast:* These are comparisons that include items with a similar classification that are compared first and then contrasted. Point-by-point comparisons describe similarities and differences alternately.

(4) *Cause and effect:* Causality tells why something happens.

(5) *Problem–solution:* A problem is presented, followed by its solution. An understanding of chronology is necessary to comprehend this structure.

(6) *Exemplification* (reason and example): The main idea is printed with supporting details (Vukelich, Evans, & Albertson, 2003).

9. Recognizes and understands features of and structures in narrative text such as
   a. *Setting:* beginning, time, place, characters
   b. *Theme:* main character's problem or goal
   c. *Plot episodes:* events leading to solving the main character's problem or reaching his or her goal
   d. *Resolution:* problem solution, goal achievement, ending

10. Engages in summarizing activities.
    a. Retelling
    b. Drawing conclusions

11. Engages in mental imagery.

12. Engages in cooperative activities, such as the following:
    a. Collaborative response groups
    b. Think–pair–share
    c. Think-alouds
    d. Literature circles
    e. Buddy reading
    f. Partner reading

13. Uses references and study skills that involve the following:
    a. The dictionary
    b. Internet searches
    c. SQ3R: survey, question, read, recite, review

14. Participates in fluency training:
    a. Echo reading
    b. Choral reading
    c. Tape-assisted reading
    d. Antiphonal reading
    e. Paired reading
    f. Reader's Theater
    g. Repeated reading

How Comprehension Strategies Are Taught

When learning strategies, children must play an active role as they respond to literature in different ways. Select narrative or informational text that relates to a child's real-life experiences and that is well structured. Narrative material contains clearly delineated settings, themes, episodes, and resolutions. Quality expository text presents nonfiction content-area information to children in the following structures: description, sequence, comparison and contrast, cause and effect, problem–solution, and exemplification.

Children practice comprehension strategies during partner reading in a private spot.

Comprehension instruction is effective when students engage in learning in cooperative settings at least some of the time. It gives them the opportunity to discuss with each other and learn from each other. Teaching comprehension strategies has been found to be most effective when using the following steps:

Explanation: The teacher explains what the strategy is, why it is important, and when it is used.

Modeling: The teacher demonstrates the use of the strategy by using it with the children.

Guided practice: The teacher provides an opportunity for the students to practice using the strategy. The teacher guides the students in how and when to use the strategy. Guided practice is a good time for students to work together so they can help each other learn.

Independent application: The teacher provides time for students to practice the strategy without guidance so they can carry it out without assistance (CIERA, 2001).

Reflection: The child thinks about how the strategy can be used in other situations. The child thinks about how good he or she is at using the strategy (McLaughlin, 2003).

In the vignette at the beginning of the chapter, Mrs. Johnson uses parts of the format described over a period of time when teaching her children about comparing and contrasting characteristics of authors and illustrators.

Comprehension Strategies

In this section, several strategies to enhance children's concepts about books and comprehension development will be described. These strategies can be introduced in whole-group settings and used repeatedly with new materials. They are appropriate for small-group instruction when explicit teaching takes place. Teachers decide which strategies to use in these reading groups based on the needs of the children involved.

All the strategies can be used with preschool-age children through third graders. They need to be adapted to the age of the children with whom they are being used.

Directed listening and thinking activities set a purpose for reading or listening and help focus students' thoughts.

The Directed Listening and Thinking Activity and Directed Reading and Thinking Activity

When children are read to or they read themselves, there should always be a purpose for the reading. The format of the **directed listening and thinking activity (DLTA)** and the **directed reading and thinking activity (DRTA)** sets a purpose for reading, thus helping to direct thought. This strategy, when internalized by children as a result of frequent use by the teacher, will be transferred and used by students when new material is read or listened to (Morrow & Gambrell, 2004; Roskos, Tabor, & Lenhart, 2004). Whatever the DLTA- or DRTA-specific objectives may be, its framework offers the listener or reader a strategy for organizing and retrieving information from the text. In the following DRTA–DLTA for *The Little Red Hen* (Izawa, 1968), Children are asked to participate in two main strategies:

English Language Learners

1. Sequencing the events of the story
2. Making inferences and judgments related to the text

In the lesson that follows, when using the DLTA, the children listen to the story; with the DRTA, the children read the story. I use a well-known story for an example since most readers will be familiar with it.

PREPARE FOR LISTENING OR READING WITH PREQUESTIONS AND DISCUSSION. Build a background by introducing the story: "Today I'm going to read a story (or you will be reading a story) entitled *The Little Red Hen.* Let's look at the pictures to see if you can tell what the story is going to be about."

Encourage children to respond as you turn the pages of the book. After they have offered their ideas, say, "The story is about a hen who wants to bake some bread and asks her friends for some help." This activity has been referred to as a *walk through the book* or a *book walk.*

Ask prequestions that build additional background that sets a purpose for listening or reading. Relate the questions to real-life experiences whenever possible: "Have you ever asked people for help? What kind of help? Did they help you? Has anyone ever asked you for help? What kind of help? Were you able to help the person? How? This story is about a little red hen that needed and asked for help while baking bread. While I'm reading [or while you are reading], try to decide if you think the little red hen did the right thing with her bread at the end of the story. Think of reasons why you think she was right or wrong. As I read [or you read], try to remember what happened first, second, third, and at the end of the story."

When the children have gained enough experience with your prequestions, you can ask them to think of their own: "Now that I've told you a little about the story, what do you want to find out when I read it to you [or when you read it]?"

READING THE STORY. Be sure to show the children the pictures as you read the story. Stop just one or two times for reactions, comments, or questions from the children. Don't interrupt the story for lots of discussion. That will come at the end. If the children are reading the story, remind them to study the pictures. Model or scaffold responses to guide them in their thinking, keeping in mind the objectives for this particular DLTA or DRTA: "Can you remember what help the little red hen has asked for so far? How have the other animals acted about giving help?" If the children do not respond, scaffold or model responses by changing questions to statements: "These animals aren't very helpful to the little red hen. Each time the hen asks for their help, the animals all answer, 'Not I.'" Also ask for children's predictions of what will happen next. Have only one or two stopping points for discussion during the story.

DISCUSSION AFTER READING. The postdiscussion should be guided by the objectives or purpose set for listening and reading: "What did the little red hen want help with first? second?" and so on. Ask children to retell the story; retelling will demonstrate their knowledge of sequence. Allow children to use the pictures in the book to help them follow sequence. Finally, focus on the second goal, making inferences and judgments: "What would you have done if you were the little red hen? Do you think she did the right thing with her bread, and why? What lesson can we learn from this story?"

A DLTA or DRTA can have many different objectives. The framework, however, is always basically the same: (1) preparation for listening or reading—prequestions and discussion; (2) reading the story with few interruptions; and (3) discussion after reading. All three steps are focused on the DLTA's or DRTA's specific objectives.

A DLTA or DRTA can focus on literal responses (such as recall of facts and sequencing), inferential responses (such as interpreting characters' feelings, predicting outcomes, and relating the story to real-life experiences), and critical responses (such as evaluating, problem solving, and making judgments). It can focus on identifying elements of story structure, whether narrative or expository text. It helps youngsters draw meaning from the print. Research has demonstrated that a DLTA can increase the story comprehension of young listeners (Morrow, 1984), just as a DRTA can increase the story comprehension of young readers (Baumann, 1992; Pearson, Roehler, Dole, & Duffy, 1992).

Developing Comprehension with Shared Book Experiences

English Language Learners

The **shared book experience** (Holdaway, 1979) is usually carried out in a whole-class setting, although it may be carried out in small groups as well. During this activity, teachers model fluent reading for children. They also help children to develop listening skills, since during the reading the children are asked to participate in some way.

Shared book reading often involves reading from a Big Book designed so that everyone in the group can see the pictures and the words clearly while it is being read. If the book is a new one for the class, the children are asked to listen during the first reading. If it is being read for the second time or is already familiar, immediate participation is encouraged. Often the teacher uses a pointer during the reading to emphasize left to right progression with younger children and the correspondence of spoken and written words.

Children's participation could include chanting together repeated phrases in the story, stopping at predictable parts and asking children to fill in words and phrases, or reading key words that are special to the story. Shared book experiences could include echo reading: the teacher reads one line and the children repeat it. Big Books and regular-size copies of the same book should be available for children to use independently after a first Big Book reading.

Shared book readings can be tape-recorded and made available in the listening station. This activity provides a familiar and fluent model for reading with good phrasing and intonation for children to emulate. Shared book experiences can be adapted to the DLTA format, with one of the objectives being to provide a participatory and enjoyable read-aloud event.

Research indicates that shared book reading benefits the acquisition of reading and writing. It enhances background information and sense of story structure and familiarizes children with the language of books (Bus, 2001; Cullinan, 1992; Morrow, 1985). A well-structured story has a setting (a beginning, time, place, and introduction of characters), theme (the main character's problem or goal), plot episodes (a series of events in which the main character attempts to solve the problem or achieve the goal), and a resolution (the accomplishment of the goal or solving of the problem and an ending). From hearing many well-formed stories, children can predict what will happen next in an unfamiliar story on the basis of their awareness of its structure. Hearing stories with good plot structures also helps children write and tell their own stories. The language of books is different from oral language and provides a model for their writing and speaking. The following sentences from two well-known picture storybooks make this evident:

> One bad day a tuna fish, fierce, swift and very hungry, came darting through the waves. (Lionni, *Swimmy*, 1963)
> The wild things roared their terrible roars, gnashed their terrible teeth, and rolled their terrible eyes. (Sendak, *Where the Wild Things Are*, 1963)

This next piece is from E. B. White's *Charlotte's Web* (1952) and is appropriate to read to first and second graders.

> At last Wilbur saw the creature that had spoken to him in such a kindly way. Stretched across the upper part of the doorway was a big spiderweb, and hanging from the top of the web, head down, was a large grey spider. She was about the size of a gumdrop. She had eight legs, and she was waving one of them at Wilbur in friendly greeting. "See me now?" she asked.
> "Oh, yes indeed," said Wilbur. "Yes indeed! How are you? Good morning! Salutations! Very pleased to meet you. What is your name, please? May I have your name?"
> "My name," said the spider, "is Charlotte."

Predictable stories are ideal for shared book experiences because they allow children to guess what will come next, thereby encouraging participation. Predictability takes many forms. I have purposefully selected well known favorites as samples to learn about these types of texts. The use of catch phrases, such as "'Not I,' said the dog," "'Not I,' said the cat," and so on, in *The Little Red Hen* (Izawa, 1968) encourages children to chant along. Predictable rhyme enables children to fill in words, as in *Green Eggs and Ham* (Seuss, 1960). Cumulative patterns contribute to predictability. For example, new events are added with each episode, then repeated in the next, as in *Are You My Mother?* (Eastman, 1960). This book repeats phrases and episode patterns as its central character, a baby bird, searches for his mother by approaching different animals and asking the same question, "Are you my mother?"

Conversation can contribute to predictability, as in *The Three Billy Goats Gruff* (Brown, 1957) or *The Three Little Pigs* (Brenner, 1972). All books become predictable as children become familiar with them, so repeating stories builds a repertoire for shared book experiences. Books that carry familiar sequences, such as days of the week, months of the year, letters, and numbers, are predictable—*The Very Hungry Caterpillar* (Carle, 1969), for instance. Books gain predictability through good plot structures and topics familiar to children. Books in which pictures match text page by page tend to be predictable to children, especially if everyone in the group can see the pictures as the story is being read.

Predictable books are excellent for emergent and conventional readers in shared book experiences, as well as in independent reading. They allow the child's first experience with reading to be enjoyable and successful with minimal effort. Such immediate success encourages the child to continue efforts at reading. (A list of predictable books is provided in Appendix A.)

We often stop reading to children as they begin to read themselves. It is crucial to continue reading to them as they get older. Reading to them in a shared book setting enhances skills already learned and motivates interest in the books featured in the classroom.

Repeated Book Readings to Enhance Readers' Comprehension

English Language Learners

Children enjoy repetition. Being familiar with an experience is comfortable, like singing a well-known song. Besides offering the pleasure of familiarity, a repeated story helps develop concepts about words, print, and books. In a study with 4-year-olds, one group listened to three repeated readings of the same story and the other group listened to three different stories. After stories were read, each time the discussions revealed that the children in the repeated-reading group increased the number and kind of responses made, and their responses differed significantly from those of the different-story group. Their responses became more interpretive, and they began to predict outcomes and make associations, judgments, and elaborative comments (Morrow, 1987a).

They also began to narrate stories as the teacher read (their first attempts at reading) and to focus on elements of print, asking names of letters and words. Even children of low ability seemed to make more responses with repeated readings than with a single reading (Ivey, 2002).

Repeated readings are important to youngsters because they can engage in the activity on their own. Children who are able to read themselves or participate in pretend reading behaviors often will select the same book to look at or read over and over again. Teachers should repeat readings of stories to children and encourage youngsters to read stories more than once. They should carry out discussions about books that have been read and discussed previously.

The following dialogue is from a transcription of a child's responses to a third reading of *The Little Red Hen*. This excerpt includes primarily the child's comments and questions and the teacher's responses; most of the story text has been omitted.

Teacher: Today I'm going to read the story *The Little Red Hen*. It is about a hen who wanted some help when she baked some bread. (The teacher begins to read the story.) Who will help me to cut this wheat?

Melony: "Not I," said the cat. "Not I," said the dog. "Not I," said the mouse.

Teacher: That was good, Melony. You are reading. (The teacher continues reading.) Who will take this wheat to the mill to be ground into flour?

Melony: "Not I," said the cat. "Not I," said the dog. "Not I," said the mouse with the whiskers.

Teacher: Very nice, Melony. (The teacher continues to read.)

Melony: I want to read that part, but I don't know how.

Teacher: Go ahead and try. I bet you can. I'll help you: The cat smelled it.

Melony: The cat smelled it and she said umm, that smells good, and the mouse smelled it, and it smelled good.

Teacher: (The teacher continues reading.) Who will eat this bread?

Melony: The mouse, the doggy, the kitty!

Teacher: You're right again, Melony. (The teacher reads to the end of the story.) Did you want to say anything else about the story?

Melony: He was bad so he couldn't have no bread. (Melony searches through the pages.) That's the wrong part.

Teacher: Show me the part you are talking about.

Melony: There it is, almost at the end. She's going to make bread and she'll say who's going to bake this bread for me? And the cat says, "Not I," the dog says, "Not I," the mouse says, "Not I." And then when she's cooking it, they smell a good thing and then they wanted some, too, but they didn't have any, 'cause they didn't plant the wheat.

Teacher: You're so right. They didn't help do the work, so they didn't get to eat the bread.

Melony: Where does it say, "Not I"? Show me the words in the book.

Teacher: Here it is. Can you find it again?

Melony: (She flips through the pages.) I'm looking for where she bakes the bread. Here it is. Yea. And he smelled it. And he smelled it. And the mouse smelled it. (She turns pages.) They're going in the kitchen. And she said, "All by myself, I cut the wheat. All by myself, I took it to the mill to get it into flour. All by myself I baked the bread. All by myself I'm going to eat it."

Teacher: That's terrific, Melony. That's what the hen said.

Melony: (She points to the dog.) The dog was not happy. Where does it say dog?

Teacher: You're right. He doesn't look happy. Here is where it says dog (pointing).

Melony: There's the word, dog, dog, dog. How does that dog look?

Teacher: He looks hungry and mad because he can't have any bread.

Melony: You're right. But it's his fault. He didn't help. And that's the end. (Morrow, 1987a)

This type of sophisticated response can only happen when a child has heard a story that has been repeated many times.

Children enjoy hearing the same book read to them over and over again. As adults we often tire of the repetition, but it has great value in early reading development. There should be a repertoire of books considered favorite stories that are read repeatedly to children at home and in school. To study emergent reading behaviors, Sulzby (1985) observed children from ages 2 to 6 attempting to read favorite storybooks. They could participate in the activity because they knew the stories so well. Although they were not yet readers in the conventional sense, the children were asked, "Read me your book." Sulzby found that, in their "reading," the children produced speech that could indeed be categorized as a first act of reading; that the speech they used as they "read" was clearly different in structure and intonation from their typical conversation; and that different developmental levels could be observed in these "oral readings."

From children's attempts at storybook reading, then, we can develop and determine particular characteristics of reading behavior. Because the activity is developmental and leads to literacy, teachers should ask children to participate in it to encourage their emergent literacy behaviors and to evaluate it as well. (See Figure 6.3.)

Figure 6.3

Sulzby's Classification Scheme for Children's Emergent Reading of Favorite Storybooks

1. *Attending to pictures but not forming stories.* The child "reads" by labeling and commenting on the pictures in the book but does not "weave a story" across the pages.

   yes ☐   no ☐

2. *Attending to pictures and forming oral stories.* The child "reads" by following the pictures but weaves a story across the pages through wording and intonation like those of someone telling a story. Often, however, the listener too must see the pictures in order to understand the story the child is "reading."

   yes ☐   no ☐

3. *Attending to a mix of pictures, reading, and storytelling.* The child "reads" by looking at the pictures. The majority of the child's "reading" fluctuates between the oral intonation of a storyteller and that of a reader.

   yes ☐   no ☐

4. *Attending to pictures but forming stories (written language-like).* The child "reads" by looking at the pictures. The child's speech sounds like reading, both in wording and intonation. The listener rarely needs to see the pictures in order to understand the story. With his or her eyes closed, the listener would think the child was reading print. The "reading" is similar to the story in print and sometimes follows it verbatim. There is some attention to print.

   yes ☐   no ☐

5. *Attending to print.* This category has two divisions:

   a. The child reads the story mostly by attending to print but occasionally refers to pictures and reverts to storytelling.

   b. The child reads in a conventional manner.

   a. ☐   b. ☐

Source: Adapted from E. Sulzby, "Children's Emergent Reading of Favorite Storybooks: A Developmental Study." *Reading Research Quarterly,* 20(4), 458–481. Copyright © 1985 by the International Reading Association.

Small-Group and One-to-One Story Readings

English Language Learners

The importance and benefits of reading to small groups and to individuals must not be overlooked. Too often considered impractical in school settings, one-to-one and small-group readings yield such tremendous benefits that they must be incorporated into school programs. The most striking benefit of one-to-one story readings at home, often called the *lap technique*, is the interactive behavior it involves, along with the direct channels of information it gives the child. It also provides the adult with insight into what the child already knows and wants to know. Very young children participate best in small-group and one-on-one readings, since they need the attention that this setting offers.

In one study (Morrow, 1988), it was determined that one-to-one readings in a school setting had positive results with preschoolers from lower socioeconomic backgrounds, even though the youngsters had little previous experience with storybook reading or interacting with adults during this time. Teachers in the study practiced interactive behaviors identified by researchers who had studied home storybook readings (Applebee & Langer, 1983; Cochran-Smith, 1984; Roser & Martinez, 1985). Teachers introduced stories by providing substantive background information before reading.

Frequent readings by teachers who followed the guidelines outlined below increased the number and complexity of the children's responses.

Guidelines | Teacher Behavior during Storybook Reading

1. Manage
   a. Introduce story.
   b. Provide background information about the book.
   c. Redirect irrelevant discussion back to the story.
2. Prompt Responses
   a. Invite children to ask questions or comment throughout the story when there are natural places to stop.
   b. Scaffold responses for children to model if no responses are forthcoming. ("Those animals aren't very nice. They won't help the little red hen.")
   c. Relate responses to real-life experiences. ("I needed help when I was preparing a party, and my family shared the work. Did you ever ask for help and couldn't find anyone to give it to you? What happened?")
   d. When children do not respond, ask questions that require answers other than yes or no. ("What would you have done if you were the little red hen and no one helped you bake the bread?")
3. Support and Inform
   a. Answer questions as they are asked.
   b. React to comments.
   c. Relate your responses to real-life experiences.
   d. Provide positive reinforcement for children's responses.

The youngsters offered many questions and comments that focused on meaning. Initially, they labeled illustrations. Later, they gave increased attention to details, their comments and questions became interpretive and predictive, and they drew from their own experiences. They also began narrating, that is, "reading" or mouthing the story along with the teacher. As the program continued, some children focused on structural elements, remarking on titles, settings, characters, and story events. After many readings, the children began to focus on print, reading words and naming letters and sounds (Barone & Morrow, 2003; Morrow, 1987a; Xu & Rutledge, 2003). Compared with one-to-one readings, reading to small groups of children seems to encourage more and earlier responses. Children tend to repeat one another's remarks, and they are motivated to respond to and elaborate on what their peers have said.

The following segments from transcriptions of small-group story readings illustrate the various questions and comments children make when they are involved in the activity and the wealth of knowledge and information they receive from the responding adult. The transcriptions also illustrate what the children already know and what their interests are, which helps teachers design instruction.

Story: *The Very Hungry Caterpillar* (Carle, 1969)
(The child asks questions about book concepts.)

Jerry: (He points to the picture on the front of the book.) Why does it have a picture on it?

Teacher: The cover of the book has a picture on it so you will know what the story is about. Look at the picture. Can you tell me what the book is about?

Jerry: Ummm, I think that's a caterpillar. Is it about a caterpillar?

Teacher: You're right, very good. The book is about a caterpillar, and the name of the story is *The Very Hungry Caterpillar*. When you look at the pictures in a book, they help you find out what the words say.

Story: *Caps for Sale* (Slobodkina, 1947)
(The child asks for a definition.)

Teacher: I'm going to read a story today called *Caps for Sale*.

Jamie: What are caps?

Teacher: A cap is a little hat that you put on your head. See, there is a cap in the picture.

Jamie: I never knew that before. I knew about hats, but I never heard about caps.

Story: *Chicken Soup with Rice* (Sendak, 1962)
(The child attends to the print.)

Chris: Wait, stop reading. Let me see this again. (He turns back to the page that talks about the month of June.) How come they're the same? (He refers to the words of June and July.)

Teacher: What do you mean?

Chris: Look at the letters, J–U, J–U. They look alike.

Teacher: Look more closely at the ends of the words. Are they the same?

Chris: Ohh, nooo, just the front part.

Story: *Caps for Sale* (Slobodkina, 1947)
(The child predicts.)

Colleen: I wonder why those monkeys took the caps?

Teacher: I don't know. Can you think why?

Colleen: Well, the peddler was sleeping and those monkeys looked at the caps, and maybe they think they're for them. Or, I know! Maybe they're cold so they want a cap.

Teacher: Those are good ideas, Colleen.

Story: *Madeline's Rescue* (Bemelmans, 1953)
(The child relates the text to real-life experience.)

Jamie: What's the policeman going to do?

Teacher: He's going to help Madeline. Policemen are nice; they always help us.

Jamie: Policemans aren't nice. See, my daddy beat up Dominic and the policeman came and took him away and put him in jail for no reason. And my daddy cried. I don't like policemans. I don't think they are nice.

The children's comments and questions relate to literal meanings, raise interpretive and critical issues by associating the story with their own lives, make predictions of what will happen next in a story, or express judgments about characters' actions. In these examples the children's comments and questions relate to matters of print, such as names of letters, words, and sounds. The same types of questions and comments occur when small groups of children read together without the presence of a teacher. Recording and then analyzing one-to-one and small-group story readings reveal what children know and want to know (Morrow, 1987a). The coding sheet in Figure 6.4 aids such analysis.

It is difficult to provide one-to-one and small-group readings in school because of time limitations and the number of children. Asking aides, volunteers, and older children to help in the classroom and with storybook reading one-to-one or in small groups can solve the problem.

Answering Questions and Participating in Discussions Generated by Teachers and Students

The benefits of reading aloud come from the interaction between adult and child. Studies carried out in school settings illustrate that active participation in literacy experiences enhances comprehension of and sense of text structure (Morrow, 1985; Pellegrini & Galda, 1982).

As children discuss text with others, at first they are interested in the illustrations and label items pictured or repeat words said by the adult who is reading (Bowman, Donovan, & Burns, 2000). Such interactive behavior leads children to respond with questions and comments, which become more complex over time and demonstrate more sophisticated thinking about printed material. Eventually, children's remarks about the content of the text demonstrate their ability to interpret, associate, predict information, and elaborate. Their remarks focus sometimes on title, setting, characters, and story events (Morrow, 1988; Roskos, Christie, & Richgels, 2003) and at other times on print characteristics, including names of letters, words, and sounds. Teachers help students to discuss and thus respond to text by

1. prompting children to respond before they do on their own.
2. scaffolding responses for children to model when they are not responding themselves.
3. relating responses to real-life experiences.
4. answering student's questions.

Figure 6.4

Coding Children's Responses during Story Readings

Child's name _____ Date _____

Name of story _____

(Read one story to one child or a small group of children. Encourage the children to respond with questions and comments. Tape-record the session. Transcribe or listen to the tape, noting each child's responses by placing checks in the appropriate categories. A category may receive more than one check, and a single response may be credited to more than one category. Total the number of checks in each category.)

1. Focus on story structure   _____

   a. Setting (time, place)   _____

   b. Characters   _____

   c. Theme (problem or goal)   _____

   d. Plot episodes (events leading toward problem solution
      or goal attainment)   _____

   e. Resolution   _____

2. Focus on meaning   _____

   a. Labeling   _____

   b. Detail   _____

   c. Interpreting (associations, elaborations)   _____

   d. Predicting   _____

   e. Drawing from one's experience   _____

   f. Seeking definitions of words   _____

   g. Using narrational behavior (reciting parts of the book
      along with the teacher)   _____

3. Focus on print   _____

   a. Questions or comments about letters   _____

   b. Questions or comments about sounds   _____

   c. Questions or comments about words   _____

   d. Reads words   _____

   e. Reads sentences   _____

4. Focus on illustrations   _____

   a. Responses and questions that are related to illustrations   _____

Total   _____

Small-group storybook reading with the teacher encourages interesting responses and elaboration of text by children.

5. asking questions.

6. offering positive reinforcement for children's responses.

GENERATING QUESTIONS. Productive discussions result from good questions. Discussions from questions must include more than a few words by participants and include questions that ask for clarification, explanations, predictions, and justifications. The following is a list of categories for asking questions:

1. Literal questions identify who, what, when, and where details. They ask students to
   a. classify ideas.
   b. sequence text.
   c. find the main idea.

2. Inferential and critical questions ask students to
   a. draw information from their background knowledge.
   b. make text to life, text to world, and text to other text connections.
   c. predict outcomes. (What do you think will happen next?)
   d. interpret text. (Put yourself in the place of the characters.)
   e. compare and contrast.
   f. determine cause and effect.
   g. apply information.
   h. problem solve.

Discussion questions should reflect children's interests and have many appropriate responses, rather than just one correct answer. Occasionally, questions with one correct answer can be asked. Most questions, however, should stimulate discussion and elicit responses that reflect what children think and feel about what has been read. These questions are asking for an aesthetic response, because children have to synthesize ideas, sensations, feelings, and images. The questions provide a model for children to pose their own. The last question asks the child to make text-to-life connections. The following questions will enable children to participate in an aesthetic discussion:

How did you feel about the story?

What did this story mean to you?

What questions do you have about the story?

What did you learn from what you read?

How will that information be useful to you?

Do you agree with what the characters did in the story? Why? Why not?

What in your life is like the story you just read?

(Gambrell & Almasi, 1994)

The efferent stance is usually taken with expository text that offers content information. Questions that ask for an efferent response require students to remember and analyze details and descriptions, sequences, and cause and effect. The last two questions deal with text-to-world and text-to-another-text connections. Some questions that will elicit efferent responses (Gunning, 2003; Rosenblatt, 1988) include the following:

What is the main thing that the author is trying to tell you?

What details, facts, happenings, or examples are used to explain the main idea?

What idea did you find most interesting?

What new ideas did you learn?

How could you find out more about these ideas?

If you could speak with the author, what would you like to ask him or her?

What else do you know about that is similar to the information in this book?

What other book(s) have you read that is similar to this one?

When asking questions, instruct students to look back into the text to find the answers to questions they cannot answer themselves. We need to help students know where to find answers that are explicit; that is, the answer to a question is stated in the text. Students need to be able to find implicit answers to questions when the answer is not exactly stated, but can be found within a few sentences in the text. Finally, students need to be able to answer scriptal questions. These answers are not in the text, but are a part of the child's background knowledge (CIERA, 2001).

STUDENT-GENERATED QUESTIONS. When they are able, we need to encourage students to engage in asking questions similar to those posed by the teacher. When they do so, they can find out if they can answer their own questions, they can practice looking for the answers, and they can work with others to find the answers.

Graphic Organizers

English Language Learners

Graphic organizers are visual illustrations or representations of text information that help readers see relationships between concepts or events in a narrative or expository writing. They can help teach many elements needed for comprehension, such as vocabulary, cause and effect, problem solving, and so on. Following are some well-known types of graphic organizers. I have also used well-known books to demonstrate, which should help the reader understand the concepts with ease.

MAPPING AND WEBBING.   Maps and webs are graphic representations, or diagrams, for categorizing and structuring information. They help students see how words and ideas are related to one another. Webs tend to be drawn using a spiderlike effect, and maps may have boxes with labels in them that connect in different places. **Mapping and webbing** strategies build on children's prior knowledge. They help the child retrieve what is known about a topic and use the information in reading and listening to text. Research has demonstrated that the use of webbing and mapping strategies is successful in the development of vocabulary and comprehension. This research has also shown the effectiveness of the strategies with struggling readers, minorities, and bilingual children (Pittelman, Levin, & Johnson, 1985; Pittelman, Heimlich, Benglund, & French, 1991).

When webbing or mapping is used to develop vocabulary concepts and definitions related to a word, the word is written on the board or chart paper. Children are asked to brainstorm ideas related to the word. For example, after reading *The Snowy Day* (Keats, 1962), the teacher asks the children to provide words that describe what snow is like. The word *snow* is written in the center of the chart or chalkboard, and the words given by the children are attached to it. A sample of a snow web done by a kindergarten class is shown in Figure 6.5.

Another web about the same story could be used to expand ideas about activities to do in the snow. In Figure 6.6 a first-grade class generated the things that Peter did in the snow in the story and then other things that we can do in the snow.

A map provides a different format for graphically presenting materials before and after listening to or reading a book. Maps deal with more complex representations; therefore, boxes for different categories are needed to present the ideas graphically. Story structures can be mapped to help children learn about the structural elements in the text. Sequences of events or studies of individual characters can be mapped also. Figure 6.7 is a map of the story *Mr. Rabbit and the Lovely Present* created by a second-grade class. The map illustrates the structural elements in the story.

K-W-L. K-W-L is a cognitive strategy to enhance comprehension. It is used mainly with expository text and can be adapted for use with narrative stories. It shares some similarities with a DRTA and a DLTA. **K-W-L** stands

---

Figure 6.5

A Web for Expanding Vocabulary

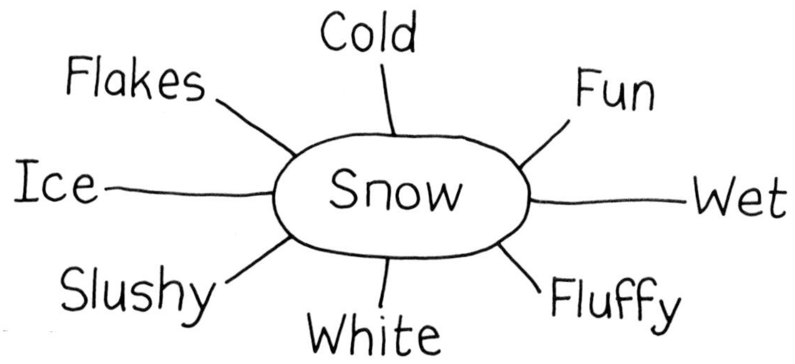

Figure 6.6

A Web for
Expanding Ideas

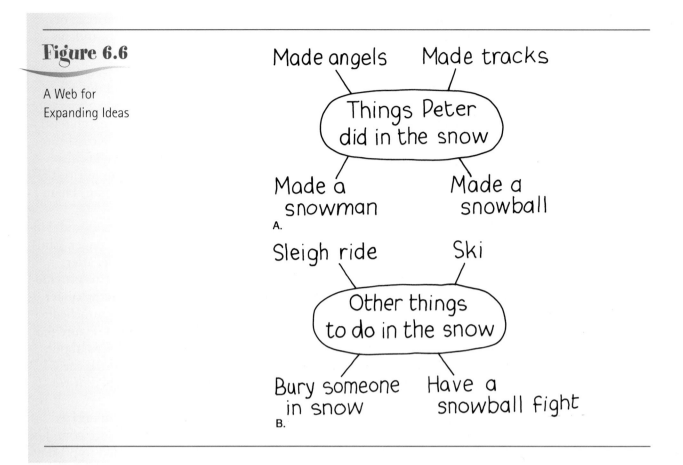

Figure 6.7

A Story Structure Map

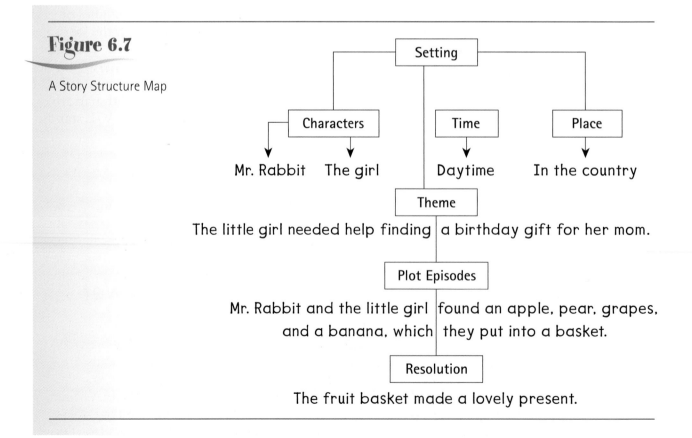

Figure 6.8

K-W-L Chart

Topic: Volcanoes

What We **K**now	What We **W**ant to Know	What We **L**earned
What they look like. Where some are. They are dangerous.	Why do they erupt? Where are all of the volcanoes? Can we stop them from erupting?	Where there are other volcanoes. Why they erupt. How hot the lava is.

for *What We **Know**, What We **Want** to Know,* and *What We **Learned*** (Ogle, 1986). With this technique students use prior knowledge to create interest about what is to be read. It helps set a purpose for reading to direct thinking, and it encourages sharing of ideas. The K-W-L chart (Figure 6.8), which lists items generated in a K-W-L discussion, is particularly useful when reading material for thematic instruction (Sampson, 2002). The following are the steps involved in putting the strategy into practice.

1. Before reading expository text, children brainstorm what they think they know about a topic. For example, if the book they are going to read is *Volcanoes* (Branley, 1985), the class would list *What We **Know*** about volcanoes.
2. children list questions about *What We **Want** to Know* before reading the book about volcanoes.
3. after reading the text, children make a list of *What We **Learned*** about volcanoes.

After reading the book, children can compare information learned from the text with what they already knew before reading the book. They can determine what they learned as a result of reading the text and, finally, what is still on the list of what they would like to learn because it was not included in the book.

VENN DIAGRAMS. A *Venn diagram* is a graphic organizer that uses two overlapping circles to show relationships between ideas. The Venn diagram helps to compare two or three concepts in a text (Nagy, 1988). When comparing two concepts, we list the main characteristics of each in the outer circles and the characteristics in common in the intersection. The Venn diagram can be used with expository or narrative text (Figure 6.9).

Ms. Anastasi read the book *Frogs and Toads and Tadpoles, Too* (Fowler, 1992) to her class. This informational story highlights the similarities and differences between frogs and toads. Ms. Anastasi drew two big intersecting circles on chart paper, labeling one "frogs" and the other "toads." Ms. Anastasi labeled the space created by the intersecting circles "similar characteristics." She asked the children to name traits from the book that were specific to frogs and then to toads. As the children responded, their teacher wrote the comments in the appropriate areas of the diagram. Then

Figure 6.9

Venn Diagram

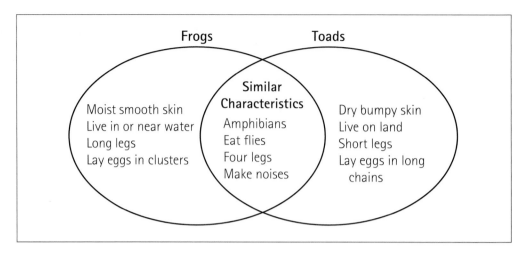

she asked the children if any of the traits were the same. If they were, she put them in the space labeled "similar characteristics." Ms. Anastasi looked back into the text with the children to look for words that would help them know that similarities or differences were being discussed. For example, words like *similarly, likewise, as,* and *nevertheless* indicate sameness, while words and phrases like *in spite of, still, but, even though, however, instead,* and *yet* indicate differences (Vukelich, Evans, & Albertson, 2003). As an extension activity, Ms. Anastasi had the students work with partners to create Venn diagrams using another expository text that included ideas to compare and contrast.

GRAPHIC ORGANIZERS FOR EXPOSITORY TEXT. Graphic organizers can help children learn text structures as well. In Figure 6.7 we illustrated a story structure map for a narrative text. Children need to learn the structures of both narrative and expository text and to summarize both. To give students more help with expository text structure, the following text structure sentences can be used over and over again:

> **Description:** A _____ is a kind of _____ that
> *An apple is a kind of fruit that is red and juicy and sweet.*
>
> **Compare and Contrast:** __X___ and __Y___ are similar in that they both, but __X___, while __Y___
> *Rain and snow are similar in that they both fall from the sky and they are both wet, but rain doesn't stick to the ground and has no color, while snow does stick to the ground and is white.*
>
> **Sequence:** _____ begins with, continues with, and ends with
> *Flowers begin as seeds, we water them, and they will grow; they continue to grow a stem and leaves, and end with the flower.*
>
> **Problem–Solution:** _____ wanted, but, so
> *The children wanted to play outside but couldn't because of the rain, so they played in the school gym instead.*
>
> **Cause and Effect:** _____ happens because
> *The car got stuck and wouldn't go because it was out of gasoline.*

Figures 6.10 and 6.11 provide graphic organizer outlines for sequence-of-events and cause-and-effect structures in expository text. According to Duke (2000; Duke & Kays, 1998), early childhood classrooms have very few non-fiction texts and spend little time dealing with informational text. Informational texts are read more often than narrative texts in adult life. It is important that children be taught how to read them. Appendix A provides an extended list of expository texts by grade to emphasize the importance of working with informational text.

Figure 6.10

Graphic Organizer for Sequence of Events

Name/s _____ Date _____

Topic: ___How Plants Grow_____

Sequence of (Important) Events

Buy seeds to plant. 1	Find a spot with dirt that gets sun. 2	Dig a hole in the ground. Plant the seed. 3
Water the seed. 4	Pull the weeds. 5	When it pops out of the ground, enjoy looking. 6

Figure 6.11

Graphic Organizer for Cause and Effect

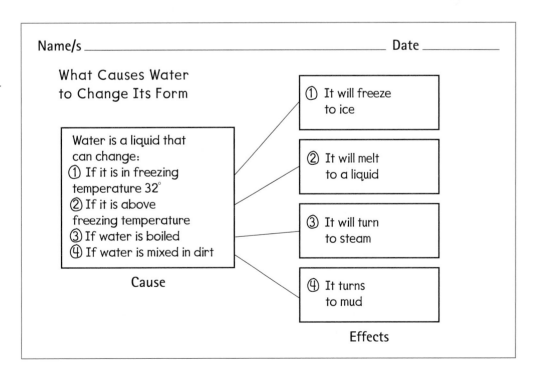

Name/s _____ Date _____

What Causes Water to Change Its Form

Water is a liquid that can change:
① If it is in freezing temperature 32°
② If it is above freezing temperature
③ If water is boiled
④ If water is mixed in dirt

Cause

① It will freeze to ice

② It will melt to a liquid

③ It will turn to steam

④ It turns to mud

Effects

Use graphic organizers in Strategies for the Classroom for Chapter 7 on pages S-31 through S-36 to help students recall expository and narrative information they read.

Summarizing Strategies for Young Children: Story Retelling and Rewriting

Letting a listener or reader retell or rewrite a story offers active participation in a literacy experience that helps develop language structures, comprehension, and sense of story structure (Ritchie, James-Szanton, & Howes, 2003). Retelling, whether it is oral or written, engages children in holistic comprehension and organization of thought. It also allows for original thinking as children mesh their own life experiences into their retelling (Gambrell, Pfeiffer, & Wilson, 1985). With practice in retelling, children come to assimilate the concept of narrative or expository text structure. They learn to introduce a narrative story with its beginning and its setting. They recount its theme, plot episodes, and resolution. In retelling stories, children demonstrate their comprehension of story details and sequence, organizing them coherently. They also infer and interpret the sounds and expressions of characters' voices. In retelling expository text, children review what they have learned and distinguish the main ideas from the supporting details.

Retelling is not an easy task for children, but with practice they improve quickly. To help children develop the practice of retelling, tell them before they read or listen to a text or story that they will be asked to retell or rewrite it (Morrow, 1996). Further guidance depends on the teacher's specific purpose in the retelling. If the immediate intent is to teach or test sequence, for instance, instruct children to concentrate on what happened first, second, and so on. If the goal is to teach or assess the ability to integrate information and make inferences from text, instruct children to think of things that have happened to them like those that happen in the selection. Props such as felt-board characters or the pictures in the text can be used to help students retell. Pre- and postdiscussion of text helps to improve retelling ability, as does the teacher's modeling a retelling for children.

Retellings can develop many types of comprehension and allows adults to evaluate children's progress. If you plan to evaluate a retelling, tell the child during your introduction of the selection that he or she will be asked to retell it after the reading. During the evaluative retellings, do not offer prompts beyond general ones such as "Then what happened?" or "Can you think of anything else about the selection?" Retellings of narrative text can reveal a child's sense of story structure, focusing mostly on literal recall, but they also reflect a child's inferential and critical thinking ability. To assess the child's retelling for sense of story structure, first parse (divide) the events of the story into four categories: setting, theme, plot episodes, and resolution. Use a guide sheet (see Figure 6.12) and the outline of the parsed text to record the number of ideas and details the child includes within each category in the retelling, regardless of their order. Credit the child for partial recall or for recounting the gist of an event (Pellegrini & Galda, 1982; Wasik & Bond, 2001; White-hurst & Lonigan, 2001). Evaluate the child's sequencing ability by comparing the order of events in the child's retelling with the proper order of setting,

Figure 6.12

Story Retelling
and Rewriting
Evaluation
Guide Sheet:
A Quantitative
Analysis

Child's name _____ Beth _____ Age ___5___

Title of story _____ Jenny Learns a Lesson _____ Date _____

General directions: Give 1 point for each element included as well as for gist. Give 1 point for each character named as well as for such words as *boy, girl,* or *dog.* Credit plurals (*friends,* for instance) with 2 points under characters.

Sense of Story Structure

Setting

a. Begins story with an introduction ___1___

b. Names main character ___1___

c. Number of other characters named ___2___

d. Actual number of other characters ___4___

e. Score for "other characters" (c/d): ___.5___

f. Includes statement about time or place ___1___

Theme

Refers to main character's primary goal or problem to be solved ___1___

Plot Episodes

a. Number of episodes recalled ___4___

b. Number of episodes in story ___5___

c. Score for "plot episodes" (a/b) ___.8___

Resolution

a. Names problem solution/goal attainment ___1___

b. Ends story ___1___

Sequence

Retells story in structural order: setting, theme, plot episodes, resolution. (Score 2 for proper, 1 for partial, 0 for no sequence evident.) ___1___

Highest score possible: ___10___   Child's score: ___8.3___

Source: From L. M. Morrow, "Story Retelling: A Discussion Strategy to Develop and Assess Comprehension." In *Lively Discussions!: Fostering Engaged Reading,* ed. L. B. Gambrell & J. F. Almasi, 265–285. Copyright © 1996 by the International Reading Association.

theme, plot episodes, and resolution. The analysis indicates which elements the child includes or omits, how well the child sequences, and thus where instruction might be focused. Comparing retellings over a year will indicate the child's progress.

The following example uses a parsed outline of the narrative story *Jenny Learns a Lesson* (Fujikawa, 1980). The parsed outline is accompanied by transcriptions of two children's retellings of the story. A retelling guidesheet follows with a quantitative analysis of the first transcription told by a child named Beth (Morrow, 1996).

PARSED STORY

Setting
1. Once upon a time there was a girl who liked to play pretend.
2. Characters: Jenny (main character), Nicholas, Sam, Mei Su, and Shags, the dog.

Theme
Every time Jenny played with her friends, she bossed them.

Plot Episodes
First episode: Jenny decided to pretend to be a queen. She called her friends. They came to play. Jenny told them all what to do and was bossy. The friends became angry and left.
Second episode: Jenny decided to play dancer. She called her friends and they came to play. Jenny told them all what to do. The friends became angry and left.
Third episode: Jenny decided to play pirate. She called her friends and they came to play. Jenny told them all what to do. The friends became angry and left.
Fourth episode: Jenny decided to play duchess. She called her friends and they came to play. Jenny told them all what to do. The friends became angry and left.
Fifth episode: Jenny's friends refused to play with her because she was so bossy. Jenny became lonely and apologized to them for being bossy.

Resolution
1. The friends all played together, and each person did what he or she wanted to do.
2. They all had a wonderful day and were so tired that they fell asleep.

VERBATIM TRANSCRIPTIONS
(Beth, age 5) Once upon a time there's a girl named Jenny and she called her friends over and they played queen and went to the palace. They had to do what she said and they didn't like it, so then they went home and said that was boring. It's not fun playing queen and doing what she says you have to. So they didn't play with her for seven days and she had an idea that she was being selfish, so she went to find her friends and said, I'm sorry I was so mean. And said, let's play pirate, and they played pirate and they went onto the ropes. Then they played that she was a fancy lady playing house. And they have tea. And they played what they wanted and they were happy. The end.

This retelling by 5-year-old Beth was transcribed when she was in the first part of her kindergarten year. To demonstrate how retellings can become more sophisticated and improve with practice and time, another retelling by this same child when she was at the end of her kindergarten year follows. The story is called *Under the Lemon Tree* (Hurd, 1980). It is about a donkey who lives under a lemon tree on the farm and watches out

Guidelines   Story Retelling

1. Ask the child to retell the story. "A little while ago, I read the story [name the story]. Would you retell the story as if you were telling it to a friend who has never heard it before?"

2. Use the following prompts only if needed:

   a. If the child has difficulty beginning the retelling, suggest beginning with "Once upon a time," or "Once there was..."

   b. If the child stops retelling before the end of the story, encourage continuation by asking "What comes next?" or "Then what happened?"

   c. If the child stops retelling and cannot continue with general prompts, ask a question that is relevant at the point in the story at which the child has paused. For example, "What was Jenny's problem in the story?"

3. When a child is unable to retell the story, or if the retelling lacks sequence and detail, prompt the retelling step by step. For example:

   a. "Once upon a time," or "Once there was..."

   b. "Who was the story about?"

   c. "When did the story happen?" (day, night, summer, winter?)

   d. "Where did the story happen?"

   e. "What was [the main character's] problem in the story?"

   f. "How did [he or she] try to solve the problem? What did [he or she] do first [second, next]?"

   g. "How was the problem solved?"

   h. "How did the story end?" (Morrow, 1996)

for all the other animals. A fox comes in the night to steal a chicken or duck and the donkey hee-haws loudly to protect them. He scares the fox away, but wakes the farmer and his wife who never see the fox. This happens frequently until the farmer can no longer take the noise and moves the donkey to a tree far from the farmhouse where he is very unhappy. The fox comes back and steals the farmer's prize red rooster. The other animals quack and cluck and finally wake up the farmer who chases after the fox. When the fox passes him, the donkey makes his loud noises again, frightening the fox, who drops the red rooster. The farmer realizes that the donkey has been protecting his animals and moves him back to the lemon tree where he is happy again.

Here is 5-year-old Beth's retelling of *Under the Lemon Tree:*

Once upon a time there was a donkey, and he was in a farm. He lived under a lemon tree close to the animals on the farm. In the morning all the bees buzzed in the flowers under the lemon tree. He was next to the ducks, the chickens, and the roosters. It was night time. The red fox came into the farm to get something to eat. The donkey went "hee-haw, hee-haw" and then the chickens went "cluck, cluck" and the ducks went "quack-quack." Then the farmer and his wife waked up and looked out the window and saw nothing. They didn't know what came into their farm that night. They said, "What a noisy donkey we have. When it gets dark we will bring him far away." So when it get darker and darker they brang the donkey over to a fig tree. And he had to stay there. He couldn't go to sleep alone. That night the red fox came into the farm again to try and get something to eat. All the ducks went quack-quack and the turkeys went gobble-gobble. The farmer and his wife woke up and said, "Is that noisy donkey back again?" They rushed to the window and saw the fox with their red rooster in his mouth and yelled, "Stop thief, come back." The fox passed the donkey and shouted "hee-haw, hee-haw." The red fox heard it and dropped the rooster and ran away. The farmer and his wife said, "Aren't we lucky to have the noisiest donkey in the whole world?" And they picked up the rooster and put one hand around the donkey and they all went home together and tied the donkey under the lemon tree.

Retellings can be evaluated for many different comprehension tasks. The directions to students prior to retelling and the method of analysis should match the goal. Figure 6.13 provides an analysis form for evaluating oral and

Figure 6.13

A Qualitative Analysis of Story Retelling and Rewriting

Child's name _____ Date _____

Name of story _____

Setting	Yes	No
a. Begins story with an introduction	☐	☐
b. Names main character	☐	☐
c. List other characters named here: _____ _____		
d. Includes statement about time and place	☐	☐

Theme

	Yes	No
a. Refers to main character's primary goal or problem to be solved	☐	☐

Plot Episodes

	Yes	No
a. Episodes are recalled	☐	☐
b. List episodes recalled	☐	☐

Resolution

	Yes	No
a. Includes the solution to the problem or the attainment of the goal	☐	☐
b. Puts an ending on the story	☐	☐

Sequence

	Yes	No
a. Story is told in sequential order	☐	☐

Interpretive and Critical Comments: Read through the retelling or rewriting and list comments made or written by students that are of an interpretive or critical nature.

Figure 6.14

Student Oral or
Written Retelling
Self-Evaluation
Form

Name_____ Date_____

Name of story_____

Setting	Yes	No
a. I began the story with an introduction.	☐	☐
b. I talked about the main character.	☐	☐
c. I talked about other characters.	☐	☐
d. I told when the story happened.	☐	☐
e. I told where the story happened.	☐	☐

Theme

	Yes	No
I told about the problem in the story or the main goal of the characters.	☐	☐

Plot Episodes

	Yes	No
a. I recalled episodes in the story	☐	☐

Resolution

	Yes	No
a. I told how the problem was solved or goal achieved.	☐	☐
b. I had an ending on the story.	☐	☐

Sequence

	Yes	No
My story was retold or rewritten in proper order.	☐	☐

Comments for Improvement:

Next time I need to include in my retelling:

---

written retellings in which checks are used instead of numbers for a general sense of the elements a child includes and to determine progress over time. Also provided in the form is a qualitative evaluation of interpretive and critical responses. Figure 6.14 provides a student evaluation form for oral and written retellings. Self-evaluation with a teacher, with a child, or alone is an important part of the learning process.

Collaborative Response Groups

English Language Learners

Strategies discussed for enhancing comprehension thus far are done in whole-group, small-group, or one-to-one settings with the teacher as director. In the following strategies, students participate in collaboration with one another, independently of the teacher. The National Reading Panel suggested that collaboration is an important strategy for developing comprehension (2000). These strategies are often referred to as **response groups** because they enable children to engage in productive and personal conversations about the text.

Response groups allow students to exchange ideas, listen to each other, refine ideas, and think critically about issues related to what they read or listened to. Because young children need the teacher to model behavior for response groups before they are able to participate in them with peers, the groups are introduced in teacher-directed settings first. A description of different response groups follows.

LITERATURE CIRCLES.   **Literature circles** consist of a group of children who have read the same book to discuss it. The children have these discussions independently of the teacher. Teachers need to model literature circle activities so that children can carry them out independently and successfully. Literature circles are organized as follows:

> Small groups are formed by the teacher, and they select one book from the list of books she provides that they will read and discuss. Groups meet regularly for their discussions.

> The teacher helps students with discussion using prompts similar to those reviewed in previous sections dealing with promoting conversations about books.

> Students are given jobs within the group, for example:

- The *discussion director* is responsible for the opening and closing remarks, reminding members to refer to their books to find support for their comments, and ensuring that everyone participates. The discussion director asks questions that the group will discuss.
- The *literary luminary* is responsible for selecting parts of the book for the group to read aloud. The selection should be funny, sad, interesting, etc.
- The *illustrator* draws something related to the reading.
- The *creative connector* finds the connection between the book read and the outside world. The connections are to the students, the book, the classroom, and their families and friends.
- The *vocabulary enricher* looks for words that are important to the book. They could be new words.
- The *summarizer* writes a summary of the reading. It should be short and to the point.
- The *investigator* finds more information about the topic of the book. (Daniels, 1994)

With young children in kindergarten and first grade, the teacher may need to lead the literature circles, act as discussion director, and ask the following:

- Tell the parts of your story you liked best.
- Tell the parts of the story you did not like.
- How might you have ended the story if you were the author?

Children can place Post-It notes on pages to remember issues to discuss. They ask the group to turn to the page as they refer to it. Children can comment on an issue, ask a question of others, or ask for clarification to help them better understand. This type of exercise requires guidance from the teacher and practice on the part of children.

BUDDY READING. **Buddy reading** is usually a situation in which a child from an upper grade is paired with a child in kindergarten or first or second grade. The child in the upper grade is instructed how to read to children. At specified times during the school week, buddies get together for storybook reading and discussions.

PARTNER READING. **Partner reading** involves peers reading together. This may simply mean that the children take turns reading to each other, or that they read sitting side by side. Teachers can structure partner reading similar to literature circles with topics posed for partners to discuss after reading to each other.

THINK, PAIR, SHARE. The **think, pair, share** strategy involves teacher-posed questions, which students are asked to think about before answering. Students are then paired with peers to discuss their answers to the questions. They then return to a larger group to share the answers they have discussed among themselves (Gambrell & Almasi, 1994).

MENTAL IMAGERY AND THINK-ALOUDS. **Mental imagery** and **think-alouds** involve children in several strategies, alone, together, and with and without the teacher. Mental imagery asks children to visualize what they see after they have been read to or have read a passage themselves. We ask children to "Make a picture in your minds to help you remember and understand what you read or what was read to you." After the mental imagery, we ask children to "think aloud" and talk about their images to peers or to the teacher. We also ask children to predict what will happen next in the story. We tell children to ask themselves questions about the story and to reread when they need to clarify ideas or remember forgotten details. We often ask them to personalize the text by asking them if they have ever been in a similar situation as the main character and what did they do. Visualizing ideas, and relating those visualizations orally, helps clarify information and increase understanding (Gambrell & Koskinen, 2002). See pages S-22 through S-27 in Strategies for the Classroom for literature circle forms and literature journals.

Fluency

A skill that needs more emphasis in literacy instruction is fluency. According to the National Reading Panel Report (2000), helping children to become fluent readers is crucial for literacy development. Fluency is a combination of accuracy, automaticity, and prosody when reading. More simply, a child who reads fluently is able to decode text automatically and accurately. He or she does not have to labor over every sound. In addition, the child reads with the appropriate pace and expression. This aspect of language is referred to as *prosody*. Prosody suggests that the student is comprehending text, since he or she is reading with appropriate expression and rate (Kuhn & Stahl, 2003). The ultimate goal for reading instruction is that students be fluent readers.

Research has shown that the following strategies are useful in helping to develop fluency:

ECHO READING. When we involve children in echo reading, the teacher or more able reader reads one line of text, and the child then reads the same line. The number of lines read is increased as the child's reading improves. When reading, be sure to model with good accuracy, pace, and expression and be sure the children are looking at the words and reading the words, instead of just listening and repeating. Ask them to look at and follow the print on the page with their finger. Try to echo read a few times a week.

CHORAL READING. When choral reading, the entire class or a small group of children reads an entire passage together along with the teacher. The teacher ensures that he or she provides a model for pace and expression. Short passages and poetry are good for choral reading. When choral reading, the child feels the correct pace and expression necessary in reading fluently. Try to choral read a few times a week.

PAIRED READING. Paired reading involves a more able reader in the same classroom or from another classroom as a model of fluent reading for less fluent readers. When they read together, the more able reader acts as the tutor. The children should read material that is easy for the child who is less fluent. The readers should take turns; for example, the tutor can read a page and then the less fluent reader repeats the same page. They can also alternate reading page by page. The tutor helps the less able reader with accuracy, rate, and expression.

READER'S THEATER. Reader's Theater is the oral reading of a short play. The children have assigned parts and practice the parts for the presentation. This provides a model of what good fluent reading sounds like. Invite parents to school to hear the class perform a Reader's Theater piece and take the opportunity to introduce them to the concept of fluency. Teach them some of the strategies by having them participate with you and their children. These activities are easy, they don't take much time, and they are effective. See Strategies for the Classroom for a Reader's Theater script and face puppet figures to use as well.

ANTIPHONAL READING. Antiphonal reading is a choral reading in which parts are taken by groups. Poetry, especially poetry with conversation, lends itself to antiphonal reading. Divide your class into two, three, or four groups. Assign each group a different part to read. Practice each part and then read together (Johns & Berglund, 2002).

TAPE-ASSISTED READING. Listening to fluent reading samples on audiotapes while following the written text is an excellent model for children. Tapes can be either purchased or made by teachers, parents, and other students who present fluent models for reading.

REPEATED READING. Read the same book three or four times a week. When a story is repeated and known, it offers the opportunity for fluent reading just because of its familiarity. When children can read a text fluently, they get a feeling for what it sounds like. On the first day, read the text to the children.

Cooperative strategies (when children read together as in partner reading and think, pair, share) enhance comprehension.

On the second day, do an echo reading. On the third day, do a choral reading, and on the fourth, a partner reading. Because you are supporting the reading of the text, use challenging books with rich vocabulary.

Children should participate in fluent reading activities daily. They are easy to do, they don't take much time, and they are fun. Fluency can be worked on with children from preschool through grade 3. Preschoolers can participate in all the fluency activities, but as listening activities rather than reading. They are exposed to the rhythm, pace, and expression involved in fluent reading. They can echo speak instead of echo read. The teacher recites, and they repeat. Choral speaking can be done with memorized pieces of poetry. They can be involved in paired listening with an older child, listening to excellent models of storybook reading on tape, and repeated readings.

EVALUATING FLUENCY. Listen to a child's reading of a passage that is at his or her instructional level. The child can read it to you, or you can tape-record the passage and evaluate it later.

1. Check the number of words read per minute in comparison with expectations at the child's grade level.
2. Do a running record or miscue analysis to determine types of errors being made that disrupt fluency.
3. Use an informal fluency tool that describes the reading, such as the following:
   - Reading is word by word.
   - There are long pauses between words.
   - Many words are missed.
   - The reading is in a monotone with little evidence of use of punctuation or sense that the text is understood.
   - The rate is slow and laborious.

The following are appropriate reading rates for first, second, and third graders:

The mean number of words read per minute for first graders in December is 54, in February is 66, and in May is 79.

The mean number of words typically read by second graders is 53 in the fall, 78 in the winter, and 94 in the spring.

For third graders, the mean number of words read in a minute is 79 in the fall, 93 in the winter, and 114 in the spring.

Have students evaluate their own fluency about four times a year. They can listen to the taped reading and evaluate the reading as follows:

Okay: Reading is word by word, slow, and choppy with some words missed and not enough expression to show an understanding of the text.

Good: The pace of the reading is slow but not choppy. Most words are pronounced properly with enough expression to show some understanding of the text.

Fluent: Reading flows smoothly at a good pace. All words are decoded properly and expression demonstrates an understanding of what is being read.

MATERIALS FOR FLUENCY TRAINING. Reading materials for reading instruction, such as basal selections or leveled books, are good for fluency training. They can be read using echo and choral reading as part of the instructional routine when new text is introduced. Books with conversation, such as fables, are good for Reader's Theater, since the characters provide parts for children to read. Short pieces of text and poems are best for choral, echo, repeated, and paired reading. A book of poems by Mary Ann Hoberman called *You Read to Me, I'll Read to You* (2001) has delightful poems with at least two characters talking to each other in every poem. The poems are in different colored print for the different characters. It is perfect for Reader's Theater, echo and choral reading, antiphonal reading, paired reading, and repeated reading. A portion of one poem entitled "I Like" is colored in purple for one character and pink for another, and blue represents reading all together.

I like soda.	*I like milk.*
I like satin.	*I like silk.*
I like puppies.	*I like kittens.*
I like gloves.	*I like mittens.*
I like to slide.	*I like to swing.*

We don't agree on anything.

Assessment of Concepts about Books and Comprehension of Text

The techniques described in this chapter are designed to develop concepts about books and comprehension of story through the use of expository and narrative text. The skills listed in the following checklist can be developed and assessed by a broad range of strategies used in various contexts. To determine how much children know about books, such as their front, back, top, and bottom; which part is print and which parts are pictures; how pages are turned; where reading begins; and what titles, authors, and illustrators are, one can observe regularly how youngsters handle books; hold one-to-one interviews with children; question and encourage response in whole-group, small-group, or individual interaction; or use any of the several other techniques described in this chapter. Children's responses can be literal, interpretive, or critical. They can reflect simple recall, detail, sequence, association, prediction, judgment, and evaluation. Children's comprehension of story can be demonstrated and evaluated through their story retelling, story rewriting, attempted reading of favorite storybooks, role-playing, picture sequencing, use of puppets or felt-boards to reenact stories, and questions and comments during storybook reading. When possible, keep periodic performance samples of activities, such as a story rewriting and audio- or videotapes of retellings.

Throughout this chapter, assessment tools for evaluating strategies have been provided. These materials should be placed in a child's portfolio to evaluate his or her concepts about books and comprehension of text. Baseline data from children should be collected early in the school year with assessment measures repeated every 6 to 8 weeks.

When Do I Teach Comprehension in the School Day? How Much Time Do I Spend Teaching Comprehension? How Do I Differentiate Instruction to Meet All Achievement Levels?

Comprehension skills are taught from PreK through college. There should be a daily lesson based on standards and your school curriculum dealing with comprehension for the entire class. Take advantage of teachable moments when they occur during the day to reinforce the skills being taught. Purposefully integrate whatever skill you are emphasizing into science, social studies, math, play, music, and art when it fits. For example, if you are reading a book about rain in a weather unit, let children talk about their own life experiences that were funny or scary or interesting about rain to make text to life connections since it is a skill you were emphasizing in the whole-class lesson earlier.

It is crucial to teach in small groups to determine individual needs. Small groups allow you to find out what students have learned and what they need to learn. Small groups allow you to differentiate instruction. When differentiating instruction you have similar goals for all children in the different groups,

Checklist   Assessing Concepts about Books and Comprehension of Text

Child's name _____   Date _____

Concepts about Books	Always	Sometimes	Never	Comments
Knows a book is for reading				
Can identify the front, back, top, and bottom of a book				
Can turn the pages properly				
Knows the difference between the print and the pictures				
Knows that pictures on a page are related to what the print says				
Knows where to begin reading				
Knows what a title is				
Knows what an author is				
Knows what an illustrator is				

Comprehension of Text				
Attempts to read storybooks resulting in well-formed stories				
Participates in story reading by narrating as the teacher reads				
Retells stories				
Includes narrative story structure elements in story retellings:				
Setting				
Theme				
Plot episodes				
Resolution				
Responds to text after reading or listening with literal comments or questions				
Can summarize what is read				
Responds to text after reading or listening with interpretive comments or questions				
Responds to text after reading or listening with critical comments or questions				
Generates questions that are literal, intentional, and critical				

Participates and Responds During

Use of graphics organizers

Partner reading

Buddy reading

Literature circles

Mental imagery

Think-alouds

Discussions

Think, pair, share

Vocabulary Development

Learns new words daily in oral language

Uses new words in writing

Recognizes and understands features of expository text:

    Table of Contents

    Glossary

    Index

    Diagrams, charts

    Expository structures such as description, sequence, comparison and contrast, cause and effect, exemplification

Teacher Comments:

but lessons are designed for the students needing more challenging or easier work. Small groups meet individual needs. Comprehension in small groups to differentiate instruction can be done easily, with more interpretive conversation for those who can engage in it and less with children who are struggling.

There is a formal time in the day to teach comprehension in whole group, there is informal teaching embedded into content-area teaching, and there is another formal time for teaching done in small-group instruction to differentiate instruction and meet individual needs. The length of lessons depends on the age of the child. They are shorter with younger children and longer with older ones. Comprehension skills should always be able to challenge the child and be easy enough for them to succeed. For example, children who need practice with connecting the text to real life will work on this in small groups, and those who are struggling with retelling will work on that. Small-group differentiated instruction is important for English language learners. In some cases differentiation of instruction may mean that a small group is so advanced or so challenged that they are working on different skills than the majority of the class.

An Idea from the Classroom

Visualizing

This third-grade activity helps develop the effective comprehension strategy of visualizing. Choose a passage or full text (either narrative or expository) that contains vivid descriptions. Have the students sit in a circle on the floor. Start the lesson by writing the word *visualizing* on chart paper or on the board. Ask students what they know about visualizing and write down their responses. Explain that visualizing involves making a picture in your mind that connects to the words you hear or read. Describe a situation in which you used visualization to understand and remember something, and ask the students to provide their own examples. Next, read the chosen text, but do not show any of the pictures. Ask the students to listen carefully and to make a picture in their minds that helps them remember the story. They can close their eyes if it helps them. After the read-aloud, have the students return to their seats and illustrate the "pictures they made in their minds," or their interpretation of the text. The students can then share their illustrations with their classmates and explain their individual interpretations. Lead a discussion of the similarities and differences in the students' various interpretations. Compare the students' illustrations with those in the actual text.

English Language Learners

Heather Casey, Third-Grade Teacher

An Idea from the Classroom

Graphic Organizers

This activity, appropriate for second or third grade, works with a variety of text structures, both narrative and expository. The creation of graphic organizers is useful for all students, especially ELL students, because it provides a concrete, visual, simplified representation of the text. I begin by reviewing different text structures and the appropriate graphic organizers that help us summarize and understand the text. I explain that the students will make their own creative graphic organizers to help them understand, organize, and remember what they read.

Students select a book from a set of texts with varied reading levels. If you are studying a particular theme, the books may all be related to that theme. The teacher helps each student select a text at the appropriate reading level. There should also be a variety of text structures, especially sequence, main idea–supporting details, cause–effect, and problem–solution, represented by the students' selections.

The students read their text and decide which structure it seems to best fit. Examples of multiple graphic organizers are written on the board. Once the students choose the structure, they summarize the text using an appropriate graphic organizer. For example, a student who reads a narrative text may do a story map with the setting, characters, problem, plot episodes, and resolution. A student who reads an expository text with a main idea–supporting details structure will put the main idea at the top of the paper, with all the important supporting details written in boxes underneath. As the students work, I circle around the room and meet briefly with each one to make sure they are on the right track. The students might want to write out a rough draft before they finalize their graphic organizer design. Students may choose to work in pairs, providing the added benefit of collaboration, or alone.

Julie Anastasi, Third-Grade Teacher

Activities and Questions

1. Answer the focus questions at the beginning of the chapter.

2. Ask a 2-, 4-, and 6-year-old to read a favorite storybook. Describe the reading behaviors they attempt. Are developmental differences evident among their performances?

3. Meet with one child between the ages of 3 and 8 years. Each time you meet, let the child practice retelling a story. Tape and transcribe each session. Using the forms provided in Figures 6.3 and 6.4, analyze the tapes for the elements of story structure, details, and sequence. Did the child improve from the first time to the third retelling?

4. Select a piece of informational text and narrative text. Prepare discussion questions that will involve children in literal, interpretive, and critical thinking. Then change these questions into activities (such as role-playing stories or felt stories) that enable children to demonstrate their comprehension of the story.

5. Prepare two different directed listening and thinking activities and directed reading and thinking activities, including pre- and postdiscussions. Select different objectives for each DLTA or DRTA. Use your plans with small groups of children.

6. Using another comprehension strategy, such as graphic organizers, create a lesson to teach the strategy with both expository and narrative texts.

7. Select a strategy to enhance fluency and create a lesson to teach the strategy. Identify selections you will use for reading.

8. Continue your portfolio assessment for the child you selected to assess for language development in Chapter 4. Observe the child using the assessment checklist in this chapter concerning the evaluation of concepts about books, comprehension of text, and other measures provided.

9. Continue the thematic unit that you began in Chapter 4. Select two objectives in the area of concepts about books, two in comprehension of text, and two for fluency. Describe the activities that will satisfy each objective using your theme.

10. **Strategies** Tear out the activities in Strategies for the Classroom for Chapter 6 and carry them out in your classroom and in classrooms where you are student teaching. Try the literature circles, the literacy journal, and the Reader's Theater script with props for the story. Use them over and over again. Use graphic organizers from this chapter and Chapter 7 on pages S-31 through S-36 to organize and recall information read.

11. The following passages describe a guided reading lesson in a small group taught by three different first-grade teachers. Each uses strategies to promote comprehension. While reading these passages, think about the following questions:

    a. Do the questions posed by the teachers foster factual or interpretive thought?

    b. Is there an emphasis on specifics or an understanding of issues raised?

    c. Is the plan flexible or predetermined?

    d. Is there time for problem solving in an interactive manner with peers?

    e. Is the atmosphere constricted, controlled, supportive, warm, or rewarding?

    f. Can children raise questions?

    g. Are students asked to predict and analyze?

    h. Is there an emphasis on higher-order thinking or literal levels of thought?

    Read Teachers A and B and then answer the questions. If you had to select just one of these teachers, which one would you choose to be and why? After answering the questions, read Teacher C and then go back and answer all the questions again.

    ### Teacher A

    Teacher A begins her lesson by introducing to the group the story they will be reading, Goldilocks and the Three Bears *(Daley & Russell, 1999). The teacher guides the children through a book walk, looking at the pictures and discussing what is happening on each page, to become familiar with the story in advance of reading. Before reading the story, she tells the children she will want them to remember the important details of the story, such as the main characters; where the story takes place; what happened first, second, and so on; and how the story ends. She writes this information on an experience chart.*

    The teacher asks the children to read the story orally together. At the end of the reading, she has the children do their own book walk to review the text. To check their comprehension, the teacher asks factual questions about the text, such as "Who are the main characters in the story?" and "What did Goldilocks do first when she got to the bears' house?" She asks similar questions all the way through the passage.

    After the discussion the children are given a worksheet to complete. The worksheet is designed to reinforce the details of the story and enhance vocabulary. It includes questions that require the children to circle the correct answer. When the children are finished with the worksheet, the lesson is over.

    ### Teacher B

    Teacher B begins her guided reading lesson by asking the students to share things they have done that they knew were wrong. After the children describe their experiences, the teacher asks why they did these things. She then introduces the children to the story they will read, Goldilocks and the Three Bears. *Before reading, she has the children take a book walk by looking at the pictures in the book. She asks the children to predict what they think is happening on the different pages and what the story is about. The teacher asks the class to think about who does bad things in the story while they read. The class then reads the story orally together from beginning to end. Afterward, the teacher asks questions designed to elicit information about the students' comprehension of the story theme by asking, "What are the main events in the story? Who does good things in the book and who does things that are wrong in the book and why? Why were they wrong or right? Was it okay for Goldilocks to go in the bears' house uninvited? Why yes or why no?" Children are asked to discuss favorite parts of the story and read these parts to the class. A discussion follows about the illustrations in the book. "Are the pictures important to the story? Do they help tell parts of the story?"*

The teacher offers the children three choices for extended activities they would like to do related to the story, for example, draw a picture about the story, act out the story, or make a felt story and tell it. The children decide to draw pictures about the story and make a class book. Different parts of the story are given to each child. They write what is happening on their page. The book is put together for the class to read.

Reminder: Answer the questions posed at the beginning of the case study activity and then read Teacher C.

Teacher C

Teacher C begins his guided reading lesson by asking the students if they have any special things at home that they like very much. He asks how they might feel if someone came and took or used their special things without asking and ruined them. He introduces the story Goldilocks and the Three Bears *and has the children do a book walk, looking for how the bears' special things were used and ruined. Before reading, Teacher C asks the children to think about what special things were used and ruined. They read the book aloud together. The teacher asks the class to discuss how they think the bears felt when they got home and found someone had been in their house. All suggestions are accepted as the teacher explains that there are no right or wrong answers.*

The teacher asks the children to create an entirely new story about Goldilocks. The teacher allows the children to decide which students they would like to work with. In pairs they brainstorm and create their new story with illustrations and text. When they complete their work, they share their stories.

Now answer the questions at the beginning of this case study activity for Teacher C and decide which teacher you would like to be now that you have read Teachers A, B, and C. Support your answer.

PEARSON
myeducationlab ᕽ

VIDEO EXERCISE

Now that you have the benefit of having read this chapter, return to the www.myeducationlab.com topic "Comprehension" and watch "Defining Reading Comprehension" and "Contextual Analysis and Story Dramatization" one more time. You may complete the questions that accompany them online and save or transmit your work to your professor, or complete the following questions, as required.

Defining Reading Comprehension (1:58 minutes)

1. How do readers derive meaning from print?
2. How does the teacher in this clip assess the students' comprehension of the reading? Choose a children's picture book and type the text into a word-processing program. Go through the story and, in bold type or a second column, add questions that you would ask students to determine if they comprehended the story. Include queries that get the students to think at a variety of levels, from basic knowledge to synthesizing the infor-

mation, such as where the authors may be going with the story or how the outcome of the story would change if one detail was changed. Summarize the activity here.

Contextual Analysis and Story Dramatization (3:36 minutes)

1. After watching this clip, how would you define contextual analysis? Name some ways that context provides clues to word meaning.
2. How does retelling the story with puppets contribute to the students' comprehension?
3. The second follow-up activity was a vocabulary lotto game, which the teacher stated had reading and writing components. What are some other writing activities that could be used as a follow-up to reading the story? What are the specific purposes these activities would serve?
4. Next step: What circumstance might hinder a reader from using context clues effectively? Is there something the teacher could do to overcome the barriers?

Focus Questions

■ Describe theories concerning how early writing is acquired.

■ Describe the categories that reflect children's early attempts at writing and compare them to the stages of spelling development.

■ What objectives are appropriate for promoting writing development in early childhood?

■ What strategies can be used for writing development from birth to 2 years of age?

■ What strategies can be used for developing writing in preschool through third grade?

■ What steps are involved in the process approach to writing?

■ What mechanical aspects of writing are important for children to learn?

■ How can writing be assessed?

■ What strategies will promote achievement in spelling?

■ **VOCABULARY:** writing workshop, narrative writing, descriptive writing, persuasive writing, expository writing, journal writing, poetry writing, functional writing, process approach to writing

■ **Strategies** Try the activities in Strategies for the Classroom for Chapter 7 in your classroom or student teaching. Reflect on how they worked.

PEARSON myeducationlab **VIDEO PREVIEW:** The Writing Process: Prewriting (3:44 minutes); Writing and Reading (3:47 minutes); Word Walls (1:42 minutes). Before reading this chapter, go to www.myeducationlab.com. Under the topic "Writing," access and watch the video "The Writing Process: Prewriting." Under the topic "Reading and Writing Connections," access and watch the video "Writing and Reading." Under the topic "Emergent Literacy," access and watch the video "Word Walls."

Writing, Spelling, and Literacy Development

Children want to write. They want to write the first day they attend school. This is no accident. Before they went to school they marked up walls, pavements, newspapers with crayons, chalk, pens or pencils, anything that makes a mark. The child's marks say, "I am."

—Donald Graves
Writing Teachers and Children at Work, 1983

At the beginning of an interactive writing session, Mrs. Brice read the story *I Know an Old Lady*. It is a nonsense tale that is read and also sung. The story is composed of rhymes, and each segment is repeated to make it predictable. The purpose of the lesson is to have children engage open-ended, problem-solving thinking, to develop vocabulary, and to use rhyme. A portion of the story follows:

> I know an old lady who swallowed a fly,
> I don't know why she swallowed a fly, perhaps she'll die.
> I know an old lady who swallowed a spider
> That wiggled and jiggled and tickled inside her,
> She swallowed the spider to catch the fly,
> I don't know why she swallowed the fly, perhaps she'll die.
> I know an old lady who swallowed a bird,
> How absurd to swallow a bird
> (the refrain is repeated)
> I know an old lady who swallowed a cat,
> Now fancy that she swallowed a cat
> (the refrain is repeated)
> I know an old lady who swallowed a dog,
> What a hog to swallow a dog
> (the refrain is repeated and additional verses are chanted).

After the story, Mrs. Brice asked her second-grade children to think of other things the old lady might swallow and what would she do or say as a result.

Tasha said, "I got one, I know an old lady who swallowed a snake, ummm, ummm, she got a big ache when she swallowed the snake." Mrs. Brice suggested she come up to the flip chart to write her idea down on the chart paper. After she wrote it Jason said, "I think it might sound better if we said what a mistake to swallow a snake." Mrs. Brice asked the class which idea they thought was best for the poem. They all agreed that they liked Jason's idea. The teacher gave Tasha the white correction tape to put over the sentence so she could write it again the way the class wanted it.

Christopher raised his hand and said, "I know an old lady who swallowed a frog, what a hog to swallow a frog." Molly said, "We can't do that, because in the real story when she swallows a dog, they say what a hog to swallow a dog." Christopher thought and said, "I know—I know an old lady who swallowed a frog, she started to jog when she swallowed a frog." "That's great," said Molly. Mrs. Brice asked Christopher to come up and write his rhyme on the chart paper.

Many of the children had ideas that were written down. Several of the ideas were improved by the group. Numerous new words popped up, and there were discussions about how to spell them and their meanings. The class agreed on 10 lines to the poem they liked for their story. Each child had paper on a clipboard to write on that they used during interactive writing. They wrote the poem on their paper as it was being created. When the chart was complete, the class chanted the poem together. When they were done, Michael said, "You know, I think what we wrote is better than the original one." Everyone nodded and agreed.

Theory and Research about Writing Development

Relationships between Reading and Writing

The purposes for reading and writing are similar. We read and write to construct meaning. Readers deal with meaning by responding to what has been read. Writers deal with meaning by constructing text (Bromley, 2003). When reading and writing, children engage in similar activities. Readers and writers

- organize ideas.
- generate ideas.
- monitor their thoughts.
- problem solve.
- revise how to think about the ideas.

Children learn about reading and writing in similar ways. They experiment and pretend play at reading and writing and engage in trial and error as they practice literacy skills they have learned. Children are inventive when learning to read and write—they decorate letters, symbols, and words; they mix drawing and writing; and they invent messages in various forms and shapes (see Figure 7.1). Similarly, when they read, they invent what they think the text may say by reading the pictures, they invent the voices of the characters in the books, and they predict outcomes in stories and create their own endings. We teach children

Figure 7.1

In this writing sample, Max, age 5, uses his writing almost as a decoration for the drawing.

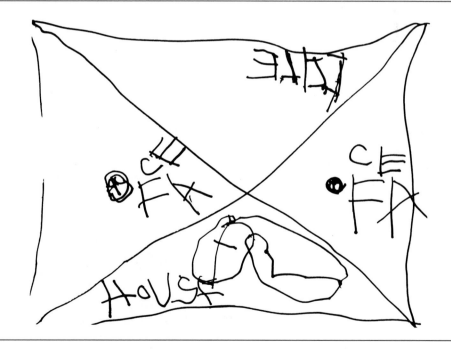

phonics skills so they can decode text independently. When children write, they need to use the same phonic skills to create their writing pieces. It is important to realize how similar reading and writing are and to engage children in both daily. When children read, they are strengthening writing skills, and when children write, they are strengthening reading skills.

How Early Writing Is Acquired

Children's early literacy experiences are embedded in the familiar situations and real-life experiences of family and community (Ritchie, James-Szanton, & Howes, 2003). In fact, we have discovered that, because these literacy events are so natural, many parents do not know about their children's writing and reading experiences until they are pointed out to them (Schickedanz & Casbergue, 2004; Soderman & Farrell, 2008; Taylor, 1983). Many things family members do on a regular basis involve literacy. They write each other notes, they make to-do lists, they send greeting cards, and they write directions.

Early writing development is characterized by children's moving from playfully making marks on paper, to communicating messages on paper, to creating texts. Children are at first unconcerned about the products of their "writing"; they lose interest in them almost immediately. However, once they begin to understand that the marks made can be meaningful and fun to produce, they are determined to learn how to write (Tompkins, 2000).

Children learn the uses of written language before they learn the forms (Bromley, 2007; Gundlach, McLane, Scott, & McNamee, 1985). In observing children scribbling and inventing primitive "texts," researchers have noted that children seem to know what writing is *for* before they know much about how to write in correct forms. The letters to friends or relatives, the greeting cards, and the signs they produce are not conventional forms of writing. Yet the children seem impelled by an understanding of the function of written texts (see Figure 7.2).

Figure 7.2

Jay, age 5, attempts functional writing in a letter to his friend, Peter.

Children's writing develops through constant invention and reinvention of the forms of written language (Calkins, 1994; Dyson, 1986; Graves, 1994; Spandel, 2008). Children invent ways of making letters, words, and texts, moving from primitive forms to closer approximations of conventional forms (Hansen, 1987; Jalongo, 2007). Parents and teachers of preschool children need to show an interest in children's early writing and accept and support their youngsters' production of the primitive forms. Children invent writing forms from their observations of environmental print and their observing, modeling, and interacting with more literate individuals who write in their presence.

Children learn about writing through explicit instruction from teachers and by observing others more skilled than themselve*s***.** Children need to be guided and taught about writing by supportive adults, and they need to observe adults participating in writing. People who are more proficient writers play an important modeling role in children's writing development (Jalongo, 2007; Temple, Nathan, Burris, & Temple, 1988).

Children need to write independently. When they write independently, they are involved in practicing aspects of writing—letter formation and differentiation, similarities or differences between drawing and writing, spelling, punctuation, and so forth. When children engage in independent writing, they become more conscious of what they know (see Figures 7.3 and 7.4).

Children need to write in social settings. When children write with each other, with a teacher, or with a more literate other, they talk about what they write, they share each others' writing, and they imitate the more literate other. Social interaction is crucial to learning to write.

Figure 7.3

Jennifer, age $3\frac{1}{2}$, practices writing through the repetition of similar letter patterns from left to right across the page.

Figure 7.4

Three-year-old Robert separates his writing from his drawing by enclosing each in a circle during self-initiated practice.

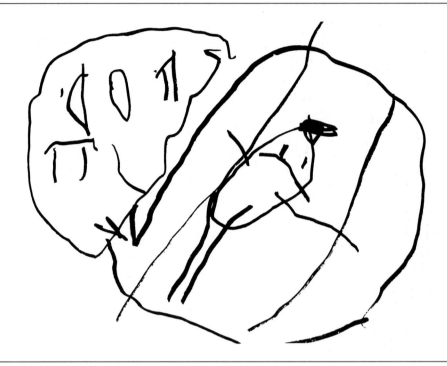

Writing development is part of a child's journey to literacy development. Literacy learning starts with drawing, then writing, and next reading (Vygotsky, 1978). Children's main resource for literacy learning is their knowledge of ways to symbolize experience and to communicate through those symbols. This theoretical framework can be summarized as follows:

1. Literacy development encompasses the development of reading, writing, listening, speaking, and viewing.
2. Literacy development involves learning to use the symbols involved in reading, writing, listening, speaking, and viewing.
3. The symbols in literacy development also include the development of social and cultural meanings.

For most children, the process for writing development occurs as a continuum. Under normal circumstances, children's early literacy development begins with learning to communicate, first nonverbally, then by talking, next with symbolic play, and finally by drawing. Each new phase is rooted in earlier phases and forms a new network of communication resources.

Literacy learning begins to develop in the interactions of family and community life. In the process, children move from playing with written language to using it to communicate. They invent and reinvent forms. When children first begin making marks on paper, most do so with no knowledge of the alphabetic nature of the written language's symbol system. Shortly thereafter, they view letters as referring to actual people or things. It is quite a bit later when children realize that writing represents language (Spandel, 2001).

The Development of Writing Ability

Children learn a lot about literacy through play, especially in literate societies where they imitate adult models by making their own pretend play marks on paper. Soon the marks become written messages from which children achieve a sense of identity in their own eyes and in the eyes of others. The continuum from playing with drawing and writing, to communicating through written messages, to writing narrative and expository text reflects the basic theories of early literacy development (Dyson, 1993; Halliday, 1975; Schickedanz & Casbergue, 2004; Turbill & Bean, 2006).

Researchers have recorded varied descriptions of the developmental stages of writing in early childhood (Dyson, 1985; Soderman & Farrell, 2008; Sulzby, 1986b; Teale, 1986; Tompkins, 2007). Most agree, though, that if there are stages, they are not well defined or necessarily sequential. Dyson (1986) describes children's writing development as having two broad phases. From birth to about age 3, children begin to explore the form of writing by scribbling. Then, as children progress from age 3 to 6, their "controlled scribbling gradually develops into recognizable objects that they name, and similarly, the scribbling gradually acquires the characteristics of print, including linearity, horizontal orientation, and the arrangement of letterlike forms" (p. 2).

Sulzby (1985) identified six broad categories of writing in kindergarten children, cautioning that these should not be considered a reflection of developmental ordering. They do, however, describe children's early attempts at writing.

1. ***Writing via Drawing.*** The child will use drawing to stand for writing. The child is working out the relationship between drawing and writing, not confusing the two. The child sees drawing–writing as communication of a specific and purposeful message. Children who participate in writing via drawing will read their drawings as if there is writing on them (Figure 7.5).

Figure 7.5

Writing via drawing: When asked to write something, James (age 2¹/₂) drew a picture and included a *J* for James.

Figure 7.6

Writing via scribbling: When asked to write, Katie (age 3) scribbled randomly. She eventually progressed to a left to right scribble and then purposeful marks that could be periods to end the sentence.

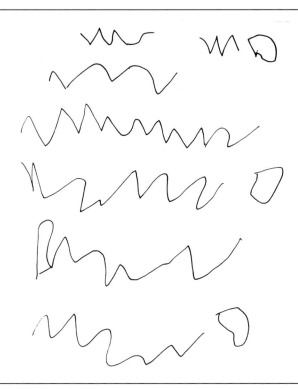

2. ***Writing via Scribbling.*** The child scribbles but intends it as writing. Often the child appears to be writing and scribbles from left to right. The child moves the pencil as an adult does, and the pencil makes writing-like sounds. The scribble resembles writing (Figure 7.6).

3. ***Writing via Making Letterlike Forms.*** At a glance, shapes in the child's writing resemble letters. However, close observation reveals that they only look like letters. They are not just poorly formed letters, though; they are creations (Figure 7.7).

Figure 7.7

Writing via making letter-like forms: Olivia (age 4) wrote letterlike forms from left to right.

Figure 7.8

Writing via reproducing well-learned units or letter strings: Written by Brian (age 4), these letters go from left to right across the page.

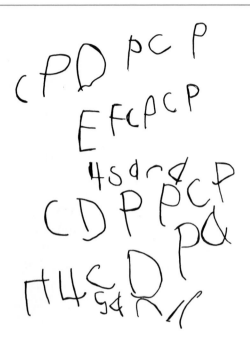

4. ***Writing via Reproducing Well-Learned Units or Letter Strings.*** The child uses letter sequences learned from such sources as his or her own name. The child sometimes changes the order of the letters, writing the same ones many different ways, or reproduces letters in long strings or in random order (Figure 7.8).

5. ***Writing via Invented Spelling.*** Children use many varieties and levels of **invented spelling.** Children create their own spelling for words when they do not know the conventional spellings. When using invented spelling, one letter may represent an entire word, and words sometimes overlap and are not properly spaced. As the child's writing matures, the words look more like conventional writing, with perhaps only one letter invented or left out.

6. ***Writing via Conventional Spelling.*** The child's writing resembles adult writing (Figure 7.9).

"Good Morning Red Group. Today is Wednesday we will Miss our mommy when (we) come at school." Iris, 5 years, 1 month.

Figure 7.9

Conventional spelling:
This story was written by
Kevin, who was in third
grade.

Little Red Riding hood

Once upon a time there
was a little girl named
little red riding hood.
No one knew why she always
walked, she should be riding
something. The next morning
Mrs. Shobert asked little Red
riding hood why are you always
walking? Then she walked
away and she was thinking
hmm that gave her an idea
to buy something. She went to
a toyota deler, She didn't like
anything. Then she went to
a bike place and said, "I
think I like that one." Now
Red riding hood rides.

This general description of early writing is helpful for teachers and parents when they are observing and describing children's writing. It should be noted, however, that these categories are not necessarily developmental or sequentially invariant.

Objectives for Promoting Writing Development

Thinking about writing development changed enormously in the 1970s. We always encouraged children to use crayons and paper to develop motor coordination in preparation for writing, but we never thought of writing to convey meaning as being an integral part of an early literacy program for children as young as age 2. We now integrate strategies for writing into the daily routines of babies, toddlers, preschoolers, kindergartners, and first graders. We consider even the youngest child's marks on paper as early attempts at writing, rather than as random marks. This perception is necessary in programs for early literacy development.

Generally, the best way to assist young children in language and literacy development is to provide instruction and create situations that are meaningful. This principle applies equally in the home, child-care center, preschool, kindergarten, and first, second, or third grade. The following objectives for promoting writing development are posed from the perspective that children learn language, including writing and reading, by using it purposefully in many situations (for example, in playing or communicating).

Objectives for Writing Development

1. Children will be provided with an environment in which they are regularly exposed to many kinds of print.
2. Children will experience print as a source of pleasure and enjoyment.
3. Children will regularly observe adults writing for work and for leisure.
4. Children will be given opportunities and materials for writing.
5. Children will be assisted in deciding what to write, but allowed to make the decisions.
6. Children's attempts at writing, whatever the form, will be responded to as meaningful communication (e.g., scribble writing, letterlike forms, random letters, invented spelling).
7. Children will be instructed in and encouraged to use writing for a wide range of purposes, such as creating stories, expository text, persuasive writing, descriptive writing, journal writing, and functional writing, such as lists, letters, signs, and announcements.
8. Children will be taught about and read narrative and expository text in a variety of structures to serve as models for their writing.
9. The use of writing will be integrated throughout the curriculum.
10. Children will experience constructivist activities prepared for them when writing in school and explicit instruction on skills in writing.
11. Teachers will evaluate student work and students will participate in evaluating their own work.
12. Children will be taught manuscript and cursive writing.
13. Teachers will take the opportunity through children's writing to point out sound–symbol correspondences as the spoken word is transformed into the written.
14. Children will be exposed to and taught the use of some aspects of punctuation: periods, commas, and quotation marks.
15. Children's invented spelling will be accepted as working toward conventional writing.
16. Teachers will provide instruction in spelling.

Standards for Writing in Early Childhood

Policy makers, educators, and others are concerned about expectations for children to accomplish specific goals at specific grade levels. The International Reading Association and National Council of Teachers of English's *Standards for the English Language Arts* (1996) outline the following general standards for writing that are not grade-level specific:

> Students employ a wide range of strategies as they write and use different writing process elements appropriately to communicate with different audiences for a variety of purposes.

> Students apply knowledge of language structure and language conventions (e.g., conventions, style, vocabulary) to communicate effectively with a variety of audiences and for different purposes. (p. 3)

States and national organizations have standards for writing development as they do for reading. Standards for writing in the primary grades include *Writing Habits and Processes.* This standard provides for children's exploration and experimentation. It suggests that students write daily in kindergarten through grade 3 to develop the desire and need to write regularly. Children should be given the opportunity to select their own topics and experiment with writing. Another standard involves *Writing, Purposes and Resulting Genres.* It notes purposes for young children's writing, such as telling stories through narrative writing, informing others with information reports or expository text, using functional writing, and responding to literature. A third standard addresses *Language Use and Conventions.* It concerns style of writing and syntax, vocabulary and word choice, spelling, punctuation, capitalization, and other conventions. (*Primary Literacy Standards for Kindergarten through Third Grade,* 1999, prepared by the National Center on Education and the Economy and the Learning Research and Development Center at the University of Pittsburgh.)

These standards suggest some explicit and systematic instruction for the specific outcomes desired. The following section outlines strategies that can be used to accomplish these outcomes.

The Writing Center

Homes, child-care centers, and preschools should provide environments for writing—comfortable spots with rugs and child-size tables and chairs—and storage for writing materials. The latter should include felt-tip markers, pencils, crayons, and chalk. There should be ample supplies and varied sizes of large unlined paper (newsprint works well) and a chalkboard. Materials should be stored consistently in the place provided for writing so that the child can learn how to select materials and put them away independently.

The literacy area in the classroom should also include a place designated for writing. It should be easily accessible, attractive, and inviting. This area can be a part of the library corner. It should be furnished with a table and chairs, plus a rug for youngsters who want to stretch out and write on the floor. Writing implements should include plenty of colored felt-tip markers, large and small crayons, large and small pencils (both regular and colored), and chalk and a chalkboard. Various types of paper should be available, lined and unlined, plain white or newsprint, ranging from 8 × 11 inches to 24 × 36 inches.

Index cards for recording Very Own Words should be stored in the writing area, as should the children's collections of Very Own Words. Each child should have a writing folder to collect samples of his or her written work during the school year. Several computers for word processing are also necessary. Materials for making books should be available, including colored construction paper for covers, plain white paper for inside pages, a stapler, and scissors. Teachers can prepare blank books, keyed to special occasions, for children to use. For example, a blank book shaped like a snowman, made of construction paper with five or six sheets of plain white paper stapled inside, provides inviting space where children can write a story, poem, experience, or greeting to a family member about winter. (See Figures 7.10, 7.11, 7.12 on preparing blank books.) Stock *bare books* (books with hard covers but no print inside) for special projects and blue books used for examinations are perfect for young chil-

Figure 7.10

Stapled book. Cut colored construction paper and white writing paper into a desired shape. Staple at the side.

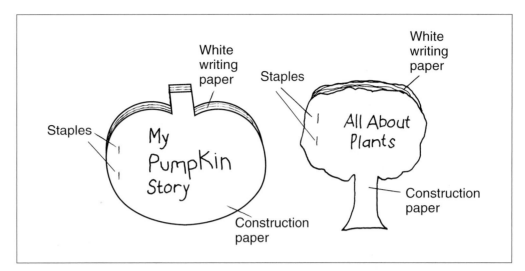

dren's writing. They can be purchased inexpensively from school supply companies. They come with 12 or 16 pages, which is usually just right for an original story by a young child. Try to purchase blue books with the name of a university or college that is close to your school or select a university well known to your students. It makes children feel special about writing in them. Keep a supply of interesting pictures, posters, magazines, and newspapers; these can stimulate, decorate, or illustrate children's writing.

An alphabet chart in easy view helps children identify and shape letters they may need while writing. Plastic, magnetic, wooden, and felt letters should be among the language arts manipulatives. These help develop eye–hand coordination and aid in letter recognition and formation. Small white slates are good for practicing new words learned and writing sentences that feature these words. A bulletin board should be available for children to display their own writing, with a space for posting notices or sending and receiving private messages. "Mailboxes" for youngsters' incoming and outgoing "mail" can be placed in the writing center. The mailboxes for a pen pal program are discussed later in the functional writing section. The writing center should be labeled with a sign that says "Author's Spot" or with a name selected by the children.

Basic implements and supplies for writing should be stocked in every other learning center in the room as well. The accessibility of these materials will encourage writing (Bromley, 2003). A child might want to record the outside temperature on a chart in the science center, protect a construction of blocks with a "Do Not Touch" sign, or copy a Very Own Word in the social studies or science area. A group might decide to turn the dramatic-play corner into a dentist's office, including in it an appointment book for recording dates, times, and patients' names; appointment cards; patients' records; and a prescription pad for medication.

The activities described for the writing center should be introduced to the entire group. They are used during writing workshop and at center time for independent writing. Since the activities are done independently, the teacher has modeled for the children how to use the materials. With this preparation, students will participate in the writing activities as a means of communication quite naturally.

Figure 7.11

Folded, stitched, and glued book

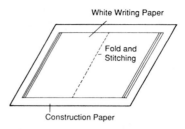

White Writing Paper

Fold and Stitching

Construction Paper

a. Sew a running stitch down the center of eight to ten sheets of eight-and-a-half-by-eleven plain white writing paper backed with a piece of nine-by-twelve colored construction paper.

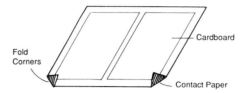

Cardboard

Fold Corners

Contact Paper

b. Place an eleven-by-fourteen piece of contact paper or wallpaper face down. Paste two pieces of six-by-nine oaktag or cardboard on the peeled contact paper a quarter inch apart, leaving about a one-inch border. Fold each corner of the contact paper onto the oaktag to form a triangle (glue if using wallpaper).

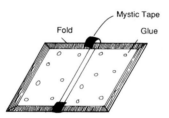

Mystic Tape

Fold   Glue

c. Fold the edges of the contact paper onto the oaktag (paste down if using wallpaper). Place a twelve-inch piece of Mystic Tape down the center of the contact paper and over its edges. Put glue on the two exposed pieces of oaktag and on the quarter-inch space between them.

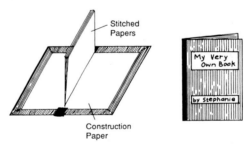

Stitched Papers

My Very Own Book

by Stephanie

Construction Paper

d. Place the folded and stitched edge of the construction paper and plain white paper in the quarter-inch glued space. Paste the construction paper onto the oaktag and over the contact-paper border to make the inside covers.

Figure 7.12

Sewn book. Punch holes into oak tag and white writing paper. Sew together with yarn.

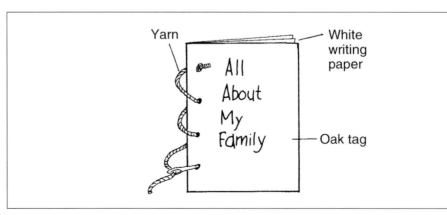

Yarn

All About My Family

White writing paper

Oak tag

Caitlin works on her page for the class book during writing centers.

English Language Learners

Strategies for Writing Development from Birth to Age 2

Earlier chapters have described strategies that parents can use to help children with oral language development and early reading. Some of these strategies can be applied directly to children's early writing development; others can be adapted. Some strategies are helpful specifically with writing development. It is crucial to remember, though, that speaking, reading, and writing are dynamically linked in children's development. When we help children with oral language, we also contribute indirectly to their literacy development by increasing their language experience. Similarly, reading development contributes to speaking and writing, and writing to speaking and reading. This understanding forms the basis for the integrated language arts approach.

I've watched my grandson begin his adventure into the world of literacy. We have large newsprint in the house and fat crayons for him to use that are always placed in the same spot. At 15 months he began to make marks on the paper. When he began scribbling, his productions sprawled all over the page. At 20 months we saw more controlled sprawls, dots, and wavy lines. He watched his parents writing often, and by 23 months his writing began to resemble cursive writing. The length of time he was able to engage in writing increased as he reached age 2. Now he could spend 10 minutes writing. He also began to babble in his own way while he wrote as if he was telling a story about what he was writing. Next he began to attempt to write letters to familiar words such as the M in McDonald's or in Mommy. It is important to observe the literacy development of a child so we can remember milestones for future reference. This attention is important for parents, child-care providers, and preschool teachers to adopt.

If we interact with children in this way, especially from their second year on, we are ready to support them when, as a part of their scribble writing, they try to write one or more of these environmentally learned letters. In fact, some children may make their first such attempts between 18 and 24 months, though most children will not begin until they are age 2 or 3.

Some children may make their first attempts at scribble writing between 18 and 24 months, though most children will not begin until they are age 2 or 3.

We can assist children in their first attempts to make marks on paper. Often, when children begin scribbling (some at 18 months), they bang on the paper with their writing implements. As they become more familiar with writing, they will begin using smoother, more deliberate and coordinated movements to make their marks. When children are in their first, primitive stages of scribbling, we can show them how to hold markers or crayons. We can guide their hands to paper, not making marks for them but helping them understand that the paper is the place for writing.

Our responses to children's early scribbling are important. It is better not to urge children to write particular things. They should make marks spontaneously and decide for themselves when these marks are intended to represent something. It is important not to press them to tell us what their marks mean or represent. It is better to say, "I like that," than to ask, "What is it?" "Can you write some more?" is also a helpful response, but do not insist if the child says no. Expressing genuine pleasure in children's early markings, whether they resemble writing or not, and seeing them as an important step in a long developmental process are positive responses that will encourage children to continue. By continuing their "writing," they will incorporate in it what they are learning about print from daily literacy events.

Beyond responding supportively to children, we can model writing for them. We can let them see us writing letters, lists, and notes and filling out forms, and we can interact with them about what we are doing. For example: "I'm writing a letter to invite your parents to school. Do you have ideas of what I should say? Do you want to write something on the paper to them?" When writing, invite the youngsters to sit with you, watch you, ask questions, and try their own hand at writing. This gives children opportunities to see how we go about writing and to begin to understand that the marks we make convey meaning.

An important way that we can support children's writing development is to provide experiences with environmental print, including print they see on television, on food cans and boxes, on signs, in stores, and on the computer. We need to talk with children about their experiences with environmental print by commenting, asking questions, and encouraging them to identify and remember signs, letters, and bits of print out of their normal contexts (for instance, an *M* used somewhere other than in a McDonald's sign).

Junk mail is a form of environmental print that can arouse interest in writing. Children enjoy writing or making marks on flyers, brochures, ads, announcements, and forms. They will write over the print and in the blank spaces. Apparently, the look and arrangement of the print gives them the model and inspiration to make their own marks.

Repeating rhymes and singing songs also can contribute to children's early writing. So can using hand puppets and playing with toys and games, such as puzzles that can be taken apart and put back together. Manipulative toys that require dexterity help with the motor development needed to shape letters. Playing with clay or play dough, finger painting, using chalkboards, and painting on easels help build motor coordination as well. Of course, reading to children not only develops oral language and promotes early reading attempts, as discussed earlier, but it also can motivate children to emulate the writing or to make their own books, no matter how crude the first attempts. Parents and caregivers in child-care centers can display children's early writings on walls, doors, and appliances, to be enjoyed and not judged or corrected.

Writing in Early Childhood Classrooms

PreK and Kindergarten

Parents and teachers can expect to see rapid development in writing in children from ages 2 to 8. As we have seen, it is during this period that most children move from scribbling to producing random letters, to writing letters, to writing words with invented spellings, to beginning to use conventional writing. They will begin to space properly between words and use some marks of punctuation. They tend to write longer pieces, and their productions often represent wider ranges of functions and forms. This is a time when children show intense bursts of writing activity, perhaps alternating these with intense bursts of reading activity. It is important, therefore, that teachers have a sense of children's writing needs and interests at this time and know how to interact with them to support their efforts, learning, and growth.

Like younger children, preschoolers and kindergarteners take more pleasure in the *process* of writing than in its *products*. The act of writing is their center of interest, although they gradually develop concern for the products. When they play waiter or waitress, for example, and take an "order," they may be concerned that others can "read" it. The same thing might happen with notes or greeting cards sent to relatives or friends. Children begin to evidence concern that recipients are able to read their messages—perhaps so they can write back. Children who have had little experience pretending to write might be reluctant to make marks on paper even by kindergarten age, possibly because they have become aware that their marks are not conventional writing and thus might not be accepted. It is important to let them know that writing that is not conventional will be accepted. Some children may request conventional spellings and will not write unless they know it is correct. They should be given the help they request.

We must realize that what young children write about and how they approach writing is more important initially than their mechanics of writing (spelling, handwriting, punctuation, and spacing). Learning to write involves learning to compose texts that convey meaning. As children gain experience with writing, they will learn the skills and mechanics of writing through practice and instruction.

When children are free to write in unconventional ways, such as using invented spellings as pictured earlier, they are enhancing phonemic awareness and eventually knowledge of phonics. When children write, they have to transform the spoken word into written language. This process fosters understanding of the structure of spoken language and how it is related to written language. The more children write, the better they become at segmenting sounds and blending them into words, which develops not only their ability to write, but also their ability to read independently.

Young children choose to write if a situation has meaning for them. If we impose on them our selection of what they should write about all the time, we are not likely to see positive results. With these basic ideas in mind, we can create strategies and appropriate environments for helping children write. One of these strategies for young children is Taking Dictation.

English Language Learners

TAKING DICTATION.   Many children in pre-K and kindergarten have a lot to say, and because they cannot write well enough yet, we often take dictation. Taking dictation from children was a common language-experience-approach strategy that was used before we realized that young children could and should write in their own unconventional way. Taking dictation, however, does play an important role in writing development. We model reading for children by reading to them before they read conventionally; we should also model writing for them by taking dictation some of the time. When teachers take dictation, children have the opportunity to grow more in their writing ability as they watch an adult model. The following ideas are important when teachers take dictation:

1. Begin with discussion to encourage ideas.
2. Write exactly what the child says, using standard spelling.
3. Make sure the child can see you write.
4. Write legibly.
5. Read the dictation back to the child when finished, tracking the print as you read it.
6. Encourage children to read the dictation by themselves, to another child, or to an adult.

Moving into Grades 1 through 3

The strategies we have discussed thus far are mostly for pre-K and kindergarten, but should be used in the first through third grades as well. Teachers often want to know how children move from one level of writing ability to another or from unconventional writing to conventional. It is somewhat individual for every child, but trends do emerge. First and foremost, we want to provide an atmosphere in which children will write. Children who are reluctant to write, because they think they cannot, can be shown work done by others of their own age so that they see that unconventional writing is acceptable. We foster acceptance so that children will attempt writing. As youngsters learn more about phoneme–grapheme correspondence, they begin to realize that their invented spelling is not conventional spelling. At this point, they begin to ask for correct spelling as they move into the conventional stage of writing. It may seem as if they are taking a step backward, because suddenly they will not be writing as much or as spontaneously as they did in the past. Their concern for writing correctly has this effect on their performance. This will last for a short time as their spelling vocabulary increases, they learn to use the dictionary, and they seek help from friends and the teacher. Conventional writing is a gradual process in which a child often goes back and forth from conventional to unconventional writing until sufficient proficiency is gained for the writing to be considered completely conventional.

Although children in grades 1 through 3 need experiences in writing similar to those in pre-K and kindergarten, they also need instruction that is more explicit and goal oriented. A definition of writing that will help us with teaching writing in these grades is this: Writing is formulating an idea and composing it into text so it has meaning and purpose, in a context that can be easily understood by others when read. Writing is a social activity since it is created for others to read. The following list will help teachers understand what they need to teach to help children become good writers. It will also help children understand what they need to learn.

- Good writers write about things they know about.
- Good writers write about what they are interested in.
- Good writers think about who they are writing for.
- Good writers write with a specific purpose in mind.
- Good writers write fewer rather than more words.
- Good writers use interesting and varied vocabulary and sentence structures.
- Good writers write paragraphs that flow from one to the next.
- Good writers write pieces that have a logical sequence of events.
- Good writers have a beginning, a middle, and an end to their work.
- Good writers make the reader believe what they have written.
- Good writing has been revised.
- Good writing has been edited.
- Good writing work includes good spelling, punctuation, grammar, and handwriting.

Through multiple strategies and experiences that are explicitly taught, modeled, and provided by the teacher, including guided writing, shared writing, interactive writing, independent writing, and so on, children will become the good writers described above. These strategies are introduced in the following sections.

The Writing Workshop

A **writing workshop** is a period of time set aside for writing instruction of any kind, such as independent writing, interactive writing, or journal writing. During writing workshop, the teacher will provide a mini-lesson, a time for writing, and a time that writing is shared. At least 30 minutes a day should be allocated for writing workshop. As children get older they should spend more time writing. In the writing workshop, a purpose for the workshop is set, there is a mini-lesson, time to write, and time to share writing. The writing may be revisited at a later date.

PURPOSE.   In writing workshop there needs to be an established purpose and audience for the writing that will be done. It should be meaningful and relevant for the children.

MINI-LESSON.   The teacher carries out a lesson to teach a particular type of writing skill, such as letter writing or writing expository text. The lesson lasts from 5 to 10 minutes. It prepares the children to practice writing with the new skill. The lesson could include a shared interactive writing experience with the teacher and children as the skills for the writing are modeled by the teacher. The mini-lesson can also be referred to as guided writing, since it is an explicit lesson about a specific writing skill. These lessons can be in a whole-class setting or in a small group. When done in the whole group, it is a skill in the curriculum to be taught to all children at their grade level. When guided writing mini-lessons are done in small groups, it is a writing skill directed toward the specific needs of a few children.

WRITING TIME.   The teacher gives the children the responsibility for writing after the group lesson. They can work with a few children or a partner, discussing what they think they will write or actually writing together. While the children are writing, the teacher offers informal guidance and will meet with children or pairs of children for a **conference** about the writing they are doing to help with the new skill learned. When working with a peer, children are encouraged to conference with each other about their work. Remember that time is needed for writing.

SHARED WRITING.   Writing workshop ends with children completing a written product, sharing their finished work with a partner or small group, or sharing a piece of writing with the class. With the sharing comes constructive comments such as "I really like the way you described that horse in your story. I could actually picture him in my mind." The comments should relate to the skill that was emphasized in the mini-lesson. In this case it was descriptive language.

REVISIT.   Sometimes the piece of writing is not finished in the writing workshop and the children go back in another session to revisit what they have written. Some writing workshops produce finished work, some do not. (Routman, 2005).

Teachers may hold writing workshops with small groups of children based on a need for the development of different writing skills. This type of arrangement is similar to the guided reading lessons described in Chapter 9. All the strategies that follow could be taught first in what would be called a writing workshop mini-lesson or guided writing lesson.

The Process Approach to Writing in Early Childhood

The **process approach** makes children realize that writing involves thinking, organizing, and rewriting before a piece is complete. They become aware that a first writing rarely constitutes a finished product. Typical steps in this approach include prewriting, drafting, conferencing, revising, and editing (Calkins, 1986; Fletcher & Portalupi, 2001; Tompkins, 2007; Turbill & Bean, 2006).

PREWRITING.   Probably the most important part of the writing process, prewriting helps students select a topic to write about, to figure out the purpose of a piece, and to decide for whom the piece is being written. In prewriting activities a decision can be made about the form that the writing will take, such as a poem, letter, or narrative. Prewriting also can involve getting the information needed to write and organizing the writing (Tompkins, 2003). Prewriting activities could involve brainstorming related to the topic, webbing ideas, and making outlines. Prewriting can take place with the entire class, a friend, the teacher, or alone.

DRAFTING.   In this second part in the process, the author makes a first attempt at writing the piece by getting the words down on paper. The lists prepared in the prewriting phase are used as a guide. During drafting, getting the ideas written is more important than spelling, punctuation, correct grammar, and so on. Rough drafts can be done on the computer or by hand. When writing by hand, write on every other line of the paper so there is space for editing.

CONFERENCING.   Conferencing can be done with a teacher or a friend. This is a time to reflect on what has been written to see whether changes are needed. The discussion about changes has mostly to do with content. To get the conference going the teacher can say,

- Tell me how your writing is coming along.
- What will you write next in this piece?
- Can you think of another way of describing the character in your writing?
- I like the way you say your character is funny; could you write some examples of how he is funny?

Children should be taught to reflect on their own work and the work of their peers. We can teach them to use some of these questions with each other.

REVISION.   This is the process of making substantive changes in ideas and finding ways to make the piece more descriptive or informative. It means changing things around or trying different ways to make them better. It means sharing the writing with a friend or a group and reading it over again and again.

EDITING. The last part of the process approach, editing, requires making minor changes to the piece, mostly attending to mechanics such as punctuation, grammatical corrections, spelling, and handwriting.

Process-writing self-planning sheets for prewriting guidance and revising are helpful for students in late first grade and beyond; see Figures 7.13 and 7.14.

Figure 7.13

Prewriting Guidance Sheet

Author_____

Who am I writing this for?

Why am I writing this?

What is being explained?

What happens:

- First
- Second
- Third
- Then
- Finally

Source: Adapted from Thomas Gunning, *Creating Literacy Instruction for All Children* (4th ed.) (Boston: Allyn & Bacon, 2003). Copyright © 2003 by Pearson Education. Adapted by permission of the publisher.

Figure 7.14

Revising Guidance Sheet

Author_____

What do I like about my writing?

- Why?

Did I:

- Tell what was being explained?
- Change the parts that needed changing?

What are the changes made?

- Make a list.

Source: Adapted from Thomas Gunning, *Creating Literacy Instruction for All Children* (4th ed.) (Boston: Allyn & Bacon, 2003). Copyright © 2003 by Pearson Education. Adapted by permission of the publisher.

CONCERNS ABOUT THE PROCESS APPROACH.   The process approach should be used cautiously and only occasionally with children in the early childhood years. The prewriting phase may be accomplished through discussion and word lists with very young children and throughout the grades. Prewriting often involves the selection of a topic to write about. We want to allow the children themselves to select topics as often as possible. Many children just cannot seem to make such choices. Having a purpose for a writing activity is helpful when trying to select a topic. For example, the writing activity should have a particular form, such as writing an acrostic poem, or the activity could be to learn about writing a well-formed expository piece. After the type of writing is identified, it is easier to select the topic. With students who are still having trouble, it is helpful when the writing revolves around a very general topic that is being studied in class, such as the rain forest. Children can then select their particular topic more easily. With this type of support, students will eventually become more capable of selecting topics on their own.

Drafting can also be done by very young children and throughout the grades, but the products of drafting will be different depending on the development of the students. A draft could be an entire written story or a series of letter strings. Conferencing, when the teacher asks children to discuss their work, can also be done at all ages and stages. Older children can be asked how they think they can change their piece to make it better. Most younger children should not be asked to revise. Editing might be too tedious for many students. It is up to the teacher to understand the developmental level of the children with whom she is working. Some children may be frustrated by revisions and editing, particularly by having to copy their work over. Be selective in choosing students with whom to use the process approach. Involve only those who seem capable of handling it. Try only one or two of the steps in the process. As children increase their skills, more of the steps can be used.

Writing conferences between a teacher and a child are times to discuss what the child has written, to encourage the child in writing, and to assess progress by observing and reviewing the writing products gathered in the child's folder. During the conference the teacher can take dictation or help the child with a word, caption, picture, or publishing activity. This is an especially good time to work with students who are capable of dealing with any of the steps in process writing and to encourage reluctant writers.

Writing programs in early childhood should be initiated at the beginning of the school year. Teachers should refer to children as authors and writers so that they perceive themselves as such. Teachers need to model writing through messages on the message board, notes to parents, thank-you notes to children, and experience charts dictated by the class. They must be supportive when working with young writers. Reluctant writers need to be encouraged to write in "their very own way" (Bromley, 2003; Martinez & Teale, 1987; Sulzby, 1986b). Youngsters need to know that their work does not have to look like adult writing. Showing them samples of other children's writing, including drawings, scribble writing, and random letters, helps them see that they can do the same thing. Adults need to facilitate young writers' attempts by taking dictation, if children cannot or will not write themselves, spelling words, showing children how to form letters when asked, and answering questions that arise during writing. Like other areas of literacy, writing requires social interaction if it is to promote development. Therefore, teachers need to offer young writers feedback, encouragement, and positive reinforcement.

English Language Learners

INTERACTIVE WRITING.   Interactive writing provides a model for children so they will know what to do when writing on their own. Interactive writing is a joint effort as the teacher and the children create the writing together. The teacher guides the lesson and writes on large chart paper in a whole- or small-group setting. Sometimes the children are writing as the text is being created either on regular lined paper or on their own whiteboards. Whiteboards work well in this activity, since there is editing along the way, and it is easy to edit on a whiteboard. Any type of writing can be done in the interactive setting, such as writing a letter, a narrative piece, or an informational piece (McCarrier, Pinnell, & Fountas, 2000). Interactive writing is for the purpose of instruction, so the goal is to end up with a well-written text in content and form.

The topic for writing is decided on by the teacher with some input from the class. It is good to select writing that has a purpose for the class and that includes a part of the writing curriculum. If the class is studying *water*, for example, it might want to make a list of the uses of water as a summary of the unit. In addition to recording what they learned, they will also learn about writing lists.

Anyone can begin the writing. When a student contributes an idea, it is written by that child on the chart and then discussed afterward. The teacher guides students almost word by word if they need help with spelling, an idea, or a better way to say something. The entire class can contribute to the conversation to improve the writing. White correction tape is used during interactive writing for errors that are made. Instead of crossing out a misspelling or incorrect form of a word, the teacher just puts the white tape over the error where the correction is made. When a child notices an error in the writing, he or she can use the tape as well.

Mrs. Jenkins wanted to teach her first-grade students about being courteous and writing thank-you notes. She wanted to teach them about the content of thank-you notes and the format. As part of their study of good health habits, a mother in the class, who was a nurse, was invited to be a guest speaker. Mrs. Jenkins used this talk as the reason for writing a thank-you note to the nurse and decided to present the lesson to the entire class in an interactive writing experience. While writing the letter, there was a discussion about the indentation of the first word in the paragraph. They discussed other things to say in a thank-you note besides thanking the person. They decided they could say what they liked about the presentation, and they thought they could ask her if she might come again. They discussed different ways to end the letter, such as using the word Love or Sincerely, and when to use one or the other. The activity accomplished two tasks, the need to teach courteous behavior and the need to learn about the content and format for thank-you notes.

Another example of an interactive writing experience is on page 234 of this chapter.

Teachers may need to take dictation for journal writing, for writing to pen pals, and so on. Eventually, children should be encouraged to do their own writing.

Teaching Children to Write in Different Genres

Children need to learn to write for many purposes. The following are types of writing that should be taught, along with experiences to help practice each writing genre.

Narrative writing involves writing original stories that are typically fiction or retelling a story that was read to children or that children read themselves. Narrative stories could be about incidents in a child's life as well. Good narrative stories have a beginning, a middle, and an end. They follow a basic story structure with

1. a setting at the beginning that introduces the characters, time, and place.
2. a theme, which is the problem or goal of the main character.
3. plot episodes, or the events that help the main character solve his or her problem or accomplish his or her goal.
4. a resolution, which involves the solving of the problem or the accomplishing of the goal and an ending to the story.

Activities that provide practice in narrative writing include the following:

1. Providing children with graphic organizers for story structure to fill in prior to writing an original story. When the story is complete, they check to see that all elements are included. (See the story structure graphic organizer map in Chapter 6.)
2. Rewriting a story that had been read to the child or read by the child and having the children check that all story structure elements were included in their rewrite.
3. Children write a story together that they discuss first. When the ideas are complete, each child takes another part of the story structure to develop completely. The story is shared and students give constructive feedback for improvement.
4. The child creates a new structure element for a well-known story, such as another setting, theme, episode, or resolution.

Descriptive writing involves writing with language that describes precisely. When we help children to describe, we ask them to be involved in using their senses: listening, seeing, smelling, touching, and tasting. We practice using many different words to tell about the same thing. Asking children to describe a flower, to compare two things, or to use their five senses when writing about a particular topic will help with descriptive writing.

Persuasive writing involves trying to get someone to have your point of view. We write persuasively when we write in an emotional or factual manner. For example, a book review may try to persuade someone to read a book. Other activities include creating a poster or advertisement for a product or writing a movie review.

Expository writing includes many types of experiences. Expository writing is usually nonfiction and uses information that might come from content-area subjects, such as the social studies or science. In this type of writing, children need to collect information and summarize it. The reports do not include personal views; they are factual. This type of writing could include providing directions to complete a task or discussing cause and effect. When we ask children to engage in this type of writing, we might ask them to write up an interview with someone, prepare a report about an informational text, summarize a unit of study, or write a biography. Expository text structures are discussed in Chapter 6. The structures that need to be taught and practiced by children are these:

Description: Gives the reader a picture of the subject of the written piece based on observation.

Sequence: Explains the steps that produce a certain product or outcome.

Comparison: This can include comparisons of items with similar classification that are compared first and then contrasted. Point by point comparisons describe similarities and differences alternately.

Cause and Effect: Causality tells why something happens.

Problem Solving: A problem is presented, followed by its solution. An understanding of chronology is necessary to understand this structure.

Exemplification: This can also be called reason and example. The main idea is presented with supporting details. (Vukelich, Evans, & Albertson, 2003):

*To help her first graders begin to write expository text, she engaged them in a lesson called "All-About Books." The children worked in groups of four, and each group had four pages for the book. The first page was called "**Different Kinds of Dogs.**" There were four rectangles on the page with two lines under each. Children were to come up with four types of dogs, and then one person in the group wrote a type of dog under each rectangle and then drew a picture of that dog. The second page was called "**Parts of a Dog.**" On this page was a picture of a dog. The children discussed the parts of the dog, and it was one child's job to fill in the words identifying parts of a dog. The third page was called "**How to Care for a Dog.**" On this page there were four rectangles with lines next to them. The children generated ideas for this page, and one child wrote the text and drew pictures for the topic. The last page was called "**How to Walk a Dog.**" The children once again generated ideas together. The child in charge of this page wrote the text on the lines provided next to a rectangle and drew the pictures. The teacher prepared a table of contents for the book. This was the story created.*

All about Dogs

Table of Contents
Chapter 1 Different Kinds of Dogs
Chapter 2 Parts of a Dog
Chapter 3 How to Care for a Dog
Chapter 4 How to Walk a Dog

Chapter 1: Different Kinds of Dogs
The different kinds of dogs we know about are poodles that have curly hair, terriers that have short, rough hair, a dalmation that has black and white spots, and a mutt that is more than one kind of dog.

Chapter 2: Parts of a Dog
A dog has the following parts. They have a head, ears, eyes, a nose, teeth, lips, legs, toes, feet, hips, tails, and a back.

Chapter 3: How to Care for a Dog
If you want a healthy dog, you need to take care of him. You should have fresh water at all times for the dog. You should have a nice cozy bed for your dog to sleep in. Select good dog food for your dog to eat and don't give him candy. Take him for regular checkups.

Chapter 4: How to Walk a Dog
Dogs need to be walked. The best way to walk a dog is to attach the leash to the dog's collar. Put a coat on your dog if it is cold outside. Take the dog outside and let him do his business. Give your dog a treat after the walk.

This structured format helps children succeed in learning how to write this type of expository text; similar lessons with different directions will help with other types of writing (Calkins, 1994).

Functional writing is writing that serves clear, real-life purposes. Class writing projects that are particularly purposeful include *greeting cards* for birthdays, holidays, and other occasions to parents, grandparents, sisters, brothers, friends, and relatives. Write *thank-you notes* to guest speakers who come to class, to adults who help on class trips, to the director of the zoo you visited, or to the librarian who spent time with the class at the public library. Prepare *lists of things to remember* to do in preparing a party, a special program, or a class trip. Make *address and telephone books* with entries from class members. Write notes to parents about activities in school. Encourage individual children to write to their parents about specific things they are doing in school.

Collecting and using Very Own Words offer opportunities for writing and copying. Using classroom environmental print in one's own writing is another good writing task.

Word walls also help with writing since children can copy words they don't know how to spell from the Wall. Some preschools and kindergartens, as well as elementary classrooms, have established *mail service* and *pen pal* programs (Edwards, Maloy, & Verock-O'Loughlin, 2003; Teale & Gambrell, 2007). Children are offered pen pals to write to regularly (once a week is reasonable). Teachers or aides may have to help children write their letters or may have to take dictation. Encourage children to use the writing capabilities that they have, even if they cannot produce conventional writing. Teachers also may have to read the incoming letters to students who cannot yet read conventionally.

The use of e-mail for pen pals (called *key pals*) is another way for children to communicate with others for functional reasons. E-mail gives children the opportunity to write to others around the world, and the sending and receiving of messages is almost immediate.

A *notice board* for exchanging messages also motivates functional writing (McGee & Morrow, 2005; Newman, 1984). Children can tack up pictures for each other as beginning messages. The teacher needs to provide a model by leaving messages for individuals and for the entire class. Notices about school or class events are appropriate. It is important to draw attention to the board when posting a class message or when leaving messages for individuals so that children will get into the habit of looking for messages and leaving them themselves. There also needs to be a place for private messages. These can be posted on the notice board in an envelope or in student mailboxes. Some teachers have taped brown bags to each child's desk for them to receive private messages. Occasionally, the teacher should check the messages to see that children are writing. One teacher found the note in Figure 7.15, written by Asia, a first-grade girl, to Andra, a boy in first grade.

Figure 7.15

A Private Message Sent by a First-Grade Girl to a First-Grade Boy

Dear Andra
look I am triing
to make this
relashtoin ship work.
I no that you are
mad at me but I
did not do anything
to you. All I did was
trie to take the
paper away from
you and you ript
it and you no that
you did. And if you
did thn wi did you
blame it all on me. Love Asia

Melissa pretends to be a nurse and writes down an appointment in the dramatic-play center designed to be a doctor's office when the class was involved in a thematic unit about good health.

English Language Learners

JOURNAL WRITING. Journal writing can be carried out successfully in early childhood rooms, with entries made daily or at least several times a week. Journals can be written in notebooks or on pages stapled together to create a book. Children are encouraged to write freely in their journals at times and to write at their own developmental levels. Thus, some children's journals might include pictures and no writing, scribble writing, random letters, or invented spelling. The teacher models journal writing, perhaps with a personal message, such as "I'm very excited today. My daughter is going to be in a play tonight, and I'm going to watch her." By example, children are given an idea about the kinds of entries that are appropriate. Some children draw or write stories in their journals, others write about personal experiences, and others write about information they have learned. Journals entries can be related to topics studied, such as recording the growth of a seed that was planted, charting daily temperature, or reacting to a story that was read. From time to time the journal can also take dialogue form, with the teacher responding to a child's journal entry with a comment. If the child writes, "I had a picnic," the teacher might respond, "That sounds like fun. What did you eat?" The length and fluency of children's journal entries show great gains when the activity is continued regularly throughout a school year (Gunning, 2003).

Because there are different names for journals, it often becomes confusing as to which one should be used. It is the concept of journal writing that is important, that is, putting one's thoughts and early writing attempts down on paper without concern for the mechanics of writing. To help differentiate the different uses of journals, several are mentioned in the following paragraphs:

Personal journals are private journals in which children write about their lives or topics of special interest to them. These are shared only if a child chooses to do so. These are never subject to correction for spelling, punctuation, and so on.

Dialogue journals can be written about any topic, but they are shared with teachers or peers. The journal is similar to a conversation, except that the conversation is done in writing instead of speaking. A dialogue journal could be shared with the teacher or a peer responding to a journal entry that is written. It can also be an actual conversation between two people in which one is writing to the other and a response is expected. The written dialogue

Dialog journals involve a conversation between children; each takes a turn responding to what the other has written.

provides students with feedback about their thoughts.

Reading response journals are those in which children respond to narrative or informational text read. They write their feelings concerning responses to the story or information. Teachers do read response journals.

Learning logs usually involve content areas, such as social studies or science. Children record information being learned, such as charting the progress of a setting hen's eggs. The more children learn about content-area subjects, the more they will have to write. The writing can take many forms, such as charting or summarizing information.

There are many other titles for journals—family journals, journals about themes, and so on. Journal writing helps students become more fluent writers, choose topics to develop, learn the mechanics of writing, reflect on ideas, and articulate them. Whatever they are called, some journal experiences should include private reflections about the life of the child, others should include responses to a child's journal writing by the teacher or peers, some should be written in response to literature, and some should be written in relation to information learned.

Children's Literature and Writing

English Language Learners

CHILDREN'S LITERATURE MOTIVATES WRITING. Children's literature is as natural a medium for encouraging writing as it is for encouraging oral language and reading (Tompkins, 2000; Vukelich, Evans, & Albertson, 2003). Reading several books by the same author or illustrator can prompt a class letter asking the author how he or she gets ideas to write or asking the illustrator what kind of art materials he or she uses. It is best to identify authors or illustrators who are likely to respond, for it is important to receive a response, even if it comes from a publisher's representative.

Old favorites and series books—those that use the same character in several different books, such as *Madeline* (Bemelmans, 1939), *Curious George* (Rey, 1941), and *Harold and the Purple Crayon* (Johnson, 1981)—can motivate children to write their own books or a class book about the character. Books such as *Swimmy* (Lionni, 1963) and *Alexander and the Terrible, Horrible, No Good, Very Bad Day* (Viorst, 1972) involve the main character in a series of adventures or incidents as the story proceeds. Children can be asked to write still another episode or adventure for the

Figure 7.16

An Example of Writing
Motivated by Children's
Literature

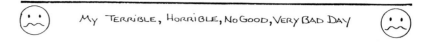

character. Such stories lend themselves to writing about personal experiences. (Figure 7.16 illustrates one child's response to this task.)

Shared book experiences and small-group story readings (described in Chapter 6) all can lead to writing experiences. Predictable books provide patterns that children can imitate in their own writing through cumulative patterns, as in *I Know an Old Lady* (Westcott, 1980); repetitive language, as in *Are You My Mother?* (Eastman, 1960); familiar sequences, as in *The Very Hungry Caterpillar* (Carle, 1969); or catch-phrases, as in *What Cried Granny: an Almost Bedtime Story* (Lum & Johnson, 1998). (See Appendix A for a list of such books.)

Heather, Kim, and Tina decided to write their story about a baseball hero they particularly liked. Heather was concerned that the information they had from a magazine was not enough. She suggested that they look in the dictionary. Kim told Heather that dictionaries are for finding out how to spell words and getting their definitions, and encyclopedias are for finding out information. The girls found additional information in the encyclopedia, copied it, and continued with their work. These students were collecting information that they would have to organize and summarize. These were skills they had learned in writing workshop about writing expository text.

SHARING WRITING MOTIVATED BY CHILDREN'S LITERATURE.   Children need to share their writing with an audience. When they know they will be sharing their work, they will write for that audience and have a greater purpose for writing. At a designated time during the day, usually at the end when the class gets together to review the day's happenings, a child can be selected as Author of the Day to share something that he or she has written (Graves & Hansen,

1983; Rog, 2007; Routman, 2005). More than one piece can be read, and more than one child can be Author of the Day. Those authors who read their writings in a particular week should display them on a bulletin board in the writing center along with photographs of themselves. When sharing work, the child can sit in a chair marked Author's Chair. Children in the audience should be encouraged to comment about their friends' work with such statements as "I like what you wrote" or "I fell and cut my knee once, too." Because at first the children may not comment readily, the teacher needs to model comments for the audience, whose young members will soon emulate the behavior.

It was Steven's turn in the Author's Chair. He sat down, organized his materials, and said:

I've been working on a series of stories. They are all about the same character, and in each one he had another adventure. It is sort of like the books about Clifford the Big Red Dog. My stories are about a cat, and the first one is called The Cat Named Buster. *I call that Part I; I already have Part II and Part III. Part II is called* Buster Meets Pretzel. *Pretzel is a dog. Part III is called* Buster Gets Lost. *I'll read Part I to you.*

After reading Part I of his stories, Philip said, "Can I read one?" Steven replied, "Sure, but you should read all of them. They go together." Philip continued, "I just want to read the first one now." Steven said, "OK, but you don't know what you're missing."

Writing Poetry

Another form of writing enjoyed by young children is poetry. With very young children, the class can write the poetry together in a shared writing experience on chart paper. Poetry that rhymes is probably the most well-known type. Many types of formula poetry are enjoyed by children. Acrostic poems are very popular. They begin with a topic word that is written vertically on the page. The word could be a child's name, a season, a place, or a thing. The poem uses the letters of the topic being written about. You can use just a word, a phrase, or a sentence. For example, here is an acrostic poem I wrote about my grandbaby James:

James

Jolly

Adorable

Magnificent

Enthusiastic

So sweet, so silly, so special

Triangle poems follow a specific formula. The first word and first line is a noun, the second line is made of two adjectives, the next two words are "ing" words, and the fourth and last line is a sentence. Here is a triangle poem about spring:

Spring
New pretty
Dancing playing
It's so nice to be outdoors

Haiku is a form of formula poetry that comes from Japan. The topics of haiku are often related to nature. There are three lines in a haiku and 17 syllables in the entire poem. The first line has five syllables, the second line seven syllables, and the third line five syllables. Here is a haiku about trees:

The trees above me
Swaying across the blue sky
Make a pretty sound

An activity that develops vocabulary and syntax and can create poems follows. Select a topic about something you are studying—for example, the rain. Make that the topic word in the poem. Brainstorm what rain is like and what it does, for example:

Rain
Heavy
Light
Cold
Warm
Falling
Blowing

This is a poem that can be chanted. To take it one step further, put the word *rain* with the words listed and chant

Heavy rain
Light rain
Blowing rain
Cold rain
Warm rain
Falling rain

English Language Learners

INDEPENDENT WRITING.   Chapter 8 discusses periods of time for independent reading and writing, which give children the opportunity to participate in literacy activities. During independent reading and writing, children can choose activities based on several options, and they choose to work alone or in collaboration with others. Since writing is time consuming, giving time for independent writing could allow children to practice whatever writing they might like to or to work on a piece in progress. Chapter 8 also emphasizes pleasurable experiences with reading and writing. It is difficult to separate reading and writing, especially during this independent time when children direct their own behavior. However, it is interesting to note when observing children during independent reading and writing periods that equal time is spent at both these literacy activities. When children decide to engage in reading and writing, it is often a cooperative effort. During this period, children have the opportunity to select from a list of literacy activities, such as the following:

Read a book, magazine, or newspaper alone or with a friend.

Listen to a story on the headsets at the listening station.

Read or tell a story using a felt-board and story characters.

Read or tell a story using puppets.

Prepare a tape story by recording your reading of a book.

Write a story alone or with a friend.

Write a story and make it into a felt story.

Write a story and record it for the listening station.

Write a story and perform it as a puppet show.

Present a play based on a story you wrote or read.

Bind a story you have written into a book and place it in the library corner for others to read.

Participate in content-area activities that involve reading and writing.

The following anecdotes describe the writing that took place during my observations of independent reading and writing periods in a second-grade classroom. It is evident how closely reading and writing are linked. So many of the things children chose to do were motivated by what they had read or what was read to them. When writing, they often looked for additional information by reading more in other sources.

After listening to the teacher read My Cat, the Silliest Cat in the World *(Bachelet, 2006), Stephanie, Jason, Kevin, and Nicky decided to make an advertisement poster for the book that showed key pictures with captions. They had learned about persuasive writing in writing workshop and were putting these skills to practice. The children delegated responsibilities. They made up a title for the poster and called it, Scenes from* My Cat, the Silliest Cat in the World. *They drew episodes from the story and wrote their own captions for the pictures. The poster took a few days to complete. (One of the characteristics of independent reading and writing is that projects can be worked on over a long period.) When the poster was complete, the children presented their work to the class. Stephanie and Jason held the poster, and Kevin and Nicky were the spokespersons. Kevin explained how the group wanted to illustrate the story in an unusual way and decided on a poster. Kevin and Nicky took turns pointing to the pictures they had all drawn and reading the captions they had written for each.*

Motivated by a story about magic, Zarah and Shakiera decided to write their own about a magical fish called Alexander. Shakiera asked Zarah to write the story, and Shakiera suggested that she would draw the pictures. Shakiera also offered to help think of the words to write. Zarah began to write the first line: "A fish called Alexander was a talking fish." Shakiera told Zarah to add to the sentence, "and he had magic."

Zarah said, "Magic, I don't know if that's the right word. I think he had powers." Shakiera said, "I think that magic and power are the same thing." The girls agreed and went on to write the rest of the story. These children were writing narrative text and discussing vocabulary issues.

Television shows, rock stars, and current events also motivated writing during independent reading and writing. Three girls created a roll movie that included biographies of each member of a well-known singing group. They used very descriptive language that they had learned about in writing workshop.

Current events and books children read motivated writing. Joey was reading a book about the U.S. Civil War. He asked the teacher to read it to the class, which she did. Joey decided to write his own book about the Civil War, and Christopher joined him. Christopher called the book "U.S. Saratoga." As they were drawing pictures, they made bombing sounds. Suddenly Joey said, "Wait a minute, this is weird. We're making airplane carriers fighting in the Civil War." The two boys changed their minds and decided to do a book about a war that could be happening now. These boys were sorting out, collecting, and organizing their ideas, which are skills they learned about writing informational text.

Julia and Katie wrote a script for a play they were going to have some children act out. It was a wedding ceremony, and their text is reproduced in Figure 7.17. Conversation is another skill being practiced here, which the students have been taught about during journal writing and narrative writing.

These episodes during independent reading and writing reveal the wide variety of topics that children focused on. We would probably never think to ask children to write about some of them. If we did, the children would never have the enthusiasm they demonstrated because they had not selected the topics themselves. We also don't know all the interests of students. Some of the topics they might select to write about are very sophisticated. Children have original ideas that they can draw on from their varied and rich life experiences. The topics they select have meaning and function for them, and therefore they write freely and enthusiastically about them.

Independent writing activities can be adapted for children with special needs. Children can write to other youngsters who may share their problems. As teachers have said, "There is something for everyone during independent reading and writing—the gifted, the child who attends basic skills classes, and youngsters who are English language learners."

Children need to participate in many types of writing experiences. A center time when children write independently is an important experience for practicing writing skills learned. Children practice different types of writing, such as functional writing, journal writing, narrative and expository text writing, and writing using the process approach. Before

Figure 7.17

A Play Written by Julia and Katie during an Independent Writing Period

We are gathd her today to jon thes two wondrfal pepel in holey matramony. Silvea Do you tak Gim to be yor offl weded hasbind, I do. Gim do you tak Silvea to be yr offel weded wife. I do. Ma we have the rins. Silvea pot this ring on Gims Finger. Gim pot this ring on Silveas finger. I now prnawns you man and wife. Yo may now kis the brid

Stephanie made her story into a roll movie.

Stephanie puts the finishing touches on the cover of a book she has written.

children engage in any type of writing, the teacher should know what is expected of them.

Publishing Children's Writing

English Language Learners

Children's work should be published. "Why publish?" almost answers the question "Why write?" "Writing is a public act, meant to be shared with many audiences" (Graves, 1983, p. 54). When children know their work will be published, they write for a defined purpose. When work is to be published, it becomes special; it needs to be done carefully. Children can publish their work in many ways. The most popular is to bind writings into books, which are placed in the literacy center and featured on open bookshelves for others to read. (Three ways of making a book are illustrated in Figures 7.10, 7.11, and 7.12.)

Strategies

Other means of publishing include creating felt-board stories or roll movies, telling stories to classmates, role-playing what has been written, or presenting the story in a puppet show. A computer can be used to type, save, and print original material. Try Strategies for the Classroom writing activities on page S-37 through S-39 with students in your class or at student teaching.

The Mechanics of Writing: Spelling and Punctuation

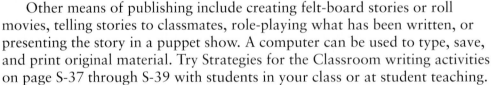

Thus far this chapter has emphasized the importance of promoting children's interest in writing and giving them opportunities to write that will prove to be enjoyable. This section deals with the *mechanics of writing*.

HANDWRITING. Writing requires dexterity. Although it is unnecessary and often unwise to teach preschoolers and kindergarteners the particulars of proper letter formation, they can be encouraged to use manipulatives such as

Figure 7.18

Forming the
Letters of the
Alphabet

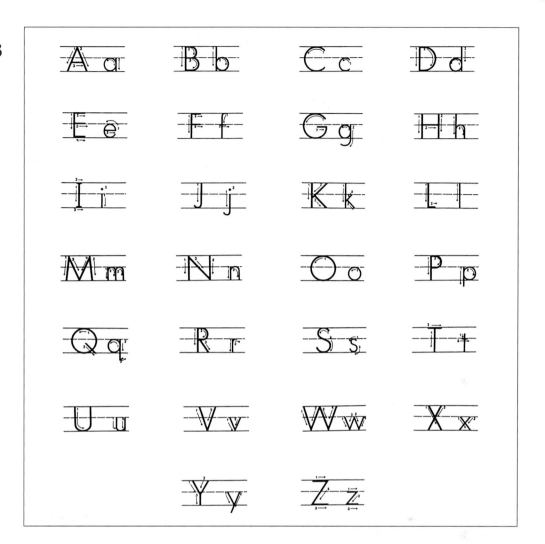

puzzles and sewing cards that strengthen their fine motor coordination. In the earlier discussion of the literacy center, other materials that help with writing and identifying letters were mentioned, including magnetic letters, letter forms to trace and copy, and whiteboard slates to practice writing letters, words, and sentences. The letters of the alphabet should be displayed at eye level for children, and the teacher can model the correct formation of upper- and lowercase manuscript (Figure 7.18). Legibility needs to be the main goal for handwriting. Learning about spaces between words is important so that words will not run into each other. There are only a few lines and shapes to learn when writing manuscript. They include a vertical line, a horizontal line, diagonal lines, a half circle with the opening on the left, right, top, or bottom, and a full circle (Figure 7.19). The straight lines in manuscript are called *sticks*. All lines are written from the top to the bottom. All circles and half circles are written from the top to the bottom. The letters *h, m, n, r,* and *u* are written without lifting the pencil off the page beginning with the stick. So to make the *h,* you start at the top of the stick and go down to the line and go

Figure 7.19

Manuscript
Forms

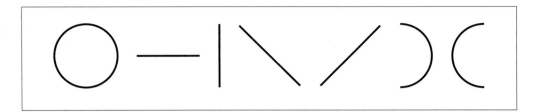

back up half of the stick to make the half circle with the opening on the bottom. The letters *b*, *d*, *g*, *p*, and *q* are made with a circle first and then the stick is attached.

Teach children about putting spaces between letters and words. A good rule is that one finger space will help to separate words. Children can and will develop their own handwriting style, but they need to learn that, whatever their style, neat handwriting is a form of courtesy for those who will be reading what they write.

Initial writing will be on unlined paper. When children have developed sufficient dexterity, they can begin to use lined paper. This level will be reached at the end of kindergarten and into first grade.

SPELLING AND PUNCTUATION. Spelling and punctuation should be taught when the need arises and in a systematic fashion during mini-lessons. Opportunities for dealing with commas, question marks, periods, and capital letters occur when reading a morning message, for example, and then the mechanics of writing are being discussed in a natural setting. Spelling and punctuation have become areas of concern with the acceptance, for example, of invented spelling in the early stages of writing. Many teachers are not sure when to begin formal teaching of spelling and punctuation and correcting invented forms. Children should be encouraged to write in any way that they can in their first attempts. However, they need to know that it is "a child's way of writing and not grown-up writing." When children are comfortable writing and do so freely in their own style of early attempts, teachers should begin to point out elements of spelling and punctuation that will help them make the transition from invented spelling and punctuation to conventional forms. Figure 7.20 outlines stages of spelling development.

The following are some suggestions for encouraging conventional forms of spelling and punctuation:

- When you take dictation from a child, you can comment on the spelling of some unusual words and appropriate punctuation.
- When children use certain consistent invented forms of spelling and punctuation in their writing, put the correct form on a 3 × 5 Very Own Word card for them to copy the next time they use that word or punctuation. Get children in the habit of asking for words they do not know how to spell on index cards to help them develop their own spelling word list.

Figure 7.20

Stages of Spelling
Development

Precommunicative Spelling

- Children use scribbles.

- Children are developing a sense of directionality with scribbles.

- Children write some letters.

- Children write random strings of letters and numbers mixed with no association of the letters, marks, or numbers to sounds (e.g., L4TZMP for house).

Semiphonetic Spelling

- Consonants begin to represent words and are related to the sounds of the words (e.g., TIMGTAK—Today I am going to the park.).

- Beginning and ending consonant sounds may be included (bg for bug; bd for bed).

- One or two sounds may be correct in a word.

Phonetic Spelling

Children spell words as they sound (e.g., sokar for soccer).

Transitional Spelling

Children use a high percentage of correctly spelled words, and the remaining words are spelled using some type of spelling generalization (e.g., afternewn for afternoon).

Conventional Spelling

Children apply the basic rules of English to spelling and correctly spell 90 percent of the words they write.

Source: Adapted from J. Johns, S. D. Lenski, and L. Elish-Piper, *Early Literacy Assessments and Teaching Strategies.* Dubuque, IA: Kendall/Hunt, 1999, pp. 139–140.

- When using Big Books and tracking print, emphasize the spelling of words or types of punctuation used.

- Use the morning message for teaching spelling and punctuation. Write new spelling words in the message for children to copy in their writing. Leave blanks for children to fill in words from a choice of the new spelling words for the week. You also can use incorrect spelling and punctuation so children can act as detectives to correct the errors. Or a message can be written in all lowercase letters for children to correct with appropriate capitals put in the right place. Use incorrect spacing between words and sentences to provide for conversation about these mechanics of writing. This activity leads to an opportunity to help children with spacing in their own writing by telling them how one finger space is used between words and two finger spaces between sentences.

- Encourage children to do free writing, which will result in improved spelling and punctuation.

- Phonics lessons, which teach about word families and sound–symbol relationships, will help with spelling. Make children aware that they should be using their knowledge of sound–symbol relationships when they spell words, and that phonograms or chunks or digraphs such as *ch* and *sh* are spelling patterns to learn.

- In writing conferences with children, take the opportunity to make them aware of editing, which includes correct spelling.
- Make children aware of spelling resources, such as the dictionary.
- Teach the children how to use spell-checks on the computer.
- Use word lists of common but difficult words to spell, such as *the*, *this*, and *but*, for children to memorize. A few words a week should be part of a spelling list to learn. The older the children, the more words that can be assigned per week. (Figure 5.2 is a list of high-frequency words.)
- Add words from theme units to spelling lists.
- Encourage children to help each other with spelling words and punctuation.

It is important to free children to write their thoughts on paper without concern for the mechanics of writing. When they are ready, it is also important to make them aware of writing that is mechanically correct. There are times for free writing and times for edited pieces. Children should know that each type of writing is acceptable, but they occur in different settings. The word-study discussion in Chapter 5 about phonics provides activities that will help with spelling through word building. The following are some spelling games that are easy to use in the classroom to reinforce spelling words being taught (Rosencrans, 1998):

Letter Box: Put five or six letters that make up the week's spelling words in a box. Students will arrange letters to make spelling words.

Mixed-up Scrambled Words: Write spelling words with the letters mixed up, and ask children to write each word correctly.

Spelling Collage: Ask children to write their spelling words randomly on a 9 × 12 paper covering as much of an area as possible with the words. With markers and crayons, have the students trace over the spelling words in different colors in a decorative manner. Display the spelling collages on a bulletin board.

Spelling Detectives: In various communications such as on word walls, morning messages, center activity directions, or job descriptions, make errors in spelling words. It is the children's job to find the errors daily.

Word Hunt: Have students look regularly for spelling words that appear in all that they do at school and at home, for example, in a math book, a science book, the newspaper, a book they are reading for pleasure, on food lists at home, and so on.

Trace a Word: Have students "write" spelling words on a partner's back using their pointer finger. The partner has to guess the word.

Hidden Words: Prepare a list of spelling words that are surrounded by other letters. Have students find and then circle or color the spelling words embedded within (example: ovisrm mx**the**uv qr**but**zi).

Assessment of Children's Writing Development and the Writing Environment

As in other areas of literacy, assessment of a child's writing should take place throughout the school year. That way the teacher can determine a child's level of development, monitor progress, and plan programs accordingly. The checklists on pages 274–276 provide a resource for the teacher to evaluate characteristics of a child's writing development and the classroom writing environment.

The assessment checklist is used to analyze individual writing samples collected all year for the specific characteristics outlined in the measure. Figure 7.21 provides another means of evaluating children's written original stories

Figure 7.21

Evaluating Oral and Written Original Stories

Child's name _____ Date _____

Name of story _____

Setting	Yes	No
a. The story begins with an introduction.	☐	☐
b. One or more main characters emerge.	☐	☐
c. Other main characters are talked about.	☐	☐
d. The time of the story is mentioned.	☐	☐
e. Where the story takes place is mentioned.	☐	☐

Theme

	Yes	No
a. A beginning event occurs that causes a problem for the main character or for the goal to be achieved.	☐	☐
b. The main character reacts to the problem.	☐	☐

Plot Episodes

	Yes	No
An event or series of events is mentioned that relates to the main character solving the problem or attaining the goal.	☐	☐

Resolution

	Yes	No
a. The main character solves the problem or achieves the goal.	☐	☐
b. The story ends with a closing statement.	☐	☐

Sequence

	Yes	No
The four categories of story structure are presented in typical sequential order (setting, theme, plot episodes, resolution).	☐	☐

Interpretive and Critical Comments: Read through the oral taped story and the written original story and record comments and responses that demonstrate interpretive and critical thought.

Checklist   Assessing Writing Development

Child's name _____ Date _____

Teacher fills out the checklist for each child	Always	Sometimes	Never	Comments
Explores with writing materials				
Dictates stories, sentences, or words he or she wants written down				
Copies letters and words				
Independently attempts writing to convey meaning, regardless of writing level				
Can write his or her name				

Check (✓) the level or levels at which the child is writing

_____ uses drawing for writing and drawing				
_____ differentiates between writing and drawing				
_____ uses scribble writing for writing				
_____ uses letterlike forms for writing				
_____ uses learned letters in random fashion for writing				
_____ uses invented spelling for writing				
_____ writes conventionally with conventional spelling				
Collaborates with others in writing experience				
Writes in varied genres:				
narrative (stories)				
expository (personal and informational reports)				
Writes for functional purposes				
Stays on topic				
Thinks about the audience				
Makes opinions clear				

Teacher fills out the checklist for each child	Always	Sometimes	Never	Comments
Gives details and examples				
Puts things in order or sequence				
Includes a beginning, middle, and end				
Uses a variety of words and sentences				

Mechanics for Writing

	Always	Sometimes	Never	Comments
Forms uppercase letters legibly				
Forms lowercase letters legibly				
Writes from left to right				
Leaves spaces between words				
Uses capital letters when necessary				
Uses punctuation correctly				

Spelling Development

Check (✔) the level or levels at which the child is spelling

_____ precommunicative spelling				
_____ semiphonetic spelling				
_____ phonetic spelling				
_____ transitional spelling				
_____ conventional spelling				

Teacher Comments:

and oral dictations of stories for sense of story structure as well as the inclusion of interpretive and critical thoughts. Qualitative and quantitative assessment measures for narrative story rewriting after reading or listening to a story read are found in Figures 6.12 and 6.13. Assessment of children's expository writing is found in Figure 7.22.

The measures for evaluating writing and the checklists in this chapter provide the teacher with information about the language the child uses, the concepts included in the writing, the purpose for writing, and the writing mechanics used. The checklists provide information about the conventions

Figure 7.22

Evaluating
Expository Text

The expository text includes some of these characteristics:	Yes	No
1. **Comparing and contrasting** Noting similarities and differences.	☐	☐
2. **Sequencing** Listing factual information that happened in proper sequential order	☐	☐
3. **Cause and effect** Describing how something happened and why	☐	☐
4. **Exemplification** Providing a reason and an example	☐	☐
5. **Description** Giving a good picture of what specific information looks like	☐	☐

of writing. They will indicate the stage of writing or spelling that a student is demonstrating, as well as the mechanics of writing used, such as capitalization and punctuation. The measures for story rewriting and writing of original stories will determine how well the child uses meaning and structure in his or her writing. All these assessment tools will help determine appropriate instruction and practice a child needs in order to progress in writing development.

CheckList   Assessing the Classroom Writing Environment

	Yes	No
Space provided for a writing center		
Tables and chairs included in center		
Writing posters and bulletin boards for children to display their writing themselves		
Writing utensils (pens, pencils, crayons, magic markers, colored pencils, etc.)		
Typewriter and/or computer		
Writing materials (many varieties of paper in all sizes, booklets, pads)		
A message board or private message area for children to leave messages for the teacher and other members of the class		
A place to store Very Own Words		
Folders in which children place samples of their writing		
Materials to make books		

Teachers should maintain a portfolio of materials related to a child's writing development, such as observation notes as the child writes, samples of the child's writing over a period of time, notes from conferences with the child, notes from conferences with the child's parents, and completed checklists. The portfolio should include the best of the child's work and samples showing need for improvement as well. The portfolio can be used during parent conferences and can accompany a child to his or her next teacher. Children should have their own writing folders in which they keep samples of their writing throughout the year. They also should be involved in the assessment process by participating in parent and teacher conferences and in conferences with the teacher alone. Figure 7.23 provides a general way for children to assess their own writing interest and ability. For kindergarteners and young children, something simpler can be used for self-evaluation. The children can evaluate with a friend or the teacher whether their work is *Wow, Good,* or *Okay.* The teacher says *Wow* with a very enthusiastic voice; *Good* is much more toned down; and *Okay* is said just that way, *Okay.* When they evaluate, they discuss why one of these words was used. The evaluation is based on their ability as well. When evaluating together, check to see whether children took time with their illustrations. Was their writing done to the best of their ability? All these suggestions support the purpose of assessment to (1) enhance the teacher's understanding of children's writing ability, (2) aid in program planning, and (3) help children and parents understand a child's progress and the processes involved to help gain more competence in writing.

The evaluation of writing is not only done in the classroom but, based on standards set by different states, tests for writing are used regularly. To evaluate children's writing, states often create rubrics. Rubrics are scoring guides

Figure 7.23

Self-Assessment about Writing for Children

Name _____

The good things about what I wrote are:

The things I don't like about what I wrote are:

I could make this writing better if I:

I used correct spelling:

I used my best handwriting:

Is writing hard or easy for me?

For me writing is (a) fun, (b) not so much fun.

Writing could be better if:

Next time I write something, I will try to do the following things to make it better:

and are useful tools for students and teachers to get a sense of what they should strive for in their writing. It is helpful for students to see writing samples that have excellent rubric evaluations to help them with their own work. These tests most often take place in third and fourth grade for the first time. However, in preparation for the test, what is being asked of the students in terms of writing performance must begin in preK. A typical standards test may provide a child with a picture and a prompt to complete a writing task in 30 minutes. The prompt may simply say "Create a story about what is happening in the picture and persuade the audience about your point of view based on the what you write." The writing is evaluated on the following:

1. How clearly and appropriately students responded to the prompts.
2. Did they support their writing with appropriate details?
3. The organization of the piece is evaluated for the inclusion of an introduction, appropriate transitions, and a conclusion.
4. The use of elaboration to engage the audience is evaluated.
5. The use of varied sentence structures and vocabulary is evaluated.
6. The use of conventions of print and literary forms is evaluated
7. The use of language appropriate to the audience is evaluated.

A rubric is used in the evaluation of these seven items. On the evaluation, for example, taken from the New Jersey Registered Holistic Scoring Rubric, each of the seven items is on a scale that rates children from 1 to 6. Children receive a score of 1 if their work is evaluated as inadequate, 2 if their writing is considered limited, 3 for writing that shows partial command on items being evaluated, 4 for adequate writing, 5 for a strong command of their writing, and 6 for superior writing. Therefore, if a sample is evaluated on how clearly and appropriately the student responded to the prompts, he or she could receive anywhere from a 1 to 6 from the evaluator. The following is a checklist for young writers to check their own work (New Jersey State Department of Education, 1998).

Checklist Self-Assessment of Writing

Did you remember to

_____ Stick to the topic?   _____ Use a variety of words and sentences?

_____ Think about your audience?   _____ State your opinion clearly?

_____ Give details and examples?   _____ Use capitals and punctuation correctly?

_____ Put things in order?   _____ Write neatly?

_____ Include an opening and a closing?

An Idea from the Classroom

Preschool and First-Grade Pen Pals

Children from a nearby preschool wrote to my first graders to find out what the elementary school was like. We wrote a class letter back answering their questions and included our pictures. One week later, we received a response. Now we had established a letter-writing routine. The children in my class took turns writing parts of each letter on chart paper. We went through the writing process steps of brainstorming, revising, editing, and rewriting for our new audience. Three children acted as scribes, while the rest of the class developed the letter. Later, three new children were chosen to revise and edit. Finally, three more children rewrote the letter. We also used e-mail to send messages that needed quick responses to pen pals. Being pen pals became a part of our writing curriculum. We invited the preschoolers for a snack and a paired-reading session and to our end of the year play. In turn, the preschoolers invited our class for a picnic at the preschool. We developed a friendship with the younger students, and our first-grade class learned the purposeful and very rewarding skill of letter writing. In addition, the preschoolers became familiar with our school, which most of them would be entering soon.

Donna M. Ngai, First-Grade Teacher

An Idea from the Classroom

Writing across Genres

One of the best ways to help students learn about the styles and purposes of different genres is to read a variety of genres and discuss the characteristics. The students should also have plenty of practice writing in different genres. In my second-grade class, we study metamorphosis, and we have caterpillars living in our classroom. I read a variety of nonfiction texts about caterpillars and metamorphosis to the class. My students brainstorm what they notice about these nonfiction texts, in terms of style and content. These expository texts are sometimes easier for ELL students to understand because they are not culturally specific and they lack English idioms. Also, big words like *metamorphosis* and *chrysalis* are often easier for students to remember because they are so distinct. I ask the students to observe the caterpillars on a daily basis and to take notes in their science journals. After their observation period, I ask them to expand on their notes and to write "as scientists" to document what they have noticed. If a student starts to write something like "Pedro was taking a nap. Pedro was happy," I explain that scientific writers need to use the word *caterpillar* instead of a first name and that they also must write only what they observed, without interpretation. I say to the student, "We are not sure if the caterpillar is happy, so let's try to think of something that we know for sure because we observed it." With guided conversations like this one, the students start to understand the differences in various genres, and their writing becomes much more specific and purposeful.

Joanne Jacobson, Second-Grade Teacher

Activities and Questions

1. Answer the focus questions at the beginning of the chapter.

2. Ask three children of different ages, for example, 3, 5, and 7, to write about their favorite food, television show, storybook, or game. Take notes on their behavior during writing, and analyze the sample of their writing to determine each child's writing developmental level.

3. Many functional and meaningful writing experiences are related in this chapter. Try to think of writing experiences not dealt with in the chapter that you could suggest for children to participate in.

4. Think of several dramatic-play themes that you could create in an early childhood classroom, such as a restaurant. For each theme, think of the writing materials you could provide for that play area for children to use.

5. Continue the portfolio assessment for the child you selected to assess for language development in Chapter 4. Observe the child using the assess-ment checklist provided in this chapter concerning the evaluation of writing development. Collect writing samples from the child over the course of several months. Evaluate them to determine the child's development in writing over time.

6. Continue the thematic unit that you began in Chapter 4. Select three objectives in the area of writing development and describe three activities that will satisfy each objective using your theme. Be sure that your activities reflect functional and meaningful writing tasks.

7. Create an activity to enhance spelling and punctuation for young children.

8. **Strategies** Use pages S-30 through S-41 in Strategies for the Classroom with children in your class or in your student teaching. Try making webs as a precursor to writing; try KWL, Venn diagrams, writing exposition text, etc.

mγeducationlab

VIDEO EXERCISE

Now that you have the benefit of having read this chapter, return to the www.myeducationlab.com topic "Writing" and watch "The Writing Process: Prewriting" one more time. Under the topic "Reading and Writing Connections," watch "Writing and Reading" one more time. Under the topic "Emergent Literacy," watch "Word Walls" one more time. You may complete the questions that accompany them online and save or transmit your work to your professor, or complete the following questions, as required.

The Writing Process: Prewriting (3:44 minutes)

1. What prewriting strategies did you see taking place in this example? Did you think they were effective? Explain your answer.
2. Create a list of five or six traits, with two or three picture books for each trait, that can be used to teach different traits of good writing.

Writing and Reading (3:47 minutes)

1. How is the relationship between reading and writing demonstrated in this video clip?
2. Explain some of the techniques this teacher uses to make the connection between reading and writing.
3. As a teacher, how might you use technology to facilitate the reading–writing connection? Describe a lesson that uses technology as a resource.

Word Walls (1:42 minutes)

1. The teacher in this clip is using three strategies to help students learn to spell some key words. What are they and why are they effective?
2. In this example, what is a word wall and what are some other ways it can be used?
3. Word walls can be very effective, but often they are not used to their best advantage. Name three ways that you, as a teacher, would use a word wall to support writing and spelling using a theme, such as space or the rain forest.

Focus Questions

■ What objectives and standards help guide the development of positive attitudes toward literacy activities, thus motivating reading and writing?

■ What are the physical characteristics of well-designed literacy centers that motivate children's use of these spaces?

■ Name and define different genres of children's literature.

■ Describe strategies using children's literature that motivate interest in reading and writing.

■ Describe literacy center activities and explain how they are organized to promote independent reading and writing.

■ How can technology enhance literacy development?

■ How can play enhance literacy?

■ **VOCABULARY:** literacy center, picture storybooks, informational books, picture concept books, traditional literature, realistic literature, easy-to-read books, fables and folktales, wordless books, poetry, novels, biography, Big Books.

■ **Strategies**   Use Chapter 8 pages S-42 through S-45 in Strategies for the Classroom to create restaurants as play centers that are equipped to engage children in literacy behavior.

PEARSON myeducationlab VIDEO PREVIEW: Creating a Print Rich Environment (3:36 minutes). Before reading this chapter, go to www.myeducationlab.com. Under the topic "Motivation," access and watch the video "Creating a Print Rich Environment."

8

Motivating Reading and Writing Using Old and New Literacies

Children who read and write only when they have to are not being taught a love of reading. The best index of the success of literacy instruction is the eagerness with which children approach reading and writing.

Love of reading and writing is not taught, it is created.

Love of reading and writing is not required, it is inspired.

Love of reading and writing is not demanded, it is exemplified.

Love of reading and writing is not exacted, it is quickened.

Love of reading and writing is not solicited, it is activated.

—Russell Stauffer, 1980
Adapted from Wilson Library Bulletin

During a period for independent reading and writing, second graders Trisha and Jessica chose a felt story of the book *Are You My Mother?* (Eastman, 1960). The following transpired as they worked together reading the story and manipulating the felt characters:

Jessica: Can I read the story?

Trisha: OK.

Jessica: (She begins reading with enthusiasm as Trisha works the felt pieces on the board.) The baby bird asks the cow, "Are you my mother?"

Trisha: (She puts the cow on the felt-board.) Mooooooo.

Jessica: Moooooooo. (Jessica continues to read the book.)

Trisha: Look at this picture. (She points to the baby bird. Both start to giggle.)

Jessica: Here I am Mother! (She reads in a high-pitched voice.) Mother, Mother, here I am!

Trisha: I like it when he says to the tractor, "You are my mother, Snort, Snort."

Jessica: Snort, Snort! I thought I had a mother. (She puts her hand to her head as she says this, using a baby bird voice and swaying back and forth pretending she is crying.)

Trisha: (She imitates Jessica by putting her hands on her head.) I thought I had a mother!

Jessica: (She points to the felt-board.) Can I do this now and you read? (They trade places, and Trisha starts reading. She speaks in dramatic and different voices for the two birds. Trisha is reading too fast for Jessica to put the characters on the board.)

Jessica: Wait, wait, will you wait a minute Trisha. (She puts the dog on the felt-board, and Trisha continues.) Wait, Wait, Wait! (She puts the mother bird on the felt-board.)

This dialogue was between two second-grade children engaged in a literacy center activity. The children were practicing literacy skills in a classroom atmosphere that promotes the desire to read and write through the use of motivating literacy activities.

Strategies for Motivating Reading and Writing

A survey of classroom teachers concerning priorities for research indicated that motivating children to want to read and write was ranked high on the list of suggestions (O'Flahavan, Gambrell, Guthrie, Stahl, & Alverman, 1992). Teachers recognize the importance of motivation in the development of children's literacy skills. They are interested in learning new ways to promote their students' interests in reading and writing. An entire chapter about this topic has been included because I believe it is an integral part of teaching children to read and write. I begin with motivation theory and then go to selected topics I believe to be particularly motivating for children in classrooms that utilize the theory. The areas discussed in the chapter are designing literacy centers and

Two second graders reading and performing a felt story together.

using them in classrooms, using children's literature in the classroom, new literacies such as technology, and literacy and play.

Motivation is defined as initiating and sustaining a particular activity. It is considered the tendency to return to and continue working on a task with sustained engagement (Brophy, 2004; Gambrell, Palmer, Codling, & Mazzoni, 1996; Guthrie, 2004) A motivated reader chooses to read on a regular basis and for many different reasons. Researchers have found that experiences that offer students (1) choice, (2) challenge, (3) social collaboration, and (4) success are likely to promote motivation.

Choice

Providing children with the opportunity to make choices about which literacy tasks they will participate in gives them responsibility and control over the situation. Choice needs to involve multiple modalities for learning; that is, the development of literacy skills may combine traditional activities that use pencil-and-paper experiences with modalities that use technology, drama, or the visual arts. However, when providing choice, only give a few; otherwise, it is too confusing for a child. Choice instills intrinsic motivation (Gaskins, 2003; Guthrie, 2002).

Challenge

Students must perceive that there is some challenge to an activity, but that it is one that they can accomplish. Tasks should be perceived as not too hard, but not too easy. When tasks are viewed as too easy, children aren't interested. If tasks are too difficult, they become frustrated (McKenna, 2001; Stahl, 2003).

Social Collaboration

Motivation is increased through activities that offer opportunities for *social collaboration*. When children have the opportunity to learn in social situations involving collaboration with the teacher or peers, they are likely to get more done than they could do alone. They also enjoy the experience of the social interaction (Guthrie, 2002).

Children participate in independent reading with peers.

Success

When students complete a task they must consider it a *success*. Often children finish a task in a way that is not completely correct, but if they perceive themselves as being successful, intrinsic motivation is enhanced (Ritchie, James-Szanton, & Howes, 2003). When a child has met with some but not total success, such as spelling the word *read* as *reed*, he or she should be acknowledged for the part of the spelling that is correct. After all, three of the four letters are right. The child's success should be noted, but at the same time he or she needs help with the correct spelling of the word. We don't want to mislead.

The information presented in this chapter is based on motivation theory. The following are objectives to help motivate the desire to read and write.

Objectives and Standards for Motivating Reading and Writing

1. Children should be provided with an environment that is literacy rich, with choices of literacy materials that are challenging but will bring success.
2. Teachers should provide models of literacy behavior for children to emulate.
3. Children need to be given the opportunity to participate in social collaborative settings when reading and writing, as well as opportunities for reading and writing alone.
4. Children should be able to choose literacy activities in which to participate.
5. Children should have the opportunity to listen to stories read by their teachers and peers in a pleasant, relaxed atmosphere.
6. Teachers should allow for response to literature through discussion, role playing, the use of puppets to retell stories, and so on.
7. Children need the opportunity to take books home from the classroom literacy center.
8. Children should experience varied genres of children's literature.
9. Teachers should help children enhance word-analysis skills and comprehension skills using children's literature.
10. Teachers need to provide literacy experiences that involve technology and play.

Standards for literacy achievement generated by various groups, states, and school districts often appear to be skills based. However, most standards are concerned with developing readers and writers who do not learn just the skills of reading and writing, but also the joys of reading and writing. The focus is on the need for children to be motivated to read and write for pleasure and information. The standards in different states and from different groups have included sections about reading and writing habits and expectations for how students will acquire these habits in kindergarten through third grade. The following are standards for reading and writing habits from the National Center on Education and the Economy and the Learning Research and Development Center at the University of Pittsburgh (1999).

Reading Habits

Good reading habits will be established when children have frequent opportunities to read independently. Books that are of high literary quality and interest, represent multiple genres, and are at a greater difficulty level than children could read on their own should be read to children. It is expected in the early childhood grades that to develop a habit of reading, children will have the opportunity to:

- read a wide range of genres in literature, such as poems and stories, functional text (signs, messages, and labels), and narrative and expository texts.
- read several short books a day at school during independent reading periods.
- listen to books read to them each day at school and discuss the books.
- listen to and read books with parents.

Writing Habits

Good writing habits will be established when children have frequent opportunities to write independently. Children should listen to each other's writing. Many different forms of writing should be practiced, such as functional, informational, expository, and narrative writing.

To develop good writing habits and thus enhance motivation to write, it is expected that in the early childhood grades children will:

- write a lot and listen to what others write.
- write independently.
- write in a wide range of genres, such as poems and stories, functional text (signs, messages, and labels), narrative texts, and expository text.
- listen to others' writing and discuss each other's work.
- write at home.

Standards for literacy achievement are important goals to attain. It is particularly important to include the standards just discussed so that we create students who not only can read, but also choose to read for pleasure and information. Time for independent reading and writing has been criticized as wasted time, since children can be off task. It is important to structure these periods to help children reap the benefits of the activities. Ideas for structuring independent reading and writing are discussed later in this chapter.

Preparing a Literacy-Rich Environment

Plato said, "What is honored in a country will be cultivated there." Teachers who honor the development of literacy demonstrate that attitude by providing within their classrooms a rich environment where the use of books can be cultivated. Their students honor literacy development by assimilating the attitudes and atmosphere presented by the teacher.

A classroom **literacy center** is essential for children's immediate access to literature. Children in classrooms with literature collections read and look at books 50 percent more often than children in classrooms without such collections. The efforts spent in creating an inviting atmosphere for a classroom literacy center are rewarded by increased interest in books (Guthrie, 2002). Morrow (1987b) found that well-designed classroom literacy centers significantly increased the number of children who chose to participate in literature activities during free-choice periods. Literacy centers in preschools, kindergartens, and first and second grades that were identified as having specific design characteristics correlated with children's use of the centers during free-choice periods. Conversely, poorly designed literacy centers were among the least popular areas during free-choice periods in early childhood rooms (Morrow, 1982). Suffice it to say, the physical features of a classroom literacy center can play an important role in motivating children to use the area.

Features of Well-Designed Literacy Centers

Classrooms need multiple centers for children to practice skills learned and to work independently. Chapter 4 describes content-area centers to meet this need. Classrooms should have literacy centers that include a library corner and writing area. The library corner in the literacy center will be described in this chapter. In Chapters 7 and 9 the writing area is discussed.

Physical Space

English Language Learners

A classroom literacy center should be a focal area, immediately visible and inviting to anyone entering the classroom. To provide privacy and physical definition, it should be partitioned on two or three sides with bookshelves, a piano, file cabinets, or freestanding bulletin boards. The dimensions of the literacy center will vary with the size of the classroom. Generally, it should be large enough to accommodate five or six children comfortably. The literacy center (Figure 8.1) should be furnished with:

- a rug
- pillows and/or beanbag chairs
- small table and chairs
- headsets and taped stories
- a rocking chair (for teachers to read to children and for children to read to classmates from trade books or their own original writing, or for invited

Figure 8.1 A Classroom Literacy Center

guests to use to read or present other information to the class). The rocking chair is the **Literacy Chair of Honor.**

- elements of softness such as stuffed animals
- books related to stuffed animals when possible, such as a stuffed rabbit next to *The Tale of Peter Rabbit* (Potter, 1902).
- a felt-board with figures of story characters
- a roll movie box (a box with a picture window that looks like a TV. A dowel is inserted at the top and bottom of the box. Use shelving paper to draw the story and attach to dowels; see photo on p. 311).
- puppets
- posters from the Children's Book Council (12 West 37th Street, 2nd Floor, New York, NY 10018; www.cbcbooks.org) and from the American Library Association (50 East Huron Street, Chicago, IL 60611; www.ala.org)
- The Author's Spot, or writing center, which is described thoroughly in Chapter 7.

Children have little privacy in school. Many children relish being alone and sometimes read in coat closets and under shelves. Because it is partially partitioned from the rest of the room, the literacy center provides some privacy. Listening to recorded stories on headsets offers even more privacy, and an oversized carton, painted or covered with contact paper, makes a cozy separate reading room.

The *Author's Spot* is an integral part of the literacy center. It usually consists of:

- a table and chairs
- colored felt-tip pens and crayons
- lined white paper and unlined paper in a range of sizes
- one or more computers
- book-making materials
- colored construction paper
- a stapler and scissors

Children should be involved in the planning and design of a literacy center. They can develop rules for its use, be in charge of keeping it neat and orderly, and select a name for it, such as the Book Nook.

The Library Corner

English Language Learners

Well-designed library corners within literacy centers have several ways for storing books. One type houses the bulk of the books, which are shelved with the spines facing out. Another type is open faced, allowing the covers of the books to be seen; this method is important for calling attention to special books. Featured books are changed regularly and placed on the open-faced shelves for easy access. An alternative to open-faced shelving is the circular wire rack, commonly found in bookstores. These racks and open-faced shelving should highlight books with the themes being studied. These books are changed with the theme and the shelving is used to feature special new selections (Tafa, 2001).

Books in the collection should be shelved by category. They can be color coded according to the type of book. Identify all animal books, for example, by placing a blue dot on their spines and clustering them on a shelf marked Animals, with a blue dot next to the label. An even simpler method is to store genres in plastic crates or cardboard boxes, with labels on the front naming the types of books in the container.

About five to eight books per child are appropriate in a classroom library, with three to four grade levels included. Books should include narrative and expository text. In the past, collections for early childhood were almost exclusively narrative stories. Nonfiction expository text should comprise one-third to one-half of the total selections in a classroom library (Moss, Leone, & Dipillo, 1997).

Books are not difficult to accumulate. They can be purchased inexpensively at yard sales or flea markets. Teachers can borrow up to 20 books a month from most public libraries, ask for book donations from parents, and hold fund-raisers for book purchases. In addition, children's paperback book clubs offer inexpensive books and free bonus books for bulk purchases.

Children's magazines and newspapers belong in the classroom library, even if they are not current. For the cost of mailing and shipping, some publishers and local magazine agencies will donate outdated periodicals to schools.

To ensure continued interest, the teacher must introduce new books and materials and recirculate others in the library corner. Approximately 25 new books should be introduced every two weeks, replacing 25 that have been there for a while. In this way, "old" books will be greeted as new friends a few months later. Recirculation compensates for limited budgets as well.

Books from the library corner should be available for students to check out and take home for a week at a time. The check-out system should be simple. Young children should have specified times to bring books to borrow to the teacher, who notes the date, child's name, and book title. Some kindergarten children have been taught to check out books themselves by copying titles and recording dates on 5×8 cards filed under their own names. Other youngsters enjoy keeping track of books borrowed and read by recording titles and dates on index cards held together with a key ring. Another method for checking out books is a loose-leaf notebook with a page for every child to record books taken out and returned. Figure 8.2 provides a sample check-out notebook page.

Books in the Library Corner

English Language Learners

Books and other materials selected for the library corner should appeal to a variety of interests and span a range of grade levels. It is advisable to stock multiple copies of popular books. Children sometimes enjoy reading a book because a friend is reading it (Morrow, 2002; Pressley, Allington, Wharton-McDonald, Block, & Morrow, 2001; Roskos, Tabors, & Lenhart, 2004). Several types of children's literature should be represented:

Picture storybooks are the most familiar type of children's literature. Their texts are closely associated with their illustrations. Picture storybooks are

Figure 8.2

Loose-Leaf Notebook Page for Checking out Books

Name Talmika Jones

Name of book	Date out	Date in
Green Eggs and Ham	Feb 10	Feb 17
Carrot Seed	Feb 20	Feb 26
Curious George	March 3	March 9
Where the Wild Things Are	March 15	March 21

available on a wide range of topics, and many are known for their excellence. The Caldecott Medal is awarded annually to the illustrator of an outstanding picture storybook. Many of these books have become classics and their authors are renowned—Dr. Seuss, Ezra Jack Keats, Tomie dePaola, Maurice Sendak, and Charlotte Zolotow, to name just a few. Every child should have the benefit of hearing some of these books read. However, emergent readers will often find the vocabulary and syntax too sophisticated to read on their own. Quality picture storybooks will include a setting, a well-defined theme, episodes closely tied to the theme, and a resolution of the story.

Informational books offer nonfiction for readers. For a while we did not include much expository text in our libraries, thinking that young children liked narratives more. As adults we read material that is mostly nonfiction; therefore, we need a lot of experience with this type of text. Informational text is about foreign countries, communities, dinosaurs, famous people, and so on. These texts broaden children's background information, help them to explore new ideas, and often stimulate a deep interest in a particular topic. Quality expository text will have a definitive structure. Good structures found in expository texts include description, sequence, compare and contrast, cause and effect, problem and solution, and exemplification.

A classroom literacy center is crucial for children's immediate access to books.

The rocking chair is the Literacy Chair of Honor.

Picture concept books are appropriate for the very young child. Most do not have story lines, though they often have themes, such as animals or toys. Each page usually carries a picture identified by a printed word. Many picture books are made of cardboard, cloth, or vinyl to withstand rigorous handling. Alphabet and number books are also considered picture concept books.

Traditional literature includes nursery rhymes and fairy tales, familiar stories that are part of our heritage and that originated in the oral tradition of storytelling. We assume that children are familiar with *Goldilocks and the Three Bears* (Daley & Russell, 1999) and *The Three Little Pigs* (Zemach, 1991), yet many youngsters have not been exposed to these traditional stories. Children who *do* know the stories welcome them as old friends.

Realistic literature is a category within picture storybooks that deals with real-life problems. *Tight Times* (1983) by Barbara Hazen, for example, describes how a family handles the problems that arise when the father loses his job. He tries to explain the situation to his son so he will understand when he calls it "tight times." Books in this category deal with issues that many children face, such as bedtime fears or problems that arise when a new baby comes into the family. These books touch on very sensitive issues, such as divorce, drugs, alcohol, and death. Many can be read to the entire class if they address issues that all share. Teachers should use discretion as to what is read to the whole class. They can recommend specific titles to families of children who face difficult issues.

Fables and folktales retell many of the myths and traditional stories that are available in picture-book style for the younger child. Many of these stories originate in other countries and cultures and therefore broaden a child's experience and knowledge base.

Wordless books carry definite story lines within pictures, but use no words. They are often thought appropriate for very young children and are confused with picture books. They are designed not for babies, but for children age 3 and older. The child creates the story by reading the pictures, some of which are intricate.

Poetry is too often forgotten in collections of children's literature at home and in school. Many themed poetry anthologies have been compiled for young children, and they are an important part of the literacy center.

Novels are longer books with chapters. We can begin reading novels to young children to expose them to the genre. They are often very attracted to them and eager to begin to read them. Children call novels *chapter books*.

Children's literature stored by categories in baskets that are labled for access.

Biography is another genre appropriate for young children. There are simple biographies of historical figures, popular figures in sports, and television performers.

Big Books are usually large versions of smaller picture storybooks or original picture storybooks in this large format. They are oversized books that rest on an easel in order to be read. The purpose of the Big Book is for children to be able to see the print as it is being read, to make the association between oral and written language, and to see how the print is read from left to right across the page.

In addition to these categories of books, young children enjoy joke and riddle books; craft books; cookbooks; participation books, which involve them in touching, smelling, and manipulating; books in a series built around a single character; and books related to television programs appropriate for their age. Magazines and newspapers should also be choices for reading in the library corner. They provide a nonthreatening format, different topics, and reading matter for diverse ability levels, and they include multicultural material. Newspapers and magazines appeal to parents as well.

Children particularly enjoy literature that is predictable, because it helps them understand the story line more easily and enables them to read along with the individual reading to them. Predictable literature contains rhyme; repetition; catch phrases; conversation; familiar sequences, such as days of the week or numbers; cumulative patterns, in which events are repeated or added on as the story continues; stories about familiar topics; familiar or popular stories; uncluttered illustrations that match the text; and stories that have well-developed story structures (setting, theme, plot episodes, and resolution).

Listings of children's literature in several categories, including books for children with special needs and multicultural books, are in Appendix A. A special emphasis is placed on informational books in the appendix, since we have neglected this type of text in the past. There is also a list of websites for locating children's books.

The following are children's book clubs and children's book awards that provide additional literature resources:

Book Clubs

Scholastic Book Clubs, Inc., Honeybee (Toddlers–4-year-olds), Club Leo (PreK–8), Firefly (preschool), SeeSaw (K–1), Lucky (2–3), Arrow (4-6), Tab (grades 7 and up), TRC (teens); 2931 East McCarty Street, PO Box 7504, Jefferson City, MO 65102-7504; 800-724-6527

Trumpet Book Club, PO Box 7511, Jefferson City, MO 65102; 800-826-0110

Children's Book Awards

Caldecott Medal. American Library Association, 50 East Huron Street, Chicago, IL, 60611-2795

Children's Book Showcase. Children's Book Council, 12 W. 37th Street, 2nd floor, New York, NY 10018-7480

Newbery Medal. American Library Association, 50 East Huron Street, Chicago, IL, 60611-2795

Other Materials in the Literacy Center

The literacy center needs to contain language arts materials for skill development. Manipulatives that help children learn letters of the alphabet, rhymes, and sound–symbol relationships of consonants, digraphs, and long and short vowels should be included in a special section of the center. These manipulatives come in the form of magnetic letters, puzzles, bingo games, and board games, to name a few. Teacher-made materials can also be used. (These types of materials are described more fully in Chapter 5, which deals with skill development.) Materials to enhance comprehension must also be available in the literacy center. Techniques described later in this chapter, such as using a felt-board and story characters for storytelling and organizing puppet presentations, engage children in demonstrating knowledge of story sequence and structure, classifying details, predicting outcomes, and interpreting text—skills that develop and enhance comprehension of text.

Reactions to Literacy Centers

Teachers and children had the following reactions to literacy centers in their classrooms that I had designed. Teachers said that they were originally concerned that there was not enough space in their rooms for literacy centers and were surprised that all the materials could fit. Eventually, teachers themselves provided more space for the literacy centers. Teachers commented that the physical presence of the literacy center made a statement to the children that literacy was valued because space was taken from the classroom to make room for the area. Teachers agreed that children were attracted to the area by the manipulative materials in the center, such as the felt-board stories and puppets.

They found that the rocking chair, rug, pillows, and stuffed animals made the center relaxing and comfortable for reading. One teacher remarked:

> *The literacy center became a place where children of all reading and writing abilities mingled. This social context seemed to provide an atmosphere for cooperative learning. The children looked forward to their time there each day.*

A child commented:

> *I liked to cuddle up on the pillows with a book, or crawl into a private spot, or rock in the rocking chair and read. You get to take books home right from the classroom center.*

Children referred to the center as a special place. They felt that the literacy center could be improved by adding more space, more books, and more time to use it. One child commented, "The only thing missing from the literacy center is a snack bar."

The Teacher as a Model to Motivate Interest

The teacher plays a critical role in influencing children's attitudes toward reading and their voluntary reading.

> *One of the clear points to emerge from research into reading failure is that there was no association between reading and pleasure. The role of teachers in stimulating voluntary reading among children and young people is potentially the most powerful of all adult influences upon the young.* (Irving, 1980, p. 7)

Programs that incorporate pleasurable experiences with literature create interest in and enthusiasm for books, which in turn increases children's voluntary use of books (McKenna, 2001). Among other specific activities in early childhood classrooms, teachers should read or tell stories to children daily. Interest heightens when stories are discussed both before and after being read, especially if they are related to issues that reflect children's real-life experiences or current school topics. Literal and inferential discussions can be introduced even at the preschool level. Skill development can easily be incorporated into storybook reading activities in pleasurable and meaningful ways. The following example describes a discussion about *Goldilocks and the Three Bears* in which inferential and critical comprehension is being developed with 4-year-olds.

After reading *Goldilocks and the Three Bears*, I asked who were the good and the bad characters. Hands waved in the air, and Jennifer answered, "Goldilocks was good and the bears were bad." When I asked Jennifer why she thought that, she said, "Well, the bears scared Goldilocks."

Another hand went up and Tim said, "No, that's not right. The bears are good and Goldilocks is bad. Goldilocks went into the bears' house when they weren't home. She ate their food and didn't even ask."

"That's right," said Megan, "and she broke their chair and went to sleep in their bed and didn't even ask if it was okay."

The library corner invites children to read, and the Author's Spot provides accessible materials for writers.

Chris chimed in, "Yeah, Goldilocks was really bad. She did a lot of bad things because she didn't ask if she could."

"Would you go into a stranger's house and do the things Goldilocks did?" I asked. The whole group called out in unison "Nooooo." I asked why not. Sara answered, "Because that is bad. It's like stealing. She was naughty. If the cops found out, I bet they would arrest her."

Discussion about authors and illustrators also arouses interest. Reading different stories by the same author or a series of books about the same character, such as *Frog and Toad Are Friends* (Lobel, 1979) or *Amelia Bedelia* (Parrish, 1970), increases interest as well. Read different kinds of literature to the class, and as often as possible coordinate stories with topics being discussed. If the topic is spring, bring a cocoon to class, discuss the life cycle of a butterfly, and follow the discussion with *The Very Hungry Caterpillar* (Carle, 1969), the story of the caterpillar's transformation to a butterfly. Read and recite poetry together regularly. Recruit older children, the principal, the custodian, the nurse, the librarian, parents, and grandparents to read to classes, to small groups, and to individuals. Encourage children to share books with one another. Books from home should be shared with the group and children should be encouraged to take books home from school.

Many popular folk songs have been made into picture storybooks, such as *Go Tell Aunt Rhody* (Quackenbush, 1973) and *Old MacDonald Had a Farm* (Quackenbush, 1972). These books are particularly good to read to children because the children are familiar with the words and want to pretend to read the books themselves. Cooking is another pleasurable activity that can be related to literature. Many picture storybooks feature food, such as *Bread and Jam for Frances* (Hoban, 1964). After reading the story, the class can make bread and jam or whatever food is appropriate. Art activities also can be motivated by story readings. After reading *The Snowy Day* (Keats, 1962), have children create a winter collage from blue construction paper, white cotton, wool, doilies, chalk, and silver foil. After reading *Where the Wild Things Are* (Sendak, 1963), ask kindergarteners and first graders to think of a wild thing and draw a picture of it. Gather their pictures into a class book. Class books become favorites and are read frequently. Children also enjoy filmstrips and videos, which motivate their interest in reading the associated book.

Story Reading and Storytelling with Expository and Narrative Text

Making Story Reading Pleasurable

Being read to helps to create positive attitudes toward reading and writing. The warmth that accompanies storybook reading by a caring adult lasts beyond the experience. It involves ritual, sharing, and mutual good feelings. Certain books take on special meanings between an adult and child through repetition or because they are favorites of the one or the other. My daughter and I have a special relationship with the book *Alexander and the Terrible, Horrible, No Good, Very Bad Day* (Viorst, 1972). I first read it to Stephanie when she was 4, and whenever things seemed to go wrong for her, I found myself saying, "I guess you're having a terrible, horrible, no good, very bad day." Soon, when things were not going well for me, she would say the same thing to me. When Stephanie was in the seventh grade, she came home from school one day wearing only one sneaker and looking generally distraught.

"What's the problem?" I asked.

She replied, "Someone stole one of my sneakers, I got yelled at for talking when my friend asked me a question in class and I answered her, I have tons of homework, and I lost my assignment notebook."

"I guess you're having a terrible, horrible, no good, very bad day," I said.

She smiled and said, "You're right, so I think I'll move to Australia."

"Some days are like that, even in Australia," I replied. We both laughed.

A more recent ritual started with my grandson James and the book *What Cried Granny: an Almost Bedtime Story* (Lum & Johnson, 1998). In the book Patrick is sleeping overnight at his Granny's house for the first time. She says it is bedtime, but he has no bed, so Granny cuts down trees and makes him a bed. This same scenario continues; he has no pillow, so Granny collects feathers from the hens in the hen house, and so on. Each time Granny says it is bedtime Patrick finds something that is missing such as, "But Granny I have no blanket." "What!," cried Granny. Consequently, at breakfast after a sleepover, James says as we are preparing the table, "Grandma Weswey, you forgot the napkins," and I say "What!" and pretend to be running to get napkins. James giggles and giggles.

The familiar words of a familiar book can create special rituals. Good feelings gained in story readings transfer to the act of reading itself (International Reading Association, 2006; Dickinson, De Temple, Hirschler, & Smith, 1992).

In the discussion that follows, the word *story* refers to both the use of narrative and expository text. A story is the reading, telling, or reporting of an event or series of events whether fictitious or nonfiction. For quite a while narrative stories have been used almost exclusively with young children, with little exposure to expository text. Surveys of primary classrooms show that less than 15 percent of the read-aloud materials were expository (Yopp & Yopp, 2000). The concept has been that children must learn to read narrative text in the early grades before reading to learn information with expository text in the upper grades. This unnatural separation has caused difficulties for students when the focus shifts to expository text in fourth grade and children are unfamiliar with the genre. Adults read and write more nonfiction than narrative text. Yet in early childhood classrooms children are infrequently exposed to expository text. There is a misconception that 3- to 8-year-olds are too young to understand and enjoy expository books. Therefore, in the discussion that follows we are talking about story reading and storytelling with both expository and narrative text.

To make story reading as enjoyable and pleasurable as possible, select good pieces of literature. Good narrative text includes the following:

- A *setting* with well-delineated characters, a time, and place described
- A well-designed *theme* concerning the problem or goal of the main character
- *Episodes,* which are a series of plot-related events that help the main character to solve his or her problem or achieve the goal
- A *resolution,* which is the solution to the problem or the achievement of the goal

Quality expository text should be selected for reading as often as narrative and include a definitive structure. The types of expository text that children should be exposed to include the following:

- *Description:* Description gives the reader a picture of the subject based on story observation.
- *Sequence:* Sequence explains the steps that produce a certain product or outcome.
- *Compare and contrast:* Comparisons are usually made in two ways. In block comparisons, two items (with a similar classification) are compared and then contrasted. In point-by-point comparisons, similarities and differences are compared alternately.
- *Cause and effect:* Causality tells why something happens.
- *Problem–solution:* A problem is presented, followed by its solution. An understanding of chronology is necessary to comprehend this structure.
- *Exemplification* (reason and example): The main idea is presented with supporting details (Vukelich, Evans, & Albertson, 2003).

Good expository and narrative texts include clear and uncluttered illustrations, catch phrases, rhyme, and repetition.

A teacher should read to youngsters in a relaxed atmosphere in a location designated for such readings. Each day let a different child sit close to you while you are reading, with the other children in a single or double semicircle. If you have a rocking chair, use it as the place where you sit when you read. Because children enjoy seeing illustrations in books during story reading, hold the book so it faces the group or turn the book at appropriate pauses so its pictures can be seen. Before reading a story to a group, practice reading it aloud to yourself.

Be expressive in your reading, change your voice and facial expressions when a different character speaks, and highlight special events. A story reading is like a dramatic presentation. Read slowly and with a great deal of animation. Record or videotape your readings so that you can evaluate and improve your technique. Begin a story with an introduction like the following:

> *Today I'm going to read a story about a little girl who wants to get her mother a present for her birthday. She can't think of anything and asks a rabbit to help her. The title of the story is* Mr. Rabbit and the Lovely Present *(Zolotow, 1977). The author's name is Charlotte Zolotow, and the illustrator is Maurice Sendak. While I read the story, think of which part of the present you like the best. When you have finished reading the story, begin a discussion with a question such as "Who would like to tell me which part of the present you liked best?"*

Creative Storytelling Techniques

English Language Learners

Storytelling strongly attracts children to books (Ritchie, James-Szanton, & Howes, 2003). It has a power that reading stories does not, for it frees the storyteller to use creative techniques. It also has the advantage of keeping the storyteller close to the audience. Telling a story produces an immediate response from the audience and is one of the surest ways to establish a rapport between the listeners and the storyteller. Long pieces of literature can be trimmed so that even very young children can hear whole stories in one sitting. Considered an art, storytelling can be mastered by most people. Storytelling is an extremely important technique for our classrooms filled with children from diverse backgrounds. Many of these children come from cultures where storytelling as opposed to storybook reading is more the norm. This strategy will be a comfortable one that they will enjoy and learn from.

It is not necessary to memorize a story, but be sure you know it well. Use all the catch phrases and quotes that are important to the story. Use expression in your presentation, but do not let your dramatic techniques overshadow the story itself. Look directly at your audience and take their attention into consideration. Storytelling allows you to shorten stories as you go if attention spans seem to be short. It is important to have the original book at hand when you have finished telling a story so that the children can see it and enjoy it again through its pictures and printed text.

Creative techniques help storytelling come alive. They excite the imagination, involve the listeners, and motivate children to try storytelling themselves and create their own techniques. Take clues for creative techniques from the

Children act out *The Three Little Pigs* using face puppets.

story. Some stories lend themselves to the use of puppets, others are perfect for the felt-board, and still others can be worked up as chalk talks.

Felt-boards with story characters are a popular and important tool in a classroom. You can make characters or purchase them. Prepare your own with construction paper covered with clear contact or laminate. Attach strips of felt or sandpaper to the backs of the cutouts so they cling to the felt-board. Narrative and expository texts that lend themselves to felt-board retelling are those with a limited number of characters who appear throughout the story or a limited number of ideas.

Puppets are used with stories rich in dialogue. There are many kinds of puppets, including finger, hand, stick, and face puppets. Shy children often feel secure telling stories with puppets. Such stories as *The Gingerbread Boy* (Galdone, 1983) and *The Little Red Hen* (Pinkey, 2006) are appropriately told with puppets because they are short, have few characters, and repeat dialogue. An informational book can be retold by a puppet.

Sound-story techniques allow both audience and storyteller to provide sound effects when they are called for in a book. The sounds can be made with voices, rhythm instruments, or music. When preparing to tell such a story, first select those parts of the story for which sound effects will be used. Then decide on each sound to be made and who will make it. As the story is told, students and storyteller chime in with their assigned sounds. Record the presentation, then leave the recording in the literacy center with the original book. Among books that adapt easily to sound-story techniques are *Too Much Noise* (McGovern, 1992) and *Mr. Brown Can Moo! Can You?* (Seuss, 1998).

Prop stories are easy to develop. Simply collect stuffed animals, toys, and other articles that represent characters and objects in a story. Display the props at appropriate times during the storytelling. Three stuffed bears and a yellow-haired doll aid in telling *Goldilocks and the Three Bears* (Daley & Russell, 1999). Several toy trains aid in *The Little Engine That Could* (Piper, 1990) and could be used with an informational book about trains as well.

Chalk talks are another technique that attracts listeners. The storyteller draws the story while telling it. Chalk talks are most effective when done with a large chalkboard so that the story can keep going in sequence from beginning to end. The same technique can be carried out on mural paper hung across a wall; the storyteller simply uses crayons or felt-tip markers instead of chalk. The chalk-talk technique can also be adapted to easel and chart paper or an overhead projector. Choose a story with simple illustrations. Draw only a select few pictures as you tell the story. Some stories have been written as chalk talks, including an entire series, *Harold and the Purple Crayon* (Johnson, 1981).

Headsets with taped stories are also popular materials in the literacy center. The stories are most often read, but can be told on a tape for children to listen to and follow along in the text. They are helpful with English language learners because they provide a model for correct English. They are also good for struggling readers who can follow along in the text while listening to a fluent reader. Have parents, the principal, teachers, the nurse, the superintendent, and others record the tapes. Eventually, children can make tapes for others as well.

Because numerous techniques for storytelling have not been mentioned, you can add to this list. All the materials discussed need to be modeled for children, who will then want to become storytellers themselves. After modeling children can do the following:

- Tell the story that the teacher modeled with one of the techniques the teacher used.
- Create a technique for presenting a piece of literature they know well that has been selected by the teacher.
- Present the completed project to the class.
- Write an original story and create a technique for presentation. When it is complete, the children who worked on the project can present it to the class and then place it in the literacy center for others to use.

Storytelling activities involve children in literal comprehension because they must know the sequence, details, and elements of the story. They must problem solve as they create the materials, deciding what parts of the story to include or delete. They interpret voices of characters as they make a presentation of their finished project to the class.

The teaching of specific skills can be embedded into teacher presentations of storytelling techniques. For example, if you need to teach letter-writing skills, the story *A Letter to Amy* (Keats, 1998) is a perfect selection. The story is about a boy who wants to invite a girl to his birthday party, but he worries that his friends might laugh. He sends her an invitation and wonders if she will come and what will happen. The book contains a lot of discussion about the letter. A student of mine taught letter writing and introduced it by telling a felt-board version of *A Letter to Amy*. One of the items in the story for the felt-board was an envelope with a well-written letter having the appropriate heading, format, and so on. Children used this model to write letters of invitation to others.

Story Reading and Storytelling: Vignettes from the Classroom

I had the opportunity to work with several first- and second-grade teachers who practiced sharing literature with children in pleasurable ways. The teachers read and told stories and made manipulatives for storytelling to use in their classrooms. These teachers incorporated many of the strategies discussed earlier, and one of them commented about these strategies:

> *The children enjoy being read to, and they never grow tired of this activity. I thought that in second grade, reading to youngsters wasn't that important anymore; however, the benefits of read-aloud sessions became quite evident as I involved my children in them more and more. The stories generated sophisticated discussion; we'd relate them to the students' own life experiences. We discussed authors, illustrations, and elements of story structure. Through these story readings and discussions, I found that my students seemed to appreciate literature more, they became more aware of the different genres of children's literature that exist, and vocabulary and comprehension were enhanced as well. I realized how important it was for me to model reading to children and in many different ways. I read using felt characters, roll movies, chalk talks, and so on. I learned how to make reading more appealing for the children. Consequently, I saw an increased desire in my children to read as they modeled my behavior in reading stories I had read to them and used the storytelling props.*

Second graders who listened to the teacher tell stories and use story techniques were asked what they learned and liked. They commented:

> *I like it when the teacher reads to us. She uses such good expression, you can learn to read better yourself by listening to her. The teacher reads and tells stories in many different ways so it is always interesting, and you can learn to do it the way she does.*

One day during a story-reading session in a second-grade class with a focus on making comparisons between styles of illustrators, Ms. Payton told the children that she was going to read two picture storybooks that they had heard before. She asked the children to concentrate on the pictures or illustrations as she read the stories and to note their styles so that the children could describe them. After she read the stories, she asked if the children thought that the books were illustrated by the same individual. They all said no because they looked very different. Ms. Payton identified the illustrators (and also authors) of the books, who were Ezra Jack Keats for *Peter's Chair* (1967) and Dr. Seuss for *Green Eggs and Ham* (1960). Then she asked the children to describe the illustrations for each book.

Tamika said, "Well, in *Peter's Chair* the illustrations look like a painting. They are made like they are real. I think Ezra Jack Keats is a very good drawer. I like the colors he uses."

Ms. Payton explained that not only does Mr. Keats paint his pictures, but he also uses collage as a technique. When you look closely at his illustrations, you see bits of wallpaper, newspaper, doilies, and so on blended into his pictures.

Ms. Payton asked if someone would like to describe the style of the other book. Marcel raised his hand. He said, "Dr. Seuss is very different from Keats; he uses lots of lines and sort of fantasy little shapes. He uses colors on people and things that aren't what we usually expect. His drawings look like cartoons, and the other ones look like real things."

The discussion was followed by the children's illustrating stories they had written. They were told that their illustrations could be their own original styles or that they could use the style of an illustrator in a storybook that they knew. Ms. Payton walked around to talk about the work the children were doing. Magda decided to make her drawings similar to those of Dr. Seuss, and Ms. Payton said to her, "Magda, if Dr. Seuss came through our door he would think that he illustrated your story, your work looks so much like his." Magda is a child with limited English proficiency. The positive reinforcement in this situation started a conversation about her work with the teacher.

Reading and Writing Independently

ELL

English Language Learners

Research has shown that the amount of free reading done by children, both in and out of school, correlates with reading achievement. In a large-scale investigation of elementary school children, it was found that students who reported reading 2 minutes a day outside of school scored at the 30th percentile on standardized reading tests. Children who read 5 minutes a day scored at the 50th percentile. Those who read 10 minutes a day scored at the 70th percentile, and children who read 20 minutes a day scored at the 90th percentile (Anderson, Fielding, and Wilson, 1988; Taylor, Frye, & Maruyama, 1990). Children who read voluntarily develop lifelong, positive attitudes toward reading.

Sustained silent reading and DEAR time (Drop Everything and Read) have been defined as a quiet time for children to engage in silent reading. Everyone in the classroom selects a book, sits alone, and reads. Silent reading is important because it allows children to practice skills learned and to concentrate on understanding what is read. However, these periods have been criticized because children spend a lot of time selecting a book, and when they finally sit down to read, they often flip through the pages and do not do much reading. In addition, there has been no accountability for what is read.

To be more productive, independent reading and writing periods can focus on a content-area theme that is being studied in the classroom, an author or illustrator, or a particular genre of children's literature. For example, if children are learning about animals, the teacher can explain that their book selection for independent reading and writing can only be about this topic. The teacher should separate these books from others on the shelf. There can be a special spot for independent reading books on the shelf, or they can be in a special basket. Limiting the number of books helps to make the selection task easier and quicker for the child. (Ritchie, James-Szanton, & Howes, 2003). For the purposes of accountability to help keep children stay on task, they can keep a log of the number of pages read during independent reading and writing time, write one sentence about what they read, or copy a sentence from the book they liked. Keep the task very simple and one that will take very little time. But with this task, children are more likely to concentrate on their independent reading rather than have their minds wander. Teachers need to set rules and review them before independent reading and writing begins. Some appropriate rules follow:

- Select your book quickly.
- Read only one book in a period.

- Record the name of the book and the date it was read in your log.
- Write a one-sentence note to the author about what you liked about the book.

Literature Activities Initiated by the Teacher

Literature activities need to be modeled and initiated by teachers to encourage children's interests. The following is a list of motivating suggestions to use on a regular basis:

Carry Out on a Daily Basis

1. Read or tell narrative and expository stories to children.
2. Discuss literal and interpretive issues in stories read.
3. Allow children to check books out of the classroom library.
4. Have children keep track of books read.
5. Have children keep the library corner neat and organized.

Do Several of the Following Each Week

1. Have the principal, custodian, nurse, secretary, or a parent read to the children at school.
2. Discuss authors and illustrators.
3. Write to authors.
4. Have older children read to younger children.
5. Have children read to each other.
6. Show DVDs of stories.
7. Use literature across the curriculum in content-area lessons.
8. Use art to respond to books (e.g., draw a mural of a story using art techniques modeled after a particular illustrator).
9. Tell stories using creative storytelling techniques.
10. Have children tell stories with and without props.
11. Have children act out stories.
12. Prepare recipes related to stories (e.g., make stone soup after reading the story of the same name).
13. Read TV-related stories.
14. Make class books and individual books; bind them and store in the library corner.
15. Sing songs that have been made into books and have the book on hand (e.g., *I Know an Old Lady*).
16. Make bulletin boards related to books.
17. Have children write advertisements for good books they have read.
18. Discuss proper ways to care for and handle books.

Children use the literacy center first thing in the morning when they arrive at school.

19. Read, recite, and write poetry.
20. Have a 10- to 20-minute independent reading and writing period a few times a week.

Carry Out on a Regular Basis

1. Feature and introduce new books on the open-faced bookshelves.
2. Introduce new books added to the library corner.
3. Circulate 25 new books into the library corner every 2 weeks.
4. Have a bookstore in the school where children can buy books regularly.

Carry Out a Few Times a Year If Possible

1. Give bookmarks to children.
2. Give each child a book as a gift.
3. Have a young authors conference (share books children have written; bind books; invite authors, illustrators, storytellers, poets).
4. Have a book fair for children to purchase books.
5. Have a book celebration day (e.g., dress up as book characters, tell stories to each other, show movie and filmstrip stories, have stories told creatively).
6. Have children order books from a book club.
7. Invite an author or illustrator to speak to the children about their work.

Activities for Parents Related to the School Literature Program

1. Provide a newsletter a few times a year about book-related activities in school.
2. Ask parents to participate in some literature-related activity at school (e.g., reading to children, helping with book binding, raising money to buy books).
3. Have a workshop for parents that describes the importance, purpose, and activities of the school literature program.
4. Have a workshop for parents describing how they can participate in independent home reading programs.
5. Provide booklists for parents with suggestions for their home library.

Motivating Reading and Writing with Literacy Center Time

The literacy center is an important part of the classroom that acts as a source for motivating reading and writing. It is used in many ways.

1. The literacy center is used to engage children in productive literacy work as soon as they arrive at school.
2. When children finish their work before others, the literacy center is used to engage in interesting activities and reinforce strategies learned.
3. The literacy center engages students in productive independent work, freeing the teacher to work with small groups of students in guided reading instruction, one-on-one teaching, and assessment.
4. The literacy center allows students to select and enjoy literacy activities in a social setting during periods set aside to read and write for pleasure and information. The purpose of these activities is to develop lifelong voluntary readers and writers.

Elements that help motivate children include choice, social interaction, challenge, and success. When children work in the literacy center, they have a choice of activity. These activities are most often done with peers in a social setting. The activities are challenging, but designed to allow for success.

Organizing Literacy Center Time

During literacy center time, children make decisions about what they will do and with whom they will work. Some guidelines for children to follow are shown in Figure 8.3. These are posted in the classroom and reviewed before each session.

Figure 8.3

Rules for Using Materials during Literacy Center Time

1. Decide with whom you will work or if you will work alone.
2. Choose a reading or writing activity from the literacy center.
3. Do only one or two activities.
4. Use the materials in or outside the literacy center.
5. Handle the materials carefully.
6. Speak in soft voices; people are working.
7. Put materials back in their places before taking out others.
8. Try activities you haven't done before.
9. Try working with people you haven't worked with before.
10. Be ready to share completed activities with the class.
11. Record completed tasks in your log.
12. Keep the literacy center neat.

Figure 8.4

Rules for
Cooperating
in Groups during
Literacy Center
Time

Helpful Things to Do When Working in Groups

- Select a leader to help the group get started.
- Give everyone a job.
- Share the materials and take turns talking.
- Listen to your friends when they talk.
- Stay with your group.

Helpful Things to Say When Working in Groups

- Can I help you?
- I like your work.
- You did a good job.

Check Your Work

- Did you say helpful things?
- Did you help each other?
- Did you share materials and take turns?
- Did you all have jobs?
- How well did your jobs get done?
- What can we do better next time?

English Language Learners

In addition to rules pertaining to the use of materials, children are taught cooperative skills that are practiced and posted as shown in Figure 8.4. These include helpful things to say and do for each other during literacy center time (Morrow, 1997).

When the literacy center is first used, some teachers assign children to groups of two or three, determine the activity in which children will participate, and appoint a leader to help organize the project. As a result of participating in the assigned groups with assigned tasks, children eventually can make these decisions about what to do on their own. To help children select activities, things to do during literacy center time are posted and reviewed, as illustrated in Figure 8.5. In addition, cards that explain how to use each activity are also posted (see Figure 8.6).

For children who are beginning readers, teachers often include pictures representing activities on the activity cards to help with reading rules and roles. However, teachers need to review these lists so that children will learn what they say and begin to read them.

At the literacy center, children practice skills learned and learn to participate in reading and writing activities independently. Early in the program, some children do not stay on task. Within a few weeks, most of the children will be able to complete activities.

Figure 8.5

Things to Do during Literacy Center Time

1. Read or look at a book, magazine, or newspaper.
2. Read to or share a book with a friend.
3. Listen to someone read to you.
4. Listen to a taped story and follow the words in the book.
5. Use the felt-board with a storybook and felt characters.
6. Use the roll movie with its storybook.
7. Write a story.
8. Draw a picture about a story you read.
9. Make a book for a story you wrote.
10. Make a felt story for a book you read or a story you wrote.
11. Write a puppet show and perform it for friends.
12. Make a taped story for a book you read or a story you wrote.
13. Check out books to take home and read.
14. Use activity cards with directions for the task you select.

Figure 8.6

Activity Card

Tell a Story Using the Felt-Board

1. Select a leader for your group.
2. Select a book and the matching felt-story characters.
3. Decide who will read or tell the story and who will use the felt characters.
4. Take turns reading and placing the felt figures on the board.
5. Be ready to present the story to the class.
6. Record the activity in your log (see Figure 8.7 for a log sample).
7. Check your work:
   How well was the story presented?
   How well did the group work together?

Children often spend a good deal of time on projects from the literacy center, which may extend over a few days. When center time ends and a child has not completed an activity, a place is provided for projects to be stored. Each child fills in a log at the end of literacy center time to show what he or she accomplished during that period (Figure 8.7).

Teachers should share center materials from other classrooms to increase their supply. Children can be involved in making materials for the literacy center. They can record taped stories and make felt stories and roll movies for others to use in the listening center. They can create original stories and make

Figure 8.7   Log Sample

Log: Circle, draw, or write about what you did during literacy center time

Name _____

Activity _____   Date _____

| Read by myself | Read to a friend | Told a roll movie | Listened to a taped story |

| Told a felt story | Wrote a story | Made a felt story, roll movie, or picture | Other |

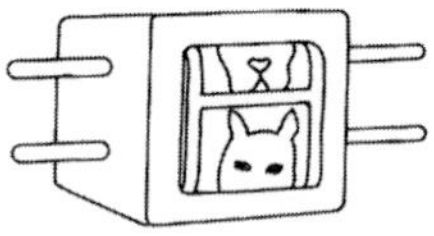

Write or draw what you did:

Source: Adapted from *The Literacy Center: Contexts for Reading and Writing*, 2nd ed., by Lesley M. Morrow, copyright © 2002, with permission of Stenhouse Publishers.

them into books for the classroom library. Participation in these activities promotes a feeling of ownership and respect for the area (Morrow, 1997).

The Teacher's Role during Literacy Center Time

Besides preparing the literacy center environment, the teacher also plays an important role before and during literacy center time. The teacher models the use of literacy activities before they are ever put into the center so that children are familiar with them. He or she helps children to get activities started and participates along with the children in their activities when they need assistance. The goal for this period, however, is for the children to be self-directed in the activities undertaken.

During literacy center time, children may choose to tell a roll movie story or listen to a book on tape. All activities are literature related and are accompanied by the original book.

The effort to help children be independent when using the literacy center will be extremely beneficial when teachers work with small groups for guided reading instruction. During such instruction, all children, except for a few who are working with the teacher, need to be productively involved in independent literacy activities.

Skills Developed during Literacy Center Time

The data collected in several research studies of students who participated in literacy center time revealed that students participated in many different activities (Morrow, Sharkey, & Firestone, 1994). The activities were self-directed and involved the children in making decisions about what work to do and how to carry through with their plans. Children read books, wrote stories, and engaged in projects, such as creating puppet presentations for pieces they had written or read. Most activities were done in groups of two or three and involved peer cooperation and peer tutoring. The groups were composed of single and mixed genders. Children took charge of their learning and demonstrated the use of oral reading, silent reading, and writing, while demonstrating their comprehension of text in literal and inferential discussions.

Literacy center activities expose children to reading and writing in many forms and give them the opportunity to make choices. These activities constitute a positive approach toward activating interest in reading and writing and provide a time to practice and learn skills. Because of the element of choice, there is something for everyone: gifted, average, and children with special needs. Children from different backgrounds work together on similar interests. Children with language differences are welcomed as members of groups doing puppet shows and felt stories and are given roles by which they can participate.

I work with teachers regularly to implement programs similar to those described here. I visit the classrooms often. Mrs. Lynch had a second-grade class in an urban district that I had been working with for an entire school year. I visited her room on the last day of school to say good-bye to the children.

Mrs. Lynch and I shared a sense of pride while observing the children during a literacy center time. We saw some children curled up on a rug or leaning on pillows in the literacy center with books they had selected themselves. Louis and Ramon were squeezed tightly into a rocking chair, sharing a book. Marcel, Patrick, and Roseangela snuggled under a shelf—a "private spot" filled with stuffed animals. They took turns reading.

Tesha and Tiffany were on the floor with a felt-board and character cut-outs from *The Gingerbread Boy* (Galdone, 1983), alternately reading and manipulating the figures: "Run, run as fast as you can! You can't catch me, I'm the Gingerbread Man!"

Four children listened on headsets to tapes of Maurice Sendak's *Pierre* (1991), each child holding a copy of the book and chanting along with the narrator, "I don't care, I don't care."

Tyrone had a Big Book and gave several other children copies of the same story in smaller format. Role playing a teacher, he read to the others, occasionally stopping to ask who would like to read.

Leon read a story he had written to Tamaika. When he finished, she suggested acting out Leon's story with puppets, which they did. Throughout the dramatization, Leon behaved like the director of a play. He knew his story and his characters and wanted them to act in a manner that reflected his intent.

Much of the information discussed here represents the results of studies that involved classroom observation and intervention in kindergarten through second grade. Children in these classrooms participated in literacy programs that included activities that have been described in this chapter. These youngsters scored significantly better on tests of reading comprehension, the ability to retell and rewrite stories, and the ability to create original oral and written stories by including elements of story structure than children in classrooms that did not participate in the program. Children in the treatment classrooms also showed significant improvement in use of vocabulary and language complexity (Morrow, 1990, 1992; Morrow, O'Connor, & Smith, 1990).

Reacting to Literacy Center Time

Teachers and children were interviewed to determine their attitudes toward literacy center time and the program in general.

Teachers commented that the children particularly like literacy center time because they are able to

- choose activities they want to do.
- choose the books they want to read.
- choose to work alone or with others.
- choose manipulatives, such as puppets and felt stories.

Teachers said that children learned the following during literacy center time:

- To work together and cooperate with each other
- To be independent and make decisions
- A sense of story structure from the stories they listened to and read
- New vocabulary

- A better understanding of what they read or what was read to them
- An appreciation for books and knowledge of different genres of children's literature
- That their peers could teach them and were willing to do so

By participating in the program teachers said they learned that

- the social family atmosphere created at center time was conducive to learning.
- children are able to collaborate and work independently.
- there is something for everyone, advanced and slower children, in the literacy center. Allowing children to work in the literacy center made the teachers more flexible and spontaneous. They became facilitators of learning rather than always teachers.
- children who do not readily participate in reading and writing did so during literacy center time. It may be because they are making the decisions about what they do.

In the student interviews, children were asked what they learned in the literature program, and they answered:

- You learn that reading can be fun.
- You learn to read and write better because you read a lot.
- You learn to understand what you are reading, and you learn a lot of new words.
- You get to learn how to read better because kids who know how to read well help you.
- You learn about authors and illustrators and that they are people like you, and you think that you could be one. (Morrow, 1992)

Evaluating Literacy Center Time

A major concern of literacy center time is helping children who are not on task. Typically about 85 percent of a class will work well independently. One good thing about literacy center time is that you can see who is off task. When we teach whole groups, we never know. Children learn to look like they are involved. To help with on-task behavior, structure activities for those having difficulty. Be sure activities include a completed task to give to the teacher.

During literacy center time, teachers observed their classes to notice which children were on task, which children needed help getting started, and what activities the children were choosing to participate in. They periodically made changes in the management of literacy center time to help enhance productivity.

Teachers recorded anecdotes of activities and collected writing samples. They made audiotapes and videotapes of the groups at work and of performances of completed tasks. Children were involved in evaluating their literacy center time activities. They discussed how they cooperated and the quality of their completed tasks. When completed activities were presented, peers offered constructive criticism. Children were asked about their suggestions for improving the program and identified materials and books they wanted added to the centers.

Teachers discussed literacy center designs and how they might be improved to increase student productivity. Teachers moved the center from one area of the room to another, because they found a space that was bigger, brighter, or quieter. They added books and manipulatives to provide more choices for children. Figure 8.8 provides an evaluation form for assessing your literacy center.

Use of Technology to Motivate Literacy Development

English Language Learners

New literacies involve print materials that deal with computers, the Internet, and technology in general. Technology is important in the early childhood classroom; it is a part of our lives and a source of motivation for literacy instruction. Technology offers young children opportunities to develop literacy skills. Computers allow children to construct knowledge in social or independent literacy settings in which they deal with word study or with the meaning of text (Labbo & Ash, 1998). For example, electronic books have been found to motivate children to read and enhance their achievement in analyzing words, recalling details of stories, and acquiring a sense of story structure (Kinzer & McKenna, 1999; Stine, 1993).

The Internet connects children to limitless sources of information from around the world. As teachers of young children, we need to be aware of what computers can do so that we can help our students use the technology to enhance their literacy development.

Computer Software

Software programs are one of the most common ways for teachers to use computers with children. The following general rules should be followed when selecting software for use (Wepner & Ray, 2000):

Instructions for children are concise, clear, and easy to follow.

The activities are engaging, promote active participation, and will hold the attention and interest of children.

The content matches and expands on what children are learning within their school curriculum.

The program provides practice for concepts being learned.

The text is narrated and highlighted for children to be able to deal with the activities independently.

There is a guide for teachers for introducing and using the software.

Assessment is provided.

Quality software is available for every type of literacy skill, such as the development of phonemic awareness, phonics, comprehension, writing, and vocabulary. According to Wepner and Ray (2000), the following criteria

Figure 8.8 Literacy Center Evaluation Form

	Yes	No
1. Children participate in some phase of the library corner design (develop rules, select a name for the area, develop materials, etc.).	☐	☐
2. The area is placed in a quiet section of the room.	☐	☐
3. The area is visually and physically accessible.	☐	☐
4. Part of the area is partitioned off from the rest of the room.	☐	☐
5. Bookshelves are available for storing books with spines facing outward.	☐	☐
6. There is an organizational system for shelving books (e.g., color coding by topic).	☐	☐
7. Open-faced bookshelves are available for new featured books.	☐	☐
8. Five to eight books are available per child.	☐	☐
9. Many books are available representing three to four grade levels and of the following types: (a) picture books, (b) picture story books, (c) traditional literature, (d) poetry, (e) realistic literature, (f) informational books, (g) biographies, (h) novels, (i) easy-to-read books, (j) riddle and joke books, (k) participation books, (l) series books, (m) textless books, (n) TV-related books, (o) brochures, (p) newspapers, (q) magazines.	☐	☐
10. New books are circulated every 2 weeks.	☐	☐
11. There is a check-out/check-in system for children to check out books daily.	☐	☐
12. There is a rug.	☐	☐
13. There are throw pillows.	☐	☐
14. There is a rocking chair or beanbag chair.	☐	☐
15. There are headsets and taped stories.	☐	☐
16. There are posters about reading.	☐	☐
17. There are stuffed animals.	☐	☐
18. The area is labeled with a name selected by the class.	☐	☐
19. There are a felt-board and story characters and the related books.	☐	☐
20. There are a roll movie and related book.	☐	☐
21. There are materials for writing stories and making them into books.	☐	☐
22. There is a private spot in the corner, such as a box to crawl into and read.	☐	☐
23. There is a system for children to keep track of books read.	☐	☐
24. The area occupies about 10 percent of the classroom space, and five to six children can fit comfortably.	☐	☐

Computers should be a part of early childhood equipment and provide a source for literacy development.

should be used to select quality software to develop reading skills such as phonics and phonemic awareness: (1) Skills are introduced in a predictable sequence; (2) feedback is focused and immediate; (3) there is opportunity for repetitious feedback; and (4) children are engaged in an active manner with the software.

Another type of software is the electronic book. Electronic books use the best children's literature and present stories to children in a variety of ways. Images move on the screen, books are read aloud, and the text is clearly shown. Because these stories are animated, they are motivating to children. Another advantage to electronic books is that embedded in the book are skill development techniques such as K-W-L, emphasis on development of story structure, and the use of a directed reading and thinking activity format (Wepner & Ray, 2000).

Software to develop writing is helpful for beginning writers, children whose fine motor control is not well developed, and children with physical disabilities involving their hands. Quality software for writing development supports text that is generated by children and encourages students to expand on, revise, and edit what they have written.

When using software, be sure that you are familiar with it and that children know how to use the computer and the program. Software can be introduced to the whole class by projecting it onto a TV monitor or projecting with a data processor so that all can see. Your purpose will determine how you choose to use the software, but most of the time software is used for practicing skills already taught. The work is done alone or with a peer, independently of the teacher. Similar to a center activity, computer work is a perfect activity for children when teachers are engaged in guided reading groups for explicit instruction. There should be a time for students to discuss problems they may have with the software and to share accomplishments on the computer.

Many commercial companies have created entire reading programs for computers; more effective, however, and more common are programs for intervention for struggling readers and programs for practice. In these programs the children are tested and their needs assessed, and computer activities are selected based on their needs. The computer, however, cannot take the place of the teacher.

The Internet

Another way to use new literacies in classrooms is to take advantage of the Internet. This affords endless possibilities. Pen pals correspond instantly all over the world using e-mail. The World Wide Web is an unlimited resource for information related to whatever children are studying. For example, when studying outer space, the teacher can get a collection of titles of fiction and nonfiction books from the Internet and where to locate them for her classroom. She will help children locate an appropriate website for them to use as a source for more information. There are sites for children to review books before reading them, review software they are using, and access electronic books. In addition, schools and classrooms can create their own websites for various reasons. Figure 8.9 is an example of a website prepared by a second-grade teacher to welcome her class at

Figure 8.9

A Website Created by a Second-Grade Teacher

Welcome to Second Grade!

I Am So Excited to Begin Our Year Together!

We are going to have so much fun together! On our first day of school there will be many surprises for you! We have a special pet that can't wait to meet you! A yummy delicious treat will be on your desk! A bag of goodies will be waiting for you! I could go on and on, but I really want you to be surprised!

What Should You Bring on the First Day?

The first day is such a special day. It will be a day spent getting to know each other and the classroom. I thought that a fun way for us to get to know each other a little bit better is to make bags about ourselves. Let me explain. Take any bag that you have around your house. Fill it with things that would help us to get to know you better. You might include a family picture, your favorite book, a special stuffed animal, or anything else that you dream up! We will each get a chance to share our special bags!

A Little Bit about Me

I have always wanted to be a teacher ever since I was in the second grade. I used to set up my dolls and pretend to teach them. Now I have real live students! (They are a lot more fun!) I am married and have three cats—Forest, Cleo, and Michina. I love to read, write my own stories, travel, cook, spend time with my family, go to the movies, rollerblade, and jog. I feel that I am the luckiest person in the world because I get to do my favorite thing every day—teach!

Source: Loredana McFadden, 1999, second-grade teacher, Colts Neck, New Jersey.

the beginning of the school year. Children's work can be posted on websites, newsletters can be sent home to parents, and websites can provide a space for discussion out of school about what is being studied.

It is the teacher's responsibility to help students find websites that will be useful for them and to help them learn how to find others on their own. A helpful reference book is *1001 Best Web Sites for Kids* (Kelly, 2004). When selecting websites for children, Wepner and Ray (2000) advise the following considerations:

- The website loads quickly.
- The title page presents a thorough overview of the contents.
- The contents of the website fit with your purpose.
- There are icons that link to pages on the site needed and possibly to other relevant sites.
- The graphics are attractive and enhance the concepts.
- The narration is clear and enhances the concepts to be learned.

The computer with software and the Internet with all its capabilities for correspondence and retrieval of information must be included in daily routines for learning. Children will need to function with a computer on a daily basis. Appendix C provides a list of software and websites designated for specific skill development.

Use of Play to Motivate Literacy Development

English Language Learners

A curriculum area we must continue to use is motivating literacy learning through play. In play settings, children interact and collaborate in small groups. When designed to promote literacy behaviors, the dramatic-play area is coordinated with a social studies or science theme that is being studied to bring meaning to the experience. Materials for reading and writing are provided to support the play theme, and during play children read, write, speak, and listen to one another using literacy in functional ways.

Although early childhood educators have realized the value of play for social, emotional, and physical development, in the past it has not been viewed as a place or time to motivate literacy. Play has gained greater importance as a medium for practicing literacy behaviors because it provides repeated, meaningful, functional social settings. Literacy development involves a child's active engagement in cooperation and collaboration with peers, builds on what the child already knows, and thrives on the support and guidance of others. Play provides this setting. During observations of children at play, one can see the functional uses of literacy that children incorporate into their play themes. Children have been observed to engage in attempted and conventional reading and writing in collaboration with other youngsters (Morrow, 1990; Neuman & Roskos, 1992; Roskos & Christie, 2000). To demonstrate the importance of the social, collaborative, and interactive nature of literacy development, let us visit a classroom where the teacher, Ms. Hart, has designed a veterinarian's office to go along with an animal theme with a concentration on pets. The dramatic-play area was designed with a waiting room; chairs; a table filled with magazines, books, and pamphlets about pet care; posters about pets; office hour notices; a no-smoking sign; and a sign advising visitors to "Check in with the nurse when arriving." A nurse's desk holds patient forms on clipboards, a telephone, an address and telephone book, appointment cards, a calendar, and a computer for recording appointments and patient records. Offices contain patient folders, prescription pads, white coats, masks, gloves, cotton swabs, a toy doctor's kit, and stuffed animals to serve as patients.

Ms. Hart guides students in the use of the various materials in the veterinarian's office, for example, by reminding the children to read to pets in waiting areas, fill out forms with prescriptions or appointment times, or fill out forms with information about an animal's condition and treatment. In addition to giving directions, Ms. Hart also models behaviors by participating in play with the children when the materials are first introduced.

The following anecdotes relate the type of behavior that was witnessed in this setting, which provides a literacy-rich environment with books and writing materials, models reading and writing by teachers that children can observe and emulate, provides the opportunity to practice literacy in real-life situations that have meaning and function, and has children collaborating and performing reading and writing with peers.

Jessica was waiting to see the doctor. She told her stuffed animal dog Sam not to worry, that the doctor wouldn't hurt him. She asked Jenny, who was waiting with her stuffed animal cat Muffin, what the kitten's problem was. The girls agonized over the ailments of their pets. After a while they stopped talking and Jessica picked up a book from the table and pretended to read *Are You My Mother?* to her pet dog, Sam. Jessica showed Sam the pictures as she read.

Jennie ran into the doctor's office shouting, "My dog got runned over by a car." The doctor bandaged the dog's leg; then the two children decided that the incident must be reported to the police. Before calling the police, they got out the telephone book and turned to a map to find the spot where the dog had been hit. Then they called the police on the toy phone to report the incident.

After examining the stuffed bear, this young veterinarian in the dramatic-play center wrote, "This teddy bear's blood pressure is 29 points. He should take 62 pills an hour until he is better and keep warm and go to bed."

Figure 8.10   Forms to Write on for the Veterinarian's Office in the Dramatic-Play Center

---

Appointment Card

Name: _____

Has an appointment on _____

☐ Mon. ☐ Tues. ☐ Wed. ☐ Thurs. ☐ Fri. ☐ Sat.

Date _____ at _____ a.m. p.m.

Prescription

Patient's Name:

Prescription:

Refills: Instructions:

                    Franklin A. Morrow, D.V.M.

Patient Record Form

Patient's Name: _____   Type of Animal: _____

Owner's Name: _____   Date of Visit: _____

Address: _____   Telephone Number: _____

  History and Physical Findings: Treatment:

Preston examined Christopher's teddy bear and wrote out a report in the patient's folder. He read his scribble writing out loud and said, "This teddy bear's blood pressure is 29 points. He should take 62 pills an hour until he is better and keep warm and go to bed." While he read, he showed Christopher what he had written so that he would understand what to do. He asked his nurse to type the notes into the computer.

Figure 8.10 shows forms that may be used in the dramatic-play center when it is designed as a veterinarian's office during a unit on animals.

The type of play just discussed sets the stage for excellent opportunities for ELL children and those from diverse backgrounds. They will learn about functioning in real settings with other children. With the props and the informal nature of the experiences, they will feel more comfortable participating.

Additional play settings that encourage reading and writing at different grade levels follow:

1. *Newspaper Office:* Includes telephones, directories, maps, computers, paper, pencils, and areas that focus on sports, travel, general news, and weather.

2. *Supermarket or Local Grocery Store:* Can include labeled shelves and sections, food containers with their labels left on, a cash register, telephone, computers, receipts, checkbooks, coupons, and promotional flyers.

3. *Post Office:* Can be used for mailing the children's letters and needs to include paper, envelopes, address books, pens, pencils, stamps, cash registers, computers, and mailboxes. A mail carrier hat and bag are important for delivering the mail by reading names and addresses.

4. *Airport:* Can be created with signs posting arrivals and departures, tickets, boarding passes, luggage tags, magazines and books for the waiting area, safety messages on the plane, and name tags for the flight attendants. A computer is used to get onto the Internet to make plane reservations.

5. *Gas Station and Car Repair Shop:* Can be designed in the block area. Toy cars and trucks can be used for props. There can be receipts for sales, road maps to help with directions to different destinations, auto repair manuals for fixing cars and trucks, posters that advertise automobile equipment, and empty cans of different products that are sold in stations (Morrow & Rand, 1991).

For materials to be used for literacy to their fullest potential, teachers need to use props that are natural and from the child's environment. The materials in the setting created must serve a real function and be familiar to children. Do not set up several dramatic themes at once. Have the dramatic-play area match a theme being studied. Change the area when you begin to study a new theme. Teachers need to guide the use of materials initially by modeling their use (Barone, Mallette, & Xu, 2004; Neuman & Roskos, 1993).

The materials in dramatic-play areas should be clearly marked and be accessible. All levels of literacy development should be accepted, and reading or writing attempts should be recognized as legitimate literacy behaviors. Teachers might find it useful to record anecdotes about literacy activities engaged in by children.

In the discussion of play, I have concentrated on cooperative learning to encourage literacy development. Play is typically thought of as a preschool and kindergarten activity; however, play can be used with first, second, and third grades as well. Older children engage in more sophisticated literacy behaviors when participating in play. For example, the Internet can be used in many play settings as a source of information, for news stories, for air travel routes, and so on. See Strategies for the Classroom for materials to create play settings.

 **Strategies**

Assessing Children's Attitudes toward Books

Direct observation of children's behavior while they are listening to stories, reading, or looking at books independently is an effective method for assessing their attitude toward books. How much attention do they give to the books they are looking at or reading? Do they simply browse? Do they flip through the pages quickly, paying little attention to print or pictures? Do they demonstrate sustained attention to pictures and print throughout (Martinez & Teale, 1988)? You should also note how frequently children select looking at books when faced with other options. In occasional interviews with individual children, asking what they like to do best in school and at home might reveal interest in reading. During conferences, ask parents if their children voluntarily look at books or pay close attention when they are read to. At the same time, ask parents how often they read to their children. Gather facts about the home literacy environment that will help you understand the child's attitude toward books.

A checklist for assessing attitudes toward reading and writing is provided on page 323, and a motivation interview for a child's portfolio of assessment materials appears in Figure 8.11. They are useful tools concerning children's interest in reading and writing.

Figure 8.11   Motivation Interview

Directions: Tell the child that you would like to find out more about what kids like to do and how they feel about reading and writing. Ask each question in the interview and read the multiple-choice responses.

1. How often would you like your teacher to read to the class?

   (2) every day   (1) almost every day   (0) not often

2. Do you like to read books by yourself?

   (2) yes   (1) it's okay   (0) no

3. 2. Which would you most like to have?

   (2) a new book   (1) a new game   (0) new clothes

4. Do you tell your friends about books and stories you read?

   (2) a lot   (1) sometimes   (0) never

5. How do you feel when you read out loud to someone?

   (2) good   (1) okay   (0) bad

6. Do you like to read during your free time?

   (2) yes   (1) it's okay   (0) I don't read in my free time

7. If someone gave you a book for a present, how would you feel?

   (2) happy   (1) okay   (0) not very happy, disappointed

8. Do you take storybooks home from school to read?

   (2) almost every day   (1) sometimes   (0) not often

9. Do you read books out loud to someone in your family?

   (2) almost every day   (1) sometimes   (0) not often

10. What kind of reader are you?

   (2) I'm a very good reader (1) I'm okay   (0) I'm not very good

11. Learning to read is

   (2) easy   (1) a little hard   (0) really hard

12. Do you like to write?

   (2) yes   (1) it's okay   (0) I'd rather do something else

13. Do you write in your free time?

   (2) a lot   (1) a little   (0) not at all

14. What do you like to read best?

   (2) books and magazines   (1) schoolwork   (0) nothing

Source: Adapted from L. B. Gambrell, B. M. Palmer, R. M. Codling, & S. A. Mazzoni, "Assessing Motivation to Read," *The Reading Teacher* 49(7):518-533. Copyright © 1996 by the International Reading Association.

CheckList   Assessing Attitudes toward Reading and Writing and Amount of Voluntary Reading and Writing

Child's name _____ Date _____

Teacher evaluates child.	Always	Sometimes	Never	Comments
Voluntarily looks at or reads books at school				
Asks to be read to				
Listens attentively while being read to				
Responds during book discussions with questions and comments on stories read to him or her				
Takes books home to read voluntarily				
Writes voluntarily at home				
Writes voluntarily at school				

Teacher Comments:

An Idea from the Classroom

ELL
English Language Learners

I created the following experience when I was teaching children in a mixed-age-grouping primary classroom. The story is particularly suited to diverse classrooms because it deals with self-esteem, or liking who you are.

Felt-Board Story

I wanted to introduce my students to the use of the felt-board as a means for retelling stories and creating their own original stories with characters. I selected a story that was easy to illustrate and a theme that would generate interpretive conversation, and I encouraged the opportunity to write additional episodes for it. The name of the story is *A Bunny Called Nat,* an anonymous tale. The story is about "a bunny named Nat, who was sassy and fat, and he could change his color, just like that." This is a repetitive rhyme in the story, and at the end of the rhyme, fingers are snapped. The bunny in the story is a gray bunny who does not like his color because it is so plain. He is able to change his color, but each time he does, he has an unpleasant adventure.

When I introduced the story to the children, I asked them to listen for the different colors that Nat becomes and the problems he faces each time. I then told the story, using the different colored bunny characters on the felt-board to help. When the story was over, we discussed Nat and his different colors. We also discussed the ending of the story and its meaning, trying to relate it to the experiences of the children. We discussed whether they ever wanted to be anyone other than themselves and why and whether it would really be better.

After the discussion, I asked the children to think of another color that Nat could become with an adventure attached to it as in the real story. I then asked them to write their story and draw and color a bunny to add to the felt story we already had. The bunnies were made of construction paper, and felt strips were glued onto the back to make them stick to the felt-board.

Seven-year-old Lindsey wrote the following:

> *"I'm a bunny named Nat, I'm sassy and fat, and I can change my color just like that." And suddenly Nat was a red bunny. Red like an apple, red like a cherry, and red like a fire truck. Suddenly a group of bees was coming. They saw Nat in the red color and they were thinking that Nat was an apple. The group of bees was going where Nat was sitting, they wanted to eat him. Then Nat saw the bees. He ran and ran but the bees followed him. So he said as he ran, "Being red is not so good, but I'm a bunny called Nat, I am sassy and fat, and I can change my color, just like that."*

In this activity children are involved in the discussion and creation of a story. The theme of the story, concerning self-image, is an important topic for conversation and can help children understand each other's strengths, weaknesses, and needs. The story, *A Bunny Called Nat,* and a pattern for the bunny (Figure 8.12) follow.

Figure 8.12

Felt Figure for Story A Bunny Called Nat

An Idea from the Classroom

Sample Felt-Board Story

A Bunny Called Nat (adapted version of an anonymous tale)

As the story is being told, hold up and then place a new colored bunny on the felt-board as each bunny is named.

Materials

Five bunny characters drawn identically, but in the following colors: gray, blue, green, yellow, and orange. The bunny pattern is found in Figure 8.12.

Once upon a time there was a little gray rabbit and his name was Nat. One day he looked around and saw that all his brothers and sisters, cousins and friends were gray, too. He thought he would like to be different from them. So he said:

I'm a bunny called Nat,
I'm sassy and fat,
And I can change my color
Just like that. (Snap your fingers.)

And suddenly Nat was a blue bunny. He was blue like the sky and blue like the sea. He was blue like the twilight and blue like the dawn. It felt nice and cool to be blue. He decided to take a look at himself in the pond. He hurried to the edge and admired his reflection in the water. He leaned over so far that SPLASH! he fell into the pond. Nat fell deep into the blue water and he couldn't swim. He was frightened. He called for help. His friends heard him, but when they came to the pond they couldn't see him because he was blue just like the water. Fortunately, a turtle swam by and helped Nat get safely to shore. Nat thanked the turtle. He decided that he didn't like being blue. So he said:

I'm a bunny called Nat,
I'm sassy and fat,
And I can change my color
Just like that. (Snap your fingers.)

And this time, what color did he change himself to? Yes, he was yellow—yellow like the sun, yellow like a daffodil, yellow like a canary bird. Yellow seemed like such a happy color to be. He was very proud of his new color, and he decided to take a walk through the jungle. Who do you think he met in the jungle? He met his cousins the lion and the tiger. The lion and the tiger looked at Nat's yellow fur and said, "What are you doing in that yellow coat? We are the only animals in this jungle that are supposed to be yellow." And they growled so fiercely that Nat the bunny was frightened and he ran all the way home. He said:

(Repeat poem.)

And this time what did he change his color to? Yes, he was green. He was green like the grass and green like the leaves of the trees. He was green like a grasshopper and green like the meadow. As a green bunny, Nat thought he'd be the envy of all the other bunnies. He wanted to play with his other bunny friends in the meadow. Since he was the color of the grass in the meadow, he could not be seen and his friends just ran and jumped about him not seeing him at all or mistaking him for a grasshopper. So Nat the bunny had no one to play with while he was green. Being green wasn't much fun. So he said:

(Repeat poem.)

And what color was he then? Right, he was orange. He was orange like a carrot, orange like a sunset, orange like a pumpkin—he was the brightest color of all. He decided he would go out and play with all his brothers and sisters and friends. But what do you suppose happened? When his friends saw him, they all stopped playing and started to laugh, "Ha-ha, whoever heard of an orange bunny?" No one wanted to play with him. He didn't want to be orange anymore. He didn't want to be a blue bunny because if he fell into the pond no one could see him to save him. He didn't want to be a yellow bunny and be frightened by the lion and the tiger. He didn't want to be a green bunny because then he was just like the meadow and none of his friends could see him. And so he said:

(Repeat poem.)

Do you know what color Nat the bunny changed himself into this time? Yes, you're right. He changed himself back to gray. And now that he was gray all his friends played with him. No one growled or laughed at him. He was gray like a rain cloud, gray like an elephant, gray like pussy willows. It felt warm and comfortable being gray. From that time on, Nat the bunny was always happy being a gray bunny, and he decided that it's really best being just what you are.

Activities and Questions

1. Answer the focus questions at the beginning of the chapter.

2. Select a literacy skill to teach that is grade appropriate for you. Select a piece of children's literature that provides an example of that skill and choose a creative storytelling technique that seems appropriate for the story and skill (e.g., felt characters, chalk talk, sound story). Create materials for the story and tell it to a group of children or to your peers. Evaluate your performance according to the criteria for storytelling discussed in the chapter and how well the skill was taught.

3. Evaluate the literacy center in an early childhood classroom using the form in Figure 8.8. List all the characteristics of the center that reflect criteria described in this chapter. List items that need to be included.

4. Observe an early childhood classroom on three different occasions. List all the literacy activities carried out by the teacher that you believe contribute to developing motivating positive attitudes toward reading and writing.

5. Continue your portfolio assessment for the child you selected to assess. Observe the child using the assessment checklist provided in this chapter concerning the evaluation of his or her attitudes toward writing and reading. Interview the child using the motivation survey (Figure 8.9).

6. Create a play experience for second and third graders that will develop literacy.

7. Write a lesson plan that requires children to use the Internet to find information. Be sure that children are using literacy skills in the assignment.

8. Continue the thematic unit that you began in Chapter 4. Select three objectives for building positive attitudes toward reading, and describe three activities using your theme that will satisfy each objective.

9. **Strategies** Use Strategies for the Classroom pages S-42 through S-45 to create a restaurant in your classroom or where you are student teaching. Real-life literacy will occur.

myeducationlab

VIDEO EXERCISE

Now that you have the benefit of having read this chapter, return to the www.myeducationlab.com topic "Motivation" and watch "Creating a Print-Rich Environment" one more time. You may complete the questions that accompany it online and save or transmit your work to your professor, or complete the following questions, as required.

Creating a Print Rich Environment
(3:36 minutes).

1. Identify two reasons why exposure to print is important for children's literacy development.
2. Identify two additional examples of how print can be used in the preschool classroom.
3. Briefly identify two activities parents can do at home with their young children to demonstrate the use of print in everyday situations.

Focus Questions

- Describe classroom environments that are rich in literacy materials and support optimal literacy instruction.

- What is meant by integrating literacy learning into content areas through the use of themed units?

- How can literacy development be integrated into the following content areas: art, music, math, science, social studies, and play?

- Identify different grouping methods or organizational arrangements for working with children to meet their individual needs.

- Describe a language arts block that incorporates all aspects of a balanced literacy program.

- How can literacy learning be integrated into activities throughout an entire school day?

- **VOCABULARY:** thematic unit, literacy center, library corner, writing center, content-area centers, whole-group instruction, small-group instruction, one-to-one instruction

- **Strategies** Use center cards in Strategies for the Classroom for Chapter 9 on pages S-46 and S-47 to identify these areas in your classroom or in your student teaching room.

PEARSON myeducationlab VIDEO PREVIEW: Using Centers (1:45 minutes). Before reading this chapter, go to www.myeducationlab.com. Under the topic "Organizing for Reading Instruction," access and watch the video "Using Centers."

9

Organizing and Managing the Literacy Program

What is honored in a country will be cultivated there. In classrooms in which teachers honor literacy development, it will be cultivated as an integral part of the school curriculum.

—Plato

Mrs. Green wanted to integrate literacy activities in content-area subjects. Her second-grade students often found science boring with only the textbook, because it did not feature real-life situations. She decided to use selections of children's literature that related to different topics in science to make them more relevant.

The children were learning about "The Changes in Our Earth," a unit that focused on topics such as hurricanes, glaciers, and the composition of Earth. Mrs. Green found several excellent selections of children's literature for this unit. Two of them were *How to Dig a Hole to the Other Side of the World* (McNulty, 1979) and *The Magic School Bus Inside the Earth* (Cole, 1987). Both books combined good literature with factual information about the topic. These books motivated a great deal of enthusiasm and discussion in class. Mrs. Green asked the children to write a narrative story similar to the literature she shared—that told a story, but included many science facts they had learned. This proved to be a difficult task for the children. Most of them wrote expository pieces that gave facts about the composition of the inside of Earth and what a volcano is and does. Those who wrote narratives did not include very many science facts. Mrs. Green decided to have the children write a whole-class science story by having the students generate science vocabulary and concepts they learned and use these ideas to write the story together. The story they wrote follows.

Our Class Adventure

One sunny day in Sacramento, California, our class went on a camping trip to a mountain. We put down all our bags and set up the tents. Kevin, Alex, Jason, and Keri went to the stream to catch fish for lunch. Antoinette and Emily went to get wood for a fire, since it was cold on the top of the mountain. While the other kids were setting up their tents, a bear came out. The bear saw some fish, ate them, and went away. Two hours later, our class decided to go for a hike. Along the way we saw a river and rocks that were weathered. We also saw two glaciers which were blocking a river. Suddenly, everything started to rumble and shake and everyone fell to the ground. Little and big rocks tumbled down the mountain. Smoke started coming out of the mountain and everyone started to yell. Amber started running around in circles. Then what we thought was just a mountain blew its top. Lava started coming down out of the volcano and an earthquake started. It was a good thing we brought our earthquake survival kits. We all ran to our camp for cover, but the camp was destroyed. The survival kits were fireproof and lava proof, so they were okay. Inside there were tools which we used to fix up the camp. We fixed it up so well that it looked like new.

The success of any program depends to a large extent on how it is organized, designed, and managed. Even creative and knowledgeable teachers have difficulty without careful planning, preparation of the environment, organization of lessons, and management of daily routines. This chapter ties together the prerequisites for successful implementation of the ideas described earlier in this book. Specifically, it focuses on

1. Preparation of the physical environment, including selection of materials and their placement in the classroom
2. Integration of literacy activities throughout the school day in all content areas
3. Grouping practices to meet individual needs

4. A suggested outline for a school day that provides literacy experiences throughout.

The chapter is concerned with the teaching of children from age 2½ to 8 (preschoolers, kindergartners, and first, second, and third graders). (Chapter 10 addresses home literacy environments and daily routines appropriate for infants and toddlers. Child-care centers for children from birth through age 2 need to organize rich literacy environments, routines, programs, and activities similar to those described for homes.)

Preparation of the Physical Environment

The physical design of a classroom has been found to affect the choices children make among activities (Jalongo, 2007; Morrow & Tracey, 1997; Morrow & Weinstein, 1986; Otto, 2006). The design of the room should accommodate the organization and strategies of the teaching that occurs there. Programs that nourish early literacy require a literacy-rich environment, an interdisciplinary approach to the development of literacy, and recognition of individual differences and levels of development.

The following example shows children participating in functional literacy activities in a classroom environment prepared with materials and space that stimulated reading and writing.

Mrs. Shafer's kindergarten is learning about workers in the community. While discussing news reporters, the children decided they would like to have a news office in the dramatic-play area where they could publish their own newspaper. Their teacher helped create the center where they placed writing paper, telephones, phone directories, a typewriter, and a computer. There were pamphlets, maps, and other appropriate reading materials for the different sections of the newspaper, such as sports, travel, weather, and general daily news. The class completed their first newspaper, and Yassin was in charge of delivering the paper the first month. He had a newspaper delivery bag, and each paper had the name of a child on it. As the delivery person, Yassin had to match the names on the papers to the names on the children's cubbies. He also delivered the papers to the principal, the nurse, the secretary, the custodian, and all the teachers in the school. Later, when the kindergartners read their newspapers, they shared them with great enthusiasm. Each child had contributed something to the paper, for example, a drawing, a story, or a group poem. The newspapers went home to be shared with parents.

Theory and Research Concerning Literacy-Rich Physical Environments

Historically, theorists and philosophers who studied early childhood development emphasized the importance of the physical environment in learning and literacy development. Pestalozzi (Rusk & Scotland, 1979) and Froebel (1974) described real-life environments in which young children's learning could flourish. Both described the preparation of manipulative materials that would foster literacy development. Montessori (1965) depicted a carefully prepared classroom environment intended to promote independent learning, and she recommended that every material in the environment have a specific learning objective.

Piaget (Piaget & Inhelder, 1969) found that children acquire knowledge by interacting with the world or the environment. Ideal settings are oriented to real-life situations, and materials are chosen to provide opportunities for children to explore and experiment. Dewey (1966) believed in an interdisciplinary approach. In other words, learning takes place through the integration of content areas. He believed that storing materials in subject-area centers encouraged interest and learning.

Based on these discussions, any classroom designed to provide a literacy-rich environment and optimum literacy development will offer an abundant supply of materials for reading, writing, and oral language. These materials will be housed in a literacy center. Literacy development will be integrated with content-area teaching reflected in materials provided in content-area learning centers. Materials and settings throughout the classroom will be designed to emulate real-life experiences and make literacy meaningful to children. They will be based on information children already possess and will be functional so that children see a need and purpose for using literacy. Careful attention to a classroom's visual and physical design contributes to the success of an instructional program. Preparing a classroom's physical environment is often overlooked in planning instruction. Teachers and curriculum developers tend to concentrate on pedagogical and interpersonal factors, but give little consideration to the visual and spatial context in which teaching and learning occur. They direct their energies toward varying teaching strategies, while the environment remains unchanged. The environment needs to be arranged to coordinate with and support program activities; otherwise, instruction will not be as successful as it could be (Weinstein & Mignano, 2003).

When purposefully arranging the environment, teachers acknowledge the physical setting as an active and pervasive influence on their own activities and attitudes, as well as those of the children in their classroom. Appropriate physical arrangement of furniture, selection of materials, and the visual aesthetic quality of a room contribute to teaching and learning (McGee & Morrow, 2005; Morrow, 1990; Morrow & Tracey, 1996; Morrow & Weinstein, 1986; Tompkins, 2003, 2007). For example, design of spatial arrangements alone affects children's behavior in the classroom. Rooms partitioned into smaller spaces facilitated verbal interaction among peers, fantasy, and cooperative play more than did rooms with large open spaces. Children in carefully arranged rooms showed more productivity and greater use of language-related activities than did children in randomly arranged rooms (Moore, 1986; Reutzel & Cooter, 2004).

Studies that investigated the role of literacy-enriched dramatic-play areas based on themes being used in the classroom found they stimulated increased language and literacy activity and also enhanced literacy skills (Morrow, 1990; Neuman & Roskos, 1993, 1997). These researchers also have found that dramatic play with story props improves story production and comprehension, including recall of details and ability to sequence and interpret.

English Language Learners

Preparing Literacy-Rich Physical Environments

Research that has investigated the physical design of classrooms strongly suggests that, by purposefully arranging the space and materials, teachers can create physical environments that exert an active, positive, and pervasive influence on instruction. Educators must think of their classrooms as places to project a visual atmosphere that communicates a definitive message. The following sections describe the visual presentation of a literacy-rich physical environment to motivate reading and writing based on the research discussed in previous chapters.

English Language Learners

PRINT IN YOUR CLASSROOM.   Literacy-rich classrooms are filled with functional print that can be seen easily. There are labels on classroom items and signs communicating functional information and directions, such as *Quiet Please,* and *Please Put Materials Away after Using Them.* There are charts labeled *Helpers, Daily Routines, Attendance,* and *Calendar,* to name a few (McGee & Morrow, 2005; Schickedanz, 1993). Labels identify learning centers and each child's cubby. When the class has children from diverse backgrounds, it is a good idea to label in more than one langague.

A notice board placed prominently in the room can be used to communicate with the children in writing. Experience charts and morning messages are used to display new words generated from themes, recipes used in the classroom, and science experiments conducted. Word walls display high-frequency words learned, new spelling words, sight words, and words that feature phonics elements being taught. Teachers discuss and use the print in the classroom with the children to ensure it is noticed. Children are encouraged to read and to use words from the print in their writing (Ritchie, James-Szanton, & Howes, 2003).

The outdoor environment also should accommodate literacy development. In addition to the usual playground equipment, new materials that reflect unit instruction add to the interest of outdoor play. Where climates are seasonal, for example, flowers should be planted in the spring, rakes are provided in the fall for leaf gathering, and pails, shovels, and other digging and building equipment are provided in winter for snow play. Creative materials, such as crates, boxes, plastic containers, boards, ropes, and balls, give children incentives to play creatively. The materials generate language during play and in class discussions and provide information for writing experience charts and class books.

THE CLASSROOM LITERACY CENTER.   The literacy center, which includes the library corner and a writing area, should be the focal point in a classroom. Children's immediate access to literature and writing materials increases the number of children who participate in literacy activities during the school day. Both areas in the literacy center need to be obvious and inviting, but also should afford privacy and be clearly defined. The areas should accommodate four to five children comfortably. The center says to children that as teachers we value literacy by making it an important part of our classroom. The materials range in difficulty to meet individual needs and the different developmental levels of the children. Each set of materials has its own place and is to be respected. The literacy center includes materials for reading,

A sight-word chart of high-frequency words helps children to read and write independently.

writing, oral language development, and developing word-study skills. The different parts of the center have already been discussed in other chapters (the library corner in Chapter 8, the writing center in Chapter 7, oral language center materials in Chapter 4, and materials to develop word study in Chapter 5). The library corner and writing center will be described again here to pull the area together.

English Language Learners

THE LIBRARY CORNER.   The library corner should house books on traditional shelves with only their spines showing. Shelve books by category, and use some sort of coding system. Coding introduces the idea that books in regular libraries are organized systematically for easy access. Other shelves should be open faced to display full covers, thus calling attention to them. Use the open-faced shelving to feature books about themes being studied, and rotate in new books every few weeks. Books can be stored in plastic bins labeled by genre. We also store leveled books in plastic bins labeled by level of difficulty. To ensure there is something for everyone in the center, include five to eight books per child at three or four grade levels representing different genres of children's literature. Stock multiple copies of popular stories. Children enjoy reading the same book together.

Furnish the area with a rug and pillows. Include a rocking chair representing the Literacy Chair of Honor, where the teacher and others read to the children. This area is where children read for pleasure, read to other children, or present stories to the class that they have written. Provide a cozy private spot for reading. Teachers have used large cartons from household appliances, painted or covered with contact paper, where children can crawl inside and read.

Posters and bulletin boards that celebrate reading should be used to decorate the area. Devise a method for checking books out of the classroom library to take home and read. Provide materials for active involvement in storybook reading and storytelling, with storytelling manipulatives such as a felt-board with story characters, roll movies, puppets, and headsets for listening to taped stories. These materials deal mostly with language and comprehension skills. Provide manipulative word-study games and activities that include making words and sorting words based on letter patterns to help build independent readers.

English Language Learners

THE WRITING AREA.   The writing area requires a table and chairs, plus colored felt-tipped markers, large and small crayons, pencils (both regular and colored), chalk, a chalkboard, and paper in a variety of sizes, kinds, and colors. Include unlined plain paper or newsprint of many different sizes. Have index cards available to record children's Very Own Words, high-frequency words, or word patterns they may need to practice. A writing folder for each child can be kept in a large box. Computers must be in the writing area as well. Book-making materials include paper, a hole punch, a stapler, and construction paper. Blank books prepared by the teacher and children can be keyed to special occasions and completed by youngsters. Display children's writing on a bulletin board. Equally valuable are *notice boards* on which messages can be exchanged among classmates or between teacher and students.

Involve children in designing and managing the literacy center. They can help develop rules for its use and keep it neat and orderly.

English Language Learners

DESIGNING CONTENT-AREA CENTERS TO ACCOMMODATE INDIVIDUAL NEEDS. Programs that motivate early literacy development require literacy-rich environments that recognize the need for an integrated approach to literacy learning and awareness of individual differences and developmental levels. These classrooms are arranged in centers designed for particular content areas. Centers contain materials specific to topics currently under study and general supplies and resources. The materials are usually manipulative and activity oriented. They are also designed such that children use them independently or in small groups. Centers are partially separated from each other by furniture that houses their materials. Centers should be labeled and their materials stored on tables or shelves, in boxes, or on a bulletin board. Each piece of equipment in a center should have its own designated spot so that teachers can direct children to it and children can find and return it easily. Early in a school year, a center need hold only a small number of items; new materials are gradually added as the year progresses. The teacher should introduce the purpose, use, and placement of each item added.

Content-area centers are dedicated to social studies, science, art, music, math, literacy, dramatic play, and block play. Centers contain materials pertinent to the content area, and materials are added that are specific to themes being studied, such as nutrition or animals. Each subject-specific center includes literacy materials as well: things to read, materials with which to write, things to listen to, and things to talk about. These materials create interest, new vocabulary and concepts, and a reason for participating in literacy activities. With each new theme studied, additional books, posters, artifacts, music, art projects, dramatic-play materials, and scientific objects can be added to create new interest. Chapter 4 describes general materials for each content-area center and then discusses additions made for the study of a particular theme. The classroom floor plans in Figures 9.1 and 9.2 illustrate this type of learning environment from preschool through fifth grade.

Notice in Figure 9.1, in the preschool through first-grade floor plan, that the art center is placed by the sink for easy access to water. In this same area are children's cubbies for storing individual work. Because the working needs of early childhood classrooms are better met by table surfaces than by desks, children should be provided with these storage areas. The contents of the various centers diagrammed in the figure were

Figure 9.1

Classroom Floor
Plan for
Prekindergarten
through First
Grade

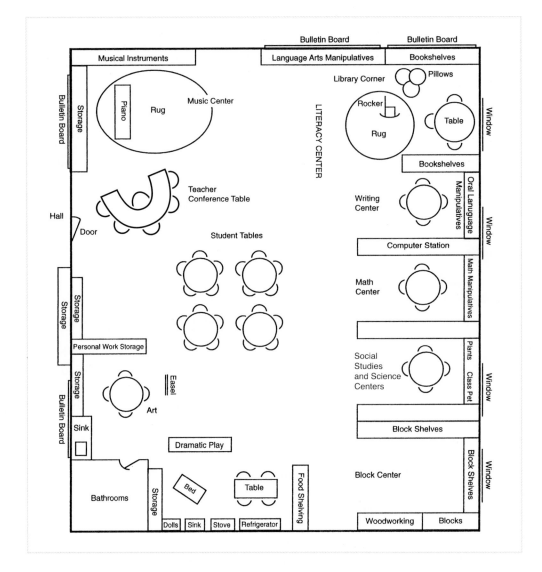

described in Chapter 4. In addition to all the materials available in them, it is important that each has books and writing materials. The music center, for example, can include picture storybooks adapted from songs, such as Maurice Sendak's *Chicken Soup with Rice* (1962). In addition to looking at the book, children may choose to copy words from the story. Certainly, social studies and science centers should hold informational books and children's literature that relate to topics being studied. The art center might have books with craft ideas, including directions and diagrams. Books are also appropriate in the dramatic-play area. If the class is discussing outer space, the area should have books about space and space stories for pretend caregivers to read to their "children." The block center can contain books that help develop ideas for building. Books that contain maps or plans of communities might motivate children to create such communities in their block play.

In addition to generating a rich literacy atmosphere and an interdisciplinary approach, the room is designed to cater to different teaching methods,

Figure 9.2

Classroom Floor Plan for Second through Fifth Grade

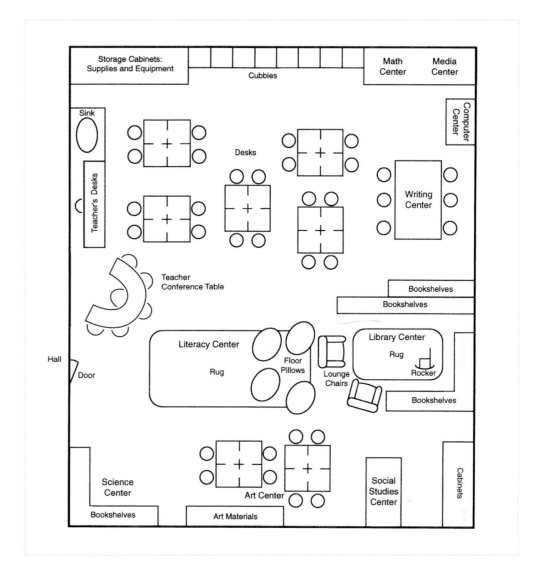

organizational strategies, and grouping procedures so that the differences among the children can be accommodated. The centers provide space for independent or social learning, exploration, and self-direction. The tables illustrated in the classroom floor plan (Figure 9.1) provide a place for whole-class instruction, as does the open area in the music center with the rug on which children can sit. The teacher's conference table is a place for individual learning or small-group lessons. All furniture is, of course, movable so that any other needed teaching arrangement can be accommodated. The centers are located to create both quiet, relatively academic areas and places for more active play. The literacy center, for example, which houses the library corner and the writing and oral language areas, is next to the math center. Because these areas generally house activities that require relative quiet, they are in close proximity. Alternatively, dramatic play, woodworking, and block play tend to be noisier activities, so they are placed at the opposite end of the room from the quiet areas. The art center can also be a noisy area and is set aside from the quieter sections of the room. The teacher's conference table is situated in a quiet area, yet allows the teacher a view of the rest of the classroom. While the teacher is involved in small-group or individualized instruction at the conference table, the rest of the class is working independently. The table's location allows the teacher to see all the children even while working with just a few.

The plan for the physical environment is used in many nursery schools and kindergartens and some first and second grades. The assumption is that it is for younger children. Teachers in first and second grade should consider these designs because they encourage literacy learning. Figure 9.3 is a planning sheet for you to fill in the general materials for your centers and the materials to add that are specific to a particular theme. Evaluate the richness of your literacy environment using the checklist on pages 340–341.

Figure 9.3

General Center Materials and Center Theme Materials

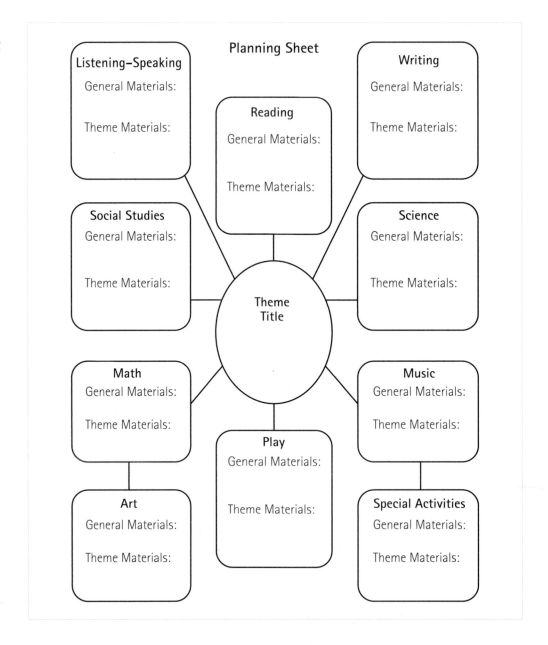

Thematic Units: Integrating Literacy Learning into Content Areas

English Language Learners

Dewey (1966) was largely responsible for bringing the concept of an interdisciplinary approach to teaching to educators' attention. This approach, or the integrated school day, teaches skills from all content areas within the context of a topic or theme being studied. The themes that are studied at school derive from children's real-life experiences and topics that they demonstrate an interest in. Learning experiences are socially interactive and process oriented, giving children time to explore and experiment with varied materials. If, for example, a class is studying dinosaurs, the students talk, read, and write about them; do art projects related to dinosaurs; and sing songs related to the theme. In doing so, they learn about dinosaurs and develop skills in other content areas.

Literacy activities can be integrated into the study of themes and into all content areas throughout the school day. Several are described here to demonstrate how the strategies to develop literacy, as discussed in previous chapters, can be used in other areas of the curriculum (Morrow, 2004; Pappas, Kiefer, & Levstik, 1995).

Objectives for Art Experiences

In early childhood, art experience should offer children the opportunity to

1. be exposed to varied art materials.
2. explore and experiment with these materials.
3. express feelings through art.
4. represent experience through visual art forms.
5. gain an appreciation for varied art forms.
6. name and discuss the content of art: line, color, texture, form, and shape.
7. experience literacy learning in art activities.

Art experiences allow children to explore and experiment with interesting materials, such as finger paints, watercolors, printing, string painting, sponge painting, colored pencils, felt-tip markers, crayons, colored construction paper, tissue paper, foil, transparent wrap, paste, scissors, yarn, fabric scraps, pipe cleaners, clay, and play dough. If children are encouraged to discuss such materials as they use them, language development flourishes. Children immersed in finger painting, for instance, use such words as *mushy, smushy, gushy,* and *squiggle.* Playing with dough or clay elicits the words *pound, squeeze, roll, press,* and *fold.* Watercolors stimulate such comments as "Oooh, it's drippy," "The paint is running down the page like a stream of water," "Look how the colors all run together. The red is making the blue turn purple," and "My picture looks like a rainbow of colors across the sky." The teacher can take the opportunity to make word lists from the language generated in art activities and to encourage the children to share and talk about what they are doing. The words that individual children generate are a source of Very Own Words.

CheckList Evaluating and Improving the Literacy Environment

Teacher uses the Checklist to evaluate his/her classroom

The Literacy Center	Yes	No
Children participate in designing the center (e.g., develop rules, select a name for center, develop materials).		
Area is placed in a quiet section of the room.		
Area is visually and physically accessible, yet partitioned from the rest of the room.		
There are a rug, throw pillows, rocking chair, beanbag chair, and stuffed animals.		
There is a private spot in the corner, such as a box to crawl into and read.		
The center uses about 10 percent of the classroom space and fits five to six children.		

The Library Corner		
Bookshelves for storing books with spines facing outward		
Organizational system for shelving books		
a. books shelved by genre	a.	
b. books shelved by reading level	b.	
Open-faced bookshelves for featured books		
Five to eight books per child		
Books represent three to four grade levels of the following types: (a) picture books, (b) picture storybooks, (c) traditional literature, (d) poetry, (e) realistic literature, (f) informational books, (g) biographies, (h) chapter books, (i) easy to read books, (j) riddle and joke books, (k) participation books, (l) series books, (m) textless books, (n) TV-related books, (o) brochures, (p) magazines, (q) newspapers.		
Twenty new books circulated every 2 weeks		
Check-out/check-in system for children to take books out daily		
Headsets and taped stories		
Felt-board and story characters with related books		
Materials for constructing felt stories		
Other story manipulatives (e.g., roll movie, puppets, with related books)		
System for recording books read		
Multiple copies of the same book		

The Writing Center (The Author's Spot)	Yes	No
Tables and chairs		
Writing posters and bulletin board for children to display their writing themselves		
Writing utensils (e.g., pens, pencils, crayons, magic markers, colored pencils)		
Writing materials (many varieties of paper in all sizes, booklets, pads)		
Computers		
Materials for writing stories and making them into books		
A message board for children to post messages for the teacher and students		
A place to store Very Own Words		
Folders in which children place samples of their writing		
A place for children to send private messages to each other		

Literacy-Rich Environment for the Rest of the Classroom

	Yes	No
The classroom should include literacy materials in all centers. Materials should be changed often to reflect the unit being studied; for example, in the science center there should be books on the unit topic and in the music area, posters of songs related to themes. Play areas should reflect units with themed play and literacy materials. All centers should contain the following:		
Environmental print, such as signs related to themes studied, directions, rules, functional messages		
A calendar		
A current events board		
Appropriate books, magazines, and newspapers		
Writing utensils		
Varied types of paper		
A place for children to display their literacy work		
A place for teachers and children to leave messages for each other		
A word wall		
Print representative of multicultural groups present in the classroom		

Content-area centers present are ☐ (circle centers)

☐ music ☐ art ☐ science ☐ social studies ☐ math ☐ dramatic play

Children are often eager to exhibit their creations. This practice is likely to result in children's asking each other how they made their projects. The resulting description provides an excellent opportunity for literacy development. Children sometimes ask to dictate or write sentences and stories about their artwork or write about it themselves. Individual works of art on similar subjects can be bound together in books that include captions, titles, or stories. Art activities also can highlight concepts such as the letter *p*, for example, through the use of purple and pink paint, paper, and play dough.

Objectives for Music Experiences

English Language Learners

In early childhood, music experiences should include

1. having intense involvement in and responding to music.
2. exposure to different forms of music (instruments, singing, types of music) to be able to discriminate among them and develop an appreciation for varied forms.
3. music experiences that involve listening, singing, moving, playing, and creating.
4. expressing feelings through music experiences.
5. experiencing literacy learning in music activities.

Music provides ample means for literacy development. Children find new words in songs, thus increasing vocabulary. Songs emphasize word patterns and syllabic patterns, which should be brought to the children's attention. Songs can be written on charts and sung, the teacher pointing to the individual words while tracking the print from left to right across the page. Picture storybooks adapted from songs, such as *Old MacDonald Had a Farm* (Quackenbush, 1972), provide predictable reading material for young children. Listening to classical music often creates images and is a rich source for descriptive language. Children can create stories about the music, describe their feelings, or describe the sounds of various instruments.

Objectives for Social Studies and Science Experiences

Social studies and science themes for the most part provide the meaning and function for learning, particularly for literacy learning. Themes provide a reason to read and write about topics of interest. Skills are learned within a context, rather than in isolated lessons for skill development.

In early childhood, social studies experiences should include

1. fostering self-esteem.
2. learning social skills for functioning, such as sharing, cooperating, and communicating with others.
3. recognizing and respecting similarities and differences in others.
4. increasing knowledge of other cultures and ethnic and racial groups.

5. increasing understanding of the nature of our social world through the study of history, geography, and economics.
6. using the content of social studies to promote literacy development.

In early childhood, science experiences should include activities that involve

1. observing, hypothesizing, recording data, summarizing, analyzing, and drawing conclusions.
2. increasing understanding in
   a. biological science, the study of living things.
   b. physical science, including the study of
      (1) astronomy—heavenly bodies and their movements.
      (2) chemistry—materials found on the earth and the changes that occur in them.
      (3) meteorology—weather and air.
      (4) physics—the nature of matter and energy.
3. using the content of science to promote literacy development.

Science and social studies are probably the two content areas that provide the greatest opportunities for literacy development. Their contents typically generate enthusiasm, meaning, and a purpose for using literacy strategies. A unit about the farm can lead to oral language development through discussions about farm work, different types of farms, and farm animals. Word lists of farm animals, crops, and jobs on the farm can be made. Pictures of farm scenes, a trip to a farm, or a visit by a farmer generate discussion, reading, and writing. To encourage positive attitudes toward books, the teacher can carefully select good pieces of children's literature about farms to read to the class. The *Petunia* series (Duvoisin, 2002) deals with a delightful goose who lives on a farm. *The Little Red Hen* (Galdone, 1973), *The Tale of Peter Rabbit* (Potter, 1902), *Barnyard Banter* (Fleming, 2001), and *Chicken or the Egg?* (Fowler, 1993) are just a few examples of good children's literature that relate to the farm. The teacher should select some multicultural trade books as well.

Science themes with experiments and interesting materials to investigate integrate literacy instruction into content-area instruction.

These books will motivate youngsters to pick up the books on their own, retell them, role play them, and share them with each other. A farm visit can be retold in stories or drawings bound into class books, recaptured in a language experience chart, or reflected in Very Own Words. The teacher can associate letters and sounds in farm words with those in children's names or in environmental print.

Science experiments and food preparation offer opportunities for discussion and an exchange of interesting vocabulary. The block center, too, can stimulate literacy activities. For instance, when introducing a unit on transportation, the teacher can add toy trucks, trains, cars, boats, and airplanes to the block corner, along with travel tickets, luggage and freight tags, maps, travel guides, tour brochures, travel posters, and signs common to airports, train stations, and bus depots, such as gate numbers, names of carriers, and arrival and departure signs.

Objectives for Mathematics Experiences

Early childhood mathematics activities should involve

1. many opportunities to handle and deal with mathematical materials and ideas.
2. movement from dependence on the concrete to abstract ideas.
3. opportunities to classify, compare, seriate, measure, graph, count, identify, and write numbers and perform operations on numbers.
4. using mathematical vocabulary.
5. using mathematics to promote literacy development.

In all other content areas, a teacher can feel confident that he or she is providing a fairly adequate program of study through the themed units used in social studies and science that incorporate music, art, play, and literacy development in early childhood. Math, however, is a specialized area that needs more attention than can be dealt with in a content-area unit. Still, many activities can bring meaning to mathematics through unit topics and include literacy as well. Stories related to numbers can be read, children can count cookies for snack time to make sure there are enough for the class, and children can be in charge of collecting and counting milk money. When studying weather, a chart of daily temperatures can be graphed to observe the variability from day to day.

When literacy skills are developed in an integrated fashion, as in the practices and approaches described here, children see purposes and reasons for becoming literate. When we teach literacy skills that do not reflect real-life experience and lack content, children are not likely to perceive their usefulness. When skills are taught in an integrated, interdisciplinary fashion, children ask for the skills they need to participate fully in experiences that interest them during their work and play at school and at home (Manning, Manning, & Long, 1994; McGee & Morrow, 2005; Purcell-Gates, Duke, & Martineau, 2007; Walmsley, 1994). During a unit on transportation in a kindergarten class of my own, children asked for even more materials than I had already made available in the several centers. Books on transportation led to requests for books on space travel and various maps of places not in the center. Many children added to their Very Own Words. Children asked for help preparing signs representing places they wanted to visit and highway signs indicating mileage to various destinations. Some dictated travel directions. The need for literacy information was created by preparing an environment that reflected interesting, real-life experiences. In such an environment, learning is to a great extent self-generated.

Objectives for Play Experiences

In early childhood, play experiences include providing opportunities for children to

1. problem solve.
2. acquire new understandings.
3. role play real-life experiences.
4. cope with situations that require sharing and cooperating.
5. develop language and literacy through play.

Dramatic play provides endless possibilities for literacy development through the use of oral and written language and reading. The materials and activities typical of dramatic-play areas stimulate considerable language, and the addition of new props and materials provides the opportunity for continued growth. Dramatic play provides realistic settings and functional reasons for using print. New units in social studies and science trigger opportunities to add print materials that stimulate reading, writing, and oral language. A unit on community helpers, a topic familiar to early childhood teachers, invariably leads to a discussion of firefighters, police officers, supermarket clerks, doctors, nurses, mail carriers, and office workers. The mention of any of these community helpers is an opportunity to add literacy materials to the dramatic-play area.

Role playing supermarket, for instance, is aided by the addition of food and detergent containers, a toy cash register, play money, note pads, a telephone and directory, store signs, a schedule of hours, advertisements, and posters for food and other products. Teachers or aides might visit a nearby supermarket to note for the classroom the print that is there and to pick up outdated signs and posters. Store managers readily give away such materials when they no longer need them. Among the materials for dramatic play about supermarkets, definitely include a bookshelf full of magazines and books "for sale." All these materials help children engage in conversation as they role play a store manager, clerk, or shopper. They read posters, books, signs, and magazines and write shopping lists, orders, and new signs when they are needed.

Many topics lend themselves to dramatic play and incorporating literacy materials. A study of health-care personnel can lead to the creation of a doctor's office. A waiting room can be set up with magazines and pamphlets about good health for the patients to read. There can be a no-smoking sign, a notice displaying the doctor's hours, and posters on the wall concerning good displaying health habits. There should be an appointment book for the nurse, a pad for writing appointment reminders for patients to take with them, a pad for writing prescriptions, patient folders containing forms to be filled out, and a patient address and phone book.

When studying transportation, the class can create a travel agency. Here there would be maps, travel posters, pamphlets about places to visit, and tickets to be issued for planes and trains.

Children enjoy role playing in these situations because the activity includes meaningful experiences. In dramatic play, children are voluntarily participating in reading and writing.

Dramatic play is considered appropriate in preschools and kindergartens; however, we seldom leave time for it in first and second grades or think of it as an area in which learning can take place. In classrooms that integrate content themes into dramatic play with 6- to 8-year-olds, extremely sophisticated productions of reading, writing, and oral language result. It is suggested that first- and second-grade teachers incorporate play into their curriculum. Technology has made it more acceptable to engage in dramatic play with second and third graders as they search the Internet for train and plane routes when role play is about travel. Children also can use the Internet to find other information for any role-playing theme featured.

Preparing a Thematic Unit

English Language Learners

Unit themes can be selected by the teacher and the children. Giving students choices concerning what they will learn is important. When a topic is selected, allow the children to brainstorm what they would like to know about. You might begin by suggesting categories to focus on and letting them fill in subheadings (Katz & Chard, 2000; Rand, 1993; Tompkins, 2003). In preparation for a unit on nutrition, I asked a class of kindergarten children to help decide what they might like to learn. I used a web to chart their ideas and started it for them with nutrition as the theme and four categories to focus on: Why is food important? What foods are good for you? Where do we get food from? and How are different foods prepared to eat? The web in Figure 9.4 illustrates the children's responses and the content to be studied for the unit.

Figure 9.4

Curriculum Web for a Thematic Unit on Nutrition

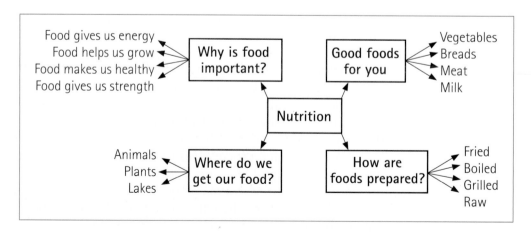

In planning a unit, the teacher needs to include activities in all content areas. Create a plan and select activities related to the unit from different content areas to schedule throughout the school day. Following is a mini-unit written by Ms. Ngai, a first-grade teacher. As you will see, she integrates content-area activities throughout the day that focus on the theme.

Thematic Instruction: Good Food

An interesting theme can make learning come alive for children. With food as our theme and popcorn as our weeklong focus, things were really "popping" in our first-grade classroom! Here are some exciting ways to make learning about popcorn fun, while tying in content-area instruction.

The Friday Before: *We planted popcorn kernels in baking tins lined with paper towels. We spread popcorn in the pans, watered the seeds, and covered the pans with plastic wrap. In a few days, the roots began to sprout* (science).

Monday: *Using a log, we recorded the growth of the seedlings over the weekend. We read* The Popcorn Book *by Tomie dePaola (1978). We discussed that the Native Americans introduced popcorn to the colonists. We used the compound word* popcorn *to trigger a list of other food compound words, such as* cupcake *and* milkshake, *which we wrote on a chart. Anytime a student thought of or came across a compound word, he or she would write it down on the chart. By the end of the week, the chart paper was full* (science, language arts, social studies).

Tuesday: *We set up an experiment chart for making popcorn. We asked ourselves, "What do I want to find out?" (How does a corn kernel change to popcorn?) "What do I think will happen?" "How will I find out?" "What actually happened?" and "What did I learn?" We answered the first two questions. We used an air popper to pop the corn and then completed the experiment chart, answering the remaining questions. We also enjoyed the popcorn for our snack. We planted our seedlings in paper cups filled with soil* (science).

Wednesday: *We made more popcorn to create an estimation lesson for math. Each child grabbed a handful of popcorn from a large bowl and guessed how many kernels were in his or her hand. Then we used a simple record sheet to log estimations. We then counted to find the actual number. We tried it a second time to see if we arrived at a more accurate estimation* (mathematics).

Thursday: *One way Native Americans popped corn was to put an ear of dried corn on a stick and hold it over a fire until the kernels popped. Another way was to throw kernels into the fire until they popped out all over the place. Still another way was to use clay pots filled with hot sand, in which the kernels were mixed until they eventually popped to the top of the pot. We illustrated the method we thought was the best and wrote a few sentences as to why we felt that way. We discussed how the Native Americans made necklaces out of popcorn. Using the popcorn from Wednesday, we gave it a try. We used large, blunt needles and heavy thread and created necklaces* (writing, art, social studies).

Friday: *As a culminating lesson, we had parent volunteers come into our classroom to make popcorn balls. We checked for any growth of our corn plants and recorded the information in our science logs* (science, cooking).

See Appendix F for a complete integrated language arts unit entitled "Animals around the World" for use in the classroom.

Organizing Instruction to Meet Individual Needs: Guided Reading and Center Activities

English Language Learners

There are a variety of strategies for organizing instruction. Children can be taught as a whole class, in small groups, and individually. Children can be in homogeneous or heterogeneous groups based on ability, needs, and interests or they can be divided into peer groups for cooperative learning. The use of a variety of organizational strategies is important, because some children benefit more in one setting than in another. The use of several different grouping schemes within the same classroom also tends to eliminate the stigmas attached to a single grouping system. Variable grouping makes it likely that children will interact with all others in one group or another.

Whole-Group, Small-Group, and One-to-One Learning Settings

Whole-group instruction is not appropriate until children are almost age 3. Younger children lack the ability to concentrate or to sit in a large-group setting and listen for any period of time. Whole-group lessons, sometimes referred to as shared experiences, are appropriate when information needs to be introduced to all the children and the presentation can be understood by all. In early childhood literacy development, storybook readings by an adult, group singing, class discussions, and brainstorming sessions are appropriate whole-group activities.

English Language Learners

Small groups are effective when close interaction with children is necessary for explicit instruction and assessment, as with guided reading and writing instruction. Small groups also are used for cooperative projects with children working independently of the teacher. Teachers should use many types of small-group formations, such as guided reading groups for explicit instruction of skills, groups based on friendships or interests, and independent reading and writing groups. In the description of the language arts block at the end of this chapter, many types of grouping configurations are included. Various group formations are for children to have experiences working with many others and to avoid the stigma attached to being associated with only one group. When using grouping, it is necessary to have children participating in many groups and for children's group placement to change from time to time.

Working with children on a one-to-one basis and allowing them to work independently are forms of *individualized instruction*. Although children need to work cooperatively with peers and adults, they also need to problem solve and accomplish tasks on their own. One-to-one instruction provides an opportunity for the teacher to offer personal attention to a child and to learn much about a child. When a teacher works with a child alone, he or she can

Whole-group and small-group settings allow teachers to vary instructional presentation.

take running records for assessment and do story retelling instruction and assessment. Children can get help with specific skills they are having difficulty with, and teachers can take story dictations or discuss a new piece of the child's writing.

I learned the value of meeting children one-to-one early in my teaching career. A mother of a child in my class told me that he liked to be absent from school. I was upset by the comment, assuming that her son was unhappy in my class. The mother said that her son liked being absent because when he returned to school he was given "private time with the teacher." I had made a practice of meeting with absentees on their return to school to share work we had accomplished when they were absent. I realized then that children enjoy time alone with their teacher. And, through private conferences, I learned a great deal about the instructional needs of my children, their emotional needs, and their interests.

Small-Group Guided Reading and Writing: Explicit Instruction of Skills

English Language Learners

Teachers need to provide direct instruction of skills for most youngsters. Direct instruction is designed for the needs of individuals and can take place in a whole group, in small groups, or on a one-to-one basis, although most often it occurs in small groups. Without the direct instruction component in literacy instruction, some children will miss learning many important skills. It is crucial that teachers be aware of the individual needs of their students and accommodate those needs with an appropriate balance of instructional strategies, both direct and open ended.

Researchers have studied learning in small groups for the purpose of more direct instruction. In small-group instruction, teachers are better able to obtain and retain students' attention. The small group offers the opportunity for more student participation (Combs, 2006; Lou et al., 1996; Slavin, 1987; Sorenson & Hallinan, 1986). In addition, teachers can change instructional methods and materials to meet the needs of each student in small groups. When groups are homogeneous, it is possible for teachers to provide more individualized instruction at the appropriate level (Jalongo, 2007; Slavin, 1987). In small groups, instruction can be paced for students' rate of learning, teaching styles can be modified to meet different learning styles, and students are easier to control (Combs, 2006; Hallinan & Sorenson, 1983).

There are some disadvantages of grouping. For example, children from minority backgrounds are often disproportionately placed in low-ability groups. If groups are inflexible, once a student is tracked in a particular group, that placement may never change throughout his or her school career. This practice affects self-esteem and the type of instruction a student receives (Antonacci & O'Callaghan, 2004; Slavin, 1987) Another disadvantage of grouping is that frequently only one measure determines a child's group placement. Often there is a set number of groups, such as three, in which all children must fit. In addition, teachers sometimes have low expectations for students in the low groups, which can lead to continued low performance for these students (Gambrell & Gillis, 2007; Hallinan & Sorenson, 1983; Otto, 2006).

Guided reading is a form of explicit instruction that typically takes place in small groups. Fountas and Pinnell (1996) define it as follows:

> In guided reading a teacher works with a small group. Children in the group are similar in their development of the reading process and are able to read about the same level of text. Teachers introduce the stories and assist children's reading in ways that help to develop independent reading strategies. Each child reads the entire text. The goal is for children to read independently and silently. The emphasis is on reading increasingly challenging books. Children are grouped and regrouped in a dynamic process that involves ongoing observation and assessment. (p. 4)

And Spiegel (1992) writes,

> The overall purpose of guided reading is to enable children to read for meaning at all times. Guided reading instruction is systematic instruction with a scope of skills and objectives to accomplish. Activities are designed to meet the objectives. Skill instruction is not left to chance; it is assured. Although there is a systematic plan, guided reading instruction should allow for "teachable moments."

Teachers select the instructional materials for small-group reading instruction based on meeting the skill needs of the children. The texts can be any type, such as those from a reading program or children's literature; however, they should be at the instructional level of the child, neither too easy nor too hard. Leveled reading books, often called *little books,* are the most common materials used for guided reading. These books have been

During one-to-one instruction, the teacher does frequent running records to determine a child's strengths, needs, and reading level.

leveled for difficulty, making it easy for teachers to select those needed for particular groups. The texts also must be at the child's instructional reading level. This means that the child can read the text with 90 to 95 percent accuracy (Clay, 1993b). If the text is too easy, there is no opportunity to teach new strategies; if the book is too difficult, children will not understand what they are reading, and the activity becomes an exercise in decoding words, rather than trying to make meaning. Leveled books for early childhood are instructional materials for teaching reading. They are created for this purpose and do not take the place of quality children's literature.

Selecting Children for Groups

English Language Learners

With such a variety of group formations, many teachers ask, "How do I select children for each type of group?" Children can make decisions about participating in some groups such as those based on friendship and interest. Small-group instruction for reading and writing is selected by the teacher because the instruction in these groups is based on children having similar needs, instructional levels, and achievement. Each group will be instructed with different materials and in a different manner from others.

Many pieces of information should be used to determine students' needs and abilities for guided reading and writing group selection. Throughout this book I have discussed several types of assessment that should form a composite picture of the child to help determine group placement. One of the most important pieces of information is teacher judgment. Other types of assessment that will help in group placement include the following:

Running records to determine text reading level, types of strengths and weaknesses in word analysis, fluency, and self-monitoring (see Chapter 2)

Letter-recognition tests (see Chapter 5)

High-frequency word tests (see Chapter 5)

Comprehension evaluation (see Chapter 6)

Standardized test scores (see Chapter 2)

Alternate rank ordering is another way to assign children to groups. This method is mainly based on teacher judgment. List all the children in your class, with the child you rank as having the highest literacy ability at the top and the others following to the last child, whom you rank with the lowest ability. To assign groups, select the top and the bottom child to start two different groups. Place the next child from the top into the group with the top child, and place the next child from the bottom into the group with the child with the lowest ability. Continue this procedure, each time asking yourself if these children are alike enough to be in the same group. When the answer to that question is no, then start a new group. You should end up with four to six groups for your class, with about five children per group. After several meetings, if the groups do not seem to be right for certain children, change their placement. As children are evaluated on a regular basis, their grouping placement could change.

Managing Small-Group Instruction during Guided Reading

In Chapter 8, I discussed organizing and managing independent periods for reading and writing, or literacy center time. The independent work during small-group instruction is very similar but more structured. The purpose of this small-group work is for children to learn to work independently of the teacher and in cooperative social settings with peers. It is a time for children to practice skills already learned. During center time, children engage in self-selected reading and writing activities that they work on independently of the teacher. The teacher acts as a facilitator by answering questions and keeping children on task if necessary. During guided reading and writing, the teacher is occupied with small-group instruction and cannot be disturbed; therefore, the children not in the small-group lesson need to know exactly what to do, when to do it, and where. The management plan in Chapter 8 for independent work is a good model for organizing and managing activity choices and rotation systems for working in independent centers to reinforce skills. However, it needs some modifications when children are being instructed in explicit small groups. A visit to Ms. Shea's second-grade classroom provides a look at the organization of independent work to suit the guided reading lesson format.

The activities that Ms. Shea models for her class for independent work are often skill and theme related. In the beginning of the school year, she spends time introducing children to the centers in the room and the types of activities they include. She has her class practice working on the different activities. At this time, Ms. Shea does not work with small groups during independent center time; rather, she helps the children so that they eventually will be able to work independently.

The children are assigned tasks and and in some cases have some choices when they complete reqired activities. The tasks engage the children in reading and writing to help with skill development. Ms. Shea assigns activities 1, 2, 3, and 4 (listed next) to all children. They work in the heterogeneous groups she has organized. These groups work at the same center at the same time. They can choose to do activity 5 or 6 after they finish the required tasks. At this time they do not have to stay with their group.

1. For *partner reading*, children pair off and read the same book together. They also may read separate books and then tell each other about the story they read. Because the class is studying animals, children are to select books from the open-faced bookshelves that include stories and expository texts about animals. Discussion about what is read is encouraged. Each child must fill out an index card with the name of the book read and one sentence about the story.

2. The *writing activity* requires the children to rewrite the story called *Ugly Fish* (LaReau & Magoon, 2006) that Ms. Shea read at the morning meeting. In their rewritings, children are to include story elements discussed, such as setting, theme, plot episodes, and the resolution. They may consult copies of the book in the classroom if necessary. Each day there is a different writing activity related to the story read.

3. For the *working with words* activity, the children are to find words around the room that have the *sh* and *ch* digraph in them. They classify these words by writing them on a sheet of paper under appropriate digraph headings. Children can look through books to find these digraphs.

4. The *listening center* has taped stories about animals. For each story, there is a sheet of paper with a question to answer about the story. Two titles on tape are *Is Your Mama a Llama?* (Kellogg, 1989) and *Arthur's Pet Business* (Brown, 1990).

5. The *art center* has magazines with many photos of animals that children can use to create animal collages.

6. The *computer center* has literacy software and writing activities.

Ms. Shea has an organizational chart that she uses for assigning children to centers. The rotations occur in coordination with the groups that she meets with for small-group instruction. If children finish before group rotations, they can start one of the optional activities or go on to the next task if there is space at the center. There is a basket for completed work, and every center has sign-in sheets and requires a finished product to be handed in.

In the beginning of the school year, some teachers start center time in a structured fashion. They assign the groups and tasks. As children learn to function independently, they are given opportunities for decision making and select groups to work with or tasks to accomplish.

The management of center time is crucial for its success. Students must know

1. how to use all materials in the centers.

2. the activities in which to participate.

3. the rules that guide participation concerning the selection of materials and what is to happen in groups or when working alone.

4. to place completed work in a designated spot when done with a particular center area.

Children can help generate the guidelines and rules for working independently. Figure 8.3 lists rules for children to follow when working independently.

Children work independently in productive activities.

Some of the rules that are important for independent work during guided reading are as follows:

Rules for Using Materials and Completing Work

- Do all mandatory tasks before you do the optional tasks.
- Speak in soft voices; people are working.
- Put materials back in their place.
- Take care of the materials so that they are in good condition for others.
- Put your completed work in a designated place.
- Record completed work on a contract form or in a log.
- If you have questions, use the "Ask Three and Then Me" rule. Seek help from other students designated as helpers before asking the teacher when she is in a guided reading group.

Rules for Cooperating and Collaborating

- Share materials in collaborative activities.
- Take turns.
- Listen to your friends when they talk.
- Offer help to others you are working with if they need it.
- When you complete an activity, ask yourself if you were helpful to others and if you shared materials.

Some teachers provide a list of activities to do during small-group reading, as shown in Figure 9.5. This list may indicate that the first few activities are mandatory and the others are optional, if the children have time. Some teachers allow children to go from one activity to the next listed on the chart. With this system, children must sign in at a center on a form provided (see Figure 9.6). They can use the center only if there is an empty chair for them, a rule that avoids crowding. When a child finishes an activity, he or she places the product in a designated spot. All independent activities must have some sort of accountability record associated with them so that teachers know what

Figure 9.5

Things to Do
during Guided
Reading

The mandatory activities are done first.

Mandatory Activities

- Read your guided reading book for review.

- Practice any skills your teacher indicated you need to work on.

- Write an informational piece about hibernating animals based on the book read during the morning meeting. Include your new high-frequency words in your expository writing.

- Select the material modeled by the teacher from the word-study center that will enable you to practice making words by blending the initial consonants with ending phonograms.

- Listen to the winter story on the headsets, and answer the questions posed on a sheet of paper provided.

Optional Activities

- Tell a felt story with the story characters and felt-board.

- Create a roll story for a book related to the theme being studied.

- Make a winter collage at the art center.

children are accomplishing. In addition, the child reports the activities completed on his or her contract (see Figure 9.7 for a student contract agreement and Figure 8.7 for a student log for readers and nonreaders).

Another way to designate independent work is through the use of a *center chart*. There are many variations on this type of system. The center chart in Figure 9.8 is an adaptation of the *Work Board* described by Fountas and Pinnell (1996). It designates several choices for three or four different heterogeneously grouped children. The chart is made of tagboard and has a row of figures representing center activities. At the top of each row is a place to attach names of children. The figures are movable, as are the name cards. They can be attached to the chart with Velcro, or the chart can have several pockets in it. (See Strategies for the Classroom for Chapter 9 for more center ideas.)

Strategies

Some teachers prefer a more structured approach to assigning independent work, especially early in the school year. A teacher may assign children to the centers and then have them rotate from one to the next as the teacher rotates her small groups for instruction. For example:

Ms. Shea's second graders sit in groups of four desks pushed together, which she calls pods. These children are heterogeneously grouped and move together from one center activity to another or from one activity to another as listed on the center chart. From time to time, Ms. Shea will change the pod groups so that children have the opportunity to work with different children. When Ms. Shea meets with her first reading group, the other children have designated center assignments. When the first small-group reading lesson ends, all children move to the next center area with their group to work on a new project.

Figure 9.6

Center Sign-in Sheet

Listening Center

Class List Date: *11/18*	Write Your Name Here:
1. Sarah Anders	
2. Barry Duke	
3. Kathleen Carin	
4. Narain Evat	
5. James Gala	
6. Megan Hand	
7. Jovaon Harris	
8. Christine Kim	
9. Dylan Kotter	
10. Kathryn Levin	
11. Irene Lopez	
12. John McNeal	
13. Andrea Penn	
14. Zachary Pierce	
15. Alyx Sax	
16. Gina-Marie Teal	
17. Micah Urani	
18. Max Valley	
19. Brandon Wimbush	

Putting a Guided Reading Lesson into Practice

Every child in every classroom is different from the next. They are different in social, emotional, physical, and intellectual abilities. They are different in background experiences and therefore what they have been able to achieve before entering school and when they are in school. Differentiating their instruction by meeting children in small groups who have similar needs is crucial.

Figure 9.7

Contract
Activities

	Contract	
Name_____	Date_____	
Things to Do	**Specific Activity**	**Done**
	Reading 	
	Writing 	
	Oral Language 	
	Language Arts Manipulatives 	
	Listening Station 	
	Math Manipulatives **1+4−2**	
	Other Activities:	

Small-group lessons should focus on a systematic sequence of skills to be developed based on the needs of the children in the group. In the lesson, many experiences are drawn on to help children with phonograms, syntactic cues, semantic cues, and writing (Reutzel & Cooter, 2004). The objectives for the lessons, like the selection of the text, depend on the students' reading achievement and needs.

Small-group reading instruction in classrooms today is characterized by the following:

1. Children are assessed regularly so that their group placement is changed when their reading ability changes and they are not fixed in one group forever.

2. The teacher purposely uses other types of groups for instruction throughout the day so that students never associate themselves only with their guided reading group.

3. The number of groups formed is not set; it is determined by the number of different ability levels represented in a given classroom. Typically, there are four to six groups.

4. Books selected for instruction meet the needs of the students regardless of their grade level.

Figure 9.8   Center Chart

Janine, Jen, Keith, Kelly, Rumon	Holly, Michael, Ben, Mat, Alexis	Darren, Tisha, Ivory, Sam, Matt	Sarah, Tim, Yassin, Josh, Kyle
Buddy Reading	Listening Station	Oral Language	Journal Writing
Journal Writing	Computer Center	Word-Study Manipulatives	Buddy Reading
Oral Language	Word-Study Manipulatives	Buddy Reading	Listening Station
Word-Study Manipulatives	Buddy Reading	Journal Writing	Computer Center
Listening Station	Oral Language	Computer Center	Word-Study Manipulatives
Computer Center	Journal Writing	Listening Station	Oral Language

All figures and name cards are removable and can be changed around.

Source: Adapted by permission from *Guided Reading* by Irene C. Fountas and Gay Su Pinnell. Copyright © 1996 by Irene C. Fountas and Gay Su Pinnell. Published by Heinemann, Portsmouth, New Hampshire. All rights reserved.

Teachers meet with guided reading groups three to five times a week for direct instruction of skills.

5. Small-group instruction is designed to provide children with strategies for becoming independent fluent readers.

6. Activities provided for children who are not in guided reading groups are often in centers. Children are actively engaged in interesting, productive work practicing skills learned in guided reading lessons. (In the past the most commonly used method for occupying children was the use of workbook pages.)

A guided reading lesson can take almost any form. The major concern is that it be designed to meet the needs of the children in the group. Some particular components are associated with the design of guided reading that follow a Reading Recovery lesson (Clay, 1991). The components are as follows:

1. The lesson begins with children reading something familiar that is easy. This creates fluent, smooth oral reading with good pronunciation, intonation, and flow.

2. The teacher introduces a new book to children by taking a "walk through the book" to build some background knowledge about it before it is read. This helps generate children's prior knowledge about the book's topic, which should help them comprehend what is read (Anderson & Pearson, 1984; Jalongo, 2007; Tompkins, 2007). Here are typical steps in the "walk through the book":
   a. Children are asked to make predictions about what they think might happen in the story.
   b. Children are asked to read the title, author's name, and illustrator's name.
   c. The teacher can give a short summary of the story.
   d. The teacher can introduce patterns in words.

3. With younger children the first reading of the book is done aloud. This is not round-robin reading with different children taking turns, nor is it choral reading. Each child reads his or her copy of the text at his or her own pace. Older children read silently after the teacher provides a good reading model by reading a portion of the selection.

4. While the children read, the teacher listens to provide guidance or scaffolding when a child cannot figure out a word. The teacher also takes notes about the children's reading strengths and weaknesses. He or she may have a different child from each group sit next to him or her during the lesson. This is the student she will take most notes about, which makes record keeping easier. The next day a different focus child will sit next to the teacher during guided reading.

The teacher arranges her guided reading groups based on achievement level and selects books for them to read based on their reading level.

5. After the first reading, children reread for fluency and comprehension, which is easier during the second reading because they do not have to concentrate on decoding as much. Multiple readings of the same text help students become better readers (Clay, 1991; Frey & Fisher, 2006; McGee & Morrow, 2005).

6. After the readings, the teacher selects specific skills to concentrate on based on the needs of the group. He or she might select a word chunk from the text that occurs frequently, such as /og/ in the word *frog*, and build other words that use that chunk. The teacher provides several activities for learning this skill, such as having children generate new words as a whole group that end with the /og/ chunk, such as *log, fog, jog*, and so on. The teacher also might give students magnetic letters with the /og/ chunk and ask them to create /og/ words on their own small magnetic board. To further reinforce the concept, the teacher may ask children to select an /og/ word and write it in a sentence, paying attention to punctuation and spelling. The teacher then cuts each sentence into separate words for students to sequence and read for practice.

7. The teacher often writes notes to parents during the guided reading lesson for children to take home. The note suggests homework for the child and how parents can help.

8. The last component of a guided reading lesson is a running record. This is usually done on an individual basis. A child is asked to stay after the lesson and read a passage to determine progress. The teacher evaluates the child's reading needs and reading level and determines whether the child should remain in his or her present group or move to a group where the work is easier or more difficult. A description of the administration and evaluation of a running record is in Chapter 2 with a sample evaluation form.

It is important to note that during the small-group reading lesson the teacher not only instructs, but also determines children's strengths and needs. Each time there is a guided reading lesson, one child sits next to the teacher for him or her to concentrate on. The teacher can take a running record as the child reads along with the group. Other types of assessment that should be collected and stored in a child's portfolio are frequent writing samples and observation notes about reading behaviors. Teachers should also use the checklists provided in each chapter in this book that deal with

Children read from books at their reading level in guided reading groups. The books are stored in a plastic baggie that is often referred to as a "book in a bag."

different aspects of literacy development. To help you further understand the use of guided reading groups, the following is a discussion and description of guided reading in Mrs. Keefe's first-grade classroom.

Mrs. Keefe believes strongly in the need for small-group instruction to find out what individual children know and what they need to learn. She has organized the class into five groups of four to five children each who have similar reading needs, are capable of similar reading skills, and are reading at about the same level. Children frequently move from group to group based on Mrs. Keefe's ongoing assessment of their progress. She meets with each group three to four times a week for about 10 to 20 minutes. A typical lesson includes (1) reading something familiar for fluency and success, (2) working on a skill involving word analysis, (3) introducing a new book and the decoding or comprehension skills associated with it, (4) reading the new book with teacher and peer support, (5) discussing the story, and (6) doing a writing activity. Mrs. Keefe assesses one or two children's reading development during each reading group by taking a running record of their oral reading and recording errors to determine skill needs and by listening to children's oral retellings of stories to check comprehension.

During a typical day, first Mrs. Keefe engages her children with independent work. When students are working well on their own, she calls on her first group for guided reading instruction. She begins her small-group reading lesson with a familiar text that each child has in his or her baggie. She calls this "a book in a bag," and every day the children bring it to reading group. She uses a familiar text for fluency, to create a feeling of success. The children enjoy the ease with which they can read this old friend.

Next Mrs. Keefe engages the children in a mini-lesson, helping them with a skill they need to learn. She wants the children to use the text along with phonic clues to decode unknown words. She writes a sentence on a small white slate, leaving one word blank. She asks the children to predict what word might make sense in the blank. She then asks them to write the word on their whiteboards. Mrs. Keefe has prepared a practice sheet with three more sentences that have words missing, but that include the first letter of each missing word. She asks the children to work in pairs to figure out the missing words.

At this time, a new book about animals is introduced from a set of leveled books selected for the reading achievement level of the children with whom Mrs. Keefe is working. She introduces some new vocabulary words on 3 × 5 cards. As the children recite the words, she places them in a pocket chart. The children copy the words on their white slates. Mrs. Keefe also has prepared sentence strips that come from the text of the new book, with the new vocabulary words left out. She places the sentence strips in the pocket chart, and the children fill in the blanks with the correct vocabulary word card.

Books stored in boxes or pocket charts are an ideal way of storing children's literature.

For the first reading of the new book, Mrs. Keefe has the entire group read the book aloud. The children are not choral reading, they read at their own rate. She listens carefully to support those in need of help. Following the first reading, she invites the children to read the book again, but this time independently. Because these are beginning readers, they are reading aloud but in soft voices. She selects a focus child for the day for whom she takes a running record. The next time she meets with this group, another child will sit by her side to be assessed.

After the second reading, the children and teacher discuss the story. Mrs. Keefe asks questions that relate to details in the text and questions that require students to connect the story to circumstances in their own life.

As the lesson ends, Mrs. Keefe writes a short note to all the children's parents about their progress, what they were learning, what they needed help with, and what their homework is. Homework can be to read a book well known to the child to demonstrate to his or her parent success or reading a new book with a parent to show progress. The parent's signature concerning the work they did with their child is required. When the group finishes its work for the day, all members put their books in their plastic baggies with their homework note. They place their materials in their own box, which sits on the windowsill, until it is time to go home.

Boxes of books leveled for difficulty are available for children to read and for use during guided reading lessons.

Mrs. Keefe then meets with another group using books selected for their reading instructional level and carries out an appropriate lesson for them. She meets with two other groups until lunchtime.

The discussion concerning the instruction in these first and second grades includes practices suggested in two documents that have made an important impact on early literacy instruction. Both documents were edited by Burns, Griffin, and Snow. One is entitled *Preventing Reading Difficulties in Young Children* (1998) and the other, *Starting Out Right: A Guide to Promoting Children's Reading Success* (1999).

Organizing and Managing Literacy Instruction: Daily Schedules

Scheduling the daily routine in nursery school, kindergarten, and first, second, and third grade must take into account the social, emotional, physical, and intellectual levels of the children. It must also reflect the best from theorists' models of early childhood education, including those of Piaget, Froebel, Dewey, Montessori, the behaviorists, and Vygotsky. The environment should be prepared so that learning can take place naturally, but with the guidance and instruction that will help children achieve their fullest potential.

Young children cannot sit for long periods, so their schedule needs to vary. Whole-class lessons that require sitting and listening must be few and short. Children need large blocks of time for exploring environments. They need play situations, manipulative materials, learning centers, and outdoor areas. Activities that require sitting and listening need to be followed by ones that allow movement. Quiet times must be followed by noisier times. To nurture literacy, the teacher must allow for rich literacy experiences throughout the day, experiences in using and enjoying language in all its forms and functions.

In scheduling the school day, be sure to include *whole-class, small-group,* and *one-to-one* settings for learning. There need to be *teacher-directed* experiences and activities that children participate in *independently*. Children should have opportunities for *oral reading* and *silent reading* from books and from their own writing. They need to have time for *shared reading* experiences and *shared writing* experiences. Time should be set aside for periods of *guided reading* and *guided writing*, as well as *reading and writing independently*. Children should have the opportunity to *read and write collaboratively* with peers and to *perform* in formal and informal settings the products of their reading and writing. Figure 9.9 provides a self-analysis form concerning the organization of instruction. The form provides space for recording lessons taught. It also asks that lessons be identified as whole-group, small-group, or one-to-one settings and as teacher-directed or independent. There is a place to record the materials used in the lesson and where the activity occurred in the classroom. If you record this information for a few days, it will help you analyze the teaching strategies you are using and identify those that you may need to incorporate.

Figure 9.9 Evaluation Strategies and Organization of Instruction

---

Planning Your School Day: Theme Topic_____

(TD-Teacher Directed, IN-Independent Activity, WG-Whole Group, SG-Small Group, 1 to 1)

CHANGE TIME SLOTS WHEN USING LONGER OR SHORTER PERIODS OF TIME

9:00 to 9:30 Activity and Content Area:	**9:30 to 10:30** Activity and Content Area:
Materials Used:	Materials:
Where Activity Takes Place:	Where:
TD or IN:	TD or IN:
WG, SG, 1-to-1:	WG, SG, 1-to-1:
10:30 to 11:30 Activity and Content Area:	**11:30 to 12:30** Activity and Content Area:
Materials:	Materials:
Where:	Where:
TD or IN:	TD or IN:
WG, SG, 1-to-1:	WG, SG, 1-to-1:

Lunch 12:30 to 1:30

1:30 to 2:30 Activity and Content Area:	**2:30 to 3:00** Activity and Content Area:
Materials:	Materials:
Where:	Where:
TD or IN:	TD or IN:
WG, SG, 1-to-1:	WG, SG, 1-to-1:

The sample schedules that follow illustrate where and when specific opportunities to promote literacy can occur. The schedules provide a routine or structure for the day that seems to make children comfortable. Keep in mind that there is no one schedule for all classrooms. These are models with content, activities, and organization that should be included. The schedules and descriptions are found in the next section and are presented in the following order:

1. Language program for kindergarten through third grade
2. Full-day preschool and kindergarten
3. Half-day preschool and kindergarten
4. Child-care centers for infants and toddlers

An Idea from the Classroom

Programs for Kindergarten through Grade 3

The following is a description of a model for organizing and managing an early literacy language arts block, from a study of exemplary first-grade teachers from the Center for English Language Arts and Achievement at the State University of New York at Albany (Morrow & Asbury, 2003). The teachers in the study were identified by their supervisors as exemplary based on observations of their teaching. The exemplary nature of their teaching also was confirmed by other teachers, parents, students, and the children's scores on literacy tests. The teacher in the description (given the pseudonym Ms. Tracey) is a composite of many we observed when trying to discover a model for exemplary teaching. This description includes many theories and strategies discussed throughout the book.

8:30–9:00. As soon as the children entered Ms. Tracey's class, they began to engage in literacy activities. They located their name and photograph on the attendance chart and turned the picture face up to indicate their attendance. Children who were buying lunch signed their names under their choices on the lunch chart. The children then focused their attention on the daily jobs chart, on which Ms. Tracey changed the children's names every day after school. Those with morning jobs quickly got busy. Damien watered the plants while Angel fed the rabbit. Patty and Ashley worked together to write the date on the calendar and complete the days of the week charts. Kelly was responsible for completing the weather graph and asked Dalton to help her. Stephanie and James were the reporters whose job it was to write one or two sentences of daily news, such as what was going to happen during the school day.

The children who were not assigned morning jobs were given a choice of three activities in which they could engage: journal writing, independent or buddy reading, or solving the daily word problem. Angelica chose to write about her upcoming sleepover. Darren finished his journal entry and began reading a book about winter, which was the content-area theme being studied. As they solved the day's theme-based word problem, David and Joel chorused, "Yes!" At 8:55, Ms. Tracey clapped a rhythm that indicated to the students they had 5 minutes to clean up and join her on the rug for their morning meeting.

9:00–9:40. During the whole-group morning meeting, math and language concepts were integrated in a discussion around the calendar and the weather. The children counted how many days had passed and how many days remained in January. They wrote the date in tallies and represented it in popsicle sticks grouped in tens and ones. Discussion about the calendar was rich with new words learned in the winter thematic unit. The two daily reporters read their news aloud.

Ms. Tracey then began to write a theme-related morning message containing news about an upcoming trip to the ice-skating rink. She modeled conventions of print and good penmanship and punctuated her writing with explanations about how print works. Because she was working on punctuation with her students, she included a question and an exclamatory sentence in her message. As a result, the question mark and the exclamation point and their appropriate use were discussed and explained.

After the message was written and read, Ms. Tracey focused the children's attention on the print by asking them if there was anything in the message they noticed and wanted to point out to the class. The *sh* digraph was a "chunk" they had discussed. David said he noticed the *sh* in *shivers* and circled it in the message. Shanaya noticed the word *ink* in the word *rink*. Ms. Tracey took the opportunity to reinforce looking for a little word you know inside of an unknown word as being an excellent strategy to use when reading. She asked the children to see if *rink* was written on their word wall under the *ink* chunk. Shanaya offered to write it on the chart along with an illustration.

Next, two children shared things brought from home with the class. In the biweekly newsletter, Ms. Tracey had explained to the parents that the children were learning about winter. She asked them to help the children choose something related on winter to bring to school and to write three clues about what they chose. The item and the clues were carried to school in a paper bag marked "secret" and "keep out." Each child removed the clues from the bag, being careful not to expose the item. As they read aloud each clue, they called on a classmate to guess the secret item.

Ms. Tracey then read a theme-related piece of children's literature, *The Wild Toboggan Ride* (Reid & Fernandes, 1992), about the last toboggan ride of the day, which becomes a zany adventure for a little boy, his grandpa, and some surprised toboggan riders. She chose this text because of its sequenced plot episodes and repeated language patterns. Before reading the story, she initiated a discussion about riding down a snow-covered hill. The children brainstormed ways to go down a snowy hill as Ms. Tracey listed their ideas. Using the cover illustration, she then explained a toboggan was a type of sled. The word *toboggan* was added to the posted winter words list.

Next, Ms. Tracey used a directed listening and thinking activity format. She set a purpose for reading by asking the children to listen while she read to learn who rides on the toboggan and why the ride is "wild." While reading aloud, she encouraged the children to join in by reading the repeated words and phrases.

After the story, the class talked about who rode on the toboggan and how they became involved in the ride down the hill. As the characters in the story were mentioned, Ms. Tracey wrote what the children said about their role in the story onto sentence strips. She then asked the children to read the strips and put them in the order in which they happened. Then she introduced the words *first, next,* and *last* as a means to express sequence in a story. She explained that the children would be writing about a time they went sledding or played in the snow. She showed the children a graphic organizer or story map they could use to help them sequence their own stories. The story map followed the model of the sentence strip activity. Copies of the map were placed in the writing center for the children's use when writing their own story response.

9:40–9:50. After engaging in shared reading and writing experiences, Ms. Tracey began what she called her Reading Workshop. She explained and modeled center activities for the children to participate in while she met with small groups for guided reading instruction. The following activities were available to the children during Reading Workshop:

Reading Alone or Buddy Reading. Children selected a book about the theme being studied. After reading alone or with a buddy, they made written recommendations about the book on 5 $\times$ 8 cards for others to read.

Writing Center. In the writing center, children wrote their responses to the shared book reading of *The Wild Toboggan Ride.* The graphic organizers that were previously modeled were in the center to help the children sequence their stories. The children collaborated with a partner while writing. They conferenced after completing the organizer to check if their stories were clearly sequenced and if their use of sequencing words was appropriate.

Listening Center. In the listening center, the children listened on headsets to tape-recorded stories. Ms. Tracey had placed several theme-based books of assorted genres in this area. Titles included *The Hat* (Brett, 1997), *Rabbit's Wish for Snow: A Native American Legend* (Tchin, 1997), *When Winter Comes* (Maass, 1993), and *Manatee Winter* (Zoehfeld, 1994). She also made available two tape recorders for the students to record and listen to their own reading of favorite stories and poems. She found this to be a motivating way for the children to develop fluency and expression. After listening to this reading, they wrote evaluations of their reading.

Word Study. A copy of the winter words list was kept in the word-study area. Today, Ms. Tracey asked the children to choose a word from the list and, using letter tiles, see how many new words they could make from the letters of the selected word. They were to write their new words on a recording sheet. Completed recording sheets were placed in a marked folder. Recording sheets "still in progress" were placed in another folder for later use.

Computer Center. Two computers were used throughout the day. This morning, two children were copying winter poems, which had been learned earlier that week.

Ms. Tracey frequently used poems along with children's books in her themed literacy instruction. She found poetry to be a rich context for teaching word chunks, high-frequency words, phonics, and rhyming. She also highly valued the joy of poetry. Many of the children had started their own books called *My Favorite Poems.* They often used the computers to write and illustrate the poems they wanted to include in their collections.

Science Center. Ms. Tracey was planning to conduct an experiment with the class later in the day. The children would be timing how long it took different frozen items to melt. She wanted the children to think about, write, and explain their estimations before carrying out the experiment. A recording sheet was provided. Their predictions would be tallied and graphed prior to the experiment and confirmed and discussed after the experiment.

Art Center. Materials for making puppets were available to the children in this area. Ms. Tracey had chosen three winter stories with well-defined, sequenced plot episodes for use during shared reading: *The Wild Toboggan Ride* (Reid & Fernandes, 1992), *Do Like Kyla* (Johnson, 1990), and *The Mitten* (Brett, 1989). The children selected characters from the stories to make as puppets, which could be used in retellings of the stories. The class was going to work on the puppet shows and perform them for the kindergarten classes at the end of their winter unit.

The children were reminded they were required to do two of the activities: read alone or with a buddy and the writing response. They had to spend at least 20 minutes on each. They then could choose which center area they wanted to work in for the remainder of Reading Workshop. Because the science experiment was to be done that afternoon, Ms. Tracey reminded those who had not yet made their predictions to do so.

9:50–11:15. While the children engaged in the self-directed activities, Ms. Tracey met with small groups of students for guided reading instruction. She had organized her class into five groups of four to five children who had similar reading behaviors, had control of like reading strategies, and were reading on the same level. It was common for the children to move frequently from group to group based on Ms. Tracey's ongoing assessment of the children's progress. She met with each group three or four times a week for 20 to 30 minutes. After each group, she selected one child to focus on and assessed reading development by taking a running record and listening to a story retelling.

This morning's first guided reading group began with a mini-lesson about attending to print. Ms. Tracey had observed that these children were attending only to the first letter of an unknown word, rather than gleaning all the information found in the print. She also wanted these children to learn to cross-check printed information by checking to see if the word they used made sense in the sentence. She wrote a sentence on a small whiteboard leaving one word blank. She asked the children to predict what word might make sense in the blank. She then asked them to predict what the word would look like by writing it onto their small writing boards. They then worked together to correctly fill in the missing word of the sentence. After doing three sentences this way, the children discussed with Ms. Tracey how this might help them when they are reading.

Then a new book was introduced to the group. Each child had his or her own copy of the story *The Crazy Quilt* (Avery & McPhail, 1993). Ms. Tracey used a set of leveled books for most of her guided reading instruction. She did, however, use a rubric to level some of her easier to read classroom books about winter. She used the books she leveled for guided reading instruction whenever appropriate. She did a page by page book walk with the children and discussed necessary background information and vocabulary so that the children could read and comprehend the book independently. Following the book walk, she directed the children to begin reading. Because these were beginning readers, they read aloud in quiet voices. Ms. Tracey listened in as they read, guiding children when necessary.

After the children read the story twice, Ms. Tracey praised the use of good reading strategies she had observed in their reading. She particularly reinforced cross-checking behaviors and attending fully to print. The children then composed a sentence that modeled the repetitive pattern of the story. The sentence was cut apart and reassembled word by word. Ms. Tracey then selected two words from the sentence to be cut apart and reassembled, again emphasizing the need to attend to all the graphophonemic information in a word. As the group was dismissed, each child placed the book into his or her book basket to be read later during independent or buddy reading time. Ms. Tracey kept records regarding the children's performance during the guided reading group on a clipboard. She wrote brief anecdotal notes during and after the group meeting. She also wrote a note to each parent letting them know what had been accomplished in the guided reading lesson, homework the child had to do, and how they could help. This all went in the child's baggie to take home. Reading Workshop ended at 11:20.

11:20–11:30. Cleanup, bathroom.

11:30–12:20. Lunch and recess followed by Reading Workshop.

12:20–12:30. When the children returned from recess, Ms. Tracey read aloud from *Little Polar Bear, Take Me Home!* (deBeer, 1996).

12:30–1:15. This afternoon's instruction began with Writing Workshop. Ms. Tracey started the workshop with a 10-minute mini-lesson about the use of capital letters and punctuation. She noticed during her writing conferences with the students that they needed review about when to use capitals. Though most students were using periods and quotation marks regularly, she wanted them to use question marks and exclamation points consistently.

She had written a paragraph from *Little Polar Bear, Take Me Home!* onto an overhead transparency. She omitted capitals and punctuation from the paragraph. As a class, the children discussed where and why capitals and punctuation needed to be inserted as they edited the paragraph. The children were then dismissed to get their writing folders and worked for the remaining 35 minutes. Many chose to write books related to the winter theme.

Because the children worked independently, they were at different stages in their writing. Some were drafting new stories; others were editing or working on final drafts at the computer. Throughout the workshop, Ms. Tracey conferenced with students individually to discuss their progress and to help them plan the next step in their writing process. Because Ms. Tracey's mini-lessons often focused on how to peer tutor, the children productively and actively engaged with one another.

1:15–2:00. After Writing Workshop, Ms. Tracey conducted the whole-group science lesson on melting.

2:00–2:45. The science lesson was followed by a 45-minute Math Workshop.

2:45–3:00. The day concluded with a 10-minute whole-class meeting in which two students' accomplishments were applauded: Paul and Linda had completed publishing their books that day and would share them with the class tomorrow. Ms. Tracey then gave last-minute reminders about homework and returning permission slips. Children packed their things for dismissal.

An Idea from the Classroom

Full-Day Program for Preschool (Ages 3 and 4)

Some preschool children cannot sit very long for whole-group lessons. During these times, provisions need to be made for those unable to participate with the help of the aide in the classroom. As the year progresses, there should be a greater expectation for participation in whole groups, especially for four-year-olds.

8:00–8:30: Arrival at school and greeting, storage of outdoor clothing. Quiet activities and short circle time to explain new centers and activities for the day.

8:30–9:30: Exploration time with learning centers and special daily activities.

9:30–9:40: Cleanup and hand washing.

9:40–10:10: Whole-group music, movement, and dramatic play.

10:10–10:30: Morning snack.

10:30–11:00: Small-group guided literacy instruction. The rest of the class works at centers on special projects.

11:00–11:30: Center play or outdoor play if weather permits.

11:30–11:40: Cleanup and preparation for lunch.

11:40–12:15: Lunch and outdoor play or other activities to develop large motor skills.

12:15–12:45: Shared storybook reading, creative storytelling, repeated story readings, role playing, shared book readings, use of Big Books.

12:45–1:45: Rest time with music.

1:45–2:20: Play at centers.

2:20–2:45: Circle time. Summary of the day's activities, planning for the next day, sharing items brought from home that are related to a theme being studied, songs, story.

2:45–2:55: Cleanup and preparation for dismissal.

An Idea from the Classroom

Full-Day Program for Kindergarten

It should be noted that full-day schedules allow for larger blocks of time and more time for learning through exploration and manipulation of materials.

8:30–9:00: Arrival at school, storage of outdoor clothing. Quiet activities.

9:00–9:30: Whole-group morning meeting, opening exercises, morning message, discussion of unit topic, songs and musical movement activity related to the unit topic, daily news, planning for the school day.

9:30–9:50: Whole-class lesson, either in language arts or mathematics, varying from day to day, with an assignment to complete that flows into the next period.

9:50–10:15: Small-group guided reading instruction. The rest of the class completes work from the whole-class lesson or works on individual contracts from small groups or at centers designated for use during this quiet period (literacy center, math, social studies, science).

10:15–10:45: Free play. All centers open, including dramatic play, blocks, and woodworking. Special art or food-preparation projects are set up in the art center once each week for small groups independent of the teacher.

10:45–11:00: Cleanup and snack.

11:00–11:30: Shared storybook reading, creative storytelling, repeated story readings, role playing, shared book readings, use of Big Books.

11:30–12:15: Literacy center time. Children use materials in the literacy center (library corner, writing area, oral language area, language arts manipulatives), including Very Own Words.

12:15–1:15: Lunch and outdoor play, if time and weather permit. Otherwise, large motor activities in the gymnasium.

1:15–1:45: Whole-group lesson in science or social studies incorporating language arts, music, or art.

1:45–2:15: Center time (literacy, mathematics, science, social studies). Special projects can be set up in any of these for small groups to rotate through in a given week. The teacher meets with small groups for instruction in math or literacy skills.

2:15–2:50: Whole-group circle time. Summary of the day's activities, planning for the next day, sharing of items brought from home that are related to study units, performance of work created by children, songs, and adult story reading.

2:50–3:00: Preparation for dismissal. Dismissal.

An Idea from the Classroom

Half-Day Program for Preschool (Ages 3 and 4)

Some preschool children cannot sit very long for whole-group lessons. During these times, provisions need to be made for those unable to participate with the help of the aide in the classroom. As the year progresses, there should be a greater expectation for participation in whole groups, especially for 4-year-olds.

8:00–8:30: Arrival at school and greeting, storage of outdoor clothing. Quiet activities and short circle time to explain new centers and activities for the day.

8:30–9:30: Exploration time with learning centers and special daily activities.

9:30–9:40: Cleanup and hand washing.

9:40–10:00: Whole-group music, movement, and dramatic play.

10:00–10:20: Snack.

10:20–10:50: Small-group guided literacy lessons. The rest of the class works at literacy centers or on special projects.

10:50–11:40: Free play or outdoor play.

11:40–12:00: Whole-group storybook reading using various strategies, including shared book experiences, role playing, creative storytelling. Summary of the day.

An Idea from the Classroom

Half-Day Program for Kindergarten

8:30–8:50: Arrival at school, storage of outdoor clothing. Quiet activities.

8:50–9:20: Whole-group morning meeting, opening exercises, morning message, discussion of unit topic, songs or musical movement activities related to unit topic, daily news, planning for the school day.

9:20–9:40: Whole-class lesson in language arts, mathematics, social studies, or science, varying from day to day, with an assignment to complete that flows into the next period.

9:40–10:00: Small-group guided reading lessons. The rest of the class completes work from the whole-class lesson; children work on individual contracts in small groups or at designated centers (literacy, social studies, science, or mathematics).

10:00–10:35: Center time. All centers open, including art, music, blocks, dramatic play, literacy, science, and social studies. Special projects may be set up at different centers, such as art or science. Children work alone or in small groups independently of the teacher.

10:35–10:50: Cleanup and snack.

10:50–11:10: Literacy center time. Children use materials from the literacy center (library corner, oral language area, writing area).

11:10–11:30: Outdoor play, if weather permits, or large motor games in the gymnasium.

11:30–12:00: Whole-group storybook reading with various strategies, including shared book experiences, role playing, creative storytelling. Summary of the school day. Dismissal.

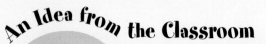

An Idea from the Classroom

Child-Care Centers

Full-Day Program for Infants and Toddlers

6:45–7:45: Arrival, caring for infants' needs (diapering, feeding). When involved in these routine activities, caregivers talk to babies, sing nursery rhymes, recite poems, reinforce babies' responses.

Activity period consisting of play (in small groups or one-to-one) with blocks, manipulative toys, books, or paper and crayons. Teacher and aides provide language models by identifying materials and talking about their use and provide positive reinforcement for such literacy activities as attempting oral language, looking at books, and using crayons on sheets of paper.

7:45–8:30: Breakfast for toddlers, accompanied by song or poetry. (Infants are fed whenever necessary.)

8:30–9:00: Free play.

9:00–9:15: Cleanup. Washing, diapering, caring for babies' needs. Adults interact with children verbally through conversation, song, or rhymes.

9:15–9:30: Morning snack.

9:30–10:30: Exploration time at learning centers. This time may include a brief whole-group lesson.

10:30–11:00: Outside play.

11:00–11:45: Lunch. Conversation involves the taste, smell, and texture of the food.

11:45–12:00: Bathroom, wash up. Babies are readied for nap time with washing and diapering.

12:00–12:15: Storybook reading.

12:15–2:15: Nap time or quiet time. Naps are begun with a song and carried through with quiet background music.

2:15–2:30: As children wake, their needs are taken care of again, and a small snack is provided.

2:30–3:40: Indoor and outdoor play. In either setting, adults work with small groups, reading stories, encouraging responses from children, pointing out print.

3:40–4:00: Teacher attempts a group session involving singing a song or reading a book aloud. The last 10 minutes of the day are spent preparing the children to leave—toileting, diapering, and general care.

As noted in the introduction to this chapter, child-care centers need to emulate as much as possible homes with rich literacy environments if they are to ensure the natural development of literacy in infants and toddlers.

Activities and Questions

1. Answer the focus questions at the beginning of the chapter.

2. Plan a school day with a balanced perspective in literacy instruction. Select a grade level of your choice from preK to third grade.
   a. Prepare the environment to provide rich literacy materials and to accommodate the thematic unit studied.
   b. Prepare a letter to send home to parents concerning the activities happening in class and inviting them to participate. Chapter 10 dealing with the family has a sample letter.
   c. Include guided reading instruction and independent center activities during guided reading.

3. Observe an early childhood classroom to evaluate the literacy environment. Use the "Checklist: Evaluating and Improving the Literacy Environment" provided in this chapter.

4. Review the sample materials you have collected in the assessment portfolio you began for a child at the beginning of the year. Write a summary concerning the child's literacy development at this time and the progress he or she has made in the months you have been collecting the materials; include suggestions you have for his or her program of instruction.

5. **Strategies** Create new center signs for your classroom or during student teaching from Strategies for the Classroom for Chapter 9.

myeducationlab

VIDEO EXERCISE

Now that you have the benefit of having read this chapter, return to the www.myeducationlab.com topic "Organizing for Reading Instruction" and watch "Using Centers" one more time. You may complete the questions that accompany it online and save or transmit your work to your professor, or complete the following questions, as required.

Using Centers (1:45 minutes)

1. What is a center? What are the different centers that are discussed in this video, and what is the purpose of each one? Choose one center and discuss what is included.

2. Choose one of the following centers or make up one of your own and write a plan for how you would set it up in a kindergarten classroom. What skills would you be targeting in this center? How would you ensure access for all children? How would you maintain order?

- Computer center
- Reading center
- Writing center

Focus Questions

- Define the many aspects of the term *family literacy*.

- What reading and writing materials should be present in a home, and where should they be placed to help promote children's literacy?

- What reading and writing activities can families involve their children in to help promote literacy development?

- What can parents do in school to help them with their children's literacy and help teachers at school?

- What are some concerns surrounding family literacy programs with diverse, multicultural populations?

- What elements make for a successful family literacy program at school?

- **VOCABULARY:** family literacy, intergenerational literacy initiatives, parent involvement programs

- **Strategies** See Strategies for the Classroom for Chapter 10 on pages S-48 through S-51 for ways to share materials with parents.

PEARSON
myeducationlab **VIDEO PREVIEW:** Involving Parents (1:59 minutes); Involving Parents in the Educational Process (5:04 minutes). Before reading this chapter, go to www.myeducationlab.com. Under the topic "Becoming a Reading Teacher," access and watch the videos "Involving Parents" and "Involving Parents in the Educational Process."

Family Literacy Partnerships

Home and School Working Together

You may have tangible wealth untold:
Caskets of jewels and coffers of gold.
Richer than I you can never be—
I had a Mother who read to me.
—Strickland Gillian "The Reading Mother"
from *Best Loved Poems of the American People*

Mrs. Bolton spread the newspaper on the floor as her two grandchildren, Adasha, 6, and Jonnelle, 4, started to put down the paint jars, water can, brushes, and paper to paint. She always used newspaper to protect the floor when the girls did something messy. As she spread the paper, she said, "Now let's see what section of the newspaper we have out on the floor today." "Oh look," said Adasha, "It's the food section. It is showing healthy food for the summer. Mrs. Bolton said, "It says fruits and vegetables are at their best in the summer and we need several portions of each a day." Mrs. Bolton always had the girls look at the contents of the newspaper on the floor. The children often would continue to investigate the newspaper and almost forget their clay or paint. Sometimes they would paint about what they had just read. Mrs. Bolton was taking advantage of the print in her environment that was a familiar part of the children's lives and was making it a pleasurable experience that would enrich their literacy knowledge.

Roxana, a student in one of my graduate courses, shared this family story:

> I don't remember being read to when I was young. What I do remember is storytelling. I remember listening to personal stories told over and over by my parents, grandparents, and relatives that had to do with funny, sad, but all real-life happenings about the family. Everyone took a part in telling the stories, adding parts they felt were missing. This was a special and favorite family tradition that took place every Sunday after church as we sat around the table having lunch in my grandmother's kitchen. I remember looking forward to it. The stories were often the same, but I wanted to hear them again and again.

Theory and Research on Family Literacy

The term *family literacy* is a complex concept. Here are some descriptions of family literacy based on several sources (Bus, van Ijzendoorn, & Pellegrini, 1995; Donahue, Finnegan, Lutkus, Allen, & Campbell, 2001; Melzi, Paratore, & Krol-Sinclair, 2000; Morrow, Paratore, & Tracey, 1994):

1. Family literacy encompasses the ways families, children, and extended family members use literacy at home and in their community.

2. Family literacy occurs naturally during the routines of daily living and helps adults and children "get things done."

3. Examples of family literacy might include using drawings or writing to share ideas, composing notes or letters to communicate messages, keeping records, making lists, following written directions, or sharing stories and ideas through conversation, reading, and writing.

4. Family literacy may be initiated purposefully by a family member, or it may occur spontaneously as families and children go about the business of their daily lives.

5. Family literacy activities also reflect the ethnic, racial, or cultural heritage of the families involved.

6. Family literacy activities may be initiated by the school. These activities are intended to support the acquisition and development of school literacy for children and families. These activities could include storybook reading, writing, and helping with homework assignments.

7. Family literacy involves parents coming to school for back-to-school night, conferences, and programs children participate in.

8. Family literacy involves parents coming to their child's classroom to observe; to read to the children; to share artifacts, hobbies, and their professions; to help with center time.

9. Family literacy involves parents in workshops at school to help them learn about and understand what they can do at home to help their children.

Family Literacy: Why Is It Important?

Family members who care for children are children's first teachers. They are also children's teachers for the longest time. Beginning at birth, children's experiences affect their success in becoming literate. The success of the school literacy program frequently depends on the literacy environment at home. Studies carried out in homes have been a major catalyst for new early literacy strategies. Because some children come to school already reading and writing, apparently without formal instruction, investigators began to study the characteristics of those children and their homes.

This line of investigation has been extremely helpful from two points of view. First, the findings reveal home practices that could be successful in school settings. Second, they provide information on the crucial role a family plays in the development of children's literacy and on how they can help.

I can attest to the vital role of the home in the development of early literacy. From the day my grandson James (4½) and granddaughter Natalie (2) were born, their parents and grandparents read to them. They were read to on a daily basis while sitting on someone's lap or in the same reading chair. They were given the opportunity to look at books. The pictures were talked about and stories read. By 5 months, James and Natalie would listen as we read to them. We chose mostly cardboard picture storybooks with only a few words on each page. From time to time, their eyes focused intently on the brightly colored pictures. They might be serious or have a wonderful smile. Sometimes they reached out to tap the book or put it in their mouths. Occasionally, they made pleasant sounds that seemed like attempts to imitate our reading voices. Because the experience was daily and positive, they became familiar with story readings and welcomed them.

As James and Natalie got older, their responses to the readings increased. Before they could talk, they pointed to pictures and made sounds as if naming objects or characters. As they acquired oral vocabulary, they labeled things in the book as they were read to. We always responded with pleasure, reinforcing their attention and understanding of the concepts. We often explained things beyond the words in the book. Book sharing was looked forward to; it was relaxing, warm, and pleasurable.

By the time each of them was about 14 months old, you would find them sitting on the floor reading a book, that is, reading as a 14-month-old child can. He or she knew how to hold the book right side up, knew which was the beginning of the book and which was the end, and knew how to turn the pages. They looked at the pictures and chanted in tones similar to the sound of reading. Except for a few words, little of their language was understandable, but from a distance one might think that they were reading. Actually, they were—not in the conventional manner, but by demonstrating emegent literacy behavior. They also had favorite books that they looked at over and over again and wanted read to them over and over again.

Books are all around their houses. Natalie and James each have an accessible shelf of books in their rooms. There is a crate of books with their toys on the floor of a closet, and they are free to use them at all times. There are books in the kitchen, the bathroom, and play areas. They see our books and their parents' books since there are all types of reading materials around: recreational reading, such as novels, magazines, and newspapers, and work-related reading. The children see their parents and grandparents reading frequently and at times join us with their own books.

In addition to books, James and Natalie have access to pencils, crayons, markers, and a supply of different kinds of paper. At the age 2, it was natural for James and Natalie to pick up a pencil and a sheet of paper, sit down and draw a picture, and even scribble write about it. I could not identify what they drew, but they talked about it. They were well aware of the difference between drawing and writing, and the squiggles of "print" looked different from the scribbles of their drawing. Although not yet capable of either drawing or writing in the conventional sense, they attempted to do both and differentiated between them.

In the house and on trips to the supermarket or post office, environmental print surrounds them as it does other children. Cognizant of its importance in early literacy development, we point out STOP signs at street corners and ask them to read as many signs as they can as we drive along. At home their parents read cereal boxes, directions for assembling new toys, letters that come in the mail, and e-mail. As a result, their awareness of the print around them and of its functions is heightened. They ask what labels say and look to print for information. We also play with language, especially when driving in the car. I say what rhymes with car, or what other words do you know that have a *J* in them like James?

When James turned 3 and now 4, our story readings became more interactive. James asks questions and comments about pictures and episodes. I respond with answers and comments that expand the discussion. He often narrates familiar stories with me as I read. Occasionally, he asks what certain words say as his attention focuses more and more on print as well as on pictures. He has a journal which we write in a few times a week about things he has done that day. We discuss what he would like to write today. He will draw a picture and tell me what to write. If he can write a letter or word, he will do so.

One day, James was sitting in the back seat of the car on the way home from a trip to the library. He was looking through one of the books he had selected and began reading it out loud. It was a humorous story called *Ten Apples up on Top* (LeSieg, 1961). The book used a limited number of words, repetitive vocabulary, and rhyme. The attractive illustrations reflected the text. As he read, I first assumed that the book was one we had read together. Suddenly I realized it was not. I pulled to the side of the road and with great excitement confirmed what I thought was true. James was reading, actually reading on his own! He had made the transition from part-reading, part-narrating stories to reading each word. James has reached this point in his literacy development gradually. The family has offered some informal instruction. Because of his constant exposure to books and print from birth, he developed a large sight vocabulary and a number of reading skills. His ability to read did not just happen. Rather, it developed within an environment that fostered literacy through the guidance, modeling, and encouragement of supportive adults. Natalie is following in his footsteps.

Today's Families Are Complex

English Language Learners

The picture painted in the preceding anecdote is the ideal situation for children to grow up in. Unfortunately, this type of environment is not always the norm. Today about 75 percent of families include both parents at work. That leaves little time to think about literacy. Many children are being raised in single-parent families, leaving the one remaining parent with so many responsibilities that time for reading, writing, and talking to each other sounds like a luxury. The number of different cultures in our country is increasing and many parents speak different languages but don't speak Engish. There are significant cultural differences in how we educate our children in the United States and how other cultures approach literacy, which makes it difficult for those children and their parents to understand our system. We also have significant numbers of family members who are not literate and therefore don't know what to do about engaging their children in literacy-rich experiences. They don't see the relevance or the importance. Those who live in poverty don't think about buying books, going to the library, or even having space for a box of books in their home (Hart & Risley, 1995). Dealing with poverty in our multicultural society is not easy when it comes to litearcy development. However, it is the job of the school and teachers to put forth the effort. What we can do is try to help parents understand how important they are in supporting the literacy development that occurs in the school and how important it is for their children to become literate to get jobs and live healthy lives. There are many things these parents can do to help, even if they cannot read themselves or speak the language. It is an issue with great frustration attached. We plan parent events at school and few attend. We make suggestions that aren't followed and feel defeated. But if we get to three parents, we have helped three families and then another and another and another. Each little success must be looked on as a large one, and we go forward from there (Christian, Morrison, & Bryant, 1998; Lonigan & Whitehurst, 1998).

Strategies That Promote Literacy Development in the Home

The information that follows is a parent involvement framework, suggesting an American mainstream approach to family literacy. The constructs are appropriate for all homes, but will be best understood and carried out in homes where school-like literacy activities are valued and understood. This approach assumes that the family members have the literacy and language ability to share the experiences discussed; however, it is also appropriate for use in the language of any family. After this initial presentation, which sets the groundwork for some basic ideas and strategies, a broader perspective will be discussed to take into consideration families who have limited literacy ability and speak a different languages. The ultimate goal is for all parents to be able to perform the suggestions in this section.

Various researchers have studied homes in which children read and write early without direct instruction (Leseman & de Jong, 1998; Morrow, 1983; Neuman, 1996). The results have consistently established that certain characteristics are common to these homes. Early readers have family members who read to them and readily help them with writing and reading. These family members read a variety of material, including novels, magazines, newspapers, and work-related information. They own or borrow books, for both themselves and their children. Reading and writing materials can be found throughout their homes. Family members in these homes often take their children to libraries and bookstores (Morrow, 1983; Morrow & Young, 1997; Neuman, 1997). The homes hold ample supplies of books and writing materials, and reading and writing are generally valued as important activities. Books are associated with pleasure, and literary activities are rewarded. The homes are well organized, with scheduled daily activities and rules and designated responsibilities for family members. They provide a setting where interactions between adults and children are socially, emotionally, and intellectually conducive to literacy interest and growth (Anderson, Hiebert, Scott, & Wilkinson, 1985).

The families of children who are likely to learn to read and write easily have homes where literacy environments have been created with books

The interactive behavior between parent and child during storybook reading involves negotiating, mediating, and constructing meaning related to the print.

Books should be available for babies in their cribs and playpens; waterproof books are available for bathtubs.

and writing materials. Children with an early interest in reading and writing tend to spend playtime at home writing and drawing with paper and crayons or looking at books. Family members in these homes enforce rules for selecting and limiting television viewing. Family membtrs talk to each other often and want to know what children are doing in school. These children are rated by their teachers as higher than average in social and emotional maturity, work habits, and general school achievement (Faber & Mazlish, 1995).

The following elements affect the quality of the literacy environment in the home: (1) the physical environment or literacy materials in the home, (2) interactions that occur during literacy experiences shared by children, family members, and other individuals in the home, and (3) positive and supportive attitudes about literacy and family aspirations for literacy achievement (Fin, 1998; Leichter, 1984).

Schools and other community agencies need to get information into homes about the need for rich literacy environments even before children enter school. Information can be disseminated at a special meeting for expectant parents, in hospital maternity wards, in obstetricians' and pediatricians' offices, and through churches, synagogues, and community agencies. A succinct handout such as "Guidelines: Promoting Early Literacy at Home" will be a helpful start and should be printed in languages found in the community in which you live. It is provided here in Spanish and English. (Booklets and pamphlets on the development of literacy at home can be found on pages 392–395.)

Materials to Read in the Home

ELL

English Language Learners

Books need to be readily accessible at home for children (Hannon, 1995; Soderman, Gregory, & McCarty, 2005). Family members can create little library areas for their children. Books can be placed in a cardboard box or plastic crate to serve as a bookshelf. In addition, books can be made available all around the house. Kitchens, bedrooms and bathrooms are important, because children spend considerable time in these places. If there is a playroom or a place for toy storage, it should contain books. Every room can hold books that are visible and accessible. Before babies are crawling or walking, books can be brought to them in cribs and play areas; waterproof books are available for bathtubs.

A variety of books should be selected for the home. For babies up to 18 months, brightly colored concept books with cardboard, plastic, or cloth pages are appropriate. They must be safe, with rounded edges, and sturdy enough to withstand chewing and other rough treatment. As the child becomes a toddler, preschooler, and kindergartener, nursery rhymes, fairy tales, folktales, realistic literature, informational books, picture books, alphabet

Babies need to explore and experiment with books.

books, number books, poetry, books related to favorite television programs, and easy-to-read books (those with limited vocabularies, large print, and pictures closely associated with the text) should be made available. Children's magazines offer attractive print material and are a special treat if they come in the mail. In addition to children's literature, print material for adults, including books, magazines, newspapers, and work-related material, should be obvious in the home. However, storytelling is as important as reading to children; discussions about the Bible and other religious books are very useful and happen often in diverse cultures.

Reading as a Home Activity

Research indicates that children who are read to regularly by parents, siblings, or other individuals in the home and who have family members who read themselves become early readers and show a natural interest in books (Bus, van Ijzendoorn, & Pellegrini, 1995; Educational Research Service, 1997). This is not surprising. Through frequent story readings, children become familiar with book language and realize the function of written language. Story readings are almost always pleasurable, and the pleasure that is experienced builds a desire for and interest in reading (Cullinan, 1992; Huck, 1992). Continued exposure to books develops children's vocabularies and sense of story structure, both of which help them learn to read.

It is clear that verbal interaction between adult and child during story readings has a major influence on literacy development (Cochran-Smith, 1984; Ninio, 1980; Vukelich & Christie, 2004). Such interaction offers a direct channel of information for the child and thus enhances literacy development (Allison & Watson, 1994; Heath, 1982; Morrow, 1987a). It leads children to respond to story readings with questions and comments. These responses become more complex over time and demonstrate more sophisticated thinking about printed material. Research on home storybook readings has identified a number of interactive behaviors that affect the quality of read-aloud activities. These behaviors include questioning, scaffolding (modeling dialogue and responses), praising, offering information, directing discussion, sharing personal reactions, and relating concepts to life experiences

Babies who are read to often take a leadership role in turning pages, babble in tones that sound like reading, and show strong involvement in shared reading experiences.

(Edwards, 1995; King & McMaster, 2000; Roser & Martinez, 1985).

The following transcription from the beginning of a story reading between a mother and her 4-year-old son Ian illustrates how the adult invites and scaffolds responses, answers questions, offers positive reinforcement, and responds supportively to the child's questions and comments. As a result of the prompts, information, and support, Ian pursues his questions and receives additional information.

Mother: Are you ready for our story today, Ian? This is a new book. I've never read it to you before. It's about a mother and her baby bird.

Ian: (points to the title on the front cover) Hey, what's this for?

Mother: That's called a title. It says *"Are You My Mother?"* That's the name of the book. See, it's right here, too: *"Are You My Mother?"*

Ian: (long pause, then points to the words) *"Are You My Mother?"*

Mother: Right, you read it. See, you know how to read.

Ian: It says, *"Are You My Mother?"* (points again with finger)

Mother: You read it again. Wow, you really know how to read!

Ian: Um, now read the book and I'll read it, too. (Morrow, 1986)

Ian's mother read the story. Each time they came to the words *Are You My Mother?*, she paused and looked at Ian, pointed to the words, and exaggerated her reading of the sentence. After two such episodes, Ian no longer needed prompting and simply read along each time they came to the phrase.

Research findings suggest that teachers should encourage family members to read to their children daily. Reading can begin the day a child is born. However, an infant's ability to listen attentively is generally limited and varies from one reading to the next. An infant may prefer to chew on the book or pound it rather than listen to it. However, babies read to from birth begin to be attentive in story-reading situations sooner than others not read to.

One of my graduate students shared this story in his class journal about his first literacy experience with his new baby. She was born during the semester he was taking a course with me.

Our First Literacy Experience by John T. Shea

When my wife and I packed for the trip to the hospital on the night before her scheduled caesarean procedure, one of the items that I included in my travel bag was my childhood copy of The Real Mother Goose, *a book my mother had given*

Fathers, mothers, siblings, grandparents, and great-grandparents should read together with young children.

back to me when she learned that she was going to be a grandmother. My first literacy experience with Casey came much sooner than I had expected.

After she was born, Casey was taken to the nursery and placed under a heat device designed to help her body adjust to the change in temperature she experienced at birth. There were some chairs set up next to the heat devices for new fathers. As I sat beside my daughter and marveled at her beauty, it suddenly occurred to me that I could read to her at that very moment. I asked the nurse if I could take a book into the nursery to read to my child. The nurse smiled and said, "You're the first father in my 20 years as a maternity nurse to make such a request. I guess it's okay."

I was with Casey for the first hours of her life in the nursery, sitting by her side, listening to her breathe, and reading selections to her from The Real Mother Goose *book. Prior to my reading she had been a bit fussy and crying, on and off. When I started reading, she became very quiet and hardly stirred.*

Reading to Children at Home from Birth to Age 8

English Language Learners

From *birth to 3 months,* a child's attention to book reading is erratic. The baby who stares at the pictures and seems content and quiet can be considered receptive. If the baby wiggles, shows discomfort, or cries, the adult might just as well stop reading until the next time.

From *3 to 6 months,* babies become more obviously involved in book readings. They begin to focus on pictures and to listen. Often, they will grab for a book, pound it, and try to put it in their mouths. As long as they seem content, they are probably involved with the reading.

Six- to nine-month-olds can be purposefully involved in story readings. They might try to turn pages. They might respond to changes in the reader's intonation or make sounds and movements to demonstrate involvement and pleasure. They sometimes begin to show preferences for books that have been read to them before.

One-year-old babies will show strong involvement in being read to. They might take a leadership role in turning pages or babble along in tones that sound like reading. They actively look in the book for familiar things that they remember from other readings.

By *15 months,* babies who have been read to can tell which is the front and which is the back of a book and if the book is right side up. They begin to identify and name characters in the book. They read along with the adult, verbalizing a great deal (Burns, Snow, & Griffin, 1999). They show book preferences at this age when they have been read to.

Fathers, mothers, grandparents, babysitters, and older siblings should all read to younger children. Let reading become a ritual, done at the same time and in the same place each day. Bedtime is a favorite time, and bedtime stories are a good reading habit to establish. Both child and family members look forward to it as a time to share at the end of the day. Reading before children go to sleep has a calming effect; it establishes a routine for the children, who will eventually read by themselves before going to bed.

Spontaneous readings are encouraged as well, and if a family member finds it easier to read at different times of the day, it is certainly more desirable to do this than not to read at all. Reading to babies requires that the infant be held in the family member's arms. When the youngster is able to sit up alone, family members and child should be close to each other, preferably with the child on the adult's lap. The book with its pictures and print must be visible to the child. Children should be considered active participants in the story reading. Their comments and questions should be encouraged and acknowledged. Family members should relate comments about the story to life experiences whenever possible and question children about familiar things in a relaxed manner to encourage their involvement.

Reading to children does not end when they begin to read themselves. This is a crucial time to continue to support and guide them in this activity. When children are able to read, the bedtime story tradition can change to the child's reading to the family member. Or it can continue with the families reading books above the reading level of the child. *Six- to eight-year-olds* are often interested in books with chapters, but are not yet ready to read them themselves. Family members can take this opportunity to share more grown-up pieces of literature with these youngsters to encourage their interest. Another important parent motivation is making sure that children have new material to read that is always accessible and of interest to them. Keep track of what your youngster has read. Sometimes we must continually put new books right in their hands, even as they grow older and seem to have the reading habit established. Be sure to let them help select what you read. It doesn't always have to be a typical narrative story. Informational books are very interesting to children, and an appropriate newspaper or magazine article is a good idea now and then.

In addition to reading to their children and reading themselves, families should make a point of providing time for the family to read together. Sitting together around the kitchen table or in the living room, each member of the family reading his or her own book, makes for a pleasant, rich literacy activity. Talking about what family members are reading is an important experience as well.

Materials for Writing in the Home

ELL
English Language Learners

Some researchers have suggested that writing develops before reading. Many children invent writing systems of their own that seem to have meaning for them. Whether reading comes before writing or writing before reading is an unsettled issue. What is known, however, is that learning to read is enhanced by concurrent experiences with writing and that the development of writing is facilitated by experiences with reading (McGee & Richgels, 2000).

One implication of these findings is that writing materials should be made available for children at home. A variety of sizes of unlined white paper is preferable, especially for babies. As children become preschoolers, smaller sheets can be added to the household supply. A child approaching kindergarten might like lined paper as well. Pencils, crayons, colored pencils, a chalkboard and chalk, and white slates and markers are appropriate home writing tools. Manipulatives such as magnetic, felt, or wooden letters are also useful. Children should be exposed to them early and have free access to them. In addition, home computers encourage writing and are appropriate for preschoolers. (A list of computer software for young children can be found in Appendix C.)

As with book reading, youngsters need to see their families involved in writing activities. Family members should communicate with their children through writing as often as possible. When children begin preschool, notes can be placed in lunch boxes that say simply, "Hi! Love, Mommy and Daddy." Notes on pillows can say "Good night" or "Good morning."

Make writing a family event whenever possible. Families can write thank-you notes and letters together. They can fill out school forms with children or make up the family grocery list together. Children will emulate family members who take opportunities to communicate through writing.

Responsive Adults Encourage Literacy

English Language Learners

The family members of early readers answer their children's questions about books and print, offer information, provide experiences that enhance literacy development, and praise children for engaging in literacy behaviors. This support system in the home encourages the development of reading. Durkin (1966) found that families who attempted to teach children were not as successful as families who simply responded to children's requests for information about reading.

Responsiveness between family members and children needs to begin early and be cultivated. Language provides an opportunity for developing responsiveness. Responsive adults answer questions and initiate activities that promote literacy. While dressing, diapering, or feeding an infant a family member should talk to the child, sing, recite nursery rhymes, and tell stories. The baby responds by smiling and cooing, thus encouraging the parent to continue, and a mutual responsiveness develops.

Environmental print surrounds children and holds meaning for them. This natural source of reading material provides literacy experiences with items familiar to children (Clay, 2000; Neuman & Roskos, 1993, 1997). Children begin to read and ask about environmental print probably before they are interested in the print found in books. When families are aware of the importance of environmental print, they will point out familiar labels and information on cereal boxes, detergent containers, and food packages. Children are naturally interested in telephone books, cookbooks, television guides, advertisements, and mail. They are particularly interested in personal letters, fliers, greeting cards, bills, catalogs, and magazines. The outside world presents a wealth of environmental print, such as street signs and names of fast-food restaurants and gas stations. Families note the environmental print that is meaningful to children and encourage them to do the same. With environmental print you can

point out specific letters in the words and sound the letters. Family members who provide rich literacy environments provide varied experiences for their children. They take them to libraries and bookstores. They talk to them a great deal, a habit that builds the children's vocabulary. Trips to zoos, fire stations, airports, and parks all foster literacy growth if they are accompanied by oral language and positive social interactions. It should be emphasized that a trip not only broadens a child's experience, but also allows verbal interactions between a family member and child before, during, and after. These interactions include providing the child with background information about the place to be visited and the things to be seen, answering questions about the experience, offering information, reading stories related to the experience, and discussing the trip afterward so that new ideas are absorbed. Suggesting that the child record the experience by drawing a picture about it and dictating a story for the family member to write will further expand literacy growth.

Television is part of our lives. To make the most of TV viewing, families should watch some programs with their youngsters, posing questions, raising critical issues, and changing passive viewing into responsive interaction. They should also choose programs that have books available, such as *Sesame Street* or *Clifford*. When specific stories are scheduled on television, such as *How the Grinch Stole Christmas* (Seuss, 1957a), families can borrow the book from the library or purchase it.

DVDs are readily availble for children to watch. If they are carefully selected and parents watch with children and talk about them, the experience can be a good literacy event. Children will use computer software and, if selected carefully and some computer games are played with an adult, it can be worthwhile. Both television viewing and playing DVD computer games need to be limited so that children don't spend too much time doing so.

In a series of informal interviews with family members whose children were early readers, it became apparent that literacy was embedded in daily activities that were meaningful, functional, and part of the mainstream of their lives. Various print materials were visible in the homes. Language was used interactively and frequently, in all its forms and in a positive emotional climate. There was praise for literacy activity and the pleasure and joy in reading and writing. When asked what they believed helped their children become literate so early, the parents found it difficult to answer, because they had not viewed the experiences they offered their children as attempts to promote reading and writing. Most of these activities had other functions, such as keeping the house running smoothly. Many of the experiences had social objectives to promote personal relationships and to teach responsibility and manners, for example. Here are some ideas related by these parents:

From the time they were very young, my children were required to write thank-you notes for gifts received. At first they dictated them and I wrote down what they said. Later they were able to write simply "thank you." One good incentive for the task was to allow them to choose their own stationery for note writing.

—Lynn Cohen

I started a baby book for each of my children from the day they were born, with information about their weight and height, and I included pictures. I reported major events, such as first words, first steps, and events of interest to me. I looked at the book frequently, and my toddler would snuggle beside me showing great interest. I've continued the books, and now they have become their own journals where they record things that happen to them.

—Stephanie Bushell

As a grandfather I don't get to see my grandchildren as frequently as I would like. In order to keep close contact, I often send them things through the mail. I'll enclose games cut from the children's section of the newspaper, which I'll ask them to complete. I send them pictures of famous people and ask them to call and tell me who they think they are, as well as questions to respond to me about.

—Milton Mandel

I started leaving notes for my children in surprise places before they could read. Somehow they managed to find out what the notes said, even at the pre-reading stage. Now I put messages in their lunch boxes. The notes often just say "hello." Sometimes I'll write a riddle or a joke, and sometimes the note may require an answer. This has become a family tradition, and lately I find surprise notes addressed to me left in the most unusual places.

—Diane Tracey

The amount of TV viewing by our three- and four-year-old children was a source of aggravation to us. To make the experience more meaningful, we read the television program guide to decide on what programs to watch and to limit the number of selections in one day. We try to watch some programs with them and ask who, what, when, *and* where *questions to elicit recall of facts. We also ask* why *questions to encourage more interpretive responses.*

—Michelle Rosen

I've always kept a journal recording my daily experiences. My four-year-old found me writing in it one day and asked about what I was doing. She wanted to do the same thing, so we started a joint journal. I'd write things that happened to me during the day, and she'd tell me what to write for her. Soon she was able to do her own writing. Sometimes I'd ask her questions about what she'd written. I did this by writing in the journal.

—Heather Casey

A rich literacy environment at home gives children a good chance to learn to read and write easily and to enjoy reading and writing as well.

Family Involvement in Your Literacy Program: What Teachers Can Do for All Parents

English Language Learners

When I speak about parents in this section I am referring to any adult or older sibling who is involved with a child at home. Teachers need to view parents as partners in the development of literacy. Every teacher has the responsibility to inform families on a regular basis about what is happening in school and how they can help their child. Teachers need to involve family members in activities at home and in school and make them feel like partners in the education of their child. They should be given the opportunity to offer input about what they would like their child to learn, to express how they feel about what happens in school, and to offer suggestions. Following are some suggestions about ways to make families an integral part of the school. Be concerned about sending home materials in the languages represented in the classroom.

1. At the beginning of the school year, send home the goals to be achieved for literacy development for the grade level you teach in a format that can be understood by all.

2. With each new unit of instruction or concept being taught in literacy, send a newsletter to let family members know what you are studying and what they can do to help.

3. Invite family members to school for informational workshops, family meetings about curriculum decisions, conferences, and school programs.

4. Invite families to help with literacy activities in the classroom, such as reading to children, helping with bookbinding, taking written dictation of stories, and supervising independent activities while teachers work with small groups and individual children.

5. Send home activities for parents and children to do together and require feedback about working together. Include activities such as writing in journals together, reading together, visiting the library, recording print they see in the environment, writing notes to each other, cooking together and following recipes, putting toys or household items together that require following directions, and watching and talking about programs on television. Participating in homework assignments is extremely important.

6. Invite families to school to talk about their cultural heritage, hobbies, jobs, and the like.

7. Send home notes when a child is doing well. Don't wait to send notes just for problems.

8. Provide lists of literature for family members to share with their children. Appendix A provides suggested books.

9. Family members should be invited to school to participate with their children in literacy activities. During center time, for example, parents can read and write with their children, see what the literacy environment is like at school, and become a more integral part of the child's literacy development.

10. Have family member and child meetings when they come to school to work together on projects.

11. Be in touch with families often through phone calls, messages sent, and conferences. Try and make these about happy news, not only bad news.

12. Include family members in helping to assess their child's progress. Provide forms for them to fill out about their child's literacy activities and things they do with their child at home. Have them contribute information about their child's progress at parent conferences. Two forms included here that can be used for this process are Guidelines: Promoting Early Literacy at Home and Checklist: Observing My Child's Literacy Growth.

13. Consult Strategies for the Classroom pages S-48 and S-49 for activities and materials for parents.

Guidelines   Promoting Early Literacy at Home

This checklist is to be filled out by parents

Your child's ability to read and write depends a lot on the things you do at home from the time he or she is born. The following list suggests materials, activities, and attitudes that are important in helping your child learn to read and write. Check off the things you already do. Try to do something on the list that you have not done before.

Materials

☐ 1. Have a space at home for books and magazines for your child.

☐ 2. If you can, subscribe to a magazine for your child.

☐ 3. Place some of your child's and some of your books, magazines, and newspapers in different parts of your home.

☐ 4. Provide materials that will encourage children to tell or create their own stories, such as puppets, dolls, and story tapes.

☐ 5. Provide materials for writing, such as crayons, markers, pencils, and paper in different sizes.

Activities

☐ 1. Read or look at books, magazines, or the newspaper with your child. Talk about what you looked at or read.

☐ 2. Visit the library and take out books and magazines to read at home.

☐ 3. Tell stories together about books, your family, and things that you do.

☐ 4. Look at and talk about written material you have, such as catalogs, advertisements, work-related materials, and mail.

☐ 5. Provide a model for your child by reading and writing at a time when your child can see you.

☐ 6. Point to print outside, such as road signs and names of stores.

☐ 7. Write with your child and talk about what you write.

☐ 8. Point out print in your home, such as words on food boxes or recipes, directions on medicine, or instructions on things that require assembly.

☐ 9. Visit the post office, supermarket, and zoo. Talk about what you saw and read. When you get home, draw and write about it.

☐ 10. Use print to talk to your child. Leave notes for each other. Make lists to do things, such as food lists, lists of errands, and lists for holiday shopping.

Foster Positive Attitudes toward Reading and Writing

☐ 1. Reward your child's attempts at reading and writing, even if they are not perfect, by offering praise. Say kind words like:

"What nice work you do." "I'm happy to see you are reading." "I'm happy to see you are writing. Can I help you?"

☐ 2. Answer your child's questions about reading and writing.

☐ 3. Be sure that reading and writing are enjoyable experiences.

☐ 4. Display your child's work in your home.

☐ 5. Visit school when your child asks. Volunteer to help at school and attend programs in which your child is participating, parent conferences, and parent meetings. This lets your child know you care about him or her and school.

Visit School and Speak to Your Child's Teacher

☐ 1. if you want to volunteer or help in any way.

☐ 2. if you want to visit your child's class during school hours.

☐ 3. if you have concerns about your child's reading and writing.

☐ 4. if you feel your child has problems with vision, hearing, or other things.

☐ 5. if you need help because the language you speak at home is not English.

☐ 6. if you need help with reading and writing yourself.

☐ 7. if you would like to know more about how you can help your child at home.

☐ 8. if you want to know more about what your child is learning at school.

Guía

Fomentar en el hogar el desarrollo temprano de la capacidad de leer y de escribir

La capacidad de su jovencito de leer y de escribir depende mucho de las cosas que hacen en casa desde el momento de su nacimiento. Usted puede hacer muchas cosas que no ocuparán mucho de su tiempo. La lista siguiente sugiere materiales, actividades, y actitudes que son importantes en ayudar a su hijo(a) a aprender, a leer y a escribir. Ponga una marca al lado de la sugerencia que usted ya practica en su casa. Procure hacer algo de la lista que no ha hecho antes.

Materiales

☐ 1. Prepare un lugar en su casa para poner libros y revistas para su hijo(a).

☐ 2. Si es posible, subscríbase a una revista para su hijo(a).

☐ 3. Coloque algunos de los libros de su hijo(a) y algunos de los suyos, incluyendo revistas y periódicos, en diferentes lugares en su casa.

☐ 4. Provea materiales, tales como títeres, muñecos, y cuentos grabados, que animarán a los niños a contar o a crear sus propios cuentos.

(continued on next page)

☐ 5. Provea materiales para escribir, tales como creyones, marcadores, lápices, y papel de various tamaños.

Actividades

☐ 1. Junto con su hijo(a), lean u hojeen libros, revistas o el periódico. Hablen sobre lo que hayan hojeado o leído.

☐ 2. Visiten la biblioteca y saquen algunos libros y algunas revistas para leer en casa.

☐ 3. Juntos, cuenten cuentos sobre libros, sobre su familia, y sobre las cosas que hacen.

☐ 4. Hojeen y hablen sobre el material escrito que tengan en su casa, tal como catálogos, anuncios, material relacionado con su trabajo, correo.

☐ 5. Sea un modelo para su hijo(a) leyendo y escribiendo en los momentos cuando él o ella le pueda observar.

☐ 6. Llame a la atención de su hijo(a) cosas impresas afuera, tales como letreros en la carretera y nombres de tiendas.

☐ 7. Escriba con su hijo(a) y hablen sobre lo que hayan escrito.

☐ 8. Indique palabras impresas en su casa, tales como las que están en cajas de comida, en recetas, en las instrucciones para medicinas, o en objetos que hay que armar.

☐ 9. Visiten la oficina de correos, el supermercado, el jardín zoológico. Hablen sobre lo que hayan visto y leído. Cuando regresen a su casa, hagan dibujos y escriban sobre estas experiencias.

☐ 10. Use la escritura para hablar con su hijo(a). Déjense notas el uno para el otro, hagan listas de cosas que hacer, tales como listas de comida para la compra, listas de tareas que hacer, listas de cosas que comprar para los días de fiesta.

Fomente actitudes positivas hacia la lectura y la escritura

☐ 1. Recompense con elogios los intentos de su hijo(a) por leer o escribir, aun cuando sus esfuerzos no sean perfectos. Use palabras bondadosas, tales como:

"¡Qué trabajo más bueno haces! Estoy muy contento(a) de ver que estás leyendo. Estoy muy contento(a) de ver que estás escribiendo. ¿Te puedo ayudar en algo?"

☐ 2. Responda a las preguntas de su hijo(a) sobre la lectura y la escritura.

☐ 3. Procure que el leer y el escribir sean experiencias agradables.

☐ 4. Exhiban el trabajo de sus hijos en la casa.

☐ 5. Visite la escuela cuando su hijo(a) se lo pida. Ofrezca su ayuda en la escuela, asista a los programas en los cuales su hijo(a) esté participando, asista a las conferencias y reuniones de padres. Esto permite que su hijo(a) se dé cuenta de que usted se interesa por él o por ella y por la escuela.

Visite la escuela y hable con el maestro o la maestra de su hijo(a)

☐ 1. ...si usted quiere ayudar de alguna manera.

☐ 2. ...si usted quiere visitar la clase de su hijo(a) durante las horas cuando la escuela está en sesión.

☐ 3. ...si usted tiene dudas acerca del desarrollo do la lectura y la escritura en su hijo(a).

☐ 4. ...si usted cree que su hijo(a) tiene problemas especiales con su visión, con su oído, o con cualquier otra cosa.

☐ 5. ...si usted necesita ayuda porque el idioma que habla en casa no es el inglés.

☐ 6. ...si usted necesita ayuda con sus propias habilidades de lectura y de escritura.

☐ 7. ...si a usted le gustaría saber más sobre cómo puede ayudar a su hijo(a) en el hogar.

☐ 8. ...si a usted le gustaría saber más y comprender mejor lo que su hijo(a) está aprendiendo en la escuela.

Checklist Observing My Child's Literacy Growth

Child's name _____ Date _____

To be filled out by parents	Always	Sometimes	Never	Comments
1. My child asks to be read to.				
2. My child will read or look at a book alone.				
3. My child understands what is read to him/her, or what he/she reads to himself/herself.				
4. My child handles a book properly, knows how to turn pages, and knows that print is read from left to right.				
5. My child will pretend to read or read to me.				
6. My child participates in the reading of a story, with rhymes and repeated phrases.				
7. My child will write with me.				
8. My child will write alone.				
9. My child will talk about what he/she has written.				
10. My child reads print in the environment such as signs and labels.				
11. My child likes school.				

Comments about Your Child:

Multicultural Perspectives Concerning Family Involvement and Family Literacy

English Language Learners

In this chapter, family literacy has been approached from the perspective of family members helping children to support their reading and writing development on their own or as a result of involvement in literacy activities at school. Many families in our country do not speak English and therefore are not able to help their children in the ways that schools may suggest. In addition, many families have limited literacy ability and, although eager to help, cannot do so with the suggestions that might typically come from school. In some cases the parent is a teenager who has dropped out of school. Therefore, when we speak of family literacy, in many situations we need to recognize that it must be an intergenerational matter in which environments are created to enable adult learners to enhance their own literacy and at the same time promote the literacy of their children. However, there is evidence that many low-income, minority, and immigrant families cultivate rich contexts for literacy development. Their efforts are different from the school model we are accustomed to. We must learn from and respect families and children from cultures in which books are not readily available, although evidence of literacy activity, such as storytelling, singing, and reading of the Bible and other religious materials with discussions, exists (Morrow, 1995).

Research shows that the types and forms of literacy practiced in some homes are different from those that children encounter in school (Auerbach, 1989; Heath, 1993; Paratore, Melzi, & Krol-Sinclair, 2003; Taylor & Dorsey-Gaines, 1988). Although literacy activity is present in one form or another in most families, the particular kinds of events that some family members or caregivers share with children may have a great deal of influence on school success. Conversely, the kinds of literacy practiced in classrooms may not be meaningful for some children outside school. As mentioned, low-income, minority, and immigrant families cultivate rich contexts for literacy development and support family literacy with exceptional effort and imagination (Auerbach, 1989; Bryant & Maxwell, 1997). Family literacy must be approached to avoid cultural bias, and intervention must be supportive rather than intrusive.

Studying the Ways Literacy Is Used by Families

Researchers are interested in advancing understanding of the ways in which literacy is used within families. In these studies, emphasis is placed on the richness of one's heritage and experiences, rather than on perceived educational deficits. In some cases, researchers are exploring literacy events that occur naturally within diverse families. In other cases, researchers are describing the effects family literacy has on children's developing concepts about reading and writing. With the knowledge gained from such studies, educators can better understand the literacies that exist in diverse families and can help make literacy instruction in school more meaningful for both family members and children.

Teachers should invite parents to school to share their cultural heritage. A father reads the Spanish version of *The Three Little Pigs* to his son's kindergarten class.

Delgado-Gaitan (1992) carried out a study to determine the attitudes of Mexican American families toward the education of their children and the roles played by these families. A major goal was to observe and describe the physical surroundings, emotional and motivational climates, and interpersonal interactions between parent and child.

Results of the study demonstrated that the Mexican American parents provided special areas for study for their children, in spite of space limitations. The parents wanted their children to succeed in school. Parents sought the help of friends, relatives, and others to assist them or their children with school-related matters. Parents punished their children for poor grades and rewarded them for doing well. Parents' attempts to help children with homework sometimes were fruitless, because they could not understand the directions and often misled their children. All parents believed that a person cannot be considered well educated through "book learning" alone, but also must learn to be respectful, well mannered, and helpful to others. Family stories about life in Mexico guided the children's moral learning.

From the findings about these families, it seems that schools need to respond in the curriculum to Latinos' concerns that children learn good manners and respect. The schools need to be aware of and help with language problems that families encounter when they want to help their children. They also need to incorporate oral history and storytelling into the curriculum, because it is an important aspect of the Latino culture familiar to both parents and children (Paratore et al., 1995).

Family Literacy: Formal Programs

Family Involvement Initiatives

English Language Learners

Family involvement initiatives include programs that are designed to involve and inform families about activities that will promote their children's literacy learning in school. Such programs involve families as agents in supporting their child's literacy development and may originate from the school, library, or other community agencies. Often they are collaborative efforts among these agencies. A basic premise of parent involvement programs is to enlist the help of families to increase the reading achievement of their children.

Running Start (RS) is an example of a family involvement initiative. This school-based project, created by *Reading Is Fundamental (RIF)*, is designed to get books into the hands of first-grade children and to encourage and support family literacy. The goals of RS are (1) to increase first graders' motivation to read so that they eagerly turn to books for both pleasure and information, (2) to involve families in their children's literacy development, and (3) to support schools and teachers in their efforts to help children become successful readers. Participating classroom teachers are provided with funds to select and purchase high-quality fiction and informational books for their classroom libraries. Children are challenged to read (or have someone read to them) 21 books during the 10-week program. A Reading Rally is held to involve the community in supporting literacy development, and families are encouraged to support their child in meeting the 21-book challenge by sharing books and stories with their children in a variety of ways. When a child meets the 21-book goal, he or she gets to select a book for his or her own personal library. Studies have demonstrated that both first-graders' reading motivation and family members' literacy activities in the home significantly increased in families that participated in the program (Gambrell, Almasi, Xie, & Heland, 1995).

Even Start is a federally funded program in which parents must come to meetings and to school to learn how they can play with, read to, and write with their children. With parents coming to school to see what their children do, they have a new awareness of how they can be and need to be helpful.

Intergenerational literacy initiatives are specifically designed to improve the literacy development of both adults and children. These programs view family members and children as co-learners and are generally characterized by planned and systematic instruction for both adults and children. Instruction may occur when family members and children work in either collaborative or parallel settings. The instruction for adults is intended to improve their literacy skills, while teaching them how to work with their children to aid their development (Wasik, Dobbins, & Herrmann, 2001).

Parents and Children Together is a nationwide intergenerational family literacy program established by the National Center for Family Literacy (NCFL) in Louisville, Kentucky. Parents who lack a high school diploma and their 3- and 4-year-old children attend school together three to five days a week. An early childhood program is provided for the children, while the parents attend an adult education program to learn reading, math, and parenting skills.

In the adult education portion of the program, parents work on improving their reading and math skills and are taught to set goals and collaborate with other parents in the program. Parent Time is a component of the program during which the adults discuss a variety of topics, ranging from discipline to self-esteem. The last component of the program is Parent and Child Together time. During this hour, families play together. The activities are led by the children. Parents find they can learn both with and from their children (National Center for Family Literacy, 1993).

What Makes a Family Involvement Literacy Program Successful?

English Language Learners

Because no two communities are the same, family literacy programs need to be tailored to the needs of the individuals they serve. Here are some tested guidelines to follow that will help programs be successful.

Objectives for Family Literacy Programs

1. Respect and understand the diversity of the families you serve.
2. Build on literacy behaviors already present in families. Although they may be different from conventional school-like literacy, most families use literacy in the routine of their daily lives. These behaviors should be identified, acknowledged, respected, preserved, and used in family literacy programs.
3. Be aware of the home languages used within the community so that materials can be translated and understood.
4. Family literacy programs should not take a "fix the family" attitude. Rather, they should view families as a supplement to the interactions that already exist.
5. Hold meetings at various times of the day and days of the week to accommodate all schedules.
6. Hold meetings in accessible locations that are friendly and nonthreatening. Transportation needs to be provided if no public transportation is available or if family members do not have a way of getting to meetings. Provide child care at meetings.
7. Provide food and refreshments at meetings.
8. Follow sound educational practices appropriate for literacy development of children and adults. Use varied strategies for literacy learning. Include writ-

ing together, reading together, and sharing materials that are fun and interesting for all.

9. You may work with family members alone and with parents and children together. There should be sharing times when parents and children work together.

10. Programs can provide support groups for family members to talk about helping their children and to find out what they want to know.

11. Family literacy programs seek not only to help with literacy development, but to improve interactions between parents and children.

12. Programs should provide family members with ideas and materials to use at home.

13. Good programs provide easy-to-carry-out functional literacy activities that families consider useful, such as talking and reading about child-rearing concerns, community life problems, housing, and applying for jobs and keeping them.

14. Programs should include the opportunity for family members' participation in school activities during school hours.

15. Portions of school and home programs should parallel each other. Activities done in school should be the same as those sent home for family members to do with children. When this occurs, family members can participate in their children's learning. Note Figure 10.3 on page 404, a newsletter to inform parents about what is being studied in school and what they can do at home.

Programs and Activities That Have Been Successful

HIGHLIGHTS PARENT INVOLVEMENT PROGRAM. Family literacy programs should promote parent–child interaction in a wide range of literacy events. Programs must view participating families from the perspective of the richness of their experiences and heritage, rather than from the perspective of their deficits and dilemmas. Home school programs need to be easy to use. Materials sent home should be introduced to children in school first. The content should be nonthreatening and culturally diverse, and the activities need to be fun. For example, a school district I worked with used the *Highlights for Children* magazine (Honesdale, PA) as the home–school connection material. Teachers featured articles in the magazine at school, and each child had a school copy. Another copy was sent home with activities for family members and children to do together that were similar to what was being done in school. The program was successful because children knew what to do with the materials. In addition, the magazine provided the following features that should be present in any home–school connection material: (1) multiple options for families to select activities from, (2) a nonthreatening format that is not school-like, (3) activities appropriate for many age levels and abilities, (4) culturally diverse content, (5) some activities that do not require the ability to read, and (6) activities that are fun and therefore engage families and children in literacy together (Morrow, Scoblionko, & Shafer, 1995; Morrow & Young, 1997).

Educators are recognizing that the family is the key to successful literacy development for both children and their families. Policymakers from a wide range of agencies need to collaborate and form partnerships in their efforts to create and support effective family literacy programs. Literacy programs in school will be more successful if they have home support; therefore, family literacy programs are crucial.

Appendix A provides a bibliography of children's literature about families for teachers and families to share with children. The books are representative of diverse cultural backgrounds. Each book illustrates some special relationship between family and extended family members. It could be parents, grandparents, an aunt or uncle, sisters or brothers, or a person who becomes like family although he or she is not actually related.

FREQUENT CONTACT WITH PARENTS: CONFERENCE, PHONE CALLS, AND THE LIKE.   Being in touch with parents often will make them feel welcome and a part of the school. This can be done in many ways. A few will be explained here.

Invite parents to school frequently. By doing so they will begin to feel more comfortable about being there and will understand better what you do in school. Make the times different so that those who work can arrange their schedule so that they can come a few times during the year (see Figures 10.1 and 10.2).

When studying a particular topic, make sure when you begin to send a newsletter to let parents know what it is about and how they can help. Figure 10.3 is an example.

Call parents on the phone. In the past if we called a parent, it was often if something really bad happened in school. The child misbehaved, was ill, and so on. However, if parents are called when good things happen, the teacher and family can build a relationship that will help everyone. Call to remind parents about a school event that is about to happen and how much you hope they can be there. Call a parent when a child has made important gains in their school work and demonstrate how excited you are about it and hope they will practice with them at home. If you call for good things, then it will also be fine to call with concerns.

Conferences to discuss progress are regularly scheduled in schools. Prior to the conference ask the parent to fill out a form such as the checklist titled *Observing My Child's Literacy Growth* on page 395. This way the parent comes with some expectations of what will happen in the conference and it can be a two-way conversation; that is, both the teacher and parent will contribute. In addition, the teacher can send home a note in advance to say we will discuss how your child is doing socially, emotionally, physically and with school work. Be sure to start your conference with many positive comments about his or her child. Some lovely anecdote about something that happened in school would be a nice touch as well. Let the parent give you information from the checklist mentioned above; then it is your turn as the teacher to share information about the

Figure 10.1

Invitation
for Family
Participation
in English

Family Members Wanted
To Visit Your Child's Class

Dear Family Members,

Please come to school and be a part of our reading and writing time. On the form below list the types of things you can do when you visit. There is a space for you to let us know the time of day and dates that you can attend. We are flexible and will arrange our time when it is convenient for you. All family members are welcome—brothers and sisters, babies, grandparents, and of course parents. Please come and get involved in your child's education and help us form a true home and school partnership.

Sincerely,
Mrs. Abere's second-grade class

- -

Please fill out the following form and send it back to school with your child:

Your name _____

Your child's name _____

The days I can come during the week are _____

The time of day I can come to school is _____

When I come to school I would like to do the following:

☐ 1. Watch what the children are doing.

☐ 2. Participate with the children.

☐ 3. Read to a small group of children.

☐ 4. Read to the whole class.

☐ 5. I am from another country and I would like to tell the children about my country and show them clothing, pictures, and books from there.

☐ 6. I have a hobby and would like to share it with the class.
    My hobby is: _____

☐ 7. I have a talent and would like to share it with the class.
    My talent is: _____

☐ 8. I'd like to tell the children about my job.
    My job is: _____

☐ 9. Other ideas you would like to do: _____

☐ 10. Give children who need it some extra help.

☐ 11. I'd like some help in deciding what to do.

☐ 12. I would like to come on a regular basis to help.
    I can come at the following times: _____

Figure 10.2

Invitation
for Family
Participation
in Spanish

Se Buscan Miembros De Familia
Para Visitar la Clase de su Niño

Ayudenos Aprender—

Comparta sus Talentos y Envuélvase con Nuestra Clase:

Observe la clase y su niño

Cuente historias

Hable de su cultura

Lea libros

Comparta su pasatiempo favorito

Traiga su bebé o animal mimado

Explique su trabajo

Cocine o traiga dulces para la clase

Venga a cantarle a los niños

Comparta con nuestras actividades de "Highlights"

Por favor ponga los días, o día, que pueda venir a la clase:

Mes: Dia(s):   Horas:

_____

- -

Devuelva este papel a la maestra de su niño.

Nombre: _____.

Visitaré la clase en esta fecha _____ y a esta hora _____.

Me gustaría compartir: _____.

Figure 10.3

Newsletter to Parents about our Healthy Bodies, Healthy Minds Unit of Study

Dear Parents:

Your child will be participating in a unit that explores what it means to be healthy in body and mind. This unit will include study of why we should eat healthy foods, the five food groups, exercise, rest, cleanliness, and the importance of self-esteem.

The good health unit will cover all subject areas—play, art, music, social studies, science, math, and literacy (reading, writing, listening, and oral language), which will be incorporated in the theme. Some of the exciting activities we do here at school may also be carried out at home with your child.

At School and at Home

Art: Your child will refine eye—hand coordination and visual discrimination skills and explore and experiment with different art materials. At school we will be creating food collages and abstract bean mosaics. At home you can encourage your child to use his or her imagination by providing these and other food-related materials for art activities. Remember that art is for exploring what can be done with different materials, rather than copying an adult model.

Science: We will be making applesauce, which will give the children an opportunity to listen, follow directions, and learn where apples come from and how they are grown, as well as how food changes as it is cooked. Making healthy snacks at home, such as a fruit or lettuce salad, and involving your child in the preparation by using simple recipes will help to extend listening skills.

Literacy: Please assist at home by labeling healthy food items with the letters *h, f,* and *b* (associated with *health, food,* and *body*) or pointing out words that have these and other beginning sounds. Read signs and point out these letters when you are outside the home as well.

Please read to your child stories, poems, informational books, cookbooks, exercise magazines, and other literature related to our theme of good health. Some books that will be featured in the unit include:

Achoo! by P. Demuth, 1997

Children around the World by D. Montanari, 2001

Gregory, the Terrible Eater by M. Sharmat, 1984

No More Baths by B. Cole, 1989

Mooncake by F. Asch, 1983

We Need Your Help

We would like your assistance with our multicultural food of the week or your favorite food at home. If you are able to prepare a snack one day and discuss it, please sign your name and tell what type of snack you would like to prepare on the attached sheet.

If you can come in and read your child's favorite bedtime story to the class, please sign your name and tell what date you are available on the attached sheet.

If you have any other materials at home related to our theme, such as empty food containers, seeds, nuts, beans, or exercise or yoga magazines that we may use in our dramatic-play area, please send them in with your child.

Other Activities to Do with Your Child

Go to the supermarket with your child. Prepare a list beforehand of the food you need to purchase. Have your child check the things off as you put them in the cart. Try to purchase food from each food group.

Plant watermelon, avocado, or carrot seeds at home. Keep a diary or record of their growth, making comparisons between them.

Make simple, nutritious recipes at home, such as fruit salad, mixed green salad, butter, or peanut butter to help our lessons carry over from class to home.

Take the time to engage in some exercise with your child each day. A brisk walk or bike ride will help your child learn that exercise is fun and should be done often. It is an activity your family will enjoy together.

Remind your child at bedtime that rest is important for our bodies. Share a special bedtime story each night with your child.

Child's Corner

Ask your child to write or draw something he or she did in school related to our theme.

Help your child keep a journal of what foods he or she eats each day. Keep track of any exercises your child does. Keep track of how many hours of sleep your child gets, writing the number in the journal. Graph the numbers. The journal can be written in a notebook, on a pad, or on pieces of paper stapled together like a book.

If you have any questions about the unit or any additional ideas, please contact me. If you are in a profession that is related to our theme, such as a nutritionist or any fitness-related career, please consider coming into class and talking to us.

Sincerely,
Lisa Lozak

I would like to prepare the following snack for your healthy bodies, healthy minds unit:

Snack: _____   Parent's Name: _____

I am able to come in on the following date for a story reading: Date: _____

Book: _____   Parent's Name: _____

child's progress. You want to touch on how children get along with others in the class and to discuss their work in all areas, with an emphasis on literacy development. You want to document comments with samples of the child's work. You want to give suggestions to the parents on how they can help support what is happening in school. At the end of the conference, review what happened at the meeting and ask if they have any questions.

More than one conference a year is important. Have one after a few months of school and one toward the end. There of course can be a conference if necessary at any time during the year.

Occasional notes, similar to phone calls, about positive behavior and growth on the part of the children and how the parent can help at home provide an important interaction between parent and teacher. Not much has to be said, but it will be remembered and appreciated. (Vukelich, Christie, & Enz, 2002)

Learning More about Family Literacy

Agencies, associations, and organizations that deal with family literacy can be contacted for further information on ways to establish, administer, and evaluate family literacy programs. A few are listed here as a starting place.

The Barbara Bush Foundation for Family Literacy, 1112 16th Street, NW, Suite 340, Washington, DC 20036, www.barbarabushfoundation.com

Even Start Compensatory Education Programs, U.S. Department of Education, 400 Maryland Avenue, SW, Washington, DC 20202, www.evenstart.org

International Reading Association, 800 Barksdale Road, PO Box 8139, Newark, DE 19714-8139, www.reading.org

National Center for Family Literacy, Waterfront Plaza, Suite 200, 325 West Main Street, Louisville, KY 40202-4251, www.famlit.org

Reading Is Fundamental (RIF), 600 Maryland Avenue, SW, Suite 600, Washington, DC 20024, www.rif.org

Resources for Families

Beginning Literacy and Your Child: A Guide to Helping Your Baby or Preschooler Become a Reader

I Can Read and Write! How to Encourage Your School-Aged Child's Literacy Development

Explore the Playground of Books: Tips for Parents of Beginning Readers

Get Ready to Read! Tips for Parents of Young Children

Summer Reading Adventure! Tips for Parents of Young Readers

Library Safari: Tips for Parents of Young Readers and Explorers

Making the Most of Television: Tips for Parents of Young Viewers

See the World on the Internet: Tips for Parents of Young Readers—and Surfers (Booklets and brochures available from the International Reading Association, 800 Barksdale Road, PO Box 8139, Newark, DE 19714)

Raising a Reader, Raising a Writer: How Parents Can Help (Brochure available from the National Association for the Education of Young Children, 1509 16th Street, NW, Washington, DC 20036)

Choosing a Children's Book (Brochure available from the Children's Book Council, Inc., 568 Broadway, Suite 404, New York, NY 10012)

Brandt, D. (2001). *Literacy in American Lives.* New York: Cambridge University Press.

Lipson, E. R. (2000). *New York Times Parent's Guide to the Best Books for Children.* New York: Crown Publishing Group.

Stillman, P. R. (1989). *Families Writing* (2nd ed.). Portland, ME: Calendar Islands Publishers.

Swick, K. J. (1994). *A Family Resource Guide for Developing Parent Education and Family Literacy Programs in Early Childhood.* Charleston, South Carolina: School Improvement Council Assistance for South Carolina's School Improvement Councils.

Thomas, A., Fazio, L., & Steifelmeyer, B. L. (1999). *Families at School: A Handbook for Parents.* Newark, DE: International Reading Association.

Trealease, J. (2001). *The Read-Aloud Handbook.* New York: Penguin Books.

An Idea from the Classroom

Family Backpacks

For this first-grade activity, you'll need to assemble a theme-based backpack with the following materials: a class journal; five to seven books that represent a variety of genres and reading levels; a folder with games, poems, songs, and/or experiments related to the theme under study; and other related items, such as videos, cassettes, and stuffed animals. Based on the cultural background of the child when applicable, place something in the backpack, such as a story or poem that relates to the unit and their background. The children take the backpack home weekly on a rotating basis. Instruct the children to share the activities and books with their family members. It may be helpful to show a backpack and model some of the activities for families at Back-to-School Night. They may also be put on display at parent–teacher conferences so that family members may become acquainted with the materials and procedures. Teachers need to go over the contents of the backpack with the children so that the parents and children can help each other with the activities.

Under family members' guidance along with the help of the child, the children respond to what is asked of them in the class journal that is in the backpack. The questions may include "Which was your favorite book, and why was it your favorite?" Or, to go along with a food theme for example, the children may be asked to share a family recipe. A music theme may include a tape recorder and blank tape to record a favorite song. When the backpack is returned to school, the child shares the journal response with the class. The kids and family members can hardly wait until it is their turn for the next backpack!

Shannon Corcoran, Graduate Student,
Graduate School of Education, Rutgers University

An Idea from the Classroom

Highlighting Family Involvement at School

Every month in our school several family involvement activities occur. These activities provide opportunities for children to bond with their own families and other families and to share their diverse cultural backgrounds with their classmates. To emphasize the importance of these activities and others, teachers in all grades began a showcase called "Highlighting Family Involvement." They keep cameras in school so that, when families participate, the teachers can take their pictures for the showcase. The following are the activities at school that help fill the showcase and bring families to the building:

Theme Nights: These evenings are devoted to different topics, such as other countries, where children and families can learn together. Families share artifacts and then read, write, and do art projects about the theme.

Cooking Nights: Families bring easy favorite recipes to share and make together. The best part is eating the goodies when the cooking is done.

Book-Sharing Evenings: Everyone brings a favorite book and reads or tells about their favorite part. The book can be in another language and, if necessary, a translator is used so that everyone can participate.

Sharing Family Photos: On this night we ask everyone to bring family pictures they want to share. We talk and write about them. Each family makes an album with the photos, and we encourage them to continue to fill the album they started at school.

Margaret Youssef, Teacher

An Idea from the Classroom

A Pajama Party: An Event to Spark School–Family Partnerships

The Pajama Party is an event in which the children, teachers, and parents come to school for the evening dressed for bed, carrying a blanket, a favorite stuffed animal, and a favorite book. (The pajamas and stuffed animal are not mandatory, but the book is). We hold this once a year for kindergarten and first-grade students and their parents and have a standing room-only crowd in the school library.

The children meet in the gymnasium to sing songs and listen to a storyteller. The parents are with the reading specialist whose goal is to help parents recognize the value of reading to their children daily and to provide good models of read-alouds. Parents are given the opportunity to ask questions and share concerns.

In the parent workshop, aside from modeling good shared reading strategies, the following are discussed:

- Importance of reading aloud

- Finding good books to read aloud

- Sharing of books with good qualities

When the parents return to the gym, they sit with their child and enjoy a story from the storyteller. Then parents snuggle up with their children and read aloud a favorite book. We finish the evening with a bedtime snack of milk and cookies.

Lynette Brenner, Reading Specialist

Activities and Questions

1. Answer the focus questions posed at the beginning of the chapter.

2. Interview members of your family or friends who are parents. Ask them to relate specific activities they have done with their children to promote literacy with natural events that arose from daily living. Collect ideas from all members of the class and put them together in a newsletter or pamphlet format to distribute to family members of early childhood youngsters.

3. Using the memories of your own home when you were a young child or the home of a friend or family member who is a parent of a young child, observe the physical characteristics and record activities done with children that promote literacy development. Determine elements that could improve the richness of the literacy environment you analyzed.

4. Select a child and his or her family to begin a portfolio of assessment materials to collect throughout the semester. Start a portfolio that you will keep in a folder for the child and provide a folder for the family. Make copies of the

Guidelines: Promoting Early Literacy at Home on pages 392 to 393 (and pages 393 to 395 for the Spanish version) for yourself and one for the family you will be working with. Ask a family member to fill out the form for themselves and a copy for you. Provide the family member with two copies of the form entitled Checklist: Observing My Child's Literacy Growth on page 395. Have them fill it out at the beginning of the semester and at the end. Be sure to get a copy for your folder as well.

5. Create a family literacy program for a familiar community. If it is a community in which families have literacy and English skills, you will probably want to develop a family involvement program; if it is in a community where families speak other languages or have limited literacy ability, you may need to engage in an intergenerational program that involves development of literacy skills for families and training them to help their children. Be sure that, whichever program you design, portions of the home and school activities are similar to each other.

6.  Using Strategies for the Classroom for Chapter 10, provide parents with a list of literacy activities to participate in and ask them to record what they do. Give parents a VIP (Very Important Parent) award (page S-50) for participating in and out of school with literacy help for their child. Create bookmarks for parents and children (page S-51).

myeducationlab

VIDEO EXERCISE

Now that you have the benefit of having read this chapter, return to the www.myeducationlab.com topic "Becoming a Reading Teacher" and watch "Involving Parents" and "Involving Parents in the Educational Process" one more time. You may complete the questions that accompany them online and save or transmit your work to your professor, or complete the following questions, as required.

Involving Parents (1:59 minutes)

1. How does this teacher involve parents in the education process?
2. How do the students, teacher, and parents benefit from this kind of classroom interaction?

Involving Parents in the Educational Process (5:04 minutes)

1. What was the first thing the principal did when he came to O'Hearn School? Why did he do this, and what might have happened if he had begun implementing changes without this process?
2. In the past, parents were welcomed into the school twice a year and very few took advantage of the opportunity. What reasons are stated on the video for this? How has this situation changed?
3. The video discusses a number of ways that the teachers and principal reach out to parents and involve them in the educational process. Name five and explain why they are effective.
4. In a small group, discuss the level of involvement of your own parents when you were in elementary through high school. Was active involvement by parents an indicator of student success overall?
5. What can schools do to encourage parents to be part of the learning community?
6. Is there such a thing as too much parental involvement?
7. Should home visits be part of staff responsibilities? Defend your answer.

Afterword

We must reignite our romance with the written word.
— Steven Spielberg, 1987

This volume has presented a theory- and research-based program for developing literacy in early childhood. It has emphasized the importance of literacy-rich environments, social interaction, peer collaboration, and whole-class, small-group, and individual learning with explicit instruction and problem-solving experiences. The activities suggested underscore the concurrent, integrated nature of learning how to use oral language, reading, and writing. The volume has outlined education that is functional and related to real-life experiences and is thus meaningful and interesting to the child. It has provided for the integration of literacy activities into content areas through units of study that are based on themes that add enthusiasm, motivation, and meaning. It has suggested careful monitoring of individual growth through direct instruction and frequent assessment using multiple measures and allowing ample space for children to learn through play, manipulation, and exploration. Attending to children with diverse needs and backgrounds is an emphasis throughout the volume.

New information about learning is constantly being generated, subsequently changing the strategies we use to help children learn. Teachers must stay abreast of the constant stream of literature that is available after they complete their formal education. Teachers need to engage in multiple forms of professional development to be up to date with the latest research, theory, policy, and practice. There are many forms of professional development to participate in.

Teachers can continue their education and receive a masters or doctorate degree or another teaching certification. They can also take a course to strengthen their knowledge in a particular area of concern. Teachers need to join professional organizations, such as those listed in Appendix D. Professional organizations have local, state, and national conferences. They publish practical and research journals with the most current information available. Some professional organizations also publish books. Through these organizations, teachers connect with others and have the opportunity to talk and reflect. In addition to these individual initiatives taken by teachers, I encourage you to work on a professional development plan with your school. The plan can be for the entire school or by grade level. It can be a 1-year plan that can continue. It is based on what teachers and administrators believe they need to work on in literacy.

Try to use a collaborative model since it has proved to work well.

1. Collaborative models involve individuals from various perspectives working together to bring new ideas to the classroom.
2. Collaborative procedures provide for teacher control.
3. Collaborative models provide support and direction from other colleagues, administrators, and/or researchers.

The goal of a professional development program in a school is to

1. Change classroom practice
2. Change teacher attitudes toward professional development
3. Create a school that is composed of a community of learners

How can this be done?

1. Focus on changing classroom practices.
2. When teachers can observe changes in student learning as a result of changing classroom practice, changes in teacher beliefs and attitudes will follow.
3. Bring in experts to model the teaching practice you wish to implement.

Components of a Good Professional Development Model

Good professional development programs include:

1. Administrative support for the project prior to beginning
2. Professional development workshops to provide information about new strategies from motivating and knowledgeable consultants
3. Goals set by teachers to accomplish
4. A coach in the school to model new strategies in the classroom and to support teachers
5. Accessible materials
6. Classroom observations by other teachers, the coach, etc. to determine progress
7. Teacher discussion groups to foster collaboration and reflection with reading materials to provide new ideas
8. Time to change

Teacher's Comments about Participating in a Good Professional Development Model

1. Teacher 1: The professional development program helped me try new ideas. Sometimes the district asks you to do new things without time to learn about them and without the help needed for implementation. The best way to foster change in teachers is to introduce ideas by having a moti-

vating and competent consultant demonstrate strategies. We had excellent support to help us understand the new ideas and implement them. We were given lesson plans that were very helpful. I also found that visiting other teachers' classrooms to see your peers doing the new strategies was extremely valuable. It is very important to realize that change happens slowly. We were not rushed. I liked our discussion groups, because we needed to talk to each other about our progress, exchange ideas, and get advice from the consultant.

2. Teacher 2: The thing that influenced me to change the most was the realization that my students' needs were not being met and therefore they were not reaching their full potential. Soon after I started to change my instruction, I began to see a change in student behavior. The students were now capable of what was being asked of them.

3. Teacher 3: I felt as though I had a lot to learn about teaching reading through small-group reading instruction, and I learned a lot in the professional development program. I intend to remain active in professional development to keep learning. I will definitely participate in meetings with the consultant and my peers. I will also be happy to help other teachers who may want to begin guided reading in their classrooms!

The Teacher-Researcher

Another area of professional development is the teacher acting as a researcher by reflecting on his or her own teaching. This can be done to discover strengths and weaknesses and to develop questions of concern to the teacher about teaching students. To be a teacher–researcher means to formulate questions about teaching strategies, child development, classroom environment, curriculum development, or other relevant topics that will clarify issues to help generate new information. Questions should be generated from your daily experiences in the classroom and be of interest to you personally. When teachers are researchers, they increase their knowledge and skill.

When an area of inquiry is decided on, the teacher should focus on collecting data that will help answer questions posed or clarify issues. Data can be collected in the following ways: Observe and record anecdotes of classroom experiences that are relevant to the question being asked; videotape classroom segments; collect samples of children's daily work over a period of time; interview children, teachers, and parents; administer formal and informal tests; and try new techniques.

As a teacher–researcher, you will always be on the cutting edge of what is current and appropriate. You will always find your teaching interesting because you will be learning about new things on a daily basis. You will enjoy your work more because you have extended your role to include additional professional activities. As a teacher–researcher, you are practicing both the art and science of teaching. The science involves inquiry, reading, observing, and collecting data. The art involves reflecting on findings and making appropriate changes. Teacher–researchers empower themselves to be decision makers and catalysts for making change in their schools. As they study questions for which they have tangible data, they are more likely to be heard when they propose new ideas or recommend changes. Rather than having change mandated based on the research by individuals outside your school district or by administrative personnel, take the responsibility for the changes that will occur by researching issues yourself. Each year that you teach, select another area of inquiry to study. When appropriate, collaborate with your colleagues on research projects. Collaboration with adults, as with children, results in projects that you might not have been able to do alone. What we have learned over the years concerning learning theory and early literacy development is due to research by college professors and classroom teachers. It must continue.

The program described in this volume is meant to be motivating for teachers and children. Motivation allows the teacher to work with vigor and enthusiasm. Motivation allows the child to associate literacy with a school environment that is pleasurable, positive, and designed to help children succeed. One of the most important elements in learning to read and write is a teacher who can encourage children to want to read and write. Wanting to read and write motivates a desire to learn the skills necessary to become proficient in literacy. With the skills develops a lifelong interest in refining and using literacy skills. The program is designed to help us "reignite our romance with the written word" (Spielberg, 1987).

Children's Literature

Sara Stofik, Kathryn Minto, Helen Giglio, and Magalena Zaremba

■ BOOKS FOR BABIES

Cardboard Concept Books

DK Books. (2002). *Things That Go*. New York. DK.

DK Board Books. (2004). *My First Farm Board Book*. New York. DK.

Dog Artlist. (2005). *The Dog from Arf! Arf! to Zzzzzz-Book*. New York. HarperFestival.

Huelin, J. (2004). *Harold and the Purple Crayon: Opposites*. New York. HarperFestival.

King, S. (2003). *On the Farm, a Magic Picture Board*. San Francisco. Chronicle.

Kubler, A. (2003). *Ten Little Fingers*. New York. Children's Play International.

Leoni, L. (2004). *A Busy Year*. New York. Knopf.

Cloth Books

Katz, K. (2007). *Baby's Day*. New York. Little Simon.

Potter, B. (2004). *Peter Rabbit Snuggle Time: A Cloth Book*. New York. Warner.

Priddy, R. (2003). *Squishy Turtle and Friends*. New York. Priddy.

Rinaldo, L. (2007). *Sleepy Farm*. Fort Huachuca, AZ. Campbell.

Ward, J. (2005). *Forest Bright, Forest Night*. Nevada City, CA. Dawn.

Plastic Books

Aigner-Clark, J. (2003). *Baby Einstein: What Floats: A Splash and Giggle Bath Book*. New York. Hyperion.

Crossley, D. (2003). *Bunnies on the Farm*. New York. Backpack Books.

London, J. (2001). *Froggy Takes a Bath*. New York. Grosset & Dunlap.

Priddy, R. (2005). *BabyHugs*. New York. Priddy.

Touch and Feel

Aigner-Clark, J. (2003). *Baby Einstein: Violet's House*. New York. Hyperion.

Brown, M.W. (2005). *Little Fur Family*. New York. HarperCollins.

Hunt, J. (2003). *Shapes*. San Diego, CA. Silver Dolphin.

Watt, F. (2004). *Fish*. DE. Usbourne.

Watt, F. (2006). *That's Not My Kitten*. DE. Usbourne.

■ CONCEPT BOOKS

Ashe, E. (2004). *Happy Horse—A Children's Book of Horses: A Happy Horse Adventure*. Chevy Chase, MD. Happy House.

Baker, J. (2004). *Home*. New York. Greenwillow.

Fleming, D. (2004). *The Everything Book*. New York. Holt.

Lehman, B. (2004). *The Red Book*. Boston. Houghton Mifflin.

McMullan, J., McMullan, K. (2005). *I Stink*. New York. HarperFestival.

Seeger, L.V. (2007). *Black? White? Day? Night? A Book of Opposites*. New York. Roaring Press.

■ ALPHABET BOOKS

Baltic, S. Goldrich, D. (2005). *I Saw an Ostrich in a Chair*. New York. Star.

Bonder, D. (2007). *Dogabet*. N. Vancouver, BC, Canada. Walrus.

Bruel, N. (2005). *Bad Kitty*. New York. Roaring Brook Press.

Ernest, L. (2004). *The Turn-Around, Upside Down Alphabet Book*. New York. Simon & Schuster.

Floca, B. (2004). *The Race Car Alphabet*. New York. Atheneum.

London, J. (2007). *Do Your ABC's Little Brown Bear*. New York. Puffin.

■ NUMBER BOOKS

Ball, J. (2005). *Go Figure! A Totally Cool Book about Numbers*. New York. DK.

Fromental, J.-L. (2007). *365 Penguins*. New York. Abrams.

Lewis, P. O. (2006). *P. Bear's New Year's Counting Book*. Berkeley, CA. Tricycle Press.

Morales, Y. (2004). *Just a Minute: A Trickster Tale and Counting Book*. San Francisco. Chronicle.

Sayre, A.P., Sayre, J. (2004). *One Is a Snail, Ten Is a Crab: A Counting by Feet Book*. Cambridge, MA. Candlewick.

NURSERY RHYMES

Denton, K. (2004). *A Child's Treasury of Nursery Rhymes*. New York: Kingfisher.

Green, A. (2007). *Mother Goose's Storytime Nursery Rhymes*. New York. Arthur A. Levine.

Grey, M. (2007). *The Adventures of the Dish and the Spoon*. New York. Knopf.

Grodin, E. (2006). *Everyone Counts: A Citizen's Number Book*. Chelsea, MI. Sleeping Bear Press.

Rescek, S. (2006). *Hickory, Dickery Dock: And Other Favorite Nursery Rhymes*. New York. Tiger Tales.

WORDLESS STORYBOOKS

Cleary, B.P. (2007). *Peanut Butter and Jellyfishes: A Very Silly Alphabet Book*. Brookfield, CT. Millbrook.

Crossley, D. (2003). *Bunnies on the Farm*. New York. Backpack Books.

Elting, M., Folsum, M., Kent, J. (2005). *Q Is for Duck: An Alphabet Guessing Game*. New York. Clarion.

Schories, P. (2004). *Breakfast for Jack*. Honesdale, PA. Boyd's Mill Press.

Sis, P. (2006). *Dinosaur*. New York. HarperFestival.

Sobel, J. (2006). *B Is for Bulldozer: A Construction Book*. New York. Voyager.

POETRY BOOKS

Donaldson, J., Scheffler, A. (2005). *The Gruffalo*. New York. Dial.

Feldman, T. (2003). *First Foil Haikus: Love*. Los Angeles. Piggy Toe Press.

Florian, D. (2005). *Zoo's Who*. San Diego, CA. Harcourt.

Kuskin, K. (2005). *Toots the Cat*. New York. Holt.

Paschen, E., Raccah, D. (2005). *Poetry Speaks to Children*. Naperville, IL. Sourcebooks Mediafusion.

Pretlutsky, J. (Selector). *The 20th Century Children's Poetry Treasury*. New York, Random House.

Rammell, S.K. (2006). *City Beats: A Hip-Hoppy Pigeon Poem*. Nevada City, CA. Dawn.

TRADITIONAL LITERATURE (FAIRY TALES, FABLES, MYTHS, AND FOLKTALES)

Aesop. (2005). *Aesop's Fables, Great Illustrated Classics*. Edino, MN. Abdo.

Gallagher, B. (2007). *Children's Classic Stories: A Timeless Collection of Fairytales, Fables, Folklores*. Essex, England. Bardfield Press.

Harrison, M., Stuart-Clark, C. (Selectors). (1994). *The Oxford Treasury of Children's Stories*. Andover, MA. Oxford.

Magee, W. (2007). *The Three Billy Goats Gruff*. Minnetonka, MN. Franklin Watts.

Mora, P. (2006). *Dona Flor: A Tale about a Giant Woman with a Big Heart*. New York. Random-Knopf.

Pinkney, J. (2007). *The Little Red Hen*. New York. Dial.

EASY-TO-READ BOOKS WITH LIMITED VOCABULARY

Cannon, A. E. (2004). *Let the Good Times Roll with Pirate Pete and Pirate Joe*. New York. Viking.

Capucilli, A.S. (2003). *Biscuit Loves School*. New York. HarperFestival.

Holub, J. (2003). *Why Do Horses Neigh?* New York. Puffin.

Juster, N. (2005). *The Hello, Goodbye Window*. New York. Hyperion.

Rocklin, J. (2003). *This Book Is Haunted*. New York. HarperTrophy.

BOOKS ABOUT REALISTIC ISSUES

Buehner, C., & Buehner, M. (2000). *I Did It, I'm Sorry*. New York. Penguin.

Davies, S. (1997). *Why Did We Have to Move Here?* Minneapolis, MN. Carolrhoda Books.

dePaola, T. (2000). *Nana Upstairs and Nana Downstairs*. New York. Penguin.

Hess, D. (1994). *Wilson Sat Alone*. New York. Simon & Schuster.

Katz, K. (2002). *The Colors of Us*. New York. Holt.

Levins, S., Langdo, B. (2006). *Was It the Chocolate Pudding?: A Story for Little Kids about Divorce*. Washington, DC: American Psychological Association.

Newman, L. (1998). *Too Far Away to Touch*. New York. Clarion.

Padoan, G. (1989). *Remembering Grandad: Facing up to Death*. New York. Child's Play.

Penn, A. (2006). *The Kissing Hand*. Terre Haute, IN: Tanglewood Press.

Richardson, J., Parnell, P. (2005). *And Tango Makes Three*. New York: Simon & Schuster.

Vigna, J., (1995). *My Two Uncles*. Morton Grove, IL: Albert Whitman.

Viorst, J., (1971). *The Tenth Good Thing about Barney*. New York: Simon & Schuster.

INFORMATIONAL BOOKS (EXPOSITORY TEXTS LISTED BY GRADE LEVEL)

PreK

Grogan, J. (2007). *Bad Dog, Marley!* New York. Harper-Collins.

Hewitt, S. (1999). *The Five Senses*. Danbury, CT. Children's Press.

Klingel, C.G., & Noyed, R.B. (2001). *Pumpkins*. Chanhassen, MI. Children's World.

Morris, A. (1998). *Work*. New York. Lothrop, Lee & Shepard.

Segal, G. (2004). *Why Mole Shouted*. New York. Farrar, Straus & Giroux.

Shulevitz, U. (2003). *One Monday Morning*. New York. Farrar, Straus, & Giroux.

Suen, A. (2004). *Subway.* New York. Viking.

Ziefert, H. (2006). *You Can't Taste a Pickle with Your Ear!* Penticton, BC, Canada. Handprint Books/RaggedBears/BlueApple.

Grades K–1

Carle, E. (2005). *A House for Hermit Crab.* New York. Aladdin.

Cuyler, M. (2001). *Stop, Drop, and Roll.* New York. Simon & Schuster.

Guiberson, B.Z. (2004). *Rain, Rain, Rain Forests.* New York. Holt.

Hewitt, S. (2000). *Nature for Fun Projects.* Riverside, NJ. Millbrook Press.

Hirschi, R. (2007). *Ocean Seasons.* Mount Pleasant, SC. Sylvan Dell.

Klingel, C., & Noyed, R.B. (2001). *Pigs.* Chanhassen, MI. Child's World.

Lewin, T., & Lewin, B. (2000). *Elephant Quest.* New York. HarperCollins.

Montanari, D. (2001). *Children around the World.* Tonawanda, NY. Kids Can Press.

Piano, M. (2006). *When Flamingos Fly.* New York. Orchard Academy Press.

Rockwell, A. (2001). *Bugs Are Insects.* New York. Harper-Collins.

Willems, M. (2005). *Knuffle Bunny; A Cautionary Tale.* New York. Hyperion.

Grades 1–2

Davies, N. (2004). *Oceans and Seas.* New York. Kingfisher.

Dussling, J. (2003). *Fair Is Fair!* La Jolla, CA. Kane.

Haskins, L. (2004). *Butterfly Fever.* La Jolla, CA. Kane.

Herman, K. (2003). *Buried in the Backyard.* La Jolla, CA. Kane.

Kerley, B. (2006). *You and Me Together: Moms, Dads, and Kids around the World.* Washington, DC. National Geographic.

London, J. (2001). *Crocodile: Disappearing Dragons.* Cambridge, MA. Candlewick.

McLiemans, D. (2006). *Gone Wild.* New York. Walker.

Murphy, S. (2004). *Earth Day—Hooray!* New York. HarperTrophy.

Schaefer, L. (2001). *Who Works Here? Fast-Food Restaurant.* Chicago. Heinemann.

Yolen, J., & Stemple, H. (2001). *The Wolf Girls.* New York. Simon & Schuster.

Grades 2–3

Animal Planet: The Most Extreme Bugs. (2007). New York. Discovery Press.

Dussling, J. (2005). *The 100-Pound Problem.* La Jolla, CA. Kane.

Hickman, P. (2001). *Animals Eating: How Animals Chomp, Chew, Slurp, and Swallow.* Tonawanda, NY. Kids Can Press.

Markle, S. (2001). *Rats and Mice.* New York. Atheneum.

Noyes, D. (2007). *When I Met the Wolf Girls.* Boston. Houghton Mifflin.

Priceman, M. (2006). *The Mostly True Story of the First Hot-Air Balloon Ride.* New York. Simon & Schuster.

Ripley, C. (2004). *Why! The Best Ever Question and Answer Book about Nature, Science, and the World around You.* Toronto, Canada. Maple Tree Press.

Sansevere-Dreher, D. (2005). *Explorers Who Got Lost.* NewYork. Tor.

Senisi, E. (2001). *Berry Smudges and Leaf Prints.* New York. Dutton Children's Books.

Wheeler, L. (2007). *Mammoths on the Move.* New York. Knopf.

Informational Text Series

Alphabet and Counting Books. Watertown, MA. Charlesbridge.

Time for Kids. New York. HarperCollins.

Wildlife Series for Kids. Tonawanda, NY. Kids Can Press.

BIOGRAPHY

Anderson, W. (2003). *River Boy: The Story of Mark Twain.* New York. HarperCollins.

Bruchac, J. (2004). *Rachel Carson: Preserving a Sense of Wonder.* Golden, CO. Fulcrum.

Carlson, C. (2005). *Dr. Seuss.* New York. Pebble Books.

Delano, M. F. (2004). *Genius: A Photobiography of Albert Einstein.* Washington, DC. National Geographic.

Demi. (2001). *Ghandi.* New York. Simon & Schuster.

Schanzer, R. (2003). *How Ben Franklin Stole the Lightning.* New York. HarperCollins.

Winter, J. (2003). *The Librarian of Basra: A True Story of Iraq.* San Diego, CA. Harcourt.

Worms, P. (2003). *Alexander the Great.* New York. Peter Bedrick.

Biographies

Biographies for Children: The Young Patriot Series. Indianapolis, IN. Patria Press.

Creative Minds. Minneapolis, MN. Carolrhoda.

Kids Who Ruled. New York. Peter Bedrick.

Meet the Author Series. Katonah, NY. Richard C. Owen.

Picture Book Biographies. New York. Holiday House.

Step-Up Biographies. New York. Random House.

MAGAZINES FOR CHILDREN

American Girl. American Girl. 8400 Fairway Place, Middleton, WI 53562 (ages 8–12).

Babybug. Canus. 315 Fifth Street, Peru, IL 61354 (ages 6 mo–2).

Chickadee. Young Naturalist Foundations. 17th and M. Streets, NW, Washington, DC 20036 (ages 4–8).

Cricket. Open Court Publishing Co., Box 100, La Salle, IL 61301 (ages 6–12).

The Dinosaur Times. CSK Publications/B&W Publications, 500 S. Buena Vista Street, Suite 101, Burbank, CA 91521-6018 (all ages).

High Five. 803 Church Street, Honesdale, PA 18431 (ages 2–4).

Kids Discover. Kids Discover. 149 Fifth Avenue, New York, NY (ages 6 and up).

Ladybug. Canus. 315 Fifth Avenue, Peru, IL 61354 (ages 2–7).

Nickelodeon. Nickelodeon. PO Box 1529, Elk Grove Village, IL 60009 (ages 6–14).

Ranger Rick. National Wildlife Federation. 1100 Wildlife Center Drive, Reston, VA (ages 7 and up).

PREDICTABLE BOOKS

Repetitive Phrases

Elliott, D. (2004). *And Here's to You.* Cambridge, MA. Candlewick.

Henkes, K. (2004). *Kitten's First Full Moon.* New York. Greenwillow.

Page, R. (2004). *What Do You Do with a Tail Like This?* Boston. Houghton Mifflin.

Sherry, K. (2007). *I'm the Biggest Thing in the Ocean.* New York. Dial.

Wilson, K. (2003). *Never, Ever Shout in a Zoo.* New York. Margaret K. McElderry.

Rhymes

Berkes, M.C. (2007). *Over in the Jungle: A Rainforest Rhyme.* Nevada City, CA. Dawn.

Brenner, B. (2003). *What the Elephant Told.* New York. Holt.

Deady, K. (2004). *All Year Long.* Minneapolis, Carolrhoda.

Hubbard, W.M. (2003). *For the Love of a Dog.* New York. Putnam.

Mortensen, D.D. (2006). *Ohio Thunder.* New York. Clarion.

Tillman, N. (2006). *On the Night You Were Born.* New York. Feiwel.

Familiar Sequences (days of the week, numbers, letters, months of the year, etc.)

Baker, K. (2004). *Quack and Count.* New York. Voyager.

Bauer, M.D. (2003). *Toes, Ears, & Nose.* New York. Little Simon.

Carle, E. (2005). *Pancakes, Pancakes.* New York: Aladdin.

Krause, R. (2005). *Whose Mouse Are You?* New York. Aladdin.

Lewison, W.C. (2004). *Raindrop, Plop!* New York. Viking.

Updike, J. (1999). *A Child's Calendar.* New York. Holiday House.

Cumulative Patterns (as the story progresses, the previous line is repeated)

Edwards. P.D. (2005). *The Bus Ride That Changed History: The Story of Rosa Parks.* Boston. Houghton Mifflin.

Ernst, L.C. (2006). *The Gingerbread Girl.* New York. Dutton.

Wilson, K., & Rankin, J. (2003). *A Frog in the Bog.* New York. Margaret K. Elderry.

Wormell, C. (2001). *Blue Rabbit and the Runaway Wheel.* New York. Random House.

Stories with Conversation

Gleitzman, M. (2005). *Worm Story.* London, England. Ladybird Books.

Herman, G. (2003). *Buried in the Backyard.* La Jolla, CA. Kane.

Krull, K. (2003). *M Is for Music.* San Diego, CA. Harcourt.

Woodson, J. (2001). *The Other Side.* New York. Putnam.

Books That Foster Critical Discussions

Edwards, P.D. (2005). *The Bus Ride That Changed History: The Story of Rosa Parks.* Boston. Houghton Mifflin.

Juster, N. (2005). *The Hello, Goodbye Window.* New York. Hyperion.

Mora, P. (2006). *Dona Flor: A Tale about a Giant Woman with a Big Heart.* New York. Random-Knopf.

Smith, L. (2006). *Jon, Paul, George & Ben.* New York. Hyperion.

BOOKS FOR ENHANCING LISTENING AND DISCRIMINATION OF SOUNDS

Krull, K. (2003). *M Is for Music.* San Diego, CA. Harcourt.

Ring, S. (2004). *Safari Sounds: Hear and There.* Norwalk, CT. Innovative Kids.

Seuss, Dr. (2003). *Gerald McBoing Boing.* New York. Random House.

Wilson, K. (2004). *Hilda Must Be Dancing.* New York. Margaret K. McElderry.

Wojtowycz, D. (2001). *Can You Moo?* New York. Scholastic.

FAVORITE WELL-KNOWN PICTURE STORYBOOKS

The following books represent a careful selection of some distinguished authors and excellent children's literature not to be missed.

Barrett, J. (1988). *Animals Should Definitely Not Wear Clothing.* New York. Simon & Schuster.

Bemelmans, L. (1939). *Madeline.* New York. Viking.

Berenstain, S., & Berenstain, J. (2002). *The Bear's Picnic.* New York. Random House.

Brown, M. W. (1977). *Goodnight Moon.* New York. HarperCollins.

Carle, E. (1969). *The Very Hungry Caterpillar.* New York. Philomel.

dePaola, T. (1975). *Strega Nona: An Old Tale.* Upper Saddle River, NJ. Prentice Hall.

Eastman, P. D. (2005). *Are You My Mother?* New York. Random House.

Flack, M. (1968). *Ask Mr. Bear.* New York: Simon & Schuster.

Galdone, P. (1985). *The Little Red Hen.* Boston. Houghton Mifflin.

Hoban, R. (1976). *Best Friends for Frances.* New York: HarperCollins.

Hughes, S. (1986). *Up and Up.* New York. William Morrow & Co.

Hutchins, P. (1989). *Don't Forget the Bacon.* New York. HarperCollins.

Johnson, C. (1955). *Harold and the Purple Crayon.* New York. Harper.

Keats, E.J. (1998). *The Snowy Day.* New York. Penguin.

Kellogg, S. (1992). *Can I Keep Him?* New York. Penguin.

Kraus, R. (1973). *Leo the Late Bloomer.* New York. HarperCollins.

Lionni, L. (1973). *Swimmy.* New York. Random House.

Lobel, A. (1972). *Frog and Toad Together.* New York: Harper & Row.

Mayer, M. (2001). *One Monster after Another.* Columbus, OH. McGraw-Hill.

McCloskey, R. (1948). *Blueberries for Sal.* New York. Penguin.

Piper, W. (1978). *The Little Engine That Could.* New York. Penguin.

Potter, B. (2006). *The Tale of Peter Rabbit.* New York. Warner.

Rey, H. A. (1973). *Curious George Rides a Bike.* Boston. Houghton Mifflin.

Sendak, M. (1988). *Where the Wild Things Are.* New York. HarperCollins.

Seuss, Dr. (1940). *Horton Hatches the Egg.* New York. Random House.

Shaw, C. (1947). *It Looked Like Spilled Milk.* New York. HarperCollins.

Slobodkina, E. (1947). *Caps for Sale.* Reading, MA. Addison-Wesley.

Steig, W. (2005). *Sylvester and the Magic Pebble.* New York. Simon & Schuster.

Viorst, J. (1972). *Alexander and the Terrible, Horrible, No Good, Very Bad Day.* New York. Atheneum.

Waber, B. (1975). *Ira Sleeps Over.* Boston. Houghton Mifflin.

Wiesner, D. (1988). *FreeFall.* New York. Lothrop, Lee, & Shepard.

Wiesner, D. (1992). *Tuesday.* New York. Clarion Books.

■ BOOKS FOR BUILDING SOUND–SYMBOL RELATIONSHIPS

Consonants

B

Blackstone, S. (2000). *Bear's Busy Family.* Cambridge, MA. Barefoot Books.

Brisson, P. (2006). *Melissa Parkington's Beautiful Beautiful Hair.* PA. Boyds Mills Press.

Chrustowski, R. (2000). *Bright Beetle.* New York: Holt.

McPhail, D. (2003). *Big Brown Bear's Up and Down Day.* San Diego, CA. Harcourt.

Walker, R. (Reteller). (1998). *The Barefoot Book of Pirates.* Cambridge, MA. Barefoot Books.

C (Hard)

Gibbons, G. (1993). *Caves and Caverns.* New York. Harcourt Brace.

Sabuda, R. (1997). *Cookie Count.* New York. Little Simon.

Stevens, J. (2004). *Carlos and the Cornfield.* AZ. Rising Moon Books.

Ward, J. (2007). *There Was a Coyote Who Swallowed a Flea.* AZ. Rising Moon Books.

C (soft)

Clements, A. (2000). *Circus Family Dog.* New York. Clarion Books.

Falconer, I. (2001). *Olivia Saves the Circus.* New York. Simon & Schuster.

Milich, Z. (2004). *City Colors.* New York. Kids Can Press.

Swain, G. (1999). *Celebrating.* New York. First Avenue Editions.

D

Bunting, E. (1995). *Dandelions.* New York. Harcourt Brace.

Hindley, J. (2002). *Do Like Duck Does.* Cambridge, MA. Candlewick Press.

Urbanovic, J. (2007). *Duck at the Door.* New York. Harper Collins.

F

Bourgeois, P. (2000). *Franklin's Baby Sister.* New York City, NY. Scholastic.

LaReau, K. & Magoon, S. (2006). *Ugly Fish.* Orlando: FL. Harcourt.

London, J. (1997). *Froggy Learns to Swim.* New York. Puffin.

San Souci, R.D. (1995). *The Faithful Friend.* New York. Simon & Schuster.

Silverman, E. (1994). *Don't Fidget a Feather.* New York. Macmillan.

G (Hard)

Berger, B. (1960). *Grandfather Twilight.* New York. Philomel.

Clark, K. (2005). *Grandma Drove the Garbage Truck*. ME. Down East Books.

Grejniec, M. (1993). *Good Morning, Good Night*. New York. North-South.

Grimm, J., & Grimm, W. (1995). *The Golden Goose*. New York. Farrar, Straus & Giroux.

Rathmann, P. (1996). *Good Night, Gorilla*. New York. Putnam.

G (Soft)

Andreae, G. (2001). *Giraffes Can't Dance*. New York. Orchard.

Brett, J. (1999). *Gingerbread Baby*. New York. Putnam.

Galdone, P. (1975). *The Gingerbread Boy*. New York. Clarion.

Peck, J. (1998). *The Giant Carrot*. New York. Dial.

Silverstein, S. (1964). *A Giraffe and a Half*. New York. HarperCollins.

H

Brett, J. (2005). *Honey, Honey Lion*. New York. Putnam.

Hadithi, M. (1994). *Hungry Hyena*. Boston. Little, Brown.

High, L.O. (1995). *Hound Heaven*. New York. Holiday House.

Hoff, S. (1985). *The Horse in Harry's Room*. New York. HarperCollins.

Wattenberg, J. (2000). *Henny Penny*. New York. Scholastic.

Yolen, J., Greenberg, M.H. (1995). *The Haunted House*. New York. HarperCollins.

J

Birdseye, T. (2001). *Look Out—Jack the Giant Is Back*. New York. Holiday House.

Saltzman, D. (1995). *The Jester Has Lost His Jingle*. Palos Verdes, CA. Jester Company.

Yang, J. (2004). *Joey & Jet*. New York. Atheneum.

Zanes, D. (2005). *Jump Up*. Boston. Little, Brown.

K

Demi. (1999). *Kites*. New York. Crown Publishing.

Larson, K. (2000). *The Magic Kerchief*. New York. Holiday House.

McKee, D. *Eleanor and the Kangaroo*. (2000). New York. HarperCollins.

O'Connor, J. (1995). *Kate Skates*. New York. Grosset.

Polacco, P. (1988). *The Keeping Quilt*. New York. Simon & Schuster.

L

Bornstein, R. (2000). *Little Gorilla*. New York. Clarion.

Bunting, E. (2003). *Little Bear's Little Boat*. New York. Clarion.

Doughty, R. (2005). *Lost and Found*. New York. Penguin.

London, J. (1996). *Let's Go, Froggy*. New York. Puffin.

Walsh, M. (2006). *Do Lions Live on Lily Pads*. Boston. Houghton Mifflin.

M

Downey, L. (2004). *Most Loved Monster*. New York. Penguin.

McPhail, D. (2001). *Mole Music*. New York. Holt.

Newman, M. (2005). *Myron's Magic Cow*. Boston, MA. Barefoot Books.

Palatini, M. (2004). *Moo Who*. New York. HarperCollins.

N

Clark, S. (2006). *Nicholas Nosh Is off to Sea*.

McDonnell, P. (2005). *The Gift of Nothing*. New York. Little Brown.

O'Connor (1997). *Nina, Nina, Ballerina*. New York. Grosset.

Shannon, D. (1998). *No, David*. New York: Scholastic.

Wells, R. (1997). *Noisy Nora*. New York: Scholastic.

P

Bynum, J. (2003). *Pig Enough*. San Diego, CA. Harcourt.

Cooper, H. *A Pipkin of Pepper*. New York. Farrar, Strauss Giroux.

Corey, S. (2003). *Players in Pigtails*. New York. Scholastic.

Dale, P. (2003). *Princess, Princess*. Cambridge, MA. Candlewick Press.

Palatini, M. (1995). *Piggie Pie!* New York. Clarion.

Papademetriou, L. (1998). *My Pen Pal, Pat*. Brookfield, CT. Millbrook Press.

Spurr, E. (2002). *A Pig Named Perrier*. New York. Hyperion Books.

Q

Arnold, M. (1996). *Quick, Quack, Quick!* New York. Random House.

Good, M. (1999). *Reuben and the Quilt*. New York. Good Books.

Holtzman, C. (1995). *A Quarter from the Tooth Fairy*. New York. Scholastic.

Johnston, T., & DePaola, T. (1996). *The Quilt Story*. New York. Penguin Putnam.

Wood, A. (1997). *Quick as a Cricket*. New York. Scholastic.

Yorinks, A. (2003). *Quack*. New York. Abrams.

R

Brown, M. (2002). *Robin's Room*. New York. Hyperion Books.

Gantos, J. (1994). *Not So Rotten Ralph*. Boston. Houghton Mifflin.

Wells, R. (2002). *Ruby's Beauty Shop*. New York. Penguin Putnam.

Willis, R. (2002). *Raccoon Moon*. Middletown, DE: Birdsong Books.

S

Arnold, T. (2006). *Super Fly Guy*. New York: Scholastic.

Capucilli, A. (2005). *Biscuit's Snowy Day*. New York. HarperCollins.

Teague, M. (1999). *The Secret Shortcut*. New York. Scholastic.

T

Bunting, E. (1997). *Twinnies*. San Diego, CA. Harcourt.

Cocca-Leffler, M. (1999). *Mr. Tannen's Ties*. Morton Grove, IL: Albert Whitman.

Dierssen, A. (2003). *Timid Timmy*. New York. North-South Books.

Griffing, A. (1999). *Trashy Town*. New York. Harper-Collins.

Manual, L. (2006). *The Trouble with Tilly Trumble*. New York. Abrams.

V

Cannon, J. (1997). *Verdi*. New York. Harcourt.

Paros, J. (2007). *Violet Bing and the Grand House*. New York. Penguin.

Rylant, C. (2005). *If You'll Be My Valentine*. New York. HarperCollins.

Williams, M. (1981). *The Velveteen Rabbit*. New York. Scholastic.

Williams, S. (1998). *Let's Go Visiting*. New York. Harcourt.

W

Brenner, B. (1995). *Wagon Wheels*. New York. Scholastic.

Derby, S. (2006). *Whoosh Went the Wind*. New York. Marshall Cavendish.

Hartman, B. (2002). *The Wolf Who Cried Boy*. New York. Putnam.

McGee, M. (2006). *Winston the Bookwolf*. New York. Walker & Co.

Milord, S. (2003). *Willa the Wonderful*. Boston. Houghton Mifflin.

Williams, S. (1996). *I Went Walking*. New York. Gulliver.

Zolotow, C. (1997). *When the Wind Stops*. New York. Harper Trophy.

X

Wells, R. (2001). *Felix Feels Better*. Boston, MA. Candlewick Press.

Wells, R. (1998). *Max and Ruby in Pandora's Box*. New York. Penguin Putnam.

Wells, R. (2002). *Max Cleans Up*. New York. Penguin Putnam.

Y

Hoberman, M. (2004). *Yankee Doodle*. Boston. Little, Brown.

Milgrim, D. (2006). *Young MacDonald*. New York. Dutton.

Seuss, Dr. (1958). *Yertle the Turtle and Other Stories*. New York. Random House.

Wells, R. (1998). *Yoko*. New York. Hyperion.

Z

McDermott, G. (1996). *Zomo the Rabbit. A Trickster Tale from West Africa*. New York. Scholastic.

Moss, L. (1995). *Zin!Zin!Zin! A Violin*. New York. Simon & Schuster.

Palatini, M. (2000). *Zoom Broom*. New York. Hyperion.

Tavares, M. (2005). *Zachary's Ball*. Boston, MA: Candlewick Press.

Vowels (long and short)

A

Arnoslay, J. (2003). *Armadillo's Orange*. New York. Putnam.

Holabird, K. (2002). *Angelina Ballerina*. Middleton, WI. Pleasant Co.

Karlin, N. (1996). *The Fat Cat Sat on the Mat*. New York. Harper Trophy.

Lachner, D. (1995). *Andrew's Angry Words*. New York. North-South.

Wright, C. (2001). *Steamboat Annie*. New York. Philomel.

E

D'amico, C. & D'amico, S. (2004). *Ella the Elephant*. New York: Scholastic.

McKee, D. (2004). *Elmer*. New York. HarperCollins.

Munson, D. (2000). *Enemy Pie*. CA: Chronicle.

Shaw, N. (1997) *Sheep in a Jeep*. Boston. Houghton Mifflin.

I

Bornstein, R. (2000). *Little Gorilla*. New York. Clarion.

Fleming, D. (1998). *In the Small, Small Pond*. New York. Holt.

Gibbons, G. (2006). *Ice Cream: The Full Scoop*. New York. Holiday House.

Hasely, D. (2006). *The Invisible Moose*. New York. Penguin.

Numeroff, L. (1998). *If You Give a Pig a Pancake*. New York. HarperCollins.

O

Falconer, I. (2000). *Olivia*. New York. Simon & Schuster.

Leonard, M. (1998). *Spots*. Brookfield, CT. Millbrook Press.

MacDonald, M. (2007). *The Old Woman and Her Pig*. New York. HarperCollins.

Parr, T. (1999). *The Okay Book*. New York. Little Brown.

Willis, R. (2002). *Raccoon Moon*. Middletown, DE. Birdsong Books.

Wilson, K., & Rankin, J. (2003). *A Frog in the Bog*. New York. Margaret K. McElderry.

U

Anderson, H.C. (1994). *The Ugly Duckling*. New York. Dorling Kindersley.

Edwards, P. (1998). *Some Smug Slug*. New York. HarperCollins.

Graves, S. (2007). *Bug in a Rug*. New York. Scholastic.

Heidbreder, R. (2000). *I Wished for a Unicorn*. New York. Kids Can Press.

Digraphs
CH

Archambault, J., & Martin, B., Jr. (1989). *Chicka Chicka Boom Boom*. New York. Scholastic.

Henkes, K. (1996). *Chrysanthemum*. New York. Mulberry.

Onyefulu, O. (1994). *Chinye: A West African Folk Tale*. New York. Viking.

Updike, J. (1999). *A Child's Calendar*. New York. Holiday House.

Varon, S. (2006) *Chicken and Cat*. New York. Scholastic.

PH

Hill, S. (2005). *Punxsutawney Phyllis*. New York. Holiday House.

Molter, C. (2000). *PH: See It Say It Hear It*. Edina, MN: ABDO Publishing.

SH

Brown, M. (1995). *Shadow*. New York. Aladdin.

Shaw, N. (1996). *Sheep in a Shop*. Boston. Houghton Mifflin.

Shaw, N. (1997). *Sheep in a Jeep*. Boston. Houghton Mifflin.

Simon, S. (1995). *Sharks*. New York. HarperCollins.

Sloat, T. (2000). *Farmer Brown Shears His Sheep*. New York. SK Publ.

Wells, R. (2001). *Shy Charles*. New York. Penguin Putnam.

TH

Marks, J. (2004). *Thanks for Thanksgiving*. New York. HarperCollins.

Munsinger, L. (1996). *Three Cheers for Tacky*. Boston. Houghton Mifflin.

Nolan, J. (2003). *Thunder Rose*. New York. Harcourt.

Simms, L. (1998). *Rotten Teeth*. Boston. Houghton Mifflin.

Word Families

Alborough, J. (1999). *Duck in the Truck*. New York. HarperCollins.

O'Connor, J. (1995). *Kate Skates*. New York. Grosset.

Seuss, Dr. (1957). *The Cat in the Hat*. New York. Random House.

Willis, R. (2002). *Raccoon Moon*. Middletown, DE. Birdsong Books.

Wilson, K., Randin, J. (2003). *A Frog in the Bog*. New York. Margaret K. McElderry.

BOOKS FOR FOLLOWING DIRECTIONS

Carle, E. (1993). *Draw Me a Star*. New York. Scholastic.

Cousins, L. (1999). *Dress Maisy*. Cambridge, MA. Candlewick Press.

Gibbons, G. (1996). *How a House Is Built*. New York. Holiday House.

Gold, R. (2006). *Kids Cook 1-2-3: Recipes for Young Chefs Using Only Three Ingredients*. New York. Bloomsbury.

Keller, T. (2007). *What's Cooking? A Cookbook for Kids*. New York. Disney Press.

Robinson, N. (2006). *Origami Adventures: Animals*. Hauppauge, NY. Barron's Educational Series.

Yolen, J., Teague, M. (2003). *How Do Dinosaurs Get Well Soon?* New York. Scholastic.

SERIES BOOKS

Bemelmans, L. (1977). *Madeline*. New York. Puffin Books.

Bourgeois, P. (2000). *Franklin*. New York. Scholastic.

Danziger, P. (2003). *Amber Brown*. New York. Putnam.

McDonald, M. (2002). *Judy Moody*. Cambridge, MA. Candlewick Press.

Parish, P. (1970). *Amelia Bedelia*. New York. Scholastic.

Park, B. (2002). *Junie B. Jones*. New York. Random House.

Rey, M., & Rey, H.A. (1973). *Curious George*. Boston. Houghton Mifflin.

Warner, G.C. (1990). *Boxcar Children Mysteries*. Morton Grove, IL. Albert Whitman.

EXPOSITORY AND NARRATIVE BOOKS RELATED TO THEMES
All About Me Books

Cain, J. (2000). *The Way I Feel*. Seattle, WA. Parenting Press.

Carlson, N.L. (1990). *I Like Me!* New York. Penguin.

Curtis, J.L. (2002). *I'm Gonna Like Me*. New York. HarperCollins.

Henkes, K. (1996). *Chrysanthemum*. New York. HarperCollins.

Kingsbury, K. (2004). *Let Me Hold You Longer*. Carol Stream, IL. Tyndale House.

Mitchell, L. (2001). *Different Just Like Me*. Watertown, MA. Charlesbridge.

Parr, T. (1999). *Things That Make You Feel Good, Things That Make You Feel Bad*. London. Little, Brown.

Parr, T. (2001). *It's Okay to Be Different*. London. Little, Brown.

Seuss, Dr. (1996). *My Many Colored Days*. New York. Random House.

Ziefert, H. (1998). *Waiting for Baby*. New York. Holt.

Animal Books

Bancroft, H., & Van Gelder, R.G. (1997). *Animals in Winter*. New York. HarperCollins.

Driscoll, L. (1997). *The Bravest Cat! The True Story of Scarlett*. New York. Penguin.

Ellwand, D. (1997). *Emma's Favorite Elephant and Other Favorite Animals*. New York. Penguin.

Hawes, J. (2000). *Why Frogs Are Wet*. New York. HarperCollins.

Hickman, P. (2001). *Animals Eating: How Animals Chomp, Chew, Slurp, and Swallow*. Tonawanda, NY. Kids Can Press.

Jackson, D. (2002). *The Wildlife Detectives: How Forensic Scientists Fight Crimes Against Nature*. Boston. Houghton Mifflin.

Jenkins, S. (2003). *What Do You Do with a Tail Like This?* Boston. Houghton Mifflin.

Markle, S. (2005). *Outside and Inside Giant Squid.* New York. Walker.

Markle, S. (2006). *A Mother's Journey.* Watertown, MA. Charlesbridge.

Weber, B. (2004). *Animal Disguises.* Boston. Houghton Mifflin.

Dinosaur Books

Carter, D. (2001). *Flapdoodle Dinosaurs.* New York. Simon & Schuster.

Diggory-Shields, C. (2002). *Saturday Night at the Dinosaur Stomp.* Cambridge, MA. Candlewick Press.

Eldredge, N., et al. (2002). *Fossil Factory: A Kid's Guide to Digging up Dinosaurs, Exploring Evolution and Finding Fossils.* Lanham, MD: Rinehart.

Gibbons, G. (2006). *Dinosaur Discoveries.* New York. Holiday House.

Kudlinski, K.V. (2005). *Boy, Were We Wrong about the Dinosaurs!* New York. Penguin.

Maynard, C. (2005). *The Best Book of Dinosaurs.* Boston. Houghton Mifflin.

Mitton, T. (2003). *Dinosaurumpus!* New York. Scholastic.

Weidner Zoehfeld, K. (2003). *Did Dinosaurs Have Feathers?* New York. HarperCollins.

Weidner Zoehfeld, K. (2001). *Terrible Tyrannosaurus.* New York. HarperCollins.

Willems, M. (2006). *Edwina, the Dinosaur Who Didn't Know She Was Extinct.* New York. Hyperion.

Yolen, J. (2005). *How Do Dinosaurs Eat Their Food?* New York. Scholastic.

Ecology

Cherry, L. (2000). *The Great Kapok Tree: A Tale of the Amazon Rainforest.* New York. Harcourt.

Cherry, L. (2002). *River Ran Wild: An Environmental History.* New York. Harcourt.

Cherry, L., & Plotkin, M.J. (2001). *The Shaman's Apprentice: A Tale of the Amazon Rainforest.* New York. Harcourt.

Craighead George, J. (1995). *One Day in the Tropical Rainforest.* New York. HarperCollins.

Fleming, D. (2000). *Where Once There Was Wood.* New York: Holt.

Green, J. (2005). *Why Should I Recycle?* Hauppauge, NY: Barron's Educational Series.

Rauzon, M.J., & Bix, C.O. (1995). *Water, Water, Everywhere.* San Francisco: Sierra Book Clubs for Children.

Seuling, B. (2000). *Drip!Drop!: How Water Gets to Your Tap.* New York. Holiday House.

Wells, R. (2006). *Did a Dinosaur Drink This Water?* Morton Grove, IL. Albert Whitman.

Five Senses

Aliki. (1989). *My Five Senses.* New York. HarperCollins.

Belk-Moncure, J. (1997). *Clang, Boom, Bang: My Five Senses Series.* Mankato, MN. Child's World.

Caviezel, G. (2005). *My Own Five Senses.* Hauppauge, NY. Barron's Educational Series.

Cole, J. (2001). *The Magic School Bus Explores the Senses.* New York. Scholastic.

Collins, B., & Cole, G.E. (1994). *You Can't Smell a Flower with Your Ear! All about Your 5 Senses.* New York. Penguin.

Miller, M. (1998). *My Five Senses.* New York. Simon & Schuster.

Romanek, T. (2004). *Wow! The Most Interesting Book You'll Ever Read about the Five Senses (Mysterious You Series).* Tonawanda, NY: Kids Can Press.

Scott, J., & Fletcher, M.B. (2003). *Our Senses (Spyglass Books, Life Science Series).* Mankato, MN: Coughlan.

Tullet, H. (2005). *The Five Senses.* UK: Tate.

How Things Work

Berger, M. (2000). *Why I Sneeze, Shiver, Hiccup, and Yawn.* New York. HarperCollins.

Cobb, A. (1996). *Wheels!* New York. Random House.

Jones, C.F. (1994). *Mistakes That Worked.* New York. Bantam Doubleday Dell.

Porter, A., & Davies, E. (2003). *How Things Work (Discoveries Series).* New York. Barnes and Noble.

Showers, P. (2001). *What Happens to a Hamburger?* New York. HarperCollins.

Voorhees, D. (2000). *Why Does Popcorn Pop? And 201 Other Fascinating Facts About Food.* New York. Carol Publishing.

Woodford, C., et al. (2005). *Cool Stuff and How It Works.* New York. Dorling Kindersley.

Insects and Reptiles

Baker, K. (1995). *Hide and Snake.* New York. Harcourt.

Berger, M., & Berger, G. (2002). *Snap! A Book about Alligators and Crocodiles.* New York. Scholastic.

Glassberg, J. (2005). *Butterflies of North America.* New York. Barnes and Noble.

Heiligman, D. (1996). *From Caterpillar to Butterfly.* New York. HarperCollins.

Holub, J. (2004). *Why Do Snakes Hiss? And Other Questions about Snakes, Lizards, and Turtles.* New York. Penguin.

Nickle, J. (2006). *The Ant Bully.* New York. Scholastic.

Orloff, K.K. (2004). *I Wanna Iguana.* New York. Penguin.

Simon, S. (2001). *Crocodiles and Alligators.* New York. HarperCollins.

Siy, A. (2005). *Mosquito Bite.* Watertown, MA: Charlesbridge.

Willis, J. (2005). *Tadpole's Promise.* New York. Simon & Schuster.

Ocean Life

Andreae, G. (2002). *Commotion in the Ocean.* Wilton, CT. ME Media.

Fuge, C. (2007). *Gilbert in Deep.* New York. Sterling.

Galloway, R. (2006). *Fidgety Fish.* Wilton, CT. ME Media.

Gilpin, D. (2005). *Life-Size Sharks and Other Underwater Creatures.* New York. Sterling.

Gray, S. (2001). *Ocean.* New York. Dorling Kindersley.

Lionni, L. (1973). *Swimmy*. New York. Random House.

Pallotta, J. (1990). *Ocean Alphabet Book*. Watertown, MA. Charlesbridge.

Osborne, M.P., & Boyce, N.P. (2003). *Dolphins and Sharks: A Nonfiction Companion to Dolphins at Daybreak (Magic Treehouse Research Guide Series)*. New York. Random House.

Pratt-Serafini, K.J. (1994). *A Swim Through the Sea*. Nevada City, CA. Dawn Publications.

Savage, S. (2006). *Oceans (Kingfisher Voyager Series)*. Boston. Houghton Mifflin.

Seasons and Holidays
All Four Seasons

Branley, F.M. (2005). *Sunshine Makes the Seasons*. New York. HarperCollins.

Gibbons, G. (1996). *Reasons for Seasons*. New York. Holiday House.

Autumn

Farmer, J. (2004). *Pumpkins*. Watertown, MA. Charlesbridge.

Hunter, A. (1998). *Possum's Harvest Moon*. Boston. Houghton Mifflin.

Maestro, B. (1994). *Why Do Leaves Change Color?* New York. HarperCollins.

Rawlinson, J. (2006). *Fletcher and the Falling Leaves*. New York. Harper Collins.

Robbins, K. (1998). *Autumn Leaves*. New York. Scholastic.

Robbins, K. (2006). *Pumpkins*. New York. Roaring Book Press.

Russell, C.Y. (2003). *Moon Festival*. Honesdale, PA. Boyds Mill Press.

Saunders-Smith, G. (1997). *Autumn Leaves*. Mankato, MN. Coughlan Publishing.

Saunders-Smith, G. (1998). *Autumn*. Mankato, MN. Coughlan Publishing.

Schuette, S.L. (2007). *Let's Look at Fall*. Mankato, MN. Coughlan Publishing.

Winter

Ehlert, L. (2000). *Snowballs*. New York. Harcourt.

Florian, D. (1999). *Winter Eyes*. New York. Greenwillow.

Frank, J. (2003). *A Chill in the Air: Poems for Fall and Winter*. New York. Simon & Schuster.

Jacques, B. (2004). *A Redwall Winter's Tale*. New York. Penguin.

Martin, J.B. (1998). *Snowflake Bentley*. Boston. Houghton Mifflin.

Poydar, N. (1997). *Snip, Snip, Snow*. New York. Holiday House.

Prelutsky, J. (2006). *It's Snowing! It's Snowing!: Winter Poems*. New York. HarperCollins.

Schulevitz, U. (2004). *Snow*. New York. Farrar, Straus, and Giroux.

Wilson, K. (2002). *Bear Snores On*. New York. Simon & Schuster.

Yolen, J. (1987). *Owl Moon*. New York. Penguin.

Spring

Carr, J. (2002). *Splish, Splash, Spring*. New York. Holiday House.

Good, E.W. (1996). *That's What Happens When It's Spring!* Kihei, HI: Good Books.

Preller, J. (1994). *Wake Me in Spring*. New York. Scholastic.

Roca, N. (2004). *Spring*. Hauppauge, NY. Barron's Educational Series.

Rylant, C. (1996). *Henry and Mudge in Puddle Trouble: The Second Book of Their Adventures*. New York. Simon & Schuster.

Spetter, J.H. (1995). *Lily and Trooper's Spring*. Honesdale, PA. Boyds Mill Press.

Thompson, L. (2005). *Mouse's First Spring*. New York. Simon & Schuster.

Wilson, K. (2003). *Bear Wants More*. New York. Simon & Schuster.

Yoon, S. (2006). *Duckling's First Spring*. New York. Penguin.

Summer

Hesse, K. (1999). *Come On Rain!* New York. Scholastic.

Perkins, L.R. (2007). *Pictures from Our Vacation*. New York. HarperCollins.

Polacco, P. (1997). *Thundercake*. New York. Penguin.

Roca, N. (2004). *Summer (The Seasons)*. Hauppauge, NY. Barron's Educational Series.

Rylant, C. (1993). *Relatives Came*. New York. Simon & Schuster.

Teague, M. (1997). *How I Spent My Summer Vacation*. Bethel, CT: Crown.

Wiesner, D. (2006). *Flotsam*. Boston. Houghton Mifflin.

Wing, N. (2002). *Night before Summer Vacation*. New York. Penguin.

Zolotow, C. (1989). *Storm Book*. New York. HarperCollins.

Space

Barton, B. (1992). *I Want to Be an Astronaut*. New York. HarperCollins.

Branley, F.M. (1999). *Is There Life in Outerspace?* New York. HarperCollins.

Davis, K.C. (2001). *Don't Know Much about Space*. New York: HarperCollins.

Gibbons, G. (2005). *The Planets*. New York. Holiday House.

Graham, I. (1998). *The Best Book of Spaceships*. Boston. Houghton Mifflin.

McNulty, F. (2005). *If You Decide to Go to the Moon*. New York. Scholastic.

Osborne, W., & Osborn, M.P. (2002). *Space: A Nonfiction Companion to Midnight on the Moon (Magic Treehouse Research Guide Series)*. New York. Bantam Doubleday Dell.

Simon, S. (1991). *Galaxies*. New York. HarperCollins.

Sims, L. (1995). *Exploring Space*. Orlando, FL. Steck-Vaughn.

Sparrow, G. (2007). *Space Flight*. New York. Dorling Kindersley.

CULTURAL DIVERSITY

African American

Bridges, R. (1999). *Through My Eyes*. New York. Scholastic.

Curtis, C.P. (1997). *The Watsons Go to Birmingham–1963*. New York. Bantam Doubleday Dell.

Hopkinson, D. (2005). *Under the Quilt of Night*. New York. Aladdin.

Kroll, V. (1997). *Masai and I*. New York. Simon & Schuster.

Rappaport, D. (2001). *Martin's Big Words*. New York. Hyperion.

Ringgold, F. (1995). *Aunt Harriet's Underground Railroad in the Sky*. New York. Crown.

Ringgold, F. (1996). *Tar Beach*. New York. Bantam Doubleday Dell.

Robinson, S. (2004). *Promises to Keep: How Jackie Robinson Changed America*. New York. Scholastic.

Steptoe, J. (2001). *In Daddy's Arms I Am Tall: African Americans Celebrating Fathers*. New York. Lee & Low.

Strickland, D.S., & Strickland, M.R. (1994). *Families. Poems Celebrating the African-American Experience*. Honesdale, PA. Boyds Mills Press.

Taylor, M. (2002). *Roll of Thunder, Hear My Cry*. New York. Penguin.

American

Bunting, E. (1999). *Smoky Night*. New York. Harcourt.

Bunting, E. (2004). *October Picnic*. New York. Harcourt.

Kuklin, S. (1998). *How My Family Lives in America*. New York. Simon & Schuster.

Lee-Tai, A. (2006). *A Place Where Sunflowers Grow*. San Francisco. Children's Book Press.

Lewis, R.A. (2000). *I Love You Like Crazy Cakes*. New York. Little, Brown.

Lord, B.B. (1986). *In the Year of the Boar and Jackie Robinson*. New York. HarperCollins.

Maestro, B. (1996). *Coming to America: The Story of Immigration*. New York. Scholastic.

Parr, T. (2003). *The Family Book*. London. Little, Brown.

Peacock, C.A. (2000). *Mommy Far, Mommy Near: An Adoption Story*. Morton Grove, IL. Albert Whitman.

Woodson, J. (2001). *The Other Side*. New York. Penguin.

American Eskimo

Bania, M. (2002). *Kumak's House*. Portland, OR. Alaska Northwest Books.

Ekoomiac, N. (1992). *Arctic Memories*. New York. Holt.

Joosse, B. (1991). *Mama, Do You Love Me?* San Francisco. Chronicle Books.

Asian

Bishop, C.H., & Wiese, K. (1996). *Five Chinese Brothers*. New York. Penguin.

Coerr, E., & Himler, R. (1999). *Sadako and the Thousand Paper Cranes, Vol 1*. New York. Penguin.

Demi. (1996). *The Empty Pot*. New York. Holt.

Lin, G. (2004). *Kite Flying*. New York. Random House.

Louie, A.L. (1996). *Yeh-Shen: A Cinderella Story from China*. New York. Penguin.

Martin, R., et. al. (1998). *The Brave Little Parrot*. New York. Penguin.

Say, A. (1993). *Grandfather's Journey*. Boston. Houghton Mifflin.

Yolen, J., & Young, E. (1998). *Emperor and the Kite*. New York. Penguin.

Young, E., & Adams, T. (2004). *The Lost Horse: A Chinese Folktale*. New York. Harcourt.

Young, E. (1996). *Lon Po Po: A Red Riding Hood Story from China*. New York. Penguin.

Irish

Daly, J. (2005). *Fair, Brown, and Trembling: An Irish Cinderella Story*. New York. Farrar, Straus, and Giroux.

dePaola, T. (1997). *Jamie O'Rourke and the Big Potato*. New York. Penguin.

dePaola, T. (1994). *Patrick: Patron Saint of Ireland*. New York. Holiday House.

Gleeson, B. (2005). *Finn McCoul*. Edina, MN. ABDO Publishing Co.

Krull, K. (2004). *A Pot O'Gold: A Treasury of Irish Stories, Poetry, and Folktales*. New York. Hyperion.

Yezerski, T.F. (1998). *Together in Pinecone Patch*. New York. Farrar, Straus and Giroux.

Italian

Creech, S. (2005). *Granny Torrelli Makes Soup*. New York. HarperCollins.

dePaola, T. (1979). *Strega Nona*. New York. Simon & Schuster.

dePaola, T. (1980). *The Legend of Old Befana*. New York. Harcourt.

dePaola, T. (1996). *Tony's Bread*. New York. Penguin.

Francia, G., et al. (2007). *Alex and Penny Ballooning over Italy*. Vercelli, Italy: White Star Publishers.

Jamaican

Hoffman, M. (1991). *Amazing Grace*. New York: Dial.

Wallace, S. *A Little Bending*. New Bern, NC. Trafford Publishing.

Jewish

Fowles, S. (2003). *The Bachelor and the Bean*. New York. Farrar, Straus and Giroux.

Gilman, P. (1993). *Something from Nothing*. New York. Scholastic.

Oberman, S. (1994). *Always Prayer Shawl*. Honesdale, PA. Boyds Mills Press.

Polacco, P. (2001). *The Keeping Quilt*. New York. Simon & Schuster.

Schwartz, H. (1999). *Journey to Paradise: And Other Jewish Tales*. Jerusalem, Israel: Pitspopany Press.

Silverman, E. (2003). *Raisel's Riddle*. New York. Farrar, Straus and Giroux.

Latino

Alvarez, J. (2002). *How Tia Lola Came to (Visit) Stay.* New York. Bantam Doubleday Dell.

Dorros, A. (1997). *Abuela.* New York. Penguin.

Ehlert, L., & Prince, A. (2003). *Moon Rope/ Un Lazo a La Luna.* New York. Harcourt.

Garza, C.L. (2000). *In My Family; En Mi Familia.* San Francisco. Children's Book Press.

Jimenez, F. (1997). *The Circuit: Stories from the Life of a Migrant Child.* Albuquerque. University of New Mexico Press.

Johnston, T., & Winter, J. (2000). *Day of the Dead.* New York. Harcourt.

Kalnay, F. (1993). *Chucaro: Wild Pony of the Pampa.* New York: Walker.

Mora, P. (1997). *A Birthday Basket for Tia.* New York. Simon & Schuster.

Reynold, A. (2005). *Chicks and Salsa.* London: Bloomsbury Publishing.

Soto, G. (1996). *Too Many Tamales.* New York. Penguin.

Native American

Bruchac, J. (1998). *The Earth under Sky Bear's Feet: Native American Poems of the Land.* New York: Penguin.

Bruchac, J., London, J. (1997). *Thirteen Moons on Turtle's Back: A Native American Year of Moons.* New York. Penguin.

dePaola, T. (1996). *The Legend of Bluebonnet: An Old Texas Tale.* New York. Penguin.

Desimini, L. (1996). *How the Stars Fell into the Sky.* Boston. Houghton Mifflin.

Goble, P. (2005). *All Our Relatives: Traditional Native American Thoughts about Nature.* Bloomington, IN. World Wisdom.

Goble, P. (1993). *The Girl Who Loved Wild Horses.* New York. Simon & Schuster.

Jeffers, S. (2002). *Brother Eagle, Sister Sky.* New York. Penguin.

Lind, M. (2003). *Bluebonnet Girl.* New York. Holt.

Lourie, P. (2007). *Lost World of the Anasazi: Exploring the Mysteries of Chaco Canyon.* Honesdale, PA. Boyds Mill Press.

Martin, R. (1998). *Rough Face Girl.* New York. Penguin.

Russian

Hesse, K. (1993). *Letters from Rifka.* New York. Penguin.

Lewis, P.P. (1999). *At the Wish of a Fish: A Russian Folktale.* New York. Simon & Schuster.

Mikolaycak, C. (1997). *Bearhead: A Russian Folktale.* New York. Holiday House.

Polacco, P. (1995). *Babushka's Doll.* New York. Simon & Schuster.

CHILDREN'S SPECIAL NEEDS

Communication Problems (Speech and Language Differences)

Cisneros, S. (1997). *Hair/Pelitos.* New York: Bantam Doubleday Dell.

Lester, H. (2002). *Hooway for Wodney Wat.* New York. Walter Lorraine Books.

Lovell, P. (2001). *Stand Tall, Molly Lou Melon.* New York. Penguin.

Reisser, L. (1996). *Margaret y Margarita.* New York. HarperCollins.

Physical Disabilities (visual, hearing, physical)

Chillemi, S. (2006). *My Daddy Has Epilepsy.* Lulu.com.

Konigsburg, E.L. (1998). *A View from Saturday.* New York. Simon & Schuster.

Meyer, D.J. (1997). *Views from Our Shoes: Growing Up with a Brother or Sister with Special Needs.* Bethesda, MD. Woodbine House.

Millman, I. (2002). *Moses Goes to a Concert.* New York. Farrar, Straus and Giroux.

Mulder, L. (1992). *Sarah and Puffle: A Story for Children about Diabetes.* Washington, DC: American Psychological Association.

Peterson, J. W., & Ray, D. (1984). *I Have A Sister—My Sister Is Deaf.* New York. HarperCollins.

Thomas, P. (2002). *Don't Call Me Special.* Hauppauge, NY. Barron's Educational Series.

Willis, J., & Ross, T. (2000). *Susan Laughs.* New York. Holt.

Learning Disabilities

Dahl, R. (1994). *Vicar of Nibbleswicke.* New York. Penguin.

Fleming, V. (1993). *Be Good to Eddie Lee.* New York. Penguin.

Gantos, J. (2000). *Joey Pigza Swallowed the Key.* New York. HarperCollins.

Gehret, J.M. (1996). *Don't-Give-Up-Kid: And Learning Differences.* Fairport, NY. Verbal Images Press.

Janover, C. (2004). *Josh: A Boy with Dyslexia.* Lincoln, NE. iUniverse.

Kraus, R. (1994). *Leo the Late Bloomer.* New York. HarperCollins.

Lears, L. (1998). *Ian's Walk: A Story about Autism.* Morton Grove, IL. Albert Whitman.

Lears, L. (1999). *Waiting for Mr. Goose.* Morton Grove, IL. Albert Whitman.

Lord, C. (2007). *Rules.* New York. Scholastic.

Shriver, M. (2001). *What's Wrong with Timmy?* New York: Little, Brown.

Smith, M. (1997). *Pay Attention, Slosh!* Morton Grove, IL. Albert Whitman.

Thompson, M. (1996). *Andy and His Yellow Frisbee.* Bethesda, MD. Woodbine House.

Quality Television Programs with Associated Children's Books

Paula Batsiyan

ARTHUR

Brown, M. (2000). *Arthur's fire drill*. New York: Random House.

Brown, M. (1999). *Arthur's new baby book*. New York: Random House.

Brown, M. (1998). *Arthur tricks the tooth fairy*. New York: Random House.

Brown, M. (1996). *Glasses for D. W.* New York: Random House.

Brown, M. (1996). *Arthur's reading race*. New York: Random House.

THE BERENSTAIN BEARS

Berenstain S., & Berenstain, J. (1997). *Berenstain Bears and the homework hassle*. New York: Random House.

Berenstain S., & Berenstain, J. (1992). *Berenstain Bears and the trouble with grownups*. New York: Random House.

Berenstain S., & Berenstain, J. (1991). *Berenstain Bears get the gimmies*. New York: Random House.

Berenstain S., & Berenstain, J. (1989). *Berenstain Bears and too much vacation*. New York: Random House.

CURIOUS GEORGE

Rey, M., & Rey, H.A. (1977). *Curious George flies a kite*. Boston: Houghton Mifflin.

Rey, M., & Rey, H.A. (1974). *Curious George takes a job*. Boston: Houghton Mifflin.

Rey, M., & Rey, H.A. (1973). *Curious George rides a bike*. Boston: Houghton Mifflin.

DORA THE EXPLORER

Beinstein, P. (2002). *Count with Dora!: A counting book in English and Spanish*. New York: Simon & Schuster.

Ricci, C. (2002). *Dora the Explorer: Good night Dora!* New York: Simon & Schuster.

Willson, S. (2002). *Dora the Explorer: Little star*. New York: Simon & Schuster.

FRANKLIN

Bourgeois, P. (1999). *Franklin's class trip*. New York: Scholastic.

Bourgeois, P. (1997). *Franklin's bad day*. New York: Scholastic.

Bourgeois, P. (1997). *Franklin rides a bike*. New York: Scholastic.

Bourgeois, P. (1986). *Franklin in the dark*. New York: Scholastic.

MAURICE SENDAK'S LITTLE BEAR

Minarik, E. H. (1984). *Little Bear's friend* (I Can Read Book Series). New York: HarperCollins.

Minarik, E. H. (1984). *A kiss for Little Bear* (I Can Read Book Series). New York: HarperCollins.

Minarik, E. H. (1979). *Little Bear's visit* (I Can Read Book Series). New York: HarperCollins.

Minarik, E. H. (1978). *Father Bear comes home* (I Can Read Book Series). New York: HarperCollins.

Minarik, E. H. (1978). *Little Bear* (I Can Read Book Series). New York: HarperCollins.

MAISY

Cousins, L. (2001). *Doctor Maisy.* Cambridge, MA: Candlewick Press.

Cousins, L. (2001). *Maisy's morning on the farm.* Cambridge, MA: Candlewick Press.

Cousins, L. (2001). *Maisy at the fair.* Cambridge, MA: Candlewick Press.

Cousins, L. (1999). *Where is Maisy?* Cambridge, MA: Candlewick Press.

MAX & RUBY

Wells, R. (2002). *Max and Ruby's busy week.* New York: Penguin Putnam.

Wells, R. (2000). *Max's dragon shirt.* New York: Penguin Putnam.

Wells, R. (2000). *Max's chocolate chicken.* New York: Penguin Putnam.

Wells, R. (1998). *Max and Ruby in Pandora's box.* New York: Penguin Putnam.

Literacy-Related Computer Software and Websites for Children

Kathryn Minto

■ WEBSITES

American Folklore

www.americanfolklore.net/

Description: This folklore site contains retellings of American folktales, Native American myths and legends, tall tales, weather folklore, and ghost stories from each of the 50 United States. You can read about all sorts of famous characters, like Paul Bunyan, Pecos Bill, Daniel Boone, and many more. According to the developer, it is a "site best viewed while eating marshmallows around a campfire under a starry sky."

Kids@Random

www.randomhouse.com/kids/

Description: Read sections of Random House books, learn about your favorite authors and characters, play games or enter writing contests. There is a multitude of things for kids to explore when they enter this site. Parents and teachers will enjoy it, too!

Kidsreads.com

www.Kidsreads.com

Description: Kidsreads is a great place for kids to find out about their favorite books, series, and authors. There are reviews of the newest titles, interviews and special features on great books, and for even more reading fun they have trivia games, word scrambles, and tons of contests.

PBS Kids

pbskids.org/

Description: This website gives you access to stories, games, songs, and contests. Kids can choose their favorite shows and either read or play along with favorite characters. Plus, there are options for teachers and parents to explore subjects that they can then share with children.

Reading Zone

http://.umich.edu/div/kidspace/browse/rzn

Description: Students can read a variety of stories and poems and research their favorite authors through links to the authors' websites. This site also provides interviews with some well-known children's authors.

Sesame Workshop

www.sesameworkshop.org

Description: This Sesame Street site provides games, stories, art, music, and the opportunity for children to e-mail their favorite characters, as well as helpful information for parents and teachers.

Between the Lions: Get Wild about Reading

pbskids.org/lions

Description: Tied to the popular PBS show, this site offers fun stories, games, and songs that all focus on literacy development. This site is also a great resource for teachers who might want to use these literacy-based games and songs in their classroom.

Intercultural E-mail Classroom Connections

www.iecc.org

Description: Students can sign up for key pals any-where in the world. Great way to promote leisure writing.

HarperChildrens.com

www.harperchildrens.com

Description: This site explains the process of how a book is made to children. It has links to the web-sites of favorite authors, contains games, features books, and contains book-related activity pages.

LiteracyCenter.Net—The Early Childhood Education Network

www.literacycenter.net

Description: This site offers games that allow children to work with letter identification, shapes, writing, word building, numbers, colors, and typing, each at the appropriate developmental level. These games are available in English, Spanish, German, and French.

■ SOFTWARE

Smart Steps

Grade 1

Description: Here is a program that offers activities in reading, math, science, creativity, and more! It features 300 nonstop learning games along with 4 interactive reading books, a word processor, and music. This child-friendly program offers kids a place to become lifelong learners.

System Required: Win 98, Me, 2000 or XP, Pen-tium 120 Mhz, 32 MB RAM, 4x CD, sound card

Availability: Global Software Publishing

Bailey's Book House

Grades PreK through 1

Description: Students learn about letter names and sounds, rhyming words, sentence building, and much more. The activities included help students commu-nicate and make sense of the world around them.

System Required: Win 98, Me, 2000 Professional or XP, Pentium II 200 Mhz, 4 MB RAM (8 MB rec-ommended), 2x CD, color monitor

Availability: River Deep

Blue's Clues

Grade Kindergarten

Description: Blue's house becomes a pretend kindergarten classroom with games and activities in

science, telling time, rhyming, art, creativity, math, and more!

System Required: Win 98, Me, XP, Pentium II 233 Mhz, 64 MB RAM, 8x CD, video card

Availability: InfoGrames

Clifford the Big Red Dog Learning Activities

Grades PreK and 1

Description: Clifford and his pals make learning really fun with this interactive learning world. Chil-dren will build skills in many areas, including word recognition, sentence structure, rhyming, critical thinking, and sound patterns and rhythm.

System Required: Win 98, Me, XP, Pentium 166 Mhz, 32 MB RAM, 8x CD, sound card, printer (optional)

Availability: Scholastic

Preschool Parade

Grade: PreK and 1

Description: Children work with clowns and ani-mals to learn the alphabet, counting, shapes, and more.

System Required: MacPlus or higher; 1 MB RAM; System 7.0 or later; hard drive; sound card recom-mended; Win 95/98/Me/2000

Availability: Nordic Software

I SPY Junior Puppet Playhouse

Grade: PreK to 2

Description: These riddles based on the *I SPY* books emphasize listening and reading skills as well as creativity.

System Required: Win 95/98/Me/2000/XP, 16 MB RAM, Pentium 90 or faster; Mac version available; sound card

Availability: Scholastic

Stickybear's Reading Room

Grade: PreK to 3

Description: This bilingual program in Spanish and English includes activities in sentence building, word matching, and word finding.

System Required: Mac DOS System 6.07 with 2 MB RAM or System 7.0 with 4 MB RAM; Win 95/98; color monitor

Availability: Optimum Resource

Professional Associations and Related Journals Dealing with Early Literacy

Elizabeth Freitag

What we have learned over the years concerning learning theory and early literacy development is due to research by college professors and classroom teachers. Professional associations hold conferences and publish journals to inform and move the field forward. This appendix provides a list of such groups and journals, along with other publications dealing with early literacy, for future study and reference.

American Library Association (ALA), 50 East Huron Street, Chicago, IL 60611, www.ala.org

American Montessori Society, Inc. (AMS), 281 Park Avenue South, 6th Floor, New York, NY 10010, www.amshq.org

Association for Childhood Education International (ACEI), 17904 Georgia Avenue, Suite 215, Olney, MD 20832, www.acei.org; journals: *Childhood Education; Journal of Research in Childhood Education*

Child Welfare League of America, Inc. (CWLA), 440 First Street NW, 3rd Floor, Washington, DC 20001, www.cwla.org; journal: *Child Welfare*

Children's Bureau, Office of Child Development, U.S. Department of Health, Education and Welfare, Washington, DC 20201; journal: *Children Today*

Gordon and Breach Science Publishers, Inc., PO Box 32160, Newark, NJ 07102; journal: *Early Child Development and Care*

High/Scope Educational Research Foundation, 600 North River Street, Ypsilanti, MI 48198-2898, www.highscope.org; publications, videos, research, professional development

International Reading Association (IRA), 800 Barksdale Road, PO Box 8139, Newark, DE 19711, www.reading .org; journals: *The Reading Teacher; Reading Research Quarterly*; brochures, pamphlets, and monographs

National Association for the Education of Young Children (NAEYC), 1509 16th Street NW, Washington, DC 20036, www.naeyc.org; journals: *Young Children; Early Childhood Research Quarterly*; pamphlets and monographs

National Center for Family Literacy, 325 West Main Street, Suite 300, Louisville, KY 40202-4237, www.famlit.org; newsletter: *Momentum*

National Child Care Information Center, 243 Church Street NW, 2nd Floor, Vienna, VA 22180, www.nccic.org

National Council of Teachers of English (NCTE), 1111 Kenyon Road, Urbana, IL 61801, www.ncte.org; journal: *Language Arts*

National Education Association, 1201 16th Street NW, Washington, DC 20036, www.nea.org; journal: *NEA Today*; magazine: *Tomorrow's Teachers*

National Even Start Association, 2225 Camino del Rio South, Suite A, San Diego, CA 92108, www. evenstart.org; journal: *Family Literacy Forum*

National Head Start Association, 1651 Prince Street, Alexandria, VA 22314, www.nhsa.org; publication: *Children and Families Magazine*

National Reading Conference (NRC), 11 East Hubbard St., Chicago, IL 60603; journal: *Journal of Literacy Research*

Office of Early Childhood Development, 717 14th Street NW, Suite 450, Washington, DC 20005

Reach Out and Read National Center, 29 Mystic Avenue, Somerville, MA 02145, www.reachoutandread.org

Reading Is Fundamental, 1825 Connecticut Avenue NW, Washington, DC 20009, www.rif.org; newsletter: *Read All about It*

Scholastic, Inc., 555 Broadway, New York, NY 10012, www.scholastic.com; publications: *Early Childhood Today; Instructor*

Society for Research in Child Development (SRCD), 5750 Ellis Avenue, Chicago, IL 60637, www.srcd.org; journal: *Child Development*

Literacy Software and Websites for Teachers

Paula Batsiyan

▨ SOFTWARE

Cloze Wizard

Description: This software lets teachers quickly and easily produce cloze passage exercises, as well as a variety of other literacy-based worksheets. Since students often must see text in several different formats to comprehend the meaning of terms and phrases used, Cloze Wizard can be used to supplement classroom instruction.

Hardware: Windows 95, 98, ME, NT/4, 2000, 2003 & XP; MacOS 9 & 10.1 or later

Availability: Rush Software

▨ STORYTOWN

Description: A great tool to promote emerging literacy, this software allows teachers to create, edit, and assign talking, animated stories or use the stories provided by the program. Students can play stories over and over and stories can be printed for in-class activities. The software also helps teachers create quizzes to test reading comprehension, which students can then take on the computer and save for the teacher to review.

Hardware: Win 98, ME, 2000, XP

Availability: Campus Tech

▨ WEBSITES

www.atozteacherstuff.com

Description: This teacher-created site provides teachers with lesson plans, thematic units, teacher tips, discussion forums, downloadable teaching materials and eBooks, printable worksheets and blacklines, emergent reader books, themes, and more.

www.songsforteaching.com

Description: This site contains an abundance of pages with ideas for integrating music into the curriculum. It contains lyrics, sound clips, and teaching suggestions. Songs from a wide variety of popular artists are presented by academic subject.

www.readwritethink.org

Description: Run by the International Reading Association, this website provides teachers with access to the most current, highest-quality practices and resources in reading and language arts instruction. It contains lessons, an overview of IRA/NCTE standards, web resources, and student materials.

www.carolhurst.com

Description: This website is a compilation of reviews of wonderful books for children, ideas on how to utilize books in the classroom, and collections of books and activities dealing with particular subjects, curriculum areas, themes, and professional topics.

www.readingrockets.org

Description: Reading Rockets presents an abundance of reading strategies, lessons, and activities designed to help young children learn how to read and to help those who can already read improve their reading skills. The website consists of resources that support parents, teachers, and other educators in working with struggling readers who require extra help in essential reading and comprehension skills development.

www.thereadingnook.com

Description: This site provides teachers with lists of grade-leveled books to help select for independent reading and guided reading.

www.dltk-tech.com/minibooks/index.htm

Description. The teacher is provided with many literacy materials, but foremost are grade-leveled books to print out and use with children.

Integrated Language Arts Thematic Unit: Animals around the World

Paula Batsiyan

■ FACTUAL INFORMATION

What Is an Animal?

Any living thing that is not a plant is an animal, including humans. There are many different types of animals, such as birds, fish, insects, farm animals, reptiles, amphibians, and mammals.

Where Do Animals Live?

Animals live all over the world in every type of *environment*. The place in which an animal lives is called its *habitat*. Animals live in many different places all over the world. For example, camels live in the desert. Lions, monkeys, elephants, and tigers live in the jungle. Bears, deer, foxes, and chipmunks live in the forest. Mountain lions, eagles, and llamas live in the mountains. Dolphins, whales, sharks, and different kinds of fish live in water. Sea lions, polar bears, and penguins live at the North and South Poles. Pigs, sheep, chickens, and cows live on farms. All types of animals, from mammals to amphibians, live in zoos. Humans and their pets, such as cats, dogs, hamsters, and small fish, live in houses.

What Do Animals Eat?

Different animals have different nutritional needs. Some animals, such as rabbits, giraffes, and elephants are herbivores; they eat plants. Animals such as lions, tigers, bears, and wolves are carnivores; they rely on eating meat for the nutrition they need. Animals such as humans and monkeys are omnivores; they eat both plants and animals. Many animals are mammals; they give birth to live young and mothers produce milk with which to feed their babies.

What Do We Call Male, Female, and Baby Animals?

Many baby animals have names different from adults of the same *species*. For example, a baby cat is called a kitten, a baby dog is called a puppy, and a baby duck is called a duckling. Baby horses are called foals; baby lions, tigers, and bears are called cubs; baby deer are called fawns; and baby geese are called goslings. Even male and female animals are referred to in different ways. For example, when we say cow we are referring to a female; the males are called bulls. The same thing can be said for seals; the females are called cow seals and the males are called bull seals. When we say lion, we are referring to a male; the females are called lionesses. Deer is the name of a species; however, the females are called does and the males are called bucks.

What Different Roles Do Animals Play around the World?

Animals live all over the world and play different roles in different cultures. For example, dogs are kept as pets, work with police and firefighters, and work as seeing-eye dogs in the United States, but are used to transport people and sleds in colder regions of the world such as Alaska. In the United States, cows are used for milk, meat, and leather, but in India, cows are subject to respect, and religious ceremonies are held in their honor. Elephants are usually seen in zoos and perform in circuses in the United States, but in underdeveloped parts of the world such as Africa, they are used as transportation, as are camels, donkeys, and mules. Insects have many functions in the United States; bees are used for honey, certain insects are used in gardens because they eat other insects that eat plants and crops, students raise insects to learn about them in school, and so on. In other parts of the world however, insects perform different roles. In many cultures across Africa, Asia, and Latin America, insects are a traditional food. In China, silkworms are used to make silk.

Were There Animals in the Past That Do Not Exist Today?

Some animals have become scarce due to hunters killing so many of them or because their natural habitats have been destroyed. Several species are now extinct, such as dinosaurs, woolly mammoths, the American lion, the American cheetah, and the Texas grey wolf. These animals no longer exist on earth. Many species are endangered or in danger of becoming extinct, such as Asian and African elephants, blue whales, panda bears, and gorillas. Zoos are very important because they try to breed endangered animals to save them from becoming extinct.

What Are Some Jobs That Have to Do with Animals?

There are many important jobs that deal with animals. Zoo keepers take care of animals that live in the zoo. They feed them, clean their habitats, and check in on the animals. Usually, each zoo keeper takes care of one particular kind of animal. Veterinarians are animal doctors. They help animals that are sick, deliver baby animals, and check the health of animals to make sure they are healthy and well taken care of. Animal trainers train animals to be around people and do interesting tricks. They often work with animals in the circus and in the movies. Animal scientists work with animals in order to learn about them. Their job is to find out where they live, what and when they eat, how and when they sleep, how they are different from and similar to other animals, how they may be able to help other animals, and the like. People working in pet stores and animal shelters are responsible for taking care of the animals, cleaning their cages, playing with the animals, and finding the animals good homes. Animal rights activists work to make sure that all animals are safe. They fight to keep animals from being killed by hunters and to keep their habitats intact.

▪ NEWSLETTER TO PARENTS ABOUT ANIMALS AROUND THE WORLD

Dear Parents:

Your child will be participating in a unit that investigates a variety of animals from around the world. This unit will consist of lessons on the different types of animals, where in the world they live, their habitats (i.e., jungle, forest, sea, etc.), what they eat, their young, and the different roles animals play all over the world. Students will also learn about endangered and extinct animals, as well as the jobs that deal with animals.

The Animals around the World unit will cover all subject areas: play, art, music, social studies, science, math, and literacy (reading, writing, listening, and oral language), which the theme will integrate. Many of the fun and exciting activities we do at school can also be implemented at home with your child.

At School and at Home

Art: Art serves as a great learning experience, improving children's hand–eye coordination and visual discrimination skills. Children will explore and experiment with various art materials while engaging in various art activities. In art, students will gain an appreciation for creativity and originality by designing collages and multicultural jewelry based on animals and their habitats all over the world. Play dough will be used to sculpt real and/or make-believe animals. Students will also make colorful masks and piñatas in the shape of animals. You can encourage your child to use his or her imagination by providing a variety of materials and mediums with which the child can create animal-inspired art at home. Encourage your child to explore with different materials, rather than supplying an adult model to copy.

Science: We will begin to investigate and understand the world of animals. Students will observe our class pets and take care of them. We will be using science kits in which students will raise tadpoles to learn about hibernation and butterflies to learn about metamorphosis. Charts and journals will be used to record observations and progress. Students will learn about the different kinds of foods animals eat and will create Very Own Word cards to help them remember what they've learned. Children will learn about the names we use for baby animals and will sort pictures of baby animals and adult animals, matching the babies to the parents, using new vocabulary learned to discuss their sorts. Afterward, students will create a class book containing pictures of adult and baby animals and the words we use for them. Encourage your child to engage in science by taking nature walks and discussing the animals you see.

Social Studies: Children will engage in several social studies skills while learning about animals. Students will learn how to use maps and about endangered animals. They will create their own postcards for the country of their choice that incorporate an endangered animal from that country. They will explore labels attached to different animal groups (i.e., dogs chase cats) and if these labels are always correct (i.e., my dog sleeps with my cat). This activity will be connected to stereotypes given to groups of people. Encourage your child to engage in social studies at home by providing informational books and magazines such as *National Geographic* and by reading and discussing them with your child.

Math: Children will use animal counting books, animal pattern cards, different-size animal figurines, pattern blocks, yardsticks, rulers, and the like, to integrate the study of animals with the study of math. Students will pretend they are farmers and/or zoo keepers and work with finances. They will come up with a budget for our class pets. Students will also create their own multicultural animal number books. We will use the rhyme *Five Little Speckled Frogs* to learn how to count backward. Children will make frog finger puppets to take home and recite the rhyme to their families. Make sure to ask your child about this! Children will also compare and classify animals using several characteristics (i.e., size, color, habitat, food, role, etc.) and use the groups they've formed to perform addition and subtraction. At home, you can count sheep with your child before bed, sing songs like *Five Little Monkeys*, and practice mathematical concepts each day.

Literacy: Your child will be reading many different genres of books and writing about animals from all over the world. Students will be encouraged to experiment with reading and writing and will have many opportunities to participate in authentic literacy activities, such as prop stories, roll movies, puppet shows, and others. Students will be encouraged to tell stories on their own and will be given time each day to read and write independently. At home you can read stories, informational books and magazines, or poems related to animals all over the world with your child. Go through magazines; discuss and cut out pictures of animals for your child to bring to class. Have your child read to you using illustrations in books and have him or her retell stories that you have read. Please do not hesitate to ask me for assistance in locating quality books related to animals.

We Need Your Help

We would appreciate your assistance with our Animals around the World theme. If you have any materials at home that would relate to our unit (e.g., small pets, multicultural costumes or jewelry, photos of animals of any kind, books or magazines about animals, stuffed animals, animal figurines, etc.) that you are willing to lend to us, please send them to school with your child. If you would like to come to school as a helper and assist with some of our activities, please get in touch with me so that we can set up a date and time. We will also need helpers for our culminating trip to the zoo and our Animals around the World Fair.

Other Activities to Do with Your Child

Take your child to a park, lake, farm, zoo, or pet store. Discuss what you see and ask your child questions. Point out environmental print such as signs (e.g., Please Do Not Feed the Animals) and have your child read the signs with you. Visit family or friends who have pets with your child and have discussions with them about taking care of their animal(s). Go on nature walks and take pictures of different animals with your child. Listen to animal songs and read books and magazines about animals.

Ask your child to write about or draw an animal he or she heard, learned, or read about in school or with you.

Help your child keep a Very Own Words box or journal related to the activities done in school and at home.

Help your child keep a scrapbook of his or her work on animals.

If you have any questions about the unit or have any additional ideas you would like to share, please contact me. If you are in a profession that is related to our theme, please consider coming to class and talking to us.

Sincerely,
Paula Batsiyan

PREPARING THE CLASSROOM ENVIRONMENT

To set the unit on Amazing Animals in motion, arrange the room so that the theme is clear to those who enter. Start with a few of the following ideas, and continue to include others as the unit evolves. Display environmental signs and labels regarding a variety of animals wherever possible.

1. *Dramatic Play:* The dramatic play center can be turned into a zoo, a farm, or a veterinarian's office. As a zoo, the center should include blocks, nets, boots, gloves, plants, pails, plastic shovels or scoops, hay, pictures of animals and zookeepers, stuffed animals, plastic animals, writing materials (such as pencils, pens, and markers), poster board, construction paper, maps, name tags, ticket stubs, and play money. As a farm, the center should include egg cartons, milk cartons, wool items, boots, gloves, pails, shovels or scoops, plants, baskets, plastic fruits and vegetables, plastic and stuffed animals, fences, aprons, a sales stand, a cash register, receipt paper, and play money. As a veterinarian's office, the center should include a stethoscope, white lab coats, rubber gloves, play syringes, cotton balls, Q-tips, Popsicle sticks, plastic jars and containers, animal treats, plastic and stuffed animals, veterinary brochures and magazines, an appointment book, a telephone, play credit cards and money, paper, pencils, and pens.

2. *Block Area:* The block area can be converted into a pet store and/or a circus. Add animal figurines, stuffed animals, balls, hoops, rope, large plastic containers, shredded newspaper, people figurines, small paper lunch bags, markers, crayons, pens, pencils, poster board for signs, ticket stubs, animal magazines, a cash register, receipt paper, and play money.

3. *Outdoor Play:* A circus can be created outside. Playground items can easily be converted into circus areas. For example, a jungle gym can become a trapeze. A balance beam can become a tight rope. Jump ropes, balls, and Hula-Hoops can be used as props. Bring out a large sack of animal figurines and have students create a ticket window, tickets, and brochures. Bring out a play cash register and play money, and play circus music.

4. *Music:* A variety of multicultural songs about animals all over the world and at zoos, farms, pet stores, and circuses can be added to the music center. All tapes and/or CDs should be supplemented by their written lyrics in both English and Spanish with colorful, descriptive pictures posted on the wall. Props to act out the songs are also great motivators. Students should also be encouraged to write, sing, and act out their own songs about animals. (For a little treat while listening to music, provide students with animal crackers to snack on and milk that comes from cows).

5. *Art:* In art, students can use magazines, newspapers, macaroni, beads, markers, crayons, colored pencils, construction paper, and other various materials to make habitat collages. Have each student pick a habitat from around the world and make a collage of animals that live there. Play dough can also be added so that students may sculpt their own real animals and/or make-believe animals and talk about their characteristics and how they are similar or different from other animals. Students can also make colorful piñatas in the shape of animals and stuff them with candy in the shape of animals, such as gummy bears and chocolate bunnies. These piñatas can be hung around the classroom and taken home at the end of the unit.

6. *Science:* Bring in one or two class pets that students can observe and take care of, such as a hamster, fish, rabbit, or turtle. Order science kits such as those in which students would raise tadpoles or butterflies. Charts and journals should be used to record observations and progress.

7. *Social Studies:* Include pictures of adult and baby animals, a map of the world, and a map of a zoo. Pictures can be attached to maps by pushpins. Include informational books and magazines in both English and Spanish on animals around the world and jobs that deal with animals as well.

8. *Math:* Include animal counting books, animal pattern cards, different-size animal figurines, pattern blocks, yardsticks, rulers, and the like. Have students pretend they are farmers and/or zoo keepers and have them work with finances. Have students come up with a budget for the class pet(s). Students can also create their own multicultural animal number books.

9. *Literacy Center*
   a. *Writing Center:* Materials should include various kinds of paper, pens, pencils, markers, crayons, pictures of animals, books about animals, index cards for Very Own words, chart paper for brainstorming activities, action pictures for picture prompts, animal-shaped blank books, and materials with which to create a class animal alphabet book.
   b. *Library Corner:* Include multicultural books and magazines of all genres that include animals (see bibliography), prop stories, roll movies, felt stories, wordless picture books, taped stories with headphones, and animal puppets.

LIBRARY CORNER BOOKLIST WITH SUGGESTED ACTIVITIES

Aliki (1999). *My visit to the zoo*. New York: HarperCollins.

Andreae, G., Parker-Rees, G. (2001). *Giraffes can't dance*. London: Orchard Books.

Andreae, G., Wojtowycz, D. (2002). *Rumble in the jungle*. London: Orchard Books.

Bancroft, H. (1997). *Animals in winter*. New York: HarperCollins.

Barrett, J. (1988). *Animals should definitely not wear clothing*. New York: Simon & Schuster.

Berger, M., Berger, G. (1999). *Do whales have belly buttons: Questions and answers about whales and dolphins (Scholastic question & answer)*. New York: Scholastic.

Brown, M. (1957). *The three billy goats gruff*. New York: Harcourt Brace.

Campbell, R. (2007). *Dear zoo: A lift-the-flap book*. New York: Simon & Schuster.

Carle, E. (1969). *The very hungry caterpillar*. New York: Philomel.

Carle, E., Whipple, L. (1999). *Eric Carle's animals animals*. New York: Penguin.

Chanko, P. (1998). *Baby animals learn*. New York: Scholastic.

Collard, S. B. (1997). *Animal dads*. New York: Scholastic.

Cowley, J., Fuller, E. (2006). *Mrs. Wishy-Washy's farm*. New York: Penguin.

Cronin, D. (2000). *Click, clack, moo: Cows that type*. New York: Simon & Schuster.

Galdone, P. (1973). *The little red hen*. Boston: Houghton Mifflin.

Hamsa, B., Dunnington, T. (1985). *Animal babies*. New York: Scholastic.

Fleming, D. (2001). *Barnyard banter*. New York: Holt.

Jenkins, S. (2006). *Almost gone: The world's rarest animals (Lets-read-and-find-out series)*. New York: HarperCollins.

Keats, R. J. (1974). *Pet show*. New York: Aladdin.

Lauber, P., Keller, H. (1995). *Who eats what?: Food chains and food webs*. New York: HarperCollins.

Lenski, L. (1965). *The little farm*. New York: Henry Z. Walek.

Lionni, L. (1973). *Frederick*. New York: Random House.

Lionni, L., Mlawer, T. (translator). (2005). *Frederick (Spanish language ed.)*. New York: Lectorum Publications.

Lewin, T., Lewin, B. (2000). *Elephant quest*. New York: HarperCollins.

Little golden book collection: Animal tales. (2004). New York: Golden Books.

Lobel, A., Lizcano, P. (translator). (2000). *Sapo y sepo son amigos (Frog and toad are friends)*. Jesus Maria, Peru: Santillana S.A.

Maguire, G. (2006). *Leaping beauty: And other animal fairy tales*. New York: HarperCollins.

Martin, B., Carle, E. (1992). *Brown bear, brown bear, what do you see?* New York: Holt.

Martin, B., Carle, E. (1997). *Polar bear, polar bear, what do you hear?* New York: Holt.

Mora, P., Cushman, D. (2006). *Marimba! Animales from A to Z*. New York: Houghton Mifflin.

Numeroff, L., Bond, F. (1985). *If you give a mouse a cookie*. New York: HarperCollins.

Palatini, M., Whatley, B. (2003). *The perfect pet*. New York: HarperCollins.

Potter, B. (1902). *The tale of Peter Rabbit*. New York: Scholastic.

Relf, P., Stevenson, N. (1995). *The magic school bus hops home: A book about animal habitats*. New York: Scholastic.

Rey, M., Rey, H. A. (1998). *Curious George feeds the animals*. Boston: Houghton Mifflin.

Seuss, Dr., Rivera, C. (translator). (1967). *The cat in the hat (Spanish Beginner Book Series)*. New York: Random House.

Seymour, S. (2002). *Animals nobody loves.* New York: North-South Books.

Staff of National Geographic, McKay, G., McGhe, K. (2006). *National geographic encyclopedia of animals.* Washington, DC: National Geographic Society.

Steig, W., Puncel, M. (translator). (1997). *Doctor de soto* (Spanish Ed.). New York: Farrar, Straus and Giroux.

Taylor, B. (1998). *A day at the farm.* New York: DK.

Wallace, K. (2003). *Trip to the zoo (DK readers series).* New York: DK.

Walsh, M. (1997). *Do monkeys tweet?* Boston: Houghton Mifflin.

Wilson, K. (2002). *Bear snores on.* New York: Simon & Schuster.

INTRODUCTORY LESSON

Objective

A written message will provide for vocabulary development and sound–symbol associations. Print will be recognized as functional because it relays a message.

Activity: *Morning Message.* Introduce the students to the amazing animals unit by writing a message on the board. The message could look something like this:

"Today, we are going to begin learning about many different kinds of animals. We will discuss where they live, what they eat, the different roles they play around the world, and how to take care of them. We will learn about places where we can see the animals we learn about and jobs that deal with animals." Provide ELL students with a translation in their language. Read the message to the class, using a pointer to track the print. Afterward, discuss the content of the message, as well as the special words, letters, and sounds. Let students add to the message and ask questions. Do a morning message daily to inform students of special unit-related activities and to pose questions related to the unit for students to discuss and think about.

CONCEPTS ABOUT PRINT

Objective 1

Increase oral and sight vocabulary through a discussion involving the seeing and writing of Very Own Words. Knowledge of animal habitats will be gained.

Activity: *Very Own Words.* Before reading *The Magic School Bus Hops On: A Book about Animal Habitats,* ask students to brainstorm where they think animals might live and write

their ideas in a K-W-L chart under what students already know. Ask ELL students to name different habitats in their home language. You may also want to show pictures of different habitats and discuss where in the world these habitats can be found. Then ask students what questions they might have about animal homes and list those under what students would like to know. After reading the book, the children will discuss new, interesting, and possibly surprising information they learned from the book. List students' ideas on the K-W-L chart under what students have learned. Write each child's favorite animal in the book on a 3 × 5 index card and that animal's habitat on another index card to be stored in her or his Very Own Word container. Include both English and Spanish words for English language learners.

Objective 2

Increase sight vocabulary and the ability to follow directions by using a chart with functional environmental print.

Activity: *Environmental Print.* A helper chart will be made that lists jobs for students to perform in both English and Spanish with corresponding pictures. The chart should be located in a visible area and relate directly to the animal unit. Jobs may include the pet feeders who feed the class pets, the habitat patrol that cleans the class pets' habitats, the animal charity workers who collect items to donate to a class-selected animal charity, animal fact checkers, and the like.

Objective 3

An alphabet book that reviews many animal words learned in the unit will be created. Knowledge of letters, both vowels and consonants, and words that are identified with specific letters and sounds will be demonstrated.

Activity: *Amazing Animal Alphabet Book.* An alphabet book will be made and photocopied for each child in the class. Each letter will by symbolized by a different animal (e.g., A, armadillo; B, bird; C, chimpanzee; D, dog; E, elephant; F, fish), and a complete sentence will be written for each letter and animal (Armadillos live in _____). Have ELL students act as translators, making the book bilingual and easily read by all. The students will read the letters, words, and sentences with the teacher and with each other.

ORAL LANGUAGE

Objective 1

Speaking skills will be improved by speaking in complete sentences.

Activity: *Show and Tell.* Have students bring in different multicultural items that are related to animals (e.g., small pets, books, trinkets, jewelry, items found in nature, and stuffed animals) to display and discuss with the class. Another activity would be to have students share interesting experiences they may have had dealing with animals (e.g., a trip to the zoo, the pet store, or a veterinarian's office; a story about their pets or friends' pets; something interesting they saw on television).

Objective 2

Appropriate vocabulary for the level of maturity will be used when retelling a story.

Activity: *Story Retelling.* Read a story related to animals such as *The Very Hungry Caterpillar* (Carle, 1969) to the class using props such as a teacher- or class-made caterpillar (one that is hollow and can "eat") and plastic food found in the story, such as an apple, two pears, and three plums. Encourage participation by having different children come up and "feed" the caterpillar. After reading the story, allow the class to retell the story using the props and then place the props in the library corner for children to use.

Objective 3

Language complexity will be increased through the use of adjectives. Students will gain knowledge about the characteristics of different animals.

Activity: *Webbing and Creating Poetry.* Brainstorm the characteristics of two or three different animals and provide a graphic representation for each animal with a web (see below) on the chalkboard. List the characteristics of each animal by writing adjectives to describe it. Encourage children to assist in putting together a poem for each animal by using the information on the web. Encourage children to read the poems to each other.

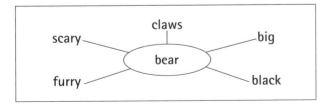

MOTIVATING READING AND WRITING

Objective 1

A story is read by a class parent to increase family literacy. Using the context of the story, outcomes will be predicted.

Activity: *Prop Story.* A story related to animals, such as *Brown Bear, Brown Bear, What Do You See?* (Martin & Carle, 1992), is read by a class parent using animal props that are in the book. Encourage participation by having the children use their knowledge of rhyme and context. Place props in the library corner for children to use.

Objective 2

A graphic organizer will be created to motivate interest and help children comprehend informational text. Students will learn about, compare, and contrast two different aquatic mammals.

Activity: *Venn Diagram.* Read *Do Whales Have Belly Buttons: Questions and Answers about Whales and Dolphins (Scholastic question & answer)* (Berger & Berger, 1999) and discuss the animal facts in the book. Next, have children work together to create a Venn diagram on the board, based on the information in the book about whales and dolphins. Afterward you can have the students make whale and dolphin stick puppets with which to act out a story that incorporates some of the information they have learned.

CONCEPTS ABOUT BOOKS

Objective 1

Learn to differentiate print from pictures and know what books are for.

Activity: *Big Book.* Create a class Big Book that contains pictures of and sentences about each child's favorite animal. Have English language learners write in both their home language and in English. When the book is completed, read the book together as a class. Place the Big Book in the library corner for repeated readings.

Objective 2

See and understand that print is read from left to right.

Activity: *Poetry Reading.* Display an animal poem (e.g., use a poem from *Rumble in the Jungle*, Andreae & Wojtowycz, 2002) on a large piece of chart paper and echo-read it with the class. Use a pointer to show that print is read from left to right. Have students act out the poem either on their own or with props, and then create a class poem to display and read in the same manner. You may want to include a Spanish poem and its translation in English for ELL students as well.

PHONICS

Objective 1

Learn about word families by singing a song about animals.

Activity: Let's Rhyme with the Animals. Sing the song "Let's Rhyme with the Animals" by Ron Brown. Ask students what word families they heard in the song. For each word family, write the animal at the top (dog, cat, pig, and cow) and its rhyming words in the song below it on the board and ask students to name some other words that fall into these word families. Have students name some other animals that belong to word families, such as fish, snake, bee, or duck, and list words that belong to the same word families. Then sing the song again, adding the word families the class came up with.

Objective 2

Learn that words are made up of syllables. Gain phonemic awareness by listening to animal words and segmenting (clapping) syllables.

Activity: Syllable Clap. Talk with children about why knowing about syllables can help them when they read and write. Ask them to clap with you as you say several words related to animals, making sure to also include words for where animals live all over the world. Begin with one-syllable words (e.g., dog, bat, fish, zoo, Spain), then move on to two syllables (rabbit, zebra, circus, Asia, Japan), three syllables (habitat, chimpanzee, Africa, Mexico), and so on. You may want to show pictures for the words for ELL students. Then ask students to say other animal-related words with one syllable, then two, three, four, and so on, and ask the class to say and clap the syllables in these words. Include a few animal words in the home language(s) of your ELL students and have them tell the class what the words mean and then have the class clap the syllables.

COMPREHENSION

Objective 1

Learn about story structure by identifying story elements (setting, theme, characters, plot episodes, resolution).

Activity: Story Structure. You will already have read *The Three Billy Goats Gruff* (Brown, 1957) in the past. Before reading the story a second time, ask children to try to remember when and where the story takes place and who the characters are. After reading the story the second time, have the children identify the three setting elements: *time, place,* and *characters.* Also have them identify other story elements, such as the *theme, plot episodes,* and *resolution.* Split the class into five groups and have each group work on a different heading for a class-made roll movie (Setting, Theme, Characters, Plot Episodes, and Resolution). Encourage each group to draw pictures and write narratives for their sections. After the groups have finished, have the class come together and have each group present their part of the roll movie. After presentations, put together the roll movie and review it with the class the next day. Put the roll movie in the library center for students to use.

Objective 2

Create a K-W-L chart (what they **K**now, what they **W**ant to know, and what they have **L**earned).

Activity: K-W-L Activity. Begin a discussion on winter and how it affects animals, as well as how animals adapt to winter. Also mention that it does not become cold in the winter all over the world and ask students to name some places that are always warm. Then ask children what they already know about animals in the winter. List their responses on chart paper under the heading "What We Know." Ask students what they might want to learn about animals in winter and list their responses on chart paper under the heading "What We Want To Know." Read a book such as *Animals in Winter* (Bancroft, 1997) that discusses animal behaviors in the winter months. After reading the book, hold a class discussion asking students to share what they have learned from the book. List children's responses under a new heading titled "What We Learned." Next, supply students with informational books and magazines in both English and Spanish (you may also want to let them use the computer) and challenge them to answer any questions under the heading "What We Want to Know" that have not been answered and to find new and interesting information to share with the class. Have students reconvene to discuss their findings and share any new interesting information they may have come across while you list their findings on the K-W-L chart. Post the K-W-L chart in the classroom for students to refer to.

WRITING
Objective 1

Learn that books are written by authors and that pictures are drawn by illustrators. Children will participate in brainstorming, drafting, conferencing, editing, and revising. An experience chart will be used as a prewriting activity.

Activity: *Book of Great Pets.* Read the books *Pet Show!* (Keats, 1974) and *The Perfect Pet* (Palatini & Whatley, 2003). Create a story web on experience chart paper as students talk about different kinds of pets and what characteristics they feel good pets should have. Each child will be writing a story about a great pet (stories can be fictional or real) while teacher conferences take place. Individual stories will be written in books with a pet store front on the cover, and children will be able to draw in the pet(s) they wrote about. This activity can be extended to other topics related to the theme, such as a circus, a veterinarian's office, or animals in a particular country.

Objective 2

Communicate through writing about animals around the world. Practice writing a friendly letter.

Activity: *Ask a Pen Pal.* Begin a discussion about the roles of different animals around the world. For example, dogs are kept as pets, work with police and firefighters, and work as seeing-eye dogs in the United States, but are used to transport people and sleds in colder regions of the world such as Alaska. Set students up with pen pals from around the world (you can use a website such as epals.com). Have them write letters to children in other parts of the world, informing them about the roles of animals in the United States and asking them about the roles of different animals in their countries. What types of animals are kept as pets? What types of animals do work, and what types of work do they do? When students receive letters

back from their pen pals, have them share new and interesting information with the class.

PLAY
Objective 1

Follow written directions and use print in a functional manner in an outdoor play activity.

Activity: *Outdoor Play: Circus.* Set up a circus with different stations that are labeled in both English and Spanish and have some students pretend be in the circus, while others pretend to attend the circus. Playground items can easily be converted into circus areas (e.g., a jungle gym can become a trapeze; a balance beam can become a tight rope). Jump ropes, balls, Hula-Hoops, and a large sack of animal figurines can be used as props. Have students come up with a name for their circus and create a ticket window, advertisements, posters, tickets, and brochures. Bring out a play cash register and play money and play circus music.

Objective 2

Engage in dramatic play, learning to listen to others, take turns, and keep talk relevant.

Activity: *Dramatic Play. Keeping Animals Healthy: The Veterinarian.* As a veterinarian's office, the dramatic play center should include a stethoscope, white lab coats, rubber gloves, play syringes, cotton balls, Q-tips, Popsicle sticks, plastic jars and containers, animal treats, plastic and stuffed animals, veterinary brochures and magazines, an appointment book, a telephone, play credit cards and money, paper, pencils, and pens. Have students name the office and make signs. Students can take on roles such as the veterinarian, veterinary assistants, receptionists, and clients.

ART
Objective 1

Create an animal mask, paying close attention to details such as color, shape, size, texture, and facial features. Perform a play using information about animals and their habitats around the world.

Activity: *Papier-mache Animal Masks.* Children will be paired up and given a blown-up balloon to cover in papier-mache (the teacher can do this prior to the lesson if desired). When the papier-mache dries, cut the balloons in half and give one half to each child. Have each child research and decide which animal he or she would like to make. Children should refer to a picture of their animal when making their masks. Supply children with masking tape and newspaper so that they may build eyes, ears, noses, and other features. Have students use papier-mache to cover the features they created and let dry. When students' masks are dry, have them paint their masks. Then attach a tongue depressor to each mask and cut out eyes so that students can use their masks to put on a play. Group students together by the animals they made so that animals from the same parts of the world are together. Then have students put on a play with masks and props that takes place in the particular habitat in which these animals live (the jungle, the forest, the farm, or other). Have students point out on a map where their plays are taking place.

Objective 2

Gain an appreciation for creativity and originality by designing collages and jewelry based on animals from around the world. Increase visual discrimination and enrich vocabulary through observation and discussion.

Activity: *Macaroni Art.* Have students create habitat collages using magazines, newspapers, macaroni, beads, markers, crayons, colored pencils, construction paper, and other various materials. Jewelry can also be made using macaroni and string. Macaroni can be dyed by placing it in food coloring and water for 3 minutes. Provide students with pictures, books, and real examples of multicultural jewelry that incorporates animals, and encourage children to design such jewelry. Students will observe and model each other's work and describe their own work to the class, pointing out on a map or globe which part of the world their art represents.

■ MUSIC

Objective 1

Learn about farm animals while refining listening skills and large motor skills in order to perform a song and improvised dance sequences. Create lyrics, recognizing and using rhyming words.

Activity: *A Place on the Farm.* Listen to "A Place on the Farm" by Jack Hartmann. Post the lyrics and track the print from left to right as children listen. Provide ELL students with a translation in their home language. Talk about farms and have children

list other farm animals they know of and come up with a verse for those farm animals to add to the song. Then assign animal roles to the children, having them work together to create a dance for each animal, and have them act out the song as they sing.

Objective 2

Increase listening skills and express feelings through musical experiences. Gain exposure to and appreciation for different genres of music and discriminate between them.

Activity: *Animal Sounds.* Read a book on animal sounds such as *Polar Bear, Polar Bear, What Do You Hear?* (Martin & Carle, 1997) or *Barnyard Banter* (Fleming, 2001). Listen to a prepared tape with excerpts of various genres of music from around the world (rock-n-roll, folk, reggae, hip hop, jazz, opera, rap, lullaby, country, rhythm and blues, classical, Latin, etc.) Ask children to describe the music. What types of instruments do they hear? Is it fast or slow? Discuss what parts of the world the music comes from. Ask children how the music makes them feel and what animals it makes them think of and why.

■ SOCIAL STUDIES

Objective 1

Students will correctly identify different countries on a map, create illustrations representing endangered animals from these countries, and create a sentence stating one specific feature of a country that they have learned about.

Activity: *Post Cards from around the World.* Read the book *Almost Gone: The World's Rarest Animals* (Jenkins, 2006). As you read the book, have students identify the countries in the book on a world map. After reading the book, have students attach premade pictures of the animals in the book to the country they come from on the map with pushpins. Have children discuss the animals and share their thoughts about what they have learned. Afterward, have students create their own postcards for the country of their choice, drawing an endangered animal from that country and writing a sentence stating something they have learned about that animal or country.

Objective 2

Understand stereotypes and their influence on interactions with others, understand feelings about self and others and how these feelings affect interactions within a group, and explore the basic need to fit in.

Activity: Animal Stereotypes. Print different names of animals that usually conflict on white index cards (i.e., dog, cat, bird, mouse, elephant, etc.). Randomly pin one animal card to the front of each student (face in), allowing only that student to see the name on his or her card and explain to the children that they are not to reveal their animal. Have children act and sound like the animal on their card and find others acting and sounding like them; have students sit together with the group they found. Discuss how they found each other and how they knew how to act or sound; record their comments on the board. Then have children move around the room reacting to the other animal groups as they might react in nature (e.g., cats may run from a dog or chase a mouse). Discuss how groups were created, the feelings linked with being in a group, and the labels attached to being in a group. Explore labels attached to different animal groups (e.g., dogs chase cats) and if these labels are always correct (e.g., my dog sleeps with my cat); record comments on the board. Connect the activity to groups of people and labels. Give the definition of and examples of stereotypes and discuss how these affect relationships between people and how people feel about themselves; record the students' reactions. Hand out blank small books in the shape of animals; using crayons and pencils, children write and illustrate a story that reflects on their experience as their animals.

■ SCIENCE

Objective 1

Understand that different animals have different nutritional needs. Create Very Own Word cards for new vocabulary learned.

Activity: Who Eats What? Have students think about animals they have seen on television or in real life and ask them to describe the kinds of foods these animals eat. Read *Who Eats What?: Food Chains and Food Webs* (Lauber & Keller, 1995). Discuss what the animals in the book eat and make a list of animals and their nutritional needs. Have students create Very Own Word cards that have the name of an animal on one side and a food that they eat on the other, illustrating the cards if they would like.

Objective 2

Increase vocabulary by discovering words we use to differentiate between adult and baby animals.

Activity: Baby Animals. Read *Animal Babies* (Hamsa & Dunnington, 1985) and *Baby Animals Learn* (Chanko, 1998). Have children sort pictures of baby animals and adult animals and match the babies to the parents, using new vocabulary learned to discuss their sorts. Afterwards, have students create a class book containing pictures of adult and baby animals and the words we use for them.

■ MATH

Objective 1

Learn backward counting while building reading fluency.

Activity: Five Little Speckled Frogs. Write the rhyme *Five Little Speckled Frogs* on chart paper and read it with students using a pointer to track the print. Have students pretend to be frogs and act out the rhyme, subtracting one from the group of frogs each time. Have children make frog finger puppets to take home and recite the rhyme to their families.

Objective 2

Relate pictures to text and see that pictures and print go together. Compare and classify animals and perform addition and subtraction operations.

Activity: Where Do I Belong? Create sorts with index cards for children that have the name of an animal in both English and Spanish and a corresponding picture of the animal on each card. Have children compare and classify animals using any characteristics they choose (size, color, habitat, food, role, etc.). Once they classify the animals, have them find and record the sum of animals in each category. After children have classified animals on a number of characteristics, have them compare groups using subtraction (i.e., How many more animals eat meat than plants?)

■ CULMINATING ACTIVITY

Objective 1

Visit many of the animals children learned about in the activities connected to the *Animals around the World* theme.

Activity: *Trip to the Zoo.* Take the children to a local zoo. Before visiting, read *My Visit to the Zoo* (Aliki, 1999) and *Trip to the Zoo (DK readers series)* (Wallace, 2003). Have children make a list of the animals they expect to see on their visit to the zoo. Take a few parents on the trip and, together, take pictures of animals. Afterward, have students create a class book about their trip to the zoo, with the pictures taken, that incorporates facts that they learned about the animals.

Objective 2

Share the knowledge gained and the products of the unit with the children's families and other classes in a fun and enjoyable way.

Activity: *Animals around the World Fair.* Invite children's families and other classes to a fair that raises money for an animal charity that the children choose. Have children create posters and

fliers to advertise the fair. Have children put on a puppet show or a skit of their favorite animal story using props they made in art lessons. Set up an "All about Animals" table that shows all the projects done during the unit, such as journals, masks, puppets, costumes, art projects, and class animal books. Set up an "Animal Games" corner with games like Go Fish, Horseshoe Ring Toss, Pin the Tail on the Donkey, and Leap Frog. Have an "Animal Art" table with various art supplies for simple projects that children can make. Set up an "Animals around the World Library" corner with different animal books and storytelling props, and encourage your students to use them with friends and family. Play animal songs and set up a refreshment stand that serves animal crackers and cookies, Goldfish crackers, a cake in the shape of an animal, animal-shaped sandwiches (cut with a cookie cutter), and the like. Have a piñata in the shape of an animal that children can break near the end of the fair.

Suggestions for Instructors

Literacy Development in the Early Years: Helping Children Read and Write is written for students in graduate and undergraduate classes in courses such as Early Literacy Development and Reading in the Elementary School, or an Early Childhood Curriculum course that includes literacy development as a major component. The book can also be used for staff development courses for classroom teachers. We suggest several activities to engage in with students. Following are a few that have been used successfully in class sessions or as assignments. Also, Appendix E includes an integrated language arts thematic unit that teachers can use as a model for beginning literacy programs in their preschool through third-grade classrooms. In addition to this brief guide for instructors, there is a handbook online that contains extensive ideas for assignments inside and outside the classroom, lessons plans, and both multiple-choice and short-answer tests. Access the instructor's online handbook using the password provided to adopters of the book.

■ ASSIGNMENTS AND IN-CLASS ACTIVITIES

At the beginning of each chapter are focus questions that students should read prior to reading the chapter. At the end of every chapter are relevant activities contributed by classroom teachers. In addition there are activities to engage in. Read the activities; you might find that some of them are appropriate for class interaction in small groups and for discussion. Be sure in all planning that a discussion about English language learners and issues of diversity are included.

Activities to participate in as you work your way through the book are as follows:

1. In Chapter 2 it is suggested that students select a child that they can study as they read the book. The child should be between 2 and 8 years old. The student should begin a portfolio for the child and meet with him or her from time to time to try

strategies and assess and describe certain behaviors. Specifically, students should obtain a sample of writing, drawing, oral language, and a story retelling from the child. In addition, several of the measures provided in the book can be used to accumulate data about the child. For example:

a. When reading Chapter 4 on language development, collect a language sample and analyze it for sentence length and numbers of different words. To elicit language from children, ask them to tell you about family, pets, TV shows they like, or games they play. Tape record the discussion and transcribe it for analysis.

b. In Chapter 5, evaluate the child's knowledge about print using the checklist included.

c. In Chapter 6, have the child retell a story that was read to him or her. Tape record the retelling and transcribe it. Analyze it Using Figure 6.12. Children can also be asked to rewrite the story. The rewriting can be analyzed with the same tool.

d. In Chapter 7, collect a writing sample from the child to determine the stage of writing and analyze it for sense of story structure, the mechanics of writing, and so forth. To elicit a writing sample, you might have the child draw a picture and write about it. Talk about ideas to write before writing. Assure emergent writers that any way they can write is fine. Show them samples of children's writing from the text so they see that one-letter or scribble writing is fine.

e. In Chapter 8, interview the child using Figure 8.11, which evaluates motivation for reading and writing.

f. When studying the family, interview the child's parents using Figure 10.1 or Figure 10.2, a checklist concerning the home literacy environment.

The Strategies for the Classroom section at the end of the book includes informal tests to administer to complete your portfolio.

2. At least three or four times during the semester, have the class break into groups to deal with special issues presented in the text. For example, in Chapter 6, the activity about Teachers 1, 2, and 3 is a good small-group activity. Have the students respond to the questions posed about the teachers and discuss which teacher each would wish to be. Discuss the pros and cons of each of the teachers presented.

3. Have students keep dialog journals about readings that have made an impression on them. They can also include incidents in class that were particularly interesting, fun, or of concern. Respond to their journals with comments of your own.

4. Have your students take a vocabulary test using words from the glossary. Teachers need to be aware of the technical language associated with early literacy when talking with peers, interviewing for a job, and explaining issues to parents.

5. Have students bring six genres of children's literature to class to share in groups. Three books should be nonfiction or informational text and three should be fiction or narrative text. This assignment gives them the opportunity to browse through lots of books and see the variety of genres available. Set the books up as if your students were going into a classroom. They will gain a sense of the numbers and types of books that should be in a literacy center.

6. Ask students to draw a floor plan for their ideal classroom using the philosophy and strategies learned. Pay particular attention to the literacy center. Be sure they create plans to support literacy instruction for whole groups, small groups, and one-on-one settings.

7. Ask each student to be involved in a storytelling project. Give students a list of early literacy skills from those outlined on the checklists provided in the book. Have them select a skill they would like to teach. Ask them to find a picture story book that will enable that skill to be taught. For example, if their skill is to teach sequencing, a story such as *I Know an Old Lady* provides a sequence of events that are easily followed. The student then selects a technique for storytelling from those described in Chapter 8, such as a chalk talk, roll story, felt story, or other techniques they create themselves. A lesson plan is developed in which the teacher presents the story and teaches the skill through the use of the material created. The material is designed for children to use to practice the skill taught. In Chapter 8 the "Idea from the Classroom for the Classroom" concerning the story *A Bunny Called Nat* illustrates this type of assignment. Students present the storytelling in class.

8. Have the students select a group to work with. Have the group select a topic for a thematic unit. Using the guide for the unit in Chapter 9, divide the sections and prepare a thematic unit for a classroom of children ages 2 through 8 years.

9. Have students participate in a teacher researcher project. Each student selects a topic dealing with early literacy and carries out a ministudy. The study should include a statement of purpose, a short literature review related to the topic, a description of methods and procedures to follow during the study, a discussion of how the data will be analyzed, a report of the results of the data collection, and a discussion concerning the results. This is a large project that is introduced to students early in the semester in order for them to have ample time to carry it out. When writing the literature review, the students should be required to consult a few articles from professional journals. Some topics for study are literacy and play, computers and early literacy, family literacy, multicultural concerns in early literacy, and early intervention programs.

10. Have students bind their own books based on the directions provided in Chapter 7. Have them use the book for their dialog journal or for writing their storytelling lesson plan.

11. Encourage students to join a professional organization such as the International Reading Association or the National Association for the Education of Young Children.

12. Encourage your students to subscribe to a professional journal and a commercial teacher magazine.

13. One important activity to offer your students is to let them experience what it would be like to be a child learning to read. For this demonstration, we have provided materials and a plan for a class experience. This activity should take about 45 minutes of class time and should be done early in the semester when you are teaching theory. The lesson involves learning how to read with an alphabet called the *Confusabet*. Following is a plan for carrying out the Confusabet. Materials needed are provided in this appendix. Photocopy them for use in your lesson plan before beginning the lesson or use the pages in the book.

■ THE CONFUSABET LESSON

Objective: To experience how it feels to learn to read and write.

Materials

Confusabet alphabet and translation

Confusabet sight words and translation

Confusabet worksheets

Confusabet reading book and translation (books must be assembled)

Procedures

1. Before the lesson, ask students to think about and write answers to the following questions during the experience:

    a. What methods were used to teach reading? Which worked well and which did not work well?

    b. What emotions did you experience while learning to read and write the Confusabet?

    c. What strategies did you use to teach yourself how to read and write?

2. Hand out or turn to the Confusabet alphabet and pictures that have the names of the Confusabet characters on them.

3. Name the characters and have the students repeat their names.

4. Hand out or turn to worksheet 1. Ask students to find the character's name among other Confusabet words.

5. Hand out or turn to the list of Confusabet words. Provide students with context clues for each word. For example: The color of the traffic light that means you should stop is _____. Have the students fill in the word and point to the Confusabet word that is *red*. Context clues are provided in the translations at the end of Appendix G.

6. Follow this step for all words and provide your own context clues.

7. Repeat the words with the students. You may repeat them all together, call on those who raise their hands, and call on students who do not raise their hands.

8. Turn to or hand out worksheet 2 with the Confusabet words just introduced and ask students to underline and name the word in each list that is the same as the word at the top of the list.

9. Turn to or distribute the Confusabet primer. Call on students to read a line or a page at a time. Try round-robin reading as well.

During the Confusabet lesson, role-play as if you are a teacher of six-year-olds. Praise students for doing well. Provide some positive reinforcement and use some positive teaching techniques. Also try punitive techniques and phrases, such as "If you don't get this work correct, you won't get to take the book home to your parents" or "You weren't listening; that's why you don't know the words" or "If you don't stop talking, you'll be sent to the principal's office."

During the Confusabet exercise, students should talk to each other naturally to try to work things out. When they do so, say, "Please do your own work and keep your eyes on your own paper" or "Don't help each other; you have to learn to do it yourself" or "It's too noisy in here" and "We can't wait for you even though you haven't finished your work." When students have answers and are very anxious to give them, say, "You've already had your turn; give someone else a chance" or "Please settle down; you are disrupting the rest of the class." When students look ahead to preview materials handed out, say, "Please wait for me to tell you when to turn the page" or "Don't go ahead of me; we aren't up to that yet." This type of role-playing allows students to experience even more how children feel in the classroom, where these types of comments often occur.

10. After reading the Confusabet materials, ask students to write their names and then the sentence "I like to read and write" with Confusabet symbols.

11. At the end of the lesson, repeat the questions posed at the beginning:

    a. What methods did you use that worked well? What methods did you use that did not work well?

    b. What emotions did you experience?

    c. How did you teach yourself to learn to read?

    d. How did you go about learning to write?

Students will express that they experienced fear, anger, and frustration when they were having trouble. They will suggest that they wanted to tune out and not participate. Those who were succeeding will suggest that they were excited, they wanted to continue, and they wanted to share their excitement. Frequently students who are succeeding will be greeted with remarks such as "You've already had a turn, settle down and let me give someone else a chance." When asked how they felt about this response, they will say that their feeling of excitement was cut short.

When students discuss the strategies they used to learn to read, they will often make comments similar to the following:

1. I used my past experience with knowledge from our real alphabet to help. For example, the Confusabet words have the same number of symbols as our alphabet. They also resemble some of the letters of our alphabet, and I was able to make associations.

2. I used the picture clues.

3. I used surrounding words or the context to figure out the word (contextual and syntactic clues).

4. I memorized symbols from one page to the next.

5. Some words were long or had an unusual shape, which helped me to figure out a word (configuration).

6. I looked at the first letter of a word to help figure it out.

When students are asked some of the things they did to help them read, they may say:

1. I pointed to the print to help me find my place.

2. I moved my eyes around the page to try and find clues.

3. I called out words one at a time, the way young children do.

What the students realize as a result of participating in the Confusabet experience is that they rely on meaning, past experience, associative strategies, and visual clues to figure out the words more than they do on individual skills such as phonics.

The Confusabet lesson presented here is adapted from materials created by Mildred Letton Wittock from the University of Chicago.

CONFUSABET ALPHABET LETTERS

CONFUSABET STORY CHARACTERS

Directions: Instructor names the characters for the students. Students repeat the names.

▨ CONFUSABET VOCABULARY WORDS

Directions: Instructor gives a context clue for each word to help student to read it. Students repeat the words. Clues are on page 453.

1. ☿φ⌒φ   2. ♯△ⱡⱡ   3. ♀φ♀⊕φ   4. 1ⱡ△Ⅎ

5. ⱡ♁⊕⊕φ   6. ∾⊖⊜   7. ⊕⊖☿⊖   8. ▸▴ⱃ

9. ∾⊖Ⅎ   10. φ♁ʃ⊖☿⊕♯△ⱡ⊜   11. ∾♁♀

12. 1♁♀♀φ   13. ♁Ⅎ   14. ♁♁☿Ⅎ   15. φ⊖

16. ⱡ⊖⊖φ   17. φ⊖♁   18. φʃ   19. ʃφ⊖

20. △ʃ   21. △∾   22. ʃφ⊖☿   23. ⊕φ♀

24. φ♀Ⅎ   25. ⊖φ   26. 1♁♀

▨ CONFUSABET WORKSHEET 1

Directions: Circle the name of the character in the list of words under his or her name. Say the name as you circle it.

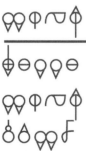

CONFUSABET WORKSHEET 2

Directions: Circle the underlined word in each column. Say the word as you circle it.

■ CONFUSABET PRIMER

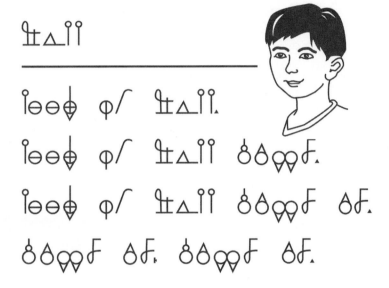

■ CONFUSABET STORY 1

■ CONFUSABET STORY 2

CONFUSABET STORY 3

CONFUSABET STORY 4

CONFUSABET STORY 5

Story Character Names

1. Mary 2. Bill 3. Nancy 4. Flip 5. Lucky

Vocabulary Translations with Context Clue Sentences

6. With my eyes I _____. see

7. Please _____ over here. come

8. , (comma) . (period) ? (question mark)

9. The top color light on a traffic signal is _____. red

10. Another name for a car is an _____. automobile

11. When I go fast on my feet I _____. run

12. A clown is _____. funny

13. When we take off in a airplane we go _____. up

14. When I play with a rope I _____ up. jump

15. The green traffic light means for us to _____. go

16. A word that rhymes with book and means to see is _____. look

17. Not me but _____. you

18. Come and look _____ it. at

19. _____ red automobile the

20. Let's get into _____. it

21. It _____ fun to ride in. is

22. I'm going over there to be with _____. them

23. Yes I _____. can

24. Come _____ play with me. and

25. When I am surprised I say _____. oh

26. When I play with my friend I have _____. fun

Story Translations for Primer

Primer Title—*Look and See*

Story 1—*Bill*
Look at Bill.
Look at Bill jump.
Look at Bill jump up.
Jump up, jump up.

Story 2—*Nancy and Bill and Mary*
Look, Bill. Look, Mary.
See Nancy.
Look and see Nancy.
Funny funny Nancy.

Story 3—*Flip and Lucky*
Come, Flip. Come, Lucky.
Come and see.
Come and see the automobile.
Come and see the red automobile.
Come, Flip. Come, Lucky.
Look and see.

Story 4—*The Red Automobile*
Look at the red automobile.
Come and look at it.
It is fun. Look at it.

Story 5—*(Without pictures)*
Jump up and run, Flip.
Jump up and run, Bill.
Look, Mary. Can you see them?

Glossary

Jennifer Kaywood and Paula Batsiyan

accommodation   Changing existing schemes to incorporate new information.

aesthetic talk   A form of conversation revolving around narrative literature in which children interpret and discuss what has been heard or read in relation to themselves.

aliterate   An individual who can read but chooses not to.

alphabetic principle   Knowing that words are composed of letters and that there is a systematic relationship between the letters and the sounds they make.

antiphonal reading   A choral reading in which parts are taken by groups.

assimilation   Incorporating information into already existing schemes.

auditory discrimination   The ability to hear, identify, and differentiate among familiar sounds, similar sounds, rhyming words, and letter sounds.

authentic assessment   Assessment based on activities that represent and reflect the actual learning and instruction in the classroom.

balanced approach to literacy instruction   The selection of theory and strategies to match learning styles of children. Constructivist and explicit strategies are both used.

behaviorist approach   A learning theory in which adults provide a model and children learn through imitation encouraged by positive reinforcement.

Big Books   Oversized books designed to allow children to see the print as it is being read.

blend   A reader's ability to hear a series of isolated speech sounds and then recognize and pronounce them as a complete word.

buddy reading   The pairing of a child from an upper grade with a younger child for storybook reading.

choral reading   A small group or the entire class reads along with the teacher, who provides pacing and expression.

chunk   Any group of letters within a word that is taught as a whole pattern; a chunk could be a phonogram, digraph, blend, etc.

comprehension   An active process whereby a reader interprets and constructs meaning about the text based on prior knowledge and experience.

conference   Meeting with the teacher or a peer to discuss work in progress.

consonant blends   Two or three letters that, when placed together, merge into one sound while retaining representations of each letter sound (e.g., *bl* or *str*).

consonants   All letters except A, E, I, O, U.

constructivist theory   A theory that views learning as an active process by which children construct knowledge to learn by problem solving, guessing, and approximating.

context clues   The use of syntax and semantic meaning of text to aid in word identification.

contracts   Assignment sheets designating specific activities to be carried out by individual learners based on their needs, interests, and ability levels.

cooperative learning   An instructional strategy in which children come together to learn through debate and discussion.

cultural diversity   Reference to the wide variety of backgrounds, languages, customs, and environments represented within the larger society or a given classroom.

decoding   Identifying words by using letter–sound and structural analysis.

descriptive writing   Writing with language that describes precisely.

dialect   An alternative form of one particular language used in different cultural, regional, or social groups.

differentiated instruction   Designing instruction to meet the achievement needs of children in the same classroom. Often the assignment is the same for all, but less is expected of the child who is struggling, that is, a shorter written story, and more of the sophisticated reader.

digraph   Consonant digraphs are two consonants that, when placed together, make one new sound unlike the sound of either individual letter (e.g., *th* or *ch*). Vowel digraphs are two vowels together that make one sound that could be the sound of either vowel or a new sound (e.g., *ie, ai, oo, ou*).

directed listening and thinking activity (DLTA) and directed reading and thinking activity (DRTA)   A framework that offers directions and strategies for organizing and retrieving information from a text that is read by or to a child. The steps in DLTA or DRTA include preparation for listening/reading with prequestions and discussion, setting a purpose for reading, reading the story, and a follow-up postreading discussion based on the purpose set prior to reading.

Drop Everything and Read (DEAR) time   Quiet time for children to engage in silent reading.

early intervention   Programs for children with special needs or those who are "at risk" in early childhood education intended to prevent potential problems in literacy development. The focus of the programs is on developmentally appropriate instruction using authentic reading and writing experiences. The program can be a pull-out or inclusion setting.

echo reading   The teacher reads a line of text and then the child reads the same line. The number of lines read is increased as the child's reading improves.

efferent talk   A formal mode of conversation about expository text used to inform and persuade.

emergent literacy   As coined by Marie Clay, refers to a child's early unconventional attempts at reading, writing, and listening.

English language learners (ELL)   Children whose first language is not English. These children can have varying levels of English ability from no English to some.

environmental print   Familiar print found in the surroundings, such as logos, food labels, and road signs.

explicit instruction   A teacher-directed strategy with emphasis on teaching a task and the specific steps needed to master it.

expository text   Text in any form that is informational and nonfiction.

expository writing   Writing that includes many types of experiences and is usually about information that comes from content-area subjects such as social studies or science. This involves collecting information and summarizing it.

expressive language   Putting words together to form thoughts or express oneself.

family literacy   Refers to the different ways in which family members initiate and use literacy in their daily living.

fluency   Level of reading ease and ability; a fluent reader is able to read on- or above-level books independently with high comprehension and accuracy.

functional print   Print for a purpose, such as informational signs, directions, greeting cards, lists, letters to pen pals, and messages for the notice board.

functional writing   Writing that serves clear, real-life purposes, including greeting cards and thank-you notes.

genre   A specific type of literature, such as picture storybook, informational book, or poetry.

gifted   Demonstrating exceptional ability.

graphemes   Letters that make up individual sounds.

guided reading   Explicit reading instruction usually in small groups based on literacy needs.

high-frequency words   Words that are frequently found in reading materials for children.

high-stakes assessment   Standardized measures whose scores might determine major decisions about school districts, such as ratings of districts and promotion or retention decisions.

inclusion   Special help and enrichment are offered in the regular classroom with the help of resource teachers and regular teachers planning together and teaching all children. This is in place of or in addition to pull-out programs for special help.

independent reading and writing periods (IRWP)   A socially interactive time wherein children select among books and other literacy-related materials.

informal reading inventory   Informal tests to determine a child's independent, instructional, and frustration level of reading.

integrated language arts   An approach to literacy instruction that links reading, writing, listening, and language skills.

interdisciplinary literacy instruction   Integration of content-area learning with literacy.

intergenerational literacy initiatives   Planned, systematic programs specifically designed to improve the literacy development of both adults and children.

invented spelling   Improvised spelling for words unknown in conventional spelling wherein one letter often represents an entire syllable.

journal writing   Written entries in notebooks by children, including *dialogue,* which is shared with teachers or peers who respond to what they read; *personal,* involving private thoughts related to children's lives or topics of special interest; *reading response,* writing in response to text reading; and *learning log,* a record of information usually involving other content areas.

K-W-L   A cognitive strategy that enhances comprehension by assessing with students what they *Know*, what they *Want* to know, and what they *Learned* before and after reading.

language experience approach (LEA)   A reading instruction method aimed at linking oral with written language on the premise that what is thought can be said, what is said can be written, and what is written can be read.

learning centers   Spaces in the classroom filled with materials for independent student activity focusing on current topics of study within content areas and including literacy materials as well.

learning disabled   Demonstrating significant difficulty in the acquisition and use of reading, writing, listening, speaking, and/or mathematical skills.

literacy center   A classroom area composed of a library corner and writing area.

literature-based instruction   An approach to teaching reading in which varied genres of children's literature are used as the main source of reading material.

literature circles   Discussion groups used to encourage critical discussions about literature among children.

mapping and webbing   Strategies for understanding text through the use of graphic representations for categorizing and structuring information. Maps deal with more detailed representations.

mental imagery   Visualization of readings used to increase comprehension and clarify thought.

metacognition   Awareness of one's own mental processes concerning how learning takes place.

morning message   A daily message about items of interest to children written by the teacher, who points out concepts about print.

narrative text   Text that describes a sequence of events or gives an account of events.

narrative writing   Writing stories.

nativist theory   The theory that language develops innately.

neural shearing   Loss of brain cells.

new literacy   A growing field of research in literacy education that investigates the impact of globalization and the increasing use of technology and new media on literacy development. The field of new literacy encompasses a wide domain of new skills that have emerged from increased computer use. New literacy tells us that literacy takes place everywhere all the time.

nonstandard English   A dialectal form of English that differs from the standard form in words, syntax, and language patterns.

one-to-one instruction   Individualized instruction.

onset   Initial letter or letters before the first vowel in a word.

paired reading   A more able reader from the same class or another class acts as a tutor while reading with a less fluent student.

parent-involvement programs   Programs designed to involve and inform parents about activities that will promote their children's literacy development in school.

partner reading   Peers reading together either simultaneously side by side or taking turns reading to each other.

persuasive writing   Writing that involves trying to get someone to have your point of view.

phonemes   Sounds made by individual letters and combinations of letters that make a single sound.

phonemic awareness   Knowing that words are composed of a sequence of spoken sounds and being able to hear and identify these sounds. Phonemic awareness includes the ability to segment and blend individual sounds. Phonemic awareness is strictly an oral activity without association to symbols.

phonics   A strategy that involves learning the alphabetic principles of language and knowledge of letter–sound relationships. Children learn to associate letters with the phonemes or basic speech sounds of English, to help them break the alphabetic code and become independent readers in the pronunciation of words.

phonogram   A series of letters that begins with a vowel, often found together (for example, *ack, ed, ight, ock, ush*).

phonological awareness   The ability to identify and manipulate individual speech sounds as well as syllables and whole words. Children can segment and blend single phonemes, syllables, and words.

poetry writing   Poems can be rhymes or can follow other formulas, such as haiku or acrostics.

portfolio assessment   A strategy for measuring student progress by collecting samples of their work that are placed into a folder called a portfolio. Materials include samples of student's written work or drawings, anecdotal records, audiotapes, videotapes, checklists, and teacher-made and standardized test results, among others.

process approach to writing   Steps involved in the production of text, including prewriting, drafting, conferencing, revising, editing, and performing.

pull-out programs   Programs in which students are taken out of their classrooms for special help in literacy instruction or enrichment.

Reader's Theater   The oral reading of a short play, in which children have parts and practice them for presentation.

reading readiness Various skills considered prerequisite in learning to read, such as auditory discrimination, visual discrimination, and motor skills.

Reading Recovery An early intervention program devised by Marie Clay in which first graders experiencing difficulties with reading receive intensive, one-on-one instruction using developmentally appropriate integrated language arts techniques.

reading workshop A period of time set aside for children to work on reading skills by reading books and conferencing with the teacher.

receptive language Ability to process, comprehend, or integrate spoken language; being able to understand what someone says to you.

repeated reading Reading the same book or story over and over until it is repeated or known. This familiarity offers the opportunity for fluent reading.

response groups A strategy for enhancing comprehension; students exchange or refine ideas and think critically about issues related to what they have listened to or read.

rich literacy environments Environments rich with materials that encourage reading and writing and support instruction.

rime Ending part of a word that contains the vowel and the remainder of the word. Onsets and rimes make up words.

rubric A rubric is a scoring guide that gives the student and teacher a sense of what they should strive for in their writing. It is an evaluation system for a teacher who ranks certain elements on the rubric, which then are listed, such as uses capitals and correct punctuation, writes neatly, stays on topic, gives details and examples, or writes things in an appropriate order.

running record An assessment strategy that involves the close observation and recording of a child's oral reading behavior. Running records may be used for planning instruction.

scaffolding A strategy in which teachers provide children with modeling and support to help them acquire a skill.

segment To divide words into segments based on their sound components; cat is "c-a-t."

self-monitoring A student's ability to read and self-correct words as they are read.

semantics Meaning that language communicates.

shared book experiences Whole- or small-group reading instruction through literature selections, in which Big Books are often used so that children can see the print and pictures. Big Books enable children to listen and participate in actual book readings.

sight words The words that are known immediately by a reader. Once a word becomes a sight word, the reader does not need to use word-attack skills to read it.

small-group instruction Close interaction occurs between teacher and child for explicit instruction, based on needs and interests and for assessment.

standardized tests An assessment measure, commercially prepared and norm-referenced, that reports results in terms of grade-level scores and percentile ranks.

standards Achievement goals that are defined at a state or national level and identify what students should know at the end of each grade level.

story retellings The recital of familiar stories, in children's own words, in written or oral form to develop and assess comprehension of story.

story structure The elements of a well-constructed story, including setting, theme, plot episodes, and resolution.

sustained silent reading (SSR) A time allocated for children to read silently.

synaptogenesis Connecting of brain cells or rapid development of neural connections.

syntax The structure of language or rules that governs how words work together in phrases, clauses, and sentences.

tape-assisted reading Listening to fluent reading samples on audiotapes while following the written text.

telegraphic speech A form of speech used by children at about 12 months of age in which content words, such as nouns and verbs, are used, for example "Mommy cookie," but function words, such as conjunctions and articles, are omitted.

thematic unit A topic of study is learned through explorations across all areas of the curriculum.

think-aloud A comprehension strategy in which children talk about what they have read or other ideas they have about a story.

think, pair, share A discussion strategy that combines think time with cooperative learning. Following teacher-posed questions, the teacher first has children *think* about their answers; then children *pair* with a partner to discuss their responses; finally, during *share*, the students share responses with the group.

t-chart A graphic organizer that helps to comprehend expository and narrative text by classifying similarities and differences in characters, facts, and ideas.

t-unit An independent clause with all its dependent clauses attached that is helpful in measuring a child's language complexity.

Very Own Words Favorite words generated by children, written on index cards, and kept in a container for them to read and write.

visual discrimination The ability to note similarities and differences visually between objects, including the ability to recognize colors, shapes, and letters.

vowels   The letters A, E, I, O, U.

whole-group instruction   Introduce information to the children with the whole class together, such as a lesson, discussion, reading a story, singing songs.

whole language   A philosophy from which strategies are drawn for literacy development. Strategies include the use of real literature, with the concurrent instruction of reading, writing, and oral language in meaningful, functional, and cooperative contexts, to help students become motivated to read and write.

word-study skills   Knowledge about print, including the use of phonics context and syntax to decipher unknown words; the development of sight vocabulary; and the use of word configuration and structural analysis.

word wall   A type of bulletin board or classroom display that features challenging and/or high-frequency words organized alphabetically.

writing mechanics   Skills related to writing, such as spelling, handwriting, punctuation, and spacing.

writing workshop   A period of time set aside for children to practice writing skills, work on writing projects, and confer with the teacher.

zone of proximal development   Based on Vygotsky's theory, this term refers to the period of time when a child has been guided by an adult and no longer needs the help. The adult retreats and allows the child to work on his or her own.

Children's Literature Bibliography

Aliki. (1974). *Go tell Aunt Rhody*. New York: Macmillan.

Archambault, J., & Martin, Jr., B. (1989). *Chicka chicka boom boom*. New York: Scholastic.

Asch, F. (1983). *Mooncake*. New York: Simon & Schuster.

Avery, K., & McPhail, D. (1993). *The crazy quilt*. Glenview, IL: Scott Foresman.

Bachelet, G. (2006). *My cat the silliest cat in the world*. New York: Abrams Books for Young Readers.

Base, G. (1987). *Animalia*. New York: Harry N. Abrams.

Bemelmans, L. (1939). *Madeline*. New York: Viking.

Bemelmans, L. (1953). *Madeline's rescue*. New York: Viking.

Berenstain, S., & Berenstain, J. (1987). *The Berenstain bears and too much birthday*. New York: Random House.

Branley, F. M. (1985). *Volcanoes*. New York: Harper & Row Junior Books.

Brenner, B. (1972). *The three little pigs*. New York: Random House.

Brett, J. (1989). *The mitten*. New York: Putnam & Grosset.

Brett, J. (1997). *The hat*. New York: Putnam & Grosset.

Brown, M. (1947). *Goodnight moon*. New York: Harper Collins.

Brown, M. (1957). *The three billy goats gruff*. New York: Harcourt Brace.

Brown, M. (1990). *Arthur's pet business*. New York: Little Brown.

Burton, V. L. (1943). *Katy and the big snow*. Boston: Houghton Mifflin.

Carle, E. (1969). *The very hungry caterpillar*. New York: Philomel.

Cohen, M. (1980). *First grade takes a test*. New York: Dell.

Cole, B. (1989). *No more baths*. New York: Farrar, Straus & Giroux.

Cole, J. (1987). *The magic school bus inside the earth*. New York: Scholastic.

Cowley, J., & Fuller, E. (2006). *Mrs. Wishy-Washy's farm*. New York: Penguin Young Readers Group.

Cronin, D. (2000). *Click, clack, moo: Cows that type*. New York: Simon & Schuster.

Daley, A., & Russell, C. (1999). *Goldilocks and the three bears*. Ladybird Books.

DeBeer, H. (1996). *Little polar bear, take me home!* New York: North-South Books.

Demuth, P. (1997). *Achoo!* New York: Sagebrush Educational Resources.

DePaulo, T. (1978). *The popcorn book*. Upper Saddle River, NJ: Prentice Hall.

DePaola, T. (1975). *Strega nona*. New York: Simon & Schuster.

DK Publishing. (2004). *Farm animals*. New York: DK Publishing.

Duvoisin, R. (2002). *Petunia*. New York: Dragonfly.

Eastman, P. D. (1960). *Are you my mother?* New York: Random House.

Fleming, D. (2001). *Barnyard banter*. New York: Henry Holt.

Fowler, A. (1992). *Frogs and toads and tadpoles, too!* Chicago: Children's Press.

Fowler, A. (1993). *Chicken or the egg?* New York: Scholastic.

Fox, M. (2000). *Harriet, you'll drive me wild*, New York: Harcourt.

Fujikawa, A. (1980). *Jenny learns a lesson*. New York: Grosset & Dunlap.

Galdone, P. (1973). *The little red hen*. Boston: Houghton Mifflin.

Galdone, P. (1983). *The gingerbread boy*. Boston: Houghton Mifflin.

Hazen, B. S. (1983). *Tight times*. New York: Picture Puffins.

Hennesey, B. G., & Pearson, T. C. (1989). *The queen of hearts*. New York: Picture Puffins.

Hoban, R. (1964). *Bread and jam for Frances*. New York: Harper & Row.

Hoberman, M. A. (2001). *You read to me, I'll read to you*. New York: Little Brown.

Hurd, E. (1980). *Under the lemon tree*. Boston: Little Brown.

Izawa, T. (1968). *The little red hen*. New York: Grosset & Dunlap.

Johnson, A. (1990). *Do like Kyla*. New York: Scholastic.

Johnson, C. (1981). *Harold and the purple crayon*. New York: Harper & Row.

Keats, E. (1962). *The snowy day*. New York: Viking.

Keats, E. (1966). *Jenny's hat*. New York: Harper & Row.

Keats, E. J. (1974). *Pet show*. New York: Aladdin Books.

Keats, E. J. (1967). *Peter's chair*. New York: Harper & Row.

Keats, E. J. (1998). *A letter to Amy*. New York: Puffin.

Kellogg, S. (1989). *Is your mama a llama?* New York: Scholastic.

La Reau, K., & Magoon S. (2006). *Ugly fish*. Orlando, FL: Harcourt.

LeSieg, T. (1961). *Ten apples up on top*. New York: Random House.

Lionni, L. (1963). *Swimmy*. New York: Pantheon.

Lobel, A. L. (1979). *Frog and toad are friends*. New York: HarperCollins.

Lum, K., & Johnson, A. (1998). *What cried granny: an almost bedtime story*. New York: Puffin Books.

Maass, R. (1993). *When winter comes*. New York: Scholastic.

McClosky, R. (1948) *Blueberries for Sal*. New York: Viking.

McGovern, A. (1967). *Too much noise*. Boston: Houghton Mifflin.

McNulty, F. (1979). *How to dig a hole to the other side of the world*. New York: Harper & Row.

Montanari, D. (2001). *Children around the world*. New York: Kids Can Press.

Neitzel, S. (1991). *The jacket I wear in the snow*. New York: Greenwillow Books.

Parrish, P. (1970). *Amelia Bedelia*. New York: Avon Books.

Pinkey, J. (2006). *The little red hen*. New York: Dial Books.

Piper, W. (1990). *The little engine that could*. New York: Platt and Munk.

Potter, B. (1902). *The tale of Peter Rabbit*. New York: Scholastic.

Quackenbush, R. (1972). *Old MacDonald had a farm*. New York: Lippincott.

Quackenbush, R. (1973). *Go tell Aunt Rhody*. New York: Lippincott.

Reid, S., & Fernandes, E. (1992). *The wild toboggan ride*. New York: Scholastic.

Rey, H. A. (1941). *Curious George*. Boston: Houghton Mifflin.

Sendak, M. (1962). *Chicken soup with rice*. New York: Harper & Row.

Sendak, M. (1963). *Where the wild things are*. New York: Harper & Row.

Sendak, M. (1991). *Pierre*. New York: HarperCollins.

Seuss, Dr. (1957a). *How the Grinch stole Christmas*. New York: Random House.

Seuss, Dr. (1957b). *The cat in the hat*. New York: Random House.

Seuss, Dr. (1960). *Green eggs and ham*. New York: Random House.

Seuss, Dr. (1998). *Mr. Brown can moo! Can you?* New York: Random House.

Sharmat, M. (1984). *Gregory the terrible eater*. New York: Scholastic.

Slobodkina, E. (1947). *Caps for sale*. Reading, MA: Addison-Wesley.

Tchin (1997). *Rabbits wish for snow: A Native American legend*. New York: Scholastic.

Viorst, J. (1972). *Alexander and the terrible, horrible, no good, very bad day*. New York: Atheneum.

Westcott, N. B. (1980). *I know an old lady*. Boston: Little, Brown.

White, E. B. (1952). *Charlotte's web*. New York: Scholastic.

Willems, M. (2004). *Knuffle bunny*. New York: Hyperion.

Yolen, J., & Teague, M. (2005). *How do dinosaurs eat their food?* New York: Scholastic.

Zemach, M. (1991). *The three little pigs*. New York: Tandem Library.

Zoehfeld, K. W. (1994). *Manatee winter*. Hartford, CT: Trudy Corporation.

Zolotow, C. (1977). *Mr. Rabbit and the lovely present*. New York: Harper & Row.

Bibliography

Adams, M. J. (1990). *Beginning to read: Thinking and learning about print.* Urbana: University of Illinois Center for the Study of Reading.

Adams, M. J. (2001). Alphabetic anxiety and explicit, systematic phonics instruction: A cognitive science perspective. In S. B. Neuman & D. K. Dickinson (Eds.), *Handbook of early literacy research* (pp. 66–80). New York: Guilford Press.

Adams, M. J., Bereiter, C., Brown, A., et al. (2002). *Open court reading.* DeSoto, TX: SRA McGraw-Hill.

Akhavan, L. L. (2006). *Help! My kids don't all speak English: How to set up a language workshop in your linguistically diverse classroom.* Portsmouth, NH: Heinemann.

Allen, R. V. (1976). *Language experience in communication.* Boston: Houghton Mifflin.

Allington, R. L., & Cunningham, P. M. (1996). *Schools that work: Where all children read and write.* New York: HarperCollins.

Allison, D. T., & Watson, J. A. (1994). The significance of adult storybook reading styles on the development of young children's emergent reading. *Reading Research and Instruction, 34*(1), 57–72.

Anderson, R. C., & Pearson, P. D. (1984). A schema-theoretic view of basic processing in reading. In P. D. Pearson (Ed.), *Handbook of reading research,* 255–292. New York: Longman.

Anderson, R. C., Hiebert, E. H., Scott, J. A., & Wilkinson, I. A. G. (1985). *Becoming a nation of readers.* Washington, DC: National Institute of Education.

Anderson, R. C., Fielding, L. G., & Wilson, P. T. (1988). Growth in reading and how children spend their time outside of school. *Reading Research Quarterly, 23,* 285–303.

Anthony, J. L., & Lonigan, C. J. (2004). The nature of phonological awareness: Converging evidence from four studies of preschool and early grade school children. *Journal of Educational Psychology, 96*(1), 1–18.

Antonacci, P., & O'Callaghan, C. (2004). *Portraits of literacy development: Instruction and assessment in a well-balanced literacy program, K–3.* Upper Saddle River, NJ: Merrill/ Prentice Hall.

Applebee, A. N., & Langer, J. A. (1983). Instructional scaffolding: Reading and writing as natural language activities. *Language Arts, 60,* 168–175.

Applebee, A. N., Langer, J. A., & Mullis, M. (1988). *Who reads best? Factors related to reading achievement in grades 3, 7, and 11.* Princeton, NJ: Educational Testing Service.

Armstrong, T. (1994). *Multiple intelligences in the classroom.* Alexandria, VA: Association for Supervision and Curriculum Development.

Ashton-Warner, S. (1959). *Spinster.* New York: Simon & Schuster.

Ashton-Warner, S. (1963). *Teacher.* New York: Bantam.

Au, K. H. (1998). Constructivist approaches, phonics, and the literacy learning of students of diverse backgrounds. In T. Shanahan & F. V. Rodriguez-Brown (Eds.), *Forty-seventh yearbook of the National Reading Conference* (pp. 1–21). Chicago: National Reading Conference.

Au, K. (2001). Culturally responsive instruction as a dimension of new literacy. *Reading Online.* Volume 5, Number 1, July–Aug. 2001.

Auerbach, E. (1989). Toward a social–contextual approach to family literacy. *Harvard Educational Review, 56,* 165–181.

Bachelet, G. (2006). *My cat, the silliest cat in the world.* New York: Abrams.

Banks, J., & Banks, C. (1993). *Multicultural education: Issues and perspectives* (2nd ed.). Boston: Allyn and Bacon.

Barone, D. (1998). How do we teach literacy to children who are learning English as a second language. In S. Neuman & K. Roskos (Eds.), *Children achieving: Best practices in early literacy,* 56–76. Newark, DE: International Reading Association.

Barone, D. & Morrow, L. M. (2003). *Literacy and young children: Research based practices.* New York: Guilford Press.

Barone, D. M., Mallette, M. H., & Xu, S. H. (2004). *Teaching early literacy: Development, assessment, and instruction.* New York: Guilford Press.

Baumann, J. F. (1992). Effect of think aloud instruction on elementary students' comprehension monitoring abilities. *Journal of Reading Behavior, 24*(2), 143–172.

Baumann, J. F., Hoffman, J. V., Dufy-Hester, A. M., & Ro, J. M. (2000). The first R: Reading in the early grades. *Reading Teacher, 54,* 84–98.

Bear, D. R., Invernizzi, M., Templeton, S., & Johnston, D. (1996). *Words their way.* Upper Saddle River, NJ: Prentice Hall.

Bear, D., Invernizzi, M., Templeton, S., & Johnston, F. (2008). *Words their way.* Upper Saddle River, NJ: Pearson Education.

Beck, I. L., & McKeown, M. G. (2001). Text talk: Capturing the benefits of read-aloud experiences for young children. *Reading Teacher, 55*, 10–20.

Bergeron, B. (1990). What does the term whole language mean? A definition from the literature. *Journal of Reading Behavior, 23*, 301–329.

Berk, L. (1997). *Child development.* Boston: Allyn and Bacon.

Berk, L. E. (2004). *Infants, children, and adolescents.* Upper Saddle River, NJ: Prentice Hall.

Blachowicz, C. L. Z., & Fisher, P. J. (2002). Best practices in vocabulary instruction: What effective teachers do. In L. M. Morrow, L. Gambrell, & M. Pressley (Eds.), *Best practices in literacy instruction* (2nd ed., pp. 87–110). New York: Guilford Press.

Bloom, L. (1990). Development in expression: Affect and speech. In N. Stein & T. Trabasso (Eds.), *Psychological and biological approaches to emotion* (pp. 215–245). Hillsdale, NJ: Erlbaum.

Boling, E. C. (2007). Linking technology, learning, and stories: Implications from research on hypermedia video-cases. *Teaching and Teacher Education, 23*(2), pp. 189–200.

Bond, G. L., & Dykstra, R. (1967a). The cooperative research program in first-grade reading instruction. *Reading Research Quarterly, 2*, 5–142.

Bond, G. L., & Dykstra, R. (1967b). *Coordinating center for first grade reading instruction programs.* (Final Report of Project No. x-001, Contact No. OES10–264). Minneapolis: University of Minnesota.

Bouch, M. (2005). *Comprehension strategies for English language learners.* New York: Scholastic.

Bowman, B. T., Donovan, M. S., & Burns, M. S. (Eds.). (2000). *Eager to learn: Educating our preschoolers.* Washington, DC: National Academy Press.

Brock, C. H., & Raphael, T. E. (2005). *Windows to language, literacy, and culture.* Newark, DE: International Reading Association.

Bromley, K. (2007). Building a sound writing program. In L. M. Morrow, L. B. Gambrell, & M. Pressley (Eds.), *Best practices in literacy instruction* (2nd ed. pp. 243–263). New York: Guilford Press.

Brophy, J. (2004). *Motivatiing students to learn* (2nd ed.). Mahwah, NJ: Erlbaum.

Brown, R., Cazden, C., & Bellugi-Klima, U. (1968). The child's grammar from one to three. In J. P. Hill (Ed.), *Minnesota symposium on child development.* Minneapolis: University of Minnesota Press.

Brownell, R. (Ed.) (2000). *Expressive one-word picture vocabulary test, 2 to 18 years.* Academic Therapy Publications: Novato, CA.

Bryant, D., & Maxwell, K. (1997). The effectiveness of early intervention for disadvantaged children. In M. Guralnick (Ed.), *The effectiveness of early intervention* (pp. 23–46). Baltimore: Paul H. Brookes.

Burke, A., & Rowsell, J. (2006) From screen to print: Publishing multiliteracies pedagogy. *International Journal of Learning.* Victoria, BC: Common Ground Publisher.

Burke, A., & Rowsell, J. (2007). Assessing New Literacies: Evaluating Multimodal Practice. *E-Learning Journal, Special Edition,* Oxford, UK: Symposium Journals.

Burns, M. S., Snow, C. E., & Griffin, P. (1998). *Preventing reading difficulties in young children.* Washington, DC: National Academy Press.

Burns, M. S., Snow, C. E., & Griffin, P. (Eds.). (1999). *Starting out right: A guide to success.* Washington, DC: National Academy Press.

Bus, A. G. (2001). Joint caregiver–child storybook reading: A route to literacy development. In S. B. Neuman & D. K. Dickinson (Eds.), *Handbook of early literacy research.* (pp. 179–191). New York: Guilford Press.

Bus, A. G., van Ijzendoorn, M. H., & Pellegrini, A. D. (1995). Joint book reading makes for success in learning to read: A meta-analysis in intergenerational transmission of literacy. *Review of Educational Research, 65*, 1–21.

Byrne, B., & Fielding-Barnsley, R. (1993). Evaluation of a program to teach phonemic awareness to young children: A one-year follow-up. *Journal of Educational Psychology, 85*, 104–111.

Byrne, B., & Fielding-Barnsley, R. (1995). Evaluation of a program to teach phonemic awareness to young children: A two- and three-year follow-up and a new preschool trial. *Journal of Educational Psychology, 87*, 488–503.

Calkins, L. M. (1986). *The art of teaching writing.* Exeter, NH: Heinemann.

Calkins, L.M. (1994). *The art of teaching writing.* Portsmouth, NH: Heinemann.

Cappellini, M. (2005). *Balancing reading and language learning: A resource for teaching English language learners, K–5.* Portland, ME: Stenhouse; Newark, DE: International Reading Association.

Cazden, C. B. (2005). The value of conversations for language development and reading comprehension. *Literacy Teaching and Learning, 9*(1), 1–6.

Center for the Improvement of Early Reading Achievement. (2001). *Put reading first; The research building blocks for teaching children to read.* Washington, DC: National Institute for Literacy.

Chomsky, C. (1965). *Aspects of a theory of syntax.* Cambridge, MA: MIT Press.

Christian, F., Morrison, F., & Bryant, F. (1998). Predicting kindergarten academic skills: Interaction among child-care, maternal education, and family literacy environments, *Early Childhood Research Quarterly, 13*, 501–521.

Clay, M. M. (1966). *Emergent reading behavior.* Doctoral dissertation, University of Auckland, New Zealand.

Clay, M. M. (1979). *The early detection of reading difficulties: A diagnostic survey with recovery procedures.* Auckland, New Zealand: Heinemann Educational Books.

Clay, M. M. (1987). Implementing reading recovery: Systematic adaptations to an educational innovation.

New Zealand Journal of Educational Studies, 22, 35–38.

Clay, M. M. (1991). *Becoming literate: The construction of inner control.* Portsmouth, NH: Heinemann.

Clay, M. M. (1993a). *An observation survey of early literacy achievement.* Portsmouth, NH: Heinemann.

Clay, M. M. (1993b). *Reading Recovery: A guidebook for teachers in training.* Portsmouth, NH: Heinemann.

Clay, M. M. (2000). *Concepts about print: What have children learned about the way we print langauage?* Portsmouth, NJ: Heinemann.

Cochran-Smith, M. (1984). *The making of a reader.* Norwood, NH: Ablex.

Cohen, M. (1980). *First grade takes a test.* New York: Dell.

Coiro, J., & Dobler, E. (2007). Exploring the online reading comprehension strategies used by sixth-grade skilled readers to search for and locate information on the Internet. *Reading Research Quarterly, 42*(2), 214–257.

Collins, N. L. D., & Shaeffer, M. B. (1997). Look, listen, and learn to read. *Young Children, 52*(5), 65–67.

Combs, M. (2006). *Readers and writers in primary grades: A balanced literacy approach K–4.* Upper Saddle River, NJ: Pearson Education.

Connell, R. W. (1994). Poverty and education. *Harvard Educational Review, 64,* 125–149.

Cook-Cottone, C. (2004). Constructivism in family literacy practices: Parents as mentors. *Reading Improvement, 41*(4), 208–216.

Cox, C. (2002). *Teaching language arts: A student- and response-centered classroom* (4th ed.). Boston: Allyn and Bacon.

Cullinan, B. E. (1992). *Invitation to read: More children's literature in the reading program.* Newark, DE: International Reading Association.

Cunningham, P. (1995). *Phonics they use.* New York: HarperCollins.

Cunningham, P. (2005). *Phonics they use.* Boston: Pearson.

Cunningham, P. M., and Cunningham, J. W. (1992). Making words: Enhancing the invented spelling–decoding connection. *Reading Teacher, 46,* 106–115.

Daniels, H. (1994). *Literature circles: Voice and choice in the student centered classroom.* Portland, ME: Stenhouse.

Delgado-Gaitan, C. (1992). School matters in the Mexican-American home: Socializing children to education. *American Educational Research Journal, 29,* 459.

Delpit, L. (1995, December). *Other people's children.* Presentation at the National Reading Conference, New Orleans, LA.

Dewey, J. (1966). *Democracy and education.* New York: First Press.

Dickinson, D. K., McCabe, A., & Essex, M. J. (2006). A window of opportunity we must open to all: The case for preschool with high-quality support for language and literacy. *Handbook of Early Literacy Research, 2,* 11–28.

Dickinson, D. K., & Tabors, P. O. (Eds.). (2001). *Beginning literacy with language.* Baltimore: Paul H. Brookes.

Dickinson, D. K., De Temple, J. M., Hirschler, J. A., & Smith, M. W. (1992). Book reading with preschoolers: Coconstruction of text at home and at school. *Early Childhood Research Quarterly, 7,* 323–346.

Donahue, P., Doane, M., & Grigg, W. Educational Testing Service. (2003). Nation's Report Card. National Assessment of Educational Progress. http://nces.ed.gov/nationsreportcard/

Donahue, P. L., Finnegan, R. J., Lutkus, A. D., Allen, N. L., & Campbell, J. R. (2001). *The nation's report card: Reading 2000.* Washington, DC: U.S. Department of Education, Office of Educational Research and Improvement.

Duke, N. (2000). 3.6 minutes per day: The scarcity of information texts in first grade. *Reading Research Quarterly, 35,* 202–224.

Duke, N. K., & Kays, J. (1998). Can I say "Once upon a time?" Kindergarten children developing knowledge of information book language. *Early Childhood Research Quarterly, 13*(2), 295–318.

Dunn, L., Beach, S., & Kontos, S. (1994). Quality of the early literacy environment in day care and children's development. *Journal of Research in Childhood Education, 9*(1), 24–34.

Dunn, L. M., & Dunn, L. M. (1997). *The Peabody picture vocabulary test: 2 years to 18 years.* American Guidance Service: Circle Pines, MN.

Durkin, D. (1966). *Children who read early.* New York: Teachers College Press.

Durkin, D. (1978–79). What classroom observations reveal about reading instruction. *Reading Research Quarterly, 14,* 481–533.

Dyson, A. H. (1985). Individual differences in emerging writing. In M. Farr (Ed.), *Advances in writing research.* Vol. 1: *Children's early writing development.* Norwood, NJ: Ablex.

Dyson, A. H. (1986). Children's early interpretations of writing: Expanding research perspectives. In D. Yoden & S. Templeton (Eds.), *Metalinguistic awareness and beginning literacy.* Exeter, NH: Heinemann.

Dyson, A. H. (1993). *Social worlds of children learning to write in an urban primary school.* New York: Teachers College Press.

Educational Research Service. (1997). *Promoting early literacy through family involvement* (ERS Information Folio No. C98-F0226). Arlington, VA: Author.

Edwards, P. A. (1995). Combining parents' and teachers' thoughts about storybook reading at home and school. In L. M. Morrow (Ed.), *Family literacy connections in schools and communities* (pp. 54–69). Newark, DE: International Reading Association.

Edwards, S. A., Maloy, R. W., & Verock-O'Loughlin, R. (2003). *Ways of writing with young kids: Teaching creativity and conventions unconventionally.* Boston: Allyn and Bacon.

Ehri, L., & Roberts, T. (2006). The roots of learning to read and write: Acquisition of letters and phonemic awareness. *Handbook of Early Literacy Research, 2,* 113–131.

Englemann, S., & Bruner, E. (1968). *DISTAR: Direct Instruction System for Teaching Arithmetic and Reading.* Chicago: Science Research Associates.

Erickson, K. A., & Koppenhaver, D. A. (1995). Developing a literacy program for children with severe disabilities. *Reading Teacher, 48,* 676–684.

Faber, A., & Mazlish, J. E. (1995). *How to talk so kids can learn at home and at school.* New York: Fireside/Simon & Schuster.

Fields, M. V., Groth, L. A., & Spangler, K. L. (2004). *Let's begin reading right: A developmental approach to emergent literacy* (5th Ed.). Upper Saddle River, NJ: Pearson.

Fingon, J. (2005). The words that surround us. *Teaching PreK–8, 35,* 54–56.

Finn, J. D. (1998). Parental engagement that makes a difference. *Educational Leadership, 55*(8), 20–24.

Fitzpatrick, J. (1997). *Phonemic awareness.* Cypress, CA: Creative Teaching Press.

Fletcher, R., & Portalupi, J. (2001). *Writing workshop: The essential guide.* Portsmouth, NH: Heinemann.

Foster, C. R. (1982). Diffusing the issues in bilingualism and bilingual education. *Phi Delta Kappan, 63,* 338–345.

Fountas, I. C., & Pinnell, G. S. (1996). *Guided reading: Good first teaching for all children.* Portsmouth, NH: Heinemann.

Freeman, D., & Freeman, Y. (1993) Strategies for promoting the primary languages of all students. *Reading Teacher, 46,* 18–25.

Freeman, Y. S., & Freeman, D. E. (2006). *Teaching reading and writing in Spanish and English in bilingual and dual language classrooms* (2nd ed.). Portsmouth, NH: Heinemann.

Frey, N., & Fisher, D. B. (2006). *Language arts workshop: Purposeful reading and writing instruction.* Upper Saddle River, NJ: Pearson.

Froebel, F. (1974). *The education of man.* Clifton, NJ: Augustus M. Kelly.

Fromkin, V., & Rodman, R. (1998). *An introduction to language* (6th ed.). Fort Worth, TX: Harcourt Brace.

Galda, G. (1995) Language change in the history of English: Implications for teachers. In D. Durkin (Ed.), *Language issues: Readings for teachers* (pp. 262–272). White Plains, NY: Longman.

Gambrell, L. B., & Almasi, J. (1994). Fostering comprehension development through discussion. In L. M. Morrow, J. K. Smith, & L. C. Wilkinson (Eds.), *Integrated language arts: Controversy to consensus* (pp. 71–90). Boston: Allyn and Bacon.

Gambrell, L. B., Almasi, J. F., Xie, Q., & Heland, V. (1995). Helping first graders get off to a running start in reading: A home–school–community program that enhances family literacy. In L. Morrow (Ed.), *Family literacy connections at school and home.* 143–154 Newark, DE: International Reading Association.

Gambrell, L. B., & Gillis, V. R. (2007). Assessing children's motivation for reading and writing. In J.R. Paratore & R.L. McCormack (Eds.), *Classroom literacy assessment: Making sense of what students know and do.* New York: Guilford Press.

Gambrell, L. B., & Koskinen, P. S. (2002). Imagery: A strategy for enhancing comprehension. In C. C. Block & M. Pressley (Eds.), *Comprehension instruction: Research-based best practices* (pp. 305–319). New York: Guilford Press.

Gambrell, L., Morrow, L. M., Pressley, M. (2007). *Best practices in literacy instruction.* New York: Guilford Press.

Gambrell, L., Palmer, B., Codling, R., & Mazzoni, S. (1996). Assessing motivation to read. *Reading Teacher, 49,* 518–533.

Gambrell, L., Pfeiffer, W., & Wilson, R. (1985). The effect of retelling upon comprehension and recall of text information. *Journal of Educational Research, 78,* 216–220.

Garcia, E., & McLaughlin, B. (Eds.), with Spodek, B., & Soracho, O. (1995). *Meeting the challenge of linguistic and cultural diversity in early childhood education.* New York: Teachers College Press.

Gardner, H. (Ed.). (1993). *Multiple intelligences: The theory in practice.* New York: Basic Books.

Gaskins, I. W. (2003). A multidimensional approach to beginning literacy. In D. M. Barone & L. M. Morrow (Eds.), *Literacy and young children: Research-based practices* (pp. 45–60). New York: Guilford Press.

Gee, J. P. (2003). *What videogames have to teach us about language and literacy.* New York: Palgrave.

Genishi, C., & Dyson, A. (1984). *Language assessment in the early years.* Norwood, NJ: Ablex.

Gersten, R., Scott, B., Shanahan, T., Linan-Thompson, Collins, P., & Scarcella, R. (2007). *LES practice guide: Effective literacy and English language instruction for English learners elementary grades.* Washington, DC: NCEE 2007-401 1 U.S. Department of Education, Institute of Education Sciences: National Center for Education Evaluation and Regional Assistance.

Gesell, A. (1925). *The mental growth of the preschool child.* New York: Macmillan.

Gollnick, D. M., & Chinn, P. C. (2002). *Multicultural education in a pluralistic society.* Upper Saddle River, NJ: Merrill/Prentice Hall.

Goodman, K. S. (1967). Reading: A psycholinguistic guessing game. *Journal of the Reading Specialist, 4,* 126–135.

Goodman, Y. (1980). The root of literacy. In M. Douglas (Ed.), *Claremont Reading Conference forty-fourth yearbook.* Claremont, CA: Claremont Reading Conference.

Graves, D. (1994). *A fresh look at writing.* Portsmouth, NH: Heinemann.

Graves, D., & Hansen, J. (1983). The author's chair. *Language Arts, 60,* 176–183.

Graves, D. H. (1983). *Writing: Teachers and children at work.* Exeter, NH: Heinemann.

Graves, M. F., Juel, C., & Graves, B. B. (1998). *Teaching reading in the 21st century.* Boston: Allyn and Bacon.

Griffin, M. (2001). Social contexts of beginning reading. *Language Arts, 78*(4), 371–378.

Gundlach, R., McLane, J., Scott, F., & McNamee, G. (1985). The social foundations of early writing development. In M. Farr (Ed.), *Advances in writing research.* Vol. 1: *Children's early writing development.* Norwood, NJ: Ablex.

Gunning, T. G. (2003). *Creating literacy instruction for all children* (4th ed.). Boston: Allyn and Bacon.

Guthrie, J. T. (2002). Engagement and motivation in reading instruction. In M. L. Kamil, J. B. Manning, & H. J. Walberg (Eds.), *Successful reading instruction* (pp. 137–154). Greenwich, CT: Information Age.

Guthrie, J. T. (2004). Teaching for literacy engagement. *Journal of Literary Research, 36*(1), 1–28.

Hadaway, N. L., & Young, T. A. (2006). Changing classrooms: Transforming instruction. In T. A. Young & N. Hadaway (Eds.), *Supporting the literacy development of English language learners: Increasing success in all classrooms* (pp. 6–18). Newark, DE: International Reading Association.

Hall, M. A. (1976). *Teaching reading as a language experience.* Columbus, OH: Merrill.

Halliday, M. A. K. (1975). *Learning how to mean: Exploration in the development of language.* London: Edward Arnold.

Hallinan, M. T., & Sorenson, A. B. (1983). The formation and stability of instructional groups. *American Sociological Review, 48,* 838–851.

Hannon, P. (1995). *Literacy, home and school: Research and practice in teaching literacy with parents.* London: Falmer.

Hansen, J. (1987). *When writers read.* Portsmouth, NH: Heinemann.

Harp, W. (2000). Assessing reading and writing in the early years. In S. Strickland & L. M. Morrow (Eds.), *Beginning reading and writing, kindergarten to grade 2,* 154–167. New York: Teachers College Press.

Harste, J., Woodward, V., & Burke, C. (1984). *Language stories and literacy lessons.* Exeter, NH: Heinemann.

Hart, B., & Risley, T. (1995). *Meaningful differences in the everyday experiences of young American children.* Baltimore: Paul H. Brookes.

Hart, B., & Risley, T. R. (1999). *The social world of children learning to talk.* Baltimore: Paul H. Brookes.

Hasbrouck, J., & Tindal, G. (2006). Oral reading fluency norms: A valuable assessment tool for reading teachers. *Reading Teacher, 59,* 636–644.

Heath, S. B. (1982). What no bedtime story means. *Language in Society, 11,* 49–76.

Heath, S. B. (1993). *Ways with words.* New York: Cambridge University Press.

Hiebert, E. H. (1981). Developmental patterns and interrelationships of preschool children's print awareness. *Reading Research Quarterly, 16,* 236–260.

Hiebert, E. H., & Raphael, T. E. (1998). *Early literacy instruction.* Fort Worth, TX: Harcourt Brace.

Hiebert, E. H., & Taylor, B. (1994). *Getting reading right from the start.* Newark, DE: International Reading Association.

Hill, S. (1997). *Reading manipulatives.* Cypress, CA: Creative Teaching Press.

Holdaway, D. (1979). *The foundations of literacy.* Sydney: Ashton Scholastic.

Hoover, J. J., & Patton, J. R. (2005, March). Differentiating curriculum and instruction for English-language learners with special needs. *Intervention in School and Clinic, 40*(4), 231–235.

Hresko, W., Reid, D. K. & Hammill, D. (1999). *Test of language development: Primary, 4 through 8 years.* Pro-ed: Austin, TX.

Huck, C. S. (1992). Books for emergent readers. In B. E. Cullinan (Ed.), *Invitation to read: More children's literature in the reading program.* Newark, DE: International Reading Association.

Hunt, K. W. (1970). *Syntactic maturity in children and adults.* Monograph of the Society for Research in Child Development (vol. 25). Chicago: University of Chicago Press.

International Reading Association. (1998). *Phonemic awareness and the teaching of reading: A position statement of the board of directors of the International Reading Association.* Newark, DE: Author.

International Reading Association. (1999). *Position statement: Using multiple methods of beginning reading instruction.* Newark, DE: Author.

International Reading Association. (2001). Association issues position statement on second-language literacy instruction. *Reading Today.* Retrieved on May 14, 2003, from http://www.findarticles.com

International Reading Association. (2006). *Reading in preschool.* Newark, DE: Author.

International Reading Association & National Association for the Education of Young Children. (1998). *Learning to read and write: Developmentally appropriate practices for young children.* Newark, DE: Author.

International Reading Association & National Council of Teachers of English. (1996). *Standards for the English language arts.* Newark, DE: Author.

Invernizzi, M. (2003). Concepts, sounds, and the ABCs: A diet for a very young reader. In D. M. Barone & L. M. Morrow (Eds.), *Literacy and young children: Research-based practices* (pp. 140–157). New York: Guilford Press.

Irving, A. (1980). *Promoting voluntary reading for children and young people.* Paris: UNESCO.

Ivey, G. (2002). Building comprehension when they're still learning to read the words. In C. C. Block & M. Pressley (Eds.), *Comprehension instruction: Research-based best practices* (pp. 234–247). New York: Guilford Press.

Jalongo, M. R. (2007). *Early childhood language arts* (4th Ed.). Boston: Allyn and Bacon.

Jewell, M., & Zintz, M. (1986). *Learning to read naturally.* Dubuque, IA: Kendall/Hunt.

Johns, J., & Berglund, R. L. (2002). *Fluency: evidence-based strategies*. Dubuque, IA: Kendall/ Hunt.

Johns, J., Lenski, S. D., & Elish-Piper, L. (1999). *Early literacy assessments and teaching strategies*. Dubuque, IA: Kendall/Hunt.

Johnson, D., & Pearson, P. D. (1984). *Teaching reading vocabulary* (2nd ed.). New York: Holt.

Johnston, P., & Costello, P. (2005). Principles of literacy assessment. *Reading Research Quarterly, 40*(2), 256–267.

Juel, C. (1989). The role of decoding in early literacy instruction and assessment. In L. Morrow & J. Smith (Eds.), *Assessment for instruction in early literacy* (pp. 135–154). Upper Saddle River, NJ: Prentice Hall.

Juel, C. (1994). Teaching phonics in the context of the integrated language arts. In L. Morrow, J. K. Smith, & L. C. Wilkinson (Eds.), *Integrated language arts: Controversy for consensus* (pp. 133–154). Boston: Allyn and Bacon.

Karmiloff, M., & Karmiloff-Smith, A. (2001). *Pathways to language: From fetus to adolescent*. Cambridge, MA: Harvard University Press.

Katz, L. G., & Chard, S. C. (2000). *Engaging children's minds: The project approach* (2nd Ed.). Norwood, NJ: Ablex.

Kelly, D. (2004). *1001 best web sites for kids*. New York: Teacher Created Materials.

King, R., & McMaster, J. (2000). *Pathways; A primer for family literacy program and development*. Louisville, KY: National Center for Family Literacy.

Kinzer, C. K., & McKenna, M. C. (1999, May). *Using technology in your classroom literacy program: Current and future possibilities*. Paper presented at the Annual Convention of the International Reading Association, San Diego, CA.

Knobel, M., & Lankshear, C. (2006). Weblogs worlds and constructions of effective and powerful writing: Cross with care, and only where signs permit. In K. Pahl and J. Rowsell's *Travel notes from new literacy studies: Instances of practice*, 72–95. Clevedon, UK: Multilingual Matters.

Knobel, M., & Lankshear, C. (2007). *The new literacies sampler*. New York: Peter Lang.

Krashen, S. (2003). *Explorations in language acquisition and use*. Portsmouth, NH: Heinemann.

Kress, G. (1997). *Before writing*. London: Routledge.

Kuhl, P. (1994). Learning and representation in speech and language. *Current Opinion in Neurobiology, 4*, 812–822.

Kuhn, M. (2007). Effective oral reading assessment (or why round robin reading doesn't cut it). In J. R. Paratore & R. L. McCormack (Eds.). *Classroom literacy assessment: Making sense of what students know and do* (pp. 101–112). New York: Guilford Press.

Kuhn, M., Schwanenflugel, P., Morris, R., Morrow, L. M., Woo, D., Meisinger, E., et al. (2006). Teaching children to become fluent and automatic readers. *Journal of Literacy Research, 38*(4), 357–387.

Kuhn, M. R., & Stahl, S. A. (2003). Fluency: A review of developmental and remedial strategies. *Journal of Educational Psychology, 95*, 3–21.

Labbo, L. D., & Ash, G. E. (1998). What is the role of computer related technology in early literacy? In S. B. Neuman & K. A. Roskos (Eds.), *Children achieving: Best practices in early literacy* (pp. 180–197). Newark, DE: International Reading Association.

Labbo, L. D., Reinking, D., & McKenna, M. (1998). The use of technology in literacy programs. In L. Gambrell, L. M. Morrow, S. B. Neuman, & M. Pressley (Eds.), *Best practices in literacy instruction*. New York: Guilford Press.

Lennenberg, E. (1967). *Biological foundations of language*. New York: Wiley.

Lennenberg, E., & Kaplan, E. (1970). Grammatical structures and reading. In H. Levin & J. Williams (Eds.), *Basic studies in reading*. New York: Basic Books.

Leseman, P. P. M., & de Jong, P. F. (1998). Home literacy: opportunity, instruction, cooperation and social-emotional quality predicting early reading achievement. *Reading Research Quarterly, 33*, 294–318.

Leu, D. J., & Kinzer, C. (1991). *Effective reading instruction K–8* (2nd ed.). New York: Merrill.

Leu, D. J., & Kinzer, C. K. (2003). *Effective literacy instruction, K–8*. Upper Saddle River, NJ: Merrill/ Prentice Hall.

Leu, D. J., Jr., Kinzer, C. K., Coiro, J., & Cammack, D. (2004). Toward a theory of new literacies emerging from the Internet and other information and communication technologies. In R. Ruddell & N. Unrau (Eds.), *Theoretical models and processes of reading* (5th ed.; pp. 1568–1611). Newark: International Reading Association.

Lindfors, J. (1989). The classroom: A good environment for language learning. In P. Rigg & V. Allen (Eds.), *When they don't all speak English: Integrating the ESL student into the regular classroom* (pp. 39–54). Urbana, IL: National Council of Teachers of English.

Lonigan, C. (2006). Conceptualizing phonological processing skills in prereaders. *Handbook of Early Literacy Research, 2*, 77–89.

Lonigan, C., & Whitehurst, G. (1998). Relative efficacy of parent and teacher involvement in a shared-reading intervention for preschool children from low-income backgrounds. *Early Childhood Research Quarterly, 23*(2), 263–290.

Lou, Y., Abrami, P. C., Spence, J. C., Poulsen, C., Chambers, B., & d'Apollonia, S. (1996). Within-class grouping. A meta-analysis. *Review of Educational Research, 66*(4), 423–458.

Loughlin, C. E., & Martin, M. D. (1987). *Supporting literacy: Developing effective learning environments*. New York: Teachers College Press.

Lum, K., & Johnson, A. (1998). *What cried granny: An almost bedtime story*. New York: Puffin Books.

Manning, M., Manning, G., & Long, R. (1994). *Theme immersion: Inquiry-based curriculum in elementary and middle schools*. Portsmouth, NH: Heinemann.

Marriott, D. (1997). *What are the other kids doing?* Cypress, CA: Creative Teaching Press.

Martinez, M., & Teale, W. (1987). The ins and outs of a kindergarten writing program. *Reading Teacher, 40,* 444–451.

Martinez, M., & Teale, W. (1988). Reading in a kindergarten classroom library. *Reading Teacher, 41*(6), 568–572.

Mason, J. (1980). When do children begin to read? An exploration of four-year-old children's letter and word reading competencies. *Reading Research Quarterly, 15,* 203–227.

Mason, J., & McCormick, C. (1981). *An investigation of pre-reading instruction: A developmental perspective* (Technical Report 224). Urbana: University of Illinois, Center for the Study of Reading.

McAfee, O., & Leong, D. (1997). *Assessing and guiding young children's development and learning.* Boston: Allyn and Bacon.

McCarrier, A., Pinnell, G. S., & Fountas, I. C. (2000). *Interactive writing: How language & literacy come together, K–2.* Portsmouth, NH: Heinemann.

McCormick, C., & Mason, J. (1981). What happens to kindergarten children's knowledge about reading after summer vacation? *Reading Teacher, 35,* 164–172.

McGee, L. (2007). Language and literacy assessment in preschool. In J. Paratore & R. McCormack (Eds.), *Classroom literacy assessment: Making sense of what students know and do,* pp. 65–84. New York: Guilford Press.

McGee, L. M., & Morrow, L. M. (2005). *Teaching literacy in kindergarten.* New York: Guilford Press.

McGee, L. M., & Richgels, D. J. (2000). *Literacy's beginnings: Supporting young readers and writers.* Boston: Allyn and Bacon.

McKenna, M. C. (2001). Development of reading attitudes. In L. Verhoeven & C. Snow (Eds.), *Literacy and motivation: Reading engagement in individuals and groups* (pp. 135–158). Mahwah, NJ: Erlbaum.

McLaughlin, M. (2003). *Guided comprehension in the primary grades.* Newark, DE: International Reading Association.

McNaughton, S. (2006). Considering culture in research-based interventions to support early literacy. *Handbook of Early Literacy Research, 2,* 113–131.

McNeil, D. (1970). *The acquisition of language: The study of developmental psycholinguistics.* New York: Harper & Row.

Meers, T. B. (1999). *101 best web sites for kids.* Lincolnwood, IL: Publications International.

Melzi, G., Paratore, J. R., & Krol-Sinclair, B. (2000). Reading and writing in the daily lives of Latino mothers participating in an intergenerational literacy project. *National Reading Conference Yearbook, 49,* 178–193.

Miramontes, O. B., Nadeau, A., & Commins, N. L. (1997). *Restructuring schools for linguistic diversity: Linking decision making to effective programs.* New York: Teachers College Press.

Montessori, M. (1965). *Spontaneous activity in education.* New York: Schocken Books.

Moore, G. (1986). Effects of the spatial definition of behavior settings on children's behavior: A quasi-experimental field study. *Journal of Environmental Psychology, 6*(3), 205–231.

Morphett, M. V., & Washburne, C. (1931). When should children begin to read? *Elementary School Journal, 31,* 496–508.

Morris, D., & Slavin, R. (Eds.). (2003). *Every child reading.* Boston: Allyn and Bacon.

Morrison, G. S. (2003). *Fundamentals of early childhood education* (3rd ed.). Upper Saddle River, NJ: Prentice Hall.

Morrison, G. S. (2004). *Early childhood education today* (9th ed.). Upper Saddle River, NJ: Pearson.

Morrow, L. M. (1978). Analysis of syntax in the language of six-, seven-, and eight-year-olds. *Research in the Teaching of English, 12,* 143–148.

Morrow, L. M. (1982). Relationships between literature programs, library corner designs, and children's use of literature. *Journal of Educational Research, 75,* 339–344.

Morrow, L. M. (1983). Home and school correlates of early interest in literature. *Journal of Educational Research, 76,* 221–230.

Morrow, L. M. (1984). Reading stories to young children: Effects of story structure and traditional questioning strategies on comprehension. *Journal of Reading Behavior, 16,* 273–288.

Morrow, L. M. (1985). Retelling stories: A strategy for improving children's comprehension, concept of story structure, and oral language complexity. *Elementary School Journal, 85,* 647–661.

Morrow, L. M. (1986). *Promoting responses to literature: Children's sense of story structure.* Paper presented at the National Reading Conference, Austin, TX.

Morrow, L. M. (1987). Promoting voluntary reading: The effects of an inner city program in summer day care centers. *Reading Teacher, 41,* 266–274.

Morrow, L. M. (1988a). The effects of one-to-one story readings on children's questions and comments. In S. Baldwin & J. Readance (Eds.), *36th yearbook of the National Reading Conference.* Rochester, NY: National Reading Conference.

Morrow, L. M. (1988b). Young children's responses to one-to-one story readings in school settings. *Reading Research Quarterly, 23*(1), 89–107.

Morrow, L. M. (1990). Preparing the classroom environment to promote literacy during play. *Early Childhood Research Quarterly, 5,* 537–554.

Morrow, L. M. (1992). The impact of a literature-based program on literacy achievement, use of literature, and attitudes of children from minority backgrounds. *Reading Research Quarterly, 27,* 250–275.

Morrow, L. M. (1995). *Family literacy connections at school and home*. Newark, DE: International Reading Association.

Morrow, L. M. (1996). Story retelling: A discussion strategy to develop and assess comprehension. In L. B. Gambrell & J. F. Almasi (Eds.), *Lively discussions: Fostering engaged reading* (pp. 265–285). Newark, DE: International Reading Association.

Morrow, L. M. (2002). *The literacy center: Contexts for reading and writing* (2nd ed.). York, ME: Stenhouse.

Morrow, L. M. (2003). *Organizing and managing the language arts block*. New York: Guilford Press.

Morrow, L. M. (2004). *Children's literature in preschool: Comprehending and enjoying books*. Newark, DE: International Reading Association.

Morrow, L. M. (2005). Language and literacy in preschools: Current issues and concerns. *Literacy Teaching and Learning, 9*(1), 7–19.

Morrow, L. M., & Asbury, E. (2003). Best practices for a balanced early literacy program. In L. M. Morrow, L. Gambrell, & M. Pressley (Eds.), *Best practices in literacy instruction* (2nd ed., pp. 49–67). New York: Guilford Press.

Morrow, L. M., & Gambrell, L. B. (2004). *Using children's literature in preschool: Comprehending and enjoying books*. Newark, DE: International Reading Association.

Morrow, L. M., Kuhn, M. R., Schwanenflugel, P. J. (2006). The family fluency program. *Reading Teacher. 60*(4), 322–333.

Morrow, L. M., & O'Connor, E. (1995). Literacy partnerships for change with "at risk" kindergartners. In R. Allington & S. Walmsley (Eds.), *No quick fix: Rethinking literacy programs in America's elementary schools* (pp. 97–115). New York: Teachers College Press.

Morrow, L. M., O'Connor, E. M., & Smith, J. (1990). Effects of a story reading program on the literacy development of at-risk kindergarten children. *Journal of Reading Behavior, 20*(2), 104–141.

Morrow, L. M., Paratore, J. R., & Tracey, D. H. (1994). *Family literacy: New perspectives, new opportunities*. Newark, DE: International Reading Association.

Morrow, L. M., Pressley, M., Smith, J., & Smith, M. (1997). The effects of integrating literature-based instruction into literacy and science programs. *Reading Research Quarterly, 32*, 54–77.

Morrow, L. M., & Rand, M. (1991). Promoting literacy during play by designing early childhood classroom environments. *Reading Teacher, 44*, 396–405.

Morrow, L. M., Scoblionko, J., & Shafer, D. (1995). The family reading and writing appreciation program. In L. M. Morrow (Ed.), *Family literacy connections in schools and communities* (pp. 70–86). Newark, DE: International Reading Association.

Morrow, L. M., Sharkey, E., & Firestone, W. (1994). Collaborative strategies in the integrated language arts. In L. M. Morrow, J. K. Smith, & L. C. Wilkinson (Eds.), *Integrated language arts: Controversy to consensus* (pp. 155–176). Boston: Allyn and Bacon.

Morrow, L. M., & Smith, J. K. (1990). The effect of group setting on interactive storybook reading. *Reading Research Quarterly, 25*, 213–231.

Morrow, L. M., Strickland, D. S., & Woo, D. G. (1998). *Literacy instruction in half- and whole-day kindergarten: Research to practice*. Newark, DE: International Reading Association.

Morrow, L. M., & Tracey, D. (1997). Strategies for phonics instruction in early childhood classrooms. *Reading Teacher, 50*(8), 2–9.

Morrow, L. M., & Tracey, D. H. (1997). Instructional environments for language and learning. Considerations for young children. In J. Flood, S. B. Heath, & D. Lapp (Eds.), *Handbook for literacy educators: Research on teaching the communicative and visual arts*, 475–485. New York: Macmillan.

Morrow, L. M., & Weinstein, C. S. (1986). Encouraging voluntary reading: The impact of a literature program on children's use of library centers. *Reading Research Quarterly, 21*, 330–346.

Morrow, L. M., & Young, J. (1997). A family literacy program connecting school and home: Effects on attitude, motivation, and literacy achievement. *Journal of Educational Psychology, 89*, 736–742.

Moss, B., Leone, S. & Dipillo, M. L. (1997). Exploring the literature of fact: Linking reading and writing through information trade books. *Language Arts, 74*(6), 418–429.

Moustafa, M. (1997). *Beyond traditional phonics: Research discoveries and reading instruction*. Portsmouth, NH: Heinemann.

Nagy, W. (1988). *Teaching vocabulary to improve reading comprehension*. Newark, DE: International Reading Association.

National Center for Family Literacy. (1993). Parents and children together. In *Creating an upward spiral of success* (pp. 6–8). Louisville, KY: Author.

National Center for Family Literacy. (2004). *Report of the National Early Literacy Panel*. Washington DC: National Institute for Literacy.

National Center on Education and the Economy & Learning Research and Development Center at the University of Pittsburgh. (1999). *Reading and writing grade by grade: Primary literacy standards for kindergarten through third grade*. Washington, DC: National Center on Education and the Economy.

National Reading Panel Report. (2000). *Teaching children to read*. Washington, DC: National Institute of Child Health and Human Development.

Neuman, S. B. (1996). Children engaging in story-book reading: The influence of access to print resources, opportunity, and parental interaction. *Early Childhood Research Quarterly, 11*, 495–513.

Neuman, S. B., & Roskos, K. (1992). Literary objects as cultural tools: Effects on children's literacy behaviors in play. *Reading Research Quarterly, 27*(3), 203–225.

Neuman, S., & Roskos, K. (1993). *Language and literacy learning in the early years: An integrated approach*. Orlando, FL: Harcourt Brace.

Neuman, S., & Roskos, K. (1994). Building home and school with a culturally responsive approach. *Childhood Education, 70*, 210–214.

Neuman, S. B., & Roskos, K. (1997). Knowledge in practice: Contexts of participation for young writers and readers. *Reading Research Quarterly, 32*, 10–32.

Neuman, S. B., & Roskos, K. A. (Eds.). (1998). *Children achieving: Best practices in early literacy.* Newark, DE: International Reading Association.

Newberger, J. J. (1997). New brain development research: A wonderful window of opportunity to build public support for early childhood education. *Young Children, 52*(4), 4–9.

New Jersey State Department of Education. (1998). *Test Specification Booklet.* Trenton, NJ.

Newman, J. (1984). *The craft of children's writing.* Exeter, NH: Heinemann.

Ninio, A. (1980). Picture book reading in mother–infant dyads belonging to two subgroups in Israel. *Child Development, 51*, 587.

O'Connor R. E., Harty, K. R., & Fulmer, D. (2005 Nov./Dec.). Tiers of intervention in kindergarten through third grade. *Journal of Learning Disabilities, 38*(6), 532–538.

O'Flahavan, J., Gambrell, L. B., Guthrie, J., Stahl, S., & Alverman, D. (1992, April). Poll results guide activities of research center. *Reading Today*, p. 12.

Ogle, D. (1986). K-W-L: A teaching model that develops active reading of expository text. *Reading Teacher, 39*, 564–570.

Ollila, L. O., & Mayfield, M. I. (1992). *Emerging literacy: Preschool, kindergarten, and primary grades.* Boston: Allyn and Bacon.

Orellana, M. E., & Hernandez, A. (1999). Talking with the walk: Children reading urban environmental print. *Reading Teacher, 51*, 612–619.

Otto, B. (2006). *Language development in early childhood* (2nd Ed.). Upper Saddle River, NJ: Merrill/Prentice Hall.

Pappas, C., Kiefer, B., & Levstik, L. (1995). *An integrated language perspective in the elementary school: Theory into action.* New York: Longman.

Paratore, J. R., Homza, A., Krol-Sinclair, B., Lewis-Barrow, T., Melzi, G., Stergis, R., et al. (1995). Shifting boundaries in home and school responsibilities: Involving immigrant parents in the construction of literacy portfolios. *Research in the Teaching of English, 29*, 367–389.

Paratore, J. R., Melzi, G., & Krol-Sinclair, B. (2003). Learning about the literate lives of Latino families. In D. M. Barone & L. M. Morrow (Eds.), *Literacy and young children: Research-based practices*, (pp. 101–120). New York: Guilford Press.

Parker, E. L., & Pardini, T. H. (2006). *The words came down: English language learners read, write, and talk across the curriculum, K–2.* Portland, ME: Stenhouse.

Pearson, P. D., Roehler, L. R., Dole, J. A., & Duffy, G. G. (1992). Developing expertise in reading comprehension. In S. J. Samuels & A. E. Farsturp (Eds.), *What research has to say about reading instruction* (2nd ed., pp. 145–199). Newark, DE: International Reading Association.

Pellegrini, A., & Galda, L. (1982). The effects of thematic fantasy play training on the development of children's story comprehension. *American Educational Research Journal, 19*, 443–452.

Pflaum, S. (1986). *The development of language and literacy in young children* (3rd ed.). Columbus, OH: Merrill.

Piaget, J., & Inhelder, B. (1969). *The psychology of the child.* New York: Basic Books.

Pinker, S. (1994). *The language instinct: How the mind creates language.* New York: Morrow.

Pinnell, G. S., Freid, M. D., & Estice, R. M. (1990). Reading recovery: Learning how to make a difference. *Reading Teacher, 43*(4), 282–295.

Pittelman, S. D., Heimlich, J. E., Berglund, R. L., & French, M. P. (1991). *Semantic feature analysis: Classroom applications.* Newark, DE: International Reading Association.

Pittelman, S. D., Levin, K. M., & Johnson, D. P. (1985). *An investigation of two instructional settings in the use of semantic mapping with poor readers* (Program Report 85–4). Madison: Wisconsin Center for Educational Research, University of Wisconsin.

Prescott, O. (1965). *A father reads to his child: An anthology of prose and poetry.* New York: Dutton.

Pressley, M. (1998). *Reading instruction that works: The case for balanced teaching.* New York: Guilford Press.

Pressley, M., & Afflerbach, P. (1995). *Verbal protocols of reading: The nature of constructively responsive reading.* Hillsdale, NJ: Erlbaum.

Pressley, M., & Hilden, K. (2002). How can children be taught to comprehend text better? In M. L. Kamil, J. B. Manning, & H. J. Walberg (Eds.), *Successful reading instruction* (pp. 33–53). Greenwich, CT: Information Age.

Pressley, M., Allington, R. L., Wharton-McDonald, R., Block, C. C., & Morrow, L. (2001). *Learning to read: Lessons from exemplary first-grade classrooms.* New York: Guilford Press.

Purcell-Gates, V., Duke, N. K., & Martineau, J. A. (2007). Learning to read and write genre-specific text: Roles of authentic experience and explicit teaching. *Reading Research Quarterly, 42*(1), 8–45.

Rand, M. (1993). Using thematic instruction to organize an integrated language arts classroom. In L. M. Morrow, J. K. Smith, & L. C. Wilkinson (Eds.), *Integrated language arts: Controversy to consensus* (pp. 177–192). Boston: Allyn and Bacon.

Rand Reading Study Group. (2002). *Reading for understanding: Toward a research and development program in reading comprehension.* Washington, DC: Author/OERI/Department of Education.

Rasinski, T. (1990). Effects of repeated reading and listening while reading on reading fluency. *Journal of Educational Research, 83*, 147–150.

Report of the National Early Reading Panel. (2004). Washington, DC: National Institute for Literacy.

Reutzel, D. R., & Cooter, R. B. (2004). *Teaching children to read: Putting the pieces together* (4th ed.). Upper Saddle River, NJ: Pearson/Merrill/Prentice Hall.

Ritchie, S., James-Szanton, J., & Howes, C. (2003). Emergent literacy practices in early childhood classrooms. In C. Howes (Ed.), *Teaching 4- to 8-year-olds* (pp. 71–92). Baltimore: Paul H. Brookes.

Rog, L. J. (2007). *Marvelous minilessons for teaching beginning writing, K–3.* Newark, DE: International Reading Association.

Rosenblatt, L. M. (1988). *Writing and reading: Transactional theory* (Report No. 13). University of California, Berkeley: Center for the Study of Writing.

Rosencrans, G. (1998). *The spelling book: Teaching children how to spell, not what to spell.* Newark, DE: International Reading Association.

Roser, N., & Martinez, M. (1985). Roles adults play in preschool responses to literature. *Language Arts, 62,* 485–490.

Roskos, K. A., & Christie, J. F. (Eds.). (2000). *Play and literacy in early childhood: Research from multiple perspectives.* Mahwah, NJ: Erlbaum.

Roskos, K. A., Christie, J. F., & Richgels, D. J. (2003). The essentials of early literacy instruction. *Young Children, 58*(2), 52–60.

Roskos, K. A., Tabor, P. & Lenhart, L. (2004). *Oral language and early literacy in preschool: Talking, reading and writing.* Newark, DE: International Reading Association.

Rossi, R., & Stringfield, S. (1995). What we must do for students placed at risk. *Phi Delta Kappan, 77,* 73–76.

Rousseau, J. (1962). *Emile* (ed. and trans. William Boyd). New York: Columbia University Teachers College (original work published 1762).

Routman, R., (2005). *Writing essentials: Raising expectations and results while simplifying teaching.* Portsmouth, NH: Heinemann.

Ruddell, R., & Ruddell, M. R. (1995). *Teaching children to read and write: Becoming an influential teacher.* Boston: Allyn and Bacon.

Rusk, R., & Scotland, J. (1979). *Doctrines of the great educators.* New York: St. Martin's Press.

Sampson, M. B. (2002). Confirming K-W-L: Considering the source. *Reading Teacher, 55*(6), 528–532.

Schickedanz, J. A., & Casbergue, R. M. (2004). *Writing in preschool: Learning to orchestrate meaning and marks.* Newark, DE: International Reading Association.

Schickedanz, J. A., York, M. E., Stewart, I. S., & White, A. (1990). *Strategies for teaching young children.* Upper Saddle River, NJ: Prentice Hall.

Schwanenflugel, P., Meisinger, E., Wisenbaker, J., Kuhn, M., Strauss, G., & Morris, R. (2006). Becoming a fluent and automatic reader in the early elementary school years. *Reading Research Quarterly, 41*(4), 496–522.

Seefeldt, C., & Barbour, N. (1986). *Early childhood education: An introduction.* Columbus, OH: Merrill/Prentice Hall.

Shaywitz, S. (2003). *Overcoming dyslexia.* New York: Knopf.

Shore, K. (2001). Success for ESL students: 12 practical tips to help second-language learners. *Instructor, 1*(110), 30–32, 106.

Skinner, B. F. (1954). The science of learning and the art of teaching. *Harvard Educational Review, 24,* 86–97.

Skinner, B. F. (1957). *Verbal behavior.* Boston: Appleton-Century-Crofts.

Slavin, R. (1998). *Success for all.* Baltimore: Success for All Foundation.

Slavin, R. E. (1987). Ability grouping and student achievement in elementary schools: A best-evidence synthesis. *Review of Educational Research, 57,* 292–336.

Slavin, R. E. (1997). *Educational psychology: Theory and practice* (5th ed.). Boston: Allyn and Bacon.

Slavin, R. E., & Madden, N. A. (1989). What works for students at risk: A research synthesis. *Educational Leadership, 46,* 4–13.

Smith, F. (1971). *Understanding reading.* New York: Holt.

Snow, C. E., Burns, M. S., & Griffin, P. (1998). *Preventing reading difficulties in young children.* Washington, DC: National Academy Press.

Soderman, A., & Farrell, P. (2008). *Creating literacy-rich preschools and kindergartens.* Boston: Pearson Education.

Soderman, A. K., Gregory, K. S., & McCarty, L. T. (2005). *Scaffolding emergent literacy: A child-centered approach for preschool through grade 5* (2nd ed). Boston: Allyn and Bacon.

Sorenson, A. B., & Hallinan, M. T. (1986). Effects of ability grouping on growth in academic achievement. *American Educational Research Journal, 23,* 519–542.

Spandel, V. (2001). *Creating writers through six-trait writing assessment and instruction.* New York: Longman.

Spandel, V. (2008). *Creating young writers: Using six traits to enrich writing process in primary classrooms.* Boston: Allyn and Bacon.

Spencer, B. H., & Guillaume, A. M. (2006). Integrating curriculum through the learning cycle: Content-based reading and vocabulary instruction. *Reading Teacher, 60*(3), 206–219.

Spiegel, D. L. (1992). Blending whole language and systematic direct instruction. *Reading Teacher, 46,* 38–44.

Spielberg, S. (1987). Acceptance speech at the Academy Award Ceremonies, Los Angeles.

Spodek, B. (1988). Conceptualizing today's kindergarten curriculum. *Elementary School Journal, 89,* 203–212.

Stahl, S. A. (2003). No more "madfaces": Motivation and fluency development with struggling readers. In D. M. Barone & L. M. Morrow (Eds.), *Literacy and young children: Research-based practices* (pp. 195–209). New York: Guilford Press.

Stahl, S. A., & Heubach, K. M. (2005). Fluency-oriented reading instruction. *Journal of Literacy Research, 37,* 25–60.

Stanovich, K. E. (1986). Mathew effects in reading: Some consequences of individual differences in the acquisition of literacy. *Reading Research Quarterly, 21,* 360–407.

Stauffer, R. G. (1980). *The language-experience approach to the teaching of reading* (2nd ed.). New York: Harper & Row.

Stine, H. A. (1993). *The effects of CD-ROM interactive software in reading skills instructions with second grade Chapter 1 students.* Doctoral dissertation, George Washington University. Ann Arbor, MI: University Microfilms International.

Strickland, D., & Schickedanz, J. (2004). *Learning about print in preschool: Working with letters, words, and beginning links with phonemic awareness.* Newark, DE: International Reading Association.

Strickland, D., & Snow, C. (2002). *Preparing our teachers: Opportunities for better reading instruction.* Washington, DC: Joseph Henry Press.

Sullivan, N. W., & Buchanan, C. D. (1963). *Programmed reading series.* New York: McGraw-Hill.

Sulzby, E. (1985a). Children's emergent reading of favorite storybooks. *Reading Research Quarterly, 20,* 458–481.

Sulzby, E. (1985b). Kindergarteners as writers and readers. In M. Farr (Ed.), *Advances in writing research.* Vol. 1: *Children's early writing,* 127–199. Norwood, NJ: Ablex.

Tabors, P. (1998) What early childhood educators need to know: Developing effective programs for linguistically and culturally diverse children and families. *Young Children, 53*(6), 20–26.

Tafa, E. (1998). *Inclusive education for children with learning and behavioral problems.* Athens, Greece: Ellinika Grammata.

Tafa, E. (2001). *Reading and writing in preschool education.* Athens, Greece: Ellinika Grammata.

Taylor, B. M., Frye, B. J., & Maruyama, M. (1990). Time spent reading and reading growth. *American Educational Research Journal, 27,* 351–362.

Taylor, B. M., Strait, J., & Medo, M. A. (1994). Early intervention in reading: Supplemental instruction for groups of low-achieving students provided by first-grade teachers. In E. H. Hiebert & B. Taylor (Eds.), *Getting reading right from the start* (pp. 107–123). Newark, DE: International Reading Association.

Taylor, D. (1983). *Family literacy.* Exeter, NH: Heinemann.

Taylor, D., & Dorsey-Gaines, C. (1988). *Growing up literate.* Portsmouth, NH: Heinemann.

Teale, W. (2003). Questions about early literacy learning and teaching that need asking—and some that don't. In D. M. Barone & L. M. Morrow (Eds.), *Literacy and young children: Research-based practices* (pp. 140–157). New York: Guilford Press.

Teale, W. H., & Gambrell, L. B. (2007). Raising urban students' literacy achievement by engaging in authentic, challenging work. *Reading Teacher, 60*(8), 728–739.

Temple, C., Nathan, R., Burris, N., & Temple, F. (1988). *The beginnings of writing.* Boston: Allyn and Bacon.

Templeton, S. (1991). *Teaching the integrated language arts.* Boston: Houghton Mifflin.

Tomlinson, C. A. (2003). *How to differentiate instruction in mixed-ability classrooms.* Alexandria, VA: Association for Supervision and Curriculum Development.

Tompkins, G. E. (2007). *Literacy for the 21st century: Teaching reading and writing in prekindergarten through grade 4.* Upper Saddle River, NJ: Pearson Education.

Tompkins, G. E. (2003). *Literacy for the 21st century: Teaching reading and writing in prekindergarten through grade 4.* Upper Saddle River, NJ: Pearson/Merrill Prentice Hall.

Tompkins, G. E. (2000). *Teaching writing: Balancing process and product* (3rd ed.). Upper Saddle River, NJ: Prentice Hall.

Tompkins, G. E., & Koskisson, I. K. (1995). *Language arts content and teaching strategies.* Upper Saddle River, NJ: Prentice Hall.

Tompkins, G. (2003). *Literacy for the 21st century: Teaching reading and writing in prekindergarten through grade 4.* Upper Saddle River, NJ: Pearson Education.

Turbill, J., & Bean, W. (2006). *Writing instruction K–6: Understanding process, purpose, audience.* Katonah, NY: Richard C. Owen.

U.S. Department of Education. (2001). *No child left behind legislation.* http://www.nochildleftbehind.gov

Veatch, J., Sawicki, F., Elliot, G., Barnett, E., & Blackey, J. (1973). *Key words to reading: The language experience approach begins.* Columbus, OH: Merrill.

Vukelich, C., & Christie, J. (2004). *Building a foundation for preschool literacy: Effective instruction for children's reading and writing development.* Newark, DE: International Reading Association.

Vukelich, C., Christie, J., & Enz, B. (2002). *Helping young children learn language and literacy.* Boston: Allyn & Bacon.

Vukelich, C., Evans, C., & Albertson, B. (2003). Organizing expository texts: A look at the possibilities. In D. M. Barone & L. M. Morrow (Eds.), *Literacy and young children: Research-based practices* (pp. 261–290). New York: Guilford Press.

Vygotsky, L. S. (1978). *Mind in society: The development of psychological processes.* Cambridge, MA: Harvard University Press.

Walmsley, S. A. (1994). *Children exploring their world: Theme teaching in elementary school.* Portsmouth, NH: Heinemann.

Walpole, S. & McKenna, M. C. (2007). *Differentiated reading instruction strategies for primary grades.* New York: Guilford Press.

Ward, M., & McCormick, S. (1981). Reading instruction for blind and low vision children in the regular classroom. *Reading Teacher, 34,* 434, 444.

Wasik, B. H., Dobbins, D. R., & Herrmann, S. (2001). Intergenerational family literacy: Concepts, research, and practice. In S. B. Neuman & D. K. Dickinson (Eds.), *Handbook of early literacy research* (pp. 444–458). New York: Guilford Press.

Wasik, B. A., & Bond, M. A. (2001). Beyond the pages of a book: Interactive book reading and language development in preschool classrooms. *Journal of Educational Psychology, 93*(2), 243–250.

Weinstein, C. S., & Mignano, A. J., Jr. (2003). *Elementary classroom management* (3rd ed.). Boston: McGraw-Hill.

Weitzman, E., & Greenberg, J. (2002). *Learning language and loving it: A guide to promoting children's social, language, and literacy development in early childhood settings* (2nd Ed.). Toronto: Hanen Centre.

Wepner, S., & Ray, L. (2000). Sign of the times: Technology and early literacy learning. In D. S. Strickland & L. M. Morrow (Eds.), *Beginning reading and writing* (pp. 168–182). New York: Teachers College Press.

Whitehurst, G. J., & Lonigan, C. J. (2001). Emergent literacy: Development from prereaders to readers. In S. B. Neuman & D. K. Dickinson (Eds.), *Handbook of early literacy research* (pp.11–29). New York: Guilford Press.

Wittrock, M. C. (1986). Students' thought processes. In M. C. Wittrock (Ed.), *Handbook of research on teaching* (pp. 297–314). New York: Macmillan.

Wylie, R., & Durrell, D. D. (1970). Teaching vowels through phonograms. *Elementary English, 47,* 787–791.

Xu, H. (2003). The learner, the teacher, the text, and the context: Sociocultural approaches to early literacy instruction for English language learners. In D. M. Barone & L. M. Morrow (Eds.), *Literacy and young children: Research-based practices* (pp. 61–80). New York: Guilford Press.

Xu, S. H., & Rutledge, A. L. (2003). Chicken starts with ch!: Kindergarteners learn through environmental print. *Young Children, 58,* 44–51.

Yaden, D. (1985). *Preschoolers' spontaneous inquiries about print and books.* Paper presented at the Annual Meeting of the National Reading Conference, San Diego, CA.

Yopp, H. K. (1992). Developing phonemic awareness in young children. *Reading Teacher, 45,* 696–703.

Yopp, H. K., & Yopp, R. H. (2001). Supporting phonemic awareness development in the classroom. *Reading Teacher, 54,* 130–143.

Yopp, R. H., & Yopp, H. K. (2000). Sharing informational text with young children. *Reading Teacher, 53*(5), 410–423.

Index

Strategies for the Classroom

Created by *Elizabeth Freitag, Lisa Fazzi, and Lesley Morrow*

Directions for using supplementary activities are on the activity pages. Tear the page out and copy it so you can use it again. When appropriate, use the activities in your own classroom, in student teaching, in a practicum, or for a class assignment.

Contents

Introduction Priorities in Teaching Early Literacy

Name:_____ Date:_____

1. List what you believe are the most important elements in the teaching of early literacy with children from ages 3 to 7. Do this very quickly and keep it brief. List 5 to 8 items.

2. After listing your items go back and prioritize them. That is, put numbers from 1 to as many items as you listed, where 1 indicates the most important.

3. At the end of the semester, fill out the bottom of the page following the directions above, but do not look at what you wrote earlier. Compare the two.

Beginning of semester:

_____

_____

_____

_____

_____

_____

_____

_____

_____

_____

_____

End of semester: Date _____

_____

_____

_____

_____

_____

_____

_____

_____

_____

_____

_____

Chapter 1   Constructivist and Explicit Behaviorist Lesson Plans for
"The Three Bears"

Photocopy, color, and laminate the figures on firm paper. Cut and then paste felt on the back
and tell the story using the felt board. Have the children retell the story as they heard it. Then
ask them to tell the story again but create a new ending.

Source: Literacy Development in the Early Years: Helping Children to Read and Write, 6th ed., by Lesley M. Morrow.

(continued on the next page)

Chapter 1   Constructivist and Explicit Behaviorist Lesson Plans for "The Three Bears" *(continued)*

Photocopy, color, and laminate the figures on firm paper. Cut and then paste felt on the back and tell the story using the felt board. Have the children retell the story as they heard it. Then ask them to tell the story again but create a new ending.

Chapter 1   Sequencing Strips for "The Three Bears"
Directions: Cut out strips and arrange them in the correct order of events.

Once upon a time, Goldilocks was wandering through the woods.

She came across the three bears' house and walked inside.

First she saw three bowls of porridge.

She tried the first bowl, but it was too cold.

She tried the second bowl, but it was too hot.

She tried the third bowl and it was just right.

Next she saw three chairs.

She sat in the first chair, but it was too small.

She sat in the second chair, but it was too big.

She sat in the medium-size chair and it was just right.

(continued on the next page)

Chapter 1   Sequencing Strips for "The Three Bears" *(continued)*

Then Goldilocks went into the bedroom and saw three beds.

The first bed was way too big.

The second bed was way too small.

The third bed was just right, so she fell asleep.

Soon after, the three bears came home.

They noticed that someone had been sitting in their chairs.

They noticed that someone had been eating their porridge.

They noticed that someone had been sleeping in their beds.

Little Bear found Goldilocks in his bed and screamed! Goldilocks woke up, ran out the door, and never came back again.

Source: Literacy Development in the Early Years: Helping Children to Read and Write, 6th ed., by Lesley M. Morrow.

Chapter 2   Reading Interview

Name:_____ Date:_____

Ask questions that are age appropriate for the child you are interviewing.

1. Why do people read or look at books? (List as many reasons as you can.) _____
    _____
    _____
    _____

2. Why do you read or look at books? _____
    _____
    _____
    _____

3. How often do you read or look at books when you are not at school? _____
    _____
    _____

4. How do you decide what to read or what book to look at? _____
    _____
    _____
    _____

5. How do you feel about reading or looking at books at school and at home? _____
    _____
    _____
    _____

6. What is the best book you have ever read or had read to you? Why did you like it? ____
    _____
    _____
    _____

7. How did you learn to read or how are you learning to read? _____
    _____
    _____
    _____

8. What have you learned from reading or from looking at books? _____
    _____
    _____

9. What do you especially like to read about or have read to you? _____
    _____
    _____

10. What kinds of reading do you like? (Ask about types that are age appropriate for the child you are interviewing.)

    _____ historical fiction   _____ fairy tales/folktales   _____ poetry
    _____ realistic fiction   _____ biography and autobiography   _____ science fiction
    _____ fantasy   _____ information books

Source: Adapted with permission from *Guiding Readers and Writers,* © 2001 by Irene C. Fountas and Gay Su Pinnell. (Appendix 46). Published by Heinemann, Portsmouth, NH. All rights reserved.

Chapter 2   Writing Interview

Name:_____ Date:_____

Ask questions that are age appropriate for the child you are interviewing.

1. Why do people write? (List as many reasons as you can.) _____
_____
_____

2. Why do you write or draw? _____
_____
_____

3. How often do you write or draw when you are not at school? Why? _____
_____
_____

4. How do you decide what to write or draw about? _____
_____
_____

5. What is the best thing you have ever written or drawn? Why do you like it? _____
_____
_____

6. How did you learn to write or how are you learning to write? _____
_____
_____
_____

7. Have you learned anything about writing from the books someone has read to you or that you have read
yourself? _____
_____
_____

8. What kinds of topics do you especially like to write about? _____
_____
_____

9. What advice would you give students in this room to help them write well? _____
_____
_____
_____

10. What would you like to learn how to do better as a writer? _____
_____
_____

Source: Adapted with permission from *Guiding Readers and Writers,* © 2001 by Irene C. Fountas and Gay Su Pinnell. (Appendix 47).
Published by Heinemann, Portsmouth, NH. All rights reserved.

Chapter 3

Spanish and English Words
These are familiar school words. Enlarge them and color or copy them on firm colored paper, laminate, and hang around the room. Talk about them before and after hanging them and refer to them often. Add to the list using clip art from the Internet.

chair

silla

books

libros

crayons

creyones

bathroom

baño

paper

papel

scissors

tijera

(continued on the next page)

Chapter 3   Spanish and English Words *(continued)*

pencils	desk
lapices	escritorio
door	computer
puerta	computadora
flag	window
bandera	ventana

Source: Literacy Development in the Early Years: Helping Children to Read and Write, 6th ed., by Lesley M. Morrow.

Chapter 3   Spanish and English Phrases

These are familiar phrases. Enlarge them and color or copy them on firm colored paper, laminate, and hang around the room. Talk about them before and after hanging them and refer to them often. Add to the list using clip art from the Internet.

Can you help me? ¿Me ayuda por favor?	 Do you speak English? ¿Habla inglés?	 Do you understand English? ¿Entiende el inglés?
 I am hungry. Tengo hambre.	Good-bye. Adiós.	Hello ¡Hola!
 Where is the bathroom? ¿Donde está el baño?	What time is it? ¿Què hora es?	How are you? ¿Cómo está?
 How do you say...? ¿Cómo se dice...?	 How much does it cost? ¿Cuánto es?	 What is the weather like? ¿Què tiempo hace?
I feel sick. Me siento enfermo.	My name is... Me llamo...	Good morning. Buenos días.

Source: Literacy Development in the Early Years: Helping Children to Read and Write, 6th ed., by Lesley M. Morrow.

Chapter 4   Stick Puppets for Oral Language Development

Enlarge, photocopy, color, or copy onto firm colored paper. Laminate and cut. Tape a tongue depressor to the back of each figure to create a stick puppet. The teacher will create an original story using the characters provided. The children will be asked to do the same after the activity has been modeled. The teacher can help the student by saying, "You can begin your story with 'Once upon a time there was a girl and a boy. They decided to take a walk in the woods and . . !'" The teacher reminds the children to include a beginning, middle, and end of the story.

Source: Literacy Development in the Early Years: Helping Children to Read and Write, 6th ed., by Lesley M. Morrow.

Chapter 5   Sorting Board

This board can be used to alphabetize letters, match pictures to letters, build words with onsets and rimes, sort pictures and words by long and short vowels, and so forth. Copy onto firm paper. Letters, pictures, vowels, onsets, and rimes appear on the pages that follow.

Source: Literacy Development in the Early Years: Helping Children to Read and Write, 6th ed., by Lesley M. Morrow.

Chapter 5   Puzzle Pieces

Use the puzzle pieces for matching. Match uppercase to lowercase letters, match rhyming words and pictures to initial sounds. Copy onto firm colored paper and write in the skill or copy letters, rhyming word pictures, and initial sounds from the pages that follow. Laminate and cut.

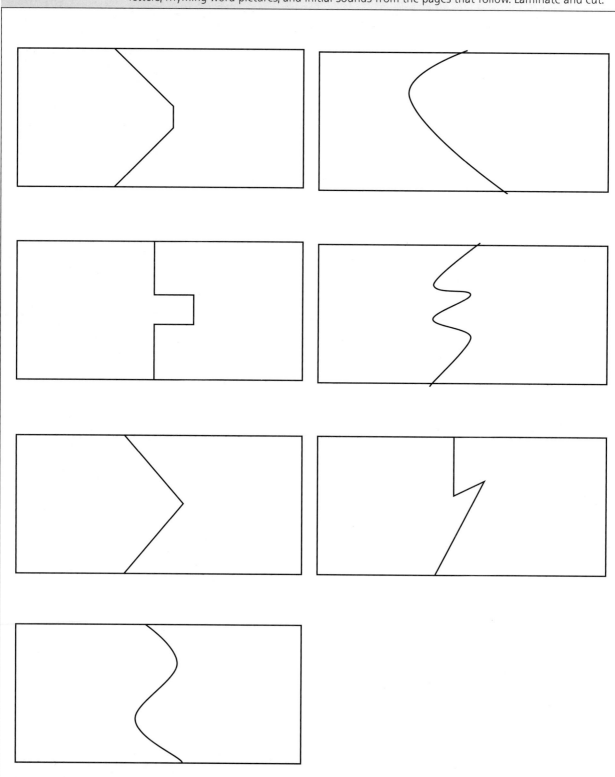

Source: Literacy Development in the Early Years: Helping Children to Read and Write, 6th ed., by Lesley M. Morrow.

Chapter 5   Initial Consonant Picture Cards

Initial Consonant Alphabet Pictures Enlarge or reduce as necessary, copy on firm colored paper, and laminate. Alphabetize, match to letters, or figure out number of sounds in each word.

Boat	Circle	Duck	Fish
Girl	House	Jar	Keys
Lamp	Mailbox	Newspaper	Paintbrush
Queen	Rainbow	Sandwich	Tennis Racquet
Van	Watch	X-ray	Yarn
Zebra			

Source: Literacy Development in the Early Years: Helping Children to Read and Write, 6th ed., by Lesley M. Morrow.

Chapter 5   Vowel Picture Cards

Enlarge if necessary, color, or copy on firm colored paper, and laminate. Use the pictures for phonemic awareness to figure out number of sounds in each word, to make rhymes, and to segment and blend. Write new words with long vowels and put them on the sorting board.

Long-Vowel Pictures

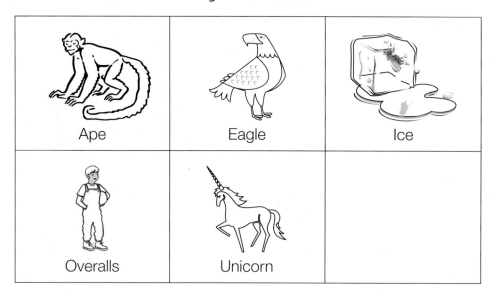

| Ape | Eagle | Ice |
| Overalls | Unicorn | |

Do the same activities with short vowels as you did with long vowels.

Short-Vowel Pictures

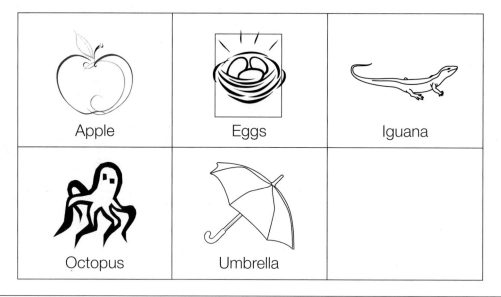

| Apple | Eggs | Iguana |
| Octopus | Umbrella | |

Source: Literacy Development in the Early Years: Helping Children to Read and Write, 6th ed., by Lesley M. Morrow.

Chapter 5   Alphabet Cards

Enlarge if necessary, copy on firm paper, laminate, and cut out. Alphabetize, match uppercase to lowercase, and match letters to picture cards.

Uppercase Letters

A	B	C	D	E	F	G
H	I	J	K	L	M	N
O	P	Q	R	S	T	U
V	W	X	Y	Z		

Lowercase Letters

a	b	c	d	e	f	g
h	i	j	k	l	m	n
o	p	q	r	s	t	u
v	w	x	y	z		

Source: Literacy Development in the Early Years: Helping Children to Read and Write, 6th ed., by Lesley M. Morrow.

Chapter 5   Building Words

Onsets and Rimes Enlarge if necessary, copy on firm paper, and laminate. Use the sorting board to build words from onsets and rimes.

b	c	d	f	g	h	j
k	l	m	n	p	q	r
s	t	v	w	x	y	z

Rimes

are	ate	ake	ame
ave	ase	ain	ap
ail	ang	ear	eat
ell	end	ent	ive
est	ine	ike	ice
ime	it	ink	ing
ip	ile	in	ot
ock	oke	op	un
unk	ump	ug	uck

Source: Literacy Development in the Early Years: Helping Children to Read and Write, 6th ed., by Lesley M. Morrow.

Chapter 5 Sorting Words

Copy on firm paper, laminate, and cut out. Put key words on the top row of the sorting board. Classify words into their correct pile. * indicates the keyword. Make new key words for additional sorts.

Pot*	Kit*	Fat*
Cat	Hot	Sit
Bit	Not	Hit
Sat	Lot	Hat
Cot	Wit	Mat
Fit	Rot	Bat

Source: Literacy Development in the Early Years: Helping Children to Read and Write, 6th ed., by Lesley M. Morrow.

Chapter 5   Identifying Digraphs Using Word Wheels

Enlarge if necessary, copy the two word wheels on firm paper, and laminate. Place the wheel with the onsets at the bottom and the rime at the top. Fill in various digraphs, blends, and chunks. Cut out the square tab. Fasten wheels together with a brass fastener. Rotate the wheel so that new words are made. Write the words you created on the sorting board. Use the word wheel pattern on the next page to make alternative digraphs, blends, and so forth.

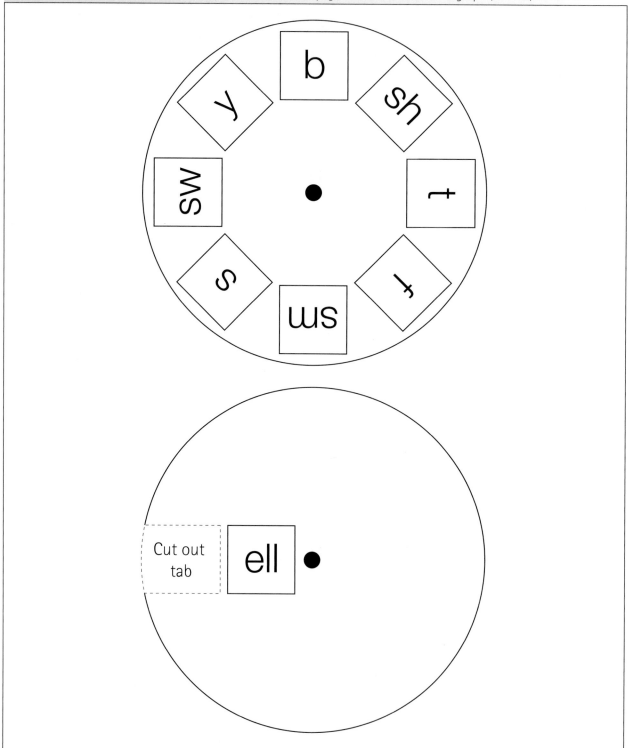

Cut out tab

ell

Source: Literacy Development in the Early Years: Helping Children to Read and Write, 6th ed., by Lesley M. Morrow.

Chapter 5   Word Wheel Templates

Enlarge if necessary and fill in phonograms or rimes in the squares of the first word wheel. Put an onset, digraph, consonant, or blend in the second word wheel. Copy the two word wheels on firm paper and laminate. Cut out the square tab. Put that word wheel on top. Fasten the wheels together with a brass fastener.

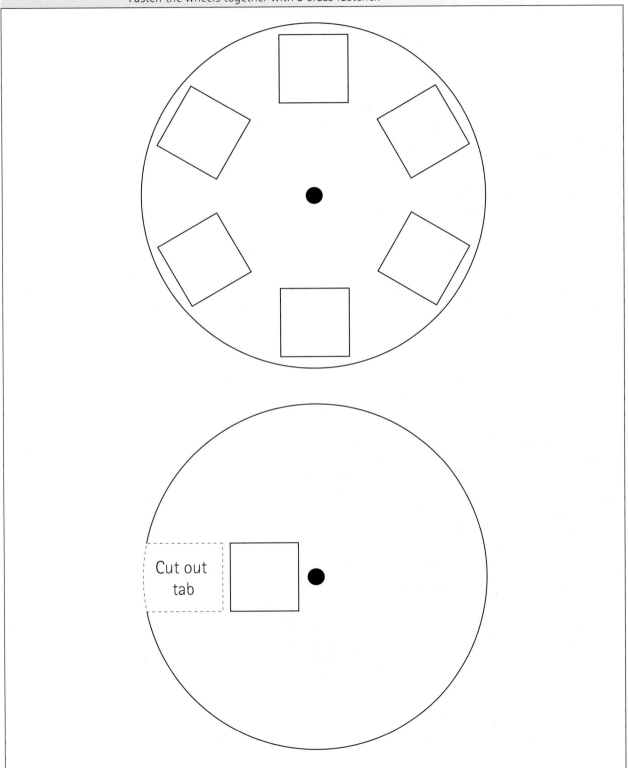

Source: Literacy Development in the Early Years: Helping Children to Read and Write, 6th ed., by Lesley M. Morrow.

Chapter 6   Literature Journal

Enlarge if necessary, copy, and cut out pages. Students fill out after reading their book. Staple the 4 pages in the top left corner to make student's own journal.

Retell the story by writing the beginning, middle, and end in the boxes below.

Beginning:

Middle:

End:

2

My Literature Journal

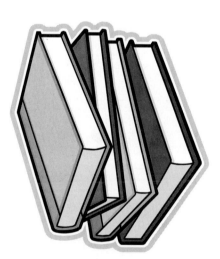

Name: _____

Date: _____

(continued on the next page)

Chapter 6   **Literature Journal** *(continued)*

Enlarge if necessary, copy, and cut out pages. Students fill out after reading their book. Staple the 4 pages in the top left corner to make student's own journal.

Draw a picture of your favorite part of the book.

4

Connections

Think about the problem in this book. How is this similar to something that has happened in your life?

Think of a book similar to the one you just read. Tell about it.

3

Source: Literacy Development in the Early Years: Helping Children to Read and Write, 6th ed., by Lesley M. Morrow.

Chapter 6   Literature Circles

Four students who have read the same book come together to discuss it. Each student takes a different role and is responsible for leading the discussion on his or her topic.

Discussion Director

You will be in charge of directing the discussion in your book club. List below who you will ask to speak first, second, and so on. Be prepared to introduce the topics with each of your member's roles.

1. _____

2. _____

3. _____

4. _____

5. _____

6. _____

7. _____

(continued on the next page)

Chapter 6   Literature Circles *(continued)*

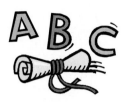

Word Finder

The word finder selects interesting and challenging words from the text and defines them for the group.

Word: _____

Definition: _____

_____

_____

Word: _____

Definition: _____

_____

_____

Word: _____

Definition: _____

_____

_____

Word: _____

Definition: _____

_____

_____

(continued on the next page)

Chapter 6   Literature Circles *(continued)*

Illustrator

Illustrate a part of the book you like a lot. Discuss with your book club members. Write a few sentences that describe what is happening in your illustration.

(continued on the next page)

Chapter 7   Writing Graphic Organizers *(continued)*
This Venn diagram may also be used for comprehension activities.

Name:_____   Date:_____

Venn Diagram

Use the overlapping circles to show the relationships between concepts and characters from a book.

(continued on the next page)

Chapter 7   Writing Graphic Organizers *(continued)*
This KWL Chart may also be used for comprehension activities.

Name:_____ Date:_____

KWL Chart

After the topic has been decided, brainstorm what you think you know about the topic, then list questions about what you want to know. After researching the topic, make a list of what you learned.

Topic:_____

What We **K**now	What We **W**ant to Know	What We **L**earned

(continued on the next page)

Chapter 7   Evaluating Each Other's Writing

Name of Writer:_____ Date:_____

Name of Editor:_____ Date:_____

Peer Evaluation

(1) Exchange your first draft with another student. Read over each other's paper. As you read, think about what you like, consider suggestions, and list any questions you might have. Record your evaluation here.

(2) Use this form for practicing **comprehension** for a story you read by answering: What I really liked about this story was.... I think the story would be better if the author.... Here are some things I wasn't sure about when I read....

Praise

I really like the way you _____

_____

_____

_____

_____

Suggestion

I think your writing would be better if you _____

_____

_____

_____

_____

Questions

Here are some things I wasn't sure about when I read your story.

_____

_____

_____

_____

_____

(continued on the next page)

Chapter 7   Writer's Self-Check List

Name:_____ Date:_____

Writer's Self-Check List

1.	Did I capitalize the first letter of every sentence?	Yes	No
2.	Do I have punctuation at the end of every sentence?	Yes	No
3.	Does my writing make sense?	Yes	No
4.	Do I have a beginning, middle, and end	Yes	No
5.	Did I use details?	Yes	No
6.	Did I indent paragraphs?	Yes	No
7.	Is my writing interesting?	Yes	No
8.	Did I use my best spelling?	Yes	No
9.	Did I use my best handwriting?	Yes	No
10.	Did I consult with the teacher?	Yes	No

What is your favorite part of the writing? Why? _____

_____

_____

_____

_____

_____

_____

What was the most difficult part of this writing for you? Why? _____

_____

_____

_____

_____

_____

_____

What would you like to write about next time? _____

_____

_____

_____

_____

Source: Literacy Development in the Early Years: Helping Children to Read and Write, 6th ed., by Lesley M. Morrow.

Chapter 7   How to Make a Booklet

Write about how to make something. List the materials on page 3 and the steps to make it on page 4. Draw a picture of what you are making on page 5. Write a glossary of new words on page 6. Then come back to page 2 and fill in Table of Contents. Enlarge if necessary.

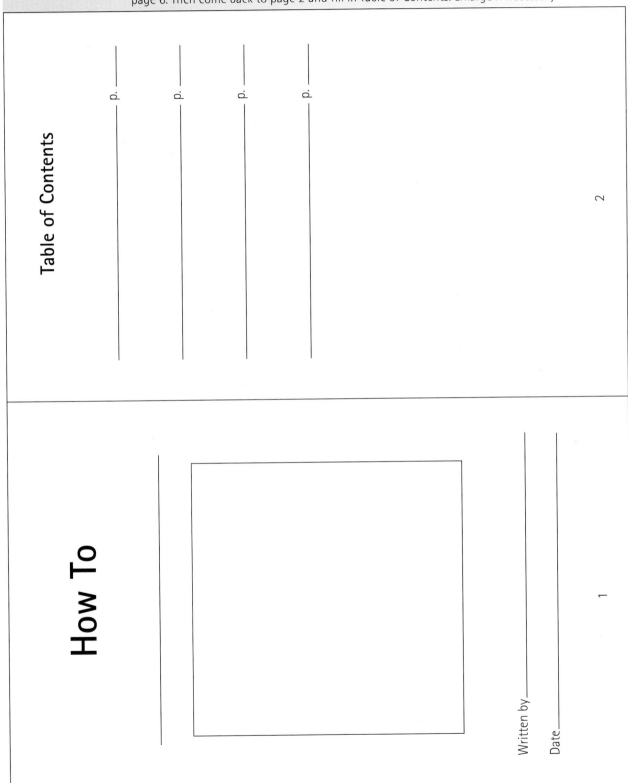

(continued on the next page)

Chapter 7   How to Make a Booklet *(continued)*

Write about how to make something. List the materials on page 3 and the steps to make it on page 4. Draw a picture of what you are making on page 5. Write a glossary of new words on page 6. Then come back to page 2 and fill in Table of Contents. Enlarge if necessary.

Sequence of steps

Write the steps and details to complete this how-to activity.

Step	Details

4

Materials

List the materials you will need to complete this how-to activity.

3

(continued on the next page)

Chapter 7 **How to Make a Booklet** *(continued)*

Write about how to make something. List the materials on page 3 and the steps to make it on page 4. Draw a picture of what you are making on page 5. Write a glossary of new words on page 6. Then come back to page 2 and fill in Table of Contents. Enlarge if necessary.

Glossary

Word: _____

Definition: _____

Word: _____

Definition: _____

Word: _____

Definition: _____

Word: _____

Definition: _____

Word: _____

Definition: _____

Word: _____

Definition: _____

6

Picture

Draw a picture of your topic in the box below. Label your picture with words.

5

Source: Literacy Development in the Early Years: Helping Children to Read and Write, 6th ed., by Lesley M. Morrow.

Chapter 7   Writing Rubrics

Obtain a writing sample from a child and evaluate using the rubric that is age appropriate.
Check items that children need to work on.

Kindergarten Writing Rubric

4   Exceptional Writer
  - Writes several complete sentences or one more sophisticated sentence.
  - Spaces between words and sentences consistently.
  - Spells some high-frequency words correctly.
  - Spells some consonant-vowel-consonant words correctly.
  - Uses capital letters to begin some sentences.
  - Uses periods and other punctuation marks to end some sentences.

3   Developing Writer
  - Writes complete sentences.
  - Spaces between some words.
  - Spells one or more high-frequency words correctly.
  - Spells beginning and ending sounds in most words.
  - Uses both upper- and lowercase letters.

2   Beginning Writer
  - Writes from left to right and top to bottom.
  - Writes one or more words using one or more letters that represent beginning or other sounds in the word.
  - Can reread the writing with one-to-one matching of words.

1   Emergent Writer
  - Uses random letters that do not correspond to sounds.
  - Uses scribbles to represent writing.
  - Draws a picture instead of writing.
  - Dictates words or sentences

2nd Grade Rubric for Stories

5
  - Writing has an original title.
  - Story shows originality, sense of humor, or cleverness.
  - Writer uses paragraphs to organize ideas.
  - Writing contains few spelling, capitalization, or punctuation errors.
  - Writer varies sentence structure and word choice.
  - Writer shows a sense of audience.

4
  - Writing has an appropriate title.
  - Beginning, middle, and end of the story are well developed.
  - A problem or goal is identified in the story.
  - Writing includes details that support plot, characters, and setting.
  - Writing is organized into paragraphs.
  - Writing contains few capitalization and punctuation errors.
  - Writer spells most high-frequency words correctly and spells unfamiliar words phonetically.

3
  - Writing may have a title.
  - Writing has at least two of the three parts of a story (beginning, middle, and end).
  - Writing shows a sequence of events.
  - Writing is not organized into paragraphs.
  - Spelling, grammar, and capitalization or punctuation errors may interfere with meaning.

2
  - Writing has at least one of the three parts of a story (beginning, middle, and end).
  - Writing may show a partial sequence of events.
  - Writing is brief and underdeveloped.
  - Writing has spelling, grammar, capitalization, and punctuation errors that interfere with meaning.

1
  - Writing lacks a sense of story.
  - An illustration may suggest a story.
  - Writing is brief and may support the illustration.
  - Some words may be recognizable, but the writing is difficult to read.

Source: Adapted from Tompkins, G. E., *Literacy for the 21st Century: Teaching Reading and Writing in Pre-Kindergarten Through Grade 4,*
2nd edition, © 2007, p. 82. Reprinted by permission of Pearson Education, Inc., Upper Saddle River, NJ.

Chapter 7   Writing Rubric for 3rd Grade through Upper Elementary Grades

Obtain a writing sample from a child and evaluate based on the criteria below.

	Inadequate Command	Limited Command	Partial Command	Adequate Command	Strong Command	Superior Command
New Jersey Registered Holistic Scoring Rubric						
Score	1	2	3	4	5	6
Content and Organization	May lack opening and/ or closing	May lack opening and/ or closing	May lack opening and/ or closing	May lack opening and/ or closing	Generally has opening and closing	Has opening and closing
	Minimal response to topic; uncertain focus	Attempts to focus May drift or shift focus	Usually has single focus	Single focus	Single focus Sense of unity and coherence Key ideas developed	Single, distinct focus Unified and coherent Well-developed
	No planning evident; disorganized	Attempts organization Few, if any, transitions between ideas	Some lapses or flaws in organization May lack some transitions between ideas	Ideas loosely connected Transitions evident	Logical progression of ideas Moderately fluent Attempts compositional risks	Logical progression of ideas Fluent, cohesive Compositional risks successful
	Details random, inappropriate, or barely apparent	Details lack elaboration, i.e., highlight paper	Repetitious details Several unelaborated details	Uneven development of details	Details appropriate and varied	Details effective, vivid, explicit, and/ or pertinent
Usage	No apparent control Severe/ numerous errors	Numerous errors	Errors/ patterns of errors may be evident	Some errors that do not interfere with meaning	Few errors	Very few, if any, errors
Sentence Construction	Assortment of incomplete and/ or incorrect sentences	Excessive monotony/ same structure Numerous errors	Little variety in syntax Some errors	Some variety Generally correct	Variety in syntax appropriate and effective Few errors	Precision and/or sophistication Very few, if any, errors
Mechanics	Errors so severe they detract from meaning	Numerous serious errors	Patterns of errors evident	No consistent pattern of errors Some errors that do not interfere with meaning	Few errors	Very few, if any, errors

Chapter 8   Creating a Classroom Restaurant

Enlarge, color, or copy onto firm colored paper and laminate. Write the name of the restaurant you are creating. For example, Our Japanese, Italian, Mexican Restaurant, Jewish Deli, etc...

Welcome To

Our _____

Restaurant

(continued on the next page)

Chapter 8   Creating a Classroom Restaurant *(continued)*

Thank You for Coming to

_____ Restaurant

Total: $:_____

Come Back Again!

The waiter or waitress fills in the Thank You form (top).
The customer completes the Survey (bottom).

Restaurant Survey

How did you like your food?

How friendly was your server?

How fast was the service?

Restaurant: _____

Restaurant Order Form and Bill for Table _____

Drinks:
$ _____
$ _____

Main Course:
$ _____
$ _____

Desserts:
$ _____
$ _____

Total: $ _____

Source: Literacy Development in the Early Years: Helping Children to Read and Write, 6th ed., by Lesley M. Morrow.

Chapter 8   Restaurant Menus

Enlarge and copy. Forms to be used during restaurant activity.

Italian Garden

Drinks	**Main Course**	**Desserts**
Milk $1.00	Spaghetti $10.00	Italian Cookies $3.00
Water FREE	Pizza $2.00	Cheesecake $3.00

Mexican Restaurant

Drinks	**Main Course**	**Desserts**
Milk $1.00	Bean Burrito $5.00	Ice Cream $2.00
Juice $1.00	Chicken Quesadilla $5.00	Rice Pudding $2.00

(continued on the next page)

Chapter 8   Restaurant Menus *(continued)*

 Bob's Barbeque

Beverages

Juice $1.00

Water FREE

Main Entrees

Hamburger $3.00

Hot Dog $2.00

Desserts

Oatmeal Cookie $1.00

Ice Cream $1.00

Create a menu for a different restaurant. Draw pictures and write in the words.

_____

Beverages

Main Entrees

Desserts

Source: Literacy Development in the Early Years: Helping Children to Read and Write, 6th ed., by Lesley M. Morrow.

Chapter 9   Center Cards
Color or photocopy on firm colored paper. Enlarge if necessary. Laminate and display.

Independent Reading

Listening Center

Science

Math

(continued on the next page)

Chapter 9   **Center Cards** *(continued)*

Social Studies

Writing Center

Poetry Center

Literature Circles

Source: Literacy Development in the Early Years: Helping Children to Read and Write, 6th ed., by Lesley M. Morrow.

Chapter 10   Integrating Literacy into the Home Environment

Do two or three of these activities with your child each week.

Top 10 Things To Do with Your Child at Home

Here are fun and easy ways you can promote reading and writing at home.

Read to and with your child. Talk about books or other literature with your child.

Leave a note in child's lunchbox.

Help your child with homework.

Talk about your day or share stories at mealtime.

Discuss or retell plots from television programs.

Keep a parent and child journal. Share writing.

Keep a chart of chores. Keep lists, such as grocery lists.

Create a library in your home and visit a library.

Cook with your family following a recipe.

Record family trips.

(continued on the next page)

Chapter 10   Integrating Literacy into the Home Environment *(continued)*

Things You Do at Home

Each time you work with your children at home, record it on the chart below.
Try doing two or three activities a week.

Activity	Date

Source: Literacy Development in the Early Years: Helping Children to Read and Write, 6th ed., by Lesley M. Morrow.

Chapter 10   Very Important Parent (VIP) Award

Give to parents who help out and participate in school activities.

V.I.P.

Very Important Parent

Great Job!

This award goes to _____

Thank you for all of your contributions to our classroom.

It is only with your continued support that we are able to have successful students!

_____
Teacher Signature

_____
Date

Source: Literacy Development in the Early Years: Helping Children to Read and Write, 6th ed., by Lesley M. Morrow.

Chapter 10   Bookmarks for the Family

Copy on white or colored paper. Paste the poem on the front and "Choosing a Just-Right Book" on the back. Laminate. Give one as a gift and make one for yourself.

Before you go to sleep tonight, read a book, then turn out the light.

Choosing a Just-Right Book

1. Look at the cover.
2. Read the title and the author.
3. Read the blurb on the back cover. (Does the book interest you?)
4. Flip through the book.
5. Read the first page and use the Five Finger Rule.

   If you come across a word that you don't know, put a finger down. Determine if this book is good for you:

   0–1 finger - Too Easy

   2–3 fingers - Just Right

   4–5 fingers - Too Hard

Source: Literacy Development in the Early Years: Helping Children to Read and Write, 6th ed., by Lesley M. Morrow.